Tales of Prison to Praise

Tales of Prison to Praise

Three Stories of Lives Transformed by God

Merlin Carothers, Valeri Barinov,
Charles Colson

Hodder & Stoughton
LONDON SYDNEY AUCKLAND

Tales of Prison to Praise first published in Great Britain in 2001

Prison to Praise
Copyright © 1970 by Logos International
First published in Great Britain in 1971 by Hodder & Stoughton,
by permission of Logos International

Jailhouse Rock
Copyright © 1990 by Valeri Barinov and Danny Smith
First published in Great Britain in 1990 by Hodder & Stoughton

Born Again
Copyright © 1976 by Charles W. Colson
First published in Great Britain in 1976 by Hodder & Stoughton

The right of Merlin Carothers, Valeri Barinov, Danny Smith and
Charles Colson to be identified as the Author of their respective
Works has been asserted by them in accordance with
the Copyright, Designs and Patents Act 1988.

10 9 8 7 6 5 4 3 2 1

British Library Cataloguing in Publication Data
A record for this book is available from the British Library

ISBN 0 340 78549 7

Typeset by Avon Dataset Ltd, Bidford-on-Avon, Warks

Printed and bound in Great Britain by
Clays Ltd, St Ives plc

Hodder & Stoughton
A Division of Hodder Headline Ltd
338 Euston Road
London NW1 3BH

Prison to Praise

Merlin Carothers

Rejoice evermore.
Pray without ceasing.
In everything give thanks:
for THIS is the will of God in Christ Jesus
concerning YOU!
1 Thessalonians 5:16–18

Contents

Introduction to the 1996 edition

When I wrote *Prison to Praise* back in 1970, I thought of it as an opportunity to encourage Christians to praise the Lord instead of grumbling. Millions of people around the world do report remarkable changes in their lives as they practise praising God. But over the years I've been astonished at the number of people who have read *Prison to Praise* and then accepted Jesus as their Lord and Saviour. Many say this is the first Christian book they have ever read.

Every day I still receive hundreds of letters from people who report changes in their lives as they read this book. Here are just a few examples:

Thank you for the tremendous influence you had on my life twenty years ago. After I read *Prison to Praise* I was, and am a completely different person. While reading, I surrendered my life to the Lord and experienced 'heavenly joy'! It has never left me to this day.

Florence

A very dear friend of mine gave me *Prison to Praise*. I can never thank her enough. I carry it in my purse and have practically worn it out. I've never been interested much in reading, but I just couldn't put this book down . . . I have since read it through many times, and it helps me more than I can tell you. I could go on for page after page telling you what *Prison to Praise* has done for me.

Betty

There are many criminal charges against me. I am twenty-one years old. When I came to jail I knew I was going to take my life. When they passed out razors for a shave, I took mine apart for the blade. I had no place to hide it except in a book that someone had left behind. When I went to retrieve the blade, I found myself reading *Prison to Praise*. By the time I had finished reading it, I had flushed the razor. I now look forward to each and every day with God.

Michael

I thoroughly enjoyed *Prison to Praise*. After reading it I accepted responsibility for my crimes and repented. Only then was I willing to accept my sentence of fifteen years and to serve my time without complaining. Others did not understand how I was able to smile. I explained and suggested they read your book. I had never before been religious, but now my mission is to learn as much as I can about the Bible and God's will.

Kenneth

A few months ago I came to the end of my rope. I could see nothing good coming out of my thirty-four years of life. My prayers didn't seem to be reaching God. I was on the verge of panic. The thought of suicide was constantly on my mind . . . Then I read *Prison to Praise* . . . Almost immediately things began turning around. My life became dear to me and now I like myself for the first time . . . Now I can clearly see the many blessings that I had all the time, but didn't see then. I know in my heart that I am secure in God's love. My needs are met.

Mark

1

Prisoner

There was the touch of cold metal against my left wrist and the harsh voice in my ear: 'This is the FBI. You are under arrest.'

I'd been relaxing in the back seat of the car with my left arm hanging out the window. The car was stolen and I was AWOL from the Army.

Being AWOL didn't bother me. It was the getting caught that hurt my pride. I'd always considered myself capable of doing my own thing and getting away with it. Now I had to suffer the humiliation of the jail cell, standing in line for lousy cold chow, back to the lonely cell and the hard bunk with nothing to do but stare at the wall and wonder how I could have been stupid enough to get into a mess like this.

I'd been a pretty independent fellow from the time I was about twelve. That's when my father died suddenly, leaving mother alone with three boys to raise. My brothers were seven and one, and mother started taking in washings and went on relief to keep us alive. She always talked about Dad being in heaven and how God would take care of us, but with the intensity of a twelve-year-old I turned in fury against a God who could do us that way.

* * *

I delivered papers after school until long after dark each night, determined to make my way in life. I was going to get the most of it. Somehow I felt I had it coming. I had a right to grab for all I could get.

When mother remarried I went to live with some of dad's old friends. I went to high school, but never quit working. After school and all summer I worked. As a food packer, shipping clerk, linotype operator, and one summer as a lumber-jack in Pennsylvania.

I started college, but ran out of money and had to go to work. This time I got a job with B. & W. Steel as a steel chipper and grinder. Not a very pleasant job, but it kept me in top physical condition. Part of staying ahead in the rat race of the world was being in top shape physically, and I didn't intend to lose out on any count.

I never did want to join the Army. I wanted to go off to sea with the Merchant Marine; I couldn't think of a more glamorous way to get into action in World War II.

To join the Merchant Marine I had to get reclassified 1-A with the draft board that had given me a deferment to go to college. Before I could make it back to the Merchant Marine, the Army inducted me. They told me I could volunteer for the Navy, which I did, but a freak incident kept me out. I failed the eye test simply because I'd been reading the wrong line on the chart by mistake! So there, against all my efforts, I landed in basic training at Fort McClellan, Alabama.

I was bored to death. The training was a breeze, and looking for excitement, I volunteered for airborne training at Fort Benning, Georgia.

A rebel at heart, my biggest problem always was in getting along with my superiors. Somehow they picked on me in spite of all my efforts to remain in the background. Once, during physical training in a sawdust pit, I spat on the ground without thinking. The sergeant saw me, and descended like a storm cloud. 'Pick that up in your mouth and carry it out of the area!' he screamed.

You've got to be kidding, I thought, but his red, glowering face indicated he was not. So, humiliated and seething with resentment carefully hidden, I picked up the spit – and a mouthful of sawdust – and carried it 'out of the area'.

The compensation came when we got our first chance to jump from an aeroplane in flight. This was living! The kind of excitement I was hungering for. Over the roar of the plane engines came the command: 'Get ready . . . stand up . . . hook up . . . stand in the door . . . GO!'

The blast of air makes you feel like a leaf in a gale – and then, as the rope attached to your parachute reaches its end, a bone-jarring jolt. You feel like you've been hit by a ten-ton truck.

Then, as your brain clears, you're in a beautiful silent world; billowing above is the parachute like a giant white arc of silk.

I was a paratrooper, and earned the honour of wearing the glistening jump boots.

Still, I wanted more excitement and volunteered for advanced training as a demolition expert. I wanted in on the war effort, and the hotter the action the better, I thought.

After demolition school I returned to Fort Benning to wait for orders to go overseas. I pulled guard at the stockade, had KP and waited some more. Patience was not my strong point. At the rate the Army was moving, I figured I might miss out on the fun altogether, scrubbing pots and pans till the war ended.

I wasn't going to sit around doing nothing, and with a friend, I decided to go over the hill.

We simply walked out of the camp one day, stole a car, and headed for any place. Just in case someone was looking for us, we dropped the first car and stole another and finally ended up in Pittsburgh, Pennsylvania. There we ran out of spending money and decided to pull a stick-up.

I had the gun and my friend waited in the car. We'd picked a store that looked like an easy job. My plan was to pull the wiring to the telephone so they couldn't call the police, but however hard I tried, the wiring wouldn't give. I was frustrated. The gun was in my pocket, the cash register was full of money, but the line to the police was still there. I wasn't about to invite disaster.

So I went back to the car to tell my buddy, and we were just sitting there, eating green apples and talking in the back seat, when the long arm of the law finally caught up with us. We didn't know it, but a six-state alarm had gone out for us, and the FBI was hot on our heels.

Our search for adventure had ended in a pretty sad flop. I was back in the stockade at Fort Benning where I'd been a guard only a few months earlier. I was sentenced to six months' confinement and immediately started a campaign to get overseas. My fellow prisoners laughed and said, 'You wouldn't have gone AWOL if you wanted to go overseas.'

I kept insisting I'd gone AWOL because I got bored waiting to be sent overseas.

At last my pleas were heard; I was placed on overseas shipment and went 'under guard' to Camp Kilmer, NJ, where I was placed in the stockade to wait for our ship to Europe.

At last, I was on my way. Almost anyway. The night before our ship was due to sail I was called to the commander's office where I learned that I wouldn't be sailing with the rest of the men.

'The FBI wants you held and returned to Pittsburgh, Pennsylvania.'

Once more I felt the cold steel of handcuffs, and under armed guard I returned to Pittsburgh where a stern judge read the charges and asked: 'Guilty or not guilty; how do you plead?'

My mother was there and her tear-filled eyes made me cringe. Not that I was sorry for what I'd done. I wanted out of there and on with some fast living, the sooner the better.

12

'Guilty, sir.' I had been caught red-handed and somehow I determined it would be the last time. I would learn the tricks and play it safe from now on.

The district attorney carefully explained my past life to the judge who asked the investigating officers for their recommendation.

'Your honour, we recommend leniency.'

'What do you want, soldier?' the judge asked me.

'I want to go back in the Army and get into the war,' was all I could say.

'I sentence you to five years in the Federal Penitentiary.'

His words hit me like a load of bricks from the skies. I was nineteen and would be twenty-four when I got out. I saw my whole life go down the drain.

'Your sentence is temporarily suspended and you will be returned to the Army.'

Saved, thank heavens! In less than an hour I was released. But first the district attorney gave me a stern lecture and explained that if I left the Army in less than five years I should report back to his office.

Free at last! I headed back to Fort Dix, New Jersey, only to get another load of bricks on my head. At Fort Dix they looked at my papers and sent me back to the stockade to serve out my six months' sentence for AWOL!

At this point I had only one thought in my head. I wanted to get into the war or bust. Again I started my campaign to get on an overseas shipment. I pestered the command until finally, when four months of my time was completed, I was released. Soon I was on my way across the Atlantic aboard the *Mauretania*.

We were piled six high in the hold, and I was lucky enough to get the top berth. That way I missed the shower of vomit those on the lower berths often received.

Not that I really would have cared. I was thrilled to be on my way, and didn't waste any time. I was out to get as much excitement and as much profit as possible out of the war effort. I had developed one talent during my confinement that now came in handy. I had become quite adept at gambling, and the days and nights of our crossing were spent in this worthwhile endeavour. I accumulated a nice little pile of money, and the only thing that reminded me of the circumstances of our voyage was a brief encounter with a German sub that tried to hit us and missed.

In England we were put on trains that took us to the English Channel. There we boarded small boats and moved out into the choppy waters of the channel. It rained cats and dogs, and on the French side we had to jump into waist-high water and wade ashore.

On the beach we stood dripping wet in line waiting for cold C-rations. Then we rushed again for a train headed east. Without stopping, we crossed France and were transferred to trucks taking us into Belgium. We got there just in time for the Battle of the Bulge with the 82nd Airborne Division.

On my first day in combat, the commanding officer saw my record as a demolitions expert and put me to work making small bombs out of a pile of plastic explosives. The pile was about three feet high, and I pulled up a log and went to work. Another soldier joined me, and I learned that he had been with the unit for many months. While he was telling me about his experiences with the 82nd Airborne, I looked across a field at incoming artillery exploding. The explosions came closer and closer to our position. Out of the corner of my eye I kept watching the other soldier, wondering when he'd give the signal to dive for cover. He had all the experience, and I was just a green replacement; I wasn't going to chicken out.

The explosions came nearer, and my fear mounted. If one of those rounds landed near us . . . the pile of bombs would make one giant crater.

The other fellow sat there paying no attention to the artillery. I wanted desperately to dive for cover, but I wasn't about to show myself a coward. At last the explosions were coming on the other side of us. They had missed!

Two days later I discovered why the other soldier had played it so cool. The two of us were walking through a forest known to be heavily mined. I carefully examined the trail for any signs of booby traps, but the other fellow was paying no attention to where he was walking.

I finally said: 'Why aren't you watching for mines?'

'I hope I step on one,' he said. 'I'm sick and tired of this rotten mess. I want to die.'

From that day I kept as much distance as possible between the two of us!

At the close of the war I went with the 508th Airborne Regiment to Frankfurt, Germany, to serve as guard for General of the Army, Dwight D. Eisenhower.

I would have liked to see more action, but the spoils of war weren't so bad either. We lived in plush apartment buildings that had belonged to top German officials.

I was still looking for excitement, and once I almost got more than I bargained for. We were loaded on aeroplanes for a parachute jump. It was to be a routine training exercise, but we were told that Marlene Dietrich, the movie actress, would be on the ground watching the jump. We were all hoping to land near her.

As soon as I left the plane I began to scan the ground below to see if I could locate the 'lady with the beautiful legs'. Suddenly I was aware that something was horribly wrong. Around me in the air were terrible screams, and the roar of an aeroplane engine seemed suddenly to burst right on top of me.

Several hundred troopers were in the air and an aeroplane had lost engine power and was diving right through us! Parachutes were cut off and men were plunging to the ground. They were falling all around the spot where Miss Dietrich was standing. My parachute was intact, and when I reached the ground there were dead men all around, and the plane was exploding in flames.

In Frankfurt I had plenty of free time. My idea of a good time usually involved a considerable amount of drinking. It happened that I drank myself into a state of oblivion and other soldiers told me what pranks I had pulled in town the night before. Once I had stretched myself flat on the floor of a German streetcar and dared anyone to walk over me. The other soldiers had roared with laughter and found the whole incident uproariously funny. It never occurred to me that my behaviour probably didn't help the image of the American Occupation Army.

I discovered that black marketeering was a quicker and more reliable source of income than gambling. I bought cigarettes from other soldiers for ten dollars a carton. With a suitcase full, I went to the black-market area in town where I could sell the cartons for one hundred dollars apiece. The black-market area was a frequent site of robberies, beatings, and murder, but I didn't care. I kept one hand on a loaded, cocked '45' in my pocket.

Soon I had a suitcase full of ten-dollar bills in military money known as scrip. The only problem was to find a way to get the money back to the United States. Tight control limited each soldier to sending home only the amount he was paid by the Army. I stayed awake nights trying to figure a way to beat the system.

At the post office I watched the men line up to convert their monthly pay into money orders. Each man had to have his finance card which listed the exact amount he had been paid. I observed one man with a pile of finance cards, a bag of money, and an armed guard. He was company clerk and was getting money orders for his entire company. I suddenly realised that all I needed was a pile of finance cards!

I located the unit finance clerk and soon learned that he

would be willing to provide me with the finance cards for five dollars apiece. I was in business.

I set myself up as the company clerk of my own private company. With the money and the finance cards I went to the post office and had the money orders made out without a hitch!

With this setup I now found new ways to accumulate the military scrip money. I learned that men coming from Berlin would give $1,000 in scrip for a $100 money order. I gladly obliged and then converted the $900 into my own money order. I was on my way to becoming very rich!

The Army announced the decision to send some men to universities throughout Europe. I took the examinations, was selected, and sent to Bristol University in England. The courses I took were far less important than the fact that we were surrounded by girls who spoke English. I soon met a cute blonde named Sadie. She was full of fun, and I fell head over heels in love. Within two months we were married, and spent exactly thirty wonderful days together in England before I had to go back to Germany. Sadie remained in England with other war brides, waiting for the airlift back to the United States.

I got to the United States nearly six months ahead of my new bride and could hardly wait for her to join me.

I received the long-coveted paper stating I was now a civilian. Free! I had no desire to ever see the inside of an Army post again. I had plenty of money, and life ahead looked rosy.

There was the problem of converting my suitcase full of money orders into crisp green bills. I couldn't very well walk into the post office in my hometown in Ellwood City, Pennsylvania, and dump the whole stack on the counter. Finally I thought of a solution. One by one I began to send the money orders to a post office in New York. Soon the money began filtering back.

My experiences with the law so far had taught me that I better get into a profession where I would be able to operate safely within every available loophole. I'd always wanted to become a lawyer, so I began the necessary steps to enrol in law school in Pittsburgh, Pennsylvania.

2

Set Free!

Grandmother was a sweet old lady, and I thought a great deal of Grandfather, but going to visit them was still an ordeal I avoided whenever possible. They made me nervous. Grandmother always found an opportunity to talk about God.

'I'm doing fine,' I'd say. 'Don't worry about me.'

But she would insist: 'You need to give your life to Christ, Merlin.'

It bugged me more than I wanted to admit. I hated to hurt Grandmother's feelings, but I didn't have time for any of that religious stuff. I'd just begun to live!

One Sunday evening shortly after I'd come back from Germany, I went to see Grandmother and Grandfather. I quickly realised I'd made a mistake. They were getting ready to go to church.

'Come go with us, Merlin,' Grandmother said. 'We haven't seen you for so long; we'd love to have you come.'

I squirmed in my chair. How could I tactfully get out of this one?

'I'd like to,' I said finally. 'But some friends have already asked if they could come pick me up.'

Grandmother looked disappointed, and as soon as I could get to the phone I began calling everyone I knew. To my dismay

I couldn't find anyone who was free to come pick me up.

It was getting close to church time, and I couldn't say to my grandparents: 'I just don't want to go.'

At the zero hour I had no choice. Off we went together.

The church service was held in a barn, but everyone there seemed to be happy. *Poor people, I thought, they don't know anything about real life out there in the world, or they wouldn't waste an evening in a barn.*

The singing began and I picked up a hymn book to follow the words. I at least had to look as if I was with it.

Suddenly I heard a deep voice speak directly in my ear.

'What – what did you say?' I whirled around to find no one behind me.

There was the voice again: 'Tonight you must make a decision for me. If you don't, it will be too late.'

I shook my head and said automatically: 'Why?'

'It just will be!'

Was I losing my marbles? But the voice was real. It was God, and He knew me! In a flash I suddenly saw it. Why hadn't I seen it before? God was real; He was the answer. In Him was everything I'd ever searched for.

'Yes, God,' I heard myself mutter. 'I'll do it; whatever You want.'

The service went on, but I was in another world. This was crazy, but I knew God!

Grandfather was in deep thought beside me. I didn't know it then, but he told me later. He was carrying on his own battle with God. For years he'd been smoking and chewing tobacco. Forty years of addiction to the weed had him hooked pretty good. Many a time he'd tried to quit, but had been seized with violent headaches and soon was back to chewing and smoking heavier than before.

Now he was sitting next to me in the meeting making his own commitment. 'God, if you'll change Merlin, I'll give up my chewing and smoking even if it kills me.'

No wonder Grandfather nearly collapsed when I went forward at the end of the meeting to make public the decision I'd made during the singing.

Years later I was by his bedside when his time came to die. He looked up at me and smiled. 'Merlin,' he said, 'I kept my promise to God.'

That Sunday night I couldn't wait to get home and read the Bible. I wanted to know God, and I read hungrily page after page. I had a wonderful feeling of excitement inside. It was even better than jumping off an aeroplane with a parachute. That night God had reached down inside me, and I was changed into a new being. I felt as if I was standing on the threshold of exciting adventures the likes of which I couldn't even begin to imagine yet. The God of Abraham, Isaac, and Jacob was still alive; the God who parted the Red Sea and spoke through a burning bush and sent His Son to die on a cross – He was my Father too!

I could suddenly understand what my earthly father had tried to tell me. When he was thirty-six years old he was confined to a bed for the first time in his life. Three days later his heart stopped. The doctor was there with an injection, and my father's heart began beating again. He opened his eyes and said: 'That won't be necessary, doctor. I am going to leave now.' He raised himself up in bed and looked around the room with a radiant glow on his face.

'Look!' he said. 'They are here to take me!' With that he lay back and was gone.

My father had known Jesus Christ as his personal friend and Saviour. He had been ready to go.

Now I felt ready too, but even as I voiced the thought to myself, I became aware of an uneasiness, a gnawing at the back of my mind. What was wrong? Show me, God!

Gradually the thought became clearer. The money! All that money. It wasn't mine; I had to give it back!

The decision made, I breathed a sigh of relief. I couldn't

wait to get rid of that money. It was like a sickness inside me, and I knew that feeling would be there until the money was gone.

I told the post office, but they said it wasn't any concern of theirs because I hadn't stolen the money orders. I could do with them as I liked.

I still had a whole bunch that I hadn't cashed in yet, so I took the suitcase into the bathroom and began to flush piles of one hundred dollar money orders down the toilet. With each flush I felt a mounting flood of joy inside.

That still left me with the money I had already cashed. I wrote the US Treasury Department and told them how I had acquired the money. They wrote back asking if I had any evidence of how I had got the money and the money orders. It was too late; the evidence was flushed down the drain! I told them I had no proof, just the money, and they advised me that all they could do was to accept the money into the Conscience Fund.

Once again I was a poor man, but I would gladly give away everything I owned for that new life and joy I felt within.

There was one more shadow of the past to be encountered. I returned to Pittsburgh and reported to the district attorney. There were three years remaining on my sentence, and I would now have to be on a parole status for these years. This meant regular reporting and supervision by a parole officer.

The district attorney received me and asked a clerk to get my records. He glanced at them and looked surprised.

'Do you know what you have received?' I knew I'd received Christ, but that could hardly have got into my record already.

'No, Sir.'

'You have received a presidential pardon, signed by President Truman!'

'A pardon?'

'That means your record is completely clear. Just as if you had never got involved with the law.'

I wanted to shout for joy. 'Why did I get it?'

The district attorney smiled. 'It has something to do with your excellent combat record.'

He explained that I was free to go and do anything I wanted to; my case was closed.

'If you ever apply for a federal job you are completely eligible.'

'Thank you, Lord.' I was overwhelmed. Not only were my sins washed away and the case closed at Calvary, but God had given me a clean start in the eyes of the United States government as well. Not that I ever thought I'd be looking for a job with them again!

But what was I going to do? My motives for becoming a lawyer had been questionable; it seemed clear that God did not want me in that profession. Soon the thought became very persistent. I was to become a minister! Me, in the pulpit. The thought seemed preposterous. 'You know me, Lord,' I argued. 'I like excitement, adventure, even danger. I wouldn't make a very good preacher.'

It seemed God had His plans for me all set. I couldn't sleep nights, and the longer I thought and prayed, the more exciting did the whole idea seem. If God could make a preacher out of an ex-jailbird, paratrooper, gambler, and black-marketeer, that would be a greater adventure into the unknown than anything I'd ever tried before.

I couldn't wait to tell Sadie. She was due to arrive in New York on a Liberty ship loaded with army brides from Europe. Somehow I hadn't been able to tell her about my encounter with Jesus Christ – it was the kind of thing I'd rather tell her when we were together.

The ship was at dockside when I arrived; there were guys hugging girls all over the place, and my heart was pounding as I searched for Sadie's blonde head in the crowd. There she was – suddenly everything seemed very different – marriage meant something more under God than when we decided to get hitched. I marvelled at the way God had held His hand over me all this time – even to the choosing of my wife before I had sense enough to ask His advice.

It was good to hold her hand in mine again; there seemed to be thousands of things to talk about . . . yet I was bursting to tell her the greatest news of all. That I was a new man. I wasn't the carefree, reckless, irresponsible guy she had married.

'Sadie,' I searched her face. 'Something wonderful has happened to me . . . I've met Jesus Christ, He's changed me, I'm a new man . . . things are going to be different now.'

She stared at me, her eyes puzzled. 'I fell in love with you the way you were, Merlin,' she said slowly. 'I don't want you to change.'

It was as if an invisible screen had gone up between us; my world had tumbled. Yet, hadn't I been where she was not so long ago? I'd rejected the Saviour too. 'Jesus,' I breathed it silently. 'Touch my wife.'

The next months were difficult. Sadie didn't like the idea of being a minister's wife at all. She kept saying that she would have to go back to England if I didn't get off my silly pre-occupation with religion.

Communications between us were nil, but I went ahead with my plans to enrol in school, praying that Jesus Christ would come into Sadie's life at the right time.

I enrolled in Marion College, Indiana, a church-related school, and I must have been the most excited student on campus. Sadie came along – bravely putting up with my exuberance.

A few months later we went home to Mother's on vacation. Mother was operating a rest home for elderly people, and a sweet old lady, the widow of a Free Methodist minister, had taken a special liking to Sadie.

One afternoon I returned home to find a tearful Sadie in the living-room.

'Oh, Merlin,' she sniffed happily. 'I understand what you

mean about being a Christian. I want us to be in Christ together.'

Together we knelt by the living-room couch.

'Thank you, Jesus,' we laughed and cried for joy.

After vacation we returned to Marion – both eager to get through school and into a full-time service for God.

To supplement our income from the GI bill, I worked six hours a day in a foundry. I wanted to get through school as fast as possible and got special permission to take twenty-one hours rather than the maximum seventeen hours allowed per semester.

I worked from 2 p.m. until 8 p.m., studied until 12 p.m., slept until 4 a.m., and then studied until 8 a.m. when it was time to go to school.

On Sunday I got my first chance to preach – in the local jail. I held on the bars and begged the men to give their lives to Christ. Every week prisoners knelt, holding on to the bars from the other side, and wept their way to faith in Christ.

I went back to school floating on a cloud.

Saturday nights were free, and I got a group of students together to hold outdoor services on the courthouse steps in the centre of Marion. To our delight people came forward to accept Christ. After the service we walked up and down the streets, urging anyone who would listen to let Jesus come into their lives.

I'd never been so busy; yet I felt as if I couldn't work hard enough for Jesus Christ. He'd saved my life; the least I could do was give Him my time.

I finished the four-year course in two-and-a-half years and enrolled at Asbury Seminary at Wilmore, Kentucky. God provided us with a Methodist circuit of four churches where I served as student pastor. Every week we drove the round trip of two hundred miles to serve our churches. For this each of them gave us five dollars a week and we were able to eat bountifully each weekend.

By squeezing everything I could into the schedule, I completed the three-year seminary in two years and at last we'd made it to our goal. I was a minister! I'd worked so long and so hard that I didn't quite know how to stop. But this was it; this was what God had called me to. We were sent to the Methodist church at Claypool, Indiana, for our first full-time assignment. I threw myself into the work with all the zeal I could muster, and slowly the three churches in the circuit began to grow. The offerings increased, the attendance grew, and my salary went up.

Young people accepted Christ in growing numbers, and our flock accepted and loved us and put up with the blunders of a young minister.

Still, I felt a growing restlessness within me. There was a void, an emptiness, almost a boredom. Increasingly my thoughts were drawn towards the Army chaplaincy. I knew the soldier, his thoughts, and his temptations. Did God want me to serve the men in uniform? I prayed about it. 'I'll go if You want me to go, Lord; I'll stay if You want me to stay . . .'

Gradually the pull towards the Army got stronger.

In 1953 I volunteered for the chaplaincy and was accepted. It couldn't have happened if I hadn't received that presidential pardon. God had known then.

After three months at chaplain's school, I was sent to join the airborne troopers at Ford Campbell, Kentucky.

At the first opportunity I boarded an aeroplane and heard the familiar words: 'Get ready; Stand up, Hook up, Stand in the door . . . GO!'

I felt the thrust of the wind and the shock as the parachute opened. It still felt like a ten-ton truck hitting you. I was back where I belonged!

3

The Search

It's exciting to be a chaplain, and it was excitement I'd been looking for. I went everywhere with the men. In the air, on the ground, climbing mountains, going on marches, undergoing physical conditioning. In the billets, offices, on the field, or in the mess hall – everywhere I had opportunities to tell men what God wanted to do for them.

I enjoyed every minute of the physical hardships. On jungle-expert training in Panama I lived in and lived off the fruits of the jungle with the men. The steaming jungle rapidly took its toll, and some men had to be carried out on stretchers. I learned how comfortable it can be to lie in a puddle of mud!

At Fort Campbell I had the opportunity to become a pilot, something I'd always wanted. With a friend I bought an old aeroplane held together mainly by chewing gum and rubber bands, it seemed. The plane had no radio equipment and we had to fly by sight or instinct. Once I got completely lost and suddenly found myself escorted by two army planes. They motioned for me to land, and I found I'd been flying over Fort Knox, Kentucky. The angry security police informed me I was lucky not to have been shot down.

Our plane came to an abrupt end when my partner crash-landed in a cornfield.

While stationed at Fort Bragg, North Carolina, I went with the 82nd Airborne Division to the Dominican Republic. This was a small police action, but thirty-nine paratroopers were lost.

Back at Fort Bragg I continued parachuting and finally received the coveted Army award of Master Parachutist.

From outward appearances all was well. My life was full and exciting and I was doing God's work. Maybe that was part of the problem. *I* was doing God's work. I didn't like to admit it, but I often became too tense when I talked to the men about God's love for them. Converting them was my business and I struggled hard.

I was always aware that I was falling woefully short of the perfection I longed for. Somehow it was always just beyond the horizon.

As a young boy I'd heard my mother and grandmother talk about the need for purity and holiness in living. They were Wesleyan and Free Methodists and spoke of the work of the Holy Spirit in the life of the Christian.

Whatever it was, I certainly lacked it. I read books about the deeper life of prayer, and went to camp meetings to hear others preach about the power of God.

I didn't see much of that power in my own life, and I desperately longed for it. I wanted to be used of God, and everywhere I looked were people in need. I just didn't have what it took to meet their needs.

A friend gave me a book about an eastern cult claiming to know the method of opening people's minds to the power of God. I learned to lie on a board with my feet elevated and to practise silent meditation.

I began to read everything I could find about psychic phenomena, hypnotism, and spiritism, hoping to find a clue to the secret of letting God's Spirit work in and through me.

About this time I went to Korea and there, in an accident, my glasses shattered into my right eye. Sixty per cent of the vision in that eye was gone. The cornea was scarred, and the doctors said vision would never return.

Now where was the power of God? Christ had walked the earth and healed the blind. He said that greater things even than He had done, those who followed after Him would do.

I went to Seoul twice for eye operations. The verdict was negative. I prayed. Everything in me rebelled against accepting a God of salvation, a God who is omnipotent creator, a God whose name I preach to men who face death on the battlefield, as a God without the power to heal. But where was the key? How was that power released through men? I had to know.

On my third flight to Seoul for a visit to the surgeon, I was sitting in the aeroplane when suddenly there was a strong sensation within me. It wasn't an audible voice, but something definitely communicated, saying: 'Your eyes are going to be all right.'

I knew God had spoken. He had spoken to me, just as clearly as He did that Sunday evening in the barn back in Pennsylvania.

The surgeon in Seoul shook his head and said: 'Sorry, Chaplain, there's nothing we can do for your eye.' Instead of feeling discouragement, I was elated. God had spoken; I trusted Him.

A few months later I had a sudden urge to go back to the doctor to check on my eye. After the examination he looked astonished. 'I don't understand,' he said. 'Your eye is perfectly well.'

God had done it! I was thrilled and more determined than ever to research every avenue of contact with His power.

I returned to the United States in 1963, went back to chaplain school for six months and was assigned to Fort Bragg, NC, in 1964.

Here I continued studying hypnosis with renewed vigour, and got involved in the Spiritual Frontiers movement led by Arthur Ford. I had heard that many ministers were drawn to this movement. In Arthur' Ford's home I saw firsthand evidence of the workings of a spirit world completely separate from our known rational world. I was fascinated.

But was it scriptural? There were pangs of nagging doubts in the back of my mind. The spirits were unquestionably real, but the Bible speaks of spirits other than God's Holy Spirit, and talks about spiritual wickedness in high places (Ephesians 6). The Bible calls these spirits our enemies, Satan's own forces, and warns us to test all spirits to be sure we aren't being manipulated by the enemy. Satan can cleverly counterfeit the work of the Holy Spirit.

I felt reasonably sure that I wasn't getting myself into a blind alley. These spirits, and the people I met in the movement, did, after all, speak very highly of Christ. They certainly recognised Him as the Son of God and a great spiritual leader who worked many miracles.

The goal for us, they taught, is to become like Christ in all things, since we are also sons of God.

I travelled many miles to talk with people who knew something about the subject, studied books on hypnotism, spoke to doctors, even wrote the Library of Congress. For here, I felt, was the avenue I, as mortal man, could use to help others.

I didn't know I was on dangerous ground, subtly, but surely I had begun to look at Jesus Christ as someone much like myself. Someone I could be like if I tried hard enough.

I had greatly underestimated the powers of the enemy. I didn't know it then, but hypnosis is potentially very dangerous spiritually, leaving the subject wide-open for impulses from the realm of Satan.

Oh yes, I was also falling into the trap of thinking of Satan as a bad character with horns from a realm of imagery. He certainly couldn't pose a threat to the sophisticated man of the twentieth century.

C.S. Lewis once said that Satan's cleverest trick is to convince the world that he doesn't exist.

My faith had become damaged and seriously undermined, although I didn't know it yet. The change was so subtle. Perhaps the fine line was crossed when I found myself talking about Jesus as teacher and miracle worker and failing to mention that He died on a Cross for us, that His Blood cleanses us from sin.

Satan quoted Scriptures even in Jesus' time. He still does, and really doesn't mind when we do. But he would like to see us forget about the Cross, the Blood, and the Resurrected Jesus.

Paul speaks about the secret of the Christian life in his letter to the Colossians, 1:27. The secret is Christ *in* us. Not that we become like Him, but that He lives in us and transforms us from within. Others may look at us and say we appear to be Christlike, but not because we have become more worthy or holy or spiritual or pure. He lives in us, that's the secret.

The subtle danger of the so-called 'Christian spiritualist movement', or 'Spiritual Frontiers movement', is that it would lead men to try to copy Christ and appropriate spiritual powers for themselves, and so commit the original sin of Satan, the fallen angel who wanted to be like God himself.

Without Christ as Saviour, without the Cross, there would be no plan of salvation, no possible way to be forgiven of sin. In fact, there would be no gospel.

I was falling into the trap. My motives were pure; I honestly wanted power to help others overcome their problems and their sicknesses of body and mind.

It took an act of God to open my eyes to the error of my ways.

4

Be Filled

For some time I'd been going to a small weekly prayer group near Fort Bragg. One evening, Ruth, a member of the group, was visibly moved during a prayer session. I'd watched her during several meetings and often thought I'd like to ask her how she had come to experience such obvious joy in her life. Unlike some of the rest of us, she seemed to be filled continuously with a joy I certainly had felt only on rare occasions in my life.

This particular evening Ruth confided in me: 'I was so blessed I almost prayed out loud in tongues!'

'You almost what?' I was horrified.

'Prayed in tongues,' Ruth said brightly.

I lowered my voice and looked around to see if we were being watched. 'Ruth, you could have ruined our group! Whatever has come over you?'

Ruth laughed heartily. 'I've been praying in tongues ever since I received the Baptism in the Holy Spirit.'

'What is that?' I'd never heard the term before.

Ruth patiently explained that it was the same experience that the disciples had at Pentecost. 'I experienced my own Pentecost,' she smiled with unmistakable radiance.

'I thought you were Baptist.' I felt shaken.

'I am, but God is moving in all denominations.'

I had heard rumours of a wave of emotionalism invading the churches, people were getting off on fads and losing faith in Christ. I'd heard some tales about Pentecostals being 'drunk in the spirit', whatever that meant, and having wild orgies. I knew Ruth needed help badly.

I put my hand on her arm. 'Be careful, Ruth,' I said earnestly. 'You're playing with dangerous stuff. I'll be praying for you, and if you need help, call me.'

Ruth smiled and patted my hand. 'Thank you, Merlin. I appreciate your concern.'

Some time later she called me.

'Merlin, a group called Camp Farthest Out is having a retreat at Morehead City; we'd like for you to go.' It sounded like something I'd better stay away from. I tactfully replied that I would go if I could, which meant that I wouldn't be able to.

Within the next week several others called. A businessman to remind me that I would need my golf clubs, a lady from Raleigh to tell me that she had arranged for all my expenses to be paid if I'd go. Someone else called to say I could bring another minister free of charge. This was too much. How could I resist all this genuine interest in my spiritual wellbeing. I said thank you, I'll go.

I got in touch with a Presbyterian minister friend and invited him to come along. He hedged.

'It's an all-expenses-paid trip at a resort hotel!'

'I'll go.'

On the way Dick said: 'Merlin, why are we going to this thing?'

'I don't know,' I said. 'But it's for free, so let's enjoy it.'

In the hotel lobby we were greeted with such warm enthusiasm from people we'd never seen that I was beginning to wonder what kind of strange beings we had fallen amongst.

The services were unlike anything we'd ever attended before.

People sang with uninhibited joy, clapped their hands, and actually raised their arms while they were singing.

Both Dick and I felt very much out of place, but agreed there was a joy here that we could learn something from.

One very cultured and refined-looking lady kept coming up to us and saying: 'Has anything happened yet?'

'No, ma'am, what do you mean?' we'd answer.

'You'll see, you'll see,' she always said.

Ruth and some of the others who had invited us urged me to have a private talk with a certain lady who they said had unusual power.

They took us to meet her, and I instantly disliked her. She quoted Scripture in a way that made me feel as if she was trying to convert me. I didn't like to have Scripture quoted to me, and especially not by a woman.

Still, our friends insisted that we have a talk with her, and since they'd paid our way there, I felt we ought to oblige.

We sat patiently as she told us what God had done in her life and in the lives of others that she knew. She made numerous references to the 'Baptism in the Holy Spirit', and went through the Scriptures to show that the experience had been a common one for Christians in the first century.

'The Holy Spirit is still doing the same thing in many people's lives today,' she said. 'Jesus Christ still baptises those who believe in Him, just as He did at Pentecost.'

I felt a twinge of excitement. Could it be that I could experience my own Pentecost? Could I see tongues of fire, hear the rush of wind, and speak in an unknown tongue?

She had finished talking and sat looking at us.

'I'd like to pray for you,' she said softly. 'That you might receive the Baptism in the Holy Spirit.'

Without hesitating I said, 'Yes.'

She placed her hands on my head and began to pray softly. I waited for 'it' to hit me. Nothing happened. I didn't feel a thing.

She went on and placed her hands on Dick's head. When she had finished praying I looked at him and he looked at me. I could tell he hadn't felt anything either. This whole thing was a fake.

The lady looked at us both with a hint of a smile.

'You haven't felt anything yet, have you?'

We shook our heads. 'No, ma'am.'

'I'm going to pray for you in a language you will not understand. As I pray you will receive a new language of your own.'

Again she placed her hands on my head. I felt nothing, saw nothing, heard nothing. When she was through praying, she asked if I could hear or sense any words within me that I didn't understand. I thought for a minute and realised that there were in my mind words that didn't mean anything to me. I felt certain that these strange words were strictly a product of my own imagination, and I told her so.

'If you said them out loud, would you feel as if you were being made a fool of?' she asked.

'I certainly would.'

'Would you be willing to be a fool for Christ's sake?' This put the whole situation in a different perspective. Of course I'd do anything for Christ, but speaking out loud such utter nonsense could mean disaster for my future. I could imagine all those people going around telling everyone that a Methodist chaplain had been praying in an unknown tongue. I might even have to leave the Army! Still, what if this was what Christ wanted me to do? Suddenly even my Army career seemed less important. Haltingly I began to speak out loud the words that were forming in my mind.

Still I *felt* nothing different. I did believe that Jesus Christ had given me a new tongue as a sign that He had baptised me in the Holy Spirit, yet the disciples at Pentecost had acted like drunk men. Obviously they had been overwhelmed by some feeling.

I watched Dick; his experience seemed to be the same as mine. He spoke words of an unknown language and believed in the validity of it, yet displayed no emotional reaction.

'Your experience is based on faith in a fact, not on feeling,' said the lady, apparently reading our minds.

I sat in deep thought – I didn't *feel* any different, but *was* I different? I looked up; an amazing realisation had just hit me.

'I *know* that Jesus Christ is alive!' I said. 'I don't just believe, I KNOW!'

Why, of course! The Holy Spirit brings witness of Jesus Christ, says the Bible. Now I knew that to be a fact. That was the source of the new authority of the disciples after Pentecost. They didn't remember a man who had lived and died and risen again. They *knew* Him in the present tense because He had filled them with His Holy Spirit whose primary purpose is to witness to Jesus Christ!

In a flash I understood the horror of what I'd been guilty of for the last several years. Not only I, but scores of so-called Christians in pulpits and in pews who dilute the message of the Cross and the central position of Christ.

Even as I saw the magnitude of my sin, I also saw Jesus Christ in all His splendour as my redeemer. I saw Him for what I'd always known deep in my heart that He was. All my recent nagging doubts were swept away by a wave of joyous certainty. It was glorious! Never again could I doubt that Jesus Christ was who He said He was. Never again could I commit the folly of thinking that He had been a mere man, a good man, an example for us to follow.

What a marvellous truth; Jesus Christ living in us, His power operating through us, He is the vine, His life pulsates through our beings.

We are nothing apart from Him, can do nothing in our own power.

'Thank you, Jesus!' I stood up, and as I reached my full height, something hit me! I was suddenly filled and overflowing with a feeling of warmth and love for everybody in the room.

It must have hit Dick at the same time. I saw the tears well up in his eyes, and without a word we reached out and gave each other a bear hug, laughing and crying at the same time.

I looked at the dear lady I had resented so fiercely just a short while ago, and realised that I loved her. She was my sister in Christ!

We went downstairs for lunch and I felt an overwhelming love for everyone I saw. I had never known anything like it before.

That evening Dick and I began to pray in one of the rooms. People came in to join us and soon the room was full. As we prayed, others were filled with the Holy Spirit. The hotel rang with shouts of joy as people experienced the fullness of Christ's presence.

At 2 a.m. Dick and I tried to go to sleep. It was no use, we were too excited.

I said: 'Dick, let's get up and pray some more.' We prayed for another two hours for everyone we knew and then praised God for His goodness to us.

5

By His Power Within You

I returned to Fort Bragg anxious to share with everyone the wonderful thing that had happened to me. I had once wondered how an experience like this would affect my ministry. How well I remembered my own reaction to the 'Pentecostal emotionalism' in the church.

Now I knew that whatever the reaction, I would not be able to keep from sharing what I had experienced.

The first day I went to our headquarters company orderly room. The first sergeant was sitting behind his desk. He was big and rough and well known for his gruff manners.

'First Sergeant,' I said, 'did I ever tell you that Jesus loves you?'

To my amazement the tears began to roll down his cheeks. He said: 'No, Chaplain, you never told me anything like that.'

I felt my face flush hot with shame. For over a year I had seen him several times a day and I had never told him anything about Jesus.

I walked into the hallway and met the supply sergeant.

'Sergeant, did I ever tell you that Jesus loves you and I love you too?'

'No, Sir, you never told me anything like that.'

Again I felt ashamed, and he said: 'Sir, do you have a minute to talk?' We went to my office and he poured out a host of problems I had never known he had. When he was through I asked if he would like to accept Christ as his Saviour. He said he would, and knelt with tears streaming down his face.

Everywhere I went, men accepted Christ. It seemed as if there was a power in me that was doing the talking for me. When I started to speak to someone, I had no idea what I was going to say, but whatever came had a new power that drew men to Christ.

It was easy to serve God this way. The old tension was gone and I could laugh. Preaching was no longer something to labour over. It became pure joy just to let His thoughts pour through me.

All Army personnel must attend a character-guidance class once a month. Teaching this class as chaplains, we are not allowed to preach. As carefully as I could, I one day told the class that the God of our country is still alive and daily answers prayers. After the class a private came up to me, and with his nose six inches from mine, rather insolently said: 'You really believe all that stuff, don't you?'

'Yes, I do,' I said.

'Do you mean that if you prayed now, God would answer?'

'Yes,' I said, 'I know He will.'

'Do you think it is wrong to smoke?'

The question was an unexpected one. 'For some it may be wrong, for others right,' I said evasively.

'I've been smoking since I was fourteen,' the private said. 'Now I smoke three packs a day and the doctor told me this morning that if I don't stop it will kill me.'

I said: 'There's no question about it; for you it is wrong to smoke.'

'Then you ask your God to make me quit!'

How could I pray like that? The obvious pat answers were swirling through my head: God helps those who help themselves, he could pray that God would help him want to quit. But that wasn't what he'd asked me.

'God,' I prayed silently, 'help me know what to do.'

Immediately I felt a strong impression: 'Pray in your new language!'

'Out loud?'

'No, just silently.'

I began to pray in the language I had received at the retreat. Then I paused.

There came another impression: 'Put your hand on his shoulder and pray.'

I obediently put my hand on his shoulder. 'Pray what?'

'Silently pray in your new language.' I did. Then came the impression again: 'Translate it into English.'

Without thinking, I opened my mouth and out came the words: 'God, don't let him smoke again as long as he lives.'

What a prayer! If the man ever smoked again he'd be convinced that God didn't answer prayer. I felt utterly confused, and just turned on my heels and left.

In the days that followed, I asked God repeatedly if I had misunderstood. Would my mistake make that man disbelieve? Again and again came the impression: 'Just trust me.'

Trusting God apparently meant going out on a limb without anything to hold on to but faith. With new eagerness I dove into an intensive study of God's Word. If I was going to operate on faith, it would have to be faith in the integrity and very nature of God. I had to *know* Him, and I found that the more I read, the stronger I believed. Bible reading had never been this exciting before. From the pages rose a new knowledge of God the omnipotent who promised that we could do all things in Christ. Who says that the power within us is the same power that raised Christ from the dead!

In Ephesians 3:20–21 Paul wrote: 'Now to him who by his power within us is able to do infinitely more than we ever dare to ask or imagine – to him be glory in the Church and in Christ Jesus for ever and ever, amen!' (J. B. Phillips translation)

Carefully, I studied Paul's instructions to the church at Corinth. He lists the various ways the Holy Spirit was known to operate through men: there were speaking in tongues, interpretation of tongues, healing, miracles, prophesying, preaching, wisdom, knowledge, faith, discernment.

How could I know what 'gifts' God wanted to express through me? Had He given me any special gifts?

Again the verse from Ephesians came back to me: '*He* who by *His* power within us.' No, I didn't have any gifts. All I could do was to be willing to let God operate through me.

In other words, my job was strictly that of being obedient to the impressions or urgings I felt within me. It said that He could do far more than we dare ask or imagine. Obviously, there was no way I could anticipate or know what God wanted to do.

One evening in our prayer group, I talked about God's power to heal our bodies. One lady spoke up. 'Why don't you ask God to heal one of us then?'

I felt a bit shaky. Of course I knew God could and would hear prayer for the sick. But would he hear and answer me?

'Okay,' I said, with a sudden release of faith. 'Who wants to be prayed for?'

'I do,' said the same lady. 'One of my eyes had been weeping tears for several months. Medication hasn't helped. Please pray about it.'

I held my breath, placed my hands on her head, and prayed, mustering all my faith to believe that God was healing her right then. When I was through, her eye was still weeping. Had I done something wrong? Again came the prompting within. 'Trust me.' All right, faith means believing something you don't see. All the stories I'd read in the Bible had made it very plain; the difference between victory and defeat was always a matter of faith. God couldn't do a thing when the Israelites refused to believe. The promises in the Bible are plentiful to those who will only believe.

'Thank you, Lord,' I said out loud, 'for hearing our prayer.'

That night the lady called me. 'Chaplain, guess what happened?' Her voice was bubbling with excitement.

'Tell me!'

'I was sitting here reading when I suddenly realised that something had happened to my eye. It is completely healed!'

I was thrilled. 'Thank you Lord,' I said. 'I get your point. I'll do the trusting; You'll do the rest.'

A local Presbyterian minister who had been filled with the Holy Spirit had been reluctant to tell his congregation. He invited a member of our prayer group to give her testimony during a Sunday evening service, and several of us in the group came along to be in prayer.

As she told how she, a Southern Baptist, had been baptised in the Holy Spirit, there was dead silence in the church. It was evident that God was speaking to the people. At the close of the service the pastor called on me to pronounce the benediction. I stood up, but instead of giving the benediction, I began to speak the very first words that came into my mind: 'Everyone who wants to come to the altar and surrender his life to God, please come forward.'

Dead silence! There had never been an altar call in the history of that church. Then one by one, people began to come forward, falling on their knees.

I walked over to the first one. I didn't know what to pray. I didn't know why he had come forward. I bowed my head. Within me I prayed silently: 'Show me how to pray, God.' I heard 'Pray in the Spirit.' I silently prayed in my new language.

'Now begin to translate what you have said.'

'Lord, forgive this man for his drunkenness, his dishonesty in business.' I was shocked at my own words. What if I had misunderstood? I could really mess things up for my minister friend.

I walked over to the next person and followed the same procedure. 'Lord forgive this man for his vile temper, his ugly disposition, and his selfish treatment of his family.'

I went from one to another, and with my hands on the person's head prayed as I was prompted to pray, prayers of repentance and confession.

By the time I was through I knew I had really crawled way out on a limb in complete trust.

After the benediction the people came to me one by one. With tears of joy they said: 'You prayed for exactly what I needed, but how did you know my problem?'

Days later the minister told me that the congregation had been revolutionised. Many of the people who had come forward that night were elders and officers in the church. Now the entire congregation was overflowing with enthusiasm, zeal, and joy.

I felt like shouting. I hadn't known the problems that beset the men and women of that church, but God had. He knows the heart and mind of all of us, and can speak through us in a power that will directly minister to the exact needs of every individual. If people respond, it isn't our doing, but His. If they refuse, again we do not get blamed for a failure.

Every day and wherever I went it was the same. People responding to Jesus Christ. Whenever I fell back into the habit of trying to think beforehand what I would say to someone, the results were immediate. I became tense; the power and presence of God simply didn't flow. The principle of letting go and letting God was valid. All I had to do was relax in the presence of God, letting my mind go blank and opening my mouth in faith to speak whatever God impressed on me. Always the words spoke directly to a need, always the person was wonderfully helped.

I marvelled. I'd been a pastor for many years and worked hard at it, yet I'd never seen so much happen in the lives of so many in the short time since Jesus Christ invaded my being in the fullness of his Spirit.

Without the pressures of having to preplan and organise and research and write sermon notes, I found that I had much more time to spend in Bible reading and prayer. It seemed as if I suddenly had more energy than ever before, and I never had the frustrating experience of wasting time on projects that turned out to be ineffective.

As long as I rested in Christ, it seemed that God took my days, and every detail, every appointment, every happening began to fall into place in a perfect whole. No longer did I experience confusion and conflicts of appointment or schedules.

My only regret was that I wished I'd discovered this experience of yielding myself fully to God many years before.

About this time, Oral Roberts came to Fayetteville. A huge tent was set up, and night after night thousands came to hear him preach and pray for the sick. I wanted to meet him personally so I found out what local minister would be in charge of the service. I went to see him and volunteered to do anything I could to help.

He was amazed that a Methodist chaplain would want to be involved. He'd never been able to get anyone but Pentecostal ministers to assist before.

From the opening night, I was on the platform in uniform. I was there next to Oral Roberts as he prayed for the sick, and I saw physical changes take place as bodies were healed! What a tremendous joy!

My chaplain friends began to hint that if I continued appearing in such places and being associated with men like Oral Roberts, I might as well forget about ever 'getting any-place' in the Army chaplaincy. They were probably right, but I'd rather be obedient to God and see His power clearly demonstrated than be seeking the temporal approval of men.

The next week I was casually leafing through a list of

chaplains who had been selected for promotion to lieutenant colonel. I hadn't been a major long enough to be considered, but there, on the list, was my name! Later I found that the Army has the authority to promote five per cent of its officers before they are eligible under the ordinary rules.

All I could think was, 'Thank you Lord for showing me that I can trust You to look after all my needs.'

Obedience sometimes meant going against the expressed wishes of the people who came to ask for help.

A young Army lieutenant brought his wife to see me. 'She would like a prayer for the Baptism in the Holy Spirit,' he said.

I had a most unusual feeling within. I just knew that this girl had already received this experience. She hadn't said a word since they entered my office; yet I knew this was so.

I said: 'You have already received the Baptism, you don't need to be prayed for again.'

'How do you know that?' she looked surprised. 'I've tried to believe ever since I was prayed for.'

'I know because the Holy Spirit tells me,' I said. 'He also says that before you stand up you will receive the evidence of speaking in a new tongue.'

This was really way-out, I thought. What if nothing happened? Her faith would surely be shaken. Yet within I felt a certainty. I invited both of them to join me in a prayer of thanksgiving for what God had already done.

Before I finished, I could hear her softly praying in her new language. She was so filled with joy that she nearly floated out of the office.

One day a young private showed up in my office. I remembered the prayer I'd prayed for him: 'God don't let him ever smoke again.' He was beaming all over his face.

'Sir,' he burst out, 'you'll never believe what happened to me after you left.'

I'd seen enough amazing happenings in the last month to believe anything.

'Yes, I'll believe,' I said. 'Tell me.'

'When you turned and left, I laughed and thought, *This will be easy. All I have to do is smoke, and I'll prove that God doesn't answer prayer.* I went into the latrine and lit up a cigarette, took a big drag, and immediately started to vomit. I figured that was a coincidence, probably something I ate, and later that afternoon I tried smoking again. The same thing happened. For the next three days, every time I tried to smoke I vomited. Now, if I just think about smoking I feel like vomiting.'

I was overjoyed. Jesus Christ promised that the Holy Spirit would be with us to guide us into all truth. I hadn't misunderstood His instructions.

A few days later the private came back.

'Sir, would you pray one more prayer for me?'

'I surely will!'

'Please pray that God will forgive my sins and help me to accept Christ as my Saviour.'

Within minutes we were on our knees together and he joyfully accepted Christ.

Months later I told about this incident in the First Baptist Church of Columbus, Georgia. After the service a man came up to me and said: 'I was in *Admin* company of the 82nd Airborne Division when that happened. That man was going all over the company telling about the chaplain who had fixed him so he couldn't smoke!'

What a wonderful truth! Not only does God save, He means business when He says He can remould us and make us into His image. He can literally take away our old habits and hang-ups and impure thoughts and renew us from within!

I had received the Baptism in the Holy Spirit only a couple of months ago, yet it seemed I'd already lived a lifetime in this new dimension.

Now I was in for an encounter with the enemy in force. I was suddenly the victim of an unusual affliction. All my life

I'd been strong as a horse and in top physical condition. Now every time I exerted myself in the least, my heart began to beat rapidly. I was weak and ached all over. Reluctantly I went to bed for a week. My condition didn't improve at all. I went to the hospital to see what the medical verdict would be, and they immediately slapped me on a stretcher and hustled me off to bed. Test after test gave no clue to what ailed me. I felt wretched, weak, and in pain, and it seemed to get worse instead of better. At this rate I'd just as soon be dead; all my energies seemed depleted, and the outlook was indeed bleak.

Then suddenly one night when I wondered if the end might be near, there was the strong impression: 'Do you still trust me?'

'Yes, Lord.' I whispered it into the darkened room.

A quiet peace began to move through me, and I fell into a deep sleep.

The next morning I felt much better. The doctors insisted I stay in bed for a while, and I was grateful for days of prayer, praise, and study.

One day I was reading one of Glenn Clark's books, and I suddenly felt the voice within me ask: 'Will you now live like Jesus?'

I could only answer: 'Yes, Lord.'

'But what about your thoughts and desires, are they pure?'

'No, Lord.'

'Do you want them to be?'

'Oh, yes Lord. All my life I've struggled to overcome impure thoughts and desires.'

'Will you give me all your impure thoughts?'

'Yes, Lord.'

'Forever?'

'Oh yes, Lord. Forever.'

Suddenly it was as if a heaviness had been lifted from me, as if a mist had parted and everything looked clean and pure. The door to the ward opened and a young nurse walked through. I followed her with my eyes. She was a beautiful young nurse, and all I could think was: 'What a beautiful child of God!' There was not even a fleeting thought of temptation!

Back home from the hospital, I went to our prayer group and felt a strong impression to ask them to pray for me. I had always been the one to pray for others. Now I sat in the chair in the centre of the group and they prepared to pray for me. 'What do you want us to ask God to do?'

I thought for a moment. 'Ask God to use me more than ever,' I said. They began to pray, and I suddenly saw in the Spirit, Jesus kneeling before me. He was holding my feet and rested His head on my knees. He said: 'I don't want to use you. I want you to use Me!'

It was as if a door had opened into a new understanding of Jesus. He wants to give Himself for us each moment of our lives just as completely as He gave Himself on the cross. We have nothing to give Him; we have only to receive of Him!

6

Vietnam

In 1966 I received orders to go to Vietnam with the 80th General Support Group, then stationed at Fort Bragg.

We boarded ship in San Francisco, and as we left the bay moving out to sea, I stood at the railing feeling the peace of God within and around me. This was His will for me, I knew.

On board I immediately started a prayer group, a Bible study, and regular worship services. We spent twenty-one days at sea and each day several men accepted Christ.

The devil would frequently whisper in my ear that they were just doing it because they were going to Vietnam and their decisions weren't really honest.

Months later I had proof of how much of a liar the devil is. Many of the men who made decisions for Christ were with a unit that left us as soon as we reached Vietnam. One day I walked into their unit and one of the sergeants saw me. I almost exploded with joy. 'Praise the Lord, Chaplain Carothers.'

He told me of all the things God had been doing. Together we went to see others in the unit who had accepted Christ aboard ship, and they told me about the Bible classes they were holding and of the men they had led to Christ.

'Do you remember Lieutenant Stover?' they asked.

'Yes, I do.' I remembered the afternoon he stood on deck

and told me how he had been running from God all through college. He had given his life back to Christ right there and told me that as soon as he got out of the Army he would answer the call to a full-time ministry.

'He has started a tremendous choir and the men really enjoy singing with him.'

They took me to meet the lieutenant and we had a joyful reunion.

As soon as I arrived in Cam Rahn Bay I organised a Saturday night prayer group. Soon there were twenty-five men meeting each week. I began by challenging them to believe that God would answer our prayers if we would just believe Him.

For several weeks I asked for specific prayer requests. Finally one evening a warrant officer spoke up:

'Well, sir, I sure would be pleased for you to pray for my wife. We have been married for six years and she is so against religion that she won't even let us have prayer at the table. I don't think it will do much good to pray for her, but I'd be glad for you to try.'

I thought this was an unusual request to start with, but I was learning that God knows His business. I asked the men to hold hands in a circle, and we began praying for our first miracle.

None of the men had ever tried believing for a miracle, but they were willing to try. I had been sharing with them all the wonderful things God had been doing in my life since I received the Baptism in the Holy Spirit.

Near the battlefront in Vietnam they were far from the distractions at home and ready to start grasping the deeper things of the Spirit.

Two weeks later the warrant officer came to the prayer group with a letter in his hand. Tears flowed down his face as he read the letter to us:

Darling, you will probably find it difficult to believe what has been happening here at home. One week ago I was standing at our kitchen sink on a Saturday morning. I began to have a most unusual experience. A big white sign began flashing through my mind. On it in big black letters was the word 'REVIVAL'. I couldn't get it out of my mind. No matter what I tried to think about, the sign stayed in front of me all morning long. By noon I was really upset. I called your sister and asked her if there was a big revival sign some place in town. I thought I might have seen it some place. She said there was no such sign, but they were having revival at their church. 'Would you like to come?' she asked me.

I said, 'You know I never go to such things.' But the sign stayed with me and by evening it was so strong that I called your sister and asked if I could go with her. During the service an invitation was given and I went forward. I've waited a week to write you about this for I wanted to be sure that I really was giving my life to Christ. But darling, it is true! I was baptised today and am thrilled. I can't wait for you to come home so we can have a real Christian home.

'Chaplain,' said the officer, 'do you know what time it was here when it was Saturday morning at home?'

I shook my head.

'Saturday night when we prayed for her. That's when she began to see the sign. And do you remember Sunday morning?'

'Yes, I remember.' He had come forward when the invitation had been given at the close of the morning worship service. I had said that I thought he already was a Christian and he answered: 'Yes, I am, sir, but I was standing back there and got the strongest feeling that if I came forward it would somehow help my wife.'

Now he looked at me, tears flowing freely. 'Chaplain, do you realise what time that was back home?'

Then it dawned on me. It had been Saturday night. The

night his wife accepted Christ. An electric thrill went through our prayer group. Tears rolled down many cheeks. The men were learning for themselves that God does answer prayer.

Sitting next to the warrant officer was a Negro sergeant. I could see that he was deeply troubled. 'What's wrong?' I asked.

'Sir, my wife is like this, she won't accept any kind of religion in our home. I've been realising that if I had just a little faith two weeks ago we could have prayed for my wife too, and maybe the same thing would have happened to her.'

What a coincidence! Far away in Vietnam were two soldiers with the same unusual problem. 'Let's pray for your wife right now,' I said with enthusiasm.

'Sir, I believe I missed my chance. I just don't have faith to pray now.'

'You don't need to depend on your faith alone,' I said. 'Just believe in our prayers, and we will have faith for you.'

We joined hands and began to pray. There was a new fervour among the men. They had begun to see for themselves that God hears and God answers.

The next morning I was in my office when the sergeant came bouncing in with a letter in his hand and a big smile.

'Don't tell me you got an answer already,' I said jokingly.

'I sure did!'

He was nearly in orbit and suddenly the words flashed into my mind: 'Before they call I will answer.' Could it be?

'What does the letter say?'

It was nearly a duplication of the one we had heard the night before. The sergeant's wife too had been saved, baptised, and was already teaching a Sunday School class.

'Oh, God,' I breathed, 'I love you, I love you, I love you!'

One Saturday night a new officer came to our meeting. He was obviously not in sympathy with our approach to prayer.

'Chaplain, if God is actually answering prayer, why doesn't He do something important?'

'What would you consider important?' I asked quietly.

'From the first day our little son was able to stand up he would look at his feet and cry out in pain. We have taken him to every doctor and specialist in the area. We have had special shoes, casts, braces, wrappings, and nothing helps. He is seven years old now and every night my wife has to put his feet on a pillow and rub them before he can go to sleep. Why doesn't God do something for him?'

Under my breath I asked God to show me how to pray; then I said: 'We will pray and God will heal him!' I felt very certain. 'You don't believe, but we do, and God will heal him. Join the circle with us and let's pray.'

The men prayed with renewed hunger to see God move. Here was a third request for someone back home. I knew God had sent it.

Two weeks later another letter arrived:

Dear:

I've waited for a week to tell you about something that is almost too good to be true. One week ago I noticed that for the first time in his life, Paul didn't mention his feet once during the day. He went to sleep that night without a pillow under his feet. I wanted to write to you right away, but was afraid of raising your hopes. The next day it was the same. It's been a whole week now, and he hasn't complained about his feet hurting!

'Chaplain, it's hard for me to believe,' said the officer struggling to hold back the tears. 'But the day my boy's feet stopped hurting is the day we prayed for him!'

For months afterwards, every time I saw this officer, he would raise his arms and say, 'His feet don't hurt yet!'

From then on our men began to grow in faith. More and more prayers were answered. Other men came to our group to hear about the amazing things that were going on. I began to read letters and reports of answered prayers from the pulpit

Sunday morning and daily men would wave to me and yell, 'Any new miracles, Chaplain?'

Often I called back: 'The greatest miracle of all; another man has accepted Christ and received eternal life!'

As the Spirit of the Lord moved among us, many men were drawn to Christ.

On a Sunday morning I had given an invitation to accept Christ and many had come forward to pray. After the service I went into my office to spend a few minutes alone with the Lord. I was preparing to leave when a sergeant suddenly burst through the doorway and fell on his knees in the middle of the floor.

'Please, pray for me,' he cried in obvious anguish.

He then began to confess sins of immorality, addiction to alcohol and drugs, neglect of his children and wife. One after another they poured out of him with tears of repentance. When he was through, I told him how God loved him and had sent Jesus Christ to die on the cross for every one of the sins he had confessed. 'All you have to do is accept Christ as your Saviour and God will give you eternal life and complete pardon,' I said.

'I do, I do,' he sobbed, and a smile of peace and joy flooded his face as he began to thank and praise God.

Later he told me what had brought him running to my office. Earlier that morning he had walked by the chapel on his way to the post exchange. Suddenly he felt an urge to step inside. 'This is crazy,' he thought, 'I haven't been inside a church for six years; I don't have any reason to go now.' He went on to the PX, but something kept pulling him back. Finally he decided to go to the chapel where the service was just then getting under way. He sat through it all and when the congregation stood up to sing the last hymn he realised he was shaking so badly that he couldn't stand without holding on to the chair in front of him.

He was afraid that at any moment he would fall to the

floor, and he felt a powerful urge to walk to the front and give his life to God.

'I just can't,' he told himself and began to leave the chapel. Outside in the street his legs began to give way and he knew that he wouldn't be able to stand up much longer. A voice inside told him that now was the time. He must obey God or else God would let him die. Without waiting any longer he turned and ran back to the chapel and burst through my doorway.

One of our chaplains was a Southern Baptist. We were good friends and he loved the Lord, but he was scared to death of my emphasis on the Holy Spirit. The ideas of faith healing, casting out of demons and evil spirits, being filled with the Holy Spirit, and experiencing the gifts of the Spirit were completely strange to him. He came to one of our prayer groups and then asked to be excused from ever attending another.

He was particularly worried about the way one of us would sit in a chair in the middle of a circle while others would place their hands on him and pray that God would meet his particular needs. He had never seen this done before, and it seemed like something unchristian to him.

Through the men who kept coming to the group, he heard of things happening. Men who were discouraged, defeated, and ready to give up would ask to be prayed for. They told him of how they had experienced total release from their burdens. After sitting in the chair and having others pray for them with the laying on of hands, they had been filled with a peace and joy that stayed with them. They told how Christ had become more real to them from that moment on.

Little by little, these things were affecting the chaplain. He began to realise that God works in many ways, even in ways much different from what he had seen and experienced before. Then something unexpected happened.

A chaplain in another front line unit was killed. My friend

was called to take his place immediately. He felt naturally a little apprehensive and came to my office to say good-bye. Haltingly, he confessed that the ministry through our prayer group had come to mean a great deal to him. Then he knelt on the floor with tears flowing. He took my hands and placed them on his head.

'Merlin, please pray for me the way you pray.'

Quietly I began to pray for him in tongues, and as I prayed he began to be filled with joy and peace. Laughing through tears he told me how all his fears were gone. He was ready to go into the battle lines.

A few weeks later he called me to say that he had been nearly killed in a helicopter accident the first day he arrived in his unit.

'Even then I could only feel an overflowing love and trust in Jesus Christ,' he said.

My unit moved north to Chu Lai and joined the Americal Division. We were now in the very thick of the battle along with the Marines. More and more I saw evidences of God's power protecting His children. When we trust Him, no power on earth can touch us unless it is God's will.

On several occasions when I was scheduled to go to certain places I felt a last-minute urge to change my plans. Later I found that each time I obeyed such an urge, I had avoided an incident that could have got me killed.

Once I was scheduled to hold a service on a beach for men who were unloading five-hundred-pound bombs. At the last minute I was strongly impressed to cancel the service. At the exact time and place where we would have met, an explosion set off the bombs. If we had gathered there, many of the men would have been killed.

An old friend, Chaplain Burton Hatch, was division chaplain of the Americal Division. He invited me to hold a Sunday evening service, and at the close of the service several men came forward to accept Christ. I prayed with each one of them.

The next morning one of the men came back to the chapel. He looked a mess, with clothes dripping wet and dirty and hair plastered down his forehead. But his face shone and he kept saying: 'Praise the Lord; thank you Jesus!'

Early that morning he and five others had been fully equipped with a combat assault load: hand grenades, bandoliers of bullets around their necks, and heavy flack vests. They boarded the helicopter and headed north along the coast and over the China Sea. The pilot was flying too close to the water, and a sudden large wave hit the skid of the chopper. With a mighty jerk, the helicopter tipped over and dived straight into the sea. Men were thrown in all directions.

The young soldier suddenly realised that he was under water and going down, fast. He tried to swim towards the surface and managed to get a breath of air before going under again, weighted down by the heavy equipment. He tried desperately to free himself, but couldn't. As he began to sink, he told me, he suddenly remembered that he had accepted Christ the evening before. He was ready to die and suddenly was filled with a great peace of heart and mind. It really didn't matter if he couldn't free himself from the heavy gear. Once more he came to the surface and again he sank under. The third time he came up, he realised that his strength was gone and he would soon be with his Lord. At that very moment he felt the equipment slide from around him! He came to the surface and was free. He began to swim to shore and there he found that he was the only survivor.

After several months at Chu Lai I was transferred south to Quin Yhan to serve with the 85th Evacuation Hospital. Men who had been wounded only a few hours before were brought to us. Over and over I saw the power of God working. These men were ready to accept Christ. Man after man told me how he had been saved from death by a power beyond his understanding.

'What was it?' I asked.

'I can't explain it,' they would say. 'All of a sudden, when I knew I was going to die, I became aware of a great power surrounding me. I was then sure I was safe. I knew it was God, and that He didn't want me to die.'

Often the men asked me why God had chosen to save them. I told them that He had some special purpose for their lives and He would reveal it as they listened to his voice.

I went from bed to bed talking to the boys and was often overcome with emotion. They were torn, bleeding, and in some cases, dying. But I never heard anyone complain. They were confident that the job they had been doing was important, and that for some reason they were saved from death. I saw nurses turn away in tears as they saw the strength and courage of these men. No matter how great the pain, they would grin and say 'I'm fine.'

One night a nurse called me to the hospital to see an Army major. When he saw me he began to weep. He was covered in bandages, and for ten minutes I stood there while he tried to stop the flow of tears. I wondered what the problem was. Had he been told that his legs would have to be amputated? They were covered by heavy bandages and looked as if they were badly hurt.

Perhaps he had received word that someone at home was seriously ill.

Finally the major gained control of himself and began to tell me an amazing story.

Just a few hours earlier he had been a passenger on a helicopter. They had been hit by ground fire and crashed into the thick jungle. Six men had been scattered over the side of a mountain. When the major came to, he realised he was injured too seriously to move. He could hear the cries of other men who were also unable to move. In the distance he could hear rifle shots. The Viet Cong were converging on the position where they had seen the aircraft go down. They were moving in to capture the Americans.

The major suddenly realised he had reached the end. The VC would not attempt to carry out the wounded Americans. They would probably practise the cruel sport of torturing them to death.

He tried to pray, but realised he didn't know how. He had attended church all his life, but he'd never really talked to God. But all at once he 'felt' someone say: 'Just ask and believe!'

With a burst of anguish, and in new faith he cried:

'Oh, God, please help me!' He realised that for the first time in his life he had talked to God. Still, he could hear the VC move in closer.

Miles away, another army helicopter was flying north. The pilot later told this story: He felt a sudden, overpowering urge to turn and go east. *But why?* he reasoned. His destination was north. Contrary to all military rules he made a ninety-degree turn and headed east. He then felt an even stronger urge to fly lower and slower. This was even less logical than his first urge and contrary to all rules of flying over hostile territory. He should be flying either high or low and fast. But the urge was so strong that he went down to treetop level, and somehow knew that he was looking for something. There it was! He suddenly spotted the remains of a helicopter scattered over the jungle.

He had no idea how long it had been there, but he felt compelled to check it out. The jungle was so dense that it was impossible to land. While he hovered over the treetops, a member of his crew lowered himself by means of a winch. When the crewman reached the ground he found the wounded men. One by one he secured them to the winch and raised them into the helicopter. When the last man had been lifted to safety, he secured himself and was pulled up. Just as he left the ground, the VC arrived and started firing at him. The pilot saw what was happening, and as soon as the man was clear of the trees he moved the chopper up and out.

In a few minutes the wounded men were safe in the hospital.

When the major had finished his story he grasped my hand and said: 'Chaplain, I just wanted you to come and help me thank God for His goodness to me. I'm going to serve Him the rest of my life!'

7

Rejoice!

I returned from Vietnam in 1967 and was sent to Fort Benning, Georgia. Twenty-three years earlier I had left there, a handcuffed prisoner. Now I returned as chaplain! It was hard to even remember how I had felt then.

I was assigned as brigade chaplain for the twenty-one officer candidate companies and the twenty-one non-commissioned officer candidate companies. What an opportunity to lead future military leaders to Christ!

It was an exciting challenge, yet I was ever aware of my own shortcomings. I had come to see God's power and presence in and around me, but I was often a reluctant vessel.

I experienced days of discouragement and knew that this was not God's will and plan for me.

I searched the Scriptures for clues. In John 17 I found Jesus praying to the Father for us, His followers. He prayed: ' . . . that they might have my joy fulfilled in themselves.' That's what I wanted. The joy of the Lord, not just when things were going good, but always. Jesus prayed that I might have it, then what was keeping me from experiencing it continuously?

In Matthew 25:21 I read: ' . . . thou hast been faithful over a few things, I will make thee ruler over many things: enter thou into the joy of thy Lord.'

So it was a matter of my entering in. I had to do it; it wasn't given me just automatically. But how do I enter in, Lord?

In Luke 6:23 Jesus tells us that we are to leap for joy. He even describes when we are to leap for joy: When you are hungry... when men shall hate you... when men shall reproach you... when they cast out your name as evil... rejoice in that day, and leap for joy. I hadn't noticed that in the Bible before.

'How do you expect me to leap for joy under those circumstances, Lord?' It didn't make much sense, but the more I read my Bible, the more Scriptures I found saying the same thing. Was there a principle involved?

I read Paul's second letter to the Corinthians. In chapter 12:9–10 he says: 'Most gladly therefore will I rather glory in my infirmities, that the power of Christ may rest upon me. Therefore I take pleasure in infirmities, in reproaches, in necessities, in persecutions, in distresses for Christ's sake: for when I am weak, then am I strong.'

Infirmities were the very things that up till now I had not been enjoying. I didn't like it when people turned against me; I didn't like it when accidents happened and things went wrong.

But over and over again I found the words in my Bible: 'Rejoice! Thank God for everything.' The Psalmist continually spoke of joy in the midst of troubles. 'Thou hast turned for me my mourning into dancing,' says David in Psalm 30.

I was willing to try, but how?

One evening in a small prayer group, I began to laugh. I laughed for fifteen minutes, and while I was laughing I felt God speaking: 'Are you glad that Jesus died for you sins?'

'Yes, Lord, I'm glad, I'm glad.'

'Does it make you feel good to think of His dying for your sins?'

'Yes, Lord, it really does!'

'Does it make you feel happy to know that He has

given you eternal life by His death for you?'

'Yes, Lord, it does!'

'Do you have to strain or try hard to really be filled with joy that He died for you?'

'No, Lord, I'm filled with joy.'

I knew that God wanted me to understand how easy it was to be glad that Christ died for me. I could clap my hands, laugh, and sing with thanksgiving for what He had done for me. Nothing in my life was more important, nothing could give me more joy.

I continued laughing, but everything inside me had become very silent. I felt as if God was about to teach me something I'd never known before.

God said: 'It really makes you glad that they took My Son and drove nails into His hands. It really makes you glad, doesn't it? It makes you glad that they took My Son and drove nails through His feet. It really makes you glad that they drove a spear through His side and the blood flowed down His body and dripped on the ground. It makes you very happy and you laugh with great joy because they did this to My Son, doesn't it?'

Everything became very silent. I didn't know how to answer.

'It makes you glad that all that was done to My Son, doesn't?'

Finally I had to say: 'Yes, Lord, it does. I don't understand it Father, but I am glad.'

For a moment I wondered if perhaps I had given the wrong answer, perhaps I had misunderstood.

Then to my great relief I heard Him say: 'Yes, my son, I want you to be glad! I want you to be glad!'

I laughed on, and the joy within me increased as I realised that God wanted me to be glad. Then everything became very quiet again, and I knew I was about to learn something.

'Now listen, my son. For the rest of your life when anything ever happens to you that is any less difficult than what they did to My Son, I want you to be just as glad as you were when

I first asked you if you were glad Christ died for you.'

I said: 'Yes Lord, I understand. For the rest of my life I am going to be thankful. I'll praise You, I'll rejoice, I'll sing, I'll laugh, I'll shout, I'll be filled with joy for whatever You permit to come into my life.'

It was easy to promise to rejoice right then; I was having a wonderful time in prayer, and the joy was just flowing over me and through me like a stream.

The next morning I was sitting on the edge of my bed when I heard a voice: 'What are you doing?'

'I'm sitting here wishing I didn't have to get up!'

'I thought we made an agreement last night.'

'But Lord, I didn't know You meant things like this!'

'Remember what I said, "in everything".'

I said: 'But Lord, I've got to be honest with You. I've been sitting on the edge of my bed every morning for twenty years wishing I didn't have to get up. I've been thinking how wonderful it would be if I could just lie down for five more minutes.'

But the Spirit said: 'You are supposed to be thankful that it is time to get up.'

'Lord, that's a little beyond my comprehension.'

The Lord is always very patient and kind: 'Are you willing to be made willing?'

'Yes, Lord, I really am.'

That night I went to bed praying: 'Lord, this is a rough one, You're going to have to do it for me. I'll get up anytime You tell me to, but I don't know how to be thankful that it is time to get up.'

All I could hear was: 'Are you willing?'

'Yes, Lord, I am.'

The next morning I woke up and the first thing that popped into my mind was my right big toe. I heard: 'See if you can move it.' I could.

'Are you thankful that you can move it?'

'Yes, Lord.'

'Now try your ankle – are you thankful?'

'Yes, Lord.'

'Now your knee – are you thankful?'

'Yes, Lord.'

'Now see if you can sit up.'

'Yes, Lord, I can. But I've got to be honest with You; I still wish I could lie down and go back to sleep.'

Very patiently He said: 'See if you can stand up – are you thankful? Now see if you can walk to the bathroom. Look into the mirror. Are you thankful you can see?'

'Yes, Lord.'

'Now say something.'

'Hallelujah.'

'Are you glad you can speak and hear?'

'Yes, Lord.'

Then everything became very silent. I knew again that out of the silence I was to learn something from God.

'My son, because I love you I am going to teach you to be thankful for everything. You can learn standing right there with all the things you are thankful for, or I can let you go back to bed and not let you move, see, or hear until you learn.'

I jumped two feet into the air and said: 'Lord, I understand! I am thankful! I will always be thankful.'

The next morning and the next, and the next, the first thing I thought when I woke up was, 'Lord, I'm thankful.' Never again have I been sorry it is time to get up.

Paul said, 'Most gladly therefore will I rather glory in my infirmities.' Getting up in the morning had been an infirmity for me. God told me to take it and reverse it from pain into joy, and when I did, the power of Christ and His joy came upon me.

I couldn't wait to share my discovery with others, but the Spirit said no; first I had to learn for myself beyond any doubt how to turn every difficult situation into joy.

I memorised and said over and over to myself the verse

from I Thessalonians 5:16–18. 'Rejoice evermore. Pray without ceasing. In every thing give thanks: for this is the will of God in Christ Jesus concerning you.'

One day as I was nearing a stoplight, it turned amber, but I managed to get through, legally. As I did, a smile of thanksgiving came on my face. I felt the presence of God and He said: 'Freeze.'

So I froze with that smile on my face.

'Why are you so happy?'

'Lord, I made it through the light, thank You.'

'What would you have done if the light had turned sooner, and you had to stop?'

'Lord, I probably would have grumbled a little and wished it had waited for me to get through.'

'Don't you know that I control the stoplights? I control the universe and time itself? The next time a light turns red you must be thankful. You will know it was I who made it turn red.'

The next time the light turned red I pulled up and asked God what He wanted me to do with the time.

'See that man walking across the street? He desperately needs your prayers. Just sit there and pray for him.'

We say we believe in God. But do we really believe that He controls every detail of our lives, or do we think He's off on more important business? Jesus said that God knows how many hairs we have on our heads. So why can't we believe that He is more intimately concerned with every detail of our lives than we are ourselves? I certainly don't know how many hairs there are on my head!

God is controlling everything and working everything that happens out for good for those who love Him. (Romans 8:28)

I was beginning to trust God more, but what about Satan? Can't he sneak in and attack us against God's will?

God permitted Satan to enter into Judas to betray His Son. God permitted Satan to make Peter so weak that he denied having known Jesus. He permitted Satan to enter the hearts of the men who plotted and schemed and crucified Jesus Christ. At any moment God could have stopped them. He could have sent ten thousand angels to sweep aside every plan of Satan. But God didn't stop it. Because He knew that when all the sin and suffering passed through Jesus, it would come out as pure joy, praise, and victory.

Satan can't do a thing to us unless he first gets God's permission. Remember God allowed Satan to test Job. The only time God gives him permission is when God sees the tremendous potential in the thing passing through us and coming out as joy, pure joy!

When we begin to realise this, God can bless our lives. The power of the resurrected Christ is in us. Miracles, power, and victory will all be a part of what God does in our lives when we learn to rejoice in all things.

One morning I got into my car to go to work. It wouldn't start. In the Army there is no excuse for being late to work. I said: 'Okay, Lord, here I am. You must want me to learn something, so I thank You that this car won't start.'

After a while someone came along and helped me get it started.

The next morning the same thing happened. 'Thank You Lord, I know You have some wonderful reason for having me sit here, so I'm going to be filled with joy and praise You.' Again I was able to get it started.

Later that day I took the car to the post garage. I told the manager my problem. He said: 'I'm sorry, Chaplain, but the man who works on that kind of car has had a heart attack and is in the hospital. I hate to tell you this, but you'll have to take it to a civilian place.' He had a pained expression on his face as he said it. 'Chaplain, they know our mechanic is sick, and they'll really sock it to you. They've been doing that to everyone I've sent there.'

As I drove towards the 'civilian' garage, a voice tried to whisper to me: 'Isn't it terrible that those civilians would take advantage of us Army people?'

I told that thought to go back to where it came from, and continued thanking the Lord that He had worked out this whole incident for my personal benefit. I said: 'Lord, I know You are in this and I praise You for it.'

I pulled in to the garage, and the manager came over with his writing pad in his hand. With a glint in his eye he said, 'Can I help you, sir?'

I explained my problem to him, and he went through a list of things that 'might be wrong'.

'We can't repair that part here, so we'll have to send it to another shop. This however, may not be the problem so we may have to do something else. It could be several different things, but we'll keep looking till we find the trouble.'

'How long will it take?'

With a smile he said, 'I'm sorry, sir, but I have no idea. It just depends.'

I could imagine the cash register pounding away.

'How much will it cost?'

'I'm sorry, sir, I have no idea what it may cost.'

Our post garage was right. They were ready to get every-thing out of me if they could. 'Thank You, Lord; You had a good reason for this.'

I agreed to bring the car back the next morning to leave it there until they could find and fix whatever might be wrong.

I then managed with much difficulty to get the car started. I put it in gear and began to move forward. Just then the manager quickly stepped up and grasped my arm. 'Wait a minute! I've just thought of what may be your trouble. Turn off the engine!'

With that he opened the hood and began to poke around with a screwdriver. In a few minutes he said: 'Now try it and see how it works.'

I stepped on the starter and the engine purred away like it was new.

'Wonderful! How much do I owe you?'

'Not a thing, sir, glad to do it.'

'My son, what I wanted you to know was that you never again have to worry whether anyone will overcharge you, hurt you, or mistreat you unless it is My will. Your life is in the palm of My hand and you can trust Me for all things. As you continue to thank Me in all circumstances you will see how perfectly I work out every detail of your life.'

'Hallelujah, Lord!' I bounced up and down on the seat for sheer joy. 'Thank You, Lord! Thank You for showing me all these wonderful things.'

I rejoiced, and realised that if I had grumbled and complained the entire incident would have profited me absolutely nothing. How many opportunities I had passed up to let God teach me how much He loves me! Most of us go around carrying these opportunities as heavy burdens, but God has ordained through Christ that all of these things can be revolutionised as they pass through us and come out as joy!

How glorious to know that at this very moment God wants to fill our hearts with overflowing joy. Not because of our goodness or our righteousness or our sacrifice. It depends on only one thing, on believing the Lord Jesus.

On believing that if the chair collapses under me it is His will. If the coffee is too hot or the toast soggy, it is His will.

When we begin to really believe that, the power of God begins to break loose in our life. That's what Jesus tried to explain to us when He said, 'Leap for joy when they persecute you. When you are poor. When you have sorrow.'

For many years I had suffered with painful headaches. I seldom complained about it, I just thanked God that I wasn't as bad off as some people. One day He said: 'Why don't you try praising Me *for* the headache?'

'*For* it?'

'Yes, *for* it.'

I began to lift up my thoughts in thanksgiving that God

was giving me this headache as an opportunity to increase the power of Christ in my life. The headache got worse. I continued to thank God, but with every thought of praise came increased pain. I realised that Satan and the Spirit of Christ were at war. The pain reached an overwhelming state; I held on to thoughts of praise and thanks and suddenly I was being flooded with joy. Joy seemed to pour over every cell of my body. I had never experienced such power in joy! I was certain that if I took a step I would rise clear up into the air. And the headache was completely gone!

For fifteen years I had suffered with hay fever at least six months out of the years. Many weeks were so bad that I sneezed and coughed and held a handkerchief to my nose all day long. I had taken shots, tried medicine after medicine, prayed, fasted, and prayed some more. I went to everyone I knew or heard of that would pray for me. Nothing helped.

Why did God let me suffer? Didn't He care that I felt so miserable?

My friend, Chaplain Curry Vaughan, had told me I should believe with him that God would heal me. I avoided seeing Curry when I had one of my attacks because he always kept telling me to go on believing. I had tried believing for fifteen years and didn't know what more I could do.

One day I was scheduled to speak to a noon meeting of men in a local Methodist church. As I drove into Columbus, the water started pouring out of my nose and I sneezed so hard that it was difficult to keep on driving. The thought came: 'Praise me!'

I began to think of how good God was to let me have this infirmity of the flesh. He was permitting me to have it to teach me something. It wasn't an accident of nature that I was allergic to so many things. God had planned it this way for His glory and for my good. 'Thank you, Lord, for Your goodness. If You want me to have this I'll just trust You to heal me whenever You want to.'

'What do you want me to do?'

'Heal me, Lord.'

'Heal you or take away the symptoms?'

'Aren't they the same, Lord?'

'No, they are not.'

'Okay, Lord, then just heal me and I won't pay any attention to the symptoms.' With that I knew that God had showed me something new and wonderful. Every time I had prayed for healing in the past and tried to believe, I had always been defeated when the symptoms persisted. Now I knew that the symptoms meant nothing. Faith in God's promise was all I needed; then Satan could fake all the symptoms he wanted!

When I arrived at the meeting place my nose was still running like a tap, and I was sneezing uncontrollably.

I said, 'Lord, if you want me to make a fool of myself, I'm willing. I'm leaving my handkerchief here in the car and I'm going in to speak for You.'

As I walked towards the church I began to feel better. When the meeting was over I suddenly realised that I had no symptoms of hay fever.

Day after day there were no symptoms. Then one evening as I was preparing to go to a prayer group, my nose started running.

I thought: 'Lord, I can't go to the prayer group. Those ladies will think I've done something wrong and You've taken away my faith. They'll gather around and urge me to believe so You can heal me. But Lord, I know You've healed me so I thank You for these symptoms.'

At the prayer group one of the sisters began to exhort me to believe.

'But God has healed me,' I insisted.

'Then why are you sniffing?'

'I don't know, but God knows, and I'm just praising Him.'

On the way home I was continuing to thank Him for running my life just as He wanted to. If He wanted Satan to get in a few licks at me He must have a good reason. He had permitted His own Son to suffer for me.

'Son?'

'Yes, Lord.'

'You've been faithful. You will never again have even one symptom.'

Once again I bounced up and down on the seat. Never again would I pray for healing for the same thing twice. God says 'Ask, and you will receive, that your joy may be full.' (John 16:24)

8

Praise Him

Discovering the power in praise was one of the most exciting experiences I'd ever had; yet every time I wanted to share it with someone, it was as if God was saying: 'Hold it, this isn't the time.'

When Ron came to see me about his problem he was the picture of misery and despair. 'Chaplain, you've got to help me. When I was drafted my wife tried to commit suicide. Now I've received orders for Vietnam and she says that if I go she'll kill herself. What can I do?'

Ron was an attorney and a member of the bar association. But he had been drafted and preferred to join the Army as a private. Now he was obviously distraught and unable to handle the situation with his wife.

'Ron, have your wife come in to see me, and I'll see what I can do.'

Sue was a picture of misery. Her body was frail and she sat on the edge of a chair trembling from head to foot. Tears flowed uncontrollably down her face.

'Chaplain.' Her voice was barely audible. 'I'm scared; I can't live without Ron.'

I looked at her and a wave of compassion brought the tears to my eyes. I knew Sue's story. She'd been adopted as a baby, was estranged from her adopted family, and had no one in the world except Ron. The two of them were very much in love and I knew that if Ron went to Vietnam, Sue would stay alone in a rented room in a strange town.

I prayed silently for wisdom to comfort her.

'Tell her to be thankful.' I shook my head in disbelief. I must have heard wrong.

'Her, Lord?'

'Yes, you may begin to share with her!' I looked at Sue's tearful face and my heart sank.

'Okay, Lord, I'll trust You.'

'Sue, I'm glad you came,' I said, smiling with a confidence I didn't feel. 'You don't have anything to worry about. Everything is going to be all right.'

Sue straightened herself, wiped away her tears, and managed a trembling little smile.

I continued: 'What I want you to do is to kneel here with me and thank God that Ron is going to Vietnam.'

She looked at me in blank disbelief. I nodded. 'Yes, Sue, I want you to thank God.'

She immediately began to weep almost hysterically. I calmed her as best I could and began reading to her from the Bible the verses I had learned to trust in over the last few months.

'. . . In everything give thanks, for this is the will of God in Christ Jesus concerning you . . . All things work together for good to them that love the Lord.' Carefully I tried to show her the wonderful truths I had found to be real.

Nothing seemed to help. Sue believed in God and in Christ, but in her despair her belief was of no comfort. Finally she left my office crying, with no peace of mind and certainly no joy.

'Lord, have I completely misunderstood you? That girl wasn't helped a bit.'

'Patience, son. I'm working.'

The next day Ron came to the office. 'Chaplain, what did you tell Sue? She is worse than she was before.'

'I told Sue the solution to her problem and now I'll tell you. I want you to kneel down and thank God that you're going to Vietnam and that Sue is so upset that she is threatening to kill herself.'

Ron didn't see my point either. Carefully we went over the Scriptures. '. . . This is the will of God concerning you.'

Ron said: 'Now I understand why Sue didn't understand. I don't understand either.' And he left.

Two days later they came back. 'Sir, we are desperate. You must do something to help us.'

They were both hoping that I as chaplain would be able to put in a plea for another assignment for Ron.

Again I explained to them the only solution God was letting me hold up before them. 'All things work together for good to them that love the Lord.'

'If you can only believe that God is really working this thing out for the best for both of you, then all you have to do is trust Him and begin to thank Him – regardless of what the situation looks like.'

Ron and Sue looked at each other. 'What do we have to lose, honey,' Ron said. We knelt and Sue prayed:

'Lord, I thank you that Ron is going to Vietnam. It must be Your will. I sure don't understand, but I'll try.'

Then Ron prayed: 'Lord, this is very strange to me too, but I trust You. Thank You that I am going to Vietnam and that Sue is so upset. Thank You that she might even try to hurt herself.'

I had a feeling Ron and Sue were not as convinced as I was, but I thanked the Lord that they were trying.

They left my office and later I heard what had happened.

Ron and Sue had gone into the chapel and knelt together at the altar. There they had turned their lives and each other over to God in a deeper commitment than ever before and now Sue had the strength to pray: 'God, I thank You that Ron is going to Vietnam. You know how much I will miss him. You know

I don't have a father or mother or brother or sister or family of any kind. I will trust You Lord.'

Ron had prayed: 'God, I do thank You. I give Sue over to You. She is Yours and I'll trust You to take care of her.'

With that they rose from the altar. Ron went through the chapel and headed for his unit while Sue came back to the waiting room next to my office. She needed to sit quietly and collect her thoughts. While she sat there a young soldier came in and asked for the chaplain. Sue told him that I was busy. 'But if you wait a little while, I'll tell him you're here,' she offered.

'I'll wait,' said the young soldier. He looked distressed and Sue asked: 'What is your problem?'

'My wife wants a divorce.'

Sue shook her head: 'It won't do much good to see *that* chaplain,' she said, but the soldier wasn't easily discouraged, and while they were waiting he took out his wallet and began to show Sue pictures of his wife and children. When he turned to the next picture Sue screamed: 'Who is that?'

'That's my mother.'

'That is *my* mother,' said Sue shaking with emotion.

'That couldn't be,' the soldier replied. 'I don't have a sister.'

'It is, I know it is!'

'What makes you think that?'

'When I was a little girl I happened to find a piece of paper in my parents' desk that showed I was adopted. In the upper right-hand corner was a picture of my real mother. That's her. It's the same lady.'

And it was.

Further checking revealed that Sue had been promised for adoption before she was born and her natural mother had never seen her. She had no idea where Sue was and had never heard anything about her since the day she was born.

Now Sue had a brother, a real brother, and with him came a whole family.

Was it coincidence? There are more than two hundred million people in the United States. What would be the odds against that particular soldier walking in the door to my office just as Sue had made a covenant with God to praise Him for her loneliness and lack of family.

But that wasn't all. As Ron walked back into his unit, he ran into an old friend from law school who was now a legal officer.

'Hi, old buddy, where are you going?' he said as he met Ron.

'Praise God, I'm going to Vietnam,' Ron answered. They talked some more, and the friend persuaded Ron to ask for a transfer so that he could work with him in the legal office.

Ron and Sue did not have to be separated. And no longer did Sue have to cling to Ron in fear of losing him. She had come to have a joyous confidence in Jesus Christ and went about everywhere praising Him.

Later an officer candidate came to my office. He openly wept for a long time. 'Sir, you must help me. My wife has been asking for a divorce. Her lawyer has just sent me the papers to sign. I just can't keep on with the officer candidate programme. I don't even want to stay in the Army. Please help me.'

'I know just how to get your problem solved. Let's kneel down and thank God that your wife wants a divorce.'

He didn't understand any better than Sue and Ron did. Carefully we went over the Scriptures together. At last he decided he might as well try it. We knelt and he prayed, turning the whole situation over to God and thanking Him for having allowed it to happen.

When he returned to his unit he was so shaken emotionally that they gave him the rest of the day off. He went to his bed and lay there, repeating over and over, 'Thank you Lord, that my wife wants a divorce. I surely don't understand it, but Your Word says I should thank You for all things, so I'll do it.' All day long he thought the same things over and over. That night he couldn't sleep and so he went on thanking God. The next day he went through training in a daze. 'Lord, You know I don't understand, but I thank You anyhow.'

That evening he was sitting in the mess hall having dinner. As he was eating, it suddenly hit him. 'Lord, you really *must* know what is better for me, much more than I do. I *know* all of this must be Your will. *Thank* You, Lord; now I understand!'

At that moment another candidate tapped him on the shoulder and told him to come to the telephone.

In all the weeks he'd been a candidate, no one had ever wanted him on the phone.

When he lifted the receiver there was someone weeping on the other end. 'Honey, can you ever forgive me? I don't want a divorce!'

A lady came reluctantly to see me. One of her friends had almost dragged her into my office. She told me that she had seriously been considering suicide, but didn't see what good it would do to talk about it.

Little by little she gave me the details. Her husband had fathered an illegitimate child by another woman. The child was being kept by her husband's parents. Every time she went to visit her in-laws, there was the child. To make things worse, the child's mother usually showed up at the same time. Even though they were having financial difficulties, her husband was sending money to his parents to help take care of his illegitimate child. She couldn't live with this constant pain inside any more.

'Don't worry,' I said to her. 'You won't have to; there is a solution to your problem.'

She looked up, rather surprised. 'What is it?'

'Let us kneel here and thank God that your husband fathered this child.' Again I went over the Scriptures on thanking God for all things. Wiping away her tears, she finally agreed to try it. We prayed, and she left the office determined to let God work out the problems in her life.

The next morning I called to see how she was doing.

'Wonderful!'

'You are?'

'Yes, sir, I got up this morning just filled with joy!'

'What happened?'

'When I got home yesterday I began to think what I could do now that I am thankful for my husband's baby. I decided that if I was really thankful, I ought to do something about it. So I sat down and wrote a cheque to my in-laws and told them to use it for the baby. This morning I feel absolutely glorious.'

The next day I called her again, and she said: 'I feel even better than yesterday.'

'What have you done now?'

'I started thinking of a lady who lives near me who has a retarded child. I went to see her this morning and asked if I could help with the child. She was so amazed she didn't know what to say. I stayed and started to do what I could.'

'Do you know what to do for a retarded child?'

'Yes, sir. I have a master's degree in working with special children.'

'Have you worked with children since you graduated?'

'No, sir. This is the first child I've ever worked with.'

'Now do you understand why God permitted that thing to happen in your life?'

'Yes, sir, I do, and now I really praise Him!'

From that day on she was a changed woman. Those who knew her before said she had always looked and acted as if she was in great pain. Now they say she looks and acts as if she has discovered some wonderful secret and people are being drawn to Christ through her radiance and joy.

Jesus didn't promise to change the circumstances around us, but He did promise great peace and pure joy to those who would learn to believe that God actually controls *all things*.

The very act of praise releases the power of God into a set

of circumstances and enables God to change them if this is His design. Very often it is our attitudes that hinder the solution of a problem. God is sovereign and could certainly cut across our wrong thought patterns and attitudes. But His perfect plan is to bring each of us into fellowship and communion with Him, and so He allows circumstances and incidents which will bring our wrong attitudes to our attention.

I have come to believe that the prayer of praise is the highest form of communion with God, and one that always releases a great deal of power into our lives. Praising Him is not something we do because we feel good; rather it is an act of obedience. Often the prayer of praise is done in sheer teeth-gritting willpower; yet when we persist in it, somehow the power of God is released into us and into the situation, first in a trickle perhaps, but later in a growing stream that finally floods us and washes away the old hurts and scars.

One Army wife came to me with a problem she was convinced had but one solution.

Her husband had developed an excessive drinking problem and for the past several years had been an alcoholic. Often he would pass out drunk on the living-room floor where the wife or his teenage children would find him, stark naked. In this condition he'd also been found in the hallway of the apartment house where several other families lived.

In final desperation the wife decided to take the children and leave. Friends persuaded her to at least come talk to me first.

'Whatever you say, Chaplain, don't tell me to stay with him,' she said. 'I just can't do it.'

'I don't really care whether you stay with him or not,' I said, 'I just want you to thank God that your husband is like he is.' Carefully I explained what the Bible had to say about thanking God for all things and that if she tried it, God would be able to solve her problem in the best way.

She thought it sounded ridiculous, but finally agreed to kneel while I prayed that God would release in her enough faith to believe that He is a God of love and power who holds the universe in His hand.

At last she said, 'I do believe.'

Two weeks later I called her.

'I feel absolutely marvellous,' she said. 'My husband is a different man. He hasn't had a drink in two weeks.'

'That's wonderful,' I said. 'I'd like to talk to him.'

'What do you mean?' She sounded surprised.

'I just think it would be good if I talked to your husband about the power that is working in your lives.'

'Didn't you tell him already?' She sounded puzzled.

'No, I haven't met him yet.'

'Chaplain, this is a miracle,' she cried out. 'The day I was in your office he came home from work and for the first time in seven years he didn't go to the refrigerator for a beer. Instead he went into the living-room and talked to the children. I was sure you had talked to him.'

Our prayer of praise had released God's power to work in another person's life. The wife was openly crying over the telephone.

'Praise God, Chaplain,' she sobbed, 'now I know God works out every detail of our lives.'

A young soldier collapsed with a serious heart problem and was taken to the Fort Benning Hospital. He was released, but had to come back for frequent check-ups and eventually was scheduled to go to another hospital for heart surgery. The news filled him with despair, and he began drinking. His despair increased until he decided to leave. He stole clothes from some of the men in the barracks and took off in the first sergeant's car, which he wrecked totally.

The unhappy soldier was caught and put in the stockade to await trial. There another soldier led him to Christ. I went to see him, and he was still feeling depressed and afraid that he had messed up his life so thoroughly that he couldn't be of any use to anyone.

'Your sins are forgiven and forgotten,' I said. 'Don't think of your past as a chain around your neck. Thank God for every detail of your life and believe that He has permitted all of these things in order to bring you to the place where you are now.'

Together we searched the Scriptures for God's word on all things working out for those who love Him.

'And that doesn't just mean things that happen after you've asked God to take over your life,' I said. 'God is able to use even our past mistakes and failures when we release them to Him with thanksgiving.'

He understood, and began to thank God in earnest for everything that had happened. As his trial neared, his defence attorney told him the best he could hope for was a five-year sentence and dishonourable discharge. The soldier remained undaunted and insisted that whatever happened, God had full control of his life and would work out whatever would be for his good.

The General Court-martial had a surprise ending. General Court-martial is never held unless the military authorities believe that the crime warrants severe punishment. This soldier was sentenced to six months in the local stockade and no discharge from the Army.

With Chaplain Curry Vaughan I went to visit him in the stockade. We thought we were there to encourage him; instead he encouraged us. He was filled with joy and it was catching. Soon the stockade rang with our laughter. The young soldier couldn't stand still; he laughed and sang and skipped around the visiting-room.

Before we got ready to leave we asked how he was feeling physically. He had been scheduled for heart surgery and medically speaking was still in need of attention. He confessed that he felt very weak physically and often his heart was troubling him. But he said: 'It is wonderful. God is taking care of me.'

We asked if he would like prayer for healing and he said:

'Please do, I believe God will heal me.'

We placed our hands on him and believed that God, through Christ, was right there healing him. The soldier smiled radiantly and said: 'I believe it is done.'

A few weeks later I talked to the man's company commander.

'I believe it's a waste of government money to keep this man in the stockade.'

'Why, Chaplain?' he said.

'He isn't the same man who stole clothes and a car and wrecked it. He's completely changed.'

The commander agreed and had the man released. A week later I asked him how he felt.

'Chaplain, I used to get tired after walking one hundred yards. Now I can run and I never seem to get tired. God has healed me.'

Wherever I went I now shared what I had discovered about the power of praise. I was beginning to learn that praise was not just a form of worship or prayer, but also a way of waging spiritual warfare. Often when someone began to praise God for the problems that faced them, they found that Satan increased his attacks and the situation appeared to become worse instead of better. Many who tried the way of praise became discouraged and were unable to hold on to their belief that God was in charge.

Others simply didn't understand and refused to try praising God for unpleasant things. 'It just doesn't make sense,' they'd say. 'I'm not going to praise God for something I just don't believe He's got anything to do with. How can God have anything to do with my broken arm or my wrecked car or my husband's horrible temper. I'd be foolish to thank Him for something like that.'

Of course it doesn't make sense. The question is does it

work? It didn't make much sense when Jesus said leap for joy when you are hungry or poor or persecuted. Yet He very definitely told us to do just that. In Nehemiah 8:10 I read:

'The joy of the Lord is your strength.'

The enemy's arrows just can't penetrate the joy of someone who is praising the Lord. In II Chronicles 20 we read how a whole army was defeated when the Israelites simply praised the Lord and believed Him when He said that the battle wasn't theirs, but His.

The message is just as clear today. The battle isn't ours, it is God's. While we praise Him, He sends our enemies scurrying.

It was discouraging and sad to see those who refused to praise the Lord. My heart ached for them in their hopeless situations of suffering and misery. I asked God to give me wisdom to understand why they couldn't accept the way of praise, and also asked Him to teach me better ways of leading others to praising Him.

Nearly seven months after I first had the experience of laughing with joy in the Spirit, I went to a Camp Farthest Out Retreat. I was looking forward to a time of resting and rejoicing in the fellowship of brothers and sisters in Christ.

While I sat in the back of the auditorium during a healing service, I closed my eyes and on the screen of my inner vision God painted a picture.

I saw a beautiful bright summer day. The air was filled with light and I had a sense of everything being very beautiful. Up above was a heavy, solid black cloud beyond which nothing could be seen. A ladder extended from the ground up into the black cloud. At the base of the ladder were hundreds of people trying to get a chance at climbing the ladder. They had heard that above the blackness there was something more beautiful than anything a human eye had ever seen, something that brought unbelievable joy to those who reached it. As person after person tried to ascend they quickly climbed to the lower edge of the clouds. The crowd watched to see what would happen.

In a short while the person would come wildly sliding down the ladder and fall into the crowd scattering people in all directions. They reported that once they got into the blackness they lost all sense of direction.

My time finally came, and as I made my way up the ladder into the blackness it grew so intense that I could feel its power nearly forcing me to give up and slide back. But step by step I continued upward until suddenly my eyes beheld the most intense brightness I had ever seen. It was a brilliant whiteness too glorious to describe in words. As I came out above the dark cloud I realised that I could walk on top of it. As I looked into the brightness I was able to walk without difficulty. When I looked down to examine the nature of the cloud I immediately began to sink. Only by looking at the brightness could I stay on top.

Then the scene changed and I was back looking at all three levels from a distance.

'What does it all mean?' I asked, and the answer came:

'The bright sunshine below the cloud is the light that many Christians live in and accept as normal. The ladder is the ladder of praising Me. Many try to climb and learn to praise Me in all things. At first they are very eager, but when they get into things that they don't understand they become confused and cannot hold on. They lose faith and go sliding back. As they fall, they injure other people who have been hoping to find a way to live in continual joy and praise.

'Those who make it through those difficult times reach a new world and realise that the life they once thought of as normal cannot be compared to the life I have prepared for those who praise Me and believe that I carefully watch over them. He who reaches the light of the heavenly kingdom can walk on top of difficulties no matter how dark they may seem as long as he keeps his eyes off the problem and on My victory in Christ. No matter how difficult it may seem to trust God to work in every detail of your life, keep clinging to the ladder of praise and move upwards!'

I was half-dazed by the vision and the explanation and wondered how soon God would let me share it with someone.

At the camp I met a woman who was faced with difficult problems at home. There was illness and family difficulties and she found it hard to believe that praising God was going to do any good.

Inwardly I asked for guidance and God said, 'Tell her!'

So I told her. 'You'll be the first one to hear this,' I said, and as she listened I could see how the heaviness literally left and her face and eyes lit up with a look of joyous expectancy.

In Ephesians, chapters one and two, I found my vision described in slightly different words by Paul:

'. . . Blessed (Praised!) be the God and Father of our Lord Jesus Christ, who hath blessed us with all spiritual blessings in heavenly places in Christ: . . . he hath chosen us in him before the foundation of the world, that we should be holy and without blame . . . To the praise of the glory of his grace . . . that in . . . the fullness of times he might gather together in one all things in Christ . . . That we should be to the praise of his glory, who first trusted in Christ . . . that you may know . . . what is the exceeding greatness of his power to usward who believe, according to the working of his mighty power, which he wrought in Christ, when he raised him from the dead and set him at his own right hand in the heavenly places, Far above all principality and power, and might, and dominion . . . And hath raised us up together, and made us sit together in heavenly places in Christ Jesus . . .'

Jesus Christ is raised above all the powers of darkness, and according to God's word, our rightful inheritance is right there *above* the darkness together in Christ. The ladder is praise!

I was becoming more aware of the power of praise, but also aware of some of the enemy's snares.

At the time I began to seek my Bible for insight into praise

I was also led to Scriptures describing the power we have received in Christ over the forces of darkness. I had long been aware of the passage in Mark 16 where Jesus speaks of the signs that will follow those who believe in Him: 'In my name shall they cast out devils; they shall speak with new tongues; They shall take up serpents; and if they drink any deadly thing, it shall not hurt them; they shall lay hands on the sick, and they shall recover.'

I had prayed asking God to show me if this was all valid for me in the twentieth century, and if it was, when and how to use it.

I found that I often became uneasy when I was around certain people, and asking God, I got the strong impression that what was wrong with them was of a demonic nature.

I prayed that if I ever got face-to-face with someone like that during a prayer-session God would tell me what to do.

An Army wife was deserted by her husband who left her behind with three children. In desperation she tried to kill herself. She was rushed to the hospital and her life was saved. Friends brought her to see me after she got home. She was the picture of despair. Her friends had told me that for several years they had never seen her smile. I began speaking to her about the way of praising God but soon felt compelled to stop. I looked into her eyes and suddenly sensed that there was something very wrong and very evil with in her.

Within me was a sense of fear; I realised that I was actually face-to-face with evil.

'Lord,' I prayed within. 'I've come this far, I can't go back now, so I'll step out in faith trusting that You'll do the work.'

Looking straight into the woman's eyes I spoke out loud commanding the vicious spirit to get out of her in the name of the Lord Jesus Christ and by the power of His shed blood.

Her glassy eyes suddenly cleared, and she could listen as I explained that God could work all things to good if she would only trust and praise Him.

She now was free to understand, and smiled with a beautiful radiance. Jesus Christ had broken the bondage of darkness that had threatened her life.

Chaplain Curry Vaughan, Jr, had begun to experience the power of praise in his own life. Soon after he had started praising God for his difficulties, he arrived home one evening to learn that his two-year-old daughter had swallowed a glassful of mineral spirits, a type of high grade turpentine. She had already been rushed to the hospital. Curry jumped into his car and raced full speed to be with her. His mind was twirling with thoughts of fear and worry. He suddenly realised what he was doing, slowed the car to normal speed, and praised the Lord for what had happened.

At the hospital they pumped out his daughter's stomach, X-rayed her and told Curry that two things were bound to happen. First, she would run a high fever that night, second, there was a ninety-five per cent chance that she would develop pneumonia.

Curry and his wife Nancy took their daughter home, prepared to watch her very closely as the doctors had ordered.

At home Curry took his daughter in his arms and prayed: 'Heavenly Father, I know that Satan has tried to attack me once again, and I have praised You! Now I claim in the name of Jesus that Virginia will not get a fever and she will not get pneumonia.' The next morning Virginia woke up as bright and chipper as ever. She had suffered no ill-effects.

A successful businessman came to see me about his teenage daughter. I knew the family and knew that their daughter had received more than the average amount of love and care, yet she had developed a violent hatred for her younger sister. She would lash out and strike her with whatever heavy object she could find.

The distraught parents had taken her to the psychiatrist for treatment, kept her on tranquillisers and prayed for years that God would help them find a solution to their terrible problem.

They realised the danger as the violent outbursts increased.

I met with both parents and challenged them to try the one thing they had failed to do.

'What is that?' they both asked.

'Thank the Lord that He has given you this child to meet your need. Really praise Him for knowing exactly what would be the greatest blessing to your family.'

At first they thought this was completely beyond what they could do. They had tried for years to solve the problem and knew of no way to suddenly be glad that everything was exactly the way it was. We went through the Scriptures together and then prayed that God would work a miracle and help them to thank Him.

A miracle did happen. They began to feel and be thankful. They practised this daily for two weeks. Instead of constant worry and fear they experienced peace and joy.

One evening they were in the living-room. Their oldest daughter stood in the middle of the floor holding a potted flower. She looked at them, and when she had their attention she smiled and dropped the pot in the middle of the rug. Dirt, glass and flowers went in all directions. The girl stood smiling, waiting for their reaction. Both parents had given themselves so completely to the practice of praising God that they automatically said, at the same time: 'Thank You Lord.'

The daughter looked at them in amazement. Then she lifted her head and, looking towards heaven, she said: 'Thank You Lord for teaching me.' From that very moment she began to get well.

Her parents came to me rejoicing. The power of praise had worked. For years Satan had held the family in bondage through that girl. Now his spell was broken. In James we read that we are to draw near to God and resist Satan. In Romans 12:21 Paul describes how: 'Don't allow yourself to be overpowered by evil. Take the offensive – overpower evil with good!'

Some have asked me if this principle of praise isn't just

another way to talk about the power of positive thinking. Far from it. Praising God for every circumstance does not mean we close our eyes to the difficulties. In his letter to the Philippians Paul says to not worry about anything, but 'In everything by prayer and supplication with *thanksgiving* let your requests be made known to God. And the peace of God, which passes all understanding, will keep your hearts and your minds in Christ Jesus.'

Looking only at the good side of every situation is often a dangerous way of trying to escape the reality of it. When we praise God we thank Him *for* our situation, not in spite of it.

We are not trying to avoid our dilemmas, rather Jesus Christ is showing us a way to overcome them.

There is a ladder of praise and I believe that everyone without exception can begin to praise God right now in whatever situation they may find themselves.

For our praise to reach the perfection God wants for us, it needs to be free of any thoughts of reward. Praise is not another way of bargaining with the Lord. We don't say now we've praised You in the middle of this mess, so get us out of it!

Praising God with a pure heart means we must let God cleanse our hearts from impure motives and hidden designs. We have to experience the dying to self so that we can live again in Christ in newness of mind and spirit.

Dying to self is a progressive journey and I have come to believe it is travelled only through praise.

God is calling us to praise Him, and the highest form of praise is the one Paul exhorts us to give in Hebrews 13:25: 'By (Christ) therefore let us offer the sacrifice of praise, to God continually that is, the fruit of our lips, giving thanks to his name.'

The sacrifice of praise is offered when all is darkness around us. It is offered of a heavy heart, unto God because He is God and Father and Lord.

I don't believe it is possible to praise God in this way without having experienced the Baptism of the Holy Spirit. As we begin to praise Him – on whatever step of the ladder we may be, His Holy Spirit begins to fill our beings more and more.

To continually praise Him means a steady decreasing of self and an increase of the presence of Christ within us until with Peter we rejoice with joy unspeakable and full of glory.

And a voice came out of the throne, saying, Praise our God, all ye his servants, and ye that fear him, both small and great.

And I heard as it were the voice of a great multitude, and as the voice of many waters, and as the voice of mighty thunderings, saying ALLELUIA!

Revelation 19: 5–6

Jailhouse Rock

Valeri Barinov
with Danny Smith

Contents

Acknowledgements and Thanks

Playing postman in 1981, I 'smuggled' a guitar into Leningrad for Valeri Barinov; later we sent him a synthesiser, enabling his band to record 'The Trumpet Call'. When Valeri was arrested, we released the secret recordings (in English) to raise prayer and action. In 1987, through the Foreign Office, I issued a personal invitation to the Barinov family, endorsed by the British Prime Minister on her visit to Moscow. With airline tickets provided by Campaign friends, we welcomed Valeri and Tanya, Zhanna and Marina, to Britain in 1987.

Perhaps there will be another moment to pay tribute to all those people who played a part in the campaign for Valeri Barinov. Here I would like to thank those who were an encouragement while I tried to record his story.

To my family who made space in the life we share: Joan, Jessica, Rachel and Luke; Mum and Clement.

To everyone at Jubilee Campaign who continued to patrol the tower: Richard Warnes, Howard Taylor, John Anderson, Alison Halls, Rosie McLaughlin, Mark Douglas and Bob 'Slasher' Day who edited the final draft.

Thanks also to Dirk Jan Groot, Pete Fabian, Mike Rowe, Mike Morris, Mike Wakely, Bill Hampson, Sue Richards, Charlie Colchester, Lyndon Bowring, Emma Foa, Simon

Thomas, John Quanrad, Pete and Karen Titchener, Ian and Rosemary Dick, Bob Hitchings, Mark and Carrie Teddor, Pat Harpole, Heartbeat, Kevin Hutson; to those who organised the 'House Fund' – Andy Butcher, Clive Price, Gerald Coates, Brian Philips; to those who helped steer us on the final journey – Edward England, Carolyn Armitage, David Wavre; to David Alton MP, for unwavering support; to George Verwer, who reminded me of the important things in life.

Danny Smith

Prologue: Spring 1983

The jailor's keys jangle against the steel door of my cell. Footsteps along the prison corridor stop outside. Voices alert me to visitors.

I cross the room, which seems like a dark, dirty toilet, covering the distance in a couple of paces, trying to inhale fresh air through the window. Toilet number 207 on the fifth floor.

The window is a joke. It has a metal grid like a car radiator with louvre-type partitions. Iron railings run vertical and horizontal, both inside and outside, preventing sunlight from invading your inner space. It's a brisk April afternoon, and I search for a tiny patch of blue sky that might have escaped the watchman's eye.

What is it to be this time? Am I going to be allowed to contact Tanya at last? Are they coming to announce my release? Or am I to face another barrage of endless questions?

I am alone with my thoughts. My Jesus, how easy it is to be with you. I know that you are here in this prison cell. Thank you, Jesus, for your faithfulness to me. I can risk anything with you in my life.

My cell is dark and silent like a tomb. The door swings open, and light from the corridor fills the room with a strange glow. My eyes focus on the familiar blue of the KGB officer's uniform. I recognise one of the guards. It's Sasha, who patrols our floor.

He shuffles forward and stands to attention inside the room.

Sasha is aged about twenty, married with a family. From the prison grapevine I learn that he is troubled by the corruption he has witnessed within the prison system. He does not look at me.

Behind Sasha, several others march into my cell. Two military officers followed by a doctor and his assistant, who both carry black cases. The last one to enter is a middle aged, almost mild-mannered man whom I recognise as one of the chiefs of the prison. Captain Starkov is short and well-built. He is known for his efficiency; others may say his ruthlessness.

The door slams shut, a weird metallic gong that echoes in my head. The dark walls of the cell add a sinister menace to our meeting. The naked bulb dangling from the middle of the ceiling creates an eerie atmosphere in an unreal midnight world.

'Mr Barinov, the rock singer,' Captain Starkov says matter-of-factly. 'We meet again.'

With six adults closeted together between two beds, our bodies almost touch. I nod my head, acknowledging his introduction.

As though considering each word carefully, Captain Starkov speaks in a slow drawl. 'Why are you giving us so much trouble? Don't you like our food?'

'No, no, I assure you, I have no complaints about the food. Not at all.'

'Then why are you continuing this hunger strike?' the captain barks. Changing his tone almost to a whine, he continues, 'I was surprised when I was told about this. I didn't think you would resort to such unchristian methods of provocation. Are you not a believer?'

Captain Starkov's questions are pitched in a serious, puzzled manner and seem to hang in the air between us.

'But surely this is not the kind of behaviour for a Christian?'

I look directly at him and reply in a clear, calm voice. 'This is my prayer – fast to God. But you don't believe in God. For you, this must seem very strange. So maybe you will understand my action as a hunger strike.'

Stroking his jaw, the KGB officer continues, 'But why are you on hunger strike?'

'I was arrested even though there was never any evidence against me. I never broke any law. You know that I am an innocent man. Yet I have been held in this prison.'

I pause for breath. 'I know that false documents are being prepared to frame me and that I will be sentenced to prison. But who can I turn to for justice? For this reason I am fasting to God.'

The KGB chief holds up his hand to warn me to stop speaking. Now his voice has an edge to it. 'You must stop this hunger strike at once,' he insists.

'If you refuse to eat, then you give us no choice but to force-feed you.' The captain glances round at the officers cramped together in the tiny room. Their presence lends him tacit support. But I am not afraid of their schemes.

'Your hunger strike is now in its fifth day. You know that other troublemakers aren't allowed to continue their hunger strike for more than three days. This can be quite dangerous for your health. You know that Doctor Karenko, here from the prison hospital, is quite concerned for your health.'

Doctor Karenko, who until now has stood impassively by the door, confirms his assent. The captain continues to speak, now quicker than before. It seems that he is impatient to conclude our conversation. Perhaps other pressing duties await him elsewhere in the prison.

'So, Barinov, I have given you a final warning. Now the time has come for you to decide. What will you do? Will you stop this hunger strike?'

I am not afraid. I feel the inner peace of the Holy Spirit's presence. My God revealed to me in a vision that I should begin this fast so I am confident that I am in his will. He has never let me down. I must simply trust him and obey his command. I can't go back.

The Lord puts a boldness in my voice. 'I know that you are wrong. I will continue this fast to my God.'

Captain Starkov shrugs his shoulders, issues a command to the men and then moves behind them to lean against the far wall. He peers through the window grating. I wonder whether he can see the sky.

Two officers grasp my hands and place handcuffs on me. Until this moment, Doctor Karenko has remained a silent observer. Now he begins his work, removing tubes and medical apparatus from his black bag. His assistant also empties the bag he carries. The preparation is completed in silence.

The officers motion me towards the bed and I obey. Gripping my shoulders, they hold me down. From the bed I stare directly at each of the men in the room. No one will look at me.

Silently I pray to my Jesus.

Doctor Karenko stands above me and places his hand beneath my jaw. It is uncomfortable but I allow it. He expresses no emotion. In his right hand he holds a long colourless tube that snakes across the floor by his feet. He inserts the tube into my nose.

The sensation is excruciating. The pain is inside my head, a tingling all over my body. My nose leaks, tears stream from my eyes. I gasp for breath. I feel my whole body wrestle with this painful intruder.

The weight of the officers forces me down. The pain is all around and inside me. I can't identify its source.

Doctor Karenko forces the tube into my body. I can now feel it in my throat and every breath is a torment. I forget where I am or what is happening to me, and I cry out in agony without really knowing what sound is emerging. As the tube reaches down into my abdomen it seems to be ripping my insides apart. The torture seems too much to bear.

I grapple with the officers but their grip is like iron. The captain walks over and stares at me. Sounds appear distorted. Voices directed at me are coming from the ceiling but I can't hear any words. Perhaps they expect me to plead with them to stop this torture.

The tube in my stomach makes me feel nauseous and I retch continually. Perhaps five minutes have passed, it seems like fifty. Now the doctor brings what looks like a large injection. He attaches it to the tube and pumps a mixture of food into it. From the corner of my eye, it seems to be a special kind of meat. Eventually it hits my stomach with a weird sensation. The operation is repeated until my belly has been filled.

Doctor Karenko signals to his assistant. The KGB men relax their grip as he begins the humiliating task of pulling the tube from my body. The tissues inside my throat and nose are raw and I can see blood on the tube. He turns his back and the evil thing is removed from my sight. My handcuffs are unlocked.

Now I can see the captain clearly. He is enraged, not expecting me to endure the violence. 'Did you enjoy that? Think about it, Barinov! No one knows about this hunger strike. No one cares what happens to you. You're making life miserable for yourself. We'll soon have you singing another song. Stop this hunger strike!'

He storms out of the cell, followed by the KGB officers and finally Doctor Karenko and his assistant.

And then I am alone. My head is spinning. My stomach feels bloated and bilious. My nose and throat are sore from the invasion.

'Thank you, Jesus. You give me the strength to endure this torture.' I collapse backwards on to the bed, exhausted by the encounter.

Perhaps an hour had passed, maybe more. I lay on my prison bed as if in a trance. Starkov's words rang in my ears. No one knows. No one cares. Betrayal and despair lined the dark tunnel of sanity.

I had to get up off the bed. I had to resist the tide that was swamping me. The room was spinning and I felt the bile rise within me as I stood up.

The basin in my cell was cracked and filthy. I turned the rusty tap and felt the cold water gush out into my hand. For a moment the flow of the clear water pouring itself into the filthy basin catches my eye. The purity of the water as it glistens amidst the dirt seems strangely symbolic of the broken body of our Lord giving his life for us.

Scooping a handful of water into my palm I splash my face. The shock of the water to my senses is exactly what I need to revive myself. Instantly my mind is racing with questions.

How is Tanya coping? Has she found work to earn money for the family? What are Zhanna and Marina doing at the moment? Do they miss their dad?

These are the questions which the KGB exploit with vile rumours to gain the psychological advantage. But I am not afraid of the KGB or anything they can do to me. My Jesus watches over me. He protects me. My complete trust is in him.

The physical effort of raising my hands in the air focuses my mind as I pray aloud. 'My Jesus, I praise you my Lord. This trumpet call will never be silenced!'

PART I

YOUNG DREAMS

1

Childhood Island

Mama sat by the open window, her chin cradled in the curve of her arm, elbow in the breeze. A cold north wind brought a predawn chill to our room in the Pioneer Camp where we lived.

I rubbed the sleep out of my eyes, and tumbled out of bed. Mama stretched out her hand and drew me towards her. In one movement, I leapt forward and curled up in her lap.

Mama had turned her face away, but her eyes were red and I could tell she was upset.

'Mama!' I called out in surprise, 'You're crying. Are you hurt?'

Although she shook her head, I noticed that her pink, neatly embroidered handkerchief was wet through.

'What's wrong Mama?' I asked again, with all the innocence of a six-year-old. 'I won't let anything bad harm you.'

'Oh Valeri, my son, you're everything I've got,' she whispered, her voice weak and faltering. She gave me a gentle squeeze. With Mama's arm around me, I felt warm and protected.

Mama's tears didn't belong in my childhood world. She switched moods to protect me, and I was easily distracted.

* * *

Mama was the eldest daughter of a family of three. She was closest to her sister Tamara. Ura, the boy in the family, was the youngest by four years.

My grandfather was a hero in the Revolution, and served in the Chekka, the forerunner of the KGB. When Lenin died, grandfather became depressed and began to drink heavily. 'With Lenin dead, I know what will come of the Revolution,' he would comment wistfully. When Mama was sixteen he jumped from a moving tram, fell beneath the wheels, and died of his injuries in hospital.

Grandmother was a cultured lady who spoke four languages and impressed neighbours and friends with her dinner parties. She took the news of grandfather's death badly. Soon after the tragic accident, she suffered a heart attack.

Within a few weeks of each other both parents had died, leaving Mama to raise the family. Tamara was fourteen and Ura was a handful at the age of ten. Mama sacrificed her teenage years to this responsibility and undertook any job she could find.

Conditions in Leningrad were critical during the war. Thousands of families mourned the million casualties who were buried in the Leningrad cemetery. Amidst the turbulence of the war, Mama met a dashing young figure in a Red Army uniform who was to be the love of her life.

Alexander Sardonikov and Mama married after a whirlwind romance. I was a winter 'war baby' born on December 6, 1944 at Maternity Hospital No. 2 in Leningrad.

But the laughter soon faded. My father was unprepared for domesticity, and my mother was plunged into turmoil. Mama never got over the shock of coming home one day to find that my father had gone.

Mama sheltered me from everything and we became exceptionally close. I have only happy memories of sunny days strolling through the park with her, hand in hand.

I have no childhood recollections of my father and I

never called anyone papa or dad.

My mind focuses on a tall figure standing beneath a street-light. Somewhere in the distance a radio is playing. He turns and walks into the night casting long shadows in his path. I close my eyes and desperately try to remember my father. I feel as though I am walking down a long corridor and eventually stop outside a door. I knock and wait, but there is no reply. I continue to knock, now banging on the door. My hands are hurting, and my knuckles are red. But still, no one comes. The only sound I hear is the silence of loss.

My mother was attractive and took great pride in her appearance. I, too, was always dressed smartly, and Mama worked long hours, training as a professional book-keeper so that I could attend a local kindergarten as a toddler of three, and school at seven. I was oblivious to the many sacrifices that my mother was forced to make to keep us together.

Mama's sister Tamara proved a dependable stalwart in difficult circumstances, but Ura was reckless, and too much in need of discipline himself to offer any real assistance.

Mama was extremely popular, and I suspect she had many admirers, but remained infatuated by my father. Her photo album was a treasured possession, and she spent many hours staring at the visual memories of happy, carefree days.

I loved music, and at night I would sneak out of bed and sit on the steps outside our neighbour's flat and listen to music playing from their gramophone.

As a child I was very shy. When I entered a room for the first time, I would clutch Mama's skirt. But when music was played, I instinctively began dancing, swaying and moving to the rhythms. When I heard Russian choirs singing harmony, I would leap up and down, bob and weave until the music stopped. Then I would become shy and reserved once more.

I loved to sing and could quickly pick up a melody. At school concerts I was frequently given solo parts to perform. Music seemed to unlock something within myself.

Although I was a mischievous child and frequently needed discipline, I was also sensitive. As I grew older, I was aware that Mama was weary from a heavy burden. I found her crying helplessly on several occasions, a crumpled figure wounded from a broken heart.

Saddened by this unnamed sorrow, I was frequently alone and turned to the radio for comfort and companionship. Many nights I fell asleep with the light on in the room, static blasting out of the set. Even the late night station had closed down.

But Mama loved me and I cherished her.

When I was eight years old I became seriously ill. I was delirious with a high fever but I know Mama sat up all night with me holding my hand and trying to comfort me.

Mama's friend came to visit me in hospital. His black hair was streaked with silver and he talked with a soft soothing voice. He took me in his arms and prayed with me.

I hadn't responded to the treatment but was then given some herbal tablets and recovered quickly. I think the prayers helped more than anyone realised at the time.

On most Sundays, Mama would dress me up and silently we would walk to the Orthodox Church. I especially liked it if we arrived as the bells were ringing. There was something pure and uplifting about the chimes of the church bells.

Inside the church I was engrossed by the chanting and the music. When Mama walked forward for communion, I followed and sat beside her on the steps of the altar. Calmly I waited for the priest with his flowing beard and long robes to bend down and pat my head.

The strong distinctive fragrance and the brightness of the candlelit sanctuary created an atmospheric experience for a young boy who was taught at school that this charade was covering a vile deception.

I wasn't aware of any contradiction, but I knew that Mama's views on God differed from those of our schoolteachers, who taught that the concept of God was a fairy tale, an invention of wicked people who used religious ideas to exploit the poor.

Mama arranged for my baptism as a child in the Orthodox tradition. Brother Piotr Tiyetich, a family friend who was also an engineer and a devout believer, conducted the brief ceremony.

Although it was not apparent at the time, Mama's heartfelt prayer, offering her child to God, was to play a most dramatic role in my life.

As I grew wild and unruly on the streets of Leningrad, the problems increased for Mama. How could she contain the energy of such an active youth? Eventually she found a job in the accounts department of a Pioneer Youth Camp outside Leningrad.

This was to prove a popular decision. Situated by a beautiful lake surrounded by woods, the camp had numerous activities to occupy a growing lad.

Pioneer Camps are used by workers who pay monthly subscriptions entitling them to children's holidays. Each camp had an orphanage attached to it and I was permitted to stay there to continue my studies, while Mama had a room with the rest of the staff.

I had the run of the place and was given swimming lessons and learned to play several games. I was a skilful rower and won first prize in one of the competitions. I was also chosen to sing in some of the concerts organised at the camp. I grew into an enthusiastic young pioneer who wore his red scarf with pride.

Mama's room was in the attic of one of the residential blocks. She had decorated it tastefully and I would sneak in there late at night to eat biscuits or cake.

One afternoon I was with Mama in her room when she told me a secret. For some weeks she had been saving up to send me for singing lessons at the Rimsky-Korsakov Conservatoire in Leningrad. I was delighted. Mama talked avidly, plotting my future career and the different countries to which I would travel. That night I could hardly sleep for excitement.

A few days later Mama showed me a Russian doll that had been tucked out of sight, buried deep in her wardrobe. It was like those seen in tourist shops, but exceptionally large, and chipped in places with the paint peeling. Carefully I opened the doll, expecting to see a miniature doll inside. But to my surprise, wrapped up inside the secret compartment was a roll of rouble notes.

Mama's eyes twinkled as she saw my response. I glided round the room on a rollercoaster of dreams.

'Oh Mama,' I said, barely able to contain my joy. 'I'll work hard and we'll always be together!' Mama rumpled my hair and smiled.

Over the next few weeks, I spent several fascinating hours lying on Mama's bed emptying the money out of the doll and neatly folding and caressing each note.

One sunny afternoon Mama was lying in the grass with two other ladies, catching the sun and reading *Pioneer Pravda*. Mama waved across to me and I strolled over and lay on the grass beside her.

The women were deep in discussion over an article featuring a phenomenon reported by Siberian peasants who had seen a cross appear through a reflection of light in the street. After some speculation, the article dismissed the image as a trick of the light.

I lay on my back and stared up at the sky, shielding the bright rays of the sun with my hand. The sky had no end. It just seemed to go on and on. But surely it must come to an end.

After some time the other two women left to prepare for their evening chores. I snuggled close to Mama and we cuddled in the sunlight. I was the only one who knew that her enchanting smile hid a secret heartache.

Mama never really got over my father. 'He'll come back to

us one day, you'll see. Everything will be alright,' she would say. In her desperate search to find him she wrote to friends and relatives and made long journeys to visit anyone who may have remained in contact with him. If someone knew where he was, they weren't saying. But Mama never gave up hope.

At the Pioneer Camp someone suggested that she contact him through the army network. She wrote to the commanding officer of his unit, and to her surprise, this time she received a reply.

Mama seemed in shock for several days. She carried the letter around with her everywhere, reading and re-reading it.

Father had re-married but his second wife had died. The letter from the army bureau also included some startling information. An address! It was in Vyborg, an old town near the Finnish border. Ironically, he didn't live far away.

Unaware of the turmoil that Mama was experiencing, I waved her good-bye as she set off to Vyborg. Like the other kids at camp, my mind was on Sports Day, due to be held in a few days time.

I wasn't on the campsite the day Mama returned from this extraordinary journey. I had taken a boat out – without alerting its owner – on to the nearby river with my friend Alex, who was also eleven years old, but a little shorter than me with blond curly hair.

The day began peacefully. We tried fishing, but neither of us could sit still long enough to entice the fish.

Then, sometime during the afternoon, Alex called out in horror. Two angry-looking men were rowing furiously in our direction. At the camp we had all heard frightening tales of how some men had abducted children. The men's threats grew louder as they gained on us in spite of our frantic efforts to get away.

'Look Valeri, land!' Alex shouted. We hurried towards an island, with the men chasing us close behind. We couldn't understand what they said, but knew enough of life to recognise Finnish curses when we heard them.

We abandoned the boat and charged across the tiny beach. Without looking back, we scrambled into the undergrowth to hide from our assailants. As we lay on the cold earth my heart echoed so loudly in my ears that I thought anyone passing would discover us. Alex was as scared as I was, with his hands over his ears, and his eyes wide open.

We lay there for what seemed like hours. Protected by the bushes, the sounds of the wild became a source of comfort. Eventually we decided to step out of our hiding place and gingerly retrace our steps to the beach.

We gasped in surprise. Our boat had been taken by our pursuers. Trapped on the island, we considered all the ideas we could think of. Could we make a raft? Were there people living on the island, and would they be friendly? If we floated a message in a bottle would anyone find it? I knew how to swim, but Alex couldn't swim at all.

Gradually we grew daunted by the grim reality of the situation. Even if we finally managed to get back to the camp, what would they say about the boat we had stolen? Without knowing where the money would come from, we resolved to pay back the exact cost.

The cool, inviting water lapped at our feet as we lay on the beach considering our options.

Suddenly we heard a familiar noise in the distance. To our amazement, it was a motorboat. We were going to be rescued! We began to wave and shout, yelling and jumping up and down. They must see us! They must!

As the boat weaved through the water, heading in our direction I had a terrible thought. What if they were our attackers, returning to get us? But my fears were unfounded, dispelled by a friendly wave from the boat.

We had been rescued by a young Finnish couple who listened sympathetically to our story and agreed to take us back to the Pioneer Camp. 'You've been very lucky,' they said. 'There are some nasty people around.'

As we silently watched the boat glide through the greeny-blue water, my mind replayed the events of the last few hours. What a story I had to tell! Just wait till I saw Mama!

Alex and I arrived breathless back at the Pioneer Camp. Alex was hungry and went to scrounge some food in the kitchen. As I approached the wooden building where Mama lived, I noticed several people stop to stare at me. I knew I looked terrible in dirty, ripped clothes, but I ignored them and walked past.

'Valeri, where have you been?' a voice called out behind me. It was Schura, one of Mama's friends, a tall, slender lady with dark hair. She looked tired and worried and was carrying Mama's bag. Was something wrong?

'Schura, you'll never believe what happened to us,' I blurted out. I had to get to Mama to tell her what had happened. 'Is Mama in her room? I must see her!'

'Oh, Valeri,' Schura replied despondently. Her eyes welled up with tears and she put her arm round me. I felt my body tense up at this sudden expression of affection, and wriggled free from Schura's grasp. I couldn't understand why Schura was upset. Or was she merely relieved to see me home safely? Grown-ups were always worrying needlessly. I shrugged my shoulders and tried to move away.

'Valeri, I've something to tell you. Your Mama's not well.'

I stared at Schura without understanding what she was saying. Suddenly I felt tired, cold and alone, as the last rays of the sun enveloped the camp.

In the eerie twilight it seemed as though Schura was speaking from behind a thick pane of glass. I saw her lips move, but I couldn't hear the words. She explained that Mama had collapsed without meeting my father, that she was resting now and I could probably see her tomorrow if her condition improved.

Schura walked me back to my cabin, sensing my tiredness and shock. Suddenly, I turned to her and said, 'We were chased by some bad people and trapped on an island for several hours and our boat was stolen!' It now seemed something that had happened a long time ago. 'Where is Mama? Why can't I see her?'

Schura nodded and patted my arm. Everything seemed unreal. I was too tired to resist her gentle prodding and I followed her silently.

'Will you be OK, Valeri?' Schura asked as we reached the dormitory.

'Yes, I'll be fine. I just want to sleep.' I eased my shoes off and plunged headlong on to the bed.

I awoke in a sweat, still dressed in yesterday's stained clothes. The dormitory was empty and I could hear a football match going on outside. That meant breakfast had been served and I had missed it. Boy, I was hungry!

As I changed my clothes hurriedly, yesterday's events seemed like a dream. I had to get to Mama. She would sort everything out.

Schura arrived just as I reached the door of the cabin. 'You've been asleep a long time,' Schura said. 'I didn't want to wake you, you looked so tired. Mama wants to see you.'

'How is she?' I asked. Schura tensed slightly as she nodded and mumbled, 'She's tired, very tired.'

As we walked across the playing field, a rowdy game of football was in progress. I saw Alex and we waved.

Schura knocked softly on Mama's door, and I followed her in. The curtains were half drawn and I could see Mama's form as she lay in the darkened room.

'Mama,' I shouted, and raced over to her bed. As I leaned across my mother I was surprised that she didn't speak or embrace me. Her body seemed strangely crumpled. I had seen her just a few days ago and she had been bright and cheerful as ever. Just moving her head from side to side seemed to require an incredible effort.

Tears slipped down her cheeks when she saw me standing there. Schura moved round the bed and wiped the tears from her face. Mama indicated that she wanted to hold my hand so I eased my palm into hers. She tried to smile and squeeze my hand.

I wanted to tell Mama about the dramatic events of the last twenty-four hours. She stared at me and again made a valiant attempt to smile. I didn't want to leave Mama and clung to her hand. Mama signalled that she wanted me to stay with her. Schura left, and for a few moments we were alone.

I sensed Mama was trying to communicate with me. Perhaps she was praying for me . . .

Mama seemed to tire, and it was an effort for her to keep her eyes open. Schura returned and hovered in the background. Coming up behind me, she touched my shoulder and leant down to whisper, 'She needs to rest. It'll be good for her.'

I reached forward and kissed her gently. Her eyes flickered, followed by a momentary smile. And then she fell asleep again.

I walked slowly away and said good-bye to Schura. I had never seen Mama looking like that before, a pale reflection of her real self.

I found myself walking in the direction of the athletics field, where final preparations were being made for Sports Day at our Pioneer Camp. Decorations were going up everywhere for tomorrow's events. Rivalry among the campers was at fever pitch.

Misha, a thick-set Latvian youth, had spread the word: he was going to win the 200 metre sprint. Misha was a bully, and had already flattened another boy who insisted that he would contest the race. Rumour had it that Misha's father had promised him a brand-new foreign racing cycle if he won. Misha's father had connections and could pick up foreign goods quite easily.

I spotted Alex standing with a few other lads. He told me

that he had reported the loss of the boat, but it hadn't been taken too seriously, overshadowed by preparations for Sports Day.

A skinny, gangly lad named Tomas stood beside us. He had already beaten Misha in the heats leading up to the finals. Alex saw me staring at a cut on Tomas' face, and said, 'Misha's given him a black eye. He's warned him about the race.' Tomas looked really nervous now.

Everyone was talking simultaneously, but for once, I remained silent, my mind by Mama's forlorn frame.

'What's the problem Valeri?' Alex asked.

'There's no problem,' I snapped back sharply, surprised at myself. I watched Alex step back. I could tell he was hurt by my reply.

Yesterday I would have been one of the schemers, plotting Misha's demise, but now all I could do was trail after them.

Sports Day was held on June 26, 1956. We were awoken to the sound of a marching band, played through a special loudspeaker system rigged up throughout the camp. Events had been scheduled throughout the day. There was a treasure hunt in the morning, with a concert and a play (based on *Lenin Our Hero*) for the early evening. A band had been practising all summer and was due to play at several times throughout the day. A campfire sing-along would conclude the great day.

Dressed in blue silk shorts and blue cotton vest, ready for my rowing event, I ate a quick breakfast. There were still two hours to go before the games were to begin, so I decided to see how Mama was feeling.

Outside Mama's cabin I spotted Lara, a fair haired sweet-looking girl who was one of Mama's best friends.

'Hiya Lara,' I called out and waved.

Lara looked at me and stopped for a moment. She hesitated and seemed to be on the verge of telling me something. She gave me a rueful smile and put her arm round my shoulder. Lara looked upset.

'What is it Lara?' I enquired.

Lara bit her lip nervously. I proceeded towards the staircase leading to Mama's room, but Lara was now blocking my path. She touched my arm, a gentle gesture that expressed sympathy more than restraint. I noticed some people at the top of the stairs. Schura was one of them.

'Hello Valeri,' she said pensively. She gave Lara a questioning glance. I didn't see Lara's response, but I felt uncomfortable in the strained atmosphere. Something was going on, but I was being kept in the dark. I began to feel cross. When Mama recovered everything would be alright.

I walked away from Schura and Lara, planning to slip away from the Sports Day to see Mama later on.

The 200 metres was scheduled for 3 p.m. and I simply had to be there to cheer Tomas to victory. The band played as we ate lunch. There was a special menu which included chocolate ice cream. I relished every spoonful.

It was a brisk warm day, ideal for Sports Day. As we went to find Tomas and his gang, Mrs Avaloff, who worked at the medical station, came towards us, walking at a brisk pace. She looked serious and pointed at me. 'Come with me, Valeri,' she said.

I looked across at Alex and told him, 'Keep a place for me next to you. I'll be back for Tomas' race.'

As we headed in the direction of Mama's room, I realised that she must have got worse. Schura and Lara were still standing at the foot of the stairs, and talking to a man who looked like Uncle Ura.

It was Ura! He must have come from Leningrad. I went across to hug him. As he bent down to me he began weeping.

'I want to see Mama,' I declared, climbing the stairs two at a time. Ura and the others followed close behind.

Mrs Avaloff stopped me at the door. Gently touching my

shoulder, she said, 'Valeri, do you realise that people don't live for ever?'

I hesitated. Mama was dead, I just knew it. I staggered a little as the shock ripped through my body. Mrs Avaloff realised that I understood.

I'm a man, I told myself, men don't cry.

Turning the handle of the door I entered the room. Mama lay on the bed. She looked peaceful, as though in a deep sleep. Her skin looked pale and translucent. I flung my arms around her neck.

'Mama, I love you, I love you,' I cried, choking back the tears.

I lay on the bed beside her. My mind seemed empty and vacant. I was curiously aware of the silence in the room.

My precious Mama was dead. I stared at her face, memorising every detail. And I never got to tell her about our narrow escape on the island, or the Sports Day. So many things I never got to say.

The room itself was darkened and all the familiar items stood in their place, untouched, as if in mournful respect. Every corner had a memory, now tinged with grief.

After some time I was aware of Schura's presence guiding me out of the room. I felt an overwhelming sense of helplessness as I looked back at Mama lying on the bed. Then the door was closed.

Several people were discussing the funeral arrangements in a nearby room. I hear Uncle Ura say, 'I'll take the body back to Leningrad and finalise everything there.'

'What will become of the little one?' I heard Mrs Avaloff say looking across at me.

'I'm not little,' I wanted to reply. Uncle Ura spoke up, 'He's not an orphan, he'll come to live with me in Leningrad.' I didn't know why, but it was also decided that I would remain in camp and not travel to Leningrad for Mama's funeral. The details became complicated and someone suggested I should return to the Sports Day.

The athletics field was ablaze with colour and noise. Despite all the activity I felt little sense of sound. I seemed to be sleep-walking, but I could tell by the faces of the people I passed that the news had spread.

Suddenly, a shrill voice shattered my daydream. 'Valeri's mother is dead! She's dead!' Claps and shouts accompanied the declaration. Other voices tried to restore the balance. 'Quiet, shut up, you idiot!' I heard someone say.

I was caught by surprise. The words had some mystical, hypnotic power. Was this really happening to me? I heard a familiar voice call out. It was Alex.

'Valeri, where have you been? Why were you so long?'

I stared incomprehensibly at him. I started to speak but I could make no sound.

'Tomas won the race!' Alex cried out. 'He won, Valeri. Tomas won the race!' Non-plussed by my reaction, he repeated himself. 'Valeri, Tomas won. Misha came second, he's been beaten. Tomas came first.'

I managed to mumble something in reply, nodding to confirm that I had understood. Alex stared at me, his eyes narrowed, 'What's the matter?'

'My mother's dead,' I heard myself say.

Alex opened his mouth and swallowed but could find nothing to say. He held up his hand, and then let it drop to his side.

Somehow the next few hours passed. When the camp band played a sad melody, I identified with the music. I felt as though my soul itself was weeping.

Later that evening, I returned to Mama's room for the last time. All the clothes, furniture, carpets and the little trinkets on her toilet table had been packed into boxes to be returned to Leningrad. I found the Russian doll, now empty, and caressed it gently. I would keep it. No one except me knew why Mama had saved money in the doll. It was our secret and it would remain that way, an eternal expression of our love.

I felt a twinge of sadness. My thrilling musical career at the Conservatoire had ended before it began. If Mama had lived, everything would have been possible, I told myself.

'I love you Mama,' I whispered as my mother's body was carried out of the room.

I learned later that in Vyborg Mama had stood outside the flat where my father lived, unable to knock on the door. She struggled into the street and collapsed a few yards away. For two days she lay unconscious. The doctor who returned her to the Pioneer Camp explained that a blood vessel burst inside her head as a result of intense psychological pressure, resulting in paralysis. The emotional trauma of the last few years had taken its toll.

Mama's funeral in Leningrad was attended by over three hundred people, and she was remembered with great love and affection.

2

Nowhere to Run

Uncle Ura and Aunt Tamara and their families occupied a cramped three-room apartment on the fifth floor in Nevsky Prospekt, Leningrad. Although they shared a toilet and kitchen with no hot water, somehow they managed to accommodate another person.

Life at the Pioneer Camp with Mama had been magical and wonderful. Although she had struggled all her life, she had been my guardian and protector. Every patch of earth had a memory. Now I felt hopelessly alone, and at times inconsolably despondent.

When Mama died, I no longer felt a child. I was only eleven, but I resolved to grow up and be a man. Mama would have expected it of me, I reasoned.

When the camp season ended, Ura came to collect me. I loved our Pioneer Camp and it was hard saying farewell to my friends and the teachers.

For the last time I walked out of the main gates, with all my clothes and toys piled into two cardboard boxes, tied with string, which Ura carried with ease. I carried a smaller box containing Mama's shawl, the album of photographs, and the hand-painted Russian doll. I handled it like a treasure.

Aunt Tamara and her husband, Benjamin, had a son named

Slavik who was my age. Benjamin had worked as an editor for a military publication, and then in a solicitor's office. One day I was told that Uncle Benjamin had been 'bad' and was going away to be punished. He would be going far away and be gone a long time. At that age, it was all the explanation I needed.

Aunt Tamara and Slavik moved to a new flat near Voladsky Bridge. Later, she moved again to another flat in the Vyborg district and became a member of the Leningrad Baptist Church, joining the church choir.

Ura's wife, Vera, was an attractive woman whose eyes seemed to hint at some hidden fear. Their three-year-old daughter Valentina, or Valya for short, had a mischievous smile and we immediately became good friends.

After a few days in my new accommodation, I realised that there were serious difficulties. Ura had a kind heart, but had a reputation for drinking heavily. Ura's habit would cost him good jobs and consequently Vera's meagre salary kept the family in bread and potatoes.

One night, Ura began cursing the potentates in the Kremlin for all our difficulties. He composed an abusive letter to Khrushchev and read it out to us. Vera had learnt never to contest him in his moods, but I was horrified and questioned him.

To Vera's surprise, Ura was amused and laughed off my challenge. 'When you grow up, then you'll understand.'

'What do you mean?' I asked. 'Explain yourself.'

'No, you'll see for yourself,' he answered mysteriously.

What was worse, on Saturday nights Ura would stagger through the door around midnight, cursing at the top of his voice. I would pull the thin blanket around my ears in a vain effort to block out the noise, while our neighbour thumped on the wall calling for quiet.

Once I heard Ura slap Vera hard on the cheek. When I looked up, she was on the floor at Ura's feet while he tried again to punch her. Valya was up now and ran to her mother.

'Uncle Ura, stop it!' I shouted, climbing out of bed. He was outraged that I had interfered and tried repeatedly to punch me, but I evaded his blows.

Lunging at me again, Ura badly mistimed his step and smashed into a shelf. Four glasses crashed to the floor showering splinters in every direction.

'Come back here and I'll kill you!' he swore.

'You'll have to catch me first,' I shouted back.

Storming into the kitchen, Ura returned brandishing a meat axe. As I dashed for the front door I heard Vera scream, 'Run, Valeri, run!'. Valya shrieked in terror. I thrust myself into the hallway and jumped down the stairs, landing on my bottom. I could hear Ura swearing in the hall but I didn't wait to debate the issue.

I spent the night walking the streets in my thin vest and shorts, looking for a warm place to hide. By early morning the cold was too much to bear and I decided to sneak back to the flat. Vera had left the door ajar for me. Ura had passed out after further drinking and slept until midday.

It was an experience that was to repeat itself.

Vera tried her best to make the home a happy place, but everything hinged on Ura's moods, which in turn were controlled by the bottle in his hand.

As my twelfth birthday approached, Vera planned a party for me. On December 6th, she baked a special chocolate cake and my Aunt Tamara and Slavik came round. We all wore funny hats and had a happy time together. Ura was in a good mood and entertained us with animal noises. Little Valya's peals of laughter filled the room as she saw a different side to her father.

Snow had fallen early that year and the cold seeped through the walls of our flat. I didn't have many warm clothes, so I wore several jumpers. Leningrad's wintry streets were uninviting and I missed my friends at the camp, running free in the fields and the clean fresh air. When I thought of Mama, I felt a deep ache within my soul and longed to return to the places where we roamed together, hand in hand.

Fire crackers marked the New Year celebrations in Leningrad, but Vera, Valya and I ate dinner with uncertainty, waiting for Ura to return home.

Valya became cranky and Vera decided to put her to bed. Later, Vera sat on the sofa reading a *samizdat* novel written by some banned author. I was puzzled why anyone put up with reading a carbon copy passed secretly from hand to hand. Why couldn't it be published just like an ordinary book and be kept on the shelf?

I made up my bed on the floor and kissed Vera goodnight. Sometime that night I awoke to hear her scream in terror. Ura was staggering round the room hitting her all over like a punchbag. The buttons of her housecoat were ripped and with one hand she clutched it to herself to cover her body. Unable to maintain her balance, Vera collapsed backwards and Ura fell on top of her.

Valya had also woken up and began to wail. 'Stop that yelling,' Ura shouted at his daughter. Frightened and confused by his temper, Valya was unable to stop. As she ran towards her mother in short jerky steps, Ura knocked her sideways across the room. At this, Vera tried to grapple with Ura.

Valya's terrified screams served to taunt Ura, snapping the last reserve he may have felt. As he moved towards Valya with his fist outstretched, I crouched low and slipped past him, plucking Valya off the floor. She clung to me as I put my arm round her and sped towards the door.

Vera realised that I planned to rescue her daughter and moved swiftly to open the door, slamming it shut after us, locking herself and Ura inside. Clutching Valya tight I rushed down the stairs. Behind us, Ura's booming voice drowned out Vera's cries.

As we reached the fourth floor, the door opened on the floor above. 'Come here, you little bastard,' Ura swore. I wasn't sure whether he was following us, but if he caught me now I knew he could kill Valya or myself.

The back door of the building was bolted from the outside. Behind us the noise from the stairs became louder. My heart was beating like a bass drum, and we were both trembling.

I tried to open a window, but it wouldn't budge. I stood on the window ledge with my back against the dirty frame and summoned all my strength. A loud crash startled me! The window pane had smashed and I was covered with glass.

Down the hall I heard footsteps and the sound of heavy breathing, but I didn't wait to find out who it was. I reached down to lift Valya across the ledge to safety. Scrambling through the window, we raced into the night.

There had been a light snowfall and Valya was shivering, so I pulled off my tatty blue sweater and slipped it over her. What a sight we must have been as we trudged down the street! A twelve-year-old boy in a vest and trousers and a three-year-old girl in an outsized torn sweater.

I found a doorway into another building and we stepped out of the cold. The lift smelt of cigarettes and urine, but at least it was warm. I pressed a green button on the control panel and as the doors shut, Valya and I slumped down in a corner.

I looked down at Valya as I cuddled her in my arms. She looked beautiful in her innocence and I stroked her hair. Possibly it was one great adventure for her. Within minutes, I too was asleep.

I awoke to hear a shrill voice yelling at us and a dark-haired lady peering over us and wagging her finger. 'Haven't you got a home to go to?' she scolded.

The words stung me as I picked up Valya, and like tramps we stumbled back on to the streets in search of shelter. Valya was hungry, and tried to snuggle up to me as we slipped on the icy road. There was no one else to turn to. We had to go home.

With our hearts beating wildly, we stepped into the building and crept nervously up the stairs. As before, Vera had left the door ajar, meaning it was safe to return. Ura had gone out after us but had not returned.

Chairs had been smashed and a table leg was broken. Glasses and cutlery were lying everywhere. Vera's bruises showed that she had taken a severe beating. Her eyes hid her shame. She cuddled Valya and then made us some sandwiches.

Vera told me that she was going to leave Ura and would take Valya with her. She planned to stay with her brother who lived a few miles outside Leningrad. It was clear that there would be no room for me and I would have to remain behind.

Valya didn't understand what was happening, but the prospect of a train ride filled her with excitement. Vera had already packed a few clothes and within an hour she and Valya were ready to leave.

'Take care of yourself Valeri,' Vera said giving me a hug. 'I hope you'll be OK.'

Valya tugged impatiently on her mother's arm but decided she could wait an extra moment as we kissed good-bye.

Without Valya the flat seemed empty and within a few minutes I was filled with a great loneliness. By mid-afternoon Ura had still not returned. I ate the bread and vegetables that Vera had left for me. There was nothing to do alone in the flat, so I pulled on a coat and went for a walk. It was certain to snow very soon and the cold drove me back home.

Two days later, Ura returned home. He was tearfully sorry. But this time it was too late.

Soon Ura began drinking again and he would blame me angrily because there was no food in the house. Life was intolerable and I would find excuses to leave the house before he got violent. The cold made it difficult to stay on the streets for long.

Then I had an idea one evening. I knew some people nearby who owned a TV set. TV had only recently been introduced in Russia, and few people could afford it. I turned up at their door and boldly asked if I could watch TV.

'Of course,' the woman replied. The couple had teenage children who were out most of the time, and they enjoyed having young people around.

I showed great interest in everything that was screened in order to stay safe and warm. In reality, Ura was never far from my mind.

When it became late, the woman asked me if I should return home. Wouldn't someone be worried that I was out this late? 'No, no,' I assured them. 'No one will worry. They're used to me staying out late. I'm nearly thirteen, you know, almost a teenager.'

As I stepped into the flat, my eyes turned to the shelf by the window where Mama's precious Russian doll was kept.

The shelf was empty.

Once again, the flat was in turmoil with chairs overturned, books scattered everywhere, food on the floor. Suddenly my eyes fell on coloured slices of wood among the rubble. The doll had been smashed, it could never be restored. Like yesterday, it was gone for ever, a memory that could be visited only in the heart.

Filled with a silent rage, I cradled the broken doll in the palm of my hand as I sat in the ruins of Ura's life.

A week later, Ura informed me that he intended to place me in one of the local 'internats', a home for abandoned children, vagrants, and children from one-parent families. I pleaded with him to be allowed to return to the orphanage at the Pioneer Camp, but to no avail.

With only two weeks to go before I left, I thought that little could go wrong. But the weekend before I was to leave, Ura returned home with a prostitute.

She was a tall woman with short hair, dyed red. Perhaps she had once been attractive, but now she looked haggard and old.

As an observant thirteen-year-old, I had begun to notice that girls were shaped differently from boys, but the next few minutes degenerated into a sordid, embarrassing perversion. Ura behaved without shame and the prostitute was tough and callous. I was forbidden to leave the room as Ura mauled her in front of me.

I crawled into Valya's tiny bed and pulled the sheet over my head. Closing my eyes, I held my hands over my ears to block out the sounds in the room, and tried to sleep.

I had nowhere left to run.

By the time I arrived at Internat No. 10, the sense of isolation and abandonment that I had experienced after my mother's death in June was beginning to give way to a feeling of independence. Alone but no longer lonely, I enjoyed my new-found freedom.

In a curious way I missed Leningrad and Ura. I felt more pity than anger when I thought of him. Although his behaviour was deplorable, I knew that he cared for me. Ura insisted that I return for holidays and some weekends. I had no option but to agree, hardly relishing the prospect.

The internat was situated about two hours from Leningrad. Several old, grey buildings housed about a hundred children between the ages of six and sixteen. There were a lot of activities designed for energetic teenagers.

My first serious challenge faced me on the night I arrived. Some older boys had removed the blanket from my bunk and were threatening to report me to the kindly old matron. As the confrontation developed, the twelve or so boys who shared the cabin gathered round.

I might have been skinny, but I didn't lack courage as I stood up to the ring leaders of the plot. Realising I was not to be tangled with, they retrieved the blanket from a cupboard. I received a cut on the chin, but my bruised knuckles bore witness that I was not the only one bearing a scar.

I had passed the test with flying colours. After that, I hung out with the older boys, whistling at the girls and making up jokes that could only be told behind the toilets.

Within a few short weeks, I had become one of the gang leaders and was probably viewed as a troublemaker by the staff of the internat. But the girls liked us!

We found a way on to the roof and made a hideout where we would go at midnight with our girls. The cigarette ends which we dropped alerted the staff, and one night we were caught and severely penalised. But this only confirmed our resolve to be outlaws.

Kurakina Dacha Park, a large wooded area, was nearby. When the River Neva which flowed through it burst its banks, we would undertake midnight expeditions to inspect the chaos.

The park was notorious for muggings, and even murders. Most folk were afraid to go there at night. But not our gang!

The girls from the internat clung to our arms and shrieked at anything that moved. Although our hearts also fluttered at every shadow, we behaved like brave and carefree adventurers.

However, the danger was real and on several nights we were chased. One boy slipped and fell on the ice and was pounced on by thieves. They knifed him in the side, but fortunately he was able to get away.

I was always in trouble and got expelled many times from the internat. The punishment only fuelled my rebelliousness, and as an orphan they were forced to take me back.

'This place can't hold me,' I warned the gang. 'I'm going to escape, find a boat and sail far away. I'll find an island and live off the land and never have to work.'

As I repeated the notion, it took hold of me. The idea caught on, and I carefully selected five boys who pleaded to come with me. This was going to succeed with military precision. I could only take those who were trustworthy.

First of all, we found the ideal meeting place to plot our strategy. Late one night George, who was wiry and skinny, put his hand through a hole in the timber beams in the elevated base of the main building. 'Hey, this seems a little shaky,' he called out, manoeuvring a beam and squeezing inside. For a few moments we heard him scrambling around inside the structure, and then trying to get out again. Even in the dim light we could tell as we pulled him out that he was covered with dirt, dust and cobwebs.

But his mission had been an overwhelming success. Deep in the very bowels of the edifice, George had located a space large enough for all of us to meet.

The pirates managed to smuggle a kerosene lamp and other necessary tools down the hole. In a ceremony of conspiracy, we each cut the tip of an index finger and spilled three drops of blood in a circle of earth in the centre of the room. Stealth and secrecy were the passwords. Sasha kept notes of all our meetings and in closing, we drank a toast to freedom with whatever refreshment we could sneak out of the canteen.

One morning, we heard a great commotion. 'Fire! Fire!' Screams of panic came from all sides as the alarm went off. Puffs of smoke could be seen rising above the main building. The entire internat ground to a halt as staff and students filled the grounds.

'Right, where's the fire?' the chief fireman called as his colleagues jumped from their red wagon.

'That's just it,' replied one of the staff, looking confused. 'We can't seem to find it.'

Smirking at the joke, we gathered round the fire engine. Smoke was billowing everywhere as I whispered to George, 'I just hope our room doesn't burn down.'

Suddenly some activity round the other side of the building caught our attention. Firemen ran to point the hose. Suddenly it was getting serious! I stared in disbelief as a fireman began chopping at the hole leading to our hiding place. 'Yes, it's in here,' I heard him exclaim, to everyone's relief but our own.

I was dumbfounded. Our room had been discovered. It was all George's fault for leaving the kerosene lamp burning. He would be disciplined, I decided. Worse, he would be fired from the team. He had wrecked his chances of escaping with us.

Suddenly, the reality of it hit me. I tried not to draw attention to myself as I moved away from the front of the crowd. Discreetly, I signalled that we should disperse.

At dinner that night none of us felt hungry. I was determined to escape and this crisis would not hinder our plans. 'What are we going to do?' George said, somewhat alarmed. I glared at him. 'You mean what are you going to do?' I replied ominously. 'We'll meet tonight. Is that agreed?' There were nods all round. I decided to wait until the meeting to inform George of his future with the group.

As we were finishing dinner, I was startled to hear our names called out. We were commanded to report immediately to the chief of the internat. Frowning in puzzlement, I said calmly 'It's nothing. Don't be taken in by their bluff. They can't prove anything.'

The chief of the internat was a large balding man named Mr Titov who stood behind his desk as we marched in. Looking extremely serious, he went on and on complaining with boring monotony about our scandalous activity.

Did we realise that our irresponsible behaviour could have burned down the internat? As he droned on, it became clear that he knew a great deal about our plot to escape. When he asked us to confess, each of us stubbornly refused. My coaching had worked.

As Mr Titov became enraged, more details of our plan emerged. This tricky piece of negotiation had to be handled by the leader: I couldn't expect it of the rank and file. 'It's all guess work,' I began, deciding to brazen it out. 'Anyone could have gone in there. We deny everything. You have no proof.' I was totally convinced that there was no way he could catch us red-handed.

With a flourish, Mr Titov opened a drawer in his desk and cast his bounty on to the table. It was the diary, plotting our escape. Our names, dates, what we planned to do, everything!

Complete proof! Sasha must have carelessly left it behind. Gasping in shock, we hung our heads at such damning evidence.

How could I have been so stupid! I breathed a sigh of relief to think I was not going to lead these idiots in search of our own secret island after all.

The following morning, I was summoned to a meeting with the senior staff of the internat. It was agreed that I had been a disruptive and bad influence and I was issued with one final warning. If I didn't change, I would be expelled.

'I don't have a home to go to,' I argued. 'Get out of here!' Mr Titov yelled. 'I don't want to see you!'

One night, blinded by panic and the fear of abandonment, I strung my belt around a beam in the hallway, tying a noose in the soft brown leather. Believing that no one cared about me and with nothing to live for, I climbed on to a stool, strapping the noose around my neck. 'Jump,' someone in a mask was shouting inside my head.

I jumped.

A million light bulbs flashed. Car brakes squealed. Mud from the road splashed everywhere. A glass smashed against the wall. Mama's face floated across the roof of the sky.

The belt snapped and I fell in a heap on the floor, bruising my leg badly. Suicide could be a painful experience, I reasoned as I was carried to the medical centre.

Little had changed however. Wild and uncontrollable, I was expelled from the internat within a few months.

Ura received me warmly, glad of some company, I think. But the state of the house indicated that Ura had sunk even deeper in his debauchery. There was no food in the larder, clothes were everywhere, the settee was ripped apart and the bed had not been made since Vera left.

Ura had taken a job in the local park, where he earned about fifty roubles which he would spend on alcohol and prostitutes.

Returning home one night, I found Ura with a young girl. He insisted that I stay, but I slipped away again to ride the Leningrad subway. I covered every corner of the city. Where was there left to explore?

Back at the flat I found the prostitute asleep naked on the bed. Ura lay curled up on the floor in his own urine.

Seeing Ura's shame, I crept into the communal bathroom for a shower and felt the spray of water run down my body. I wanted to wash the events of the night away from me and change my clothes. Then I walked back on to the streets of Leningrad.

Somehow the day passed but I dreaded returning to the flat and rode the subway, tram cars and trolley buses again. I had learnt how to slip unnoticed through the ticket barrier without paying, and took the tram to the last stop on the line. I headed for Labour Square and then into Theatre Square. Slinking along the backstreets I watched the shining neon lights beckon, as smartly dressed foreigners visited the theatre and ballet, walking arm in arm with ladies in bright coloured dresses.

My feet led me down to the waterfront of the Neva River. Everyone had a home to go to, but I walked the streets with nowhere to turn.

Old men with walking sticks sat admiring the scene. I could see the coloured lights of some ships docked further along the river and crossed the bridge turning left along the bank.

I found myself hurrying along the pavement and soaking in the refreshing, exhilarating atmosphere. The military ships caught my eye with their flags and cannons. I climbed up on to the harbour wall above the blue-grey water to get a better view of the sailors, who looked so dashing in their uniforms. I couldn't think of anything more exciting than to serve our country in the navy.

I returned night after night to the waterfront, totally fascinated. One evening, I could hear music and laughter coming from the pier. A group of young people had gathered round three sailors playing the accordion and singing traditional songs. After a few choruses I felt as if I belonged to the group, who were impressed by my enthusiasm and my high ranging vocals.

They asked if I knew any songs. 'Sure,' I replied and serenaded them with a bawdy song I had picked up at the internat. The sailors laughed hilariously while the girls blushed and giggled.

I was an immediate hit. The sailors smuggled me on board and I slept in an empty cabin, waking the next morning full of excitement. I was given a guided tour of the ship and then ate a hearty breakfast. I also got my first taste of coffee. The ship had been docked opposite a submarine, fuelling my mind with romantic escapades of the sea.

One group of sailors who served on the smaller pilot boats based in the harbour became my special friends. I told them I was an orphan, and could I spend my school holidays with them? The captain consented, providing me with the holiday of my dreams.

I began to panic when I learned that Ura had alerted the police to my absence. It wasn't long before my 'holiday' came to an end.

Ura was insistent that I return to the internat. I landed in trouble on my first day. It was only a matter of time before I was expelled again, without regrets on either side. Ura's annoyance was obvious but his own life was careering out of control, so what hope did he have of taking charge over this fourteen-year-old punk?

And so I went from orphanage to Ura to internat and then back to Ura again. I felt like an unclaimed parcel in search of an owner.

I found Ura collapsed on the floor with a whore going through his wallet. It was empty. She insisted that she was only taking what she was owed for services rendered. Shoving her out of the flat, I tried to move Ura to his bed, which was difficult because of his size. Taking one last look at the flat, I called out, 'Goodbye Uncle Ura.' His snoring confirmed that he couldn't hear me and I left.

This time I had a plan! I knew that some ships hired youngsters for short-term periods and I was determined to become a sailor. A rugged sailor named Duke negotiated a position for me aboard his ship.

The idea of a ship's boy had captured the sailors' imagination and they took up a collection for me to purchase the uniform I needed, but I was unable to find naval boots in my size. They consoled me by saying I was a modern sailor with civilian shoes.

I was even given an identity card with my photograph, bearing the ship's official seal. My assignment lasted from May to September and I was treated like a regular sailor.

On my first parade I saluted with my head held high. The captain received me with a twinkle in his eye. I could see the others grinning, but I took it seriously.

Soon I knew every corner of the ship. I loved to feel the rough salty sea water spray my clothes as I polished the brass bells and ornaments.

On one occasion I was ordered to paint the anchor and chain, located in a deep, dark corner of the ship. To make matters worse, it had to be painted black! As I struggled in the dark I slipped and upset the balance of the chain, which disentangled and spun around, rolling over me. As I lay pinned under the heavy chain, I felt the sticky paint on my hands and hair.

For several hours I shouted for help, but it was my absence at the meal table that alerted the crew. As the sailors peered into the darkness, my pathetic cries enlisted laughter rather than pity. This was one occasion when I never shared the joke!

I was given the top bunk in Duke's cabin. He was a tall, powerful man but he loved me and nicknamed me 'the kid'. One night when Duke was on duty I fell out of my bunk.

Sleepily, I crawled back into bed and went back to sleep. Duke was alarmed when he saw me in the morning. 'What happened? Have you been in a fight?'

'It's nothing,' I replied although I did admit to having a headache. Duke insisted that I should see the doctor. I was not going to be cheated out of my turn to be 'the flagman'. This was one of my favourite duties, signalling to the ships that sailed past.

'I can't do that, I don't have time this morning,' I replied with annoyance. 'Besides, haven't I got the right to fall down?'

Duke may have been amused, but he looked really serious. 'You'll go straight to the medical room, young man,' Duke warned, gripping my arm and thrusting me in front of the mirror. No wonder I had a headache! There was a deep cut on my head and bruises all over my face. Reluctantly, I agreed to visit the doctor, who signed me off sick for two days. Those days were the ones I regretted most of my five-month trip.

Some weeks later, our ship passed two uninhabited islands in the Baltic Sea called Moishne and Gogland. From the ship we could see bushes, so the ship's chef sent a team to collect berries for making juice and puddings. It was agreed that I should go too, and as we climbed into the dinghies I was warned that this was a serious responsibility.

At first I worked hard. I decided that I should also sample some to test the quality. If they were not ripe, we would be wasting our time, I reasoned.

But they were delicious! My trips to empty my container became fewer and fewer. Finally, it was time to return and we passed our work load up to a round of applause.

As we climbed aboard, the chef slapped my shoulder. 'We know how hard you've been working, don't we!' Everyone on deck laughed, but I resented his insinuation that I hadn't worked hard.

I decided to shower, and as I undressed, I caught a glimpse of my reflection in the mirror. To my horror, my lips were completely black! The crew's laughter rang in my ears as I prepared to face them at dinner. When the berry juice was passed round I winced and said seriously, 'I've had enough, thank you,' much to everyone's amusement.

The ship would return regularly to Kronstadt pier in the months I served. One day I was given the responsibility of steering the small launch ferrying people to the shore. Another motor-launch followed us on our route, which was marked by tall wooden posts indicating the depth. I made a game out of guiding the boat as close to the posts as possible, which the officer on board found amusing.

The launch following us began to do the same, however, the pilot took his eye off the target for an instant and began to swerve into a post. Realising the danger, one of the officers reacted quickly by grabbing the wheel.

When we finally docked, safe and dry, the officer on board my boat congratulated me on my skill. 'I can tell that you were born for the sea!' he remarked. I experienced an over-whelming sense of joy as I saluted him. This was a compliment indeed, as the officers were strict with me and made no allowances for my age.

I felt very proud whenever I went ashore with the sailors. I looked like everyone else, just a little shorter! When friends in Leningrad caught sight of me, most were amazed. The first time I returned to Ura's flat, I saw his eyes widen in surprise.

I was crestfallen when September came around. My last night was marked by a special party on board. Somehow I got through that winter shuttling back and forth between Ura's flat and the internats around Leningrad. I lived for next summer, when I could return to sea.

I got a postcard from Duke who told me to look up a friend of his. Through this contact, I was able to obtain another summer posting and sailed the Russian coast once again from May till September.

At the end of that period, I was forced to make a decision.

I was no longer 'the kid', and finding ships to sign me up was not easy. Getting into the navy required qualifications and formal training. Finally I was forced to admit that I would have to dry-dock all my seafaring dreams, at least for the moment.

I had learned to operate a film projector during my days at sea, and was hired at the Sputnik Cinema on Nevsky Street. I had tried to study, but found it difficult to concentrate. As a street-wise sixteen-year-old, the cinema seemed more true to life.

The Sputnik Cinema, named after Yuri Gagarin's rocket ship with which we had beaten the Americans into space, screened foreign films dubbed into Russian. Among the favourites were John Wayne and Humphrey Bogart. Musicals such as *Seven Brides for Seven Brothers* and *Oklahoma* were also popular. I particularly liked the up-tempo music of Glenn Miller films like *Sun Valley Serenade*, and learnt to sing 'Chattanooga Choo-Choo' but never understood the words. It became a personal mission to meet foreigners just to find out what the songs meant.

Many people made illegal recordings of the films' soundtracks, and the tapes would appear on the black market all over town. One night someone loaned me some pirate tapes recorded from foreign stations such as the BBC or the Voice of America.

Listening to these new rhythms was like receiving an electric shock. I had never heard anything like it before. Elvis Presley, Bill Haley and the Comets became instant legends. Boogie woogie, rhythm and blues, twist. I loved it all.

When the cinema showed a rock and roll documentary it caused a sensation. I sneaked my cousins Slavik and Valya in through the back door. It was an astonishing moment. Few of us could understand the words, but there wasn't a communication problem.

I watched every performance with my eyes riveted to the screen. Soon I found I could sing along with the group on celluloid. See you later, alligator!

One night I saw someone squinting continually at me as the film was rolling. He walked across and I heard a familiar voice say, 'Valeri, is that you?'

I stared hard for a few moments, 'George?'

It seemed unbelievable. George! On stage Bill Haley was leading his Comets into a frantic version of 'Shake, Rattle and Roll', as in his audience a joyful reunion of two pirates who were going to escape from the internat together was set to music.

I had bought an accordion and George played the flute, so we formed a band by adding a trumpet, bass and drums to the line-up. We played songs learned from foreign radio broadcasts and found loyal fans in Slavik and Valya who always hung around.

But we were teenagers and took nothing very seriously. The jam sessions drifted into drinking bouts. Bad company and a weak will made it easy to live on the wild side of life. I was soon an eighteen-year-old rebel who had tasted the bitter-sweet fruit of life and had begun to challenge the established order.

Music held a mirror to my heart, the passage of release. It drew from my soul that which I couldn't reveal to anyone else. Bright, buoyant music set my foot tapping and my thoughts roaming. Melancholic music left me desolate. Why am I so lonely? Why did Mama have to die? What am I living for? The questions seemed too solemn for a teenager like me.

'Why should I live any differently?' I once questioned George. 'Who knows where I'll be tomorrow? Today is all I have.'

With little reason to change, I had become like a railway carriage detached from an express train. Now devoid of guidance or stability, I was hurtling down the tracks at great speed, wild and free with nothing in sight.

And wham! As if from nowhere everything changed. A letter from the army ordered me to report for duty. From being an aimless drifter, I was now to be drafted into a lifestyle of rigid discipline, forced on to me like a ball and chain.

3

Red Army Blues: 1963–1972

Private Barinov! It seemed like a fantastic dream. At eighteen, I would have given everything for the motherland, but all that was asked of me was two years of my life, so I signed up without hesitation. I treated every night as a farewell party and got blind drunk. I'll change when I'm in the army, I promised myself.

The day before I left, Aunt Tamara invited me for a farewell dinner with Slavik, Valya and George among the guests. Tamara loved me dearly and tried to care for me after Mama's death, but had her own difficulties and I was unable to share my heart with her.

During the meal I kept everyone amused by taking a swig from a bottle of spirits whenever my aunt's back was turned. Tamara knew something was up, wagging her finger at me, half in jest, scolding, 'Valeri, you're drunk!'

After the meal we crowded on to the balcony, singing songs, and swapping stories. I picked up my accordion and everyone joined me in the chorus of 'Good-bye dear mother, I'm off to war'. As we lingered in the cool evening, arm in arm, Tamara said wistfully, 'If only your mother could see you now, she would be proud of you, Valeri.'

She went on to talk to me about God. Smiling and nodding

my head, I maintained my image as a level-headed, serious-minded teenager. The others had all gone indoors to listen to the radio, leaving me as Tamara's captive audience.

'God exists, Valeri,' she stated emphatically. 'When you're in the army you will hear lots of talk about God. Don't argue, because you don't know who he is. If you have a problem, pray to God with all your heart, and he will hear you. He is a God of miracles but to some people, he is a mystery. You will know him by his action. You can see God in nature. This world didn't just happen. God exists!'

There were no pauses as she continued in hushed tones and I listened out of respect. Her words mingled with the traffic noise from twelve floors below. Like a farmer sowing his seed in a field, her words were carried into the evening air, sprinkled into the atmosphere.

I had mixed emotions as I walked into the army barracks. I loved my country, and carried my rifle with pride, but I would still have preferred to be in the navy.

With my shaved head and starched uniform, I was posted to Riga under Colonel Sergei Sekunov, a renowned disciplinarian. I was commended for my marching skills and selected for special parades welcoming visiting dignitaries.

However, my behaviour was far from that of a model soldier. In exasperation, Colonel Sekunov said to me one day, 'Barinov, I love you as a son, but I hate you as a soldier.' I remained at attention and replied, 'Yes sir! Thank you sir!'

I trained as an assistant radio operator, and late at night I listened to foreign broadcasts. In this way I first heard the extraordinary music of the Beatles. Recalling our pirate tapes at the Sputnik Cinema, I set about producing tapes of their songs as well as the Rolling Stones and Bob Dylan.

One day I decided to liven up the army camp. Usually a drum roll and bugle call roused us from our slumber. Bringing a modern touch to this 5 a.m. army ritual, I woke the entire camp with Bill Haley's 'Rock around the Clock'. The volume of this amplified alarm call was only matched by the blasting I received from Colonel Sekunov later that morning.

I loved animals, and made special friends of our tracker dogs, Rex and Boxer. When our unit was on night patrol around our base they waited for me to get drunk and then ate up all my food rations.

I was selected for the coveted position of projectionist, and a sergeant in my unit became jealous. In a vendetta designed to break me, he subjected me to a continuous series of humiliating tasks. His favourite was forcing me to clean the toilets all night long. He tried to engineer my dismissal, frequently putting me on the punishment list.

I found myself fearing the future, confused and depressed. On night patrols the stillness of the stars in the velvet sky created a backdrop for my restlessness. Then a new thought crept into my mind.

Valeri, you have no future here. This world is enemy territory. End it all. It's the best you can do. The logic of this solution found a foothold in my heart.

However, next weekend wasn't any different, and we ended up at an all-night drinking party. Maxim was a burly youth who always knew where to find another bottle, and I was always around to help him empty it. Perhaps it was the cheap wine, but Maxim was in a talkative mood. Aware of my depression, he said, 'Life is what you make of it, Valeri. The world is out to screw you, so don't trust anyone and screw them first! Live fast and live for the day, be sure to have a good time.'

'Yes but isn't there any real love in the world?' I asked without looking directly at him.

The word sent Maxim into giggles. 'Ha! What is love? And how much does it cost? That's the real question. Ask the whore on Karl Marx Avenue. She'll tell you the price of love.' Then with finality, Maxim said, 'There's no such thing as love, not real love. It's just a word kids carve on trees, you know what I mean, Valeri loves Anna!'

'But what about God, Maxim? Is there a God?'

'Oh, Valeri, what a joke. That's just a fairy story taught by old ladies. What did our great hero Yuri Gagarin see – God? Of course not!' Then speaking slowly to emphasise each word, Maxim said, 'There is no God, Valeri. N-O G-O-D!' Maxim was not keen to waste any drinking time on serious talk.

In bed that night I lay awake. If anyone knew anything, it was Maxim, but this time I didn't believe him.

A few weeks later I was standing guard over a supply depot with Gregor, who was considered boring company. 'Live a little,' people told him, 'Don't take it all so seriously. America might bomb us any minute, and it will all be over in a lightning flash.' We spent the hours talking to keep each other awake.

'Do you believe in God?' I asked, surprising myself with the question.

'I just don't know, Valeri,' Gregor replied, taken aback. 'I don't think there is conclusive proof of the existence of God. But when you consider the galaxy and the interplanetary system, and the spectacular beauty of nature,' he paused again before continuing, 'and then the complexities of the atom, and nuclear energy . . .'. My question had obviously touched something deep within. 'And the mystery of childbirth . . .' his words tailed off into the night.

'It does make you think,' Gregor continued. 'I can't say there is a God, but I think there is something there. Don't ask me what it is because I don't know.' The question never left my mind.

I had known many women but Viktoria, or Vikki, was my first real love. We met at a dance in town where my army buddies all vied for her, but she only had eyes for me. She worked in a fabrics factory near the base, so it was all too easy to sneak away to see her.

Young and pretty, Vikki wanted us to marry, but I wasn't ready to be tied down. Going AWOL had its penalties, as I soon learned, but it was worth it just to be near her.

The army ranked patrol duty as more important than night manoeuvres with Viktoria, and by the end of my second year, in 1966, I was facing a spell in the military prison.

The army's patience with this wild kid from Leningrad was running out. This time, my foolish erratic behaviour brought me before a court martial which threatened to terminate my career.

One night in the prison cell, in despair, I found myself reviewing my life. What was the point of it all? I lost everything when I lost my mother. I missed her world of love and warmth, and recalled memories of sunny Sunday mornings at the Orthodox Church where we shared communion regularly.

Although still young, my experience of life had left me with no illusions about people. Everyone else seemed as lost and confused as I, filled with lies and deceit. The Communist revolution had resulted in a country without justice or free-dom. These basic rights were replaced with mass corruption. It was a one-way street to destruction, with no exit.

If my search for truth and love was to be in vain, perhaps it would be better to kill myself and kiss this world good-bye. I thought I had decided my future, and I grew morose and depressed as I tossed and turned that night.

But two days later when I returned to my cell at sunset after my duties, I noticed a tall grey building through the prison window. At the top stood a cross. As the sun was sinking, the dim light revived a sudden flood of memories of a conversa-tion with my Aunt Tamara.

Against all the odds her words had returned to my mind, 'Valeri, if you forget everything else I've said, just remember one thing. God exists!'

GOD EXISTS! GOD EXISTS! GOD EXISTS!

Repeating the words to myself gave the idea life in my heart.

Yes, I thought to myself, maybe there really is a God.

I knelt down on the cold concrete floor desperately trying to recall how to enter the secret world of prayer. Long ago I had seen people cross themselves in church and tried to repeat the action, but what was the correct procedure? Startled by the complexity of this ritual, I suddenly found myself saying:

> Oh God,
> If you really exist, then you will help me
> because I'm pleading to you with all my heart.
> But if you're not there and if you only exist
> in people's minds, then you can't help me,
> and you will remain silent.

That night I fell into a deep sleep.

The next morning I remained remarkably calm as I waited outside the judicial enquiry office for my tribunal to begin. To my surprise and delight, I was cleared of the charges.

I had prayed and the answer had come. God exists! I accepted this as a promise, the first step along my journey.

At last! Eleven days after my twentieth birthday, on December 17, 1966, I was officially discharged from the army. As I loaded my rucksack into the jeep to leave, some nervous-looking teenagers tumbled out of the army bus. I smiled to myself and thought of my first days as a recruit.

An official escort put us on the train to Leningrad, but I got off at the next stop and made my way back to Riga, straight to Viktoria's arms. Vikki was impetuous just like me. In an impulsive moment we made plans for the future, but three weeks later, stirred by an inner restlessness, I kissed her good-bye and caught the train to Leningrad again.

Valya had grown up fast with long flowing hair and a winsome manner. I was sorry to learn of Uncle Ura's death, and Valya clung to me in a tearful embrace. I understood the tensions she had faced as a young person living in a family at war.

My first few nights in Leningrad were not spent in wild drinking sprees at the familiar haunts. George and my other friends couldn't understand what was going on.

Tamara moved elegantly through the room, dusting the flat. Perhaps sensing that I wanted to talk to her, she called out, 'Valeri, do you want some tea?'

We sat in the kitchen sipping strong tea with slices of lemon.

'I can't explain how I'm different, but I know I am because I feel like a new person,' I said almost in wonder.

'I know what you mean,' Tamara said. 'The scriptures tell of such experiences. That's what Jesus meant when he said, "You must be born again".'

'I want to be born again,' the words shot out of my mouth. 'That's how I feel. There's a tingling in my heart and senses.'

'The way to God is through Jesus. He is the door. Once we know him he will never leave us.'

'You mean, it's possible to experience God wherever you are?'

'Yes, Valeri, God is a spirit and he can be with us everywhere, in every circumstance. Even in this kitchen, he is with us.'

I nodded my head, although somewhat mystified by the theology. I was hungry for information and my mind was racing with questions.

How could I be sure I was born again? Did Christian believers really sacrifice their children live on the altar, or was this propaganda? Did Jesus really exist as a historical person, or was the Bible full of fairy stories? Did Jesus really rise from the dead? And finally, could Jesus really change my life? Tamara fielded my questions which tumbled out the more she tried to explain. My response was enthusiastic. 'I want it! I want it!'

Perhaps mistaking my reply for youthful zeal, she explained

mysteriously, 'You're young, you have your life ahead of you. You have time to decide.'

But God looked at my heart. He could see that I really wanted to be his servant. Leaning across the table, clutching my aunt's hands in mine, I spoke in earnest. 'Auntie, tell me what I should do. I believe that God exists. I believe in the holy sacrifice of Jesus. I believe that he died for me. Tell me what I should do now.'

'It's very simple,' Aunt Tamara replied. 'Just give yourself completely, all that you have to Jesus. He knows what you need. He will lead you through life by his Holy Spirit.'

I stared imploringly at her. Almost at once I began to pray secretly in my heart, 'Lord, let her go from this house leaving me alone here with you.'

To my amazement, Tamara pushed back her chair and said, somewhat embarrassed, 'Excuse me Valeri, I must go and do some shopping now because we have guests for dinner and I need to prepare some food.'

The very instant the door slammed shut, I knelt down and cried out to God, 'Oh Lord, from this very second, I want to be completely yours.'

I was like a shipwrecked sailor who catches sight of a steamer sending out a rescue boat.

Although the earth did not move and there were no miraculous signs, I did feel peace in my heart as I rose. I recognised this as the same peace that I had experienced as a child when my mother recited the Lord's Prayer. I was aware of a spiritual awakening within myself. I knew things would be different and I felt a mounting sense of excitement.

When I awoke early the next morning I thought my heart was going to burst with joy. 'Now I really am a child of God,' I told myself. 'I was an orphan but now I have a daddy in heaven. Praise God!' I wanted to dance through the streets and cartwheel along the pavements yelling, 'People of

Leningrad, why do you live without God?'

Crowding into George's front room where the new Beatles album was playing, I tried to join Paul McCartney's voice on the chorus, 'Good day sunshine, Good day sunshine, Good day sunshine!' The gang were amused that I talked about God instead of cursing and swearing. It was all a big joke. When they realised I wasn't drunk, they thought I was crazy. I related my experience in the army, 'I had a problem and I prayed to God. I escaped punishment even though I deserved it. It was a miracle. I know it's true, God exists!'

I had immediately stopped smoking and drinking, and with the bravado of youth, felt I knew all I needed to know about the spiritual life. I had 'arrived'. But there were many lessons to be learned.

How could I explain that God lived in my heart, and that I was filled with peace and joy? One night alone in my room, I prayed, 'O Lord, give me a mouth so that I can share your holy love with everyone all over this world.' It took me several years to understand the significance of this simple prayer.

God cradled me in his loving arms for two months. But I was impatient to prove my own capability and independence. I told him, 'Lord, I am ready. I will do anything for you, and go anywhere for you. Look I've already stopped smoking and it's been two months since I've touched a drop of vodka.'

And the Lord said, 'OK, my son.' And still cradling me, he placed me on the ground. Of course I was still a child, and as I reached the ground and tried to stand on my own, I tumbled down. Thinking myself to be sufficient in my own strength, it wasn't long before I fell into temptation.

One night I was talking about the Lord with George and the gang but continued to swig from the bottle each time it came round. Somehow I managed to stagger home but collapsed in the alleyway by my aunt's home.

In the frolic my shirt and trouser buttons had been ripped

off, and I had picked up an old bugle on which I blew a bawdy bar song.

I awoke in the flat with a hangover, and the little I could remember about the night before made me squirm. Aunt Tamara found me sitting in the kitchen sipping tea. She didn't speak and I was content to ignore her. However, I couldn't escape her probing eyes.

'They're selling winter coats at the corner. Do you want to come with me and see if there's anything you like?' she remarked. Winter coats in summer or swimming gear in winter weren't a surprise. Soviet production has no marketing strategy. Things suddenly appear in shops, street corners and the backs of cars and you buy them while you can. It was all crazy.

I didn't really want to go, but I didn't want to cause an argument. Besides, I knew that Tamara wanted to speak to me about last night and I couldn't evade that conversation.

Leaving the flat we stepped almost straight into our neighbour, a stout woman named Galina. She was a firm atheist, and nothing I said to her seemed to make any impression.

She plunged straight for the weak spot. 'What was that song you were singing last night, Valeri? A new song about Jesus?'

Tamara was silent. I stared at my shoes.

Galina was relentless in her pursuit. 'Where is your god now? Is this how Christians behave, keeping us awake at night? What a joke.' Her mocking laugh rang in the stairwell as we left.

I hung out with the same crowd that night. Within the next few days I couldn't keep up the pretence of a changed life and soon slid back to my old ways. How I shamed Aunt Tamara.

Two months later, Galina confronted Aunt Tamara about my drunkenness. Tamara was remarkably calm, and told Galina, 'God knows everything. Our lives are in his hands. We will all have to answer to God personally. Valeri will, I will, and you, Galina, will also have to answer to God.'

I was in the flat with my ear pressed to the front door as my aunt dealt with our nosy neighbour. I knew I was in the wrong, but how could I change my ways?

I apologised to Tamara and told her how wretched I felt. 'I think the best thing I can do is to leave Leningrad.'

Although Tamara was shocked, she quickly regained her composure. 'Yes, maybe you're right, Valeri. But where would you go?'

I already knew of an expedition leaving shortly for Siberia to complete a topographical survey for a planned new airfield, and the group needed an assistant. After a few calls and a brief interview, I was hired. The group was leaving in two days.

I couldn't handle a farewell party, so I only told George I was leaving. Tamara had mixed emotions about me being away all summer. On my last evening at home, I solemnly packed my few clothes and belongings into my army rucksack. Tamara cooked my favourite fried-chicken dish for me, but although we laughed and joked, somehow the sparkle was missing.

'God bless you, Valeri,' Tamara said as we embraced for the last time. I loved her so dearly and was distressed that I had hurt her. I knew I would miss Tamara and everyone else in Leningrad.

I was leaving under a dark cloud. A sense of disgrace and loss dominated my final hours. But I felt I had no choice. I knew that if I stayed longer, I could not survive.

Siberia. The thought sent a chill through me. What did the future hold?

4

Tanya the Redhead

About 2,000 km from Leningrad lies the mining town of Uray in the heart of Siberia. It is near Turmin, an old city to which the enemies of the Tsar were banished. Siberia itself has come to symbolise a land of prisoners in a never-ending winter of exile, of isolated communities of log cabins which never appear on any maps.

Progress and the twentieth century were catching up with Siberia's rich unexploited reserves of oil, gas, coal and iron ore. The expedition on which I was an assistant produced site plans and data for architectural drawings for the airport to be built at the developing centre of Uray.

Although the Saturday-night dance was never mentioned in the newspapers, the unofficial grapevine ensured that everyone in Uray was there. An hour before the doors opened, there were kids hanging around at the entrance.

A dance band with homemade instruments played traditional songs but tried to jazz it up a bit.

After playing for an hour, the band took a break and I introduced myself to Jan, the leader of the group. Before I knew it he had insisted that I join the group on stage.

I sang the Beatles song 'All my loving', and immediately several of the girls clapped in time to the music. News of the rock and roll revolution had obviously spread, as the dancers were inspired to further improvised movements. By the end of the song, a crowd had gathered below the stage and everyone in the hall seemed to be clapping and cheering.

Jan gave me thumbs up. 'Great. Great,' he shouted. 'By the way, do you know any other songs?' We may not have won any musical awards, but we were having fun and I launched into another Beatles song.

My hair was long, and I wore a Beatle-style jacket. As I was from Leningrad, the group expected me to know the latest pop songs and fashions. No one else in the town had tried anything like this, and we were considered daring. During my time in Uray, we gained a reputation for playing rock and roll.

On completion of the airport plans, it was time for the expedition to move on to Annaderth, a remote settlement nearer Alaska than Moscow. At this point I requested permission to stay in Uray. The leader was a kind man who agreed and said, 'Perhaps music is your life.'

I not only missed Leningrad, but also my girlfriend Viktoria from Riga. I sent her the money for an airline ticket to join me in Uray, but I suspected something was not right from the letters she wrote. In spite of her excuses for delaying the trip, she never came.

One day I was drunk and decided to speak to Vikki immediately, so I staggered to the post office. The sweet red-haired girl behind the counter placed the call, and finally I heard her voice on the telephone.

'Vikki, when are you coming to see me, my love?' I yelled down the phone, much to the amusement of the other customers. Vikki seemed detached and vague, and the call was over much too soon.

The girl at the counter tapped her desk to attract my attention. I sauntered over and called out, 'I'm in love but my girlfriend is in Riga!'

'Never mind your girlfriend,' the redhead replied, 'you owe

me ten roubles for your phone call.'

'What's your name?' I asked the girl.

'Tanya.'

She was attractive, but the people behind me were no longer amused. 'G'bye!' I called, and staggered out of the post office.

I decided to surprise Vikki by visiting her unexpectedly a few days before my birthday. No one was home, so I had to wait half an hour on a bench outside her block. When I saw her we rushed into each others' arms as if in a romantic movie.

We spent the next few days in a lovers' daze, and celebrated my birthday. When the vodka ran out, Vikki's friend Katya took me to a backstreet 'fixer' to buy some alcohol. In the taxi, Katya turned to me and said, 'Vikki doesn't deserve you. Did you know she has a lover?'

I couldn't be sure if Katya was a troublemaker or making a play for me, but I dared her to give me proof. Directing the taxi-driver to a high-rise block, Katya took me to a nondescript apartment. We rang the bell and a tall bearded youth answered the door.

'Katya . . .' he stammered. 'What are you doing here?'

Katya was forthright. 'Are you Vikki's boyfriend?'

'Yes,' he blurted, not giving the word a second thought, ushering us into an untidy room. His name was Leo, and he freely admitted that although Vikki and he were lovers, they weren't all that serious about each other.

As we looked at photographs of Leo and Vikki caught in a lovers' embrace, the proof burnt my eyes. What really hurt was the way she looked at him.

Leo hung his head sheepishly as Katya and I walked to the door. Back at the flat, Vikki immediately knew something was amiss. 'What happened to you?' she asked. 'I was worried.'

'It's no use, Vikki, he knows,' Katya replied. 'I just couldn't hide the truth from him anymore.'

Vikki crumpled into my arms. 'Oh Valeri, I'm sorry. I tried to tell you. I'm so confused.'

'It's my birthday party,' I said, trying to sound cheerful. 'This is a time for laughter not for tears. Don't stop the celebrations.'

But among the empty vodka bottles that lined the kitchen floor, I felt dazed and alone. Vikki clung to me as though I was some sailor on his last night in port. The cassette player seemed to be playing songs just for me, as I tried to hide my heartbreak. Vikki lifted a vodka bottle to her lips to drown her tears.

Somehow we made it through the night.

The next morning when I awoke I couldn't find my suitcase among the sleeping entwined bodies in the flat, so I threw my belongings into a cloth sack. Vikki looked peaceful as she lay on the bed, moving slowly in her sleep. 'Good-bye, Vikki,' I whispered, and walked from the room.

A wave of loneliness washed over me as I closed the door, and Riga suddenly seemed an unfriendly town.

But I couldn't forget Vikki. Back in Uray I began drinking more heavily than before. I tried to pray, insisting that I would turn from my old ways, but I was powerless to change.

I shared a flat with our bass guitarist Boris, and Pavel our drummer, and we became close friends and drinking partners. One night, Pavel saw a religious tract that my aunt had sent me. 'What are you doing with this?' he joked.

'I'm a Christian,' I replied.

Pavel began to joke about my lifestyle, not realising I was serious. This annoyed me, so I retorted, 'My life will change. I love Jesus. I will stop drinking.'

'If someone else told me that, I would believe it. But not you, Valeri!' Pavel laughed even more. 'I can't imagine what you'd be like without a drink.'

I woke up in a sweat after a vivid dream. Uncle Ura was standing in the middle of the room and I approached him burdened with guilt. He looked at me and said, 'Clean your feet!' I then looked down and realised that my feet were muddy and that I had left a trail of dirt behind me as I walked into the room.

Understanding the dream immediately, I didn't hesitate to kneel beside my bed. 'Jesus, without your help, I will perish,' I whispered, deeply moved by the experience. 'Lord Jesus, I surrender to you. Help me!'

I felt a release and a sense of cleansing. Although I had turned away from God, he had not abandoned me. I was lost and searching for a way out, but God knew this moment would come, as he continued to work in my heart.

I carried on praising God as I rose from my knees and walked to the window. I also prayed for a girl to share my life. Outside the street seemed tranquil in the silky moonlight. I understood that I was a solitary pilgrim tramping through this world.

For the next few days, I walked a tightrope between conscience and corruption. Boris and Pavel understood that I was caught in an internal conflict, but they were powerless to help.

On Saturday night, 27 April, we joined Pavel at a wedding reception to which he had been invited. We were used to gatecrashing.

We arrived in time to wave good-bye to the happy couple as they left for a holiday on the Black Sea. Minutes later I bumped into the bride again, who had completely changed her appearance and now served wine and wedding cake to the guests! Astounded by the transformation, I soon realised the answer was much simpler.

The bride and the girl were twins.

There was a flicker of recognition as I thanked her for the wine. In a flash, I remembered an embarrassing episode at the local post office. I knew that she had recognised me as well.

There was a sparkle in our encounter and we were hardly out of each other's sight over the next hour.

For once I declined Boris and Pavel's invitation to join an impromptu band. The group began to play Elvis Presley's 'Love me tender' as I manoeuvred Tanya on to the floor for a slow dance together. Holding her tight, I guided her towards the verandah as the song was drawing to an end. Still cuddling and giggling like teenagers on a first date, we walked to the end of the porch hand in hand.

I put my arms around her and gave her a squeeze. She seemed to respond. Seize the moment, I thought. Closing my eyes, I planted a kiss on her lips.

Was it an earth tremor after just one kiss? No! It was Tanya's mother jerking us apart. I guess she didn't want to lose two daughters in one night. 'I know your kind,' she barked. 'My daughter isn't going to be led astray by someone like you.'

I knew a potential mother-in-law would not see me as an ideal prospect with my long hair and tight black clothes. Risking her wrath I hung around the party for another hour, joining the jam session.

Surreptitiously I arranged to see the redhead after work at the post office during the week.

I just couldn't get her out of my mind. Tanya! Tanya! Tanya!

Although she had a temper to match the legend of the fiery redhead, I found her shy, unassuming and delightful. I discovered that she wasn't impressed by the number of Beatles songs that I could sing in English. Incredibly, she didn't even like the Beatles.

I found that I could relax with her and over the next few months a serious attachment formed between us.

Tanya's mother worked at the local factory and was strict with her children, rarely allowing them out at night, and extremely particular about the boys they dated. In a small town like Uray, gossip spread quickly.

Tanya wasn't a Christian and found it hard to understand that someone who played rock music, wore jeans and loud clothes could also believe in God.

Tanya's family were involved with occult practices, and she had her mother's gift of foretelling the future. 'I see you have Baptist eyes,' she said to me one evening. Tanya feared Christians, believing that they sacrificed their children in some weird ritual. I tried to explain the Christian faith to her, but she had been steeped in superstitions from childhood, making it difficult for me to speak about Jesus. But I looked for an unlatched window into her soul.

Like everyone else, Tanya loved to listen to the radio and believed everything she heard. After listening to Radio Moscow for half an hour, I returned the set to Radio Monte Carlo. It was a Bible study on the fifteenth chapter of John's Gospel. Soon I could sense Tanya's growing impatience.

'I can't believe that people listen to this in the twentieth century,' Tanya finally interrupted in exasperation. But I didn't budge and replied firmly, 'I listen to it.'

Somewhat surprised, but not wishing to offend me, Tanya covered her tracks, 'Oh! I just thought no one listened to this kind of religious broadcast.'

Sensing a break in the cover, I moved in. Tanya's eyes widened as I explained to her how Aunt Tamara's influence had led me into a personal relationship with God. She didn't share my convictions, but she listened to me.

Despite our differences of belief, I was convinced that we were destined to be together. I telephoned my aunt and shared my feelings. 'If you are sure about it Valeri, then go ahead. Don't put your trust in the counsel of man. Learn to listen to the heart of God. He will guide you. It may be a dangerous route, but it will be the best one.'

I prayed and asked God for direction. *What should I do, Lord?* Tanya returned to my consciousness at every possible moment. She was more than a weekend romance.

Tanya was dreamy and I cradled her in my arms as I asked her the question of a lifetime. Both of us remained silent for a few moments with our private thoughts.

Then with a mischievous look, Tanya said, 'You mean you are prepared to marry someone who doesn't even like rock music?' We collapsed in giggles.

Tanya's parents were understandably reluctant. They found me unpredictable and were horrified by my religious views.

Tanya's mother tried to talk her out of the wedding. 'Why do you want to marry Valeri?' she persisted.

Tanya replied, 'Because he has a tender heart.'

We both felt that we should be married immediately. We hit on December 27, 1968 for the registry office requirements, and the wedding was to follow soon afterwards in the New Year. Tamara agreed to come from Leningrad for the wedding and she wrote a short note of congratulations to Tanya.

One week before the wedding, disaster struck. Tanya developed a large painful boil on her face, and I had lost my red internal passport, a document needed for the registry office. There wasn't enough time for me to apply for a new passport, and Tanya became extremely worried. Her mother hinted that I had hidden the document to get out of the marriage.

Without a word of explanation to Tanya, I bowed my head and prayed, 'Lord Jesus, if it's your will that this wedding should take place and that we are meant for each other, please help me to find my passport.

'Please touch Tanya's body and heal this abscess,' I continued, 'prove to Tanya that you have a wonderful future for both of us.'

Tanya didn't know what to do. It was her first experience of prayer. I assured her that God was interested in the details of her life.

This simple and somewhat naïve prayer had an electric effect. Tanya awoke the next morning feeling considerably better and in much less pain. In two days the boil had vanished without even a scar.

The day after we prayed, I was at home learning the guitar

with Boris. We had just heard the latest Beatles song 'Hey Jude' on the BBC, and I was trying to play it. The doorbell rang, and I was perplexed to find a militiaman standing in the doorway. Reaching into his briefcase, he held out a small red document.

My passport!

At the time, Uray was gripped by 'the great freeze'. That winter was unusually cold even for Siberia, and life effectively stopped as the town was wrapped in a blanket of snow fifty to sixty degrees below zero.

For several days there were no flights in or out of Uray. It seemed unlikely that Aunt Tamara would be able to make the journey from Leningrad in time for our wedding, and I began to be concerned.

Curiously, Tanya seemed to understand the significance of Tamara's presence at our wedding. I comforted her by saying, 'If it's the will of God everything will be OK.'

No one knew what would happen. The day before the wedding the air thinned slightly. We heard on the radio that the area was still enveloped by the freeze, but a patch of clear weather was predicted for Uray. Abruptly, the conditions changed, turning from minus sixty degrees to minus six.

We borrowed a car and somehow made it through the snow to the airport. We didn't even know if Tamara had caught the plane from Leningrad. 'Just pray,' I told Tanya. The airport staff knew nothing in the chaos of cancelled flights.

After two hours, spontaneous applause broke out in the arrivals hall as a flight from Leningrad was announced. Then a few minutes later, Tamara herself walked through the barrier.

Dragging Tanya with me, I raced to hug Tamara. 'We didn't know if you'd make it.'

Tamara laughed with a twinkle in her eye, 'God brought me here.'

Ironically, the freeze returned on the day that Tamara left

again, on 29 December. It seemed that even nature had conspired to celebrate our union.

Tamara brought the wedding rings, the veil, and Tanya's shoes with her. Although she had never seen Tanya before, incredibly everything fitted and Tanya was pleased with my aunt's choice.

On the wedding day Tanya looked beautiful in a fashionable white mini-skirt she had sewn herself. I wanted to whisk her away and carry her into the sunset.

It was hard to get flowers because of the cold weather, but we were able to locate a tiny patch of earth that preserved a delicate bunch of wild flowers, timed to perfection. Tanya clasped the flowers, looking angelic as the moment to make our vows drew near.

The registry office clerk smiled. I was twenty-four and a man of the world. But Tanya looked an innocent eighteen-year-old maiden. As I handed over the red passport and gave Tanya's hand a squeeze, the lady behind the counter gave us a cheeky smile. 'This is your last chance!' she said with the fatal rubber stamp poised over our marriage certificate.

But Tanya clutched my arm tightly and proudly declared, 'I wouldn't change him for anyone else. I love him.'

Later that evening according to traditional custom, we were brought bread and salt on a silver platter. We were required to dip the bread into the salt and eat it together as a symbol of our union. Then we drank a toast to our marriage and smashed the glasses against the fireplace to a great roar of approval from our friends and family.

I was spellbound when I opened Aunt Tamara's present to us. Inside the cardboard box was a large heavily-bound Bible. This was the first Bible I had ever seen. I opened the book and gently turned its pages. This is God's book, I thought to myself. From that moment I read it avidly.

I prayed continually that Tanya would come to know God, and asked my aunt to explain the danger of spiritualist practices to her. I felt that Tanya listened to Tamara and that the foundation of our relationship was a good one.

We held a party in one of the rooms at the sports hall, and with Tanya and me seated on the stage, the toasts were proposed. As the wine was sipped, our friends roared 'Bitter!'

I took Tanya in my arms and kissed her, prompting another sip from the wedding glass, and another roar from the crowd, 'Sweet!'

'One-two-three-four-five-six-seven'. The count continued as Tanya and I were locked in a lovers' embrace, oblivious to everything around us.

We spent our honeymoon in a rented dacha, thirty days of togetherness. I never touched Tanya until our honeymoon. It seemed quite natural, even though my friends had been amazed at my restraint.

Zhanna, our daughter, was born the following October, weighing six pounds and twelve ounces. She was a delightful bundle of joy, and I sat for hours cuddling her and whispering into her ear. A special bond developed between us that has remained through the years. Zhanna was a blessing from God on our family.

I had found work as a driver and was taking an advanced course in professional driving. Late one night as I returned from an assignment, I reflected on how I had met very few Christians in Siberia, and there was no church to attend. It was as if the land was covered with a spiritual darkness.

Approaching the lights of Uray I felt strangely distanced from all that I saw. God had answered my prayer for a girl to share my life, and had given us a beautiful daughter. But I still felt as if I didn't belong in this dark world. I started to pray, 'All I have in this life is a sinner's world, God and myself'.

I found that I was repeating this prayer as I drove. Then through his Holy Spirit, God began to tell me, 'Valeri, this is your world.' On the unlit road the dark night seemed unfriendly and foreboding. I replied, 'No Lord, this isn't my world.'

Again I felt the presence of God. 'Valeri, this is your world.' The message was strong and urgent, and would not leave my mind. I struggled to resist it.

'No Lord,' I insisted, 'this isn't my home. Not this world.'

'Then Valeri, why have I placed you here?'

I had no answer to the challenge.

PART II

ROCK PREACHER

5

Love at the Crossroads

Tanya and I decided to settle in Leningrad, but first I had to return alone to my home town to explore accommodation and job opportunities.

I found myself taking the trolley bus to Labour Square, and drifting towards the Neva River. All I could see were the flashing lights of the harbour, all I could hear was the rustling of the leaves. A dog barking, somewhere in the distance, the sound of an accordion playing a sad refrain.

I strolled along the bank and peered into the swirling river, catching a fleeting glance of my reflection in the water.

A fourteen-year-old waif stared back at me.

Over a decade ago I had sought refuge here from Uncle Ura's anger, curled up under a tree, a homeless runaway, an orphan in the storm.

Reliving a moment from yesterday, I was on the verge of retracing the steps of another poignant journey into the past. Like Mama, I had written to the army resettlement office requesting the current address and whereabouts of a certain Red Army soldier, Alexander Sardonikov.

The contents of a nondescript brown-manilla envelope confirmed that he still lived in Vyborg, near the Finnish border, 270 km from Leningrad. I had written before to Father at this address from Uray, enclosing photographs of his grand-children, but the letters had been returned, with no explanation given.

Perhaps it wasn't my father. Maybe Alexander Sardonikov of Vyborg had never been a soldier.

I simply had to know the answer.

The house on Kraypostnaya Skaya was an old Finnish-style building and the Sardonikov apartment was on the third floor.

On the brink of abandoning my secret mission, memories of the past made me tremble. Battling against my trepidation I climbed to the third floor.

The name on the door looked imposing: ALEXANDER SARDONIKOV.

But no one was in. Undecided, I shuffled along the hallway and knocked at a neighbour's door. Staring intently at the jittery youth fidgeting in front of her, she appeared to recognise me when I mentioned the name Sardonikov. 'Andrew, his son, is here. Ask him.'

Fifteen minutes later, a young teenager charged up the stairs. Something in the way he moved, the way his hair fell on his face, the glint in his eye, told me this was Andrew.

I used my cover story. A man named Alexander Sardonikov had been my driving instructor and now I was tracking him down. The student had come in search of his master.

Andrew responded with buoyant enthusiasm and welcomed me into an elegant room with a beautiful fireplace. The rapport with Andrew was immediate and within minutes we had discovered some striking similarities in taste and personality. To the kid's surprise, we even looked alike.

But I had to be sure.

'Do you have any photographs of your father?' He sprang to his feet and passed me a photo album. I felt as though I had been dowsed with a bucket of ice-cold water. Here was an old sepia photograph of a dashing young soldier. Mama had cherished this same photo.

It was Father!

The next photo was of a group of soldiers on a troop train.

'Don't tell me which one is your father, let me guess,' I said to Andrew, who was captivated by the game.

It didn't take a second.

I asked if there were any duplicate copies of the recent photographs. 'Of course,' he smiled, and handed one over.

The front doorbell announced another visitor to the Sardonikov home. A family friend from another town had come visiting for a few days.

'Mama will be home soon,' Andrew explained. The woman introduced herself, staring curiously at both of us, glancing back and forth. 'Which of you is Alexander's son?' she teased.

Andrew found this hilarious. 'Guess!' he posed the challenge. 'And we have so much in common, it's amazing.'

Without warning the front door opened and a straight faced woman, aged about forty, entered the room. Andrew jumped up and exclaimed, 'Mama, this is Valeri! He's a student of Papa's, but we're so alike it's unbelievable,' Andrew chuckled. The woman's piercing gaze seemed to peel away the veneer from my story.

Andrew's mother embraced the other visitor and both of them sat talking together on the settee. Every few minutes she glared across at me. Every second I stayed in the room seemed to increase the tension, so I rose to my feet and headed for the door.

Andrew argued, insisting that I should stay. 'You haven't even seen my train set.' 'I always wanted a train set,' I admitted, 'but I really must go.'

I didn't want to leave, but I knew I couldn't stay.

At Vyborg railway station, the train to Leningrad was an hour late. When it finally pulled in, I searched out an empty carriage and huddled in the corner, pressing my face against the glass. I watched the landscape float by as the train picked up speed. Like pouring rain in a thunderstorm, a thousand thoughts assailed my mind.

But I had found my Father!

In March 1971, five months after Zhanna's birth, I moved back to Leningrad. Three months later, Tanya and Zhanna joined me. Tanya was apprehensive about moving to the big city, but I was able to allay her fears. I had found work as a driver and some modest accommodation for our first home together.

I had obtained a room in a ground-floor flat in a six-storey building in Babushkin Street. There were three rooms in the flat, each of them occupied by another couple, with shared toilet and kitchen facilities. Such flats are common in Leningrad and Moscow.

Marina our second daughter was born a year after we moved to Leningrad and once again I experienced that incredible moment when the nurse says, 'Congratulations, you've got a girl!' I was a proud dad and paraded our tots around the local park delighting in other people's enthusiasm for our girls.

Our cramped living conditions were not the only problem we encountered. I enjoyed my job driving senior executives around town in a luxury Volga car, but the hours were long and the hundred roubles barely covered our food bill each month. Some nights we went to bed hungry.

There were also the usual difficulties faced by newlyweds of growing accustomed to each others' ways. But the tensions increased between us when I started to attend the Registered Baptist Church on Poklonnaya Street.

I tried to attend every meeting at the church, and soon my knowledge of the Bible increased. I found it easy to speak about how Jesus had turned my life around and was asked to share my testimony with the entire church. I couldn't stop speaking about Jesus. In September 1971 I was baptised and became a member of the church.

To my surprise, I had become a respectable member of society. I cut my hair and dressed in a suit and tie. Sometimes I even wore a hat. I stopped drinking, sold all my Beatles records and for two years hardly listened to any rock music.

I was sincere in my pursuit of Jesus but the religious path was a slippery one. I found it easy to judge others, comparing their response to mine. I had confused an appearance of religion with the freedom Jesus gives.

But Tanya wasn't impressed.

One night after a Bible study, I shared with Brother Boris the conflict that Tanya and I were facing over my interest in the church. I respected Boris because of his knowledge of scripture and his position as an elder in the church.

'Will you come and talk to my wife?' I pleaded. 'Maybe you can convince her.'

Brother Boris pointed out the scripture exhorting us not to be linked with non-believers.

'But I'm sure that my marriage to Tanya was made in heaven,' I insisted.

Brother Boris was not amused. He arranged to visit our home on the following Tuesday at 7.30 p.m. Promptly to the minute, the doorbell rang. It was Brother Boris, dressed in a suit and tie. I greeted him and introduced Tanya, who smiled nervously. The table had been prepared carefully with cakes and pastries made by Tanya during the afternoon.

Strutting into the tiny room, the church leader surveyed our home. His eyes fell on some wine glasses in a cabinet, a wedding present from Pavel who had played in the band with me in Uray.

'What are they?' he questioned, peering at the glasses. Surprised, I didn't know what to say.

Turning slowly, he gazed at the television set in the other corner of the room. 'What is that?' he asked again.

'We have a small child. She likes to watch TV,' I stuttered. Brother Boris smiled sarcastically as he continued his inspection. This time, a carpet hanging on the wall caught his attention. This was a wedding gift from Tanya's aunt. It was light brown with an intricate pattern woven into the fabric, like the ones made by skilful Uzbek craftsmen, and bought from gypsy traders.

From his questions I understood that Brother Boris assumed that we were wealthy. I sought to explain to him how God had blessed us, but I knew from his condescending manner that he disapproved. He moved on to deal with the matter in hand in a superior tone that made him sound as though he had just returned from a private audience with God.

Then he looked at his watch and announced that he had business elsewhere and he must leave us. We shook hands solemnly at the door and then he was gone.

I helped Tanya carry the cups and plates to the communal kitchen to be washed up. Neither of us said a word. Finally Tanya broke the silence.

'Never speak to me about Jesus again. I don't want to become like those religious people.' She had an edge to her voice and a finality in her words. The meeting had only lasted an hour, but the whole evening was a disaster.

Over the next few weeks my efforts to repair the damage led instead to constant bickering and arguments. Tanya was miserable and I could find no peace.

One night after a bitter quarrel I said, 'It's no use, Tanya, we can't go on like this. When fish and crab both swim in opposite directions, the current forces them to swim together.'

It was late and as I lay on my bed my mind wandered over Brother Boris' eventful visit and a message I had heard in church once about prayer. I recalled that when Jesus took three of his best men to pray, he went on ahead to pray alone. But how did he pray, I wondered to myself. No one knows.

In my simple way I understood that even a church leader can be a stranger to God, like a tourist in God's country. I knew instantly that it was more important for the heart to move freely, than to be wrapped in a religious disguise.

I fell asleep and in a dream, God urged me to trust him in this situation with Tanya. After that I prayed, 'Lord help me.' But I sensed God saying, 'Do you trust me? If you trusted me, you'd have peace.' This was a turning point in my prayer life as God challenged me to have faith.

But full breakthrough was preceded by a barrier.

A few days later I was determined not to allow an argument to flare up. Tanya was annoyed, but struggled to contain her feelings. Suddenly she exploded. Her eyes blazed defiantly as she brushed her red hair back and vowed, 'I'll never believe in Jesus.'

'You've lost,' a little voice whispered as her words stung deep within my soul. 'You've lost!' But I resisted replying to Tanya and prayed, 'Lord, I need victorious faith now!' I was reminded of a scripture which I had read, 'He and all his family were saved.'

Calmly I tried to relay this message to Tanya. To my surprise she listened. I knew then that Tanya was on the brink of belief in God.

I had been maintaining the guise of a valiant spiritual warrior. But behind the façade, the enemy had attacked and I was spiritually ill. I knew I could cover my sin but in God's eyes, every secret will be uncovered. And how could I make my wife well, when I was ill? The contradiction disturbed me. I felt that humility was the source of strength. I decided to confess my mistake to Tanya.

'Tanya, I know I have told you that my life has changed. Maybe you think I'm an angel, but I'm not.' Tanya's eyes widened. What was this? 'Don't be surprised,' I continued, 'God has shown me that I am nothing at all. When I met you, I was at the bottom and you were at the top. But I changed, and maybe I have made you feel that I am superior. Well, I want you to know that I'm not the angel you think I am.'

I didn't know how she would react, but I knew that my

redemption lay in humbling myself before my wife. Tanya stared at me, listening intently.

'Even though I have failed, I want you to remember one thing. I love Jesus. Nothing else matters to me. Jesus gives me strength to go on.'

The Lord had softened Tanya's heart and instead of ridiculing and taunting me, I sensed a new-found respect in her attitude. The experience helped me to mature and taught me that the power of humility was a fundamental principle in God's kingdom. It was to be the turning point in our relationship.

Slowly, Tanya began to change. She was an unbelieving witness to God's intervention in our lives. A seed had been planted and in an invisible way faith began to grow in Tanya's heart. I decided to avoid confrontational situations whenever they arose.

Two months later, Zhanna became seriously ill with an extremely high temperature. We grew worried as she became weaker. Cradling Zhanna tenderly in my arms I could feel her body warm with fever as she seemed to wrestle feebly with me.

'Lord,' I prayed, 'we are your children. Heal this little one of her fever. It's easy for you, Lord.' I continued to pray for Zhanna while Tanya tried to sleep. Perhaps half an hour passed. I was then conscious that Zhanna was much cooler. She calmed down and quickly fell into a deep sleep. Gently, I laid her in her cot. Tanya stirred. 'How is she?' she enquired.

'She's going to be OK,' I said grinning. Tanya sat up and felt our daughter's cheek.

'She's cool,' Tanya said, somewhat puzzled. 'I'm sure her temperature is down. What happened?'

'Tanya, God healed Zhanna. I prayed and God touched her,' I said.

Tanya raised her eyebrows. 'Are you joking?'

'It's true, Tanya,' I confirmed.

The next morning, Zhanna had made a dramatic recovery. Tanya couldn't doubt the evidence before her eyes.

Tanya had witnessed the power of God in our home. When either of the girls fell ill again, it was she who asked me to pray for them. Poised on the precipice of faith, all she needed was a little push to believe.

Tanya's mother was urging her to return home so that she could see Marina for the first time. It was decided that Tanya would take both girls early in August and plans were finalised for their departure. As a concession, Tanya agreed to visit the Baptist Church with me before they left, to ask God's blessing on the trip.

It was a moving experience which encouraged my soul. Zhanna and Marina sat perched in the front row while old ladies passed mandarins and sweets forward to them, forming a human chain of kindness which the girls watched with enthusiasm.

The pastor of the church was a kind man who prayed over our family, laying hands on Zhanna and Marina. I bowed my head and prayed, 'Jesus, our lives are in your hands.'

At the end of the service Aunt Tamara came over and kissed Tanya. Several friends greeted us and remarked on our beautiful children, making me feel very proud.

At the airport the next day, Zhanna and Marina were excited about the journey and oblivious to everything else. When finally it was time to say good-bye, I hugged Tanya but felt a coldness in her kiss as she brushed my cheek.

'I'll miss you,' I said.

'I'll miss you too,' she replied.

I felt a solitary figure as she turned to wave, picking up Marina so she could see me, and then was gone.

The next few days dragged. I missed Zhanna and Marina terribly and consoled myself with their photographs. Tanya was always on my mind, and I reflected on the past few years with her. 'How can we live together?' Tanya had cried one night. 'You love Jesus, but I'm not interested.' I knew that Tanya's mother would try to talk her into remaining in Siberia. But despite this fear, I had decided not to prevent them going home.

Returning to a cold and empty room each night was a reminder of how much I loved and missed my family.

At the end of September I got home to find a telegram pushed under the door, postmarked Siberia. Ripping it open I read, 'Arriving September 30th. Children well.' It was brief but the news was thrilling. I took time off work to pick them up at the airport. The children seemed to have grown much taller even in two months. Tanya was friendly, but somehow I felt a distance in our relationship.

About three weeks after they returned, Tanya said that she wanted to talk with me. It was 10 o'clock and the children were asleep.

Tanya was sombre. With a clearly rehearsed script she began, 'Valeri, I'm not unhappy being married to you and we have had some good times; but we've reached a crossroads in our life. I can't go on like this. You must choose either to live with me and the children or to continue with this Jesus business. You can't have both.'

I stared at her, and then asked, 'Are you serious?'

Tanya looked across at me and said, 'Yes.'

Although she looked intently, I felt she was following her mother's advice. I recalled the scripture which says, 'If you love anyone more than me, you are not worthy of me.' But I also knew that it wasn't God's way to ignore your relatives.

I reminded Tanya of the events which had led me to believe in God. 'Do you remember how I wanted to kill myself when I was in the army? But I was rescued by God. He showed me what this world is really like. I believe that God gave you to me and that we were meant for each other.'

I took her hand and held it gently. 'I really love you Tanya, and I love our children. If two people lose each other in the forest, one will call out and the other will hear the cry. We're like that couple Tanya, we're lost in the forest and we need each other. We've got to stick together.

'You know the old saying, "God gives and God takes away." If you want to leave me, it's not possible for me to stop you.'

Tanya was close to tears. I felt her body relax against me and we cuddled. In a few days it would be Zhanna's fifth birthday and we were planning a little party. Tanya said she would call a truce until after the party and contemplate my words over that period.

Zhanna's birthday was fun. We played games and wore silly hats. Tanya had made a cake in the shape of a farmyard with lots of little animals. I mimicked animal noises and everyone laughed, including Tanya.

That night, as we tidied up together, I gave Tanya a cuddle. 'Thanks for working so hard and making it such a lovely day.' She smiled and threw her arms around me. We swayed back and forth for a few moments and then I moved her back towards the old sofa against the wall. Tanya was receptive and I kissed her tenderly, passion burning in our hearts. Playfully the evening passed into night.

Later that night I reflected on the ultimatum Tanya had hoisted on to the future of our life together. Usually, if lovers fall out and want to dismantle a relationship, they are poised like enemies across the great divide. Tanya hardly looked like an enemy. I knew that the move had not been of her own design.

A week later I came home early from work to find that the girls had gone out to play with some friends. As we were alone I asked, 'What have you decided, Tanya? The deadline has passed.'

Tanya seemed troubled. 'We'll live together but lead separate lives.'

'You're treating our relationship like a child's toy,' I replied.

'Our life together is the most precious thing we have. Either we live together happily or we separate.'

Tanya was serious. She looked really pretty standing in the kitchen surrounded by dirty pots and pans. I recalled the first time I had seen her in the post office. Her cheeky yet shy smile had captivated me.

Tanya looked up and smiled. 'OK, we'll live together.'

In a rush we threw our arms around each other. Neither said a word as we held each other tightly. I heard someone cough. Taken by surprise, Tanya and I leapt back. Jonas, who lived in another room in the apartment, looked sheepish. 'Sorry, sorry, I didn't mean to interrupt anything. Don't worry, it's quite legal what with you being married and everything.'

Back in our room we collapsed in a heap of giggles. Like doves cooing on a window ledge, Tanya and I kissed and cuddled recreating the romance of our courtship.

I didn't realise it at the time, but an invisible pattern of faith had begun to grow in Tanya's heart. Like a map of the world, first the outline was drawn, and then as each day passed a little more detail appeared, rivers and streams, valleys and hills.

6

'You Christians Should Be Shot'

The car depot where my job was based was on Ispolkomskaya, a short ride on the subway from our apartment. It was attached to an export office controlling shipments to the West. Not everyone warranted the attention and personal transport given to these export officials. The higher up in the Party structure, the greater the luxury.

I was proud of my Volga car and arrived early to clean it, and to check the oil and tyres. I was the youngest driver and got on well with everyone at the depot. 'Hey kid,' another driver would joke, 'come and clean my car after you've done yours!'

I was naïve about my faith. 'I'm a Christian,' I would announce. 'Do you have any questions about the Christian faith?' Most people were amused by my youthful fervour and played along. When I was stumped by a difficult question, I would reply with great confidence, 'Oh! If you ask my aunt, she'll be able to answer that one. She knows everything.'

Each week I had to transport an accountant to the finance department of one of the company's factories. One of the typists, a chirpy blonde named Rita, would give me a cup of tea and tease me about the stern requirements of the religious life.

'I could never be a Christian,' Rita told me one day. 'I could never keep all the rules!'

'But Christianity isn't a rule book,' I argued, 'it's a way of life.' This made Rita giggle. 'You'd be shocked if you knew about my life, Valeri.'

I replied, 'It doesn't depend on where we've been, but where we're going.'

Rita considered this for a moment and then said, 'No, Valeri, not for me.'

Our discussion was joined by others who both agreed and disagreed, a welcome distraction on a boring day. I was told, 'You should talk to Mrs Agrova. She's a convinced atheist.'

'I'll face anyone, anywhere, anytime!' I replied to the challenge.

Unknown to me, my presence in the office had been reported to Mrs Agrova. Suddenly the atmosphere in the room changed. Everyone looked attentively at their desks, papers rustled, pages were turned to great effect.

Mrs Agrova was a hefty stern-faced woman, much taller than me. As chief factory accountant and communist official she was an authoritative figure.

'Who is the preacher?' she barked.

'I am,' my voice squeaked.

She looked at me with contempt.

'Maybe you have some questions?' I asked meekly.

Hands on hips, Mrs Agrova asked with natural dismissiveness, 'If God exists, why is there war?'

I answered seriously, 'I believe in God but I also believe in the devil. The devil has blinded us, covering this world with darkness. And in the darkness we confuse good with bad. In the darkness we find brother fighting brother, the bad man stealing from the upright, the wicked cheating the innocent. No one is satisfied with what he has, and we'll fight and kill to get what we want.'

Mrs Agrova continued the assault. 'Why do so many children die?'

I found the question difficult. 'There's only one thing certain in this life and that is we will all die,' I explained. 'Children have a special place in God's kingdom, so if children die, they will be in paradise, and it's good to be in paradise.'

This reply infuriated her. 'If God exists, where is he?' she taunted. 'Have you seen God? Does he have a long white beard?' There were a few chuckles around the room. 'Science proves there is no God and that's a fact!'

I was quick off the mark. 'Many scientists believe in God, even our legendary mathematician Mendeleyev, whose work is studied in every school. He knew we weren't just dangling in space.'

'He was just a crazy old man,' she said dismissively.

I pounced, 'That's a very unpatriotic remark about a loyal citizen. I would have expected you, above all others, to be more complimentary.'

'But scientists have to deal with facts, the Bible deals with myths and legends.'

'That's not true,' I replied, 'The accuracy of the Bible has never been seriously disproved. But scientists are forced to admit their text-books are obsolete when new discoveries are made.'

Mrs Agrova now appeared to be on the defensive. 'Oh, you are so slippery. You never answer my questions directly, you're being so evasive.'

Her face flushed with anger. It was humiliating for a woman of her authority to back down to a young upstart. 'I can't stand around talking to people like you. I have important work to do.' She turned to face the room where the staff were hanging on every word. 'Back to work everyone! Back to work!'

Mrs Agrova strode purposefully to the door, then scowled at me, 'Have you finished your work here?'

Before I could reply, she barked, 'Out! You've wasted enough time already!' The door reverberated behind her as she stormed out.

I hesitated. Rita looked up with a twinkle in her eye, 'Well! The preacher and the dragon!' Around us there were roars of laughter followed by louder appeals for quiet from those fearing Mrs Agrova's return.

Nonchalantly I strolled over to the door and felt its handle. Grimacing in feigned anguish, I jerked my hand away as though it was boiling hot. Rita stormed across the room in an exaggerated impersonation of Mrs Agrova and announced, 'The end of the world has come, preacher.' She opened the door and barked, 'Out!'

Tipping my imaginary hat to everyone in the room, I walked through the door. Rita grinned at me, 'What a performance. You should be an actor rather than a preacher!'

I danced down the stairs and waved to the people standing at the factory gates, who looked somewhat bemused.

As I prayed in the Volga on the drive back from the factory, I knew I hadn't said anything unusual but it had clearly been an unprecedented event for that finance department. I felt that God had given me great power in my witness.

Everything else had gone from my mind and I raced up the stairs into the central office whistling a cheery tune. Nikolai, the depot chief, sat at his desk and beckoned to me. Another assignment, I figured. He worked with an efficiency that was remarkable and highly unusual for Russia, where no one seemed to care what happened.

I stood before him with my hands behind my back. It was like being in the army.

'We've had a complaint about you,' Nikolai said looking directly at me. I was genuinely surprised, and it showed. What could it be? My mouth hung open in shock. Nikolai didn't prolong the suspense, but read out a scribbled note. ' "We asked for a driver, you sent us a preacher." Do you know who complained?' he asked, raising his eyebrows.

'I can guess,' I replied. 'Mrs Agrova!'

I decided not to say anything as I was guilty.

Nikolai considered the situation for a moment, but then chuckled. 'I know the woman. It must have been quite a confrontation. She can usually take care of herself.' Nikolai looked at me sternly, screwed up the paper and tossed it into the bin, dismissing me with a wave of his hand.

I nodded and made a quick exit. As my next assignment was not for another hour, I decided to head outside. I wanted to pray for Mrs Agrova and for the impressionable girls such as Rita who had heard the conversation.

I felt as though I was floating down the street, a little confused, but it felt so wonderful to pray like a child to God. I found that my very soul was lifting itself in praise and the hour seemed to pass in just a few minutes. It was easy and natural that my experience with Jesus should become part of my everyday life.

Some weeks later I was to transport a senior Party official from his luxury apartment in Lenin Square to the export marketing office in the city centre.

Dressed in a smart western suit, Mr Latvin slouched back in the car and chain-smoked. The Volga's windscreen-wipers clattered back and forth to clear a light drizzle, and pedestrians hurried away to avoid the spray of brown slush.

After ten minutes or so, Mr Latvin became irritated by the weather. 'Just my luck,' he moaned.

Sensing an opening I volunteered, 'I don't believe in luck. God has a plan for my life.'

'God!' Mr Latvin spat out the word.

I said brightly, 'Oh, I see you believe in God.'

'Of course not,' he said mockingly. 'There is no God. That's official.'

Perhaps Mr Latvin had never been face to face with a real Christian before, so I responded to his abuse with a barrage of questions which he eventually found impossible to answer.

'I don't want to hear any more of this rubbish,' Mr Latvin

erupted. 'You Christians should be shot! We could have wiped
you out. Like that.' He snapped his fingers in a threatening
gesture behind me and continued, 'We have spared you because
of our greater cause. We have to spread socialism and communism throughout the world. Nothing must get in the way. But
your time will come.'

Mr Latvin settled back in the car, grunting and puffing on
yet another cigarette. He barely spoke to me after that. At the
factory I stepped out to open the car door for him, but he was
too quick and brushed me aside.

'God bless you, sir,' I said in farewell. He stared at me and
cursed furiously. I could imagine Nikolai drumming his fingers
on his desk as he noted the latest complaint.

I never saw Mr Latvin again but I prayed for him and the
experience did not discourage me at all. Rather, it had
the opposite effect. Like a boxer analysing his strategy I asked
myself, how could I improve my technique? Should I
have been more cautious in my approach? I knew that just
having the right words was useless without the blessing of God
on my life.

It took a day for Mr Latvin to catch up with me. Nikolai
was annoyed. Mr Latvin was a far more serious case than
Mrs Agrova.

Two days later I was required to transport a KGB colonel,
an energetic young man who sat smartly in the passenger seat.
I didn't know what problems talking about Jesus would cause
me. But I knew I had no choice.

To my surprise, the KGB officer seemed eager to talk to
me about God. He told me that although the Party's line
was that God didn't exist, he had been guilty recently of
dissident thoughts. He even dared wonder if there could be a
God, after all.

Regrettably, we only had a short journey together, and as
we arrived I said, 'I know one thing. Once I was a sinner
but Jesus saved me. My life has been changed.' The colonel

remained in his seat for a minute outside his destination in Nevsky Prospekt. 'Very interesting,' he remarked and patted me on the shoulder.

Two weeks later, I sat drinking black tea with the other drivers when Nikolai called out to me. My surprise turned into delight as I learnt that the KGB colonel had again requested me as his driver. 'He asked for "The Preacher",' Nikolai said. 'I assume that means you. I could check if anyone else wants to go.'

'No, no,' I replied. 'That's OK with me.'

Once again, we did the same short journey to Nevsky Prospekt which was over in a flash. The colonel continued to question me although we had parked. We remained in the car outside a grey nondescript building with no obvious markings or signs.

A traffic policeman strolled by and peered into the car. Recognising the familiar KGB uniform the militiaman nodded and walked on. Finally, the colonel said, 'Fascinating. But I must go. I'm late for a meeting.'

Handing him his initialled attaché case as he stepped out, I saluted. 'God bless you, sir!' He seemed surprised as he acknowledged my salute.

'You asked God to bless me,' he said wistfully. The idea seemed to mystify him. He smiled, turned on his heel and walked into the anonymous building.

I couldn't explain why, but I knew this had been an important meeting. *Praise you, Jesus!*

I had been thinking about it for some time. I knew I could borrow the Volga for a long weekend to make the journey to the Finnish border. Then, in the autumn I had an opportunity.

Setting off before dawn, it took about four hours to reach Vyborg. I knew I was close as all the houses looked different. It was a clear morning and old women with long brooms piled the leaves up by the side of the road.

Outside the house I sat preparing myself. Peering up at the third-floor flat, I could see the curtains were open. Someone was in. I got out of the car and walked up the stairs, pausing at the door. There it was. SARDONIKOV.

I pressed the bell lightly, startled by the harsh loud ring. Abruptly, the door opened and a portly, elderly man stared at me.

'Hello, can I help you?'

'Can I see Alexander Sardonikov please?' I replied.

'It's me,' the man replied, 'Who are you?'

I repeated my name, but no sound could be heard, the words froze somewhere in my throat. He looked tired and old. I couldn't take my eyes off his face. It seemed as though he might disappear and never return. I couldn't turn away.

'Oh! It's you. Do you still live with Schura? I suppose she told you where I was, and that's how you found me,' he said grumpily.

'No, no, Schura didn't tell me,' I said, somewhat in a daze. 'I found your address through the army's resettlement office.'

I heard voices and suddenly Andrew appeared. 'Valeri? It's you!' At least he seemed pleased to see me. 'Come in! Come in! What a surprise.'

Andrew dragged me into the house and said, 'Dad, this is my friend, the person I told you about. Do you remember?'

'Yes, yes, I remember,' the old man said dismissively. We talked for a few moments but he was clearly uncomfortable in my presence. Making some excuse, he claimed that he was late for an appointment and had to leave the house immediately.

'Perhaps I can help you?' I volunteered, 'I could drive you there.'

He seemed flustered, 'What? Oh no, no, that won't be necessary.' As he picked up a coat and walked to the door, I explained to him that I also had to leave. 'I was only passing through.' Andrew looked disappointed.

I wanted a few minutes alone with my father. We walked

down the stairs and into the street. He eyed the Volga and said, 'It's a nice car.'

'Yes,' I smiled. 'Are you sure I can't drive you somewhere?'

'No thanks,' he replied.

I might never be given another moment. 'I know life is complicated,' I began. 'It doesn't matter about the past, I just wanted to see you myself.'

My father brushed his hand across the back of his head and looked down at his shoes.

I explained that I had been close to suicide in the army but God had given me a new life.

Father mumbled a little and then looked at his watch. 'OK, I must go.'

We shook hands and Father turned and walked slowly down the street. In the rear-view mirror of the car I watched his reflection disappear into the distance.

As I drove back to Leningrad I didn't know what to think. I tried to remember his face and the surprised look he gave me at the door. It had all happened so fast. And then he had turned and walked down the street. We had spoken together and then parted like travellers sharing a railway compartment for a few moments.

Some days later a letter arrived, postmarked Vyborg. With mounting anticipation, I saw that it was from Father.

The handwritten note read:

Valeri,
I really knew your mother but I don't want to talk about that relationship because it belongs to the past. I don't think it's a good idea to write to each other and certainly not good to meet. I don't feel that you are a relation of mine. You seem more like a stranger to me.

There was no hello and no good-bye. Across the bottom of the page he had scrawled his signature. Alexander Sardonikov.

I was broken. I felt like a plastic cup floating about amongst the debris on the Neva River. For a few days I carried the letter everywhere with me. It was a heavy burden to bear.

But as I prayed, God reminded me that I had been reborn into his family and now had brothers and sisters all over the world. When my real father had rejected me, my heavenly Father had loved me.

This was the real miracle.

7

Superstar

One day in the New Year I was drinking tea with some other drivers when I heard my name on the garage Tannoy system, 'Valeri Barinov, report to the transport union office at once.'

Something was wrong, but what? I prayed for help, and as I walked up the stairs I felt a calming presence come over me. Remember, I told myself, God's Spirit is your constant companion. He will provide words for you to speak.

I sensed tension in the air. The union chief was joined by the depot's personnel officer, a union activist and the chief of another garage. They all had notebooks ready in front of them and looked deadly serious as I walked into the room and was offered a chair facing them all.

The union chief began. 'Valeri, I must warn you that you face some serious charges and very likely a prison sentence. But we wanted to question you ourselves before turning you over to the police.'

I didn't know Mr Adas as I wasn't an active union member. He wore thick horn-rimmed glasses and a navy-blue suit. His hair was greased back, neatly combed in place.

'You see Valeri,' he went on, 'many people have complained about your religious activity. It's one thing if you keep it to yourself, but you are forcing your beliefs on everyone else.

Such propaganda is forbidden in our constitution. It's dangerous. What if other people were influenced by your ideas?'

The depot's personnel officer shook his head in agreement as Mr Adas continued, 'You see, we sent someone to question you secretly and have all the evidence we need on tape.'

Mr Adas frowned and waited a moment, as though they all expected some kind of confessional outburst. 'Yes, we have it all on tape. Why, you told everyone in the garage to visit the Baptist Church.' Mr Adas looked deeply hurt and offended that this outrage had been perpetrated under his own roof.

'Praise the Lord that you have it on tape,' I enthused.

Mr Adas and the others were completely non-plussed by my response.

'I'll explain everything to you,' I said, adopting a confidential tone. 'You see, when people ask me a question about my faith in Jesus, I reply. Why, it's the least a decent citizen should do for his comrades, provide an honest reply to their questions.

'All I'm guilty of is answering questions,' I asserted, sounding equally mystified that I should be threatened for such innocent behaviour. 'Do you know what I think?' I asked, leaning forward in my chair and lowering my voice.

Mr Adas was clearly perturbed, 'What do you mean?' he stammered.

'I think you should forbid the others in the garage from asking me about Jesus. That would solve the problem, wouldn't it?' I said harmlessly, as if that provided a neat solution to the conundrum.

'As for all that talk about visiting church,' I gesticulated with my hands, 'do you know where it is?'

Mr Adas reached for his pen. 'Where is it?' he said quickly and sat poised to write down the address.

'Why, we Christians believe in a personal God with whom we can form a personal relationship and who lives with us. There's really no need to go to a building because if God lives within us, then we ourselves are a church,' I declared boldly. 'My advice is: don't go to church, come to Jesus!'

The personnel officer held up his hand. 'We're not here to listen to your advice. Remember, you're the one facing serious charges.'

Mr Adas dared me, 'Would you become a member of the Communist Party?'

'Oh yes, certainly,' I replied, taking them by surprise once again. 'I know communism has a high moral code, and a real communist is someone who lives selflessly for his neighbour.'

I leaned forward, getting even more excited. 'Don't you see? That's what Jesus was talking about, that's true Christianity. I know that when I tell everyone in the Communist Party about this similarity, they will be pleased. Why, it will be a great privilege to preach the Gospel to the Communist Party. Thank you for inviting me.'

Before I'd even finished speaking, Mr Adas jerked forward and interrupted. 'No, no,' he cried, waving his hands from side to side. 'It's not possible. You can't preach at a Party meeting.'

Mr Adas addressed me with a new-found respect, realising he couldn't trap me. However, he told me that I could not continue working at the depot, and I left the enquiry feeling exhausted.

Tanya was naturally concerned about how we would survive, 'Don't worry,' I comforted her, 'God will provide. A loving Father cannot abandon his children, can he?'

I took a job as a labourer, then as a cleaner, and later as a driver again. I was given a huge lorry to drive. It had a broken gearbox and unreliable brakes, but was not dissimilar to other vehicles in the depot. It was clear that if I complained, someone else would be given my job.

I continued to speak openly about Jesus at the garage. Soon I was under pressure for 'anti-Soviet propaganda', which encompasses anything from pornography to the Bible, so it came as no surprise when the manager called me to his office. Another driver had become annoyed with me and complained that I was spreading sedition.

As I was leaving the manager's office, I saw his secretary look up and beckon to me. 'Valeri,' she whispered, 'I want you to know that I'm a secret believer also.'

Rema was about forty years old, tall, attractive and well educated. For a few minutes she counselled me about the risk involved in speaking openly to the other drivers. 'You'll only get into trouble,' she warned.

I knew that God had called her to be a secret believer, so I decided not to argue with her. Some weeks later Rema caught my eye, and when the coast was clear I slipped into the office. 'My son is back from the army,' she said. 'Would you like to come to our flat tomorrow evening?'

As I stepped through their front door I knew that Igor and I would be friends. He loved rock and wanted to play in a band. All evening we listened to the albums he had brought home with him, one of which was to set me thinking in a dramatic new way.

Although the British musicians Andrew Lloyd Webber and Tim Rice were relatively unknown to us, *Jesus Christ Superstar* was inspiring as it traced the life of Jesus in a rich musical pageant incorporating several different styles. We played the album until the grooves were wearing out.

One night when driving the lorry back to the garage, the musical themes from *Jesus Christ Superstar* kept returning to my mind. I was filled with a deep sadness.

Lord! Even the stones cry out to you! You cause this world to praise you even though it doesn't recognise your authority.

Why did Christians abandon artistic traditions to an ungodly world? Why were the pop charts filled with anti-God songs? Why did Christian musicians settle for church audiences instead of taking their songs to the streets? Where were the

Christian bands who would challenge the Beatles and the Rolling Stones?

God had given me musical talent but I hadn't done much with it. In recent months I had played a few gigs at communist youth clubs and hung out with musicians. Everyone knew I could sing rock songs in English and I had an audience whenever I wanted one. But what songs would they hear me sing? The question disturbed me.

I prayed and asked the Lord what he wanted me to do. Follow me, he replied, one step at a time.

Meanwhile the difficulties at work had increased. The garage manager had a dispute on his hands and I was pressured to quit.

We heard through one of Tanya's friends that Ambulance Service No. 7 needed drivers. I was hired and impressed the manager by looking after the beat-up old vehicle I was given to drive. Two months later it was replaced with a brand new ambulance.

We served several hospitals in the area and were called out both day and night. Sometimes people in the street would hail us, slip the doctor some money, and we would make unscheduled house calls. On an emergency call I knew all the short cuts through the backstreets of Leningrad.

I carried a transistor radio with me and tuned into Radio Monte Carlo. Also in the glove compartment I kept a portion of the Bible – incomplete because I had rescued it from a fire. The pages were singed and entire books were missing, but it didn't matter. Sometimes just a few sentences were enough to convey the presence of God.

I was frequently on night patrol which lasted until nine or ten the following morning. But I liked the hours because I could spend time with Zhanna and Marina.

One cold night we were called out to Kalinsky Prospekt to find a woman waiting with her eleven-year-old son in the hallway of her tower block. The doctor on duty that night was himself suffering from a cold. 'Don't worry,' I assured him. 'You stay in the van and I'll check that we have the right passengers.'

The couple were shaking with cold. Too nervous to stay in their apartment in case they missed the ambulance, they had waited over half an hour.

'Where are you going?' I asked the woman.

'My son needs an operation,' she replied. He was clutching his stomach and leaning against the wall. He seemed to be on the verge of tears.

'Everything will be fine. I'm a Christian, would you like me to pray for you? God will bless you.'

The woman's eyes lit up. 'Yes,' she pleaded. 'Yes please!'

'But first let's get you into the ambulance.' I carried the boy to the van and we sped off to the hospital. As I lifted the boy into a wheelchair in the reception area, the woman touched my sleeve gently, thinking I was about to depart. 'Don't forget,' she whispered.

'What's that?' I asked.

'You promised to pray for my boy,' the woman replied.

'No, no,' I chuckled, 'I'm not leaving before I pray.' I wheeled him into the corner of the room, put my hands on his head and prayed healing into his body and blessing for his life. When I had finished praying, his mother was in tears. 'Thank you, thank you,' she cried.

As I turned to move away I could see that the doctor had been watching everything. But the woman tugged my sleeve again. 'Wait,' she said wiping her eyes, and pulled out an apple from her bag. 'It's my last one but I want you to have it. Please take it.'

I didn't know what to say. I knew apples were expensive but I didn't want to offend her by not taking it. She reached out and placed the apple in my hand. The decision had been made.

The doctor asked me what was going on, so I explained. Rather than the ridicule I had expected, he was curious.

Over the next few weeks I felt an inner strength about my witness. When I prayed for patients their condition improved remarkably; many were simply encouraged or lifted from bouts of depression. I was gaining a reputation among the drivers and doctors. 'I don't know if it's voodoo magic, but Valeri's prayers seem to make a difference.'

However, I was an enigma for most people who assumed that religious believers wore sombre suits and never seemed to smile or have fun. When they found out that I loved the Beatles and the Rolling Stones and even played their songs with a band, the contradiction was complete.

Dr Zakharova was an elderly lady who practised as a paediatrician, and so most of our calls were to children's homes. Once when I was waiting for her to return from a house call, some kids who were kicking a ball around in a nearby playground came over to the ambulance. My attention was drawn to a pale-faced boy, aged about eight. He was shy at first, but I asked him if he'd ever driven an ambulance? From the way his eyes lit up, I knew we had made friends.

When I showed him my tattered Bible, he told me that his grandmother used to tell him Bible stories although he had never seen a Bible before. I urged him to put his faith in Jesus. 'Try it,' I said, 'you'll be surprised.'

The doctor returned and as we pulled away from the curb, I waved to the boy. 'I see you've made friends with Misha,' Dr Zakharova remarked. 'It's a sad case. He's got leukaemia, poor lad. He's only got a few months to live.'

I was moved and realised that God had sent me to him. I knew that God chose the people he brought to me.

Dr Zakharova had been baptised as an orthodox Christian and had some knowledge of the faith. Although she wasn't a practising believer, she recognised that God was in my life. 'There is something about you, Valeri,' she told me one day. 'If I could have your faith, then I think my life would change.'

'But faith is a gift from God,' I reasoned. 'Anyone can have it. It's that simple. Try it. Test it.'

'I don't know,' she argued. 'Let me think about it.'

We were called to an internat in Leningrad. A great sadness filled me as I walked in past boys and girls hanging around aimlessly, unwanted and abandoned. We were directed to the sick bay, where boys with dirty faces and runny noses and girls with long matted hair and torn dresses followed us around.

I think we heard the problem before seeing it. A skinny boy aged about two was writhing on the floor, yelling and crying. Dr Zakharova could find no clues to the child's obvious discomfort.

I asked if I could hold the child and was promptly handed a ragged, noisy parcel of arms and legs. Cradling the wailing baby, I paced the floor and prayed within myself, ignoring the noise. The boy had soon calmed considerably, and after ten minutes actually stopped crying.

The sick bay nurse was amazed. 'What did you do to him?' she gasped.

Dr Zakharova explained, 'He's my driver. He's a Christian and he prays.'

The nurse looked baffled. She kept her eyes trained on the child as if averting her gaze would trigger another bout of yelling.

Dr Zakharova quickly prepared an injection for the child I was holding. The boy cried out in surprise, stung by the prick of the needle. I handed him to the startled nurse who was able to restore calm easily. After checking a few other patients, Dr Zakharova turned to leave and pointed to the boy, now sleeping peacefully in a cot.

'I don't know what you do, Valeri, but your prayers seem to get answered,' Dr Zakharova remarked.

'You shouldn't be surprised, there's nothing special about me,' I asserted. 'You know what I mean, don't you?'

Contemplating what she had seen, Dr Zakharova didn't answer me. There was nothing else I could say to convince her. It was now a matter of prayer.

That summer, Tanya and I took the girls away on holiday. It was good to be together as a family and Zhanna and Marina enjoyed playing with their crazy dad. Tanya and I found time to be together strolling along country lanes and cuddling in front of the log fire.

Back in Leningrad the holiday was quickly forgotten as the ambulance depot was plunged into a gruelling work schedule. There were staff shortages and I volunteered for overtime, figuring we could use the extra money.

I was assigned to work for Dr Medvedev. He was a highly trained physician, aged thirty, but extremely proud and arrogant. He began to quiz me about Christianity. 'I hear you're an expert,' he said haughtily.

'Not an expert in theological dogma,' I replied. 'But I know one thing for certain – Jesus is alive!'

Dr Medvedev found this highly amusing. He then proceeded to ask me several questions. Each time I started to reply, he cut me short and gave his own answer. Soon I decided to remain silent.

'A preacher who has stopped preaching,' Dr Medvedev taunted. 'What a shame! Maybe you've nothing left to say?'

'But you won't let me finish speaking,' I reasoned with him.

'You have nothing to say to a modern man like me,' he gloated, leaning back in his seat.

'Dr Medvedev, I lived your life, but you haven't experienced my new life with Jesus,' I replied.

This made him laugh, his head rolled back and he slapped his leg. 'Poor preacher,' he chortled, 'what do you know about life?' Still laughing derisively, he opened his case and produced a magazine. 'I'll tell you about life. Look Mr Preacher! This is life.' The magazine was filled with explicit photographs depicting outrageous sex acts.

'Don't crash the car,' the doctor joked, amused by his own humour. As he proceeded to relate a running commentary of each lurid scene, I realised how corrupt his heart was.

At last we drove on in silence but I continued to pray for Dr Medvedev. Back at the ambulance depot that evening, a few of the drivers stood by the entrance to the building. As we approached them, Dr Medvedev cracked a joke about Christians and looked mockingly at me.

To my surprise Ivan, one of the younger drivers, came to my defence. We didn't know each other all that well, but I saw from his reaction that he wanted to protect me. 'Why ridicule him just because he's a Christian? Sometimes you doctors can do nothing, but when Valeri prays, people are healed. How can you explain that?'

'Yes, that's true,' some of the other drivers agreed.

The doctor started to argue. I knew it was impossible to reason with him but after a few minutes, I joined the fray, answering his questions but intending to reach the other drivers. Sensing he was outpointed, Dr Medvedev withdrew and walked into the building somewhat disgruntled.

But the discussion was far from over and during the next two days Ivan quizzed me at length about how I came to faith in Jesus. My advice to him was, 'Try it out. Test Jesus.'

One week later Ivan came to me. I knew instantly that something had happened. And it wasn't my imagination. The other drivers had noticed it.

'I tested God and the experiment worked,' Ivan told me. 'God exists!' He seemed surprised by his own discovery. In the ambulance depot he was an outspoken witness to the extraordinary change in his life and he became a good friend, visiting our family and attending the church.

I knew it was a matter of time. Eventually the manager of the depot questioned me after work. Someone had complained that I was spreading religious propaganda. I denied the accusation and insisted that I should be judged by my work record. Nothing further was said, but I would have to be careful.

8

Moonwalk

The quaint tram-cars of Leningrad were always popular with the tourists who queued to visit the museums and galleries, marvelling that such masterpieces as Picasso and Da Vinci could have been hidden away in Russia.

Few of them saw the backstreets and alleys where the hoods and pimps patrolled, or the upstairs apartments where any blackmarket deal could be struck. Leningrad was full of desperate people on the run from informers, kids strung out on drugs, teenage runaways, and child prostitutes.

The Moonwalk Club was situated in a notorious side street not far from where we lived. With the right connections you could pick up anything you wanted. But it wasn't the place to ask questions. The only warning ever given was the glint of a blade in the shadows.

Events at the club were organised by a stocky, dark-haired woman named Valentina who had a good heart, but no ability to maintain any kind of order. She was somewhat disappointed to find that I was not a potential volunteer, but soon perked up when I offered to play a gig at the club. She seemed relieved to learn that we weren't asking to be paid, and our premiere performance was immediately scheduled for the following Saturday night.

I learned that Valentina lived near us, so we took the same bus home that night. As she locked up and stepped into the street, her demeanour changed.

'What's the matter?' I asked.

'This is a terrible area. Two nights ago someone was stabbed just round the corner, and last week one of the girls at the club was raped by three men. Even the police don't know what to do,' Valentina explained.

'I've got a secret weapon,' I said cheekily.

'What's that?' Valentina enquired.

'Jesus!' I replied.

'I don't believe in God,' she said. 'Anyway what can he do for us here?' I told her about God's protection on the bus home, and she seemed moved.

The band were excited about the gig and we worked out six or seven songs which we knew would be popular. Valentina enthusiastically arranged the loan of a sound system, which I picked up in the ambulance. George, my friend from the internat took charge of the equipment, assisted by Rema's son, Igor.

Boys in leather jackets hung around at the entrance with girls in tight mini-skirts. The sound check ensured that at least we would be heard.

No one knew what would happen. About sixty kids crowded into the hall to hear us. The four-piece band was ready. Playing rhythm guitar on a homemade instrument, I struck an E-chord, walked up to the microphone, and opened my mouth. 'It's been a hard day's night, and I've been working like a dog . . .'

We knew instantly that we were a hit. In half an hour we had plundered our entire repertoire, but still they wouldn't let us stop playing. The band looked to me for guidance as the cheers and whistles grew louder. 'Jam session!' I announced.

The kids were calling out songs that they wanted us to play. 'Chuck Berry!' someone yelled. 'Play Chuck Berry songs!' I launched into 'Rock and Roll Music' and somehow the boys behind me did an admirable job of maintaining the driving beat.

An hour or so after our jittery start I announced that we would make 'Let it be' our last number. I sang with a minimum of accompaniment, but surprisingly the hall was silent. The applause at the end of the song was deafening. Finally I made a space through the barrage of noise.

'I love the Beatles,' I began and with that a ripple of applause spread among the audience. 'Shhh!' I cried, 'I've got something really important to say.'

'I love that song,' I repeated, 'but I also love the message behind the song. It's a message I want you to consider. When you have a problem and you don't know where to turn to, when you think no one understands you. When you reach the edge of life and there doesn't seem to be anything more to live for . . .' I paused as my voice bounced off the walls of the club.

'Hey!' I shouted. 'Anyone out there know what I'm talking about?'

Instantly a wave of cries burst out. I knew I had hit a nerve. 'Well if that's how you're feeling tonight then I've got news for you.'

Again I paused as the sea of faces peered up at me. 'You see I was trapped on that island of despair and thought I would be marooned for ever. But do you know who rescued me and changed my life?'

I paused for a moment, and then shouted the answer, 'Jesus!'

A buzz ran through the crowd. Questions and curses were yelled out. 'Get off!' a tall girl with a long pony tail at the side of the stage cried. But someone near her shouted her down, 'No! No! We want to listen to you.'

The attention paid to our music was transferred to my closing comments. I suggested that we call another meeting at the club for those who wanted to hear my story. But no one wanted to wait. They wanted answers now!

We moved away from the stage area so that the sound system could be dismantled and loaded back into the ambulance. The questions were hurled like spears as I stepped into the crowd.

'You don't understand,' a petite blonde told me, almost in tears, 'I've got nothing to live for.'

My throat was dry and someone brought me a glass of water which I gulped down. The music had united our hearts in an unusual way, and the kids listened to me as though I was a minstrel prophet. At 1.30 a.m. about thirty teenagers still hung around, caught up in intense discussion.

Valentina was thrilled by the amazing success of the evening although she could get into trouble because the club's closing time had been exceeded. 'Could you play every Saturday night?' she asked.

The Moonwalk Club became the turf we patrolled. The kids looked up to us as heroes. Some were drawn by the magnet of music, others were disturbed and needed help.

Lita was sixteen years old but you would never have guessed. For two years she had been passed like a bag of sweets from hand to hand, living with anyone who would keep her. Her face had been scarred by a drug dealer to whom she had owed money, and to support her habit she had turned hooker.

'I'm going to change, Valeri, I really am,' Lita told me one night after a gig. 'Will you pray for me?'

No one could believe that Lita would make it, but it was the turning point. She took a job washing dishes in a hotel and struggled to kick the drugs that had ravaged her body. One rainy night at three o'clock I answered our doorbell and was just able to catch Lita as she fell into my arms. The drug dealer had stalked her, beaten her badly, and she was soaked to the skin. She stayed with us for the next few days. Tanya and I were often up all night swabbing her face with a cold sponge.

A month later, Lita told me she had decided to contact her family and would I go with her? It was an emotional reunion as they welcomed her back. 'My baby,' her mother sobbed. 'We thought you'd gone for ever.'

When she returned to the club it was to join us in talking to the other street people. One night on the stage, Lita declared, 'Jesus rescued me . . .'

It was a powerful statement because everyone knew it was true. There was no greater testimony to the truth than Lita, standing before the Moonwalk Club, her heart shining like a torch.

Word got around at the garage that I was playing in a band and that the ambulance I drove was being used to transport musicians and instruments. The trade union chief Mr Markarenko questioned me about it. I admitted that we now had a 'rock and roll ambulance'. Mr Markarenko told me that his daughter had heard us at the 'Young Communists' Club' on Lenin Street. 'You've got a loyal fan,' he joked. 'My daughter has good taste, of course!'

One night Igor visited me at the garage to show me a new guitar he had made. A few drivers hung around and we listened to a Voice Of America broadcast. When the programme ended, I twisted the dial and located Radio Monte Carlo.

The programme that night was less than inspiring. Ten minutes after it began, Mr Markarenko walked past. We must have made an unusual sight: young guys with long hair, modern clothes and a brand new guitar, all huddled round a wireless listening intently to some dreary hymn sung by an uninspiring choir.

The next day when I saw Mr Markarenko he asked, 'Valeri, I didn't know you had such a good band. But who is the Christian in your group?'

'I am!' I replied with a smile.

'Don't joke, I'm serious,' he said. 'I need to know.'

'I'm not joking,' I explained, still smiling.

'You! I'm astounded.' Mr Markarenko's surprise became

annoyance, 'No!' he exclaimed, and walked away from me. Although he had always been cordial, he never spoke to me again. I knew I had made a dangerous enemy.

The Moonwalk Club crowd were really rocking. We could have sung the names of Kremlin Politburo members and they would have applauded us. Then through the clamour someone called, 'Sing "Jesus Christ, Superstar".'

It was a piercing cry that stopped me in my tracks. Somehow we made it through the verse and the entire club joined us in the chorus.

'Jesus Christ, Superstar! Who do you think that you really are? Jesus Christ, Superstar!'

At the end of the song, I unstrapped my guitar, signalling the end of the gig. The catcalls and whistles were urging us to continue playing, so I turned to the guys on stage with me, 'I've had it! Play some riffs for them. Sorry guys, I've just got to stop!'

The night air would clear my head, so I walked into the darkness, following my feet. Leningrad was settling down for the night as drunks staggered across my path and car doors slammed. The subway ride seemed to take for ever, but finally I was home. Everything was quiet, Tanya asleep, the girls snuggled tight. The tranquil end of a long day.

But I couldn't sleep. I retreated into the kitchen and closed the door. Like a soundtrack from a film, the words haunted me. 'Jesus Christ, Superstar' replayed itself continually in my head.

Even the stones cry out, but my people are silent!

I paced the floor as though it was on fire, crying out to God. 'Jesus, I have nothing to bring you, no offering but myself. I want to praise you Lord. I want to cry out to this city of Leningrad about you. I want to praise your name throughout this land, all over this world. Jesus, show me what you want me to do.'

How could we reach people who never came to church? How would they hear about Jesus? What about the kids from Club 47 and the other communist youth clubs where our band played?

Even the stones cry out but my people are silent!

If songs like 'Jesus Christ, Superstar' could have such an effect, surely God's people could produce songs of greater power? The idea took hold. All at once I visualised the potential for a musical performance telling the true story of Jesus of Nazareth. It should not be an album of individual songs, but a concept album, with every part contributing to the big picture.

A million ideas sprang to mind. But what should I do? I knew that prayer and fasting was the best preparation, so for three days and three nights I prayed and fasted, experiencing the very real presence of God.

My mind was a clear blue sky across which ideas floated like clouds. As I prayed it seemed clear that my mission should be to tell people that Jesus was coming again.

People get ready . . .

No expense was to be spared in telling the whole world about Jesus.

People get ready, Jesus is coming soon . . .

Step by step I prayed my way along the pathway. I would sound a trumpet every human heart would hear.

People get ready, Jesus is coming soon, very soon . . .

I picked up the guitar that lay beside me and strummed a few chords. 'This trumpet must sound!' It felt right. I repeated the phrase over and over, repeating it prophetically, praying for God's anointing. We would be a trumpet voice crying out to a lost world.

Tanya brought me down to earth by reminding me that I hadn't been to work for three days. 'What are we going to do?' she cried, 'that means even less money this month!'

I couldn't wait to tell the band. We're going to trumpet our message around the world! Fantastic! What message? What music? There was a small detail I had neglected. I hadn't actually written anything down as yet.

I spent the next few months composing the music. Sometimes I created bits of the melody while on ambulance duty, sometimes I'd wake up in the night, tiptoe into the kitchen and slip another piece of the jigsaw into place. Some ideas would remain, others were discarded. Sometimes I felt the presence of God filling our humble kitchen and couldn't do anything but bow my head and bask in his glory.

I absorbed myself in the music which was at times bluesy, dark, melancholic, moody. And then bright, rough, rock and roll.

Later on, I heard Paul McCartney explaining how he wrote a lot of his music. He would begin playing and the music flowed. It was the same for me, I would pick up the guitar and the music flowed. I wanted it to sound very contemporary, and at the time heavy rock dominated the airwaves, so I styled the album around these trends.

By spring 1974 the music had been composed, and I completed the lyrics that summer.

'Cry out you trumpet voice!' it began. I was determined that this trumpet would sound beyond the mountains of Russia and into the West, where ironically it was considered naïve and outdated to talk about Jesus although there was complete freedom to do so.

I knew I would have to create an English version of the musical, but how could this be done?

An affectionate, motherly woman called Galina who led a prayer group at the Baptist Church had once said unexpectedly to me, 'Valeri, have you ever studied English?'

Startled, I had replied, 'English? Oh no!'

'Learn!' she stated emphatically, raising a finger like a stern schoolteacher.

'Why?' I asked, puzzled by the task she had set me.

Galina had never explained and I forgot her comment. Three months later I saw her at the Baptist Church, and as we walked to the bus stop again she exhorted me, 'Did you start learning English?'

I shrugged my shoulders. 'No, Galina, I just don't have time to do it.'

But Galina was adamant. 'Valeri,' she insisted, tugging my arm, 'Listen to me. Study English. We prayed for you and God showed us a vision: you will go to England, not now, but during the last days.'

After that someone gave me a cassette player and the Gospels on tape in English. The tapes were recorded from the King James Version, and when I practised my English with foreigners they were amused. But I knew I would be blessed. Not only was I learning another language, but I was also memorising the word of God!

Remarkably Galina had been right. I would need to know English.

I met an English tourist at the Hermitage Museum and struggled to tell him what I was doing. He explained that 'Trumpet Voice', although technically correct, didn't quite convey the idea I had. 'Trumpet Call' would be more appropriate. Through his words, God confirmed in my heart that this should be the name of the musical.

I was elated. I felt I was making progress. I had a title!

9

'Lord, Don't Let Our Dog Die!'

The years went by and I didn't know how it would be possible to record our music. Early in 1980, two of the best musicians in the band received their call-up papers for the army. I played with other musicians, but not everyone shared my vision.

Having talked about trumpeting around the world, now I didn't even have a band. I was being ridiculed. Valeri the dreamer! Time had passed, and musical styles had changed.

But I knew that my Daddy never lied.

A friend from Chicago brought me a beautiful leatherbound Bible. I prayed and opened the scriptures at random. My eyes fell on Matthew, chapter 24, verse 31: 'He will send his angels with a loud trumpet call . . .'

The words seemed to leap out of the page. I almost fell off my chair. A loud trumpet call! I had never read this verse before and it was a tremendous encouragement from God which strengthened my resolve.

After church that Sunday, I saw two young girls, clearly foreigners, talking to some of the young people. I introduced myself to them in English that King James himself would have been proud of, 'How long willst thou stayeth in Leningrad?'

The girls giggled and said, 'Two months.'

This was it! 'God sent you to me!' I replied.

Again they laughed. These volatile Russians!

'But I prayed, and God sent you here to meet me!' I invited them home for tea to meet Tanya and to enable me to explain to them exactly what I wanted.

Lorna Waterton and Sally Carter didn't know if they had the time to translate the Russian text of 'The Trumpet Call' into English, but agreed to try. Two months later, I was given several pages written in English. None of it made sense to me, but I held it in my hands as though it was a map of treasure island.

The English lyrics of 'The Trumpet Call'.

I never prayed for things for myself. Secretly, I desired a pair of jeans but they were only obtainable on the black market, and we could never afford it. One night as I was praying, God said,

'Why don't you ask your Daddy for jeans?' I squirmed, 'Jeans are my desire, and I would like to have them, but only if you want me to have them. I want to serve you Lord!'

One night before Lorna and Sally left, they brought me a present: a pair of Wrangler jeans! The jeans were old and worn, with wide flares, but I was stunned. When they left our room, I hopped and danced like a little child.

Daddy! Daddy! You love me so much you even gave me jeans. And you commanded these English girls to hand them over!

I wore the jeans every day. Ripped at the knees, I assured Tanya that this was trendy. Frayed at the edges, I was convinced that this was how heavy rockers dressed. When the seat disintegrated, Tanya insisted it was time for action. 'You are not going out like that and I don't care who says it's OK.'

Reluctantly I agreed, and the jeans were shredded to make kitchen towels. Over the next few months Tanya secretly saved roubles in an empty Nescafé tin. For my birthday that December she presented me with the cash. 'To buy jeans,' she said.

One of our former band members, Sasha, had a friend who had a reputation around Leningrad for being a brilliant tailor. As a friend of Sasha's he would make my jeans at a 'bargain price'.

Sergei Timokhin was a tall, gentle giant. We shared the same musical tastes and immediately became friends. He played bass and was keen to join a band. Sergei didn't believe in God, but after meeting a few times to fit my jeans, Sergei bowed and prayed, 'Jesus, if you are true, reveal yourself to me.' By the time my jeans were ready, Sergei had found faith in Jesus.

Sasha and Sergei were both baptised together in church, a powerful declaration of how God can change the lives of those who surrender to him.

The next few months were painful. Sasha developed cancer and left Leningrad to rest in a country house. But the house was damp and his condition worsened. One evening his mother called at our home with the news that Sasha had died.

Sasha's death was a great sadness for our family, and I couldn't believe I would never see him again. Zhanna and Marina loved him and he had always had a lot of time for them. With tears welling up in their big brown eyes they came to me. 'Papa, we're sad. Why did Sasha have to die?'

I sat them on my lap and explained that in the circle of life, there is death. 'Maybe he would have suffered badly if he had lived? We wouldn't have wanted Sasha to live in pain, would we?'

Marina wiped a tear from her eye. Zhanna whispered, 'No, but we are sad that we won't be able to play with him again.'

'I'm also sad because he was my friend. But this should teach us to value the friends we have,' I explained. I didn't really feel like handing out lessons-for-life at that moment, but I wanted my daughters to understand the fragility of life and to realise that people are precious.

When Marina was born we knew that our cramped

apartment would make life difficult, so we lodged a request with the municipal authorities for a flat. Seven years later, we still waited to be re-located but with several high-rise apartment blocks newly erected around town, we decided to re-apply immediately.

When I called at the Municipal Housing Department I was given a ticket, meaning I would have to queue. There were nine people in front of me. Within an hour, the queue stretched all the way down to the ground floor and into the yard outside. No one knew when the office would open, so we just waited. I didn't want to miss such a good opportunity of sharing the good news of Jesus with so many people, so I listened for my chance.

A tall man aged about forty stood tapping his feet on the step in front. Ahead of him, a middle-aged woman was lamenting America's decision to boycott the Olympic Games being held in Moscow that year. They agreed it was a diabolical act of defiance and spite. Sport, they insisted, must be free of interference and political manipulation. The Americans had behaved shamefully!

'But can you expect anything better from the Americans?' the woman mused, philosophically.

'I suppose not,' the man said mournfully.

This was my moment! I emphasised that the heart of man was the same. 'Russians, Americans, it doesn't make any difference, we are all sinners!'

Queuing is a national pastime in Russia and I had just submitted a significant contribution. Something to do while we waited.

I knew it was controversial and risky. If someone in the building reported me, I could lose all hope of a new apartment. But everyone seemed to be playing into my hands, insisting that I explain what I meant. I agreed.

The hecklers were silent. Convinced that I spoke the truth, some nodded their heads, listening intently.

Finally, the office opened and slowly the queue snaked forward. I gave my personal details and was told that an apartment would be made available. I could hardly wait to see Tanya's face when I told her the news.

Tanya couldn't believe it was true, and was moved to tears. Zhanna and Marina leapt up and down. Our own flat! In August we moved into a three-roomed ground-floor flat in a large high-rise apartment block in one of the northern city suburbs. It was conveniently close to Aunt Tamara and not far from the Baptist Church.

After living in such cramped quarters, three rooms seemed luxurious. The girls ran from room to room. 'Mum, come and see this,' we heard Zhanna yell.

'Zhanna, where are you?' Tanya called after her, amused at the luxury of space. Laughing together we moved from room to room thanking God for this provision for our family.

Tanya was delighted to have her own home and took pride in keeping it clean and tidy. Her diligence and adaptability were always a surprise. Even though her purse was usually empty, there were always flowers on the table and when friends visited, her legendary Russian salad was prepared. No matter what time of day or night, Tanya was always there.

Zhanna and Marina had both been pleading for a pet dog, and we promised to review the situation after we moved into our own flat. It wasn't long before the girls reminded us of the promise we had made.

'Pray!' was the only thing I told the girls.

Tanya and I agreed that a dog would make a great companion for the girls and an appropriate confirmation of our home. But how could we afford to buy one? We just didn't have enough money.

Someone had given me an expensive electronic watch that could be sold privately for at least five hundred roubles. This was the only way we could afford a dog. A few days later, I asked the girls if they had been praying.

'Yes!' they exclaimed in unison. 'Well your prayers have been answered,' I replied.

Leningrad's unofficial market was an open secret. Held every Saturday and Sunday on Kandratevsky Prospekt, the police knew that it was illegal, but nothing was ever done to close it down. In an open field behind one of the city's largest housing estates, you just turned up and displayed whatever it was that you were selling. There were clothes, electrical goods, birds, animals, even cars and motor bikes for sale. Anything not on display could probably be found in one of the flats on the estate. All you had to do was ask.

We found a woman who had several pups in a homemade pen. The girls wanted a male pup, so we agreed a price with the woman, and she reached into the cage and produced a cute black pup.

As I cradled the pup in my arms, he seemed completely at home, eyes twinkling and tail wagging. Within a minute, he started licking my face, indicating his seal of approval on the purchase!

Zhanna and Marina squealed with delight.

As we walked away from the market to the bus stop, I felt a trickle of water running down my arm. My new friend looked innocently up at me. This was a great joke for Zhanna and Marina.

On further investigation, we discovered that the woman had sold us a female pup, not a male one. For a moment the girls registered some disappointment, but the pup had already won our hearts.

Zhanna and Marina conferred for a minute or so and then Zhanna spoke up, 'You know, Dad, it's probably best that we keep this little one and not return her. You see, we wanted a boy,' she continued solemnly, 'but we prayed to God and now we have been given a girl. This must be what God intended for us, don't you agree?'

'Yes, I think you have both made the right decision,' I

reflected. 'Anyway, she seems to have relaxed and made herself quite at home,' I added, shaking my wet arm in the breeze to dry it out.

We called her Panthera because she pranced and leapt about like a black panther. At night, we all snuggled into bed together, Zhanna and Marina tucked tightly under the covers with Tanya and me, and Panthera wriggled past each of us.

Five months after we bought Panthera, she became gravely ill and for three days she could neither eat nor walk. A neighbour who saw her in this pitiful condition advised us to put her to sleep. 'Your dog is going to die and this is the kindest thing you can do.'

Panthera peered up at us almost too tired to move her head. The girls were in tears and Tanya and I were equally upset. Panthera had become part of the family and we loved her dearly.

I decided to talk to the girls. 'Do you believe that God is our Daddy?' I asked them. 'Yes,' they replied. 'Do you believe that God can heal?' I enquired again. 'Yes, we do,' Zhanna and Marina confirmed. 'OK,' I said, forcing myself to sound cheerful, 'let's pray and ask Daddy to heal Panthera.' I felt a lump in my throat as I spoke.

Zhanna, Marina and I knelt together on the floor beside the blanket where our dear Panthera lay helpless. I placed my hand on the dog. Then Zhanna and Marina laid their tiny hands beside my large hand, resting them on the puppy's back.

I didn't know what would happen, but we were placing our confidence in the healing power of God. I found myself praying, 'Jesus, we know you can do anything, and the prayer of our family is that you restore our dear dog Panthera to full health.' It was a simple childlike prayer.

Zhanna and Marina had their eyes closed and I felt a slight tremor run through their bodies. In a simple expression of faith which wrenched my heart, they declared, 'Yes, Lord, we so love our Panthera. Please don't let her die.'

That evening Panthera struggled to her haunches, for the first time in three days. Gently sipping milk from a bowl, she was clearly pleased with the affection placed on her.

The very next day, Panthera was able to walk and regained her appetite. Tanya queued for hours to buy some meat for the ailing puppy. As each day passed, Panthera grew stronger, and our faith as a family increased. I had always told Zhanna and Marina that God cared for us and was interested in the intimate details of our lives. Now they had evidence that this was true and we praised the Lord together.

Sergei Timokhin visited our home shortly after this crisis to discuss the possibility of playing bass with a new band which I was interested in forming.

'Where is your fancy new watch?' Sergei asked me.

I pointed at Panthera who responded with a friendly bark. Zhanna and Marina sat on my lap and showered me with affectionate kisses. They knew that I loved my watch but had sold it as a declaration of my love for my daughters. They have never forgotten it. Such moments have tied our family in a bond of love that no power on earth can separate.

I opened the ambulance logbook and prepared to alter the mileage. It was customary practice to change the number of miles and add something extra, selling the petrol on the side. Everyone did it without a second thought. But over the past few weeks my conscience had convicted me that I was participating in something illegal.

I knew I had to make a stand but I was caught in a dilemma. If I entered the correct mileage then I would be exposing all the other drivers and the entire crew would face an investigation. The drivers were wrong to siphon off the petrol, but further up the line, we all knew that the bosses were on the take.

Troubled by this crisis of confidence, I reasoned that my confession would cause a great upheaval but change nothing. It was the system that was corrupt.

I prayed that night. If I couldn't change the system then I wanted to change jobs. I believed that God was calling me to be an evangelist and that I should extricate myself from the entanglements of corruption.

The mileometer incident was a turning point.

The following March was a cold month. I turned my collar up and tugged my black hat down over my ears. It felt good to be in the open air. It was 8.25 a.m. and Nevsky Bridge, under which the ambulance depot was located, thronged with people hurrying to work.

In front of me a portly man slipped on the ice and went tumbling down. He looked astonished as he sank down on the ground. The black bag he carried fell a few feet away from him and his hat blew off his head.

As I heaved him back on to his feet, an elderly woman passing by scolded him, 'Comrade, it's too early for vodka!'

The man looked startled. 'I'm not drunk, you silly woman,' he panted.

Obviously disorientated by the experience, he grabbed his bag from me as I handed it to him. I thought I was going to be scolded for interfering. He muttered under his breath while the other passers-by chuckled. The woman walked on but turned round wagging her finger. 'Russians who drink but can't hold their liquor should be ashamed!' she continued. 'Better to pack them off to the West. That'll teach them a lesson!'

The man stomped off in embarrassment, with his hat askew. 'God bless you!' I called out. Looking more perplexed than ever he hurried off in the direction of Moscow Station.

This had been an amusing diversion, but my thoughts returned immediately to Vladimir Solovyov, the chief of our station, who had summoned me to his office. I had my suspicions about why he wanted to see me.

I prayed and asked the Lord, 'If he is going to fire me, let him tell me directly. I don't want him to degrade and harass me.'

Vladimir Solovyov twisted uncomfortably in his chair, took a long drag from his cigarette and said, 'Sorry, Valeri, you know I respect your religious views . . .' Again he faltered, 'Valeri, you must understand me. Please leave us.'

I understood the backroom scheming that had forced him to take this decision. 'OK, I agree to leave,' I replied. 'Can you complete my documents so that I can leave from tomorrow?'

Immediately he replied, 'Yes, certainly.'

Usually employees must work a one or two month dismissal period, but when Solovyov waived this requirement, the pressure of the manipulation he was under became clear to me. I waited in his office while his secretary scampered around the building collecting the required signatures and collating my dismissal papers.

Within an hour it was over.

'Here you are, Valeri,' Solovyov said, handing me a file containing the documents I needed. He looked embarrassed but relieved. I felt he wanted to say something else to me but held himself in check as he shook my hand.

Once again I had to break the news to Tanya. I knew she worried about money for the family. I always reassured her that we were in the hands of God. He knew all our needs and would never allow us to fall, no matter how perilous the trail.

As the depot gate closed behind me I felt a weight off my mind. The noise of the road seemed a strange solace. I recalled the mileometer incident and smiled. Perhaps God had answered my prayer . . .

I headed back towards Nevsky Bridge and the cool air stirred something within. *Thank you Lord*. At least the dismissal was instant. I would tell Tanya of God's provision for our family. I must obey Jesus. Nothing else mattered.

As I crossed the bridge I felt the presence of God, and a

conviction that the dream he had placed in my heart would become a reality. We would form a rock band and record the album. I didn't know how, but I was convinced it would happen.

Tanya was startled when I turned up at home and became nervous about the future. 'This is the work of God. We must trust him for everything,' I comforted her.

Within days I had found shift work at another garage servicing broken-down vehicles. I worked two nights every four days, leaving me four days free.

About this time I met an American, Mike McGibbon, who worked for a Christian organisation in the West called Living Sound. When Mike heard my idea, his response was immediate. 'We can help you with recording equipment. I'll arrange for someone to contact you.'

True to his word, someone came to visit me to discuss details of the recording, but I quickly understood that this man from out of town had received a command from someone in the West, and didn't really want to record my music.

Was this the moment the trumpet would sound?

10

Secret Recordings

I had to make my move. It was a question of time before the KGB picked up my tracks again. At work I had become suspicious of a young mechanic who had recently joined the garage. Leonid appeared innocent and naïve, and therefore inquisitive. I couldn't be sure that he wasn't an informer.

Having talked things over with Tanya and Sergei Timokhin, who had agreed to play bass on the project, three weeks before I was due to leave for the recording, I disappeared.

In fact, I stayed at home finalising the lyrics and music of 'The Trumpet Call' and practising my English vocals. I was missed almost at once. Strangers arrived at church and at work asking if anyone had seen me. They received the same reply: the truth. No, we haven't seen Valeri Barinov. We don't know where he is. He's vanished.

Two weeks after I had gone underground we got the first of our callers at home. I was busy rehearsing a line that required a sense of drama, and paced up and down the bedroom repeating the words: where evil reigns – love grows cold.

The doorbell rang and I heard Tanya hurry to answer it. Silently I moved behind the bedroom door which was ajar.

Muffled voices at the door. Footsteps along the corridor. Into the kitchen and then out again. A flurry of activity in the corridor. Panthera's bark sounds dangerously loud. Tanya's enquiry is dismissed. More conversation and the front door is slammed.

Tanya paused by the door. A few minutes passed and the house was totally silent. Then Tanya cautiously entered the bedroom, followed by Panthera.

'The gasman!' she said in an exaggerated voice. Tanya was dismayed that we were now treated like criminals. The 'gasman' had been more interested in peering into every room in the house than in checking the gas meter.

That evening Tanya replayed the scene for Zhanna and Marina, who laughed hysterically as she mimicked our 'gasman' racing through the house. On the fifth or sixth time round, I pounced on Tanya and wrestled her to the ground yelling 'I've caught the gasman!' Panthera joined the merriment, licking our faces in the bundle.

Days later Tanya was confronted at the door by someone wanting to check the electricity meter. Once again, the intruder showed more interest in the rest of the house, barely glancing at the meter in the kitchen. Tanya was tempted to ask him, 'Do you know our gasman?'

More unexpected visitors arrived in the next few days, but each time I was able to evade them. The joke was over as we realised the sinister implications of these visits by our gasman and his accomplices. Our house was under surveillance and I was on the KGB's wanted list.

The night before I was due to leave Leningrad, George and Igor collected my guitar and suitcase from our home. We arranged to meet at the railway station the following evening in time for the 7 p.m. train. As they left at midnight, we embraced and prayed together, asking for God's protection and power to perform his holy will.

Unknown to me, a car nearby sat waiting with its lights on, and George and Igor were followed as they left. Their ordeal in the backstreets ended at 4 a.m. that morning when they eventually shook off their pursuer by hiding in the shadowy courtyard of some large installation.

I knew I would have difficulty in leaving the building, but I was ready for this moment. After preparations lasting an hour, my disguise was complete. My long hair had been rolled up with Tanya's hairclips under an old hat. Dark brown spectacles and ill-fitting clothes created a staid, formal image. As I emerged from the bedroom, everyone had to look twice and even Panthera eyed me suspiciously.

The disguise worked. I slipped out of the rear entrance and headed for the bus stop. I didn't look round but concentrated on walking along the icy pavement. One slip and I risked more than a tumble.

George and Igor arrived on schedule clutching my suitcase and guitar. I was really excited. At last we were going to record. The impossible was coming true.

Three days later at the secret location, the leader of the underground organisation appeared tense and nervous. 'The KGB won't stop until they have hunted you down,' he moaned. 'If they track you to our hideout then our work will be stopped.'

I was stung by his words. What could I say? We shook hands and the meeting was over. I couldn't believe it. Why was I being stopped?

As I settled down on the sofa to spend a troubled night before catching the 7 a.m. train back to Leningrad, a wave of disappointment washed over me. A voice in my head whispered, 'You will never record this music. Never! Never! Never! Everyone will laugh at you.' Had God brought me this close to have the door slammed in my face?

In Leningrad Tanya shared my dismay. But the KGB were still hunting me and she was pleased to see me back safely.

'That's the end of that wild idea,' Tanya stated emphatically.

'No, Tanya, I've gone too far to let go now,' I argued.

'Valeri,' she replied, 'Can't you take "No" for an answer? It's not your fault. You've tried, but it's just not meant to be.'

'Tanya, I don't know how, but I believe that we will record "The Trumpet Call",' I insisted.

Tanya pointed out the risks that our family and friends were running just because of me. 'You need your head examined,' Tanya shouted furiously. 'No one from this world would attempt the impossible.'

'But I'm not from this world,' I replied. I sympathised with her, but God alone had placed the dream in my heart.

Tanya was not amused.

At the garage Leonid expressed disappointment to hear that the secret recording had been aborted. He tried his best to find out which town I had visited and details of the underground organisation.

I went to the chief's office. Valentin was a tall young man with red hair and a full beard.

'Barinov! Where have you been?' he called out as I entered the room.

'I'm sorry,' I smiled, 'I had to go away.'

Valentin grunted and shuffled some papers about. 'Many people came here looking for you.'

'Not ordinary militia,' I replied knowingly.

He nodded.

'KGB,' I said.

'Yes,' Valentin replied. 'Unfortunately.' He drummed his fingers on the desk.

I could read the signs. I knew that I was at fault for being absent without leave. Classified as a 'parasite' my job options were reduced and I could warrant a prison term. Valentin was not being vindictive but merely following orders. He had no choice but to dismiss me.

That evening we prayed together as a family, 'Lord, we need your help. We are your children. We know that you will never abandon us.'

I decided to try to find work in a large vegetable store near us. Some years before, over a hundred people had been arrested for operating a black market from the store, so there were always vacancies. A stoker was needed to operate their furnace. It was hard work for little money.

At the interview I told the truth and explained why the secret police were hounding me. The boss was a tall thin man with a dark drooping moustache which he stroked constantly. Although quite surprised by my story, he said 'OK, you told me the truth. I respect you for that and I will honour it. Go and work!'

The next few months passed quietly, and in retrospect I began to see the design. Curiously, perhaps since my last meeting with Leonid at the garage, the KGB had lifted their surveillance on me. I was a spent force, a dreamer with empty words.

Seven years had passed and still the trumpet's call was a well-kept secret. Some laughed at the dream, others forgot the idea. As I listened to Bob Dylan's album *Slow Train Coming*, one line scorched itself into my heart: 'God don't make promises He don't keep!' I found that the store had a toilet with excellent acoustics, so I continued to practise my vocals in English and never surrendered the vision God had given me.

I worked night shifts with Anatoly, a slim young man with long brown hair. He also liked rock music and we became good friends.

Anatoly had drifted into drugs and now found there was no exit. He was hooked. I shared my faith with him and one day he took the plunge. Anatoly had opened an attic window allowing God inside his life. He never knew how things could change, but he started to feel different. I told him that when he was hooked on Jesus, drugs would lose their grip.

Anatoly tried an experiment. He cut down the amount of drugs he was using, trusting in Jesus. To his amazement, he found that within a few weeks he had jumped off the 'drugs express'.

'I can't believe it,' Anatoly told me. 'Who would have believed that I could be free from drugs?'

I was not surprised. I knew that there is no force on this planet that can compare with the power of God. My new brother in Christ was to play an important part in our future.

One morning I returned home at 8 a.m. as usual and went to bed. A few hours later, Tanya shook me. 'Wake up! A visitor from England is here!' I was about to hear some astonishing news.

The stranger began by reminding me of a conversation I had recently had with four visitors from the Ichthus Fellowship in South London. I had told them about 'The Trumpet Call', and they had asked me what was needed. 'Musical instruments!' I had replied, 'and your prayers.'

I nodded sleepily as I recalled the four young men.

The visitor explained that he was running a campaign for the release of seven Siberian Christians who had taken refuge in the American Embassy in Moscow. On behalf of his four friends he had brought us a gift on his journey to Moscow. Did we still need a guitar?

The guitar had been 'smuggled' into Leningrad and was back at the hotel. Zhanna, aged twelve, accompanied our new friend back to his hotel and they returned with a brand new red electric guitar. I picked it up and stroked its glistening frame. My heart was full of praise to God.

I rang the underground group who controlled the recording equipment. They couldn't believe what I was telling them, but hastily agreed that if I had instruments, they could, after all, provide the recording equipment and an engineer. The rest was up to us, and with the emphasis on secrecy we should complete the recording as quickly as possible.

We agreed some dates and I also called some of the

musicians who I thought would record with me. Sergei Timokhin confirmed immediately that he would play bass guitar. The others gasped in astonishment. 'Really? A new electric guitar? I can't believe it! I'm coming right over to see it.' Such a guitar could only have been bought on the black market for an astronomical price. However, reviewing the music, I realised that we needed a synthesiser for special effects. In some copies of the *New Musical Express* which my friend had left me, I saw synthesisers advertised. I ripped the page out and asked an American to send it to the campaign group in England.

'Are you ready to record?' the leader of the underground group asked me. I assured him that I was. 'What about the other instruments?' I told him that it was all in the Lord's hands. 'Oh no!' he complained. 'That means you haven't got everything.' I admitted that we still needed a synthesiser. I could see that he thought he was dealing with a madman.

The first meeting was planned for the second weekend in March. Still we had no synthesiser, and the underground group were only grudgingly loaning their equipment. If we were caught, they could lose everything.

Anatoly agreed to help by operating both his furnace and mine, enabling me to slip out of the store undetected.

Everyone involved on the project understood the secrecy of it. In a joyous moment, we celebrated communion together, evidence of the Lord's presence with us and the fulfilment of a prophetic vision.

The portable eight-track studio was to be moved around various secret locations in the city, and we devised a complex code for listing meetings. We planned to catch an out-of-town train sometimes, other times we would travel by tram or trolley bus, taking every care to look inconspicuous. When possible, a borrowed car would provide transport with George as a taxi-driver.

As the schedule of recording sessions got under way, mistakes and misunderstandings crept in, meaning that some forgot appointments or others came at the wrong time or to the wrong place.

First we recorded the drum parts, and then Sergei Timokhin played the bass sequences. This formed the foundation for the rest of the work. Before recording each song, I sat with the musician who was playing and taught him the melody and rhythm line. I sang along while he picked it up and played it again for the final recording.

We were now ready to record the synthesiser and again the owners of the equipment called on me to express astonishment that I was stupid enough to make risky plans to record an instrument I didn't have! Max, the engineer, had located a country house which was empty and nervously he finalised plans to record on a Friday night in April. One day before we were to leave, Zhanna was at home alone when a slim Englishman arrived with gifts for the family and a mysterious black box. When I arrived home and heard the news, my heart missed a beat. I walked over to the black box and opened it up.

A synthesiser!

With unbelievable timing, God had arranged the miraculous. Forty-eight hours later it would have been too late.

In England they had known nothing about the timing of the recording, but God had coordinated everything. I was so overjoyed that I rang Ivan, the synth-man, who reacted with total disbelief. I had to spend several minutes convincing him that the synthesiser had actually arrived. Within twenty minutes he was round at the flat looking absolutely stunned. Ivan was not yet a fully convinced believer, but God was certainly demonstrating his power to him.

Now it was a little easier for people to believe that the dream was becoming reality.

After the synthesiser was recorded, the lead guitarist was then able to hear the music and play his contribution. The extraordinary nature of 'The Trumpet Call' was that we never played together as a group. The songs were too dangerous for that, and consequently each of the instrumental tracks was recorded completely separately. Not all the musicians worked their best and some needed pressure to cooperate. However, when they heard the early mix of the English version everyone said they would have played better had they known what it would sound like.

The Russian vocals were kept for the final days of recording. This was clearly wise, as everyone would have understood the Russian words and it would therefore have been easier for the KGB to track us down.

The Russian version was nearing completion when the leader of the underground group visited me. He complained that rock music was not for Christians and that we had used the equipment for far too long. Their group had a project that needed recording and he told me, 'Our work is more important than yours.'

I pleaded for extra time to complete the recording, to no avail. He was leaving the following morning and within four hours the banks of recording equipment would disappear with him, never to be seen again.

I had a cold and fever, and was exhausted from the last few months of recording. What could we hope to do in four hours? And where could we find a place to record?

Anatoly told me he knew a house that had just been re-painted and was empty for the next few days. In one last burst of energy we hauled the equipment to the quiet suburb Anatoly had indicated. Our engineer checked out the basement of the house. He agreed that it would be suitable as the sound would be submerged in the building.

There was one problem. My throat reacted badly to the odour of paint which still hung in the air. The engineer was apprehensive about my ability to perform, but I knew that we didn't have an option. While the microphones and all the equipment were fitted into place, I prayed. This was the last chance to complete the recording of 'The Trumpet Call'. I had only one take and it had to be right.

I asked God to heal my throat and clear my voice. The engineer pointed to the microphone I should use and asked me to speak into it, to check the sound level.

'Praise the Lord!' I said into the microphone. 'This trumpet will sound!' I lifted my hands to heaven and prayed, 'I only want to praise you, my Jesus!'

The engineer signalled, the red light was shining. We're on: live!

I closed my eyes and sang with a passion I had not known before. I felt a tightness in my chest, but I urged myself onward, convinced that we were fulfilling the will of God.

The first rays of sunlight were peeping through the trees in the backstreets of Leningrad as we drove home. I felt drained of all energy and just wanted to sleep. The recording had finally been completed in one year and in five different towns. I don't know how everything held together. Only God made it possible.

But 'The Trumpet Call' was not yet complete! I needed one final choral item to conclude the album. The church choir leader gave me permission to record before the weekly practice. Although I had only five days, I somehow managed to obtain a Japanese tape recorder. Despite technical difficulties and the impatience of some choir members, the last take was magnificent.

I was thrilled. Eagerly I contacted Max and informed him that I had the final item. 'I have it on tape.' I said excitedly. 'And I taped it all myself.'

'On tape?' he said, sounding surprised. 'What speed was the tape you used?'

I stared at him vacantly but quickly regained my composure. 'What speed have you used for the rest of the recording?' I countered.

But the engineer ignored my question and went on to explain, 'You do know that tapes have different speeds and it has got to be on the same speed otherwise it'll be worthless?'

I nodded vigorously. 'Don't worry, God has directed this entire project. Don't you think he knows about the speeds of tape machines? Of course it's the same speed.'

With that I handed over the recording of the choir.

Two days later I visited the engineer. He was preoccupied and under a lot of pressure. 'I'll let you know as soon as your project is ready,' was all he would say.

I asked if he had any technical problems with my recording.

'No, no,' he said impatiently. 'All I need is a few more hours in the day.'

'What about the speed of the tape I gave you on Friday?' I asked casually.

'The speed of the tape? Yeah? What's wrong with it?'

'Is it the same speed as the rest of the recording?' I asked excitedly.

'Yes! Yes! It's the same speed!' he replied grumpily. 'How do you think I could edit your recording if it's not the same speed? Look, don't worry so much. Don't hassle me, I'll do it as quickly as I can.'

I smiled. I knew the Lord wouldn't let me down. 'Just trust me,' Max continued as he escorted me to the door.

I couldn't resist a parting shot as we shook hands. 'No, no, Max. Trust Jesus!'

11

Night Train to Moscow: December 1982–March 1983

While we were recording 'The Trumpet Call', Zhanna and Marina were growing in faith in Jesus and both of them kept asking me to arrange their baptism.

The State banned young people from being baptised in the Baptist Church, so with the help of friends in the Orthodox Church, a date was set for early January. It didn't matter to me which denomination administered the gift of baptism. The real issue was that Zhanna and Marina were sincere in their search for God.

The girls looked gorgeous as they stood in the cathedral in white taffeta gowns that Tanya had stitched. The ceremony itself had a tremendous effect on Tanya and solidified our unity as a family.

Zhanna and Marina caused a stir when news of their baptism spread throughout the school. The teachers were apprehensive but the girls' friends were curious and eventually many in their class found personal faith also.

Shortly after my thirty-eighth birthday, Sergei Timokhin and I began a fast in order to focus our minds on God. We had experienced God's miraculous intervention recording 'The Trumpet Call'. Now we had to tell the world!

We wrote and signed an appeal to the Presidium of the Supreme Soviet emphasising the non-political content of the album and requesting permission to perform our music 'in the concert halls of our country'. To ensure delivery, we registered the letter at our local post office on 17 January, but suspecting confiscation by the local authorities, we decided to deliver it personally to Moscow.

Sergei and I made plans to catch the night train to Moscow. The 'Red Arrow Express' covers the 800 km journey once a week. It was always crowded with people taking advantage of its exceptionally well-stocked restaurant carriage, where many delicacies unobtainable in the shops were for sale.

We sipped tea in Leningrad's main railway station. Thirty minutes to go. Even at this late hour, the station was busy. A couple near us were arguing loudly. All around us travellers trundled across the station floor.

I felt a tap on my shoulder. A militiaman stood with his hand outstretched. 'Let me see your papers,' he said. All at once four policemen surrounded us. Where had they come from? I showed them my identity card.

A plain-clothes officer in a smart fawn-coloured coat and trim dark-brown hat joined the group. KGB. We were escorted to the police station and into a sparsely furnished room, where a long wooden table divided the room in half. Behind the table, another KGB officer waited, his sleek black fur-lined coat slung over a chair.

'Empty your pockets,' he snapped.

'You have no right,' I countered.

'No right?' the KGB official chuckled. 'We have the right to do anything we want.'

Out tumbled keys, money, two railway tickets, photos of Tanya, Zhanna and Marina. Our bag was rifled through. Scarves, paperbacks, ten manilla envelopes containing our appeal and three unmarked cassettes of 'The Trumpet Call'.

The KGB investigator picked up one of the cassettes. 'What is this?' he asked.

'It's our Christian rock opera about the second coming of Christ,' I replied.

'What?' he appeared shocked and cursed. 'Strip!'

Here in the freezing room, Sergei and I could barely stand straight for the cold. Naked under interrogation, we endured the humiliation of a complete body search.

The militiamen picked through our clothes. Throughout the ordeal, the KGB officers swore abusively at us. Two witnesses were called in to sign a report that was in preparation. They were passengers from the station, ordinary people in the wrong place at the wrong time. Everyone knew you didn't refuse a request from the KGB.

The entire interrogation lasted two hours. 'OK, get dressed.' The KGB officer who had arrested us stared coldly at me as I pulled my trousers on. 'You're a marked man, Barinov. The next time we meet, things will be different.' Then he added ominously, 'Don't leave Leningrad.'

We picked up our personal belongings from the table. Tanya's photo had been torn and crumpled. The KGB officer leaned across and grabbed the cassettes and envelopes containing our appeal. 'I'll keep these,' he said, waving them defiantly. 'You won't be needing them for the journey you'll be taking.'

Everyone left the room except for one policeman. He said, 'You can go now, but don't leave Leningrad. You've been warned.'

Sergei and I walked out into the night. It was 2.10 a.m. The snowy street outside the station looked calm and serene. It was unreal and detached from our experience of the last few hours.

I tried not to disturb Tanya as I climbed into bed, but she stirred, tucking herself into the folds of my body. Sleepily she whispered, 'Valeri, what happened? I thought you were going to Moscow.'

'Don't worry Tanya,' I replied, 'I'll tell you about it in the morning.'

I closed my eyes and tried to sleep. The struggle had begun.

The next day, Sergei and I were summoned to the Council of Religious Affairs, the government's official body for controlling churches and religious activity.

Mr Kirov shook us cordially by the hand and settled into a comfortable leather chair. A framed photo of Lenin watched benignly over the smartly furnished office. A smaller photo of Leonid Brezhnev hung on the wall to my left.

The elegantly dressed KGB officer who had directed our arrest at the station stood by the window with his arms folded, smiling throughout our encounter. Mr Kirov's secretary carried in a silver tray with four steaming cups of coffee. 'Just what we need on a day like this,' the KGB man suggested.

'Valeri, you have recorded an interesting musical programme, this, er, what is it called, "Bugle Alert",' Mr Kirov faltered.

'No, no,' I replied, laughing at his apparent joke. 'It's called "The Trumpet Call".'

'That's right, "The Trumpet Call", of course,' Mr Kirov said, shuffling his feet under the table. 'We want to help you.'

'Yes, Valeri,' the KGB man said with a broad grin. 'Your music is very good. I understand that you want to perform in public? We can organise concert halls for you. We can even help you with equipment.'

'That would be wonderful,' I responded. 'Thank you very much.'

'Well Valeri,' he continued, dragging his words out but still smiling, 'you must understand that there is only one condition.'

'Yes, what is that?'

'Don't sing about Jesus. Change the words. We will help you with everything. I know some influential people. We can really take you to the top. But not with songs about Jesus.'

I smiled back at him. 'Well, that poses a problem, because the purpose of the band is to praise Jesus.'

Mr Kirov lectured me on the tasks of a good communist. 'It's our duty to wipe out these old-fashioned ideas about religion,' he declared.

It was clear that the discussion was going nowhere, and Kirov had another meeting to attend. 'Don't tell anyone about our little talk,' he said confidentially.

'That's difficult,' I replied.

'Why?' Kirov asked.

'You know the name of our band?' I said, amused at his growing discomfort. 'If we are called "The Trumpet Call", then we must trumpet!'

The pressure was on. We had secretly circulated 'The Trumpet Call' to anyone who wanted a copy. But I had kept one tape in a brown envelope in a drawer in our bedroom. I wanted to deliver this cassette personally.

My heart pounded as I caught the train to Vyborg. I was prepared to be turned away at the door, but Andrew opened it and grinned in recognition. 'Come in, come in,' he said.

The apartment looked the same, but Andrew had grown tall and was now married with a two-year-old daughter.

'Do you like rock music?' I asked.

'You know that I do,' he shot back.

When Andrew played the tape that I handed over, he listened in amazement, swaying to the beat and reflecting on the lyrics.

While I was showing him some photos of Zhanna and Marina, I heard footsteps in the hallway, someone climbing slowly up the stairs. It was Father. Breathing heavily like an asthmatic, he walked slowly into the room. He looked ashen, his hair turned to white.

He recognised me the instant our eyes met, but didn't say a

word. Andrew reminded Father that I was one of his students who shared a striking similarity to himself. He nodded in acknowledgment and sauntered into one of the rooms locking the door behind him.

With a growing sense of unease, I explained that it was time to return home. Andrew accompanied me to the train station. While we waited on the platform, I said to him, 'Do you want to know a secret?'

He grinned, 'Hey, that's a song by the Beatles.' I smiled in response. 'But what's the secret?'

'Andrew, did you ever wonder why we're so alike?' I didn't know how to tell him. Nothing would ever be the same again. Pausing for a moment, I said softly, 'Did you know that your father had another wife many years ago and that there was a baby from that marriage? I am that child.'

Andrew looked cheekily to see if I was joking but he realised I was serious. His smile froze across his face and his eyes narrowed in surprise.

'It's true,' I said. 'Father was married before and had a child from his first marriage.'

Andrew stood transfixed in front of me. 'Why, that means we're . . . we're half-brothers,' he spluttered.

'That's right, we're half-brothers,' I declared.

Neither of us had realised that the train had pulled into the station. It all seemed like a dream, but I had to get on the train and our meeting was ended.

Andrew edged up to the carriage as I climbed in. 'Valeri,' he faltered, 'I don't know what to say.'

Sensing his unease, I replied, 'There's nothing to say. It happened. That's all.'

The engine jostled our carriage as we pulled out. Andrew looked so young, just the way I must have been as a young man. 'Come and see me in Leningrad!' I called out.

'Yes, I will come,' he replied.

Andrew clung on to me as the train gathered speed. I

grinned. It was just the kind of thing I would have done, had our roles been reversed. Andrew jogged alongside the train until we were forced to let go of each other.

'God bless you Andrew!' I yelled into the dark sky as the hurtling train carried me into the night.

I settled down into a seat and reflected on scenes from the past. This visit to Father had been different in some way. Now, I didn't feel so restless. The sense of loss had been replaced with some measure of peace. I couldn't explain it, but I knew I had crossed a line.

After our meeting with Mr Kirov and his mysterious friend at the Council for Religious Affairs, I was called to the military commission and required to undergo a medical and psychiatric examination prior to being drafted back into the army. Again! No one could make sense of it.

But the signs were becoming easier to spot. The examination would declare me insane, and I'd be held in psychiatric hospital. If I refused the call-up, I would be imprisoned for disobeying orders. Either way, the KGB had set a trap.

How could I fight back? I would rather die than abandon the vision planted in my heart. Prayer was my only weapon.

A psychiatrist who wore wire-rimmed spectacles on the bridge of his nose conducted the interview while a nerve specialist made notes in silence.

I was questioned closely about my religious beliefs. When I indicated my suspicion of KGB pressure, the doctor simply smiled and said, 'It seems that you think the KGB are watching you?'

I was relaxed. 'I don't know if the KGB watch me or not,' I replied. 'We all have our work to do. My work is to praise my Jesus. The KGB have different work.'

The doctor smiled again and said confidentially, 'Let me tell you that the KGB called us and they did say that they have you under surveillance.'

I realised the importance of every word. If I agreed with his statement I would confirm that I was paranoid, suspicious and maybe crazy.

The psychiatrist closed the interview with words which were friendly, but an unmistakable warning. 'I'm afraid, Valeri, that if you preach about Jesus in the army, you are heading for a psychiatric ward.'

The official Soviet Army psychiatric report stated:

Valeri Barinov speaks of his role
in the working of divine providence,
of the power of Christ,
and actively preaches divine wisdom.

Miraculously I was later able to obtain a copy, which was smuggled to Keston College in England where most of my information was sent for circulation.

The doctor dismissed me with a referral note for a further examination at a clinic quite close to my home. I didn't need to be a prophet to know that the questions would be the same.

This second meeting lasted an hour and a half. Undoubtedly the medical team were convinced that they were dealing with a devious traitor.

Dr Maslova introduced herself and handled the preliminary discussions. I was then interviewed by a panel of experts who touched and prodded me, asking ludicrous questions. When I attempted to reply, each would look at each other, sometimes rolling their eyes in amusement. I was a spectacle for their derision.

Nothing I said could make any difference to their prognosis. I was crazy. Every time the doctors spoke, I heard the doors of the psychiatric prison swinging open.

The next morning, Tanya suggested that if the medical staff were given a copy of 'The Trumpet Call', they would understand why the KGB were hounding me. We prayed, and I had peace in my heart that this was a good idea, despite the obvious risks. Although Tanya was seen promptly by Dr Maslova, she was unable to engage her in any conversation.

One afternoon Zhanna came home from school and declared, 'Dad, we're being watched. Three days running I've seen the same car parked outside our house. They're still out there.'

I was furious and grabbed my coat. 'Quick, let's see what they look like.'

Zhanna and I linked arms against the cold January wind and headed for the road. Zhanna was right. There they were. A black Volga hugging the curb.

'Wait here Zhanna,' I said and squeezed her hand. Stepping carefully on to the icy street I made directly for the parked car. Barely a few paces away, I could make out the features of two young men huddled together inside. Somewhat startled, I saw one nudge the other. All at once the ignition key was turned and the car sped off into the distance.

Zhanna came up behind me. 'What would you have said to them, Dad?' she asked. I chuckled. I hadn't really thought of anything to say. 'God would have given me the words.'

All through the following months, each time one of us went out we were tailed. Even Zhanna and Marina were followed to school. When their friends asked if they were afraid, they replied, 'Of course not, we've got Jesus. He will protect us.'

Jesus gave me boldness, and I approached the black car five times. Each time it sped away.

As a result of Leningrad's extensive underground communication network, the secret recording became very well known, and many young people asked when they could hear us play.

'That depends on the Kremlin and the KGB,' I joked.

Realising the opportunity we had to communicate the Gospel to the youth of Leningrad, we planned a meeting in the official Baptist Church on February 6th.

Although the halls weren't being used, the doors remained

locked and about thirty young people were turned away. I wrote to the elders clarifying the mission of our rock band:

> 'The Trumpet Call' may seem a strange form of preaching to you, but thanks to the medium of modern music, God's word is made accessible to everyone and many young people hear the Gospel.

Five days later, Seva Novgorodtsev, a popular DJ on the BBC World Service, played extracts from 'The Trumpet Call'. He also read out our appeal requesting permission to play openly. Finally, Seva announced our home address.

The response was sensational. Young people, mostly non-believers, contacted us from all across the Soviet Union. It was evident that these kids were waking up from a spiritual slumber induced by atheism. Realising that alcohol, drugs or money could not satisfy the longings of their soul, they wrote in to say, 'We need Jesus!'

Early in March a policeman called at the door. 'Are you Valeri Barinov?' he asked.

'Yes,' I replied. 'You know it's me.'

'You must report for a compulsory psychiatric investigation tomorrow morning at 10 a.m. I have a police car waiting outside. Either you go by yourself tomorrow or come with us now. It's very important that you are not late.'

I convinced the young lieutenant that I could handle my own travel arrangements. The next morning, I left the house at dawn and spent the day visiting friends. If I returned to the psychiatric hospital according to the instructions, it would be as a prisoner, not as a patient.

On April 13th we had another visitor. 'Hello, I'm Nurse Yudina from the psychiatric hospital,' said an elderly, very experienced nurse.

'Why do I need a nurse?' I said in astonishment.

'Because you are registered as a psychiatric patient,' Yudina declared. This was news to me. After some haggling, the nurse reluctantly agreed to continue the discussion inside our apartment.

I offered her coffee, but she declined. Immediately to business. 'What medicine do you use?'

'I don't use any because I'm not sick,' I commented in surprise.

'But drugs have been prescribed. It is most important that the doctor is informed,' she insisted.

I confronted her in a quiet confident tone. 'You don't have to keep up this pretence because I know who has ordered you to come here today. I know that the KGB have set a trap for me.'

Yudina looked startled. 'What trap? Why do the KGB want to trap you?'

'Because of our Christian rock group "The Trumpet Call".'

At the mention of the group's name Yudina raised her eyebrows slightly. 'How many play in your group?'

'Seven,' I replied.

Without thinking, Yudina opened her notebook and scribbled down the number seven. Mischievously I pointed to her notebook and asked, 'Is this my diagnosis?'

Realising her blunder, Yudina yelled and cursed. She threw her notebook into her case. 'You're a traitor,' she screeched.

'Your reaction is proof that I am well. No one screams like this at ill people!' Stung by the truth of my words, Yudina stormed out of the apartment.

Tanya had heard almost everything from the bedroom and she rushed out. What more could be said? Swaying gently, we embraced in the tiny hallway, both aware of the hidden danger lurking ahead.

Two days after Nurse Yudina's visit I was summoned again to the Council for Religious Affairs. This time there were no cups of coffee or friendly handshakes.

Mr Kirov frowned at me from behind his desk as I was

made to stand before him like an errant schoolboy before the headmaster. I refused to be intimidated and extended my hand. 'Hello Mr Kirov, God bless you.'

He gave me a limp handshake and went on to talk continually for the next twenty minutes, barely allowing me to reply. He complained about the foreigners I was meeting and warned that I was acting like a traitor.

'Our prisons are full of people like you. Do you understand?' Mr Kirov glared.

'But Mr Kirov,' I interrupted, sounding puzzled. 'That means innocent people are imprisoned in our country.'

He raised his hand to cut me short. 'Slandering the Soviet State is a criminal offence. You have been warned. You'll end up in the Ural Mountains with your family!'

The Ural Mountains was a popular euphemism for the labour camps. He pressed a buzzer on the side of his desk and a young man in a crumpled suit escorted me from his office. Mr Kirov didn't wave good-bye.

I went straight to George's apartment, where I informed George and Sergei of Kirov's warning. Before I left, we clasped hands and committed each other to God's will.

I arrived home late to find a note from Tanya who was fast asleep:

Some friends arrived to see you today.
The only English word I could use was 'NO',
which wasn't very friendly. They will
return at 7 p.m. tomorrow, so come home early!!!
Goodnight, I love you, Tanya.
PS Zhanna and Marina asked me again whether
we can go on holiday this year. Can we?

The image of foreigners knocking on our door to be greeted by a Russian redhead who says, 'NO!' amused me. What would they think? Not the best advertisement for detente! I was also reminded of Kirov's warning against 'agents of western imperialism'.

Promptly at 7 p.m. the doorbell rang and two young Americans stood clutching a piece of paper with my name on it. I liked to entertain friends from the West and made myself available to take them wherever they wanted to go. This couple agreed to carry out some messages for me.

A few days later Nurse Yudina returned. I decided to surprise her to see what her reaction would be. 'I know all your tricks and soon you and your bosses will be exposed.'

'What do you mean?' She sounded outraged.

I pulled a copy of Tolstoy's *Resurrection* off the bookshelf and lifted out a piece of paper tucked inside its pages. 'This is a record of the pressure used to force me into psychiatric hospital,' I declared. 'It will be broadcast over the BBC shortly. Would you like me to read it to you?'

Yudina's rage could be contained no longer. 'You traitor!' she screamed. 'Have you no shame?'

The comic scene was re-enacted as the nurse shouted at her patient and slammed the door.

The house was silent as Seva read the statement over the airwaves. What a breakthrough! I could hardly believe it. Suddenly light had come, and the darkness could not hide it. I didn't know how the KGB would respond, but was determined to carry on as normal.

One week later, on May 6th, we celebrated Tanya's birthday. The glow from the coloured candles on the cake which Zhanna and Marina had baked created warmth and cosiness.

Tanya blew out the candles, and for a second or two the room was in darkness until someone switched on the light. 'Make a wish, Mama,' Zhanna said. 'Make a wish for the coming year.'

Tanya paused for a moment. 'I wish for a peaceful life, that's all I want.' And then added, 'But our lives are in God's hands.'

* * *

Sometimes one doesn't realise that seemingly unrelated events are actually linked like tracks on a railway line.

On May 13th, I was told by the boss at the store that he could no longer hire me. I was not fired, but no longer employable. I had entered the danger zone whereby I could be classified as a 'parasite' of the state.

The boss wasn't a bad man. He just wanted to get through the day. He didn't really want to discuss my situation with me but I pressed him. Was I a bad worker?

'Well no, that's not the reason,' he explained. 'It's just that we can't have someone working here who is registered as a psychiatric patient.'

The design became clear. He was just obeying orders. Whispers from the KGB didn't need an amplification system.

On June 22nd I was visited by a psychiatrist who conducted an ad hoc interview. Three days later I returned home to learn that a police inspector had called.

'He wanted to know why you weren't working and how long you had been unemployed,' Zhanna informed me. 'I explained that you had been fired because you had been illegally registered as a psychiatric patient.'

I gave Zhanna a hug, and she looked at me with a cheeky grin. Zhanna had inherited my humour.

The next assault came from an unexpected quarter and ripped deep into me.

I was told that the leaders of the Baptist Church wanted to see me on June 28th. I knew that they were under increasing pressure from the KGB to keep me 'under control'. The meeting was formal and the attitude of the elders was cautious. I explained that, although some people might not like our music, our aim was to share the Gospel. I showed them the letters we had received from young people in response to the BBC broadcasts of 'The Trumpet Call'. But the elders wouldn't look at the letters.

The following evening a church meeting was held. I was prepared for what was to happen and decided not to attend. Nevertheless, it hurt me deeply. My friends who were there told me of the decision to expel me from the Baptist Church.

The leaders had been intimidated by the KGB. But what a tragedy that they had compromised their responsibility as Christ's ambassadors. We were, after all, brothers and sisters of the same family. I determined in my heart that I would not judge them, but forgive them. Those who submit to a lie bear a greater burden than those who live by the truth.

The following reasons were given for my expulsion:

Firstly, my appearance. I looked like a hippie, I wore jeans, tee-shirts and a cross around my neck.

Secondly, my children had been baptised in the Orthodox Church.

Thirdly, I had not always clearly identified with the Baptist denomination.

Fourthly, we played rock music.

I decided to attend church and act as though nothing had happened. I had been judged by man, and was more concerned with the judgement of God. If God was on my side then I had nothing to fear.

For me, the issue was not where Zhanna and Marina were baptised, but whether they believed in Jesus. The leaders had neglected to mention that it is illegal to baptise anyone under eighteen in the Baptist Church. I had always considered myself a Christian rather than a Baptist, and felt at home in all denominations. As for rock music, it was hard for them to understand that our aim was to share the Gospel.

Aunt Tamara was caught in the tensions within the church and it was a difficult time for all of us.

That same day, I decided to fast and pray for a week. Sergei Timokhin joined me. I wanted to keep myself pure before God. We also received many more letters from young people who were curious about the faith so we organised another meeting.

Despite requests to use the church hall on July 10th, once again the doors remained closed. I was disappointed that we had missed another opportunity to share the Gospel with people who would normally never turn up at church.

But July was also a month of great triumph for us. Vindication was to come from a far country. Seva announced on the BBC that a British pop-singer had sent us a message of encouragement. And then Cliff Richard's message was played.

Zhanna and Marina hugged me. Tanya was beaming. Sergei clapped and cheered. I wanted to scream! What a moment of joy. God had used this moment to endorse and support our struggle when we needed it most.

The news spread like wildfire. Cliff Richard, the famous singer, had actually heard our music! The great thing was that he understood that we were trying to share the Gospel through rock music.

Late one night Tanya asked me if I had remembered being asked whether we could go away on holiday?

'Yes, vaguely,' I said.

'I think a holiday would do us all good,' Tanya said.

I agreed. The girls had also been under pressure. Tanya made preparations and we spent a few weeks in Odessa. It was a relaxing time. But I was not to know that this would be the last family holiday for several years. While lying on the beach, I remembered an earlier prophecy from God regarding seven trumpets. I had already recorded the first one and had no doubt that I would complete the others. But how? Only God knows.

When we returned to Leningrad, I found work in a local park where construction had begun on a skating rink. I was given the mindless task of hosing water on to a concrete block. But it gave me flexible working hours and urgently needed roubles.

Tanya and I, Zhanna and Marina were being drawn together in a new experience of togetherness. The Lord had strengthened our resilience and our resolve. God was uniting our hearts for the struggle ahead.

12

Psychiatric Terror

I glanced at the calendar: October 11th, 1983.

I stood in the hallway pulling on my denim jacket when Tanya called out to me from the kitchen. I couldn't hear what she said. Again she called. What did she want?

'Tanya,' I called out. 'I need some cash. Is there any money in the house?'

I couldn't find any money in our usual hiding places and went in search of Tanya. She was standing by the stove peeling potatoes.

'Tanya, have you got any money?' I asked her. Tanya looked up at me. 'Couldn't you hear me calling you?' she said crisply.

'Yes, but I'm in a hurry,' I explained. 'I'm meeting George and I'm already late.'

'I don't care who you're meeting,' Tanya insisted, 'I need to know when you'll be home, because I want us to eat together with Zhanna and Marina tonight.'

'Sorry, Tanya,' I apologised. 'You need a medal for living with me.'

'Go on,' she said, handing me a few coins. 'The sooner you leave, the sooner you'll return.'

I was going to be late, but George would wait, I reflected as I jogged through the October rain to the bus stop. He had asked me to bring the letters I had received following the BBC radio broadcast. 'I've got an idea,' he said enigmatically.

Udelnaya subway station wasn't very busy. I heard someone call my name and turned to find two policemen standing behind me. Now I've really got an excuse for being late, I thought as I showed my identity card.

'Come with us,' one of them said, sounding bored. This was surely a misunderstanding that would be soon cleared up. In my bag, bundled together were letters from young people all over the country. If their names and addresses fell into the wrong hands . . . Somehow I had to get a message to Tanya.

A young officer pulled up in a police car. 'OK, I've come for Valeri Barinov.' He produced a pair of handcuffs.

'Don't worry about me, I'm not going to run away,' I told him.

The officer seemed to be in a good mood. 'Give me one good reason why I should believe you won't try to escape?' he grinned.

'I believe in Jesus. Nothing happens to me out of coincidence, even this arrest is part of his plan. Why should I escape?'

When the officer realised I wasn't joking, I knew I had moved into a commanding position. He paused for a moment, chuckling, then slapped me on the shoulder. 'Come on Barinov! But I'm warning you, if you try to get away you'll really be in trouble.'

The officer hummed to himself as we drove through the midday traffic. I said to him, 'Do you know why you're arresting me?'

'Because you've broken the law,' he said, 'obviously.'

'But do you know what crime I have committed?' I continued.

'No,' he replied. 'I was just asked to pick you up.'

'I am a Christian rock musician. That's the reason I've been arrested,' I explained.

'Rock music and Christianity. That's a dangerous

combination,' he smiled. 'I didn't know there were any Christian rock musicians,' he continued, obviously intrigued.

'But there are many Christian musicians. In the West, of course. Cliff Richard, Bob Dylan, Donna Summer.'

We talked casually during the rest of the journey. The hunter and the hunted. Strange companions.

Clutching the bag of letters I was marched into a room occupied by three policemen, one of whom hurriedly finished a telephone conversation. His name was Uvarov. The officer I had arrived with talked with him for a few minutes and then walked across to me. 'What kind of music does your band play?' he asked.

'Don't speak with him! Don't speak with him!' Uvarov called out angrily.

The driver was taken aback, and moved away holding up his hands. He strode to the door and was gone.

An hour and a half had passed when I heard the screeching of brakes outside. Car doors slammed.

A young medical orderly dressed in a white coat and carrying a case entered and shook hands with Uvarov. 'So this is the Christian preacher,' he grinned.

Uvarov produced some forms and the orderly signed them. 'He's very quiet now,' the orderly sneered. 'But this is the man who wants to preach the Gospel with a loud trumpet call.' He emphasised the last two words.

I remained silent as he told the policeman about our Christian rock group. It was clear that he knew everything about me. 'His wish is to play Christian music,' the orderly continued, 'but I wish him a painful cross to bear.' Uvarov and the other policemen joined in the laughter.

'Do you realise that you are completely under our control?' Uvarov derided me, goaded on by the medical worker. 'No one can save you.' Uvarov walked across and prodded his finger into my chest. 'What do you think of that?' he boasted.

'I know only one thing,' I answered both Uvarov and the KGB medical worker. 'And I want to thank you . . .'

My retort was met with astonishment. 'For what?' they said almost in unison.

'Because God makes an advertisement of me through your action,' I declared.

Both were enraged. 'You swine,' the orderly swore. He was about to strike me, but drew back. The interrogation ended. I was hustled into an ambulance waiting outside and driven to the Leningrad Psychiatric Hospital No. 3.

The hospital was surrounded by a brick wall, its front gates guarded by two militiamen. I was asked to wait in the reception. The bag with the letters lay at my feet.

On the bench beside me, a woman dressed in a smart blue coat fiddled nervously with a medical card. I smiled at her and she acknowledged my greeting. She stared in disbelief as I explained briefly why I was detained.

'Oh! You are here because of your religious activity.' She added, almost to herself, 'That means I'm here because of my guilt.'

'What guilt?' I asked.

'I uncovered a plot at the pharmaceutical factory where I work. The bosses were going to steal narcotics and sell them on the black market. I informed our Party boss, and a few days later was asked to attend a medical examination. I came here totally convinced that there had been a mistake, but listening to your story, I wonder if it's because of the report I wrote.'

I sympathised with the woman. 'The Party boss must have reported you to the KGB,' I reasoned.

'But I'm a loyal Party member,' the woman confided.

'But this isn't the real Communist Party. These people are more like the Mafia!'

'I do believe that you're right.' Turning to me she said cautiously, 'Will you pray for me?'

'Yes,' I replied, fearing for her at the mercy of such evil people.

I approached a friendly looking woman and asked her, 'Could you phone this number and let my wife know I'm in this hospital?' I prayed that the note would not be confiscated.

I also beckoned to an old lady. 'I need your help. Could you get rid of this for me?' She eyed the package of letters suspiciously, but agreed. 'Just throw it away when you leave here,' I reassured her casually. Soon she had passed through the hospital entrance and was out of sight.

The registrar called my name and took me to Department 20 on the first floor.

'Doctor, why have I been brought to this hospital by force?' I protested.

He looked startled. 'What do you mean?' The doctor refused to discuss the matter and left the room locking the door behind him. A few minutes later a nurse arrived and led me to another part of the hospital where I exchanged my clothes for white robes. From there a nursing sister escorted me to an unmarked ward where the door was locked behind me.

The ward was large, gloomy, and silent. Like some children's game, all the inmates froze to their allocated site. I felt their eyes inspecting me. The room smelt of sweat and urine.

A tall man with a scraggy beard sauntered over, speaking nonsense. He carried a stick with a handkerchief tied to it like a flag. 'You don't have permission to breathe unless the commander says so,' he informed me.

'All right,' I told him.

Everyone began to speak simultaneously, shrieking and shouting, pointing at me. One young man pranced around on his haunches making animal noises and deliberately knocking into others in his way.

My hand reached out for the door but it was locked. I sat on the bed nearest the door and was immediately swooped on by an inmate who crossed the room on all fours mimicking the noise of a car. He was extremely upset so I apologised for sitting on his bed and moved closer to the window.

The bars on the window and the thick pane of glass, stained with dried food and vomit, contributed to the claustrophobic atmosphere.

Some of the inmates pointed accusingly at me and giggled. 'So you are sending signals through the airwaves?' the man with the flag shrieked, although not aware of my crime.

'What do you mean?' I asked.

'Silence. Permission to speak must be granted before you can obey,' he yelled, shoving me away from the window. He pointed to the far corner of the room and I passed through the rows of inmates uttering obscenities and gibberish.

As I prayed, concentrating on the person of Jesus, I intuitively felt constrained to check the window. Risking the wrath of the 'Commander' by moving quietly to the nearest window. Somehow my action passed unnoticed.

I looked through the window which faced the front of the building and to my astonishment I saw Tanya peering up. Several hours had passed since my arrival. Obviously my secret note had been delivered. *Thank you my Jesus*, I whispered.

I waved, praying that she would see me before my movements inside the room were uncovered. Tanya stared. Then she waved. I could see her begin to cry. I felt my chest tightening and my throat dry up. A wave of helplessness washed over me, but only for a few seconds. I blew her a kiss.

I had to signal quickly. Telephone, I gesticulated to her. I knew that the prayers of friends and pressure from the West were formidable weapons. Nothing else would influence the KGB.

One of the guards at the gate hustled Tanya away, but her haunting image lingered with me, returning at times of great despair.

This was a particularly violent hospital where many innocent people were broken. There was sadism in the wards and I pitied the genuinely ill patients. Permission was required to use the toilet, which was filthy and overflowing.

Periodically inmates were removed from the ward and returned in a daze. Finally, it was my turn.

'Do you believe in God?' the lady doctor asked, surrounded by books and charts.

'How long do you plan to keep me in this prison?' I replied.

Unruffled, she continued in a calming voice, 'Oh Valeri, it's difficult to say. Maybe one month, maybe three years, maybe twelve years. Maybe for ever.' She smiled sweetly.

Before I could reply, the professor of psychology entered the room. The lady doctor excused herself and the professor, who I believed was a Jew, continued.

'What God do you believe in?' he asked.

'The God of Israel!' I replied.

'Oh that's interesting,' he replied. 'Speak to me, speak to me.' God had found a way for me to talk with him.

After about half an hour of explaining Israel's significance in world history, the professor realised I was normal. 'Oh my, what shall we do with you?' I felt the question was addressed to himself. Despite the influence of the KGB he wanted to help me.

I was to be injected with aminazin, a drug used in schizophrenia. 'Minimum dose for this patient,' the professor instructed.

Back in the ward I couldn't stand still. I moved from my bed to the floor to the toilet and back again. I realised that the aminazin was taking effect. I tried to pray but found my mind wandering.

Three years. Tanya would have left you. Twelve years. You'll never see Zhanna and Marina again.

I leapt out of bed. Got to get out of here. I hammered on the door unaware that I was screaming.

One of the inmates crept up behind me. I heard him giggle.

'You'll never get away from here,' he said rolling his eyes. 'You're one of us now.'

Restlessness kept me from eating and sleeping. Each evening I was injected with aminazin. It was hard not losing control. I found myself repeating one word over and over. 'Jesus! Jesus! Jesus!'

I met one man who had been a loyal communist. We were able to talk reasonably except when we had been drugged. 'Why are you here?' he asked.

'Because of my Christian activity,' I replied.

'You will be here a long time,' he remarked sadly.

He had reported corruption within his factory and was detained on the order of his boss. The doctors had asked him, 'Have you been busy at work?'

'Yes,' the man had replied.

'Ah, then you must be tired. Are you tired?' the doctor enquired.

Unsure about the question, the man acknowledged that, if he had been busy, then logically, yes, he must be tired.

The doctor then told him, 'Since you're tired, by your own admission, I advise you to have a rest here in the hospital.'

Unknown to me, the BBC had broadcast news of my arrest. Tanya also protested but was told, 'Your husband's views on religion differ so much from those of ordinary citizens that he needs psychiatric treatment.'

After six harrowing days the injections were stopped. The next day I was interviewed for an hour by the hospital's Senior Medical Officer in the presence of the Jewish professor, who said nothing. After realising I was quite sane, the questions began to deal with political issues.

'Valeri, Ronald Reagan is a Christian. Yes? Then why does he increase American nuclear weapons?'

'But we have increased our own nuclear arsenal; it's not just the Americans,' I responded.

The Jewish professor escorted me back to the ward in silence. On the way we walked through a short corridor. All the doors were closed. We were alone. In a hushed voice he whispered, 'Don't speak about politics.' His finger was raised up to his mouth and he re-assumed the role of custodian.

I understood by his gesture that he wanted to help me, and I thanked God that even in this terrible place he could make people perform his will.

The next day I was summoned to continue the interview. Once again, the professor took notes in silence.

'Ah yes, Valeri, tell us whether you think Russia or America is the military bully?'

'Each side thinks an increase in weapons is justified,' I replied. 'But you know, I am not interested in the arguments of politicians. I have no interest in politics because I am a Christian. This is my life. The Bible teaches that we can only find peace with God through Jesus Christ. That's the message I want to share throughout this world.'

A few more questions followed, and this time a nurse escorted me back to the ward. That day passed peacefully with no more injections or interrogations. I remained in prayer and stayed quietly on my bed. Whenever one of the inmates came to taunt me, God enabled me to endure it.

The following day I awoke early but remained in bed. Today was October 20th. Zhanna's birthday! She would be fourteen years old. How I longed to hug her. My teenage daughter was almost a lady. I felt that my heart would break.

I prayed that Jesus would demonstrate his power. *You can do anything, Lord. Let me be united with my daughter today.*

The day passed slowly. Every hour seemed a torment.

'Barinov!'

I jerked up to see one of the nurses beckoning me. 'Come with me and bring your belongings.'

I replied calmly even though my heart had begun to race. I

wanted to charge out of hospital in my medical gown and run all the way home.

There were forms and signatures but everything was a blur. *Thank you my Jesus!* My heart was singing.

I was out!

I found I couldn't walk slowly. I was jogging down the street. I could think of only one thing. To hug Tanya and Marina and my birthday girl, Zhanna.

And then the moment finally came. When they saw me everyone was amazed. Tanya dropped the plate she was holding and it smashed on the floor but no one seemed to notice. My cousin Valya was at home helping the family, and she shrieked with joy, 'Valeri!'

'I love each of you with all my heart,' I said as we all hugged in a tearful embrace. '*Thank you Jesus for returning me to my family.*'

13

Midnight Rider:
October 1983–March 1984

The KGB weren't about to give up. Neither was I. If I compromised, my future would be peaceful, and the trials of the past ten days would be forgotten. I didn't choose to struggle with the KGB. I chose to follow Jesus. If the path of Jesus meant sacrifice, I was ready for death.

The same day I was released, Sergei Timokhin was warned that he would face criminal prosecution. The KGB were everywhere and we walked a tightrope.

Sergei told me that the Baptist Church had prayed for me while I was in the psychiatric hospital, and he himself had written a letter in my support. This was a great encouragement. When one part of the body suffers, the whole body suffers. I was greeted warmly at the church, even though the leadership didn't support me. Everyone knew they had witnessed a miracle.

'When are you going to play?' people asked continually. On November 11th we attempted another meeting at the Baptist Church. I couldn't believe it! Two hundred street people turned up, but the gates remained locked. I knew there was a clubroom on the building site where I now worked as a night watchman, so about eighty teenagers trailed after me and crammed into the hall.

Here in this illegal gathering the lost youth of Leningrad wanted to know Jesus, challenging the State's theft of God from people's hearts. Half an hour later, police and plain-clothes officers broke up the meeting and herded everyone into lorries which took us to the local police station where we were held for three hours.

Zhanna, aged fourteen, was among the group arrested, and along with Sergei Timokhin and myself, she was accused of being one of the ring leaders. I couldn't believe they would arrest someone so young. But she was a Barinov, and no exceptions would be made.

It took a week for the KGB to reach me. I was summoned to yet another psychiatric examination where I was aware that the doctors considered me 'not completely well', but allowed me to leave after an hour's questioning.

When Zhanna's schoolteachers heard that she had been guilty of 'disturbing the public order', I was asked to call and see them. I explained everything, including how Zhanna and Marina had been followed to school by the KGB. I don't know what the school authorities thought of me, but they were good people who were genuinely concerned for Zhanna's well-being. As I rose to leave, one teacher clasped my hand and said, 'Have pity on your children.'

I was moved when I heard these words but kept silent. My pity was for the teachers who didn't realise the Communist Party's greatest crime: the theft of God. Zhanna and Marina had chosen for themselves and found the truth.

During December a new rumour was circulating: that I was a drug trafficker. It was easy to recognise the fingerprints of the KGB. I knew many addicts and had shared the Gospel with them, but had never taken drugs myself. No one who knew me thought I had. Only the KGB's imagination could have stretched that far.

I didn't think there were any accusations to answer so I ignored the rumour. If the KGB wanted to arrest me, I knew the charges didn't matter. Instead, I concentrated on our mission to share the Gospel with Leningrad's drop outs. Our message was simple. Jesus has changed our lives, he can change yours!

Sergei and I spent the week up to Christmas praying and fasting for opportunities to play for young people. Many of our friends asked us when we would record a follow up to 'The Trumpet Call'. I already had ideas for other songs and albums and I longed for the day when I could work in freedom for Jesus' glory.

On January 30th, we received an ominous sign. A summons from the Leningrad Procuracy warned me that I must stop 'spreading slanderous fabrications defaming the Soviet social and state system'.

I could hear the footsteps of the KGB getting nearer.

I kissed Tanya for the last time. Zhanna and Marina stood beside us and I embraced them. 'Never forget that I love you with all my heart', I whispered.

I had explained to my family that I was going 'underground' in order to complete my next recording. The KGB had mapped out my future in Leningrad. I didn't need to be a prophet to read the signs.

I decided not to reveal everything to my family. We were crossing the danger line. If something should go wrong, my family would not be spared the demon of interrogation. If they knew nothing, they could reveal nothing.

Sergei and I had assembled our supplies in January and February: food, warm clothes, homemade skis, compasses and Finnish/English/Russian phrase books. We looked more like pirates than rock musicians.

I arrived early for the 6 p.m. rendezvous. We intended to take a train to Volkastra and change for the next section of our journey.

But Sergei was late.

I was on the verge of calling it off, when Sergei arrived, two hours later. Sensing danger, I asked Sergei, 'Why are you so late? Were you followed?'

'No, I wasn't followed,' Sergei assured me as we raced to catch a train. Sergei acted nervously and on the train we spotted suspicious characters in black leather jackets, standard uniform of the secret police.

From the map I had seen in Leningrad, Sofporog led to the border and was inside the frontier zone. But I didn't know that the town leading to the frontier zone, Kestenga, was a closed town. Only those with special passes were allowed in.

When the local authorities realised that we didn't have the passes, we were denied access to the town. Some local people eyed us suspiciously. I was in no doubt that they would inform the police about our movements.

We prayed for guidance. I told Sergei, 'I believe we should abandon our plans and return to Leningrad.'

Sergei nodded, 'I feel the same way. I think we should turn back.'

We learnt that the next train was heading north to the border towards Murmansk and not back to Leningrad. We had eighty roubles allocated for our return tickets and we counted that out carefully.

The train was due in ten minutes and an immediate decision had to be taken. We would board the train and change for Leningrad at a station further up the line. We hit on Kynazhaya, a small town en route to Murmansk.

The Murmansk train rolled into Kynazhaya at 9 p.m. that night and we headed immediately for the ticket office. The clerk informed us that the next train to Leningrad would leave at 5 a.m. 'There's a waiting room you can use if you wish,' he offered.

It had been a tiring journey, and we were exhausted. The waiting room was empty as we settled down for the night. We had brought bread, biscuits and a flask of milk. This had been the first chance that we had to eat anything. We maintained a discreet silence in case we were overheard. Now we only wanted one thing: to get back to Leningrad as soon as possible.

The railway benches were rough, and despite our ski jackets and woollen sweaters, I still felt the cold.

I must have dozed off. The next thing I recall was being woken by voices. I sat upright and was confronted by three militiamen towering over me. Sergei rubbed the sleep from his eyes.

'Papers!' one of the policemen said curtly. We complied.

'Where are you going?'

'Leningrad,' I replied.

Our passports were handed back. As they turned to leave I overheard the remark, 'It's not them.'

Sergei and I exchanged glances. Had we been betrayed from the beginning?

A few minutes later, the militiamen returned. I sensed something was wrong. Once again they asked for our documents. This time there would be no mistake.

A police van was parked outside with its engine running. Sergei and I were hustled into the back and driven to the local police station at Zelenoborsk.

About two hours later, Yevgeny Katchkin, a KGB officer from Leningrad, arrived at the station. Katchkin was the KGB's main investigator into religious affairs.

I was puzzled. How could the KGB man arrive from Leningrad in such a short time? Were we followed from the time we left Leningrad? Had he been waiting somewhere down the line?

The next day, Sergei and I were moved to a special detention centre in Kandalska, the nearest big town to Kynazhaya, where we had been arrested.

My interrogation began almost as soon as I entered the jail. I was introduced to Mr Shelimov, a mild-mannered avuncular figure. He offered me tea and seemed sympathetic to my plight.

'Tell me the truth,' he said, 'and I will do everything I can to help you. Trust me.'

'I will tell you the truth,' I replied, deciding to take him at his word. 'I wanted to travel to Finland to record some new songs and then return to our country with the tapes.'

'And what would you have done with the tapes?' Mr Shelimov asked soothingly.

'I was going to give copies of my songs to the authorities to prove that I am not a political activist and that my songs are not anti-Soviet or political,' I continued.

'Why do you write songs?' he asked. 'What is your motivation?'

'I write songs to praise my Jesus,' I replied. 'The KGB have stopped me from continuing my work in Leningrad. I was driven out of the country. I didn't want to leave. After all, my family and friends are in Leningrad,' I added. 'I wasn't going to leave for ever. If the KGB gave me permission to sing about Jesus, I would never have tried to leave.'

'But the police claim you were caught trying to escape,' he mused.

'That's a lie,' I stated emphatically. 'We had planned to cross the border but changed our minds. We were arrested while waiting for a train to Leningrad and can prove it.'

Mr Shelimov acted like a kind relative trying to resolve a family quarrel. He told me that twenty people had been caught at this border in the last few weeks trying to escape. 'Write down all the details,' he told me confidently and handed me some writing paper and a pen. 'Would you like some more tea?'

'Yes, please,' I replied.

Mr Shelimov left the room and I settled down to record the events of the last few days. I was tired but tried to concentrate. I knew that exact dates and times were important, but what should I say?

When Mr Shelimov returned with the refreshing tea, I asked him, 'Should I record the fact that I changed my mind about trying to get to Finland?'

Mr Shelimov smiled, 'I don't think that's relevant. Anyway, you couldn't really prove that in a court of law.' Then he added, 'No, I think it's best to leave it out.'

Without thinking, I agreed.

Mr Shelimov was skilful and I was weary and disorientated. The document written and signed by my own hand was just the kind of evidence that the KGB were banking on. I had fallen for the oldest trick in the book . . . trust in my interrogator.

14

KGB Headquarters

The KGB were playing straight into my hands. At last I was going to have a rest! I needed time to recover from the breakneck speed of the last few years. Now I was being provided with free accommodation in Murmansk prison. Food was also on offer. Stale bread, rotting vegetables, thin watery soup.

The jailors were vicious and the cells were dank and filthy. Sergei and I were held in separate cells and not permitted to communicate. Most of the prisoners were arrested on criminal charges.

One month after our arrest, Sergei and I were transferred back to Leningrad. The train had been designed specially to carry dangerous criminals in separate units. I heard movement behind me as I was hustled out of the carriage in Leningrad. It was Sergei. 'Hello!' I said. I was nudged in the back with a gun indicating that I should remain quiet.

I could hear the sounds of other passengers on the platform as I marched straight ahead with my arms behind my back. Nine or ten armed guards lined the path leading to a police van. Crouching down on my haunches I held on to the side of the van as it pulled away sharply, siren wailing.

The vehicle's sudden halt signalled our arrival, hurling me across the floor of the van like a cushion tossed on to a sofa.

The door opened and I took note of my surroundings. I was in the courtyard of an ochre-coloured building surrounded by a high wall. Six storeys high, there were many rooms to choose from.

So this was it! The KGB's legendary headquarters on Voinov Street near the Neva River.

I was led into a room at the entrance and told to undress as my documents and clothes were checked and then returned. While under investigation we didn't wear prison uniform.

'I want to contact my wife,' I told the guard, but this request was refused. Every time I saw a jailor, I asked them, 'Please tell my family I'm in prison.'

Wherever I looked, I could see corridors and cells on either side. A red carpet ran along the corridor and no one could hear our footsteps. I could hear voices from some cells, but others were strangely quiet.

We stopped outside cell number 274 on the sixth floor. The jailor unlocked the door and it opened wide, slamming shut behind me.

The KGB headquarters was to be my home for the next eight months. Compared to the other prisons, conditions here were like paradise. Only the most dangerous criminals were held in Voinov Street for investigation, and it was rarely full or crowded. I was moved frequently and kept for intermittent periods on each floor of the jail.

I was alone in cell 192 for several days. Prison legend has it that Lenin was also imprisoned in this room, an interesting twist in my history. How good it was to be alone with Jesus, I thought.

Each cell had two beds, sometimes with mattresses, a wash basin and a toilet. The window seemed designed to prevent light from entering the cell. A naked light bulb dangling from the middle of the ceiling was lit twenty-four hours a day, leaving me with a nagging ache in my eyes. I found that the light damaged my eyesight permanently.

About one month after the arrest, I had a vivid dream. Katchkin, my investigator, tussled with a red dog. I always interpreted dogs as friends, and surmised that the dog represented Tanya. I deduced that both of them had established contact. Months later, I learned that my dream had been correct.

The first evidence Tanya had of our arrest was on April 3rd when the KGB raided Sergei's home and mine. They stayed for eight hours, confiscating all Christian literature, and also personal letters and photographs. Katchkin told Tanya that the search was part of an investigation linked to our criminal case.

'What criminal case?' Tanya asked, shocked.

My wife was then informed that we were to be charged with illegally crossing the border at Murmansk. Over the next week, Tanya and her mother were called for questioning, as were Sergei's wife, Nina, and some of his in-laws.

I was called for the first of several interviews with Captain Katchkin. He was expecting me and I observed that my file was already open on his desk.

'Barinov,' he said, looking up at me. I couldn't tell what he was thinking. His expression wasn't giving anything away.

'When will I be allowed to see my wife?' I asked.

'I'm the one asking the questions,' he said matter-of-factly. He examined some papers in my file and asked me if I wanted to confess.

I looked at him in surprise. 'Confess? But what shall I confess? I'm an innocent man. What am I guilty of?'

'You were caught trying to escape,' he replied.

'But I was arrested on my way back home to Leningrad. Where could I have escaped to?' I answered. 'Anyway, Leningrad is closer to the border than Kynazhaya, where I was arrested.'

'I'm not here to debate the issue with you. It's been decided that you will be charged with trying to escape and I'll find the evidence to convict you. Bet on it! We'll put you in prison and throw away the key!' Katchkin paused waiting for a response.

'I want to contact my wife,' I replied calmly.

Katchkin stared at me. 'Don't you understand what I'm saying to you? You will be forced to serve many years in prison.'

I smiled. 'The only person I serve is Jesus!'

The encounter lasted fifteen minutes or so. He pressed a buzzer on his desk and a guard escorted me back to the cells. I was frequently warned that I would be imprisoned for many years and that my children would be married women when I was released.

It was unusual for prisoners to be beaten in the KGB headquarters. They usually relied on skilful psychological tactics to break you.

I was taken to a different cell and held with a company manager who had been caught smuggling things out of the country. Mr Vanou was in his fifties and had obviously enjoyed the good life. His suit was finely tailored and his nails were well manicured.

'I just wanted to make a lemon!' he said with a chuckle. 'Lemon' rhymed with million and was a colloquial expression. He didn't consider himself guilty, his only regret was getting caught. Although he was a communist, he hated the government. 'You can't do anything without bribing people all along the line,' he would say. 'It's a government without law. If they steal and cheat, why shouldn't I?'

On reflection, I could trace the hand of God in this placement. Through his experience I was able to gain insight into how to get along in prison. During the three days I shared his cell he told me, 'Don't trust the investigators. They'll tell you anything to get you to sign a confession.'

On April 18th, I started a fast and wrote an appeal to Captain Starkov, the chief of the prison, requesting permission to see Tanya, pointing out that I was falsely arrested. When the breakfast bowl arrived that morning, I refused it and asked for my message to be handed to the KGB chief.

Around 10 a.m. that morning, I was marched down to Starkov's office. He was a short stout man who took his work seriously. His eyes twinkled as he fiddled with the appeal I had written. 'Why are you starting this hunger strike?' he asked.

He looked directly at me to ensure that I understood what he was about to say. 'I must warn you that it is prison policy to force-feed you on the third day of your hunger strike. Now do you understand why this is a stupid course of action?'

I nodded and was immediately on my way back to the cells, this time in isolation on the third floor. The KGB chief thought I was on hunger strike, but I was fasting to God, building up my prayer muscles for the battle ahead.

I knew the risks in challenging the power of the dreaded KGB. But I bowed to a greater authority.

Three days passed, and then a fourth. On the fifth day there was a rattle of keys in the lock. Finally the moment arrived.

I was force-fed once a day by two KGB men and a doctor. The violence of the operation was the real torment. The doctor never checked my blood pressure or any after-effects of the force-feeding. Sometimes I could imagine him saying, 'It's routine work, nothing special. Someone has to do it.'

Within a few days I was suffering badly. As the doctor prepared to leave, I collapsed on the bed, breathing heavily. 'Stop this hunger strike or you'll die,' he snarled, devoid of concern.

Somehow I managed to continue for twenty-three days. Although the force-feeding was unbearable, God blessed me during that time. I was kept in isolation as part of the tactics to break me down, but this worked in my favour. I was never alone; I was with Jesus! This renewal gave me the strength I needed each day to face the torturers. I never resisted them, but told myself that Jesus' suffering was much greater.

Day by day I could feel my heart becoming weaker, and I was frequently out of breath. Even the KGB officers were a little nervous and the doctor was ordered to examine me. He prescribed glucose as nourishment.

I felt a pain in my heart. What would happen if I died from a heart attack? I feared that Tanya would never know the truth. She would be told that I had suffered a heart attack and died.

The next day when Katchkin asked to see me, I informed him that I was ready to end my fast. He reacted with surprise and relief. It would create an uproar if anyone died in prison. No, they would rather return you home to die.

Starkov stared at me long and hard. Finally he spoke. 'Have you been in contact with Sergei Timokhin?'

'No,' I replied. It was the truth.

'Then why does he begin a hunger strike on the same day that you are ending yours?' he enquired, his irritation tinged with curiosity. To the KGB chief this turn of events took on the appearance of an orchestrated conspiracy, and yet we had not been in contact. I was amused at God's unique timing.

Later I learned that Sergei had held out for five days, but when the snake tube was inserted into his nose, he decided to end the hunger strike.

After three weeks without food, I found that I could not eat a vast amount. We were fed three times a day, usually soup and bread, sometimes potatoes, occasionally fish and chicken, and on rare occasions, butter. The KGB headquarters knew how to look after its inmates.

The soup was cold and the bread stale, but I knew that God would use even these crumbs to nourish my body.

The KGB routine permitted one hour of exercise in the courtyard each day. A huge concrete grid occupied the inner courtyard, separated into twenty or so units. The cage was locked, and for an hour I stretched and jogged and jumped, covering every inch of the eight square metres.

I loved it when it rained. The mesh that sealed the roof allowed the water to pour into the cage. I stood with my hands raised to heaven thanking God for the raindrops, a reminder that some things never change.

I could hear the sound of trolley buses, the squeal of car brakes. Outside these walls life went on.

Once again I was moved to a different cell, and this time I had a cellmate. He introduced himself as Karl Ivashin from Riga. We shook hands formally as though we were meeting at some society function.

Karl was my height, aged about twenty-eight. He paced the cell, smoking nervously. He had been a documentary film maker and had made several trips abroad shooting footage for broadcast inside the Soviet Union.

'What kind of documentaries did you make?' I asked, interested to gain insight into the secretive world of Soviet television which was not known for its investigative research.

'We filmed negative things in the West like strikes and demonstrations,' Karl informed me. 'Things which endorsed the government's propaganda programme.'

'If people knew what the West was really like there would be a revolution,' he chuckled, 'so we just feed the lie.'

Karl had been caught smuggling pornographic videos back into Riga. 'Someone squealed,' he said sadly. 'Do you know how much you could make with an American porno film?'

'I haven't researched that subject very much,' I admitted.

Karl leaned back and a low whistle accompanied his hand as it shot up to the ceiling indicating an astronomically high price.

At that moment the hatch opened and we were offered a copy of *Pravda*. Every few days newspapers were on loan. Karl flicked through and read a news item about the forthcoming American elections. Angela Davis, a black American radical and member of the Black Panther group, was running for President.

Pravda emphasised her left-wing socialist views and suggested that Ms Davis' election was a certainty. All she would have to do was turn up on the night.

Karl believed it. 'So America will have a woman President,' he observed. 'With Angela Davis as President, maybe the United States will finally stop threatening us with the atom bomb.'

'There are several months before the election, Karl,' I reminded him.

Karl looked surprised that I should question *Pravda's* opinion. 'But *Pravda* has stated that she will be president!'

'Look Karl, in America people can choose, and they will not choose a socialist for President,' I asserted. 'Anyway, if Angela Davis knew what socialism was really like, then she herself would reject socialism.'

With time on our hands, we discussed many things. 'Tell me about yourself.' Karl listened intently as I told him about the hunger strike.

'What will you do now?' he asked.

'I will fight them,' I replied. Karl looked up with a start. 'Prayer is my weapon,' I declared with a grin.

'I think the best thing you can do is go on television and confess your guilt, even if you don't mean it.'

I felt myself tense, but didn't let my suspicion show. I looked across at Karl. He was puffing on his cigarette, apparently giving the matter grave consideration. I decided to call his bluff.

'That's interesting,' I said with mock seriousness. 'Tell me why you think that would be good.'

'Well, if you are in prison for a long time, think about the hardships for your family. Your daughters will be married, your wife would have left you, you wouldn't have any friends. You'll be an old man.'

All his reasons were the same as those given by the KGB. I suspected that the KGB had put us together in order to convince me to confess. From that moment on I had to be on my guard when talking to Karl.

A curious incident confirmed my suspicions. It started with a dream I had about selling a bass guitar. When I awoke, I understood that Sergei Timokhin had been broken by his interrogators.

Shortly after this dream, Karl returned from an interrogation looking agitated. 'Sergei is finished,' he declared. 'He has signed a confession.'

Then Karl began to laugh, 'I think he has made the right decision. It's the best thing you can do.' Karl wore his disguise well, but now I knew he was a conspirator.

Perhaps Sergei had succumbed at a low point to someone like Karl? This spurred me to pray for him.

In the next few days I was summoned by a new interrogator. He seemed friendly. Sifting through the papers on his table, he picked out a single sheet. Almost mournfully, he began, 'Sergei has confessed his guilt, perhaps you know?'

I looked him straight in the eye. 'What is the weather like now on the Black Sea? Good for a holiday?'

Taken by surprise, he answered, 'Good, good, I'm sure.'

'Have there been many mushrooms in the forest this year?' I questioned him. He stared blankly at me. I continued, 'I haven't been in the forest this year. Neither have I been fishing. I did want to go, but I had to change my plans at the last moment.'

The KGB man got the message. He leaned forward and said, 'So Valeri, I think Sergei has taken a step in the right direction. It would be best for you to do the same. If you don't, you'll be in prison until your hair falls out. I'm serious!'

'Is that all? Call the guard, I'm ready to return.' I spoke politely, but stared at the wall behind him.

Back in the cell, Karl paced up and down. 'What happened?' he snapped.

'Nothing happened,' I replied, casually.

It was evident that Karl was disturbed, and he began to berate me scornfully. 'Jesus can't save you, you fool. Why, he couldn't even save himself. Your only hope is to confess on TV. If not, you'll never see freedom again.' Then he cursed blasphemously.

'I'm in freedom now because Jesus changed my life,' I replied.

Karl began to giggle, and assuming the posture of a preacher, began to wave his arms about. 'Repent, repent,' he cried. 'Jesus is dead, you fool, don't you know?'

I lost control. The events of the last few hours had left me at breaking point. 'If you say one more word, I'll kill you.' The words had shot out of my mouth before I knew it. But Karl was laughing, 'Jesus, save me! Save me!' Then he saw the glint in my eye and realised that he had crossed the line of acceptability.

I slammed my fists against the steel door, rattling the bolts and yelling for the guard. 'Take one of us away! I don't know what I'll do to him!'

The guard opened the door and evaluated the scene. Realising that I was deadly serious, he signalled that I should prepare to move. Karl appeared disappointed rather than angry. Hoping to have gained some special favour through his influence over me, my refusal to confess had left him helpless.

Sleepless nights followed. If I did confess, I would see Zhanna and Marina, if I did confess, I would hold Tanya in my arms, if I did confess, I could walk the street of Leningrad again . . .

15

Shooting Out the Stars

'Thursday!' the guard announced, rattling the cell door. That meant showers. They were always too hot or freezing cold, but as I stood under the spray, I prayed that the doubts that nagged me about a confession would be washed away. I knew that the benefits of 'confessing' were a bitter-sweet illusion created by the KGB.

'God bless you!' I said to the guard as he escorted me to yet another new cell. The greeting was received with a stare, devoid of emotion.

I have a cellmate, and we shake hands. Vasily, or 'Vassa' has an open face and a tender heart, and we become friends. Vassa had worked on the railway, and had been caught smuggling jeans into the country through the Czechoslovakian border. 'Everyone does it, so why should I be singled out for punishment?' he complained bitterly. He believed that since only his load had been discovered, an informer had betrayed him.

When Vassa learned that I was a Christian, he admitted that he believed in a 'power', speculating whether fortune-tellers or astrologers really could read the future.

Vassa and I spent the afternoon discussing the energy forces that could have brought the universe together. While we talked, I prayed for him, realising that we had been put together for a reason.

Vasily's openness made it easy to turn the conversation towards the existence of God.

Vasily paced the cell. 'How can I believe in God?' he asked.

'Do you want to feel God's energy?' I urged him on to the threshold of faith.

'Yes,' he said, startled by the question.

Vasily and I stood in the middle of the cell facing each other. The bulb overhead created dancing shadows across the contours of our faces.

'Give me your hand. Open your palm.' Vassa obeyed the command, standing before me with his hands outstretched and his palms lifted towards heaven. 'Now close your eyes.'

I moved my fingertips lightly across his hand, stroking the air, but not touching his flesh. Then, as the tips of our fingers touched lightly, I experienced a wave of power, like a tiny jolt of electricity. 'Do you feel that?' I asked him softly.

'Yes,' Vassa replied, his eyes flickering almost in disbelief. 'I feel it.'

'That's the power of God,' I explained. 'Believe in him and he will change your life.'

'When I pray,' I continued, 'you will feel this same energy.'

Vassa was curious. 'What is it?'

'It's God's Spirit inside me,' I explained. 'Prayer is not a repetition of words or actions but enables us to communicate with God.'

With his hands still outstretched, Vassa opened his eyes. 'Valeri, I want God's Spirit in me.' His words sounded childlike, but sincere. Tears welled up in his eyes, evidence that God's Spirit was already at work in his heart. Trembling, he whispered, 'Will you pray for me?'

'Lord, reveal yourself to Vassa,' I prayed.

He began to rock back and forth. 'Valeri, what shall I do? I feel something in my heart but I don't know what it is.'

'That's Jesus!' I cried, almost laughing with joy. We knelt together on the cold floor and Vassa prayed a faltering, humble prayer to God.

The prison cell gained the atmosphere of a sanctuary as God's Spirit visited the altar of our hearts with a physical presence so real that I thought I could reach out and touch the hand of God.

Vassa and I were cellmates and brothers in Christ. We shared cells together several times, and each time it was a renewal of celebration. Our physical circumstances could not hinder or diminish our inner joy.

One night after this, I was woken by Vassa. 'Valeri, I just had a strange experience,' he said. 'I was lying in bed but couldn't sleep. You know, the light kept me awake. I found I was dreaming, but I wasn't asleep. It was a vision in which I saw you clearly.

'It was winter, very cold, snow on the ground, and I saw an aircraft on an airport runway. You walked to the plane and you waved to a crowd of people who had gathered. And then the plane was streaking through the sky, flying through the clouds.'

Without waiting for my comments, Vassa said, 'It's so strange, but I know within myself that you will definitely leave us and go to the West. I know this for a fact,' Vassa asserted.

'Thank you Vassa,' I replied. 'That's a message from God for me.'

'I've never known anything like it,' Vassa said, and still a little confused, lay down and fell asleep.

I was now the one who couldn't sleep as I tried to unravel the thread. Could this mean that I would be whisked to the West from my own prison cell? I believed this with total conviction. But when would it happen? The minutes turned to hours, and before long I was aware of the dawn's early light desperately trying to break through the barricaded window.

Instead of the journey I was prepared for, I was summoned

to a psychiatric hospital. From the grapevine I knew that conditions in hospital were considerably better than prison, and inmates were always conspiring to be sent there.

Under the supervision of armed guards, I jogged into the courtyard with my arms behind my back. Judging by the time gap before the van set off, I was not the only inmate being moved to the hospital.

Twisting and turning through Leningrad streets, the vehicle pulled up at Kresty Prison and extra prisoners boarded the van. It was going to be a full load.

When we reached the psychiatric hospital, I recognised Alex, a young fascist I had met briefly in prison.

Although we were carefully guarded and our contact was limited, there was a delay in registering the prisoners at the hospital foyer, providing Alex and me with a stolen moment together.

'Hi Valeri, how are you?' Alex whispered as we waited for the staff to sort out the blunder. Apparently Kresty Prison had sent an extra prisoner, and the guards did not want to wait while the hospital staff decided what to do. If the choice had been put to us we could have cleared things up easily. But no one was asking our opinion.

The psychiatric investigation took a month. Compared to the KGB prison, it was like a holiday camp. I was detained in a ward with ten others, only some of whom really were mentally disturbed.

One night I had a dream in which I saw a fire raging in the distance. When I awoke and considered the implications, I wondered if this meant that Tanya had been able to reach the West with news of my imprisonment.

I prayed and asked for confirmation that I had interpreted the dream correctly. Tell me something today. Give me a sign.

That day the doctor said to me, 'Did you get any letters from the West?' He looked at me with a smile, but I could tell that he understood everything.

Katchkin and the other investigators had tried to break me by insisting that no one cared. Now this hint came as an answer to prayer and was confirmation that people knew about me.

Alex was moved into our ward after two weeks. He was eighteen, very intelligent and a keen student of chemistry. As a neo-fascist, Alex was interested in European politics and believed that a new order would purge the country of the communist mafiosi who oppressed and corrupted our land.

We were joined in the ward by a dark-haired youth with round spectacles. Alex and he had shared a cell sometime in the past. Gregory was also a committed fascist who hated his mother because she had married his father, who was a despised communist.

When I spoke about Jesus, they listened intently. Gregory found the idea of forgiveness unacceptable, and although Alex endorsed the concept as a form of release and purification, he could not declare his allegiance to the formality of religion.

'But I'm not a religious person,' I argued, which took them both by surprise. 'I don't believe in religion, but the freedom that Jesus gives. I'm talking about a way of life, not an institutionalised dogma.'

One night, I awoke to hear Alex calling to me from his bed, which lay next to mine. He had been troubled with stomach pains and could not sleep. In obvious discomfort, he croaked, 'Pray for me, Valeri.'

I agreed, and then he added, 'I want to check your energy. To see if God really can do anything for me.'

'It's God's energy, not mine. If you want me to pray for you, I will, but there's no magic in my prayers,' I said quietly. 'But you pray sincerely to God and discover the truth.'

Around us, everyone slept as I knelt beside the bed. The next morning Alex found that his pains had vanished. He didn't know how to explain it, and a small flicker of faith burned in his heart.

The daily investigations were all a game, and I played along.

It was on a Wednesday that an orderly escorted me to the hospital reception. I wondered if I was going to be taken directly to the airport? Would Tanya be there?

And then I saw the familiar blue of the KGB officers' uniform, and the van awaiting me. No tearful reunion with Tanya. No holding hands with Zhanna and Marina. No Leningrad airport. No midnight flight to freedom. No sound of the trumpet call. Not this time.

Once again I am hustled up the steps into the reception of the KGB prison on Voinov Street. My records are checked. Yes, I am Valeri Barinov. Yes, we did play rock and roll. Yes, I am a Christian. No, no, it's a mistake, I wasn't trying to escape. Why, Leningrad is nearer the border than the place where I was arrested. Sorry, I wasn't trying to argue, I was just pointing out . . . Yes, I will remain silent and only answer those questions that are asked me . . .

And then, back up the stairway in solemn procession with the guard, the familiar red carpet, the rattle of the door, the cell with dim light and dirty mattress, the smell of the toilet, and the hole in the wall which could so easily have been a window, now barred, sealed, closed.

But I feel no sense of despair or anxiety. A peacefulness beyond explanation falls like a cloak around my shoulders. With a twinge of sadness, I imagine my family huddled together on the sofa in our apartment.

Jesus, you alone are worthy of this sacrifice. What a privilege you give me to sound a trumpet call about your holy name. You know my loneliness and pain. I trust you, my Jesus, and I commit my body into your hands.

I feel a physical presence surround me like a wave and lift my heart in praise to God. The shadows in the cell are transformed into dancing rays of sunlight. I forget myself and prance around the room, praising God.

Over the next few weeks the KGB moved me frequently.

My investigation must have been coming to a head because Katchkin summoned me for interrogation almost daily. I learned to judge the moods, realising that his attitude and response were merely tactics in the overall strategy to break me.

Katchkin himself had his orders. Who played in The Trumpet Call band? How did we record the music? Where was the equipment hidden? Did we have a list of people who had copies of the cassette?

During interrogations I was able to examine the documents as I stood in front of Katchkin's desk. It astounded me to learn that the police had questioned over one hundred people in many different cities and villages all across the Soviet Union. It was a costly and time-consuming exercise. In all, it totalled thousands of pages, and was bound in four separate volumes.

And then I saw it! A secret order issued from the high command of the KGB:

> The Christian rock group The Trumpet Call must be banned. None of this music must be allowed to spread in our country. This group must be destroyed and the operation kept secret.

As I skimmed the page, committing every line to memory, it became clear that I was considered an enemy of the State. Someone who spread dangerous ideas.

Katchkin regularly quizzed me about the recording of 'The Trumpet Call'. I feigned ignorance, reminding him that it had been a long time ago.

'How could you have forgotten?' Katchkin said disbelievingly. 'This is your recording, isn't it?' he demanded, holding up the cassette.

Pretending to call upon hidden memory banks, I peered closely at the tape as though I had never seen it before. In exasperation, Katchkin produced a tape recorder. 'Perhaps this will refresh your memory,' he growled.

As the opening refrain of 'The Trumpet Call' filled the investigation room, my heart was bursting with joy at the unexpected privilege of being given a personal audience here in prison.

But outwardly my face was masked in mystery, occasionally shaking my head in puzzlement. Katchkin glared back at me, confused by my lack of memory. He began to tap the table top in time with the music, but stopped himself.

Katchkin wised up to my scheme. The next time I suggested that playing the music might refresh my memory, he just scowled.

One day towards the end of September, Katchkin sat me down with him at the wooden desk. Unusually, the table in front of him was bare. No notebook and pen, not even my familiar brown file.

'Do you want some tea?' he asked, 'or maybe coffee?'

'Coffee, please,' I answered. 'Thank you.' We could have been colleagues at an office, meeting to discuss business.

'Valeri, today no investigation,' he said matter-of-factly. 'I wanted to talk to you directly, man to man.'

I smiled in response. Now he appeared friendly, no longer the intimidating investigator.

'Valeri, I saw your wife recently,' he said sympathetically. 'She's having a very hard time without you and wants you home. Your daughters are very pretty, aren't they? Very clever girls,' he said with a chuckle. 'They miss you, you know that, don't you?'

My smile froze on my cheeks. I felt my throat dry up and gripped the arms of my chair tightly. He spoke slowly to drive each point home. His remarks were like darts hitting the bull's-eye. 'Your family need you with them.'

'But you know my situation,' I answered, trying to sound normal. 'What can I do?'

Katchkin smiled. 'It's very easy. I will help you,' he said, speaking calmly. 'Confess!' the word sounded soothing and comforting. 'Tell us everything you know.'

'But I told you everything,' I replied.

Katchkin teased, 'You know what I mean. Tell me, how did you record 'The Trumpet Call'? Who were your accomplices?'

'Why do you ask me about the recording? You arrested me because I was trying to escape. Let's talk about that!'

Recognising that this would not provide a winner, Katchkin concluded, 'So, Valeri, consider carefully what we talked about today. If you want to sign a confession, call me at any time. Just ask one of the guards to contact me.'

After this interrogation I shared a cell with Vassa once again, to our surprise and delight. Vassa had many questions about the faith. Was the Virgin birth a fairy story? What about Noah's ark? Did Jesus really rise from the dead?

Vassa was also curious about such issues as baptism, and I explained that it symbolised our new life with Jesus. On the third day of our detention together, Vassa asked me to baptise him. I was amused by God's humour. Here, in the very heart of enemy territory, the secret agents of mercy were at work.

We spent the day in prayer and fasting. Not wishing to alert the attention of the guards, we kept the food that was served in one of the prison bowls. The other bowl was held in preparation for the baptism.

Vassa knew the risks. If we were caught both of us would have been punished severely. We knew that no hour was safe, as the guards checked us throughout the day and night. As we prayed I had the conviction that the baptism should be carried out at dawn the next morning.

Before dawn I heard Vassa moving around in our cell. I was awake in an instant, and could sense a genuine excitement in his eyes. He looked fresh and young. Vassa told me that one of the guards had checked about ten minutes earlier. Soon the morning bell would sound and the guards would be rattling the door. This was the time to conduct the baptism.

Vassa sat on his bed with his shirt around his shoulders. I sat opposite and reminded him that I didn't practise any special brand of magic. He was entering the presence of God, and this should remain his strength and fortress. Then we prayed together.

As we were praying, the window of our cell door was unlatched and a face appeared at the hole. Not suspecting anything, the face disappeared and the hatch was slammed shut.

'This is the moment!' I declared.

I picked up the tin bowl full of water and Vassa tossed his shirt on to the bed. We stood in silence and then prayed quickly over the water.

Vassa leaned over the bowl maintaining an attitude of prayer. I looked at Vassa and said, 'Vassa, I baptise you because of your faith in God . . . in Jesus' name!' I poured the bowl of water over his head.

I swiftly picked up the towel, and handed it to Vassa. He dried himself in short, rapid movements and sat on the bed again.

Once again we sat facing each other. Bread and water stood on a table beside us.

'Now it's time for communion,' I said. In an extraordinary way, it was like a celebration.

'Thank you Valeri,' Vassa said, his eyes brimming with tears of emotion.

'Don't thank me,' I replied, 'thank God!'

The experience had an anointing that was unprecedented. Basking in the joy of God's presence, we were brought back to earth with the familiar sound of the cell window being unlatched.

'Still in there?' the guard asked with a smirk.

'Where can we go?' I answered with a smile. But surprisingly, it didn't feel at all like captivity.

16

'My Crime Is I'm a Christian'

'Swashbucklers of Rock and Roll' appeared in *Komsomolskaya Pravda* on September 16th, 1983. The author of the article, Y. Filinov, charged the rock medium with subversive influences and identified Seva Novgorodtsev, the DJ, as a renegade. Seva was a legend among young people throughout the country. He had emigrated from the Soviet Union in 1977, and worked for the BBC's Russian Service broadcasting jazz and rock back into the USSR. Mr Filinov also charged that our band was unpopular and played badly:

> Seva Novgorodtsev, absolutely overcome, is making out that this dreadful work ('The Trumpet Call') with its wretched text is the greatest achievement in the field of music. Well what of it? Pay someone for lying, and he'll deliver the goods.

The publication of the article could not harm Seva Novgorodtsev. He lived in London. It could, however, influence my trial. It was quite customary for slanderous articles vilifying political and religious dissidents to appear in the Soviet press before their court appearances. Filinov's article was the strongest indication that my trial was imminent.

I used the time to maintain my physical discipline. I tried to keep my weary body alert with push-ups, skipping, jogging around my cell imagining I was hurtling across the park.

One day as I walked down to the exercise yard, I caught a glimpse of someone from the labour camps who was held on our floor. He was dressed in black trousers with his name and zone number marked on his jacket. He was a 'tenner', that meant ten years of hard labour, and was looked upon as a hero. Dark tales of the indescribable evil of camp life trailed along the prison network.

A sense of dread and foreboding came over me. But what of the vision and the silver bird soaring through the sky? The crowd waving farewell at the airport? Would I be spared the ordeal of labour camp?

My trial was scheduled to begin on November 23rd, 1983. A few days before, I was moved to a cell on the third floor. As I entered the cell, I barely managed to contain my joy. It was Vassa!

Vassa told me that he had been convicted of smuggling and sentenced to eight years. I quizzed him about the transfer from police van to court-room. That night I prayed, wondering if it would be possible to escape.

I wanted to send a message to friends in the West but my eyes were weak, so Vassa willingly detailed the false evidence prepared against me on a scrap of paper three inches by one. The miniature document was magnificent, but I had two immediate problems: smuggling it out of prison and getting it to Tanya or someone else who could publish the news.

Despite the pressure, there was a glint of sunlight. Vassa and I were not split up but remained cellmates until my trial. The night before, we prayed together and once again experienced the presence of God's Spirit. I felt like a gladiator waiting to be called into the arena.

But I was not afraid! I had spiritual weapons that could withstand the assaults of the enemy. Like a fighter in the ring

I pranced around the room shadow-boxing. 'I'll beat this devil!' I yelled as I lashed the air, striking a mortal blow at an imaginary enemy.

Vassa collapsed in laughter as I swung round and felled an assailant who crept up behind me with expert karate strokes. 'Take that, you communist devil!'

Vassa's eyes signalled behind me. A face peered at us through the hatch in the door. Undeterred, I stepped up the assault against the powers of the air. This duel of death required total concentration, but a glance at the door confirmed that my game had caused great mirth in the corridor. Now a new face appeared as another guard suppressed a chuckle.

November 23rd was a chilly morning. I awoke early and committed myself into the hands of God.

The shoelaces of my Adidas trainers had been confiscated in case they were used as a noose. I had made laces from a narrow strip of cloth, and this had been permitted. I hid the secret note inside the lace cloth and tied a tight knot at the top of the running shoes.

'Valeri, how is it?' Vassa asked me. I gave him the thumbs up.

Without informing the authorities, who would use it as a pretext to delay my trial, I resumed my fast. The struggle was not with flesh and blood, but against principalities and powers.

At 8 a.m. I was summoned to the investigation room and ordered to strip in order to check that I was not smuggling anything out of prison. I threw my jeans casually over my running shoes. The guard appeared easy going, but his examination was thorough. I was asked to rinse my mouth out to ensure that nothing was lodged in my throat.

Then the guard checked my clothes. I remained impassive as he picked up my shoes. He checked the heel carefully, and then the inside.

The shoes landed on the floor with a thud. 'Get dressed,' he said.

The officer waited for me to dress and then escorted me to a lorry-type vehicle parked near the prison gates. The gates were open, but six armed guards stood watching me. Two vicious dogs strained at their leashes. I loved dogs, but didn't wish to tangle with this pair.

Could I escape? There was only one way. Roll under the lorry and dash twenty yards to the gates. Would they really shoot me in the back?

I gave up the plan and climbed into the long narrow compartment. In the cage next to me I heard shuffling. It was Sergei Timokhin. We had a few moments before the guards climbed on board.

'Sergei,' I whispered, 'why did you sign a confession? It's a trick. They won't let you out.' I tried to imagine Sergei's face. He must have faced terrific pressure.

The front doors opened. One more question. 'Sergei, did you tell them about the studio and the band?'

'No!' he called back.

'Stop talking!' the guard yelled, slamming the bars with his pistol.

As we drove to the court-room, siren blaring, I tried to imagine what a small boy, pointing to the police van, might ask his father, and how his father would answer?

Our trial was held in the Central Courthouse of the Leningrad Procuracy, a huge building in a busy street. Hands behind my back, I was hurried at gunpoint into the building. Inside, people were milling everywhere, and I was led like a dog on a leash through swing doors and corridors. Keys unlocked a padded cell and I was ushered in.

A slim man with brown hair sat looking forlorn on a bench by a window. Few introductions were required.

'Murder,' he said.

'Christian,' I replied. Noticing the impact of my words on him, I enquired further. 'Is it over?'

'Yes.' At that moment my escort arrived. 'God bless you,' I said quickly.

I saw his eyes widen. To some it was just a phrase obscured by constant usage, but this doomed man received it like a letter from home. 'Thank you,' he replied.

Indicating his displeasure, the guard grabbed my shirt and pushed me into the hallway. Television cables marked our path to the court-room, where our arrival was filmed under bright spotlights.

I heard several people call out my name. I tried to acknowledge the familiar faces with a smile.

And suddenly, there was my Tanya. She looked so frail and weak although her blazing red hair and tender green eyes were just as I remembered her. She looked worried and on the verge of tears, but waved bravely. I longed to leap over the partition and sweep her into my arms like a knight in shining armour. She'd soon realise that everything would be fine.

Sometime later, I learned that Tanya hadn't been told in which court-room my trial was to be held. She had seen the cable of the TV crew and followed it to where the 'Barinov trial' was performing.

Here she found the seats filled with KGB agents, preventing her, or any of our friends, from attending. When Tanya threatened to phone the West to complain, she and some of my supporters were allowed in.

As the proceedings began I sat in the dock wondering how I was going to get the secret note to Tanya. I assumed a comfortable position with my leg up on a wooden panel in front of me, and cautiously removed the note and bunched it up in my fist.

When the court was adjourned for lunch, I was ordered to follow the guards out of the court. As I passed the rows of spectators, I casually flicked the pellet across at Tanya in a mischievous gesture.

The reaction was astounding. I heard someone scream,

'Over here!' Everyone followed the missile's flight as though a million roubles had been tossed into their midst. KGB agents scrambled across the floor. I saw Tanya looking for it.

'It's here! It's here!' someone called out.

Agents swooped on a middle-aged woman and emptied the contents of her handbag on to the floor. But the note wasn't there.

'Here it is! I have it!' One of the agents held it up, and passed it to the Procurator. He squinted and frowned at the tiny message. Addressing me, he enquired, 'What's written on this piece of paper?'

'It's a message for the West so that everyone will know that this trial has been fixed,' I declared boldly.

The judge glared at me. 'No! No! You're not permitted to send such messages to the West,' and with that he confiscated the note and included it with the accompanying documentation in my case.

During the three days of my trial, witnesses were called who had clearly been coached in their evidence by the KGB.

One witness, a cellmate from Murmansk, claimed that I had asked him to draw a map of the border and mark the best escape route. Such evidence could hardly prove my guilt. At the time we were imprisoned in the local jail!

Another witness whom I barely recognised, admitted that he was a psychiatric patient. His evidence was garbled and confused, and most people pitied him.

The next witness was a hardened criminal with whom I had shared a cell. During his obviously rehearsed testimony it emerged that he had signed a KGB statement without reading it. At hearing this, the judge appeared perplexed, and questioned why he had not read it first.

'You see sir,' the convict began, 'If they want to get you, they will. I was told to sign it and I did. It's just the KGB way.' At this, the judge called a halt and he was hustled away.

Katchkin was called upon to give evidence, and as he spoke about our arrest at the border, I challenged him. 'How did you get there so quickly? Did you fly?' I asked.

Katchkin glared insolently at me as the judge reprimanded me, 'Don't point your finger at the witness.'

Finally it was Tanya's turn. 'Tell us about your husband, Mrs Barinova,' the prosecuting attorney began.

With a trembling voice, Tanya replied, 'I know that if everyone in our country was like my husband, this would be true communism.'

With each of Tanya's answers, it became clear that the case against me was slipping through their fingers. Abruptly, she was told to be quiet and dismissed from their proceedings.

My friend Sergei Timokhin sat in court looking haggard and despondent. Under intense psychological pressure he had agreed to appear in a televised confession. It was a sad moment as he faced the cameras disconsolately and admitted his mistakes and misunderstandings of the constitution and religious law. Sergei claimed that the capitalist system had manipulated him.

I could imagine the KGB investigator convincing Sergei that this was the best way, the only way. But it was a trick.

On the final day, Sergei Timokhin and I were commanded to stand as our sentences were announced. Sergei was visibly shaken when the judge sentenced him to serve two years in a labour camp.

For daring to sound a trumpet call declaring that 'Jesus is coming!' I was not surprised to be awarded two and a half years in camp.

Tanya was in tears when she heard the severity of the sentence. The judge asked if I had any last words to say to the court? In a short speech I declared the true reason for my arrest and imprisonment, 'My crime is I'm a Christian!' It was all that I could say. But I knew I would be given another moment for the final word.

* * *

As I walked from the court-house, Tanya and our friends flocked around me. Even as I climbed into the police van to return to the KGB prison I could hear their cries ringing in my ears.

Our case had become a cause célèbre, and eventually it hit the newspapers. On November 27th, 1984, *Leningradskaya Pravda* published an article which stated:

> Even in his school years, Barinov was beyond the control of relatives and teachers alike. It was his aunt who, in the hopes of saving his lost soul, advised him to turn to God. To her surprise, he seized upon this idea.
>
> Of course, he didn't really believe. He learnt to use the name of the Almighty as a cover for anything. Barinov remained true to himself, and at the trial he stubbornly maintained the story he had thought up: voluntary abandonment of commission of the crime.

A day earlier, an official Tass bulletin had published a similar report under the title 'Leningrad Trial of Renegades'.

I decided to end my second fast on 6th December. It was a curious date. It was my fortieth birthday, I had been imprisoned for forty weeks, and I had been on hunger strike for a total of forty days. Somehow I was able to draw strength and encouragement from this knowledge.

The hatch of the cell was drawn back, and a guard called out, 'Get ready, you're going to have a meeting.' I was led out, down through an underground labyrinth of corridors that left me disorientated and into an investigation cell.

Satisfied that I wasn't smuggling any contraband, I was led into another room. As the door opened, I could see Tanya sitting behind a glass panel. All I could see was her face and chest. Beside her were Zhanna and Marina, both craning their necks to catch a better glimpse of me.

Tanya was weeping helplessly, and the sobs racked her body. The girls held her tightly, their eyes never leaving my face.

I placed my hands over my lips and transferred a kiss on to the glass partition. Instantly, hands reached out to own the kiss. For a second it seemed that we were actually touching.

'Have any friends in the West been helping you?' I asked Tanya.

'Nothing,' she replied sadly.

On looking closer, I noticed that the girls were both dressed in old clothes. My heart sank.

'Show daddy your shoes,' Tanya said. The girls leaned back and somehow raised their feet to the level of the window. The soles had been worn through, and the freezing weather had arrived. 'Even coming here today has caused them discomfort,' Tanya said, wiping away the tears.

'Don't cry, Tanya,' I said softly. 'God will lead us away from here and we'll be together.'

Tanya stared back at me and said, 'How do you know?'

'A vision from God has confirmed this,' I replied.

'A vision or a fantasy?' Tanya called back.

If she doubted God's abiding affection for us, I wanted to encourage her. I went on to explain that a cellmate who had become a Christian had a dream that I would be released and would leave the country with my family and travel to the West.

'I don't know when this will happen,' I concluded, 'I only know one thing: trust Jesus. Everything else will fail. Jesus is our only security.'

We talked about Zhanna and Marina, and details of family life. 'Panthera misses you, Dad,' Zhanna said.

At either side of the panel, KGB guards recorded our pitiful conversation in notebooks. When Tanya began to ask questions about my last six months inside 'the big house', the guards called out, 'Stop talking about prison, it's not allowed.'

After about an hour, we were informed that the meeting

was over. The guard on my right sat impassively observing the tearful scene. Turning to him, I pleaded, 'Can I kiss my children?'

'No,' he replied firmly, 'It isn't permitted.'

'Please!' I implored him.

'No!'

'Tanya, don't weep for me. You know that Jesus is my judge and I stand here as an innocent man. Why should we fear these earthly powers?'

Still sobbing, Tanya raised her hand in a futile embrace. Zhanna and Marina stood with their arms round their mother. I could tell that despite their sorrow, they were proud that daddy had remained strong and unbowed.

At the door I turned to wave at the faces at the glass. Hands waved back, smiles amidst tears were the final memories that I carried back to the cells with me.

The next hour was hardest. Images hurtled through my mind of the girls clutching Mama's hand on the cold journey home. My heart was aching for Tanya and my girls. The road was hard and darkness seemed to be all around, but there was no turning back.

Jesus, I need your strength to withstand this torture.

Alone in my cell, I celebrated Christmas. I knew that Christians all over the world would be celebrating as families united together to mark the birth of the Prince of Peace. Yet here I was, separated from my beloved wife and children.

As I prayed, I experienced the compassionate presence of God's Spirit encompass me.

My time at the KGB's 'big house' was nearing its end and I was allowed one final meeting with Tanya, Zhanna and Marina before leaving Leningrad for the labour camp.

Although we were happy to be together, the meeting was tinged with sadness, as we realised that this was to be our final hour together for at least two years.

I prayed for each one in turn and prayed that God's presence would become a daily reality.

Zhanna and Marina tried to cheer me up by telling amusing stories, and we talked about the day that we brought Panthera home from the market.

It was an unusual meeting and lasted longer than the allotted time. Good-bye seemed such an inadequate word. Lord, I prayed, how I long to hold these loved ones in my arms for one last time.

But the meeting was over. Tanya, Zhanna and Marina rose together and left. At the same time, the guard accompanied me out of the visiting area. Mysteriously, we met together as we waited for the connecting door to be opened.

But the door didn't open. I don't know what caused the delay, but I just looked across at my wife and daughters who stood a few feet away.

Suddenly, Marina left Tanya's side and flung her arms around me and kissed me. Marina had barely reached me when Zhanna followed.

The guard was too stunned to react. The last time that we had met, the KGB guard had forbidden such contact, but we had prayed and God had intervened, giving us one final embrace.

I clutched Zhanna and Marina close to me, kissed them tenderly and whispered a blessing in their ears.

In a few seconds it was over. The door was unlocked, the guard had moved me away, and the girls had returned to Tanya's side, their eyes twinkling with merriment. The memory of that moment would never leave my consciousness.

But Tanya's tears began to flow, bringing us back to the reality of the tension that we lived in. Zhanna and Marina tried to console her as I was led back into the belly of the dragon.

PART III

ANOTHER COUNTRY

17

Easter Surprise: 1985–1986

After a three-day train journey in a prison carriage full of filth and rubbish, I was taken out at a town called Vologdar. Once again, I was given an armed escort, once again my papers were checked carefully in case I was an imposter. Imagine someone desperately wanting to break into the prison network of the Soviet State. The height of black comedy, I mused.

I was held for a month in the local jail which had been built to house twenty prisoners, but was occupied by nearer fifty. The KGB prison seemed like paradise compared to this hole. The fleas leapt visibly between the two bunk beds which were supposed to accommodate four or five people.

In early March we were shunted like cattle in the freezing cold to the labour camp itself. A sign at the main gates stated:

We hope your stay here will be beneficial as we work together to build communism on earth.

We had arrived on another planet. Even the air smelt different, a dry, stale, rancid stench that was all around us. The camp was situated on a murky, infectious swamp in the Komi region, one of the Soviet Union's autonomous republics well-known for its labour camps and slave-labour gangs.

Two thousand inmates occupied the cramped facilities designed for eight hundred prisoners. A wall topped with barbed wire encircled the settlement, punctuated by searchlights and watchtowers thirty metres high.

Our first three days were spent in the quarantine area. There were five new prisoners with me from Vologdar prison, and about forty-five more joined us. Some were deserters from Afghanistan, young boys who didn't want to fight.

Keys rattled and the huge frame of a guard filled the room. He introduced himself with a mocking grin, hands on hips. 'I'm Captain Zhora, you're not going to forget me!' he barked. With that, he lashed out at a man to his left. Taken by surprise, the man fell backward, blood pouring from his mouth. Gasps could be heard around the room.

Zhora appeared amused. Everyone shrank back from him as he strutted across the room, launching into an obscene tirade of orders and commands designed to terrify the new recruits. 'Are you listening to me?' he yelled in the face of one nervous-looking man. 'What did I say?'

Before the man could reply, Zhora's clenched fist crashed down on his head. Zhora was infuriated that the man crumpled at his feet. His boots dug into the fallen man's body as he lay helpless on the floor.

No one knew what to say. Our words had been frozen.

'Now maybe you'll pay attention to me.' The front line ducked out of the way as he swung his fists. A wicked gleam appeared in Zhora's eyes. 'I want you all to get on to the top bunk bed!' he commanded, picking up a wooden broom stick that leaned against one of the walls.

Now, pinned against the far wall, we wondered how we could fulfil such an impossible and insane demand. Who would be sacrificed to quench this guard's thirst for sadistic pleasure?

It was then that I understood why this camp had been nicknamed 'Bloody Special'. We would spill our blood here at the hands of torturers and the legend of the camp would live on. Zhora had been our first introduction to life at Labour Camp No. 27. Nothing would change. We were, after all, in another country.

I sensed that the KGB had sent some secret communication about me to the camp administration and to Lobanov, the deputy commandant. 'KGB Prison,' I heard one official remark to another as my file and credentials were checked.

Zinchenko, the camp commandant, was sympathetic towards me, but he didn't want to tangle with the KGB. 'Musician,' he said, checking some of my papers. 'Rock band The Trumpet Call,' he smiled.

'Now you will trumpet here.'

There were twelve groups in the camp and the leaders were represented at this meeting to assign newcomers to their section. 'Who will take him?' Zinchenko asked. No one wanted to assume responsibility for me. Even in this pit, fear of the KGB sent them scrambling for cover.

Finally I was assigned to 'Group Twelve' in one of the two wooden barracks situated to the west of the camp and ordered to remove my clothes. The replacements were tatty, torn, and ill-fitting.

A vicious caste-system operated in camp, governed by cruelty and violence. Group Twelve was made up of the highest, most brutal category. As tough, ruthless criminals, the 'Stealers' were mostly serving life-sentences for murder and their commands were enforced.

For the 'Traitors', or informers, betrayal was a way of survival bringing meagre rewards, favours or food. The 'Workers' carried out most of the menial chores and duties. The lowest, most despised caste were the 'Homosexuals' who were merely there to be abused. It was common camp policy to punish inmates by moving them from one class to another.

'I'm Barinov, from Leningrad,' I called out. Someone looked

up, but no one acknowledged my greeting. At the end of the hall I spotted an empty bed with a ripped, filthy mattress, wrecked with fleas and other insects. I threw a tatty blanket over it and staked my claim.

The camp was about one hundred metres wide, by two hundred metres long, stretching from our barracks on the west over to the brick dining hall on the east. Beyond that the punishment cells were sited in an enclosure sealed with barbed wire. Adjacent to the arrival zone, a two-storey administrative building led to the private quarters of the camp staff.

The first day passed uneventfully, although I knew I was being watched. At around dusk, we queued five in a row to eat a dismal meal of cabbage soup, eating in shifts in order to accommodate everyone.

The cabbage smelt rotten, and I struggled to swallow it. 'Shall I help you?' asked my neighbour. I nodded, and in a flash he had emptied the contents of my bowl into his.

'First day?' he enquired.

'Yes,' I replied. 'How did you know?'

He grinned knowingly.

The 'pahan' in our group noted that I had returned to the barrack and watched me closely. Pahans or 'fathers' ran the work groups and each one was a long-term prisoner on a criminal charge.

I determined that from the outset I would serve only one authority. Jesus!

I introduced myself to the pahan as an innocent man imprisoned for my Christian activity. He seemed uninterested and instructed me that my duties in the barracks would consist of sweeping the room and cleaning the toilet. Behind him, the leaders of Group Twelve watched this exchange.

'I won't do that sort of work,' I said politely but firmly.

It was clear that the trial of strength had begun. I couldn't back down. All I could do was pray . . .

One of the gang stood up and pushed me backwards, almost

toppling me off my feet. 'Who do you think you are?' he said venomously.

'I don't really fit into any of these classifications. I'm not a worker. I believe in Jesus, I'm a preacher.'

Everyone listened to me as though I had told them I had landed on a space ship from Mars.

Someone cursed, and I felt a sharp pain on the side of my head. I never saw the blows come as my side and back were hit, with boots as well as hands. I curled up on the floor and put my hands over my head.

The side of my head felt wet with something trickling down my face. It tasted salty. I grunted as the blows ripped into my body.

I prayed for strength to endure this trial.

Someone gripped my shoulders and hauled me on to my feet. There was a tearing sound and cold air tickled my left side. I heard one of the gang issue another warning. All the words seemed to be tangled.

'Thank you Jesus,' I heard myself gasp in reply.

The contest had lasted about an hour and I faced the beating with a smile, answered every abusive salvo with a blessing. What could be done with this man of mystery? My body carried the marks, and my face had swollen up, scarred by the battering it had received.

The next evening, as we queued to enter the dining room Captain Verona, an officer in charge of personnel, eyed my bruises. He snapped his fingers and ordered me into one of the interrogation rooms. Assuming that I was seeking revenge and was therefore a prime candidate for the role of informer, he asked me, 'Who did this to you?'

'No one did it. It was an accident,' I replied.

The officer was infuriated and warned me that I would risk another beating if I didn't identify the culprit. He swung his baton perilously close to my head.

'I stumbled and fell,' I insisted.

I had made a dangerous enemy, and I reached the service area to learn that the food for our rota had gone.

Back at the barracks, one of the workers carried a message. 'Micky wants to see you.' Another contest? I hauled my aching body over to the middle of the room, where everyone on the 'inside' gathered. If you didn't belong, it was not the place to linger.

'You wanted to see me,' I said, not knowing who to address.

One of the gang stood up and placed his hand on my shoulder. His grin showed teeth stained with nicotine. 'You did well,' he said, grateful that I had not informed on them, indicating that I had passed their initiation ritual.

'Are you really a preacher?' someone asked. 'Yes,' I replied, 'it's true. I wouldn't lie to you.'

I saw that my reply caused some dismay. 'Valeri, if you want revenge, we can easily find you someone to beat up,' another blurted out in earnest.

'Don't worry, as a Christian, I don't hold grudges.'

I returned to my bunk and tried to sleep. Life was turning, and no one could predict the future. My life hung by a thread and I could be killed at any time. But I was certain of one thing. Only God determined whether I lived or died.

The next morning I was assigned to a work detail that was the envy of every inmate. We were permitted to venture out of the labour camp! Group Twelve regulated the rota of convicts sent by the camp administration to work in local forests.

I just couldn't believe it. Everything seemed so easy. The civilian driver dressed in brown overalls signalled to the guards and the automatic gate slid open.

Our task was to chop trees and saw planks of wood into manageable sizes to load onto the truck. It was hard work, but a welcome respite from camp life.

The next day I rode in the cabin and got chatting to the driver. To my surprise I learned that his brother was a Christian and he indicated that he could assist me in getting information and documents out of the camp.

'What are you whispering about?' Karl, one of the prisoners, asked.

Not wanting to compromise the driver, and aware that I could be betrayed, I replied, 'I was asking our driver if he could bring a guitar for me so that I could play and sing for everyone in camp.'

The driver didn't need any prompting. 'That's right, I think I can get hold of a guitar. I'll let you know the next time I'm on duty.'

Karl frowned suspiciously, but did not pursue the point.

Through contact with the friendly driver I was able to secure an amazing coup. His brother passed me a carefully wrapped parcel which I slipped into my parka, and tucked into the crotch of my trousers. It was a delicate balancing act.

Miraculously, I was ushered back into the camp with a cursory search from the guards at the gate. In the barrack I surreptitiously unwrapped the treasure. Five special Easter cakes, and so many Easter eggs! I counted the eggs. Seventeen!

Easter was celebrated in homes through out our land by exchanging specially baked Easter cakes and hand-painted eggs.

I couldn't sit still. 'Hallelujah! Praise Jesus!' I cried out. But the barracks weren't empty. 'What's going on?' someone called out. 'What's happening?'

'It's just the Christian,' someone else replied. 'He's a little crazy.'

The distraction passed unnoticed. Despite random searches by the guards and persistent pilfering by the prisoners, my booty remained intact.

One day after breakfast, I spotted three of the leaders of Group Twelve smoking by the side of the barracks. Piotr, Boris and Sergei were among the toughest men I had ever met. Undeterred, I strode forward. 'Did you know that today is Easter Sunday?' I asked with a grin.

The trio were dumbfounded. None of them expected to be questioned by a lowly convict. 'Is this a joke?' Piotr snapped.

I beckoned them to my bunk and unveiled my trophies. The religious symbolism of the Easter eggs and cakes evoked precious memories of childhood in the country, memories of another time, another place, when things were strangely different and innocently simple.

In stunned silence these tough, hardened criminals gazed at the treasure laid out before them.

'But it's impossible,' Piotr spluttered. 'How . . . how did you get all this?'

'Jesus is risen!' I declared confidently. 'Jesus makes the impossible happen.'

'I just can't believe it,' Piotr repeated, mystified. 'I wish my grandmother was alive so I could tell her. She was a believer, you know.'

'Take one,' I said cheerfully.

'Come over to my bed,' Boris invited. It was an honour to be included in this inner sanctum where the leaders met. Boris reached behind his pillow and produced a bottle of homemade alcohol. This clearly called for a celebratory drink.

If God had led me to this group it was for a purpose, I decided, and that was to preach Jesus.

Quickly I told my story. They stared at me listening intently to every word I said. The bottle passed from hand to hand, the cakes and eggs were munched.

'When the KGB began to persecute me,' I concluded, 'the devil whispered in my ear, "It's the end for you," but I was not afraid because God told me, "He is risen!" Everything is possible because Jesus is risen!'

While we were talking, one of the convicts had crept towards Boris' bed. With a scowl, Boris raised his fist and the convict slunk away. When I suggested that the eggs be shared among the others in our barracks, Boris asserted that they should be shared with the other gang leaders.

Incredibly, these leaders enabled me to gain access to several key figures in the camp underworld. As their ambassador, I was ushered in bearing Easter gifts and repeating my message.

Vlasenko lay on the ground behind the barracks, a torn blanket covering his crumpled form. A number had been attached to his foot and soon he would be dumped unceremoniously in the camp graveyard, essentially a hole in the ground.

A rag had been stuffed into his mouth to stifle the screams, and he had slashes all over his body as well as a gaping wound in his back. Surely someone must have seen or heard the assault? No one was talking. Rumour had it that Vlasenko had been selling information about Armenian brandy that had been smuggled into the camp.

Betrayal was in the very air we breathed. It wasn't safe to turn around. Even asking innocent questions could prove risky.

The technical group was run by a civilian who visited the camp each day. It attracted carpenters, electricians, painters, teachers; not that you had to be skilled in any of these trades. Rather, it enabled you to stay out of the killing zone. Everyone kept to themselves and got on with the work in hand.

It was here that I met Yura Taikov, a kindly old prisoner with a thick beard and a twinkle in his eye. Yura became my mentor and confidant, and was a good man to know. He was extremely shrewd in picking up on camp gossip and usually knew what deal was being struck and consequently whom to avoid.

Yura had been a mountain climber and kept me enthralled with some of his yarns. He told me that climbing was a tremendous way of maintaining concentration, but para-doxically was also good for relaxing. 'I'll take you with me one day, Valeri, and teach you to climb,' Yura kept telling me.

'Promises! Promises!' I teased. 'When are you going to do it?'

Immediately after Easter, I had an exceptionally violent dream. In the final scene, my clothes were ripped and my body was covered with wounds. But I had been victorious and the enemy lay slain at my feet.

Intuitively I knew that the warfare was spiritual and concerned an attempt by Tanya to visit me. From the dream, I understood that in spite of this 'attack' we would meet.

That morning I received a message ordering me to report to the administration block. A blond young man with shining eyes sat behind a desk piled high with papers. From his clothes, I saw that he was a prisoner too.

'I've got a surprise for you,' he smiled sympathetically. 'It's your wife,' he explained. 'She's come to visit you.'

'When can I see her?' I enquired, a smile spreading across my face.

'Right now,' he replied. 'I need to write out a pass for you. Can you wait a few minutes?'

I nodded vigorously. Yes, I had time, lots of time.

The man's name was Vadim. I prayed silently for him as I waited. He told me that Tanya had been in camp for two days, appealing for permission to see me. Although she had initially been refused, the officials had finally taken pity on her. The dream's interpretation had been correct.

Vadim handed me a document authorising a twenty-four-hour visit with my wife. 'Take this to the duty officer at the gate,' he explained. I accepted the paper gratefully as if it was a cheque for a million roubles.

Near the front gates there were rooms set aside for prisoners to meet their families, but visits were handled like rewards and punishments. Sometimes inmates would be told that their wives and children had arrived at the camp but they wouldn't be permitted to see them. This mental anguish could break your heart.

During my imprisonment, Tanya made the two thousand km journey six times, but I only saw her twice. The other times she returned home desolate and depressed without even a glimpse of her beloved.

I took Vadim's paper to the gate, where I was given my civilian clothes so that the fleas, bugs and lice would not be exported to civilisation. A body search completed the preparations, and I was escorted by an armed guard to the reception area.

Her red hair looked wild and uncombed, her clothes were crumpled and slept in, most unusual for Tanya. Head bowed, she sat nervously on the edge of her chair.

When she saw me, she sprang to her feet and rushed into my arms. Tears burst out and trickled down her cheeks. Gently, I led her across the wooden floor and down the hallway. We had room number two.

She clung to me like someone lost in a dense fog, as though she would be lost for ever if I disappeared. I understood that her distress was as great as any physical pain I had to endure. Her eyes were red, and she was clearly near exhaustion.

The room was spartan, but we weren't looking for luxuries. A cooking stove, sink, table, two chairs and a bed were somehow crammed inside.

'Why are you crying?' As the words slipped out of my mouth, they seemed absurd.

'You look so pale,' Tanya replied, equally shocked. Then she caught sight of some bruises, the result of a beating. 'What happened to you?' she asked.

I was in a quandary. 'It's nothing,' I muttered, 'we don't get any vitamins in our food here.'

'But can't you talk to the chiefs of the camp and ask for a different diet?' Tanya asked, with a puzzled look.

I nodded and agreed that I would do what I could. Tanya looked uncertain, but did not press the point.

There were a thousand things I wanted to ask about Zhanna and Marina and our Leningrad home. Tanya did her best to handle all the queries and then took charge.

She had brought me a parcel, but some things had been confiscated: two cartons of cigarettes, which were always good for cutting a deal. She hadn't resisted, but would gladly have turned over the entire contents of the parcel in exchange for a few minutes with me.

Tanya's small brown case was a veritable magician's trunk, and my eyes began to bulge. I had forgotten what eggs looked like, and I could have eaten the roll of sausages straight from the paper. Brown powder which filled the room with an intoxicating aroma. Coffee! I stared at the jar as though it contained precious jewels. There seemed no end to Tanya's box of delights: macaroni, an assortment of meats and chocolates.

Tanya is an exceptionally skilled cook, and soon she produced traditional Russian cabbage soup for the first course of our meal. I held the bowl and warmed my hands.

But I couldn't eat. After the camp diet my stomach had shrivelled and hardly matched my appetite. I don't know if Tanya completely understood, but she didn't interrogate me unduly.

Our hearts were overflowing with joy and appreciation for these precious few moments together, and as we thanked God for our food we didn't need many words to convey our feelings.

Tanya handed me a package. I carefully unwrapped the blue linen cloth, and there in my hands lay a copy of the New Testament. How had she managed to smuggle it into prison camp? Once again, God had done the impossible. As I clasped the book tenderly I felt a sense of power fill me. With this book, no force on earth could defeat me.

'Thank you Tanya, thank you,' was all I could say. One of the drivers in the town could slip the scriptures to me, as I would be searched thoroughly once I returned.

Tanya had taken two jobs, and the pressure was on. Sometimes the family went to bed with only tea to drink. Another disappointment was that some close friends in Leningrad had received help on our behalf from concerned people in the West but this hadn't been passed on to our family. I was surprised. Why don't people pray and help? Aren't we one family? Weren't we all God's children?

'Don't put your faith in people, trust only in God,' I counselled Tanya. I reached for the holy book, and flicking through its pages, I found the Psalm I wanted to share with Tanya. Clasping her hand, I began to read:

> I will lift up my eyes to the hills
>> From whence shall my help come?
> My help comes from the Lord
>> Who made heaven and earth . . .

In the stillness of the moment God's Spirit moved in our hearts. Outside our window we could hear the guards on night patrol calling to each other as their heavy boots tramped the ground. But their words seemed distant and strangely foreign.

We clung to each other that night discovering our love almost anew. I pulled the sheet over our bodies and our room breathed the peace of a sanctuary.

The sounds of camp life roused us from sleep. The pass ended at 2 p.m. and every moment of our time together seemed precious.

Tanya prepared breakfast in bed, with eggs and coffee.

'Don't expect the same back in Leningrad,' she joked as she poured me another cup of coffee and we settled down to savour the hours that remained.

Tanya told me that she'd had some visitors from the West, including David Alton, a British Member of Parliament from Liverpool. I was glad to hear that we hadn't been forgotten.

But as Tanya paused to remember other details of the campaign for us in the West, the door to our room swung open. Not quite room service, I thought to myself.

'You've got two minutes to clear out,' the young guard called, snapping his fingers.

Tanya spun round and looked at me in despair. 'No, there must be some mistake,' I said quietly. 'My wife's permit ends at 2 p.m. this afternoon. It's only 9 o'clock now. We have five hours together.'

He stared impassively at me. 'I don't know anything about that.'

'But it's true,' Tanya pleaded.

But the guard was deaf to her cries. 'Two minutes,' he snapped. 'If you're not out, I'll throw you out. Get it?'

I tried one last time. 'But we have permission, it's legal.'

'That was yesterday,' he said curtly. 'New rules today and I have my orders. Out!'

And so it was over. Tanya hurriedly packed her case and was shuffled unceremoniously down the corridor. A hand on my arm ensured that I didn't follow her. Craning our necks to be sure we didn't miss a single moment, our eyes alone were permitted one final embrace.

The torn and sweat-stained prison uniform was exchanged for my own clothes and immediately I began to itch. I was glad for this bizarre rule about changing clothes. Tanya had been spared this pathetic sight.

The snow seeped through holes in my prison boots, and the cold reached deep within, as though my bones rattled with each step I took. In this raging hour of madness I turned my face to the biting wind and followed the armed escort back to camp. In the grey sky, I saw Tanya's face, a haunting image frozen in time. Her face at the door in the closing moments of our encounter.

I tried to envisage the scene. How's Papa? How's Papa? my daughters cry. How does Tanya reply?

I can see her face. Weary from the long journey, she moves her lips. But her words are frozen . . .

I pray for Tanya, Zhanna and Marina. 'I will lift up my eyes to the hills . . .' I whisper under my breath.

A rifle butt nudges me in the back and a grunt from the

guard orders me to keep silence. The KGB doesn't even play by its own rules. They cheated us of five whole hours together, a move intended to devastate my morale. The enemy had encircled our encampment, but just being with Tanya was a victory in the battle.

The next morning, I awoke strangely elated, recalling the emotional power I had experienced when I held the holy scriptures in my hand. The New Testament was a dangerous book. With help from people outside eventually the scriptures were smuggled inside the camp.

In this pit of despair where every heart seemed to have lost hope, the word of God raised a match in the darkness. Life in the labour camp was intense spiritual warfare. Sometimes I was like a monk, praying every second, every moment, with every breath I took.

I wrote a letter to the Presidium of the Supreme Soviet appealing for an amnesty based on the fabrication of evidence and the false testimony of several witnesses. In addition, I managed secretly to obtain some of my trial documents as proof, and wrote a short message about conditions in the camp for Tanya to send to the West. I was running a risk.

I couldn't be certain, but I think it was Arkady, who played both sides of the street. I had been warned about him being a traitor, but when he asked me to read the 'Shepherd Psalm' we struck up a friendship.

I heard someone call my name and looked up at the watchtower. The sentry told me to report immediately to the administration block.

Boris lurked by the door. He scratched his chin, and with his fist clenched, his thumb went down. 'Someone's ratted on you,' Boris rasped slyly, his lips hardly moving and his eyes looking in the opposite direction.

Was it Arkady? It hardly mattered, who could you trust?

Punishment cell! The words spelt dread and terror, but they

also had a sense of unreality about them. How much worse could it really get?

I followed the armed escort into yet another bizarre nightmare world of desperate men.

18

Black Snow

There were no rules, and no one could be trusted. You could be betrayed by a cellmate for a crust of bread. A wrong turn, a word out of place, even a misunderstanding, and I would be dead. Jailors and guards would turn the other way as the jagged edge of a broken bottle lashed out. The walls were streaked with blood and the ground absorbed the tears. No one would know anything. The administration would inform my wife, 'Prisoner Barinov is dead.' That would be all.

In the ten-foot-square cell, five men eyed me suspiciously. 'Hello,' I grinned, attempting a wave.

My greeting was met with ominous silence. The cell was dark and dingy. The wooden floor felt damp, and water had collected in the corner by the window. The thick walls were lumpy, as though the cement had been slapped on at random, and filthy brown stains ran down the whitewashed surface. Every punishment cell bore the stains of its victims.

The stench in the cell came from the open toilet in the corner. Flies buzzed around, and the scratching of rats could be heard in the pipes. The drainage system was less than adequate, and frequently the toilet overflowed, turning the entire cell into a sewer.

The next few moments would seal my fate. It was easy to

spot him. Obviously the boss of the cell, the others looked to him to exert his authority over the newcomer. He stared insolently at me, like a huge machine with greasy matted hair.

The machine sauntered over to me and dabbed me in the chest. 'Who are you?' he said menacingly.

I knew there could be no compromise. If I was to die, it would be defending his name. 'I'm a Christian!' I declared boldly, smiling, and extending my hand towards him.

Someone laughed mockingly, and the uncertainty of the moment left me hesitant. The machine glared at me. He was also unsettled by the amusement my words had caused. Perhaps he figured that he should be the one to decide what was acceptable for derision. Turning round, the machine lashed out with his fists at a convict who gasped for breath and flung himself against the wall imploringly.

Turning back, he towered over me. 'Christian, eh?' he said, now a little quieter after his outburst. 'Tell me about it. I'm intrigued.' The tension in the air had eased and everyone began to relax.

'Thank you, Jesus!' I said aloud.

The machine stared at me. 'You talk to Jesus? Are you crazy? Only madmen talk to imaginary people.'

I grinned. 'Jesus is alive. He's real. He protects me even here in this labour camp.'

Calling for silence, the machine addressed the others in the cell. He commanded them to give me their undivided attention. 'I've always wanted to meet a Christian,' he said. He shunted the others off the bed and settled himself into a comfortable position, offering a space near the end to me. I declined, and he didn't move.

I had a captive audience!

Machine took a liking to me, and this ensured my safety. He was a killer who controlled the criminal network in camp, blind to his folly and not knowing any better. Yet I liked him and I sensed that his heart was tender, someone who God could reach.

We were fed three times a day, but the food looked like leftovers from someone else's plate. Machine would divide the bread and soup into three portions, insisting that he and I take the first two, leaving the others to pick apart what was left.

I picked the white of the bread, leaving the crust for last. Now it formed a bowl. 'I think I'll bake a pie tonight,' I mumbled. Rolling my eyes, I pranced over to an imaginary larder plucking invisible vegetables from the shelf. The charade captured everyone's attention and I was goaded on to continue the performance.

'Potatoes!' I exclaimed. 'Sausage!' I continued, dragging out the word, sniffing the air, as my audience groaned with appreciation.

'Salami!' The word sliced the air with a torment of things remembered.

'Salami?' I repeated with a mysterious air. 'No, not salami again!' Machine slapped his thigh, amused by my game.

'Carrots?' I chewed on a sample with an expression that conveyed the delights of a raw carrot.

I ran through every vegetable that came to mind, gaining a rollicking response from my audience. The game went on too long, but in prison things got distorted and it was hard to think rationally.

My pie was ready to be consumed. 'It smells delicious,' I confided in the group and proceeded to devour it.

Although everyone in the camp behaved like wolves, when a prisoner was held in the punishment cells, his 'family' would secretly send food and supplies to him. Machine had agreed to allow other prisoners to use his network to purchase food.

Everyone knew that one of the older guards, Boris, would do anything for the right price, and soon a deal was struck for cigarettes and a portion of the cognac. The risks of betrayal from the other guards were nevertheless high.

Machine worked on the base of one of the bars in our cell with a tin spoon during the afternoons when it was less likely that we would be disturbed.

To my surprise, once the bar was loosened, it could be swung forward to reveal a huge hole. Now the big man proceeded to reconstruct the window ledge using beige prison soap to stick together the shavings of cement which had been painstakingly collected in a cloth.

It was an astonishing feat.

Next, Machine made a hiding place in the wall, which was about three feet thick. A nest was hollowed out to about half the thickness of the wall, and a cover formed for it. Once again, soap and water were used to stick larger pieces of cement together.

The cover was delicate, and once it was in place, we crept like ballet dancers to the other side of the room, hardly daring to breathe.

Gingerly tapping the cover after allowing it time to dry, we ascertained that it would not come tumbling down. Our nest was secure.

Two nights later when Old Boris was on duty there was a voice outside the window. 'Hey! Number seven! Anyone awake in there?'

Everyone was awake, but no one dared stir, fearing a trap. Finally, Machine crunched by the window and whispered, 'Snake, is that you?'

'Course it's me, who were you expecting, Leonid Brezhnev?'

Snake quickly negotiated the clandestine delivery. 'Don't worry, you'll get your share,' he called out to Machine.

Chocolates! Meat! Tea! Vodka! Armenian brandy! Everyone entered the tantalising conspiracy, and rouble notes were rolled up in a brown handkerchief and thrown out of the window, where a disembodied voice confirmed its safe arrival.

Now we had to wait. Rags were shredded into long strips and tied together to form a rope. A full day had now passed since the money had been tossed out of the window, and the tension was mounting. What if it turned out to be a shake-down?

Without warning, a piece of paper sailed through the window and landed in a wet patch on the floor. 'Tonight at two,' it said.

It was possible that the message was designed to trap us. But sure enough that night there was a voice at the window.

'We need ten minutes to get ready,' Machine said in a throaty whisper.

'OK, I've got two other deliveries to make. But if you're not ready in fifteen minutes, the deal's off.'

Machine and I set to work on the bar, while the others sprang to remove the cover from the hole in the wall. We didn't have long to wait, and soon we heard movement outside. With that, we tossed our homemade rope up at the window. Perhaps it was nerves, but the rope didn't quite make it.

'What's happening in there?' Snake said, not attempting to disguise his annoyance.

Machine aimed more carefully, and this time it sailed through the window. A tug on the rope ensured that we were in business. 'OK, haul her up,' Snake instructed. A cloth packet appeared awkwardly at the opening and tumbled to the floor. Hands quickly ripped off the cloth. Tea!

With no time to dwell on the intoxicating aroma, it was bundled into the hole, in a sheet of *Pravda*. Snake worked away at the system, and the nest welcomed its clandestine treasure.

'Last one,' the voice called. Machine tugged at the rope.

Perhaps it hadn't been securely fastened, or Machine had jerked it awkwardly, but without warning, the parcel span around the room, erupted in mid-air, and crashed to the floor. On this short but momentous journey through space, a torrent of black jets was unleashed.

A blizzard of tea! The entire cell was covered with a trillion flakes of tea! At first it was funny, but the darker side of the drama hit home. How could we explain it to the guards? Black snow?

The bar was repositioned, and the cover to the nest re-moulded with soft soap paste, but what could we do about the tea? How much time did we have before the cell was hit, spelling disaster for everyone?

Machine's leadership was jolted by this turn of events. Suddenly he turned to me with a wild desperate look in his eyes. 'Valeri, I want you to pray to your God for help!'

I didn't know what to do, but my heart transmitted an urgent telegram to heaven. 'We must pick up every flake of tea,' I replied.

'But that will take hours,' Machine replied, 'and the guards search us every few minutes.'

Old Boris was due to finish his shift shortly, and the change of guards would mean someone would be here to check us any minute.

'If we truly seek God then he will help us!' I declared boldly.

Everyone followed Machine's lead. I had never seen the big man so contrite. I asked them all to kneel down on the ground with me as I prayed a simple prayer to God requesting his help. I ended by saying, 'In Jesus' name!' To my surprise, everyone repeated the phrase and the name of Jesus echoed around the walls of the cell.

Then, armed with a piece of cloth, everyone began to pick up each single flake of tea. The tea was on the walls, even on the ceiling. Black flakes floated in the toilet water. As we worked quickly I prayed aloud, and soon my words were being repeated by Machine and the others. 'Jesus, help us. Keep the guards away!'

I told them the Gospel story, acutely aware that my audience were probably hearing it for the first time. 'Jesus is alive. He died at Golgotha but he rose again.'

All at once we heard the familiar sound of footsteps in the

hallway. Voices of guards and boot leather scraping. Everyone looked at me. I didn't need them to fill in a questionnaire to know how they were feeling.

Someone was at the door. The rattle of keys was indisputable. We froze. It was just hopeless. Scouring around the cell, it was clear that we had made an impact, but it wasn't enough. We needed a few more minutes. Machine gave a look of total despair.

'Just pray,' I whispered, trying to sound calm.

At that moment the sounds outside the door stopped. Voices called out. The guard was summoned by an officer in the reception area. Machine's jaw dropped, and he looked disbelievingly at me. The others stared spellbound at the door.

'Quickly, let's get to work,' I insisted. 'We can do it!'

Living on borrowed time, we continued to pick up the tea leaves. My joints ached, and there were bouts of cramp. But we worked with new-found energy.

Finally, it was over. We combed every inch of the cell until we were sure that no tea remained. Exhausted by nervous tension as well as the task, we sank down.

'I've never known anything like it,' Machine marvelled. The others agreed. 'It's magic!'

'Not magic,' I cut in. 'But a God of miracles!'

Seconds later, there were keys in the lock and the door swung open. 'Cell number seven!' a harsh voice barked, and one of the guards sauntered in.

The search was only a cursory look around, but the few minutes felt like an hour. As he passed the nest, our hearts missed a beat, but he didn't suspect anything. Instead it was merely continuing the prison tradition of harassment, intimidation and torment.

As the guard turned to leave, his gaze fell on Yevgeny, an inmate from Riga. 'Why are you wearing two sweaters?' he snarled.

Taken aback by the question, Yevgeny stammered, 'I'm . . .

cold. It's damp in this cell . . . and I've been sick. I've got a . . . cold.'

'Nonsense,' the guard answered. 'You can't wear two sweaters. Take one off now!'

Keen to avoid any confrontation, Yevgeny obeyed and handed over the dark brown woollen sweater. The guard took it from him and strolled out of the cell as casually as he had arrived.

As the door slammed shut, every one was dumbstruck. Eventually Machine broke the silence, 'It's a miracle. I just can't believe it.'

His words came from the very centre of his being, conveying heartfelt conviction. At a desperate moment he had turned to God for help, and to his surprise the stone wall of silence had disintegrated and in its place, he had stumbled into a freezone, the uncharted territory of faith.

Over the next few days Machine questioned me repeatedly about Jesus. Then one night he startled me. 'Valeri, I'm going to heaven when I die.'

'How do you know that?' I said, somewhat taken aback.

With a twinkle in his eye, Machine grunted, 'Because I've lived in hell here on earth.'

'Showers! Showers!' Old Boris yelled. Cell number seven joined the queue to the changing room at the end of the corridor, and then into the showers. There were three showers, and usually the water was cold, even in deep winter.

We were allowed ten to fifteen minutes to shower and wash our clothes. Then a few extra minutes were permitted for shaving. Razors lay in the sink and everyone shared the same blade. Communal lifestyles were very influential in the planning of the Revolution but this was carrying things a little too far.

You got used to seeing the homosexuals hang around the showers. The system decreed that they were just there to be used.

On the way back from the showers, Yevgeny spotted the guard who had confiscated his sweater. Something about him looked familiar, but he couldn't quite put his finger on what. And then he saw it. A patchwork sweater using yellow, red and two shades of brown. And one of these shades was quite unmistakable.

Yevgeny couldn't help but stare. The guard couldn't help but notice.

As he walked past, the guard lashed Yevgeny across the shoulders with his night stick. Taken by surprise, Yevgeny was knocked off balance and crashed heavily against the wall. Groaning in pain, he tried to rise and then stumbled again.

The guard moved closer, tapping his stick against his side. He was sure to use it again unless Yevgeny moved quickly.

The injustice of the episode and the brutality of the guard sickened me. The camp system wouldn't tolerate any interference, so I remained silent. I prayed that Yevgeny would find strength to rise quickly and that the guard would be restrained from launching another attack.

Just at that moment, Old Boris strolled along, alerted by the commotion. 'What's going on?' he asked the guard. 'Trouble?'

'Trouble,' the guard confirmed. 'But I'll handle it. He's being insolent, so I had to teach him a lesson.'

No one said anything and Yevgeny shuffled forward, linking up with us as we returned to the cell.

But the incident was not to be buried. The next day the guard confiscated several inoffensive items from Yevgeny's belongings.

Yevgeny stood helplessly at his side. Ten minutes later, Yevgeny was taken for an interrogation, during which he was severely beaten. On the way back to the cells, Captain Zhora saw Yevgeny and asked what had happened. 'He fell,' the guard replied.

But Zhora wasn't a fool and quickly realised what had

happened. Smiling, he said, 'You've got to be really careful here. These cells are so slippery.'

Back in the cell we tended Yevgeny's wounds. He was due for release in two days' time, having served the usual fifteen-day term, but to his dismay he learned the following morning that he had been penalised for the recent 'indiscipline'.

An additional fifteen days!

Sentences could be extended at anyone's whim and we feared for Yevgeny's safety. Weakened by the prison diet, his spirits sank lower than ever. Yevgeny feared that the guards would kill him.

'Your only hope is getting to the hospital,' Machine counselled. 'And you know what that means.' Yevgeny looked despondent but nodded his head, indicating that he understood the coded message.

That afternoon, Yevgeny told Machine, 'I'm ready. Will you help me? Will you break my arm?' he added chillingly.

The brisk efficiency with which Machine went to work made it clear that this was not the first time that he had engineered such an operation. He soaked a towel in water, squeezed it dry, and wrapped it around Yevgeny's left arm. Already a loose floor board had been removed and lay on the bed.

One of the other prisoners stood on the end of the bed and peered through the window above the door. He gave Machine the thumbs up sign. Yevgeny was given a rag which he inserted in his mouth, and sat next to the bed.

Machine picked up the plank and placed it across Yevgeny's arm on the bed. Then he poised himself.

'Stop!' It was Yevgeny who broke the silence. Turning to me, he cried, 'Valeri, if I don't get into hospital I am going to be killed. Will you pray that my arm is broken?'

It was a heart-rending appeal. I had seen the sadistic way the guard tortured our cellmate. I had to respond to the plea for help. I nodded my head and lifted my arms, inviting God to take charge of these desperate moments.

Crack! A light snapping sound. It reverberated through my body, rocketing around my brain.

Tears streamed down Yevgeny's face as his teeth pierced the rag in his mouth. A trickle of blood appeared where he must have bitten his lip. His whole body wriggled in anguish, thrashing from side to side.

The arm hung limply at his side. Sneaking a glance, Yevgeny whimpered in torment, 'Ah! That's good! That's good!'

Swiftly the props were all replaced, and then Machine hammered on the prison door, yelling for the guards. Eventually someone arrived and the door was unlocked. Yevgeny lay crumpled on the floor, his broken hand twisted across his fallen frame.

'What happened?' the guard asked. 'Anyone see what happened?'

'No one saw anything, unfortunately,' Machine volunteered a reply for us all.

The guard bent down beside Yevgeny who squinted in pain. 'What happened?'

Yevgeny groaned and chose his words carefully. 'I fell,' he said, adding, 'These cells are so slippery.'

Two days later the doctor arrived at our cell and confirmed the diagnosis. At last Yevgeny heard the word he longed for. 'Hospital.'

'Valeri, thank you for praying for me,' Yevgeny said when the doctor had left. One hour later a prison orderly arrived to escort Yevgeny to the hospital. Yevgeny grinned at us. We had saved his life.

19

Zhora the Terrible

I lay awake, unable to sleep. I kept thinking about Tanya and prayed for her. My thoughts drifted to my daughters Zhanna and Marina. I knew that in spite of the outlaw image that the government had imposed on me, my girls were proud of their dad.

The night played tricks with my mind. I closed my eyes and in the darkness vivid images danced in the prairie moonlight. Tall grasses blew gently in the breeze, the stars twinkled like diamonds on soft dark-blue velvet. She glided towards me, her smile as hypnotic as ever. Behind her were the sounds of children playing. The sound of a brook gently flowing into the stream.

I could hear her speak, but the words were vague and distant. I felt a weight pressing down on me as I lay on the ground.

Is it her?

I awoke with a start. For an instant I thought I could hear Tanya moving around in the other room. No. The punishment cell, the stench from the toilet. But I was aware of another noise, moving in short jerks across my body.

A rat!

Racing across my stomach and hurtling over my chest,

aiming for the contours of my face, its squeal rang loudly in my ears.

With a start, my arm jerked forward, blocking the advance of the rat and knocking it off me. I leapt to my feet, and to my astonishment, two rats fell off me hitting the ground with a thud, yelping.

My hand fell to my side. The rats had gnawed their way through my pocket, nibbling on the bread I had saved from dinner. I removed the bread from my pocket and placed it on the window sill. I still heard the sound of rats scratching in the prison wall and had little confidence that they wouldn't mount another offensive before daybreak.

Moments later I was fast asleep and unaware of any intruders.

My fifteen days in the punishment cell was drawing to an end. Two days to go. The dank conditions and appalling food had drained my strength and left me debilitated.

The next day the cell door opened and the guard led a youth into the cell. Looking weary and exhausted, he had the appearance of someone with a major illness.

The prison rituals to which he would normally have been subjected were waived. Sergei was about eighteen years old, but prison had aged him. His skin was bruised, with eczema and bites, and like over half the prisoners in camp, he was suffering from tuberculosis.

Sergei should have been in hospital receiving treatment, but instead he was forced to maintain a rigorous work schedule. Unable to work, he fell behind the daily quota and found himself in the punishment zone. Machine undertook to help Sergei so that his food and safety were guaranteed.

In a curious way the degradation of the punishment cell had bound us together in an unspoken pact. I could never forget my cellmates or the excruciating moments we had shared.

Intuitively I knew that I would not escape further spells in the punishment cell. I would not seek this way through labour camp, but I could not ignore the inevitable.

In a few moments the guard would arrive to escort me out of here. From one hell to another. There was nothing to say. Machine looked at me and nodded. I smiled. Sergei was propped up against the wall staring into deep space. The others in the cell were silent, each meditating on their own thoughts.

Back in the camp nothing had changed. Nothing, except that during my stay in the punishment block four people had died and been dumped in holes in the ground marked with a numbered stick. One had hanged himself, another had been stabbed, someone else had died of malnutrition. The very air we breathed seemed to have been polluted with a sense of doom. It felt as though everyone had been alerted to some collective piece of bad news.

As always the first task of the day was to pick the fleas, lice and bugs off our clothes. All you really had to do was to stand up and jump around, and the trespassers fell in a heap on the ground. Ninety per cent of prisoners had lesions on their bodies from flea bites. Some of these had turned into septic open wounds, and blood trickled through the dirty rags used as makeshift bandages.

One cold rainy night we huddled close listening to the rain ricochet off the roof and drip into our barracks. As we heard the clatter of the food trolley even the prospect of soupy water seemed to offer us hope by its very warmth.

We should have known better.

'Hot soup on a cold night? Whatever for?'

Taking a decanter full of cold water, Captain Zhora poured its contents into the soup bucket.

'Why did you do that?' the guard pushing the trolley enquired.

'Let them die!' Zhora snarled. 'That's all they can hope for in this life.'

After leaving the punishment zone and re-entering camp life, I learned that I was no longer allowed to work with Group Twelve. This was a blow. Most of the 150 people belonging to Group Twelve linked up with Group Seven and were allowed to work outside the camp.

But the camp administration had decided to limit my contact with the outside world and I was transferred to Group Eleven. I realised that I had to exert extreme caution in this new group, as I could be betrayed by traitors and informers in order to win favour with the bosses.

But I also made a friend in Group Eleven. It was Vadim, the young man who did clerical work in the office and had issued me with the pass to see Tanya.

I was assigned work producing nets. Each prisoner's daily production quota was twelve nets, on completion of which the camp administration gave a reward. With this money, one could buy cigarettes, chocolates and selected foodstuffs from a special general store that was open for a few hours each day.

But in the given time and bad work conditions, it was only possible to produce three nets, meaning that every work shift failed to avail itself of the camp administration's generosity. This was a punishable offence.

I refused to work on the nets and declared a hunger strike that lasted about two weeks. During this time I noticed some discarded slices of bamboo on the floor in the technical centre. As I polished them a sheen appeared on the surface and the transformation was remarkable. Using twine, I tied the bamboo slices together to form a cross.

I wore the cross to remind myself that although my body had been trapped behind the red barbed-wire, my heart was free. I was not a captive of the godless Soviet system, but a servant of Jesus.

Captain Zhora's eyes were drawn to the cross like magnets and he stared at me in virtual disbelief. It was as though I had pulled a revolver on him. Striding across to me, he grabbed the cross and tugged it viciously from my neck. Feeling the full force of his strength, the twine snapped and Zhora crushed the cross with a curse.

The officer was in a fury, but I maintained an outward calm, perceiving the violence of the seizure to be an act of confession.

Weakened by the fast, I was sentenced to the punishment cells for failure to work. When fifteen days were over, I learned that I was to be transferred for a psychiatric examination and that my sentence in the cells was to be extended.

'But if I'm crazy,' I argued, 'then why am I imprisoned in a labour camp? I should have been sentenced to a psychiatric hospital. It doesn't make any sense.'

But the doctor wasn't there to make any sense out of it. His job was to find me guilty!

The hospital itself was located between two labour camps, and there were many prisoners there under treatment. The prisoners looked just like the patients, haggard and ill.

My interrogation lasted nine days. In frustration, the doctors decided to abort their assignment. It was all over in a flash and within an hour, I was in a police lorry.

Back to camp. Back to the cells. Back to normal.

'You're quite a celebrity in the West aren't you, Barinov?' Lobanov the deputy commandant grinned and puffed on his cigarette.

The hair on the back of my neck began to bristle. 'I don't know what you mean,' I replied nonchalantly.

'Well the BBC seem to be taking an interest in you and we get these cards and letters from people in the West.' Lobanov sounded mystified.

Again, I sounded non-committal and shrugged it off, but inwardly I felt a surge of strength rush through me. Lobanov had inadvertently confirmed that my friends in the West had not forgotten me, as the KGB had warned would happen. On the contrary, there seemed to be an active campaign being waged on my behalf.

I was thrilled and wanted to learn more, but Lobanov wouldn't be drawn. Instead he began to scold me for spreading sedition among the prisoners.

Again, I felt a spiritual victory. I wanted to praise the Lord and dance, but I had to conceal my joy. Lobanov's questions confirmed my suspicions. The camp authorities knew that my New Testament was in circulation and had tried to ban it, but they couldn't track it down.

'It must be your book,' Lobanov insisted. 'We never had this problem with anyone else.

'Barinov,' he continued, 'you've got to stop preaching or you'll never get out of here alive. Do you want your wife and children to visit your grave here in the Komi Mountains? Is that what you want?' Lobanov pointed to the door, terminating the interview.

I spent the next two evenings in the camp library composing letters of appeal. Squinting hard, I wrote a letter to Tanya urging her to inform the West of my plight. I also wrote to the Presidium of the Supreme Soviet, believing that if anyone in authority took time to study my case, they would realise that I was innocent.

To remain alive in camp I would have to remain silent about Jesus. I just couldn't do it. The risks were considerable. If the camp underworld came to learn of Lobanov's threats, I wouldn't last a day.

Two days later, as I queued for bread and tea, I stood next to someone from Group Twelve who worked outside the camp. His name was Nikolai but I didn't know much else about him. Like everyone else, he was imprisoned for 'economic crimes'.

'Do you want my bread?' I asked him.

'Sure,' he said. 'Aren't you hungry?'

'Yes, I'm hungry but I'm fasting to God today,' I replied. He looked startled, so I explained that I was a Christian and that prayer and fasting tuned my senses towards God's Spirit. Taking him into my confidence, I told him that I needed help in sending a message out of camp. He came into contact with local people. But could I trust him?

He looked around, speaking quietly. 'I may be able to help you. But what's in it for me?'

He wanted cigarettes, food, or cash, preferably all three. We hit on a deal and agreed to meet in two days' time allowing me to gather the required items.

Some of the younger guards were quite impressed that I could sing rock songs in English. They were in a relaxed mood, and after half an hour I had collected twenty cigarettes.

The songs were also popular among the prisoners. Others wanted me to read the scriptures. 'I'll do that for you anyway,' I joked. I also traded food and tea to boost my cigarette stash.

I was still uncertain about my new-found collaborator. What if he took my cigarettes and then turned me in, collecting a reward from the guards as well?

The next morning I asked Nikolai, 'Are you sure you can get this message to my wife?'

'Don't worry about a thing,' he replied confidently, accepting the cigarettes. 'It's best that we don't meet again,' he told me, sipping his tea.

'But how will I know what happened to my letter?' I enquired.

'You will know,' Nikolai grinned. 'You will definitely know.' He was right, I would know. Sooner than I thought.

In the dinner queue that evening Captain Zhora caught my eye and signalled to me with his index finger.

'We know your tricks!' he growled. 'There's an urgent message for you at the office.'

I hesitated, but Zhora thumped me in the chest knocking me backwards and winding me. 'Go at once,' he ordered, raising his voice.

Within minutes I was confronted with the evidence of my

crime. In my appeal I had requested that the Soviet authorities give me permission to leave the country. This was taken as confirmation that, given the chance, I would try to escape.

The camp authorities proposed to solve the problem in the old familiar way: the dreaded punishment cell!

I still had the New Testament on me when I was arrested, but as I was searched, the guards in the punishment cells were distracted by some innocent scribblings.

'It's the lyrics of a song I'm composing,' I explained.

The guard looked at me to see if it was a joke, but I told him I was a rock musician and this provided a strategic distraction as it concluded the search.

The New Testament was in the punishment cell!

The book gave me strength and was fascinating for my cellmates who insisted that I read extracts from the 'holy book'.

One night at around midnight I was awoken by a disturbance in the cell directly opposite ours. Someone was hammering at the door crying for help. I climbed on to the bed and peered in vain through the window above the door.

There were scuffles and blood-curdling screams, 'Help me! Help me! They're trying to kill me!' It was Zardok, who had assisted Snake in selling supplies to Machine.

The guard strutted unhurriedly to the scene. He ignored the dispute, refusing either to negotiate an honourable peace within the cell or offer Zardok any protection.

From the prison grapevine we learned that Zardok had died from the terrible beating he received. The guard could have prevented his death, but had instead abandoned him to his fate.

I could never have imagined anything worse than this labour camp, stranded on an island on the edge of the world, drifting to hell.

I was transferred to a makeshift medical unit for a psychiatric examination and tested for 'delusions of grandeur'. A man in a grubby white coat questioned me, 'You want to be a rock musician so that you can be famous?'

'No, I want to sing not for fame and fortune,' I corrected him, 'but for Jesus!'

'It's a puzzling case,' he remarked. 'I think you need further examination and professional help. A lot of help!'

Back in the punishment cells I was warned that such examinations could have severe repercussions. I learned of other prisoners who had been sentenced to ten years in psychiatric hospitals. 'If you're not crazy then they make you crazy.'

Over the next few days I was moved constantly. A cold north wind blew in through the windows and I caught a chill. Without warm clothes I found myself getting feverish.

The guards mauled me, and I sensed that it was 'open season' on the rock musician from Leningrad.

I must have been an enigma to the guards. Every time they shoved me, I said, 'Thank you! God bless you!' It was not easy, but as I took the first step, the next ones followed and my security came from knowing that I was fulfilling God's will.

As fifteen days drew near, the bread ration was halved without warning. We declared a hunger strike against the food that was dished out. The word spread and other prisoners in the block agreed to join us.

When the guard doling out bread and soup was met with a cacophony of tin bowls banged against the doors, Captain Zhora stormed out of his office swearing furiously. 'You'll be sorry,' he raged, 'you'll all be sorry.'

For Captain Zhora the protest had turned into a 'riot', and he was determined to punish the culprits.

Within an hour he was back, accompanied by a tough prisoner named Black. Zhora's holster was unstrapped and his revolver glinted ominously. In his left hand he held a spray can.

Zhora ranted about the 'riot' and named the three criminals he considered culprits. I was among them.

I remained silent. To protest my innocence was to betray the others. And in any case it was a spontaneous protest that could be resolved by giving us food.

I refused to sign Zhora's document confessing the crime of inciting a riot. Black witnessed my refusal and initialled the document. Zhora informed me that it would be placed in my file.

Zhora grinned at me. 'Your days are numbered, Barinov!'

Raising his right hand to his neck, he ran his finger slowly across his throat. There was no mistaking his message.

Without warning the officer raised his left hand and sprayed me in the face. Taken by surprise, I couldn't move fast enough and the jet of tear gas caught me full in the face.

I crouched down on my haunches, my arms flaying from side to side. I tried to dust the air, but it was hopeless. My eyes were streaming as I gasped for breath. Both my cellmates were coughing furiously as they turned away. As Zhora sprayed me, Black lashed out with his feet as though I were some irritating insect, a pest that he had to destroy.

Trapped in a time-warp, the tear gas assault seemed to go on for several minutes, yet it must have been over in seconds. The burning sensation lingered for many hours, but Captain Zhora's words lasted longer.

My cellmates were alarmed, assuming me to be a dangerous criminal. 'If they mark your card, there's nothing you can do,' one said sadly. The next day I was moved yet again, and they both sighed with relief.

'Good luck,' they said in unison as I prepared to leave.

'I don't believe in luck,' I told them. 'Things don't just happen by chance. Just pray to God. Take a step of faith,' I said speaking quickly, aware that I could be moved at any second and never see them again. Both seemed gripped by what I had said and asked me to pray for them. As the words tumbled out of my mouth, the door to our cell swung open.

'Barinov . . .'

20

Red Stripe

'Barinov! I've got something for you,' Captain Zhora snarled. Then he tossed me a cord about one and a half metres long. As I grabbed it, I noticed that he had tied a crude noose on one end.

'Do something useful,' he chuckled. 'Use it!' For several minutes Zhora and another officer laughed at their own joke. I could smell liquor on their breath.

'I'm not afraid to die,' I told them. 'When I die I know that I'll be in paradise.'

They stared at me for a moment. 'This man is crazy,' Zhora muttered.

My fifteen days in the punishment cell had been extended by a second term, but there was little point in appealing against this injustice. Every time I moved cells, I carried my New Testament with me like a passport, and the other prisoners would listen transfixed as I read from its pages.

When the guards discovered the Holy Book, I argued that I hadn't smuggled it in, just carried it in. 'Anyway, I told them confidently, Lobanov has given me permission.'

At the mention of the camp's second in command, questions ceased. The guards knew that I was an unusual prisoner and that Lobanov had indeed issued a confidential directorate concerning me. Perhaps he had also allowed me to keep this religious book.

To my surprise, Lobanov himself carried out an impromptu inspection of the punishment zone, and an enthusiastic guard asked him, 'Sir, did you give prisoner Barinov permission to keep a New Testament in the cells with him?'

Lobanov's denial was emphatic, and he demanded furiously that I hand the scriptures over. I had no choice but to hand the well-thumbed book reluctantly to the guards.

God had given me supernatural power to resist the tactics employed to break me, and I didn't think the pressure on me could be increased. But it was.

I was placed among the hard-regime prisoners, the toughest criminals in camp, and a vicious rumour was spread among them by the authorities. 'Barinov is a KGB agent, an informer, sent to spy on the prisoners.'

It was a plan that could not fail, as the KGB were hated by everyone in the camp. How better to strike back at the system than by taking revenge on the secret police plant? I didn't have a chance.

I was watched closely, and my story of Christian activity must have seemed like a stupid cover story. When the jailors brought me food, I always thanked them, and one day 'Gypsy', one of the gang leaders, challenged me directly.

'Why are you thanking them?' he threatened. 'Are they friends of yours?'

'No,' I said calmly, 'I'm a Christian, and this means I must love even those who hate me.'

'Who do you think you are? The Pope?' another prisoner named Ivan began.

The confrontation reached its climax on the third day when the beatings started. I was pinned against the wall and hit, slapped, kicked, without respite and without cause. I had taken a stand as a Christian and knew that if I backed down my authority as a preacher would be broken. It would confirm their fear, that I was a KGB plant.

I slumped against the wall, collapsing in a heap on the floor. Now my own blood mingled with the stains on the wall. I had pain in my kidneys, bruises all over my body, and it felt as though I had several broken ribs.

I didn't know how long I could bear the attacks. Fearing that I was near breaking point, I recalled a scripture, a promise from God: he would not let me suffer more than I could bear.

Gypsy, Ivan and the others were surprised by my resilience and determination. 'Admit that you're a KGB spy and we'll stop beating you,' they promised, surrounding me.

'I am a Christian,' I replied and prepared for their bunched fists to hurtle down into my body.

One night as my battered body kept me awake in pain I prayed, 'Lord, perhaps it is better if I lose consciousness and enter your presence. Then this pain will end.' Then I added quickly, 'But Lord, I just want to perform your will.'

The assault to discover my true identity went on for about thirty days. This was the signal for the respite: Gypsy restrained another of the inmates from a punch aimed at my head.

'Enough,' Gypsy declared, clutching his cellmate's wrist. It was the word I had waited to hear. I didn't know what had brought this change of heart, but my heart sang praises to God.

'Don't be afraid,' Gypsy told me. 'Now we believe that you are not a KGB agent, but that God sent you to us.' Before I could say anything he put his hand on my shoulder and announced, 'I have something important to ask you.'

'Valeri, tell me,' he began hesitantly, 'will your God punish us for what we have done to you?'

There was a hushed silence as everyone waited for my reply. 'Of course not.' Everyone relaxed visibly. Then half-joking, I added, 'God will not punish you if you receive Jesus into your heart, and I can tell you more about him.'

The response was immediate. 'Of course we want to hear

about Jesus.' Once again, God had extricated me from the trap that had been set, replacing it with a captive audience. During the next three months those prisoners who had been set up to be my executioners turned out to be my protectors.

Special honour was afforded to those convicts who had endured 'hard regime' sentences. When I finally emerged from the punishment zone, I found a reception committee waiting to welcome me back to camp.

In the barracks, special food had been laid out for me. To my astonishment, there was tinned fish and meat, chocolates, and an assortment of drinks, berry juice, milk and tea.

I quickly caught up on the camp gossip. Someone told me that I had been one week too late to partake in some unusual food. I recoiled in horror at learning that a dog had strayed into camp and never got out alive. It had been caught one night and stewed by several prisoners, deprived of real food.

Strangely, I lost my appetite.

My hand tapped my leg in an insistent rhythm as I stood behind the locked door. I could hardly wait. Behind the door was Tanya. Haunting images of her blazing red hair and tender green eyes floated across the room. The last time we had been together was tinged with the bitter-sweet memory of our parting, cruelly separated although we had permission to meet.

How I longed to take her in my arms and cradle her tenderly, wiping away the tears that would flow.

As I was ushered into the adjoining room I bumped awkwardly into my escort, who turned to scold me. Like a schoolboy on his first picnic, my enthusiasm could not be quenched.

But there was to be no private reunion. Dealt another blow by the authorities, I found myself in a large hall with several other prisoners sitting in front of a glass partition.

Then I saw Tanya wave, and rushed over to her, pressing my hand on the glass. Now it was her turn. Tears streamed down her face as she moved her hand to clasp mine. All I felt was the cold pane of glass which separated us.

'I love you,' I said, full of admiration for the woman who had stood by me and shared my suffering. Sometimes, even when she hadn't agreed with my plans, her devotion to me had swept her along.

When words are inadequate, the eyes dance and God binds us together in an everlasting embrace.

Tanya held up some photographs of Zhanna and Marina, and I squinted through the thick, grubby glass at the beautiful young girls in the pictures. I couldn't help smiling, but I felt an ache deep within me.

'They miss you,' Tanya said amidst the bustle of the visiting room. 'And they love you!' At this my spirits lifted.

Tanya confirmed once more that a campaign was being waged in the West on my behalf. Although there were no exact details, I was encouraged, and sensed that prayers were being offered up for me.

There was so much to say, but time was restricted and behind us the guards stood, ensuring that we did not betray 'state secrets'. It had been rough for Tanya, and slowly her story unfolded.

Tanya had suffered a breakdown due to the pressure of supporting the family, and had been hospitalised. But through it all, she had experienced God's intervention. The KGB had coerced her boss to fire her from her office job when articles about my criminal activity appeared in local newspapers. Although her superior, Vassily, was not a Christian, he was sympathetic to Tanya's situation and had defended her vigorously.

'Why punish the wife for the behaviour of her husband?' Vassily argued. 'Why should I dismiss her? Think of the two children, they are the future of our country. We can't treat families like this.'

And so this courageous man defended his decision despite sustained harassment, and remained a very real protection to

Tanya throughout my imprisonment. Tanya told me that he had become very interested in the Christian faith in recent months.

'He'll be the first person we invite for dinner as soon as I'm home,' I told Tanya, and thanked God for this man of strong principles in such a strategic position.

'I'm counting the days for you to come home,' Tanya smiled, wiping away the tears. I nodded in agreement. 'Pray. Just pray. God knows everything. My life is in his hands.'

During our meeting, Captain Zhora walked past. 'These are our re-education instructors,' I told Tanya humorously. She didn't manage to find it funny.

It felt as though only ten minutes had passed, and there were so many more things to say. But an arm on my shoulder told me that it was time to go.

'One twenty-one!' I shouted out to Tanya. She nodded, recognising the Psalm that had brought encouragement and strength. We pleaded for extra time, but it was useless. I would have given anything for one embrace, one kiss.

The sorrow of parting seemed to overshadow the joy of anticipation that I had felt. Once more, we didn't know when we would meet again.

I was a dangerous high-risk prisoner, and would be shot if caught trying to escape. Public enemy number one!

In case there was any doubt, my photograph was hung at strategic locations throughout the camp. The picture was marked with a diagonal red stripe – a distinction which was seen as an award among the prisoners, and which I shared with the most violent criminals who really were hellbent on breaking out.

Lobanov, a committed atheist and loyal communist who took his job seriously, told me that there were new rules that applied to me because of the threat I posed.

'I'm a Christian,' I explained, 'I'm not going to escape.'

But Lobanov refused to open the subject for debate and informed me, 'You will have to report to the duty officer every two hours. If you fail to report on time, then you will be put in the punishment cell.'

In an unguarded moment, Lobanov said to me, 'We know that you are a troublemaker because Katchkin told me about the problems you caused in the KGB headquarters in Leningrad.' There it was, proof of his KGB liaison.

I asked innocently, 'Oh! So you know Katchkin?'

Without thinking, Lobanov replied, 'I've known Katchkin for years.'

From this, I deduced that Katchkin was not unaware of my present difficulties, and Lobanov was probably taking orders from him.

Soon I realised that the red stripe had considerable benefits. The authorities had inadvertantly guaranteed my protection, among some of the prisoners at least.

It also meant that I had total freedom to travel anywhere in the camp, which was separated into several zones with barbed wire. Normally special permission was needed to go from one zone to another. Now I found I could slip through the zones by identifying myself and I used this free access to the full.

'It's Prisoner Barinov,' I explained to the guards on point duty. 'I'm a red striper.'

The guards came to know me and they all assumed that as I was due to report every two hours to the camp office I would be given special tasks to perform. In fact I spent most of my time speaking about Jesus to the other prisoners, among whom I found a deep spiritual hunger.

At night, the guards would check to see that it really was me under the blankets trying to sleep.

Gypsy, my friend from the hard-regime cell told me that one of his friends was curious about Jesus. Mikhail was about thirty-five, with tattoos all over his body. He had been convicted of killing his wife, whom he had tied to some concrete and dumped at sea. But under interrogation he had broken down and confessed. Here in camp he was troubled by his crime, plagued with guilt and remorse.

'I belong to the devil,' Mikhail admitted soberly.

'The devil may own your past,' I argued, 'but he doesn't control your future. When you turn to Jesus, God will give you a new future and a new plan for your life.'

Mikhail sobbed like a baby, dropped to his knees, and asked God to give him a new life. It was a thrilling moment as I witnessed the remarkable transformation.

'Thank you Valeri, thank you,' he repeated.

In the excitement of the moment, the time for me to check in had become long overdue, and it was already about 11 p.m. Captain Verona met me on my way to the office.

'What are you doing out so late?' he asked, somewhat amused.

It was a clear night and stars twinkled in my defence. 'I was just out for a stroll breathing the fresh night air,' I said gallantly.

My remark caused him to chuckle. 'Well, let me invite you to breathe some air in the punishment cell.'

I was awarded twenty-four hours in the punishment cells, but as I recalled the events leading up to it, I praised God. It had all been worthwhile.

In Captain Verona's absence it was Vadim's duty to check me off in the camp office.

'It's Prisoner Barinov. I'm here to tell you that I haven't run away.'

Vadim nodded, not bothering to pick up the file. He just grinned at me. We had met frequently in this fashion so a rapport had developed between us and I had been praying for him.

Today the office was empty. 'Yes, I'm in charge of the labour camp today,' Vadim declared. 'Any special requests?'

'Only one,' I replied.

Vadim understood and we didn't pursue the point. We were both prisoners and the concept of freedom was too painful to discuss.

About twenty-one, tall, intelligent and skilful in the ways of camp life, Vadim had engineered himself into a coveted position: a desk job in the administration block.

With time on our hands, Vadim expounded his theories of philosophy and life. His mother, of whom he was proud, had a mathematics degree, but he also told of his father's criminal record. Vadim spoke like a fascist, with deeply-held convictions.

'Do you want some tea?' he asked.

'Sure,' I grinned. It was an amusing scene. Two prisoners of the Soviet Gulag sipping tea, engaged in intellectual pursuits. But I had to be careful, as it was possible that Vadim could be a traitor.

Vadim opened a drawer and for the next few moments proceeded to twist a Rubik cube in dizzying combinations. 'It's driving me crazy,' he confessed. 'I just can't work it out. Something like life, isn't it?' he said with a grin, looking up at me.

Vadim confided in me that he had written an article summarising his philosophy, and he offered it to me. 'Read it quickly,' he said. Even though Lobanov and Verona were out of the office, the other camp officers could walk through the door at any moment.

In this rambling mixture of fascism, nihilism and folk theology, Vadim acknowledged an anonymous deity. Life was absurd and meaningless, but maybe someone was waiting round the corner with a pack of cards that could tell the future.

'What do you think,' Vadim cut into my thoughts as I skimmed the last page.

'Interesting,' I sighed, stroking my chin. 'but I met two fascists in the KGB prison who had exhausted this idea. Even they agreed that it didn't really work.'

We discussed fascism as an opposition movement to communism for a few minutes, and then I asserted, 'But I believe in a greater truth.'

Vadim's eyes widened. 'What do you mean?'

'God,' I stated.

'I don't believe in God,' Vadim shot back.

'But do you believe in justice, truth and love?' I asked.

Vadim fidgeted, nodding his head slowly.

'That's God,' I explained.

'Now I understand why Lobanov calls you Public Enemy Number One,' Vadim chuckled.

'It's a revolutionary idea,' I continued, 'but there's greater power in God than in the communist revolution.'

Vadim's questions came in quick succession and in the intensity of the moment, the truth found a foothold in his heart. The Rubik cube lay untouched on the table beside him.

'Valeri, I want to believe,' Vadim whispered.

Like a deer edging cautiously towards the riverbank, Vadim stepped nearer the kingdom of heaven.

Shortly afterwards, Vadim was transferred from the administration office and placed in charge of the camp library. One informer told us that he had heard Verona remark that, 'Vadim spends too much time with the Christian preacher.'

Vadim and I became close friends and over the next few weeks I watched an astounding transformation in his life as he set off as a pilgrim on the road to find truth, justice and love. He became fascinated with the idea that God could heal our sick bodies, and when some months later his mother visited him in camp and he learned that she had a severe headache, he insisted on praying with her. Within half an hour she had made a remarkable recovery and questioned him closely on his new wave of beliefs.

'What are we going to do with you?' Lobanov said, perplexed at the thought of devising new forms of punishment. 'You'll never leave camp alive if you carry on spreading these ideas!' he thundered.

Zinchenko, the camp commandant, joined the debate, and eventually it was decided that I should be sent back to the work force assembling net bags for sale in local towns.

There were three shifts: 8 a.m. to 4 p.m. with a short lunchbreak, 4 p.m. to midnight, and midnight until 8 a.m. These schedules lasted about a month each followed by a move to the next time slot and so forth.

The nets were produced on the second floor of a brick building about twenty-five metres long and ten metres wide. There was no proper ceiling, merely a plastic covering giving a tent-like appearance. The plastic was old and tatty, and rain dripped on us. In summer, we caught the raging heat of the sun, causing several prisoners to faint. In winter, we could barely sit on the wooden benches without shivering from cold.

The front rows nearest the toilet were occupied by the lower ranks of prisoners. In keeping with camp custom, the place was actually run by prisoners while the camp authorities maintained a general oversight.

Sitting eight to ten on a bench, three or four hundred people would cram into the hall on each shift. It was hard to believe that so many people could squeeze into a hall that size. The stench from the toilet combined with the dust from the nets was overpowering, and many prisoners became ill from in-haling this dust, coughing violently.

The tough guys sat at the back of the hall smoking and talking among themselves while their 'slaves' and 'homosexuals' did all the work. With clockwork regularity they would pounce, stealing completed bags so that they would meet the otherwise unattainable production quota. The workers handed over their nets, the gang bosses collected the money, and the camp paid out. That was the way the game was played.

The more I thought about it, the more outrageous it seemed. What a great opportunity it would be to preach to a large company of people. Yet another captive audience. And so I put Lobanov's warning aside. This was too good a chance to miss.

It was a daring plan, and I soon found some co-conspirators with the audacity it required. The first step was to get rid of the guard. This was achieved by offering him cigarettes and tins of meat. Gypsy and other gang leaders assured him that they would take charge of the group in his absence.

With the guard out of sight, Gypsy stepped back into the hall and yelled out, 'Who wants to spend the afternoon sewing nets, boys?' This was greeted with a chorus of boos and hisses. 'OK, who wants to hear Valeri speak about Jesus?' A few hands were raised, and there was a murmur of 'Anything but nets!'

'Tell some jokes!' someone called out.

Lev, one of the gang leaders with a scar running down the side of his face, was not amused. He had been instrumental in setting up the meeting and he wasn't going to have his plans upstaged. 'Who said that?' Lev called out sharply and stepped in the direction from which the voice came.

A tall gangly youth stood up, holding his hands in the air, pleading, 'No, no, I was only joking. Let's hear Valeri tell us about Jesus. We're desperate to hear about Jesus, aren't we comrades?' He looked round imploringly, seeking support.

Confirmation spread, 'Yes, we want to know about Jesus!' There was no doubt that these people were curious about God. A watchman was posted at the window and I was summoned to the front.

Without waiting another second, I began, 'Comrades . . .'

21

The Power of Love

These clandestine encounters proved phenomenally successful. Carried along by the enthusiastic support of my audience, I sometimes found myself preaching for two hours without a break. I knew it couldn't last, but I had decided to take it to the limit.

When I was arrested there wouldn't be time to return to the barracks. I always wore extra clothing so that I would be kept warm in the punishment cell. I kept waiting to hear my name called. Any moment now, I thought . . .

Then finally, one rainy afternoon, 'Prisoner Barinov, report to the main desk.'

Zinchenko was furious. 'You'll never learn,' he swore.

Cell No. 10 was freezing cold, and I was glad of my extra clothing. There were three others in the cell, and although we had never met before, one of them asked me, 'The holy one?' I nodded my head.

Late one night, with the wind rattling our window, we huddled under our blankets. 'Valeri,' one of the prisoners called out softly, 'are you awake?' I raised my head, and he continued, 'Do you know the Christian's prayer?'

As usual the cell was bathed in a dull glow from the bulb fixed over the door. Wrapped in a faded grey blanket, all I could see were two eyes twinkling in the shadows.

'The Christian's prayer,' I mulled over the request. 'Yes, it talks about God being our Father. I never had a father,' he said wistfully.

I nodded my head.

'Say it for me, Valeri, say this prayer for me,' his voice was sober and sincere.

In the silence of the night, with the shadows falling softly on the wall, I repeated the prayer that I had learned as a child. The words reminded me of the carefree years with Mama in the Pioneer Camp:

Our Father,
Who is in heaven,
Blessed and holy is your name,
May your kingdom come
May your will be done
On earth as it is in heaven.
Give us this day our daily bread,
Forgive us our sins
For we have forgiven those who sinned against us,
Don't allow us to be tempted,
But rescue us from evil.

The cold had driven a quiver into my voice, but the words took on a power and presence of their own as they hung gently in the air. We lay awake in the dark, listening to the howling wind outside, watching the shadows dancing on the wall, reliving precious memories.

It was hard to believe that one year had passed since I had arrived at labour camp. It would be Easter in a few weeks, and my mind recalled the extraordinary way in which we had celebrated the death and resurrection of Jesus last year with Easter eggs and cakes.

How different this Easter was to be. I had a cold that didn't get better, and a painful cough which seemed to tear my insides apart. I felt tight pains around my chest as I sneezed and shivered.

All the time my temperature was rising, and for two weeks I had a fever and was delirious. The cell seemed to spin round in a whirl, and my legs were too weak to stand.

Once again, Machine and I were captives together. My cellmates pleaded with the guards to call a doctor. At first their requests went unheeded. Then Zhora came to check me. After studying the thermometer and seeing the precarious situation I was in, he tossed some headache tablets into the cell.

'This is all you need,' he said casually.

But Machine and the others pleaded with him to send a doctor.

'Don't argue with me,' he warned, slamming the door.

Every time a guard went past, my cellmates called for a doctor, and eventually their diligence was rewarded. The 'doctor' was dressed in military uniform, and when pressed, admitted that he was a soldier first and a doctor second. He, too, prescribed pain-killers. 'No, this man does not need hospital treatment,' was his verdict.

My cellmates collected some wooden planks and made a makeshift bed, insisting that I sleep on it. Despite this kind gesture, I could feel a cold breeze creep through a gap in the planks.

A few nights later, my fever rose yet higher. Machine banged on the door, yelling through the hatchway. He had learned that the doctor was visiting the punishment zone. 'Bring the doctor here, Valeri needs him,' he cried.

Zhora opened the door to our cell and demanded an explanation. Despite my condition, the doctor wouldn't examine me and Zhora couldn't help. His chilling words were delivered in a curt, business-like manner: 'The administration has ordered the doctor to stay away from Prisoner Barinov.'

'Let us break your hand, and you'll be in hospital,' Machine suggested, when I had regained consciousness.

'That's not God's way,' I told him, coughing violently.

'But they want to kill you, Valeri,' he said, with a note of alarm in his voice. 'Zhora has vowed that you will rot in here.'

'God knows, God knows,' was all I could muster.

My frail body became a magnet for all the prison insects. I was too weak to resist them, so Machine and the others picked the fleas and bugs from my flesh. The toilet was another torment. Without water or privacy, it was the last humiliation. I would lapse into unconsciousness, delirious and deranged.

On the worst nights, my cellmates would huddle close to me to preserve my body heat. I could feel my life flowing out of my body, and for two weeks, I balanced between life and death. The only words I could feebly whisper were, 'Jesus! Jesus! Jesus!'

Desperately weak, I crossed the line. 'God will deliver me from this place today,' I announced. Machine and the others stared at me in disbelief. Was I hallucinating? Did I mean that death would be the ultimate release? I began to sift through the blankets and clothes, handing back whatever had been loaned to me during the worst moments of my illness.

Around 3 p.m. the cell door opened, and a guard told me to report to the camp 'medicine point'. Zinchenko had apparently been monitoring my situation, and somewhere in the bureaucratic jungle a decision had been taken. Hospitalisation!

'How did you know this was going to happen?' Machine asked, incredulously.

'I had a vision,' I replied calmly.

'I should have taken bets on it. I'd be a rich man now,' Machine remarked, an inveterate gambler.

A Jewish friend of mine, Alex Zelichenok, had been hospitalised one week before me, but had returned to camp on the day I left for hospital. He was an older man who had become very dear to me. We would quote Psalms to each other, and share the God of Israel together, usually in English, much to the annoyance of the guards. Alex's wife, Galina would sometimes accompany Tanya on the 2,000 km journey from Leningrad, and they became good friends.

Alex and I had crossed en route, and Galina visited Alex a few days later. Through their meeting, news of my plight reached the West. In a strong physical way, I sensed the prayers of God's people. It was an exhilarating feeling to know that all over the world, people were sharing my ordeal.

From the medicine point I was bundled into the back of a lorry with twenty-five other patients from various labour camps in the region. As we jolted towards the hospital, I introduced myself as a Christian to my neighbour, a defector from the Red Army in Afghanistan.

This drew an immediate response. 'We had a preacher just like you in our camp,' he said. 'He was also from Leningrad.'

'What was his name?' I asked.

'I don't know,' he replied. 'Everyone called him "the holy one".'

I marvelled at the wisdom of God. Instead of putting us together, we had been put in separate camps so that we could bring light to the darkness around us.

The staff at the hospital were local people who probably had little idea about conditions in labour camp. Here the rooms were clean, the food was an improvement, and most significantly, we were treated like ordinary people.

After registration, I was led into an ante-room where a tall bearded doctor conducted the interview. I had contracted pneumonia and pleurisy, and malnutrition was also diagnosed. The doctor stared curiously at the notes. 'I see you've been under psychiatric treatment,' he commented diplomatically.

'Yes, special psychiatric treatment by the KGB,' I said pointedly.

The doctor winked knowingly. He scribbled something on

my card and said, 'I don't think we can improve on KGB techniques, so you won't need any further psychiatric treatment here.'

That evening we were given chicken to eat. You could actually chew on the flesh, unlike the strange bony lumps which appeared from time to time in camp soup. I was given vitamins and penicillin, and began to feel better immediately.

As I was finishing dinner, I felt a hand on my shoulder. It was Yevgeny. His arm was still in a sling, but he was grinning, and I remembered how I had prayed that he would be hospitalised.

Yevgeny confirmed that hospital facilities were superb. 'I would have died in that camp,' Yevgeny said confidently. 'Please take my advice. Break your arm. That's the only way you'll survive your sentence. You know they want to kill you.'

I grinned and shook my head. 'Valeri, it's best, believe me. Join the company.'

Yevgeny turned his head and I followed his gaze around the room where the inmates were finishing dinner. I was surprised at how many left arms there were in slings.

'I only have one choice, and that is to follow Jesus,' I told Yevgeny.

'Yes, I know,' he said in a subdued tone. 'But Valeri, if you change your mind, call me and I'll be the first to help you. You know what I mean?' he implored.

The guard on duty in the hospital looked strangely familiar. I recognised him as a friend of old Yura Taikov, called Nikolai. He had clashed with Lobanov and been transferred from our camp to the hospital. Yura once told me that Nikolai's mother had been a Christian, and that a sense of justice and fair play had been instilled into him as a child. On one occasion Nikolai's mother had saved Yura from a beating, and it was evident that he wasn't going to have a promising career in this profession.

Nikolai led me into an alcove along the corridor and looked over his shoulder to see if we were alone. 'Valeri, be careful,' he whispered.

He saw my eyes widen in surprise, and then added, 'We were expecting you. The hospital administration received a call yesterday. We were told to patch you up and send you back to camp as quickly as possible.'

Our meeting ended abruptly, and I was left wondering what God was saying to me. I resolved to receive the medical treatment on offer, but to trust God for the healing of my body.

As each hour passed, I felt energy and strength flow into my limbs. After one week I attempted simple exercises, and soon after that Nikolai showed me an inner compound where I could jog without interference during the afternoon.

Within ten days, God had restored my health. Even my hair, which had fallen out, began to grow again. The doctors were impressed with the transformation.

It was customary for hard-regime prisoners to work as orderlies, and these hardened criminals were recognised by a stripe on their sleeves. Surprisingly, the 'stripers' were the most interested in Jesus, and many of them asked me to write down scripture verses for them as they had never seen a Bible. In return, they arranged for me to receive extra portions of food.

One of the stripers was an elderly Tartar of the Muslim faith. 'I am also religious like you,' he told me. 'You call your God Jesus, and we call ours Allah. As the saying goes, "All roads lead to the Kremlin." '

We established a genuine friendship and enjoyed several intense discussions together. 'Christianity has its own doctrine and rituals,' I explained to the Tartar, 'but there's a difference between religion and Jesus. Jesus is a real person and through him you can find new life. When you believe in Jesus, you feel as if you've been born a second time.

'Actually, I'm not a religious person,' I confided in him.

'Religion can be a covering that in fact keeps you from God.'

The Tartar confessed that he had killed a man in camp who had betrayed him. 'The traitor deserved his fate, but I still feel guilty.'

We talked about forgiveness, and gradually, like a child, he seemed to receive faith into his heart and began to pray to Jesus. The transformation was striking, and even the guards asked what had brought about the change.

'Jesus!' he declared boldly.

The hospital ward was a twisting corridor with rooms leading off it, each of them locked and bolted, but with a barred window above the door. One night the Tartar announced that I would be speaking about Jesus, and for over an hour I stood on a chair and spoke through the window to everyone else in our ward. This provoked numerous questions, and whenever I met anyone after that, the talk inevitably turned to discussions about the faith.

While in hospital, I also met Old Pasha, a 'lifer', first arrested during Stalin's regime and now over sixty years old. 'I don't agree with you, but I admire your courage and zeal,' he said.

We made an odd couple, the lifer and the Christian rock musician. But I think he felt at ease with me because he identified with my outspokenness. He hated all politicians and the administration hated him because he spoke out fearlessly. 'I've got nothing to lose. They locked up my body in prison years ago and threw away the key. But they can't lock up my mind.'

One day he turned to me and said, 'Why does God punish the Russian people?'

I likened Russia to Israel. 'God allowed disaster to fall because they rejected the Messiah.'

The old man found this hard to comprehend. 'But Russia is a religious country,' he argued.

'Worshipping icons can detract you from recognising the one true God,' I explained. 'Some priests have kept this treasure hidden from the people, disguising the truth with a complex book of rules and rituals. To discover the truth you must come as a child to God and experience freedom in Jesus.'

'I'll write to you,' Old Pasha said, clasping my hand tightly with the warmth of a father to a son.

'I'll wait for your letter,' I replied. The friendships formed in prison forged a bond that could not be forgotten and I knew that a letter would await me should I return to Leningrad.

Without warning one Tuesday morning after breakfast about a month after I had arrived at the hospital, an orderly gave me this message: 'Prisoner Barinov, report to the duty officer.' I was led directly to the quarantine section and handed back the squalid prison clothes. Somehow the very uniform evoked the camp atmosphere and shedding the soft linen hospital clothes was like leaving a part of our life behind.

If I had thought I was forgotten in Camp No. 27, I was in for a rude surprise. 'Barinov!' Captain Zhora greeted me with a laugh. 'We've kept cell number seven reserved for you in the punishment block.'

My expression must have spoken a million words. Zhora patiently explained the situation, delighting in every nuance. 'You see, when you left for the hospital you were serving a fifteen-day sentence, and there are still six days to run.' He could control himself no longer and broke out in a loud guffaw.

'We never forget,' he said, ordering me forward with a tap on the back.

It was raining hard, and I arrived at the cells dripping wet. My boots were cardboard-thin, and my socks were sodden.

Back in the cells, three faces turn to gaze at me. Nowhere to run to, nowhere to turn. Time, so much time. But this is my mission, my territory. I remember the Tartar, and Old Pasha back at the hospital, and their words ring in my ears like the chimes of freedom.

This trumpet must never be silent.

After six days of dry bread and cold soup, Group Eleven welcomed me back to camp with the customary fruit, food and drinks.

'Did you hear about Alex?' Yura Taikov asked me. Yura himself was shortly to leave the camp to spend the rest of his sentence in exile.

Yura went on to tell me the sad news about my dear friend, Alex Zelichenok. As he had received permission to be transferred from our camp to another, his wife Galina arrived to accompany him because of his ill health. But the administration sent him with common criminals and so he was severely beaten. He had been hospitalised, and Galina feared he would not survive.

'The godless Soviet system must not be allowed to get away with this,' I said. 'We must pray for Alex and Galina.'

Yura was equally concerned, but sceptical. 'Valeri,' he said with deep sincerity, 'what good can it do to repeat some words of prayer? How do you know this reaches any further than the ceiling?'

'Prayer is the weapon we must use,' I exclaimed with total conviction. 'You see, we don't fight against the administration, but against the kingdom of evil, the sinister forces behind the structures that exist.

'These people aren't the real enemy, but have fallen victim to a greater evil. The greatest resistance that we can bring against men such as Zhora is the power of love. When they persecute us, we must love them. If we can do this, their resistance will crumble.'

'I'd like to believe you, Valeri,' Yura said slowly, 'but I just don't know how this can be possible.'

I shook my head, understanding his dilemma. 'With God all things are possible. We can't do it alone.'

I realised that these were merely words. The test would come when we were face to face with men like Zhora.

* * *

'Valeri!' Yura yelled, 'I almost forgot.'

'What is it?' I asked.

Yura chuckled and slapped me on the back. He told me that while I was in hospital, a new batch of prisoners had arrived in camp, and among them was a musician named Sergei Markov. He had heard 'The Trumpet Call' broadcast over the BBC and 'Voice of America' and was astonished to hear that I was imprisoned in the same camp.

Under cover of darkness, I evaded the guards and arrived at his barrack hut around midnight.

Sergei was young and highly intelligent. 'Economic crimes' had led him to jail, while his collaborators avoided prison. For Sergei it was particularly frustrating, as he lived in the region and yet was prohibited from stepping outside the camp. Our musical interest founded an immediate relationship between us.

I shared a secret with Sergei: that I had been composing a follow-up concept album while in labour camp. I could tell that he was excited, and I began to hum a few of the melody lines to him, improvising the bass line, guitar licks, and the synthesiser's moody images.

'Maybe we will be able to play together? Jailhouse rock!' I said with a smile.

'You mean a concert here in camp?' Sergei's jaw dropped in surprise at the outrageous suggestion. 'You've got to be joking!'

'Just pray,' I told Sergei.

Sergei reacted immediately, 'But Valeri, I can't pray. I'm not a Christian.'

Over the next few weeks we hung out together. Sergei's mind had a childlike openness, and blessed with such an attitude, it was easy for him to absorb new ideas and I watched faith grow in his heart. When he questioned me about God, I replied, 'Try God. Pray, and see if he answers.'

22

Gulag Serenade

The criminal subculture operated an effective underground network in camp. A city within a city. At the right price and with the right connections you could get almost anything.

One gang used the facilities of the technical workshop to produce a variety of items that were smuggled out of camp and sold in the local town. These were mostly pens, lighters, rings, and similar objects for quick sale. Brass fillings for teeth were always popular, despite the acute shortage of qualified dentists. Tattoos were also in demand among the prisoners.

Once an imitation gun was produced in camp. 'With an assembly-line in fake revolvers, we could stage a mass break-out,' someone joked.

But it wasn't a joke, and a few weeks later a real gun was made and smuggled out to be sold on the black market.

I was never under threat from the gang bosses who said I was on 'a mission from God', and although it always prompted a chuckle there was a degree of seriousness about their tone.

Sergei Markov and I hung out with Vadim in the camp library. Sometimes the back room was used to negotiate a deal, and one evening I walked in on Tomas, one of the gang bosses, bargaining with someone from Group Twelve who travelled out of the camp. He was holding five or six watches in his hand while the other convict counted out a bunch of notes.

I had seen too much. It wouldn't have taken a child long to work out what was going on. I decided not to assume any disguise. I bowed my head, held my hands up, and walked backwards out of the room.

Vadim immediately understood that something was wrong, but it didn't always pay to get involved.

A few minutes later, the door opened and the Group Twelve leader made a hasty exit. Tomas peered round the door and called me in. We stared at each other for a few seconds. Tomas broke the silence. 'Are you OK?' he asked.

'Praise God, I'm fine,' I replied.

Tomas eyed me carefully. 'Weren't you in the cells and then hospitalised?'

'That's right, but my God healed me,' I nodded.

'Valeri,' Tomas faltered, 'look after yourself. We wouldn't want anything to happen to you.'

Tomas gave meaning to his cryptic words: 'You have a message for our people. A message they must hear.'

I relaxed, grateful that the back room business was over with. 'Yes,' I said, 'I believe that God will make it possible for this trumpet call to cry out to our people, and to people all over this world. Maybe.'

'Maybe,' he agreed.

A few days later I saw Tomas at breakfast and we arranged to meet that evening at the library. 'I've got something for you,' he said enigmatically.

Tomas pointed to the back room and I followed him. 'Making good use of the Party's paper,' he said with a grin and pulled a crumpled issue of *Pravda* from his pocket.

Tomas unwrapped the package with great care. 'There's only one person in camp who could use this,' he said proudly. I couldn't imagine what it was going to be.

In his hands he held a carefully crafted cross.

My face registered surprise. 'Thank you Tomas, thank you,' I repeated.

I received it joyfully as a sign of God's abiding presence during the final six months in camp. Although the enemy would hurl poison arrows at me, I would not be harmed. Tomas refused to accept any payment for the cross. Instead, he asked me to write out some 'words of Jesus', and I agreed.

I was careful to tuck the cross under my clothes, but on close inspection, it was visible.

The shop in camp was run by an elderly woman who lived locally. A few days later, I stopped to buy some chocolates, and as I reached into my pocket, the cross swung free. Her eyes widened in surprise and she cautioned me in a whisper, 'Why do you wear a cross? It's bad for you. You'll have trouble, my son.'

'No, no, it's all right. I'm a Christian.'

But she wagged her finger disapprovingly at me. In a low voice she recounted an incident that happened in 1982. 'There was a man like you, a holy one, and he carried a cross despite repeated warnings. One night the guards beat him mercilessly and crucified him on one of the posts. They actually nailed him to the post. He was hospitalised for a very long time, and after that, I don't know what happened to him.'

The woman's deep brown eyes looked imploringly at me, 'Please, my son, don't wear the cross.'

'I know that I am a marked man, but my safety lies in obeying God.' I explained.

A new officer, Captain Pushkin, had arrived in camp. Young and intelligent, he played strictly by the rules with a no-nonsense approach. Pushkin's first few days were eventful, and the gamblers in camp were taking bets on how long he would last.

Captain Pushkin was patrolling the camp one night when he saw the lights on in the kitchen block. Thinking some of the convicts had broken in to steal food, he was surprised to stumble on an extensive bootlegging operation. The network was an open secret, run by hard-regime prisoners who paid the guards to keep silent.

Pushkin immediately arrested everyone, forcing Lobanov and Zinchenko to take a stand by extending their sentences. The camp administration were concerned that the gang would lead a revolt, and doubled the guard in the punishment zone.

The gang leaders were ruthless men with nothing to lose, and a contract was put out to get Pushkin. One evening the library went quiet as he walked in. He paused in front of me and called out, 'What is it?'

His gaze had fallen on the cross around my neck.

'What is it?' he repeated.

'It's a cross,' I replied calmly.

'Remove it now,' he ordered. 'This is forbidden by Soviet law.'

I pleaded with him for permission to wear the cross but he was adamant. 'No!' It was emphatic and beyond debate.

He received the offending item with a shake of his head, turned on his heel and left the room.

I had committed an offence for which I could be punished severely. One week later I was summoned to Captain Pushkin's office. Predictably, it was clean, neat and orderly. Without preliminaries, Pushkin began, 'So, Barinov, you believe in God?'

'Yes,' I replied simply.

He smiled, 'It's funny to find someone like you in the twentieth century. You believers are like dinosaurs. You belong to the prehistoric age.'

I sensed that Pushkin wasn't merely mocking Christians, but sincerely believed the truth of what he was saying. When I realised that he disliked religious people, he was surprised to hear that I was not religious.

'No, I believe that Jesus brings freedom. Even here in labour camp, I have experienced freedom of the spirit.'

'But how can intelligent people believe in something they have never seen?' Pushkin insisted.

'But can you see electricity?' I asked him pointedly.

'No, I agree, but we can experience the effect of that power.'

'You can experience the power of God,' I smiled.

Two hours had passed. 'I'm pleased that we talked,' Pushkin said.

I couldn't be sure that I wasn't being manipulated, but there was a growing conviction in my heart that Pushkin was genuinely seeking the way of truth. I prayed for him continually.

Three days later a guard ordered me to follow him. 'Captain Pushkin wants you in his office. Hurry up!'

Pushkin acknowledged the salute my escort gave him, but when the door was closed, he relaxed. 'Take a seat,' he said, pointing to a chair in front of his desk.

'Do you want some tea?'

This spontaneous question, although quite natural between friends, seemed to startle both of us. Pushkin was aware that I was running a risk by being with him. Only traitors and informers formed such liaisons, and our cosy chat could have serious repercussions.

Pushkin took some papers out of his desk drawer and spread them out. 'If anyone interrupts us, we'll need a cover for our dangerous words,' he said, amused at his own ingenuity.

The labour camp captain leaned forward, with a steaming cup of tea at his elbow. 'Now Valeri, let's talk about Jesus!'

Pushkin called me a third time to his office. This time he was less talkative, and I could tell that he had something on his mind. He reached under his desk and pulled the bottom drawer open.

He looked up at me and said, 'Valeri, I'm sorry I took your cross away and threw it in the rubbish. It was a terrible thing to do. It was the action of a blind man. Over these last few days I feel as though I have caught a glimpse of God through what you have told me. I know that you truly believe in Jesus, and I want to give you something.'

With that, Pushkin pulled a large heavy cross out of his drawer and handed it to me. 'Please accept this as a gift for the one I destroyed.'

Stunned and deeply moved by this gesture, I knew I could not accept the cross. To Pushkin's surprise, I declined his offer, and the cross lay on the desk between us.

'Why won't you take the cross, Valeri?' he said dolefully. 'Are you angry with me?'

'Not at all,' I said quickly. 'No! When you took the cross away, I took that to be a symbolic gesture that God would also take me away from labour camp. I know that the camp administration are plotting against me, but I now believe they will be unable to hold me here.

'I am confident that I will be released when my sentence is over,' I declared. 'No, I'm not angry, in fact I want to thank you for playing a part in this.'

Pushkin returned the cross uncertainly to his drawer. Then he brought out another package and said with a prophetic ring of truth in his words, 'I brought this food for you. Eat! You must be strong, and the struggle isn't over.'

Sergei was shaking. 'I can't believe it. I can't believe this is happening.'

We stood side by side at the morning assembly where prisoners lined up to hear camp news. A list of names for the punishment block was read out.

Then another announcement confirmed that a historic event was to take place in two weeks' time. A concert!

Our names were among the six or seven performers taking part. The news sent a buzz through the crowd. 'A concert? What did he say? What kind of concert? Is this some kind of joke?'

Through the prison network, we had been able to obtain a trumpet, a bass drum, and a homemade guitar. Sergei had learned of a few other musicians in camp and we had secretly rehearsed the popular *Varyak March*, the story of a battleship sunk during the war. In an outrageous move, we had sneaked a meeting with Zinchenko, and performed it for him. Somewhat dumbfounded, Zinchenko found himself agreeing to this ragged bunch of musicians playing for the camp drill and organising a concert.

The news spread like wildfire. I saw Machine that night at dinner and he grabbed my arm. 'What's all this about a concert?'

'It's true, we're going to organise a concert,' I replied.

'You're crazy,' he said, thinking I was hiding something from him.

I could hardly believe it myself. But the duty officer confirmed it the next morning. Only God's intervention made this possible, and I told that to everyone who asked.

The concert was held at the assembly point, and was an unprecedented moment in the life of the camp. The guards wandered around non-plussed and were caught up in the excitement of the moment. In the punishment zone, the convicts crowded round the cell windows as the music wafted across the courtyard. Even Zinchenko and the other camp chiefs attended for a few minutes.

My songs combined old nostalgic folk tunes, Beatles numbers, and a rhythmic Hebrew rag called 'Jerusalem'. I sang a few Christian songs ending with the 'Prisoner Song'. There wasn't a single person listening who couldn't identify with the lament of a captive.

Before leaving the stage I told everyone that by popular demand, the final item was to be 'The Christian's Prayer'.

To my surprise, the men listened in silence, overwhelmed by the occasion and the power of the words. As we walked off the stage to thunderous applause, Sergei turned to me. 'It's a miracle!' he said emotionally.

All around people congratulated us. For a few minutes we had brought a moment of hope into the despair of camp life.

Snake, and a long-timer called Mickey who was inside for armed robbery tapped me on the shoulder. 'I didn't know you were a rock singer,' Mickey said.

Before I could answer, Snake butted in, 'His music has been broadcast on the BBC and Voice of America, yes indeed,' he said proudly.

Mickey's eyes widened in amazement. It was all the endorsement that was needed. Snake and Mickey were music enthusiasts, and I promised them copies of 'The Trumpet Call'. In a wild moment we began to make plans for meeting up in Leningrad and arranging further concerts. Snake envisaged himself as an entrepreneurial concert promoter.

'We could make a lot of money,' he said excitedly. It was like talking about launching a rocket from our labour camp, but it was hard not to get swept along with the enthusiasm of the moment.

With childlike wonderment we began to make plans but gradually the reality of our plight hit home. We weren't in Leningrad, we were in labour camp. But no one said anything to break the spell.

Snake stopped abruptly, and his eyes flickered. 'Valeri,' he said 'that prayer you closed the concert with . . .' his voice tailed off uncertainly.

'It's the prayer Jesus taught his disciples,' I explained.

'Could you write the words down for me?' he asked.

Mickey interrupted, 'That prayer was really powerful. It reminded me of something my mother taught us, but that was such a long time ago and so much had happened in my life since then.' His head dropped down. 'That prayer left me in tears. Could you write the words down for me also?'

Snake turned to him and snapped, 'Wait a minute, I asked Valeri first.'

'Hey, I can write the words down for both of you,' I grinned.

'That's not the point,' Snake said, disgruntled. 'You see, I don't want you to give the words to anyone else, only me,' he said uneasily.

Snake saw a flicker of understanding in my eyes. A piece of paper materialised in one hand and a gold-capped pen in the other. 'I'll share the profits with you,' he said sheepishly. 'Everyone wants a copy, and they're all coming to me because they know I'm a fixer.'

'Profits?' I questioned. 'Look Snake, thanks for the offer but I can't sell the prayer. It's not right.'

'But Valeri,' he coaxed, 'we could really clean up.'

'No,' I said firmly, 'I'd like to help you, but not this way.'

'But Valeri, I really do want the prayer for myself.'

I promised both Snake and Mickey that I would have copies for them the next day, praying that the words would have a powerful impact on their lives.

Snake was right. The prayer had caused a stir, and not only among the prisoners. Two days later I was on a work assignment with Sergei Markov carrying supplies to the kitchen when Viktor, a new guard aged about twenty-two, beckoned to me.

'Weren't you the singer from the concert?' he asked. 'What was that prayer you used at the end of the show?'

'It's a prayer that Christians say,' I explained.

'Are you a real Christian, a believer?' he emphasised every word. 'Or merely a Christian in name?'

'I am a Christian believer,' I confirmed. 'In fact, I am imprisoned here for my Christian activity.'

Viktor was startled. 'No, no, there must be some mistake. You wouldn't be sentenced for such a thing. But I'm curious that people can believe in Christianity when you can't prove that there is a God.'

'On the contrary,' I answered, and crouching down I drew a circle on the ground with a stick. 'Assume that this is the total knowledge a man can possess.'

Viktor nodded, and I continued, 'Do you have access to this total knowledge?' He grinned and shook his head. 'Who knows everything?' he laughed.

'Then how much knowledge would you claim to possess?' We agreed that a smaller circle within the full circle would be more realistic.

'In your life you say you have no experience of God, but what about in the total knowledge and experience outside of your own? If you don't claim to know what happens in the area of knowledge outside of your own, then how do you know that God does not exist?'

Viktor grinned and scratched his head. 'I guess this does prove at least the possibility of God's existence.' I could tell that Viktor was struck by our conversation, and I was impressed by his sincerity. It was clear that God had already begun to work in his heart as he thought about these questions.

I always found it easy to pray wherever I was, and as I returned to the job of unloading gunny sacks, I immediately prayed for Viktor.

Oleg, one of the convicts, nudged Sergei in the ribs as he heard me praying. 'What's the matter with him? Is he crazy?'

'He believes in God and he's praying to Jesus,' he commented.

Oleg rolled his eyes upwards. 'Then he is crazy.'

'Why is he crazy because he believes in Jesus?' Sergei said. 'I also believe in Jesus.' I smiled to hear Sergei go on to explain to Oleg the steps that had led him to faith in God.

I knocked lightly on Captain Pushkin's door. I heard him call out and stepped inside. Pushkin was by the window talking with another officer. He looked at me sternly so that his colleague would suspect nothing and said, 'Wait there. I'll deal with you in a minute.' I bowed my head in a suitably subservient manner.

A few minutes later the officer left the office briskly. Pushkin yelled, 'Now then Barinov, what's all this I've been hearing about you?' When I stepped into the room, I saw that he welcomed me with a smile.

He beckoned me forward and spoke in a hushed voice, 'I've only got a few minutes, but I wanted to warn you that Lobanov and the others are furious about the concert. They are angry with Zinchenko for giving you permission to perform.'

He went on, 'They are planning to add five years to your sentence so that you won't be able to leave in three months' time.' Pushkin stared at my face, which didn't register any dramatic emotion. 'Did you hear what I said?'

'Yes, I did,' I replied, 'but how can their plots change the will of God?'

'No, you don't understand,' Pushkin went on, still staring at me. 'They are collecting false documents to frame you. With Andropov's new law they can add an extra five years to your sentence on evidence from someone like Captain Zhora. They can do anything they like. Who's going to stop them?'

At that moment the door opened and another officer strolled in. Pushkin assumed an authoritative air and pointed angrily at the door. 'Out!' he shouted, 'And don't forget my warning!'

In fact, his warning stirred me deeply. Time was running out. I believed that my safety lay in obeying God, rather than staying one step ahead of Lobanov's conspiracies. Soon my belief would be put to the test.

Three months. Ninety days. I imagined the moment when I would hold Tanya in my arms again and stroke her cheek, when I would pick up Zhanna and Marina, one on each arm, and collapse in a joyous embrace. I couldn't wait. But the KGB trap had been set. I asked to see Zinchenko, and waited outside his office in the hour allocated for prisoners' enquiries. He spoke to me uneasily, as the concert affair had put him under intense pressure.

'Yes, what is it?' he said sharply.

'Sir, I have three months left here in camp . . .'

'Yes, yes, I know,' he interrupted, 'so what, I can't do anything.'

I knew at that moment that he was aware of the plot to extend my term. I continued, 'But prisoners with three months left in camp are given permission to grow their hair. I'm asking for permission from you, sir. Will you let me grow my hair?'

I could almost see Zinchenko's brain whirring as he debated the complex issue. If he said yes, then it would soon become visually obvious to the whole of camp that I would be leaving in three months. If he said no, then the sinister intrigue would have a public face.

Zinchenko stammered and lost his temper. 'I can't be bothered with such matters. No, no, I can't give you permission.'

I questioned why not, and he shouted, 'I don't have to answer to you. Remember I'm the boss.' Zinchenko called for the guard and terminated our encounter.

I felt that I had gained the advantage. By forbidding me to grow my hair, their conspiracy had become public. They had lost the initiative.

What should I do next? It was my move.

Stay low. Keep out of sight, Don't try anything risky. It sounded right. Yes, that's what I would do. Stay out of sight. Become the invisible man.

And then late one night, Vadim, Sergei Markov and I were talking about faith.

'Valeri, will you baptise me?' Sergei said quietly.

I could feel my insides rumble.

Vadim peered at me and said in a husky whisper, 'And me. Valeri, will you baptise me also?'

I had been informed on and sentenced to the punishment block the last time baptisms had been planned. If the KGB could catch me red-handed conducting baptisms here in camp I would be giving them all the necessary evidence for them to lock me up and throw away the key.

I looked at Sergei and Vadim, marvelling at the transformation God had done in their lives. Lord, what should I do? In a flash, the answer was clear.

Trust me!

I smiled at them both and heard myself say 'Yes, I'll baptise you. Let's make a plan!'

23

Dancing in the Dragon's Jaw

Lobanov leaned back in his chair staring into space with his hands behind his head. His eyes looked bloodshot and his tousled, greasy hair fell across his forehead. A table lamp on his desk was switched on, although his room was bathed in sunlight.

I stood unperturbed in front of him. I understood the rules, I had played the game before.

'She's a pretty woman.' His words were issued without warning. His gaze finally came to rest on me. 'Red hair. They're supposed to have fiery tempers, or so the saying goes.'

I recognised what his opening gambit would be.

'Does she?' he said, sounding genuinely curious.

I expressed bafflement.

'Your wife, the redhead, does she have a fiery temper?' Lobanov had made his move. It was important to stay one step ahead to beat the dealer.

My face showed the anguish that Lobanov had hoped to see. I watched his lips quiver with a smile of accomplishment. The target was in his sights.

I played the game. 'Well yes, she does have a temper, that's right.'

Lobanov opened a drawer and shuffled around until he

found a matchbox. He leaned across the desk and began to pick his teeth. I was right, he had been drinking. I could smell his breath from where I stood.

'Shame,' Lobanov muttered. 'Shame.' He stared at me and scowled, shaking his head. 'She's going through hell for you.'

I felt the blow in the pit of my stomach, but I didn't let on. I just stared back at him.

'And those girls of yours,' his words slurred slightly, 'they're really pretty.'

There it was again. An ache inside. A smashing blow that came hurtling down.

'Don't you care what happens to your family? What kind of a man are you?' he spat the words out contemptuously.

I started to pray within my spirit. This was my only defence.

The blows came fast and furious. Lobanov had obviously received recent information from Leningrad about my family. Twisting the knife with the expert skill of an experienced interrogator, Lobanov spelled out in graphic detail the humiliation facing my family.

'They'll be ruined,' he said sympathetically. 'And all for nothing. That's the real tragedy.'

Then he laughed a lowdown cackle deep within his throat. 'And no one cares. If only you knew that. You resist, but it's all in vain,' he said, drawing out the words.

'God knows everything,' I replied. 'My life is in his hands.'

Lobanov slammed his hand on the desk. 'Don't you understand? We can do anything we want with you. I heard you wanted to grow your hair.'

'That's right,' I replied. 'My sentence ends in a few weeks.'

'You'll stay here until we've finished with you,' Lobanov said with finality. 'Do you know the law of the labour camp?'

I nodded, and in response, Lobanov bunched his fist and shook it at me. 'This is everything.'

But Lobanov had tired of his game, pressed a button beneath his desk to call the guard, and terminated the interrogation. The whole time he eyed me closely, picking his teeth and spitting on the floor.

'God bless you,' I said as I turned towards the door.

Infuriated by my remark, Lobanov cursed me. 'Don't think you're going to get away, Barinov,' his voice boomed out across the room. 'Remember Moshinsky!'

Moshinsky had believed that if the Party Boss knew how the camps were run everything would change, and so he drafted an appeal to the Kremlin. However, a traitor had handed his appeal over to Captain Verona, negotiating his own exchange. Two days later Moshinsky was caught in the showers and subjected to a brutal sexual assault. He was then held in the cells and continually abused by some of the homosexual prisoners from the hard regime. This went on for over two weeks, until Moshinsky was released from the cells as a broken man.

Lobanov watched my face for a reaction. Just the sound of Moshinsky's name was enough to sting.

The back room in the library was used by fences and dealers. Why shouldn't it be used for Jesus? With some wine, we could even celebrate the Lord's supper after the baptisms.

'Viktor can get us some wine,' said Vadim, 'but he wants to see you.'

I met Viktor behind the barracks. He pretended to search me, and he made me stand with my legs apart and my hands up.

'What is it Viktor? Do you want us to pay for the wine?' I knew we only had a few minutes together.

Viktor shook his head vehemently. 'Of course not, don't be absurd.' Then he blurted out, 'Valeri, don't baptise them without me!'

I didn't know what to do. Was it a trick? He appeared to have a great interest in Jesus. Vadim had sought me out to answer some of the questions Viktor had asked. What was baptism of the Spirit? Was it possible to lose our salvation? Was it possible never to sin again?

I said to Viktor, 'You live in freedom. You can go anywhere you like, to any town, and be baptised. Why do you want to be baptised here?'

'I have met some priests,' Viktor confessed, 'who are priests only by profession. They keep God hidden from people. But I have watched you and I know that you are a real Christian.'

I felt privileged and humbled by Viktor's words. He was running an extraordinary risk, and I was surprised by his bravery. I decided to baptise him by his desire for faith.

The next few days were spent in prayer and fasting. If something went wrong, I knew I would not leave this camp and see Tanya and the girls again. Not for a very long time.

Zinchenko's office on the first floor of the administrative block had a commanding view of the woods behind the camp. It was rumoured that he took long walks in the woods, seeking the tranquillity which evaded him in the turbulence of camp life.

I had lain awake for much of the previous night, wondering what the tactics would be, plotting a strategy, determined to be strong. But now, strangely devoid of anxiety, I strode into the room knowing that God was my only shelter, my only peace.

'I'm an inspector from the Police Procurator's Office in Leningrad,' Zinchenko's visitor explained in a city accent. He was tall, neatly dressed, and in his mid-twenties.

The inspector confirmed with Zinchenko that the interrogation would take the entire day, and Zinchenko waved his hands expansively, putting all facilities at his guest's disposal. 'Let me know if there's anything else you need,' he said, collecting a few of his own papers in a slim brown file and closed the door behind him gently.

The inspector got down to business. He looked like a career officer who would play by the rules. His smart black attaché case bulged with papers, files, documents. I was obviously a 'high priority' criminal.

As we traced the criminal trail of Valeri Barinov, using KGB Bureau notes, transcripts from the trial and interviews with witnesses inside camp, it became clear from the investigator's remarks that his brief was to compile sufficient evidence to secure a second conviction.

The morning passed without incident.

Skimming a report detailed by Captain Zhora, the inspector mused, 'This case is puzzling.'

'It's not that puzzling,' I said slowly.

'What do you mean?' the inspector asked.

'The State hates Christians,' I continued. 'My only crime is that I'm a Christian. That is why I am threatened with an additional sentence even though my time is nearly up.'

The inspector paused, reflecting on the mass of document-ation on the case. 'I just can't believe the accusations you make against the State. After all, everyone claims to be innocent,' he said.

'But sir, you have read my documents. You have all the evidence there in front of you,' I said quietly.

'Then if what you claim is true, the entire Soviet judiciary system and institutions such as these corrective re-education camps have been a waste of time,' he exclaimed, clearly troubled.

'Re-education camps?' I cried. 'We receive a criminal educa-tion here. Good people come here to be corrupted.'

The inspector shook his head and was silent. 'There must be something to warrant your criminal record,' he continued.

The inspector confirmed that the orders had come from high up. That meant the KGB in Leningrad. All that was required was to rubber stamp the evidence. But where was the evidence? What was he going to tell Zinchenko? Far more importantly, what was he going to tell the KGB General back in Leningrad?

I began to pray. The inspector shuffled through the documents once more. The most damaging evidence was a note indicating that I had been interned in the punishment cell. 'Why were you in the hard regime? There's no reason listed on the charge sheet. By law you should have signed this and it should have been countersigned by the commanding officer.'

It was 4.30 p.m. and time was running out. Briefly, I tried to explain the laws of the labour camp. Rather, the lack of them. Yes, I had been dumped in the hard regime without reason.

'I know they want to kill me,' I continued. 'Extending my sentence is part of the plan.'

The inspector leaned across the desk. 'Do you realise what's happened? Your punishment in the hard regime could probably be used to extend your sentence by an additional five years. Captain Zhora would testify against you. But the document is unsigned. Without your signature it is worthless.'

The inspector rose to switch on the light in Zinchenko's office. This movement heralded the change to follow. 'I'm going to complete your documents and authenticate them with the Leningrad Procuracy's seal. This means that nobody will be able to alter the file or add anything to it.'

The procedure was undertaken with professional skill. Each document was sealed and initialled by the inspector, and a final form placed at the front of the file noted that it contained thirty-seven pages. The inspector signed the document, and pressed the seal of the Leningrad Procuracy on the top right hand corner.

In a court of law, this document compiled within the final half hour of the business day would be my protection from a second sentence. But would it really serve as protection here in 'Bloody Special' Camp No. 27?

It had been a long day. The inspector was staying overnight in the local town and flying back to Leningrad in the morning. As though reading my thoughts, he said, 'It'll be your turn soon. You'll be on the way back to Leningrad. Just be careful during these last few days in camp. Do you know what I mean?'

'Yes,' I said, 'I know what you mean.'

The inspector shook my hand and reached for the door. As an afterthought he said softly to me, 'Perhaps God sent me to you?'

The second investigation was conducted in a casual manner by a KGB officer from Leningrad who wore a patch over one eye. Merely a formality that required my signature on the document that lay on the table between us.

'I'll have to notify the authorities of your refusal to assist with this investigation,' he declared.

I shrugged my shoulders. 'Do whatever you have to do.'

The official sighed. 'You're making life very difficult for yourself. You've only got a few weeks left in camp. Don't make waves. Don't you want to get out?'

Never stated, always implied, the judgement could be lifted with a stroke of a pen. His pen, my signature. But I won't sign.

'Do you believe?' I said gently to Sergei as he knelt in an attitude of prayer.

Sergei's eyes revealed the secrets of his heart as he looked up at me. There was a flicker of emotion in his voice as he whispered, 'Yes, I do believe.'

I made the sign of the cross and the secret ceremony commenced. 'Sergei, because of your faith, I baptise you in the name of the Father, Son, and Holy Spirit.'

The cascade of holy water made Sergei flinch as it crashed down on his naked frame. The water trickled down his body and into the drain in the corner.

Bathed in warm candlelight, the ante-room to the showers behind the library was strangely transformed as we experienced the presence of God with us. I felt a tingle in my heart. Sergei shook the water out of his hair and reached for a towel.

Smiling, Viktor quickly unbuttoned his uniform and knelt on the cold concrete floor. As I baptised him, I knew that he would never forget these moments in the quietness of our makeshift sanctuary.

Vadim was last, and as the jets of water raced down his body, he declared, 'Praise God! Praise God!'

While Vadim was drying himself and dressing, we quickly moved the candles to a central location and spread a mat on the floor. Viktor placed the wine and some fresh bread beside the candles, and we huddled close to share communion together.

Emotions were running high as we ate the bread and drank the wine which had been provided by the guard, now our brother in the family of God. Smiles marked our coming together with a joyousness that I have rarely experienced.

Viktor unpacked another cardboard box. Fruit and chocolates. The celebrations continued for a few more minutes as we clasped hands together and prayed the Lord's Prayer.

It would be difficult meeting Viktor in the morning and having to refrain from charging after him in the camp street. He had to leave us to prepare for the early morning shift, but Vadim, Sergei and myself stayed behind for another hour.

But with Zhora on duty, anything could happen. Finally we locked the library door and climbed out of the rear window, cautiously setting off to our barracks.

It had been an extraordinary, unbelievable moment in our lives.

'You have to sign these documents,' Lobanov said abruptly. 'It's all to do with the end of your sentence. It ends in a few days. You know that of course?'

'Yes, I will leave camp soon,' I replied, but he hadn't really heard me.

Like a magician Lobanov flashed the papers past me, placed them face down on his desk and covered them with his left palm. With his right hand he shoved a blank piece of paper over to me and said curtly, 'Sign it.'

Lobanov's hair was rumpled and he looked tired. Cigarette butts littered the floor of his office. 'Show me the other documents,' I said confidently.

Lobanov looked up at me. I could see the rage building up in his eyes, 'You don't believe me?'

'If I can't read the documents, I won't sign this blank piece of paper,' I replied.

Lobanov bunched his fist and glared at me. But I stood my ground, locked for an instant in this jangled war of nerves. Lobanov was the first to break.

Perhaps he had promised to trick me into signing some false document intended to frame me. 'You will die in here!' he yelled, and shouted for the guard. 'Take him away,' he snarled.

Lobanov's fury erupted and he hurled abuse at me. He looked on the verge of bounding across to hit me.

'You will die here!' Lobanov repeated his threat as the door slammed shut behind me.

24

Final Hours

I had dreamt of these moments a million times or more. I could almost taste the fresh air of freedom, feel the warm embrace of Tanya and my girls.

I didn't need a calendar. My inner clock had been set. It was September 3rd. Tomorrow, I would walk free. And yet danger overshadowed every footstep I took.

Evening roll call for the last time. Borodin . . . Zamyatin . . . Popov . . . punishment block, fifteen days. A groan went up from the crowd, and Captain Verona scowled at this expression of comradeship.

No one paid attention to the monotonous notices which followed. And then the release list. Nobody moved. Not a sound. It seemed as though life itself had stopped. Just the names.

Yevshenko . . . Marchenko . . . Yakhimovich . . . Zakharov . . . Vedeneyev . . . Golubyatnikov . . . Andzhaparidze . . .

There must have been twenty names. Every time a name was announced, there was a gasp. From the front. From the side. There next to me.

Barinov!

Finally!

Astonishingly, a ripple of applause erupted after my name.

Someone cheered. It seemed as though the entire camp were rejoicing. It was common knowledge that I had been threatened with extra time.

I smiled, with the joy of triumph in my heart. 'Jesus, I praise you, you really are the victor!'

Captain Zhora paced restlessly at the front. 'Dismiss, dismiss, that's all,' he yelled, driving us away like a flock of pigeons.

Vadim signalled, holding up two fingers. I understood and winked back. So, two hours later, tea and choice foods materialised as guests arrived to say farewell.

'You don't know me, but I've heard about you,' said a gaunt figure, hand outstretched, 'Give my love to Leningrad.' And then as an afterthought, he said proudly, 'I've got God's Book for this week.'

The New Testament was still around, passed regularly from hand to hand. It could never be stopped. You can arrest a man and jail his body, but how do you imprison an idea?

Vadim, Sergei, Machine, Snake, Mickey, Gypsy. It was hard to say good-bye. We had shared the bitter cup together. We could never forget.

The next morning was a cool grey autumn day. I was allowed to shower, and to wear my civilian clothes. They were loose and baggy.

Zhora caught my eye as I stood in the reception area. The atmosphere was tense. A document signed by Zinchenko allowed me to walk to the main gate where my personal items and internal passport, confiscated at Murmansk two and a half years ago, were handed back. I stared at them as though they belonged to a stranger.

The duty officer pointed me to the 'box' located at the main gate. One final humiliation.

As I walked, I turned back to peer at the camp. The marshy swamp, the barracks where the rats prowled, the cells with water running down the walls. And the faces, the haunted, doomed eyes of witnesses tramping through the cold wilderness. The scene was caught, as by a photographer's lens, frozen in time, from some forgotten far country.

A guard opened the box, and I stepped inside, a tiny wooden hut where I sat huddled with two others. No one said a word. Then the other two were summoned, transferred by van to another prison.

But I was going to walk free. I knew. Jesus had told me.

An hour passed.

I rattle the door.

'What is it?'

'It's me. I'm still here.'

Silence.

'If there's a woman outside with red hair, tell her I'm still in here. She's waiting for me.'

Silence.

Another hour passes.

The rollercoaster of emotions. I pray aloud.

I will lift my eyes to the hills . . .

It's after 11 a.m., four hours after I arrived at the reception area. Without warning, the door opens and I'm tossed my own coat. Tanya must have brought it with her. It hangs loosely on my shrunken frame.

A hand points the way. It's now quite warm in the midday sun. I press my palm against the gate, ensuring that my fingerprints remain.

There she is, red hair blowing gently in the breeze. Tender eyes express relief when I appear, as if from nowhere. My arms go round her and she clings to me. It's exactly how I knew it would be.

I made it. I'm outside the gates. I'm with Tanya.

But we're not alone.

A green-grey Moskvich saloon car was parked at the gates, driver ready, engine running. A lieutenant leaned against the vehicle puffing on a cigarette.

'Barinov.' Not a question, more a command. 'Get in,' he said, gesturing to the car's open door.

'Not this time,' I called back. 'Now I'm free. Why should I listen to you?'

The officer looked stern. 'Take a look at those prison gates. One wrong move and you'll be back so fast your feet won't hit the ground.' He pointed to the car. 'I've got orders to escort you to the railway station. We've got tickets reserved for you.'

Tanya interrupted. 'But my luggage is back at the hotel in Uktah.'

'No problem,' the officer replied. 'Give me your room number and we'll send your belongings on to you. But I must put you on the train.'

Tanya gripped my hand. The KGB were sending us a telegram to get on the train. Perhaps they had negotiated an 'accident' further down the track?

In a flash, the officer gripped my arm and moved me towards the car. 'Let it be,' Tanya whispered, as we were shoved on to the back seat. Tanya sat huddled next to me, holding my hand. I gave her a peck on the cheek and she smiled.

Ten minutes later the driver braked sharply, pulled up outside the railway station and we were hustled out. There were no tickets. 'Buy them on the train,' the officer insisted, as the train pulled in.

'But why the rush? Why can't I take the next train?' I argued.

'Don't give us any trouble,' the lieutenant replied, urging us across the platform. Tanya climbed aboard, and I followed. The officer slammed the carriage door shut and yelled his farewell speech, 'Obey what we tell you, or we'll throw you in prison again.'

As the train picked up speed we prayed for guidance. Both of us felt that to stay on the train would be playing into the hands of the KGB.

'Let's find the conductor,' I said to Tanya. He was in the next carriage, a tall man with a full bushy beard.

'I am a Christian,' I declared. 'The KGB put me in prison and I was released today.'

He stared at me and nodded. Could he possibly understand just what we had gone through? 'Christian?' he said, pulling the edge of his beard. 'Hmm, that's interesting.'

'Tell me,' I asked, 'where does the train stop next? Is it soon?'

'Next stop, hmm,' the conductor repeated my question thoughtfully. 'Not for a few hours, I'd say. Let me check the timetable for you.'

A few hours. Anything could happen. The inspector held on to the window rail and tried to peer out. Trees and bushes went charging past.

I stared at Tanya. She felt it too. The track led straight ahead, no bends or curves in its path. Tanya turned to me and stuttered incredulously. 'The train is slowing down.'

Within minutes the train had stopped. The conductor peered at the signals ahead. 'Can't understand what's happening up there.'

Tanya and I stared at the door. 'Could we get off here?'

The conductor looked non-plussed. 'Certainly!' he replied, scratching his head. 'Just be careful. There isn't a platform and you're in the middle of nowhere.'

'That's all right,' I said as I jumped out and helped Tanya step down.

It really was the middle of nowhere. Pine trees and railway track were all there was, and like children we held hands and tripped along the track delighting in our dance of release. This was the first burst of freedom I had experienced in two and a half years. The energy of our joy kept us going, and Tanya produced some chocolate and two apples from her bag.

This was the first chance I'd had to talk to Tanya and catch up on news about the girls and our friends. About eight kilometres down the track towards Uktah, we hit a small provincial station at Yarega. The station was deserted, but I recognised the area. Group Twelve used to drive through it from the camp on the way to chop trees.

We followed the dirt track until we saw a bus stop, and within half an hour, the bus pulled in. Tanya and I stood to one side as a few passengers disembarked. I recognised the second man to step down. He had helped me obtain the Easter eggs, and his brother worked as a driver for the camp.

'Hello, Valeri,' he said, taken by surprise. 'What are you doing here?'

'I'm free,' I replied. But I couldn't contain the disappointment I felt. 'Why didn't you help us in camp? Why didn't you bring us scriptures?'

I could see he was startled. 'But Valeri . . .' the excuses rolled off his tongue.

For a dazzling second, I felt as though I could look inside his soul and feel the fear pounding in his heart. For that instant, he came to symbolise the Christian church, asleep, bound, afraid, peeping through the window, hiding behind the door.

I was imprisoned, but free. He walked everywhere he wanted, but was imprisoned by fear.

The bus pulled out and wound its way along the track. Yarega is a small town, and the people we encountered had a richness and purity, arranging their lives in an uncomplicated mode. During our brief moment there, I felt a deep affection for this hidden country and its simple folk.

In Uktah, we slipped discreetly into the hotel and recovered Tanya's luggage. As we climbed down the creaky, wooden stairs and headed for the main reception to return the room key, I noticed a military officer enter the hotel. 'He's come for your luggage,' I whispered to Tanya.

'Where are the people from Room 717?' the militiaman called out to the hotel clerk.

'Perhaps you came for me? I am Valeri Barinov,' I called out to the officer.

His expression changed and he looked serious. 'Why aren't you on the train? You must be on the train!'

We knew that this officer was merely following orders, but like all bureaucrats, when the situation changed he became perturbed and didn't know what to do.

'Why did you leave the train? That route would have taken you direct to Leningrad,' the officer charged.

I smiled at him and said nonchalantly, 'No, you're mistaken. That route would have led me direct to prison.'

He stared at Tanya and me, uncertain as to what his next move should be. I resolved the issue by seizing the initiative. Tanya handed back the key and paid her bill. Together we crossed the hotel's foyer, our every move watched by a confused military officer and an uncertain hotel clerk.

What a strange sight this couple must have been. I walked like a criminal, my eyes darting from side to side, alert for any sudden move. By my side, Tanya walked like a lady, her head held high, her eyes bold and courageous.

It was getting dark and the town wasn't safe, so we jumped in a taxi to the airport. I didn't turn back to see if the officer was still at the hotel and we weren't followed.

The airport at Uktah was like any provincial depot. There were lots of people milling around, but no one knew what was happening. The young dark-haired girl at the counter informed us that the Leningrad flight had departed several hours ago.

'When is the next flight to Leningrad?' I asked, trying not to sound alarmed.

She pondered for a moment and then replied somewhat uncertainly, 'Tomorrow.' She smiled courteously and then added cheerfully, 'Probably.'

'Thank you,' I said, struggling to hide the growing concern. I realised that it wasn't her fault. This was how the system operated in our land.

'When does the next plane leave?' I asked her, on the spur of the moment.

The girl checked her watch and said brightly, 'Ten minutes.'

I watched her for an instant, recognising the signals. 'Probably,' we said together, chuckling.

Tanya hurriedly counted out forty-eight roubles and handed them over the counter. The girl had followed the transaction and reached out for two airline tickets.

'Oh, where's the flight going?' I added curiously.

'Moscow,' the airline clerk replied.

'Thanks!' I called out as we raced across the terminal building. The plane was on the concourse with its passengers all on board as Tanya and I strode breathlessly on to the aircraft. We found two seats together near the rear of the plane and sank down.

Within minutes of clicking our safety belts into place, the engines started up and the 'No Smoking' sign appeared.

We were airborne.

I reached out and took Tanya's hand. 'We've been so busy I forgot to tell you that I love you.'

Her eyes twinkled and she rubbed my palm against her cheek. 'It's been the longest day of my life,' she said with a sigh.

I peered through the window. There was nothing to see except the profound darkness of the night. Both Tanya and I were relaxed and calm.

We had got away.

Polkova airport in Moscow was deserted. The next flight out was not until the morning, and we couldn't be sure of getting on it. There was nothing to do but wait.

Weary and exhausted, we collapsed on the nearest bench that would accommodate our prostrate forms. Tanya was unwell, suffering from high blood pressure, so we prayed together for healing and then settled down to sleep. It was clear that Tanya had matured spiritually during my time in prison. In the morning she awoke feeling no discomfort and we were able to book tickets on the second flight out to

Leningrad. We tried to sleep on the long journey across the country.

Leningrad. I looked down at my hometown as the plane descended. It seemed that nothing had changed, as though I had never been away. As we stepped from the plane I felt a surge of energy flow through me.

But I couldn't wait to get home and we took a taxi from the airport. The driver was a young lad dressed in a trendy denim jacket, obviously obtained from a foreigner. Observing my short haircut and gaunt appearance he assumed that I had been 'inside'. When he learned that I had been imprisoned for Christian rock music, he shouted, 'Not "Trumpet Cry"?'

I laughed, 'You mean "The Trumpet Call".'

He looked flabbergasted. 'You mean you're the guy who recorded and sang "The Trumpet Call"?' He spun round to catch a better glimpse of me. With only one hand on the wheel, the car zigzagged, swerving recklessly as it hurtled along.

'Look out. We're going to hit that car!' Tanya shrieked.

The kid spun round and calmly turned the wheel to avoid a head-on collision. The journey home was a series of nailbiting near misses as he questioned me about 'The Trumpet Call'. When we reached Khudozhnikov Prospekt where we lived, I invited the driver into our home, 'I'll give you a copy of "The Trumpet Call".'

He grinned, 'No thanks, I've already got a copy. In fact, I've been giving copies to all my friends.'

The key in the door. The narrow hallway. Panthera, my faithful dog, stared cautiously, circling the intruder. Could it be him?

Suddenly, Panthera pounced, leapt, almost knocking me over, her black tail lashing the air furiously. She went wild and charged through the apartment in a frenzy. As I hugged Tanya, Panthera forced her way between us, showering me with affection, slurping my face with her long wet tongue.

A figure rushed from the living room and embraced me tightly.

Amidst the tears and flowing long brown hair, I recognised my cousin Valya.

'Valeri, thank God you're safe,' she sighed.

Tanya's mother appeared and kissed me on both cheeks. 'Sit down, I'll get some tea,' she said. 'You must be hungry.'

'Where are the girls?' I enquired.

Tanya's mother checked the clock. 'They're still at school,' she remarked. 'They will be home soon.'

Tanya and I settled down on the sofa, her mother served tea and cakes that she had baked to celebrate my homecoming. There was so much to do, so much to catch up on, but I wasn't in a hurry, curiously at peace.

Tanya handed me a photo album and I flipped through it. I stared at these beautiful young women. 'Which one is Zhanna?' I asked. I could not believe that they had changed so much.

Then Tanya opened a drawer and pulled out bundles of postcards and letters that had arrived from around the world. London. New York. Paris. Amsterdam. Frankfurt. Dublin. Brussels.

'I knew that people were praying for us and thinking of us,' she said softly. 'Somehow that gave me strength to carry on.'

I could tell that the family had struggled without me and that things had been hard.

As I flicked through the mail, a tall young girl with dark hair cascading down her back appeared at the door. I couldn't imagine who this could be as she walked into the room and came over to me.

'Zhanna!' I stammered.

At that same instant a second, slim, beautiful girl entered the room. She was even taller than the first young lady.

'Marina?' I gasped in shock.

I had left them as girls, and while I was in prison they had grown up into mature young women, aware and attracted by the fashions of this world. I thanked God that they had not succumbed to the corruption and temptations of life.

Zhanna and Marina were collectively responsible for the storming of my memory banks. Both girls fell on top of me, their hands locked around my neck, hugging and kissing me.

It was a moment beyond words.

'Never leave us again, Daddy,' Zhanna whispered amidst the tears and the laughter.

We were such a close family, and our lives had been locked together, sharing every experience. But Jesus came first. Zhanna and Marina understood and supported my struggle for faith and freedom, and within that understanding, we would find grace together.

'No, I'll never leave you again,' I replied, and I knew it would always be this way.

25

Television Exclusive

September 6th, 1987! I was home!

Like a child in a sweet shop, I wanted to taste everything – all at once! I had two and a half years of living to catch up with, but I was weary from the journey, and slept a straight nine hours that night.

The next morning, Tanya surprised me with a jar of Nescafé. It had been so long since I had tasted strong, black coffee. The pungent aroma confirmed that I hadn't been dreaming.

Tanya said she'd cook some fried chicken, but I didn't want her to leave my side. And so we ate food prepared by Tanya's Mama and Valya.

Friends phoned continually during the day to welcome me home. Some time that afternoon a husky male voice said, 'Barinov?'

'Yes,' I answered, 'it is me.'

'Turn on the television in half an hour,' the voice instructed.

'What do you mean?'

'Just watch the television,' the voice said confidently.

'Who are you?' I asked the mystery caller.

'You know who I am,' the voice said and hung up the phone. Tanya had been staring suspiciously throughout the encounter. 'Who was that?' she asked.

'Probably the KGB,' I pondered. 'They wanted me to watch television,' I explained, finding it difficult to disguise the surprise in my voice.

We soon found out why the Secret Police had alerted us. The television programme entitled *Pharisee* accused Bible smuggling operations of dealing with pornography and other vile publications. Juxtaposed with this was footage shot at my trial, carefully edited so that I was shown to be an unreliable witness. The film also included the 'confessions' of Sergei Timokhin, my friend and 'collaborator'.

All through the film, friends rang to alert me of its screening. 'Thanks, I knew it was going to be shown,' I told the callers, one of whom was George. 'You knew?' George asked incredulously. 'Then why didn't you tell me?'

We took the phone off the hook and watched the rest without interruption. The phone rang again as soon as we replaced the receiver. It was Lita, one of the girls we knew from the Moonwalk Club. 'Valeri, it's you! I'm so glad you're home. You won't believe it, but there's been an amazing film on TV!'

There was no food in the house, so I volunteered to walk to the corner to see what was available. As I stood in the queue to buy fish, brussels sprouts and potatoes, two men in their thirties stared at me.

'What happened to your hair?' the first man said. 'You were on TV just now, weren't you?' the other one called out.

Soon a crowd had gathered. Someone said, 'Is it him? He looks so thin. I'd heard he wasn't coming home.'

I explained what had happened, and immediately there were expressions of sympathy.

'Communist mafia!' someone yelled after I had finished speaking, and everyone laughed.

Two weeks after that, the film was repeated on television. I was impressed with the project and discussed it at length with Tanya and our friends.

Someone had obviously paid close attention to detail and orchestrated the preview to coincide with my release from camp. The same authority must have had access to the television network's programme scheduling. As all media were controlled by the State, this wasn't hard to achieve. But who could have engineered such an operation? There were no prizes for the answer to that question.

The film made a remarkable impact in Leningrad, and wherever I went, people recognised me and shouted their congratulations. 'We heard your music on the BBC,' one teenager in torn jeans and a punk hair style told me on the subway. 'Don't let them beat you down,' he said, touching my arm in sympathy.

One old lady stared at me in the street. 'Aren't you the Christian whose trial was shown on TV?'

'Yes, it's me,' I grinned, 'I'm the guilty man.'

She smiled and held out her hands. 'Let me give you a hug.' Then she said, 'I hope God keeps you on this path, my son.' Tears formed in her eyes and it was clear that she had lost loved ones in the Gulag. 'I fear that they will hunt you down,' she sighed.

But I smiled and tried to cheer her, 'Don't worry about me. I belong to Jesus.'

'But you don't know these wicked people,' she remarked. 'They'll do anything to get you.'

'But Jesus has the victory over the devil,' I told her confidently.

The next few months were spent relaxing at home, lying in Tanya's arms, holding Zhanna and Marina close. Every time they walked out of the room, I felt restless and uneasy, waiting for the moment when I would see them again.

Some nights I couldn't sleep, and after tossing and turning I would take Panthera for a walk. Usually the streets were deserted, peaceful and serene. Everything seemed so normal, but to me even these everyday occurrences took on special significance. It had been so long since I had lived normally.

It was just like old times. Friends called in, some brought tapes of new singers. In three years styles had changed so much. To my delight, Zhanna and Marina were modern teenagers who loved the new rhythms. They learned the words to Sting's song 'Russians love their children too.' Although they didn't understand all the lyrics it was great fun.

I jogged every day, exercised regularly, and over the next few weeks I could feel myself growing strong. My strength wasn't the only thing that was growing. My hair, which had fallen out in clumps and had been trimmed to a bristle, was soon down to my neck.

It was like being given a new life, like being born again. I even looked different.

Several days were spent in monastic-style communion with God. I couldn't name the day or the exact moment, but a feeling had grown and been confirmed. I knew what had to be done.

It was just after seven in the evening when the doorbell rang. 'That'll be Zhanna and Marina,' Tanya said, going to the door. Then I heard her call, 'Valeri!' Her voice was heavy with emotion, and I knew something was wrong.

It was the police. No explanation was offered as I was bundled into the back of a police car and driven to Police Station No. 14. The duty officer refused to volunteer any explanation for my arrest but filled out the warrant card and I was shuffled into the cells.

Forty-eight days had passed since I had been released from camp. By 2 a.m. the dingy cell was full of thieves, prostitutes and criminals arrested that night.

One drunk tugged my sleeve and began to tell me his sad story. After he lost his wife, his children had married and moved away, and he lived alone. In despair, he had turned to drink and had frequently been picked up by the police. 'But this time,' he complained, 'I wasn't doing anything. Why did they arrest me? What am I living for? What am I doing here?'

I placed my arm around his shoulder and spoke quietly, 'I know why you are here.' His eyes bulged as he stared at me. 'You are here to meet me,' I exclaimed.

Slowly I explained that the presence of Jesus in his life could help him overcome his loneliness and despair. I handed him my address and asked him to visit me.

The next morning, as mysteriously as I had entered the cells, I was released. 'No charges,' the duty officer at the front desk told me, 'You're free to go.'

The incident clarified my thinking. I couldn't remain silent. I had to tell everyone about Jesus. This was my mission. A few days later I wrote an appeal to General Secretary Mikhail Gorbachev requesting permission to continue my work, using rock music to share the life-changing message of Jesus with young people. I concluded my appeal with the words, 'Please grant me permission to preach the Gospel or allow our family to leave the country so that I can live for Jesus' glory and share this message all over the world.'

I gave copies to friends from Britain and was encouraged to learn that those who had campaigned for my release were standing with me in this new venture of faith.

Towards the end of the year, I visited my old adversary, Mr Kirov of the Council for Religious Affairs. I explained to his receptionist that I was 'Valeri Barinov of "The Trumpet Call".'

Suddenly his door opened wide, 'Oh, "Trumpet Call"? Come in, come in.

'You look thin,' he said with a chuckle.

Seated in a comfortable leather chair, Kirov reviewed his guest. 'So you're going to have a rest now?' he said, sounding cheerful.

I responded with equal optimism, 'No, no, I've had a long

rest. Two and a half years of rest. Now I want to work.'

Kirov jerked forward in his chair. 'No! No! Please don't! Please don't!' Kirov sounded alarmed and urged me to consider my family's welfare.

We discussed my options and the risks that I ran by continuing to work among young people. 'I don't want to leave Leningrad,' I told Kirov, 'but I must fulfil my mission.' He reflected on my dilemma and then said, 'Do you know where the "big house" is? That's the best place to discuss the subject,' Kirov answered confidently.

At their headquarters on Voinov Street, the KGB were unprepared and the interview was dismissive. All they could suggest was that I consult the Ovir (emigration office) who in turn confirmed that it was impossible to leave the country without a personal invitation from a blood relative.

The underground communications network in Leningrad had spread the news that I was still alive and back from camp. Every day someone new called in to see me.

Sergei was a thin, gaunt, long-haired hippie I dubbed 'Lennon' because of his resemblance to our favourite Beatle. He was an Orthodox believer who understood that icons and rituals didn't hold any magic power. I gave him a Bible and over the next few weeks we spent a lot of time together.

Café Saigon on Nevsky Prospekt was popular among the city's street people and we took to hanging out with the punks, hippies and dropouts. Within a few weeks we had gained a following of about three hundred people, many experiencing the power of God in their lives. But meeting together proved problematic.

For a few weeks, we met in Gatchinar, a half hour train ride away from Leningrad where an active church opened its doors to us. The meetings were extraordinary as old women shared hymn books with punk rockers.

But tensions within the church and pressure from the authorities closed that door. We suspected that the group had been infiltrated by informers and some of the leaders of our 'unofficial church' were being watched and followed. 'Lennon' summed up the situation, 'This is God's work. Nothing is going to stop us now!'

The gypsy congregation moved from street to street with Café Saigon serving as the cockpit of communication.

After observing several empty church buildings, I visited Kirov trying to obtain permission for our group to meet in one of them. This turned out to be a lost cause.

Early in March, Jubilee Campaign in Britain told me that they had succeeded in sending a copy of my appeal to Mrs Thatcher, and that they had received assurances that she would raise my case during her meetings in the Kremlin. I knew that the telephone was bugged, and it was difficult to speak freely on an open line.

When I told Tanya the news, we both chuckled with laughter. How would our telephone 'bug' file this conversation in his report to the KGB? Meanwhile, other contacts in the West tried to dissuade us from leaving Leningrad. This puzzled us for a while, but we decided to follow God's direction rather than the advice of men.

Gorbachev's doctrine of Glasnost was creating widespread speculation throughout the world. Inside the country we learnt of the changes through personal experience.

The British Prime Minister's visit was phenomenal. By all accounts, the openness surrounding her visit was unprecedented in the history of the Soviet Union.

However, for the duration of her visit, our activities were severely curtailed, and padlocks were placed on the doors of the hall where we usually met with our unofficial church of young people.

About ten days after Mrs Thatcher left Moscow, I was called to the emigration office. In a complete U-turn, they told me that if I wanted to, I could pack my suitcase and leave the USSR the following day.

'But I haven't got an invitation,' I stammered.

'That's all right,' the Ovir inspector told me. 'Just fill in these forms and return them. We'll do the rest, and you'll be on your way to Israel.'

'But I don't want to go to Israel,' I argued, 'I want to go to Britain.'

'Just take the documents and fill them in,' he said in exasperation. I left the office deep in thought. This was clearly a political decision: the British Prime Minister's intervention had resulted in a change of policy regarding my case. But did I really want to leave my homeland?

What I wanted was to fulfil my mission. I wanted to tell the world about Jesus. This was the trumpet call that I had been entrusted with.

On the spur of the moment, I decided to catch the overnight express to Moscow and seek help from the Baptist Organisation there.

Alexei Bychkov, the denomination's General Secretary, greeted me warmly in the old tradition with a kiss on both cheeks. 'What are you doing here?' he said jovially. 'You should be in the West.' From this remark I understood that he knew a lot about me even though we had never met.

When I explained that the emigration office told me that I could leave immediately, Rev Bychkov said, 'Yes, go, go.'

His response took my by surprise. 'But that's why I wanted to talk with you,' I explained. 'We are Russians, yes?'

'Yes,' Rev Bychkov replied.

'Then where is it best to work?' I posed the question that had been preying on my mind.

Bychkov squirmed in his chair. He then began a rambling discussion about the dangers of operating outside official structures. He would be unable to assist me in obtaining permission to register our group of young people. He had one reply to all my questions.

'Go!'

I found it difficult to understand why the leader of the Baptists wanted me out of the country.

Bychkov checked his watch. 'One thirty!' he exclaimed, rising to his feet and taking my arm. 'Come with me, let's get something to eat.'

As we walked to the dining room, I spotted Rev Letuyenka, the Baptist President, standing near the entrance to the hall. I had met him previously in Leningrad and we had clashed over the medium of modern music. 'Rock music is from the devil,' he had said dismissively.

Abruptly, Bychkov excused himself for a moment and I found myself alone with Rev Letuyenka. 'Greetings from Leningrad,' I called out to him. To my surprise, he walked away without saying a word.

As I waited for Bychkov's return, a tall well-built man appeared and ushered me into his office. He told me his name and embraced me warmly. 'Valeri,' he said, 'Oh, it's so good to see you! When you were in prison, I prayed regularly for you.'

Then he said quietly, 'Do you want some Bibles? Could you use them in your work?'

'Bibles?' I repeated the word. Despite all the news reports, Bibles were still hard to find. 'Yes please!'

'How many would you like?' he asked.

'How many have you got?' I countered. 'I'll take them all.'

We arranged a secret rendezvous and my new friend smuggled the Bibles out of the Baptist centre for me. I knew that everyone at the Café Saigon would want one.

Bychkov called my name, and I slipped out to meet him. The dining hall was crowded, but I was given an honoured place at the top table and we were served a generous portion of borsch.

Bychkov turned to me and said, 'Valeri, you know who sat in this chair before you? Billy Graham, as well as many other famous Christians from the West.' Bychkov repeated other well-known names and related some personal backstage incidents indicating that he knew these celebrities intimately.

But I didn't consider this an honour. I was in prison when Billy Graham visited the Soviet Union, and I found it hard to understand how such people could come to our country and remain silent about the persecution of their brothers and sisters. Perhaps he spoke privately, but I considered such moves to be powerless gestures. I was disappointed that he appeared to make no effort to signal his public support for the persecuted Church.

As I sat with Bychkov at the dining table, I became uneasy, not wanting to remain in this privileged position any longer. I perceived it to be the place of people who had compromised this godless system.

I preferred to be among lowly, ordinary people.

I left the Baptist headquarters in some confusion and headed back to Leningrad. As the overnight express hurtled through the night I prayed, *Jesus, what should I do?*

I considered going underground in order to carry on the work of our group. Many Christian leaders had been forced to live this way, hunted from house to house, rarely seeing their families.

I had been approached by a mysterious group who claimed to have a secret recording studio in the mountains. Did I want to record a follow-up album to 'The Trumpet Call'? But the deal, shrouded in secrecy, didn't work out. Yet another door had been slammed shut.

When the train pulled into Leningrad around 9 a.m. I found the house empty. The girls were at school and Tanya was at work. Weary from the journey and tired from yet another sleepless night, I tried to rest but tossed and turned. I got out of bed and paced the floor, a prison habit that I had been unable to shake off.

An hour later, I sank on to the bed exhausted. Once again, I prayed, *Jesus, what should I do?*

Every door seemed to be closing. Yet in my heart I felt a

compulsion to continue sharing my experiences with young people, not just in our own country, but throughout the world.

I fell into a deep sleep and experienced a vivid dream.

In the dream, I saw an Orthodox priest moving among the people in the Baptist Church. This was highly unusual, as denominations didn't mingle. I called out to the priest, and he came over to me immediately because I was the only one in the church who called for him. I knelt before him and said, 'Please pray for me. I want God's blessing on my life.' The priest placed his hand on my head and said, 'In the name of the Father, the Son, and the Holy Spirit.' As he did that, I experienced a great blessing of God flow through me.

I awoke immediately and recalled every detail. Only fifteen minutes had passed. But I couldn't understand the dream.

Why did you bless me, Lord? I had prayed to ask the way ahead, but was still uncertain about the future.

I suddenly realised that the front doorbell had been ringing, and hurried to open the door. It was the postman with a registered package for me. I ripped off the brown manilla covering and stared at the contents, hardly believing my eyes.

The package was from the British Embassy in Moscow. It contained a personal invitation from my friend in Britain, issued through the British Foreign Office.

My throat felt dry and parched. A tight band had formed around my chest, and I breathed in short spurts.

In the solitude of my apartment I lifted my hands to heaven, recalling the vision. Instantly I felt God's blessing flowing through me, just as it had in the dream.

This was the way!

I mailed Bibles to my friends in labour camp. It seemed such a great distance away, like a planet dangling in deep space. But when Yura Taikov and Alex Zelichenok visited me, I knew that labour camp had not been a hallucination.

One evening a tall haggard man rang my doorbell. I knew immediately that he was from the camps. He had that haunted look of a man who had travelled to the moon. But he smiled kindly and his eyes were alive. I realised that he was the Christian that I had heard about from the other prisoners. We prayed together and I told him how pleased I was that we were held in separate camps.

Viktor, the guard, also visited me and together we went to some of the meetings at Café Saigon.

The emigration papers and documents from the British Embassy were kept neatly folded in the sideboard drawer.

That summer, I travelled to several towns and cities all across the country. Without an itinerary or money, I moved as God prompted me. Everywhere I observed the amazing fruit of 'The Trumpet Call' broadcasts. When I arrived in one town with no contacts, God led me to take a taxi from the airport to the town.

'Do you know any Christians?' I quizzed the taxi-driver when he asked me where I was heading.

'Not really,' he replied, 'but my brother is a Christian.'

When the driver learned that I was the creator of 'The Trumpet Call', he swung the vehicle over to the side of the road and we talked for an hour. This led to a series of meetings in clubs, bars, and halls where many people followed us round asking to know more about God.

In one city we held an open air meeting that lasted for three hours and was attended by hundreds of people.

In one town, about six people from the KGB joined a group of young people who had come to listen to me and I was able to share my views about Gorbachev. I said that he was a special man brought by God on to the stage of history. I drew attention to the birthmark on his forehead and explained prophecies from the Bible about the Kremlin, Lenin and Gorbachev.

In Moldavia, I met many gifted musicians and together we organised a Christian Rock Festival. The KGB tried to stop us and closed all entry roads leading to the park where the event was to be staged.

The festival went ahead and was a phenomenal success, attracting more than a thousand young people, hippies, punk rockers, heavy-metal fans and other dropouts.

About sixty people were arrested and held in custody for a few hours. Many local Christians lived in fear of the KGB, but I exhorted them to be courageous.

This missionary tour was a remarkable odyssey as I criss-crossed the country. My new-found friends would collect money for me and drop me at the airport. In the terminal building, I prayed, *Lord, where should I go next?* Sometimes I had just enough money to buy a ticket on to the next destination.

I returned to Leningrad at the end of that summer. While I had been away, Lennon and the others had kept in contact with the group of young people we called the gypsy church. We were still dogged by the same problem. We had nowhere to meet together to pray and sing.

After witnessing some astonishing open air meetings on my journey, the idea of holding a public meeting in Leningrad was compelling. We found ourselves working at an extra-ordinary moment in Leningrad's history.

The meeting was scheduled for Friday, October 3rd outside the Museum of Atheism, an orange building on the busy Nevsky Prospekt. The museum was formerly Kazansky Cathedral, but now stood desolate, glorified only in its desecration.

I asked our friends from the music group Winter Garden to play, and as a crowd gathered I moved to the front and preached the Gospel, intent on restoring God's Spirit within the Museum of Atheism.

The meeting was so successful that we returned the following night, assisted by active Christians from several different churches.

The open air meetings continued whenever possible until the inevitable happened. I was arrested, held overnight, and fined fifty roubles. Some people questioned the wisdom of these open air meetings and were dismayed by the fine. But I argued, 'We must force glasnost to its limits to prove that it works. Anyway, I'm happy to pay the fine,' I said, addressing the issue directly. 'It's only fifty roubles. If we hired a hall for meetings, it would cost us three hundred roubles. Brothers, it's cheaper this way!'

Lennon and I still visited Café Saigon. Whenever we announced a meeting, the place was packed out. Teenagers with mohican haircuts, leather jackets and torn jeans told us they were hooked on drugs and homemade booze. Girls with pink eyebrows no older than seventeen who sold sex in the doorways and the back seats of cars told us they wanted to slam the door on the past. Boys with homemade switchblades told terrifying tales of crime and violence as they asked if Jesus could really change their lives.

'We're bored. We've got nothing to live for. We have no hope.' This plea was heard wherever we went. The message was simple. If you trust Jesus, he will radically transform your life.

Flick-knives were tossed to the front and drugs flushed down the toilet as conviction swept the group.

Lennon emerged as a gifted leader with pastoral insight who was trusted by everyone; he supported the decision that had been taken regarding our departure, as did all the others.

Although I believed that God was directing our family to leave Leningrad, I couldn't understand what this would really mean.

Leaving Leningrad!

Leaving my hometown, my friends, the gypsy church and the ministry that God had given me among Leningrad's street people. I wasn't leaving for a holiday in the West. I knew that the spiritual warfare might be more intense but I had to obey

God. Several prophecies had confirmed this dramatic move leading us away. It was clear that I could help our people more by leaving. Now the moment had come to act on the conviction that God had placed in our hearts.

26

Rainbow's Edge

When Tanya's Mama died, the final block to us leaving Leningrad was lifted.

Zhanna and Marina did not want their teenage romances to be broken up, but they acknowledged that their first allegiance was to Jesus.

But the saddest farewell was reserved for Panthera, who would be unable to travel to the West with us. She had become part of our lives, and the house seemed empty without her.

The night before we left Leningrad, I preached my last message. Coincidently, our meeting was arranged soon after the annual celebrations of the Communist Revolution. 'We in Leningrad have been celebrating seventy years of the Soviet system, but we are about to see the end of the godless empire.' It was an emotional time as we celebrated communion and baptised several young people who had come to faith in Christ. 'I'm not leaving you behind,' I explained, 'but I'll be able to serve you best by continuing our work in the West.'

The authorities played a cat-and-mouse game until the end. Although a political decision taken in Moscow had granted us permission to leave, we were hassled everywhere. We were prevented till the last moment from collecting airline tickets to London that had been provided by friends from the British Campaign group.

The airport was crowded with friends, who gave us a raucous send-off with songs and prayers. It seemed that all of Leningrad had turned out to say one last good-bye.

Sergei Timokhin was there, and clasped my hand tight. George, my childhood friend, threw his arms around my neck. 'Send me your address! I'll try to visit you,' he said impetuously. My cousin Slavik embraced me. 'For Holy Russia!' he said emotionally, and kissed me on both cheeks.

Valya stepped forward and clutched me tightly. I could hardly believe that once we were like tramps on the street with nowhere to run.

Her eyes were wet as we embraced one last time. 'I'll never forget,' she whispered amidst the tears.

'Neither will I,' I said and kissed her tenderly.

I had already said good-bye to Aunt Tamara, who was unable to make the journey to the airport.

Someone grabbed me from behind and tossed me like a ball in the air. The KGB men with their cameras clicked away, documenting our parting scenes for the KGB files.

It was hard saying good-bye to Lennon and the others. 'I'll never forget our gypsy church,' I said. 'You'll always be on my mind, but the world must be our mission field.'

'Don't worry, Valeri, we'll continue your work,' he assured me.

The final farewell was an emotional reunion with many whose lives we had touched in passing.

Zhanna and Marina had their own friends who lined up to say good-bye. Leaving Leningrad was a traumatic experience for Tanya, who feared the uncertainty of the West.

I couldn't believe that this moment had come. The sea of smiling faces seemed like a movie's final scene.

It had been snowing, and we stepped from the airport bus

on to a carpet of white to reach the silver jet parked on the runway.

In my mind's eye, I saw a bald haggard man sitting in a prison cell, who prophesied that I would leave for the West when snow was on the ground. 'Praise you, my Jesus!' I said aloud, as the cold night wind cut through me like a knife.

I looked up at the plane, shining in the night, illuminated by a lone spotlight from the tower. The British Airways sign reassured me. I was pleased that our flight out of Russia was not to be on an infamous Aeroflot aircraft. 'One of God's little jokes,' I whispered to Tanya.

Inside the plane, I peered through the cabin window. Down below us, a worker with a giant shovel swept the snow away from the enormous wheels of the plane.

He paused for a moment to peer up at the aircraft and then went back to his task on the ground.

But in that fleeting instant, I saw the faces of our poor Russian people reflected in his haunted image. I had seen that look all across our land. Everyone looked as if they had lost something, as though they needed something.

'Good-bye, my friend, God bless you!' I whispered as the labourer slipped from view.

Good-bye my poor Russian people. Good-bye KGB, perhaps one day you will understand how Jesus led me away and helped me cross the red barbed-wire.

As we were lifted into the night sky above Leningrad I reflected on the extraordinary events that had led to this precious moment.

Beside me, Tanya held my hand tight.

My heart felt heavy as I sensed the spiritual oppression that had fallen like a shadow across the land. God's special gift to man was the river of life, but the godless Soviet system stood against this stream by stealing God from our people. These bandits spread communism like poison all over the world. Those who tried to reveal the truth were hunted down like

411

animals. How could people be so blind as to believe these lies?

But even the KGB couldn't chain the hearts of the Russian people.

A young stewardess welcomed us on board and asked if we wanted a drink. 'You can have wine or cognac. Anything you like,' she said in a foreign accent.

'How much is it?' I asked. I only had a few kopeks in my pocket, as we had spent our money on gifts for friends in Britain.

'No, no, the drinks are free,' the British Airways stewardess replied with a smile straight out of charm school.

'Free? Why?' I asked, perplexed. She explained that the aircraft's cooling system had developed a problem and the captain had ordered free drinks for everyone to compensate for the discomfort that some passengers might experience.

Immediately, I understood that we had reached freedom. This would never happen inside the Soviet Union.

Tanya requested a glass of wine, and I ordered cognac. Together we raised our glasses and toasted our new life in freedom.

The British Airways 707 soared through the sky. But for me, time had stopped.

I found myself praying for the KGB, for Katchkin, my investigator, and Starkov in the KGB headquarters in Leningrad, Captain Zhora, Lobanov and Zinchenko in the labour camp.

They tried to kill me, but I escaped. Adrift in a labyrinth of prisons, labour camps and psychiatric hospitals, a virtual kingdom of evil, I became a prisoner of Jesus. Captured by his love, I could never be free of my bonds. My guards were the captives, imprisoned and chained by the lies and deception that had come to rule over them.

The labour camp was like a small country on some remote

island. A town without law and order, an island drifting off the coast of hell.

I hadn't known if I would ever return alive from the camp. I had seen many broken bodies adrift in anonymous space.

But I dared to live, to resist the terror that I had witnessed. Yet some things I wanted to forget. To shut my eyes and banish the image from my mind. But like a demon in the night, the darkness of the netherworld was lit by a flare out of hell. I was condemned never to forget.

Tanya's frozen smile, fading in the distance, growing dim and faint, like some old sepia photograph. The train pulling out of a station, figures huddled on the platform. Hands waving, and then a blur.

Zhanna and Marina, my babes in arms, who grew tall and beautiful while I was sewing nets and pulling lice and bugs and fleas from my body.

The pain of separation between a man and his family, the wound that cuts the deepest. Memories became the gifts I cherished. Standing alone, naked, I hid them deep in my heart.

But many others shared my experiences. Vladimir Bukovsky, who trod the treacherous path before me, estimated that almost a third of the Soviet population has passed through the camps. Bukovsky built a castle inside his cell, every detail, from the foundations, floors, walls, staircases, secret passages right up to the pointed roofs and turrets. Sharansky also withstood every assault and remained a tower of strength.

For me there was no doubt that the power of Jesus kept me alive.

Like a bullet blazing out of the midnight sky, the silver bird circled London's Heathrow airport. The lights of the city twinkled below us, a trillion glittering stars in a dazzling cavalcade of shining streets and neon boulevards.

Beside me, Tanya's grip on my hand tightened. I gave her a little squeeze. Zhanna and Marina leaned over the back of their seats. 'Daddy, Daddy, we've arrived,' they squealed excitedly.

'Ladies and gentlemen, we are approaching London's Heathrow Airport,' a friendly voice announced. 'Please extinguish your cigarettes and fasten your safety belts.'

My heart seemed to reach bursting point, overflowing with a profound sacrifice of praise.

I didn't know what would happen in the next few days. What did the future hold?

Only one thing mattered as we took our first few steps in freedom.

My Jesus!

Postscript

In 1989 the Barinov family moved to Bognor Regis, West Sussex and are members of a local parish Church. In 1990, Zhanna married her Russian boyfriend, Maxim, in Chichester.

Valeri has plans to record new albums and is preparing for an international 'Jesus March' which includes a visit to the Soviet Union.

Jubilee Campaign worked for Valeri's release, and also worked with the Women's Campaign for Soviet Jewry to free Alex Zelichenok who is now in Israel.

If you would like to help others like Valeri Barinov and Alex Zelichenok, please write to: Jubilee Campaign, P.O. Box 80, Cobham, Surrey KT11 2BQ.

Born Again

Charles Colson

To my Dad – whose ideals for my life I have tried, not always successfully, to fulfil – and whose strength and support is with me today.

To Patty – the gentle spirit who comforts me when I fail, keeps me humble in success, giving of herself always – in love.

The butterfly is nature's most visible illustration of rebirth. Once drab and earthbound as a caterpillar, the butterfly emerges from its cocoon in beautifully radiant colours, soaring upward into the sky. Free — BORN AGAIN — just as each of us can be when we are, through Christ, born again in the Spirit.

Contents

Foreword to the 1995 Edition

In the summer of 1974 I sat in a tiny prison cell watching a small, black and white television set as the President of the United States, whom I had served faithfully for three and a half years, resigned his office. It was one of the most desolate experiences of my life.

In one sense I had lost everything – power, prestige, success, money, the prosperous law firm that I had founded – but in another sense I had found everything, all that really matters: a personal relationship with the living God. My life had been transformed by Jesus Christ.

In the dark and dreary confines of that prison, I began to scribble notes, trying to describe the dramatic change in my life and what it meant to go from the White House, the most powerful office in the world, to prison. I had all kinds of lucrative offers to write political memoirs, but instead I felt compelled to tell people the simple story of what God had done in my life.

So I began to scratch out on a yellow pad the story which later became *Born Again*. I had no idea that there was even such a thing as a Christian publishing industry. All I knew was that I had a story I must tell, a story that might bring hope and encouragement to others.

Little did I dream that the book *Born Again* would become an international bestseller with millions of copies in print, or that tens of thousands of people around the world – from prisoners who sat in dark cells, to prime ministers and princes who sat in palaces – would read it and have their lives transformed by the power of God. Through the late seventies I received thousands of letters from people who had come from the darkness into the light, who had discovered a new life as a result of this book.

I rejoice that Hodder and Stoughton has elected to reissue *Born Again*. It is in one sense an old story of American politics in the most convulsive era in America's history – the Watergate scandal. In fact it is a much older story than that, one that has echoed through the centuries. It is a story of truth, hope, and the wonderful Good News of Jesus Christ's power to change a human life.

It is the Good News I hope you will encounter in the pages that follow.

Charles W. Colson

Before We Begin . . .

The origins of this book go back to a sultry late-summer day in 1974. President Nixon had only recently resigned; the government was in disarray and the country, exhausted by the convulsions of Watergate, was in numbed shock. I was languishing in an Alabama prison, a casualty of the greatest political upheaval in American history.

My own spirit was crying out in agony. How could all this have happened? My mind wandered back over two decades from the days when I was a crew-cut Marine lieutenant to the years when I sat in the Oval Office at the side of the President of the United States. I had served all the time with a burning idealism about my country.

How could we who had the trust of the nation have strayed so far afield? There must be lessons for my life – for others – for an anguished nation. What was the redemptive answer?

Around me in the dreary confines of that prison were hundreds of men trapped as much by the circumstances of their own lives as by their captors' chains. On their sorrowful, forlorn faces were written countless tales of human tragedy. I reflected back on the men with whom I served – Haldeman, Ehrlichman, Mitchell, Nixon. They had been trapped as well

– by their own pretensions of power, victims of their own human frailties.

As I kept probing for the deeper meaning of what had happened to me and to so many others, I began writing – pages of copy evaluating the men and events, forming conclusions, groping for corrective ideas. My focus was on institutions and the words as I reread them day after day seemed heavy, ponderous, and wide of the mark.

Prayer was still new to me. In my own inadequacy I sought God's help. First of all, was I supposed to write a book? There were offers – one very attractive – to write about the Nixon years. But the more I prayed and searched, the more my thoughts centred about my own experiences. What had I discovered in my own life?

Then answers were supplied in unexpected ways. As I wrote letters to my new Christian friends in Washington, I tried to tell them how real God was to some of us in prison. Somehow the Lord helped me make the words in my letters come alive. Convictions deepened. Yes, I was to write a book – but only if I sought His guidance as I wrote.

What form was it to take? Again I prayed for help. Again the answer came through events. As I recorded more of my prison experiences in letters to my friends, I felt God's hand on my shoulder. 'Put aside all their theories for now,' I seemed to hear. 'Tell the story of one life – yours.'

But who was I to moralise, to preach to others? I'd botched it, was one of those who helped bring on Watergate and was in prison to prove it. Yet maybe that very fact, plus some unusual things which had happened to me, could give me some insights that would help others. Could there be a purpose to all that had happened to me?

And then I began to see it. The nation was in darkness; there was anger, bitterness, and disillusionment across the land. While my inclination was to think in terms of grandiose reforms, God seemed to be saying that the renewal of our national spirit can begin with each person – with the renewal of individual spirit. *If you want to do something, submit yourself to Me and I will guide you* were the words implanted on my mind.

Submit yourself. Our founding fathers had built a nation on this principle, that fallible men are nothing unless they learn to depend upon God. It was to establish a true community of believers that the Puritans came to this continent. Somewhere at sea, aboard the *Arbella,* John Winthrop articulated the vision: 'The God of Israel is among us . . . we shall be as a city upon a hill.' They saw their destiny, not as political conquerors but as disciples of Jesus Christ.

'With a firm reliance on the protection of Divine Providence . . .' are the solemn words of the Declaration of Independence. And our greatest President – Abraham Lincoln – humbly acknowledged that without God, 'I must fail.'

How magnificently has God honoured the covenant of our forefathers. How richly has He blessed our nation. So deep are our religious roots, but so far have we strayed.

As I wrote, it became clear to me that Watergate could work a healthy cleansing in the nation if it is understood for what it truly is. Were Mr Nixon and his men more evil than any of their predecessors? That they brought the nation Watergate is a *truth*. But is it not only part of a larger *truth* – that all men have the capacity for both good and evil, and the darker side of man's nature can always prevail in any human being? If people believe that just because one bunch of rascals are run out of office all the ills which have beset a nation are over, then the real lesson of this ugly time will have been missed – and that delusion could be the greatest tragedy of all.

Watergate has raised so many questions. Can humanism ever be the answer for our society? There is an almost sanctified notion that man can do anything if he puts his will to it. This was once my credo. Having seen through Watergate how vulnerable man can be, I no longer believe I am master of my destiny. I need God; I need friends with whom I can honestly share my failures and feelings of inadequacy.

It was in this framework that I wrote this book: an inexperienced writer and a baby Christian, but in submission to the Almighty, praying that others might find hope and encouragement from my experiences. Out of prayer has come the help needed from experienced editors and publishing specialists.

From prayers answered by events came the title, which may amuse those who believe that *Born Again* is an overworked Protestant cliché. While accompanying my wife at her Roman Catholic church one Sunday, Patty flipped open the hymnal, smiled and nudged me. We both knew at that moment that after long weeks of searching and rejecting hundreds of ideas, the title was on that page; the hymn was 'Born Again.'

For me it is anything but a cliché suggesting that someone has arrived at some state of spiritual superiority; it means only a fresh start at putting my life in order – but it had come with the renewing of my spirit.

I have prayed especially for honesty in my writing, knowing only too well that my basic nature would want to present myself in the most favourable light. As I have fallen down, picked myself up, and fallen down again during the past few years, I am learning how God can break us in order to remake us. And through my dependence on Him has come a surprising sense of freedom – and an exhilaration in my spirit.

I have been given a tremendous eagerness to share all this with others. As you travel with me through these pages, my hope is that you will ask for God's hand on your life. And my most sincere and humble prayer now in this time of judgement is for a revival of the flagging national spirit. It can come in only one way – as each of us bows in submission to Him and as the Almighty leads us from darkness into light – so that once again we might stand together, truly one nation under God.

Charles W. Colson

1

Something Wrong

I stood there with my wife, Patty, and son Wendell, puzzled. This night – election night, 1972 – should have been the proudest of my life. Certainly a Victory Party was called for – the landslide re-election of Richard Nixon to the Presidency of the United States.

Nothing was amiss about the setting. The high-ceilinged ornate ballroom of Washington's Shoreham Hotel was packed with distinguished grey-suited men, elegant ladies in rich furs. Yet the picture was out of focus. Something wrong.

I stood there thinking that, unlike any celebration I had attended in twenty years in politics, there was no air of triumph here. The faces before us were unsmiling, looking, in fact, disappointed and even imposed upon. Around the big boards where the continuing returns were posting record-breaking margins for Nixon, there was scarcely a ripple of excitement.

My mind went back to the comparable scene four years before at the Waldorf in New York. What a contrast! That 1968 Victory Party had been alive, high drama indeed. I recalled the scene so vividly – the Waldorf ballroom jammed with eager young people who had worked so hard for months to oust the Democrats. All that long night as the brass ring neared their grasp, the excitement mounted until the sweet smell of victory filled the air. As the vote count on the big boards edged up, precinct by precinct, how they *oohed* and sighed and laughed and slapped one another on the back and roared their approval.

But tonight?

Patty turned to me. 'What's wrong, Chuck? You're so quiet.'

'I don't *know* what's wrong. Just exhausted, I guess.' With a nod and a gesture I indicated the throng pushing and shoving four deep around the bar. 'The only thing these people seem to care about is the free booze.'

'Let's walk around,' Wendell suggested. 'See what people are saying.' In only two weeks as a campaign volunteer, Wendell had learned a lot. Now he sought further insights to take back to his political-science course at Princeton.

And I wanted insights, too.

In the VIP area the comments were griping ones . . . Where was Nixon? Shouldn't their $25,000 contributions entitle them to at least a handshake on election night? Then we were cornered by Senator Bob Dole, the Republican national chairman. Angrily he jabbed his finger at me: 'The President didn't even mention the Committee in his speech.'

After that a group of dour-faced party hangers-on surrounded us. 'I want to see you about my job,' one old stalwart said unsmilingly as he clutched my arm. None of the other senior White House staffers were there, and in minutes I was being swamped with requests.

No, I wasn't imagining the sour mood. But something was also wrong in me. My insides were as deadened as the air in the room and the slow beat of the music. My lack of exhilaration made no sense. Being part of electing a President was the fondest ambition of my life. For three long years I had committed everything I had, every ounce of energy to Richard Nixon's cause. Nothing else had mattered. We had had no time together as a family, no social life, no vacations. So why could my tongue not taste the flavour of this hour of conquest?

430

Just then my little beeper, the radio receiver which I snapped to my belt whenever I was out of telephone reach, went off. There was a shrill whistle. Then as I lifted the gadget to my ear, came the command, 'Colson, Colson, report to the White House operator.'

It was the President. He wanted me at once in his office, the operator said when I called in. A limousine sped Patty, Wendell, and me through the darkness, past nearly deserted Rock Creek Park, to downtown Washington, and at last through the iron gates to the White House grounds.

A blue-suited officer, his braid glittering in the glow of floodlights, snapped a salute and told me that Mr Nixon was in his 'working' office in the Executive Office Building, called the E.O.B. Nixon used the traditional Oval Office in the west wing of the White House chiefly for formal meetings, preferring to work in the quiet intimacy of the denlike office in the E.O.B. across the alleyway. This mammoth grey Victorian structure bristling with gingerbread, arches, and turrets had once held the entire State and War Departments, but now housed only the White House staff.

When we got there we found one lone Secret Service agent in the marble-floored hallway. He waved us in and watched while I deposited Patty and Wendell in my office next to the President's. 'I'll only be a few minutes,' I told them. 'Then we'll go home to bed.'

Back in the darkened hall, the Secret Service agent spoke softly: 'He's waiting for you, Mr Colson.' I swung open the ten-foot-high door to find Richard Nixon reclining in his favourite easy chair, smiling and puffing contentedly on his pipe. The President was wearing the light-blue checked sport jacket he always slipped on when in the privacy of his office and I blinked a little at the eye-blurring combination of blue checks with the dark-blue pinstripe of his trousers.

A few feet away Bob Haldeman, Nixon's chief of staff, was sitting at a small antique table poring over election returns.

His back was to the door and he never looked up as I walked in.

The President greeted me with a big grin and, 'Good job, boy, good job.' Haldeman still did not look up.

'Sit down, Chuck, and have a drink with me,' he said. The President rang for Manola, his Cuban valet, who scurried in with two Scotch and sodas.

Haldeman never drank, and I imagined Nixon had been anxiously awaiting my arrival. 'Here's to you, Chuck. Those are your votes that are pouring in, the Catholics, the union members, the blue-collars, *your votes*, boy. It was your strategy and it's a landslide!' Nixon lifted his glass to me and then gulped almost half its contents in one swallow.

'The way the votes are piling up, you are going to top 61 per cent, Mr President. That's a record,' I said and then reminded him of a modest bet we'd made the day before.

Haldeman was still busy totalling up numbers, once snatching the phone beside him to berate his young assistant, Larry Higby, for not providing the latest figures. Watching Bob's scowling face, I saw a replay of the faces at the Shoreham. From Bob's attitude, I could have thought we were losing the election.

'Bob and I were just talking before you came in, Chuck,' the President rambled on. 'It was ten years almost to the day that they wrote us off. We were 'dead' in California, finished, all through. Look at us now – on top – biggest vote ever,' he chortled. 'I guess we showed 'em! Right?' He smacked a fist into his outstretched palm.

Nixon drank again, emptying his glass, then went into the large lavatory off the far side of the room. I turned to the grim-lipped Haldeman. 'What's eating you?'

Bob's eyes, blue and steely cold, darted up from his papers, meeting mine for the first time, a deep frown on his forehead. His short crew cut seemed to bristle, too. 'I'm trying to add the actual figures – don't be giving him your guesses,' he snapped.

Haldeman, I assumed, was tired. Perhaps he was also resenting the fact that I was sharing this moment of victory with the President. Of course there were always petty jealousies in the White House.

'What's wrong, Chuck? Why aren't you celebrating?' Nixon asked, returning to his chair.

'I guess I'm a bit numb, sir.'

'This is a night to remember. Have another drink. Let's enjoy this.' I had always followed Nixon's orders, but you can't order somebody to be happy.

The President then began composing one draft after another of a telegram to send to his vanquished opponent, Senator George McGovern. It was now close to two in the morning. McGovern had conceded hours earlier. By the rules of the game Nixon's response was long overdue. Yet as fast as the words rolled off his tongue, he would reject them. 'How can I say something nice after he kept comparing me to Hitler?'

Haldeman handed him a draft written by another aide. Nixon scanned it. 'No, I won't say that.' He flung the sheet of paper across the little table between Haldeman and myself.

That he could show no charity in this hour of his greatest triumph dramatised the paradox of Richard Nixon. In 1960 evidence suggested that the cliff-hanger had been stolen from him. 'Demand a recount,' his aides urged. But Nixon had refused: it would create uncertainty, be bad for the country, and it was his job to help unite the electorate behind the man who defeated him. Noble in defeat, he was now without grace in victory.

Time and again I had seen the President show rare courage when others around him shrank in fear. For this he had won my deepest admiration. Since I had come to respect the President for what he was in his best moments, I learned to accept him for what he was in his worst. I suppose loyalty, like love, creates its own image of what we see.

If someone had peered in on us that night from some

imaginary peephole in the ceiling of the President's office, what a curious sight it would have been: a victorious President, grumbling over words he would grudgingly say to his fallen foe; his chief of staff angry, surly, and snarling; and the architect of his political strategy sitting in a numbed stupor. Yes, the picture was out of focus. If this was victory, what might these three men have looked like in defeat?

Nixon told Manola to find us something to eat. That meant waking up a couple of the White House stewards. Shortly before 3:00 a.m. they appeared, sleepy-eyed, carrying three plates of fried eggs and ham. I wished that they had brought some food for Patty and Wendell next door, but decided not to trouble the tired stewards further. The President was chattering on about one Senate race after another, on such a reminiscing kick that we could easily be there until dawn. How could I rescue Patty and Wendell?

The answer came in a report from Haldeman's assistant; both the Associated Press and United Press wire services had shut down for the night; there would be no more vote totals until morning. That welcome news plus my drooping eyelids must have convinced the President to call it a night.

As we were leaving, Mr Nixon paused at the top of the long flight of grey cement steps leading to the driveway. Directly in front of us the chalk-white mansion rose up majestically in the darkness. 'Chuck,' he said, 'I just want you to know – I'll always be . . .'

Knowing how hard it always was for him to show emotions, I interrupted. 'Thank you, Mr President. Tomorrow will be a good day.'

With that he turned and started down the steps, with the Secret Service agent in front of him, glancing mechanically from side to side. I stood for a moment, watching the Thirty-seventh President of the United States, now with the greatest mandate in history by which to govern, slowly descending before me. Lights still burning in a few windows cast an orange glow over the green shrubs and velvety lawns. The night air was clear. In the background rose the Washington Monument, tall and proud, a sight which had never ceased to thrill me. But tonight not even this could penetrate the deadness inside me . . .

The shrill sound kept hammering at my eardrums. I pulled the blanket from over my head, rubbed my eyes and stared at the clock – 8:00 a.m. The ringing came from the White House phone beside my bed. I nearly knocked the phone off the nightstand fumbling for the receiver.

'Chuck, sorry, but he wants you in his office right away.' It was Steve Bull, the President's scheduler and office aide-de-camp.

'Come off it, Steve; I've only had four hours of sleep. The election is over, and the top of my head is coming off.'

'Sorry, but the President wants you.'

A few shaving nicks and two cups of coffee later, I was on my way, blurry-eyed, with a throbbing head. When I arrived at the White House, the senior staff was already assembling in the Roosevelt Room for a meeting with the President. *If the President wanted to thank us,* I thought to myself, *why doesn't he do it by letting us sleep late?* He ought to be walking on air; the morning vote totals were confirming our most optimistic projections – a record-breaking 49 states for Nixon, 61 per cent of the total vote.

The assembled staff, most red-eyed like myself, rose to their feet when the President entered, applauding enthusiastically. Nixon smiled and waved for us to be seated. The clapping continued and the chief dropped his eyes for a moment, gripping the back of his chair at the end of the long conference table. Richard Nixon looked fresh, surprisingly rested, in fact. He was precise, crisp, and to the point.

'I believe men exhaust themselves in government without realising it,' he began. Turning to a favourite period in history,

the mid-nineteenth century in England, Nixon recalled that
Disraeli defeated Gladstone immediately after Gladstone's great
work in reforming the British government. Gladstone was 'an
exhausted volcano,' Disraeli had charged. The parallel as Nixon
meant it was clear: We had done well, but were we exhausted
volcanoes with no fire left for the battles ahead?

The President turned to Bob Haldeman, who was glaring
sternly at the rest of the staff. 'Bob will explain the procedures
we've worked out. We need new blood, fresh ideas. Change is
important.'

Why is he doing this? I wondered, as my eyes quickly scanned
the still figures around the table.

'You are my first team,' he continued, 'but today we start
fresh for the next four years. There are great goals to be
achieved for the country and we must not lose a day. Bob, you
take over.' With that, he smiled and headed for the door
leading to the hall. It took a long painful moment for us to
realise the President was through – it had taken exactly twelve
minutes – and the applause, more restrained now, had scarcely
begun when he was gone.

Haldeman was blunt. 'I will expect resignations from every
member of the staff to be delivered to the staff secretary by
noon on Friday, from each of you and each person who works
for you. Also submit memos stating your preferences for new
assignments.' He cleared his throat, paused, and added, 'That
is, of course, the courtesy customarily extended a President at
the start of each new Administration.' He then passed out
envelopes filled with detailed instructions and forms.

His last point did not altogether take the sting out of the
chilling announcement. *Okay, Bob,* I thought, *everyone
appointed by a President serves at his pleasure. But why this, so
soon and so crudely?* I had forbidden my staff any vacations
during the election year, promising them instead a rousing
celebration, good vacations, and help in finding better positions if we won. Now, according to Haldeman, I was to

convene all thirty men and women in my office and inform them they were to look for new jobs.

I told myself that I didn't care. I had already told the President in July that I was leaving his staff after the election to return to my law practice. Even so, I felt surprisingly let down. Perhaps I had thought that the out-of-focus picture of the night before would disappear with the bright morning light. It was a shock to encounter the same sourness in this room.

Men stared at one another in disbelief, dazed by the suddenness of it all. Then the grumbling began, first only murmurs of surprise, soon everyone seemed to be talking at once as anger replaced incredulity. Herb Klein, the long-time loyal press aide who had been with Nixon for twenty-five years, quietly left, his head bowed and the bounce gone from his short quick steps.

Just as the din in the room was reaching a crescendo, Steve Bull summoned me to the President's formal Oval Office. Ill at ease. Mr Nixon explained that I was not in the same category with the others. Before he left that day for Key Biscayne, he said, he wanted to ask me again to reconsider my resignation.

I convened my staff and assured them that notwithstanding the formality of submitting letters of resignation. I would assist each of them in locating the right positions in the new Administration, and told them to take vacations.

But the mood was subdued. The victory that had come as the result of such long months of gruelling work now seemed tasteless.

I saw Nixon off that afternoon, watching as *Marine One*, the Presidential helicopter, lifted gracefully from the South Lawn. Then I headed back to my office, walking slowly through the west wing. It was always calm when the President was travelling because half the staff went with him. Normally there would be a few secretaries typing, workmen in the halls repairing lights, a few staffers standing around chatting. But this afternoon, there was only one lonely uniformed policeman, standing at the open door of the Oval Office. The emptiness was unreal, the stillness haunting – as if some deadly plague had swept through . . . I could almost hear the muffled drum-roll of distant artillery.

The President had spoken of great goals, and at long last they seemed within reach. For the first time in years, there was stability in the country. The war in Vietnam was nearly over and we had won an overwhelming vote of public confidence. What was it that was now unsettling us, invading our midst, right here at the heart of governmental power?

Bringing the question closer to home, what was spoiling inside of me? Just tired? Or was there something very wrong?

2

'Good Enough'

The afternoon papers headlined the huge Nixon victory and already contained speculation about personnel changes. Briefly I thought about my own decision. Always in the past it was the drive to climb new heights which gave life meaning. But what happened when there were no more mountains to scale? I was only forty-one. Surely there must be other stiff challenges. But what? What could I do next that would ever be as fulfilling as helping elect a President, being one of the small handful of men who each day made decisions that shaped the future of a nation?

Yet I knew I must move on. I was one of those 'exhausted volcanoes' the President spoke about in his strange speech. Back to my law practice? It was the obvious thing to do and right for my family. This way I could replenish the bank account we had drained while living on a government salary. But money – is that any real goal in life?

No, the more I thought about it, the more one word seemed to sum up what was important to me. *Pride*. Richard Nixon's deep sense of pride in his office was the quality which I most admired. In fact, pride was at the heart of the Nixon Presidency in its reach for historical importance and greatness. And pride had been at the heart of my own life, too, as far back as I could remember . . .

It was a sunny day in early June 1949 for graduation ceremonies at Browne and Nichols, a small private school in Cambridge. Rows of wooden chairs were stretched across the football field on the banks of the gently flowing Charles River. A half-mile away were the ivy-covered, Colonial brick buildings of Harvard Yard. Editor of the school newspaper, voted most likely to succeed by my classmates, and an honour student, I was elected to give the valedictory for the graduating class. Seated behind me on a raised wooden platform were my forty classmates, over half of them ready to take their places in the fall as Harvard freshmen.

Pride was the keynote of my speech. 'We are proud, very proud, of the lessons we have learned in democracy – of the school – of our class.' As I looked out over the rows of distinguished Bostonians, there were no faces in the crowd more filled with pride than those of my mother and dad, who had sacrificed to send me to school beyond our means or status.

My parents' example moulded my early life. Dad had to drop out of high school before earning a diploma, in order to support his mother and sister after his father died in the influenza epidemic which followed World War 1. He married my mother, then spent twelve years in night school, first accounting, then law, all the while holding down a thirty-two-dollar-a-week job as a bookkeeper in a meat-packing plant. How impressed I'd been at age eight, sitting in the crowded auditorium watching my father in black cap and gown, graduating from Northeastern Law School.

When Dad wasn't studying, maybe late on a Sunday afternoon, we would talk. 'Work hard, study hard; nothing comes easy in this life,' he used to say. 'There are no short-cuts. No matter how menial the job you have, the important thing is to do it well.' It was the Puritan-inspired work ethic. And then he would always add: 'Tell the truth – always – lies destroy you.' I'd tried to follow that and always did with him.

Our home was a walk-up rented apartment in an old Victorian house in Winthrop, a small middle-class town on a jetty of land north across the harbour from Boston. By depression standards, we lived fairly well; my mother saw to that, always spending slightly more than my dad earned. Moderately comfortable, we were also moderately in debt. When bills mounted too high, Mother would hold sales of our furniture and other possessions. I remember the shock of coming home from school one day, seeing perfect strangers carrying chairs out of our living room. Being in debt, being unsure where next month's rent would come from, created an insecurity which, combined with my father's exhortations, doubtless fuelled my later drive to achieve.

With his law degree my dad shot ahead in business, but his success was soon curtailed by poor health. He was forced to quit his job with General Foods, the company which had acquired the meat-packing plant he once worked in. By the time of my graduation, Dad was struggling to make it as a lawyer practising on his own in a city whose legal fraternity, like most of its institutions, was tightly controlled by Harvard men. Only by a stroke of good fortune was my father able to land a small case in the spring of 1949 that enabled him to pay my last tuition instalment at Browne and Nichols. Without it I would not have graduated.

Though so bursting with pride on that day in June that I was straining the seams of my new blue double-breasted suit, I was also filled with uncertainty over how I would possibly meet the tuition payments in college. Every summer since I was eleven I had worked to help with school expenses. But college would be exactly double prep-school costs. I took the highest-paying job I could find that summer as a messenger for a Boston brokerage firm and anxiously awaited the results of scholarship applications I had filed at Harvard and Brown.

Brown was the first I heard from – a notification that I had been accepted for a full Navy ROTC scholarship, plus fifty dollars a month for living expenses. Then in early June I was invited for an interview with the dean of admissions at Harvard.

Promptly at the appointed hour I was ushered into a handsome corner office in the two-hundred-year-old administration building looking out over the quiet Harvard Yard on one side and bustling Harvard Square on the other. The office had a slightly musty smell, the patina of fine antique brass, glowing random-width floorboards. An elegant old Colonial desk sat between sagging bookshelves filled with memorabilia of Harvard. The dean, perfectly cast for his role, wore a baggy tweed coat, with wiry grey hair close cropped and the unmistakable air of fine breeding essential for Harvard men of those years.

'I am very happy to inform you, Mr Colson – you are a fortunate young man – that the Board of Overseers has granted you a full scholarship to Harvard University.' He paused a moment for me to express my elation.

I felt it, all right, but I was aware of a second reaction deep inside me: resentment built up over the years to the superior attitude of the whole Harvard academic establishment, the condescension of aristocratic men to those who came out of less fortunate backgrounds. I thanked him politely and waited.

There was a pause as he lighted his pipe and took a long puff. 'Well, I assume you have a lot of questions, the house you will live in, and of course your academic schedule,' he said.

'But I haven't really decided, Dean, whether I will be coming to Harvard,' I said.

He stared at me for a moment, openly nettled. 'I can't imagine anyone turning down a scholarship to Harvard,' he said.

Pride. As a boy I used to stand on the pebbly beach looking across the grey-green waters of the harbour at the city then run by the Brahmins, the Beacon Hill establishment which traced its ancestry through generations of Harvard classes back to the *Mayflower*. We were neither the new ethnics – Italians, Irish Catholics just seizing political power in the wards of Boston – nor old stock. 'Swamp Yankees,' we were called. Acceptance was what we were denied – and what we most fervently sought. Now in this one moment, I had it – admission to the elite. And in my pride I believed I had something better still – the chance to turn them down. It was warped pride, no doubt, but the resentment against Eastern intellectualism stayed with me and shaped some of the tumultuous events of my later life.

And so that September, with twenty dollars in the pocket of my blue graduation suit. I headed for Brown University in Providence, Rhode Island, which Harvard men looked upon as a poor Ivy League cousin.

Pride – mixed with a deep-seated patriotism I'd felt since a small boy – was also the reason for my joining the Marines. With the Korean War at its height during my sophomore year at Brown, and the Marines needing volunteers, a strong recruiting pitch was made on our campus. A senior in my fraternity whom I greatly admired, also in the NROTC, Bill Maloney, had decided to take his commission in the Marine Corps. Bill talked about the Marine Corps with such pride and feeling that a week later I found myself standing before the desk of a Marine recruiting officer, a tall arched-backed first lieutenant named Cosgrove.

'Midshipman Colson, sir,' I said. 'I'd like to inquire about the Marine Corps.'

Cosgrove, a Naval Academy graduate, frowned, looked me up and down, and snapped, 'You are a bit premature, Colson. First, we will have to see whether you are *good enough* for the Marine Corps.'

I stood before his desk speechless for a long moment. What did he mean – 'good enough'? I ranked high in my class in all military attributes. For the next two months I smarted over

Cosgrove's putdown. One day a week NROTC students wore uniforms to class and afternoon drill sessions. From then on, the night before I spit-shined my shoes, polished my uniform brass, studied every detail of the next day's drill. I began to try to walk like Cosgrove, back straight, chin in. At every drill session I noticed Cosgrove watching me.

Finally, one day in the spring, I found a typed notice on the bulletin board: 'Midshipman Colson, report to Lt Cosgrove.' My heart fluttered for a moment; I never had really decided I wanted the Marine Corps; I just wanted to be 'good enough'.

When I stood stiffly at attention in front of Cosgrove's desk, he leaned back in an old wooden swivel chair, twirling his pencil in front of him. Finally he sat upright and scowling fiercely said, 'Colson, we think you're good enough.'

Before he could continue, I interrupted with – 'Where do I sign up, sir?' I later discovered that the Marine Corps was under its allowed quota and needed recruits badly.

How different the world around me looked from inside the suit of Marine green, with the globe and anchor on my cap. As a young platoon commander, I was assigned to the division led by General 'Chesty' Puller, the salty old warrior whose heroic exploits made him the only man in history to earn five Navy Crosses. The gruff-talking Puller was a Marine's Marine; though he led men to die, they loved him. Like thousands of my comrades I would have walked off a cliff if he so ordered me and, in fact, one day almost did.

On one training exercise in the Caribbean (the Korean War having ended) my platoon was landed on a small stretch of beach on the mountainous island of Vieques. There were two routes to our assigned objective: one around a long circuitous path over relatively flat terrain, the other straight up a craggy cliff rising sixty feet in the air. The order came: 'Up the cliff.'

For a few moments I couldn't believe it. It was only a training exercise and as I stared at the menacing volcanic ash, I thought it was not only foolhardy but impossible. *Someone, maybe me, would get killed. But Marines can do anything,* I reminded myself, and then led my forty-five men up and over the cliff, clawing every inch of our way with picks, ropes, and bare hands. When we got to the top I looked back at the beach below, the sea beyond, and in that instant realised that Puller was right; when a man throws everything into it, he can do the impossible.

It was that same summer of 1954 when orders came to me at Camp Lejeune: 'Report at once with seabag, an emergency.' Within hours my battalion was loaded aboard an old World War II 'rust bucket,' the USS *Mellette.* With several tons of ammunition in the hold beneath us, we headed for Guatemala, then in the midst of a Communist uprising. Our overt mission was to protect American lives. Off the rocky coast of the tiny Latin American republic, live ammunition was handed out to the troops while I and other platoon leaders were briefed on landing plans. Final orders were to come from Washington.

The sea that night was like glass, the air heavy and hot. As I stood on deck everything was blackness except for the red and green running lights of other ships in our task force and the thousands of stars flickering in the sky. I'd never seen so many stars, a shower spray of tiny pinpoints of light, like a Fourth of July sparkler.

It was almost midnight and I was fearful about what might lie ahead, how I would handle myself, realizing that I was responsible for the lives of forty-five men. I felt suddenly insignificant staring out into the universe, knowing that I was but a tiny dot standing on a slightly larger dot, floating on a sea that was huge and endless to me, but was only another dot compared to the vastness around me. *Where does it all end?* I wondered.

My parents had taken me to an Episcopal Sunday school and church as a boy, but it had never made much impression on me. That night I suddenly became as certain as I had ever been about anything in my life that out there in that great starlit beyond was God. I was convinced that He ruled over the universe, that to Him there were no mysteries, that – He somehow kept it all miraculously in order. In my own fumbling way I prayed, knowing that He was there, questioning only whether He had time to hear me.

Later that night the emergency was cancelled: the pro-US regime in Guatemala beat back the Communists without our help, though we stayed for six weeks just to be sure. And my awareness of God faded as personal interests crowded my life.

Feeling I had proved myself in the Marines, eager for new challenges, I resigned and switched my commission to the Reserves. Law school beckoned. Also politics. A job in a much-heralded management intern programme in the Navy Department in Washington enabled me to work days and go to law school at night at George Washington University.

The first year in Washington I met the senior senator from Massachusetts, a grand old patrician gentleman, Leverett Saltonstall, who offered me a job in his office and two years later, despite my youth and inexperience, named me his chief assistant.

Saltonstall was a towering and respected figure in the Senate but he'd neglected his political fences back home in a state whose politics were changing fast as the Italians and Irish displaced the Old Guard. John F. Kennedy, the junior senator, was the rising star and leading candidate for the Democratic Presidential nomination.

Since 1948, when I became a volunteer worker in the losing effort of Massachusetts Governor Bradford, I had been getting an education in practical politics, Boston-style. I learned all the tricks, some of which went up to and even slightly over the legal boundaries. Phoney mailings, tearing down opposition signs, planting misleading stories in the press, voting tomb-stones, and spying out the opposition in every possible way were all standard fare.

As the 1960 elections approached, Saltonstall asked me to

manage his campaign. The polls showed him trailing the popular Democratic governor, Foster Furcolo, the first Italian-American to occupy the executive mansion in the Bay State. It looked like a hopeless uphill struggle, particularly with Kennedy leading the ticket on the other side. So the challenge was appealing.

We encouraged Tom O'Connor, the young, obscure mayor of Springfield, to run as a Democratic primary candidate against Furcolo. He did so well that he upset the governor and to our shock then appeared even more formidable in the polls than Furcolo had been.

We went all out. When your candidate is of the integrity and standing of a Saltonstall, the shrewd campaign manager sees that his man travels the high road and doesn't know what his manager is doing down on the plains of battle. After several bogus mailings, plus inciting a taxpayers' revolt in O'Connor's hometown, we pulled neck and neck.

A late September poll showed that we were gaining among the Irish bloc whose votes held the key to the election. That information dictated a special tactic. I secretly rented a few rooms in a third-rate Boston hotel, installed new locks on the doors, and packed it with young campaign volunteers who began addressing plain envelopes to every Irish-sounding name in the phone book, some three hundred thousand families. Then we inveigled six prominent Irish Democrats to sign a letter endorsing Kennedy (running against Nixon) for President and Saltonstall for the Senate. The two senators, though in opposing parties, had worked together for so many home-state projects that the Saltonstall-Kennedy hyphenation was synonymous with every federal goodie that had come to Massachusetts. The letter was a blatantly provincial appeal to help Saltonstall ride in on the Kennedy vote. Saltonstall knew nothing of the ploy. In his speeches, of course, he continued to back Nixon.

The Friday night before the election I visited the hideaway

hotel rooms. Twenty nearly exhausted volunteers were hand stuffing the mountain of envelopes. At midnight we'd scheduled two station wagons to arrive at the back-alley entrance; the kids would load box after box into the wagons and then drive them to an out-of-the-way post office where a friendly postmaster would process them for us.

There was only one hitch. A Harvard freshman named Tom, in charge of the secret project, asked to see me alone. We stepped out of the room and walked together down the dimly lit corridor. 'Chuck,' he said, 'I'm worried about one of our girls. Her father is an avid party man and she thinks we're being disloyal to Nixon. I overheard her talking about going to Republican headquarters to tell the chairman what's going on here.'

'Oh, no,' I moaned. 'That'll blow us right out of the water. Any publicity and this will boomerang. Nixon hasn't a chance in this state and I've told his people what we're doing. We're trying to save a Republican senator, that's all.'

I stood with my head down staring at the grease-stained carpet, a sick feeling in my stomach. We couldn't let anyone know that Saltonstall's committee was behind the mailing. It had to look independent, a genuine letter from Kennedy supporters. The election could be riding on this one last-minute appeal which our opponent would never have time to rebut.

'Tell you what, Tom,' I looked up into his tired eyes. 'Take this.' I handed him ten crisp ten-dollar bills, all I had in my wallet. 'Take the girl out tonight and get her loaded. Keep her diverted, whatever you have to do until Election Day.'

Tom, a ladies' man, happily followed orders. The letters arrived in three hundred thousand Irish homes across the state the next Monday morning. Saltonstall, securely attached to Kennedy's coat tail, was re-elected handily by that many votes.

Heady over my success in managing the Saltonstall campaign, I spurned the senator's urgings to remain his administrative assistant, a secure, well-paying job for the next six years. I turned down bids to join a number of Boston law firms. Instead, with five thousand dollars representing my accumulated savings, I joined forces with Charles Morin, a brilliant young lawyer I'd met in my political travels and who was soon to become my closest personal friend. Charlie, though Harvard educated, was a Catholic of Canadian and Irish descent, like myself an outsider to the establishment, striving to make it. We opened a Boston-Washington law practice. I manned a two-room Washington office; Morin, a three-room Boston suite.

Fortunately, the clients began to come before the last of the five thousand dollars was gone; by mid-year we had even hired our first lawyer, a bright young man named Joe Mitchell, recommended to us by our close friend, Elliot Richardson, who was then the US Attorney. Joe was exceptionally well qualified and would have been snapped up by any firm but for one small drawback: he was black. Two months after Morin and I hired him and it was obvious he hadn't 'hurt' our business, several law firms in Boston were bidding for him. We not only had gotten a gifted lawyer but had broken the colour line among the Boston Bar as well.

The firm grew fast, but not without anxious moments. Shortly before Christmas of 1962, Charlie and I spent a long evening in our Boston office, shirt sleeves rolled up and the ledger books of our young firm spread out on a rented conference table. Sometime after midnight Morin, anxious furrows across his brow, summed it all up: 'We still owe ten thousand dollars for the furniture, the payroll is up to twenty thousand dollars a month, we are hiring too many people, the big firms are putting the blocks to us, and I don't see enough business to get us through the spring.'

I couldn't argue with a thing Charlie said. We had moved fast, maybe too fast. The next day, flying back to Washington, I found myself staring out of the window of the DC–6 at the snow-covered countryside below. But I wasn't seeing sleepy New England towns, rather blue Caribbean water, an expanse of white beach, and the craggy cliff I had scaled eight years before. The adrenaline started flowing. I began a long hand-written memo to Charlie.

'Next week I will see my friend at Grumman Aircraft. I feel sure he will retain us. With one trip to California, there are two companies . . .' I went on for several pages, listing the new business I knew we could get – if we threw everything into it. Charlie kept the memo for years; we landed every one of those accounts.

Although I refused to admit it, my personal life was suffering from my preoccupation with politics and business. Nancy Billings, a lovely Boston-bred girl, whom I married the day I graduated from college, shunned the excitement I found so fulfilling in the political arena, spending all of her time tending our three young children – Wendell, born in 1954, Christian, born in 1956, and Emily, born in 1958. As the years passed we found less and less in common. Her parents' fine home and social standing, the correct wedding, had been, however sub-consciously, important to me in my eager drive for acceptance; but the insecurity of my college days had long since given way to assurance, the certainty that I was totally self-sufficient. After a few years' separation, divorce came in January 1964.

Later that year I married Patty Hughes, a wholesome and warmhearted girl from Springfield, Vermont, whose radiant smile and winsome ways made her one of the best-liked secretaries on Capitol Hill. Her zest for life and love of politics were like mine. Descended from Irish Catholic immigrants, her religion created our one problem. Patty, a one-time Cherry Blossom Princess with scores of friends, had to forego a formal wedding; we were married in a simple civil service at an Army chapel adjacent to Arlington Cemetery. For a while I studied Catholicism, but my divorce appeared an insurmountable barrier to the blessing of her church and in time I dropped it.

Several years later Patty and I, with no children of our own, filed an application with a Washington adoption agency. The matronly interviewer suspiciously probed every facet of our lives. 'You seem to have a very successful record, Mr Colson. Why do you feel you need more children?'

After some sparring back and forth I realised she was implying that I was too busy for children and that I probably hadn't done a very good job with the first three. I explained how much I loved Wendell, Christian, and Emily, how we spent every minute possible together, but that Patty and I wanted children of our own as well.

'You're very clear about what you want, aren't you? I suppose you don't think you have ever failed in anything in your life,' she said.

'That's right, I haven't,' I replied loftily.

'Don't you think your divorce was a failure?' she pressed on.

The question stung. Deep down I knew I had failed but I couldn't admit it to myself or anyone else. The turndown by the agency could have been a valuable checkpoint for me: a chance to take a hard look at the person I was becoming. But it wasn't. I blamed it on the baby shortage, the pill, and liberalised abortion. The tough exterior coating that I had layered over myself during all the years of driving and succeeding was impenetrable.

I first met Richard Nixon when he was Vice-President during the Eisenhower Administration. My brushes with him over the years impressed me; here was a man of uncommon intellect and capacity, with visions for his country and party which I enthusiastically shared. In the late spring of 1964 the two of us sat alone in his austere corner office on the twenty-fourth floor of Twenty Broad Street in New York City while I tried to persuade Mr Nixon that only he could save the Republican Party from the debacle that would surely follow a Goldwater nomination.

'Okay, go ahead,' he told me. 'Get on the phones and see how many delegates we can count on.'

Though he tried to appear casual about it, his eyes lit up at the thought of the campaign. 'Johnson would have to debate me wouldn't he, Chuck? I mean, after all, I agreed to the debate with Kennedy.' He turned and stared wistfully out of the window at the skyline of his newly adopted city.

Nixon and I understood one another – a young ambitious political kingmaker and an older pretender to the throne. We were both men of the same lower middle-class origins, men who'd known hard work all our lives, prideful men seeking that most elusive goal of all – acceptance and the respect of those who had spurned us in earlier years.

'But it will be tough this year,' Nixon mused. 'The whole establishment is against us. If we don't go this time, well, there will always be . . .' His voice trailed off.

And of course there was no way that year to stop the Goldwater nomination and the subsequent November disaster for the Republicans. But for Richard Nixon and me the dream remained vividly alive.

I was, predictably enough, in the middle of his 1968 campaign, much to the distress of my clients and the law firm from which I took a four months' leave of absence. 'This race is too important to the country. The country needs Nixon right now. I will be back after the election,' I promised my partners, yet knowing in my heart where my deeper interest lay.

At the beginning of the Nixon Administration my old friend, John Volpe, former governor of Massachusetts and now Secretary of Transportation, asked me to take a post in his department. Under Secretary of State Elliot Richardson asked me to become an Assistant Secretary. I hedged. I was waiting for the one call, the one telling me that the *President* needed *me*.

It came in the late fall of 1969 – a call from the White House.

'Right this way, Mr Colson.' A tall ramrod-stiff Navy commander with a gold-braided aiguillette draped around his shoulder, was beckoning me toward what appeared at first to be the white plaster wall of the office occupied by the President's appointment secretary. Then I saw the faint outline of a small door etched in it; a piece of the wall itself, moulding, chair rail and all, forming a private entrance used only by the staff into the President's formal Oval Office.

As I stepped for the first time into the sun-filled, stark-white, curving walled room, my heart was beating so hard I wondered if it could be heard. I walked over a huge blue and gold oval-shaped rug, the Great Seal of the United States colourfully embroidered in its centre, directly beneath a matching white plaster seal moulded in the ceiling. In front of the floor-to-ceiling windows looking out across the South Lawn, the President sat at a large mahogany desk.

He was leaning back in his chair, sun streaming in over his shoulders revealing the first specks of grey in his hair, intently studying the pages of a large brown leather folder propped in his lap. He glanced up, peering over reading glasses I never knew he wore, and flashed a broad, quick grin: 'Sit down, boy. Good to see you again. I'll be with you in a minute.' With that his eyes returned to the brown notebook on which I could read in gold embossed letters: DAILY INTELLIGENCE SUMMARY and below that simply: THE PRESIDENT.

The President. Not the person I'd known for so many years, but *the* President – and in this room constructed during Theodore Roosevelt's Presidency, where so much of the high drama of the twentieth century had been enacted. Just to be in the room was exciting enough, but now I was here alone with *the* President, the single most important man in the world, and here as a member of *his staff.* My life, the whole thirty-eight years of it, was about to be fulfilled.

3

'Break All the — China'

To most of the White House staff, I was suspect from the beginning, Ivy League educated, and from the citadel of liberalism, Boston. To make it worse, I was the original booster of Ed Brooke, the only black then in the Senate. Bob Haldeman's Orange Country California Conservatives therefore regarded me as just another 'Eastern lib.' An early interview with a young reporter from the *Boston Globe* didn't help.

One of the questions asked me was about Attorney General John Mitchell and his southern strategy for selection of Supreme Court Justices. Having had a run-in with Mitchell in the 1968 campaign and some questions about his judgement, I effusively praised Nixon and 'no commented' Mitchell.

The resulting headline was a minor disaster: *Mitchell No Hero: Colson.* For months after the story appeared, the Attorney General would not return my phone calls. No one in those days challenged Mitchell privately, let alone publicly; one word from Mitchell and men were summarily dismissed. Perhaps Mitchell was so taken aback by my brashness, which he didn't know was unintentional, that he failed to call Nixon to have me unceremoniously dumped out onto Pennsylvania Avenue. By the time he did try – a year later in the fall of 1970 – I'd become firmly entrenched. For years afterwards at the mere mention of my name, Mitchell would grunt and puff furiously on his pipe until the bowl glowed red-hot.

On the job I began doing what I'd always done in politics and government – jump into the middle of situations. First the postal reorganisation plan which was pigeonholed in Congress, later a threatened postal strike. The key union man was a friend; we hammered out compromise legislation and I brought him in for an off-the-record chat with Nixon cementing the deal and incidentally planting the first seeds of a new political alliance with labour.

One Friday afternoon early in 1970, Nixon flew into one of his angry tirades against the federal bureaucracy. For a year he had been asking for a simple executive order to create a commission to study ways to help Catholic schools. It was a campaign pledge. Several aides had been stalling on it. Mitchell questioned the constitutionality. The public-education lobby was death on the idea. I had brought in a group of Catholic-school educators to meet Nixon that morning; they told him of their needs and reminded him of his campaign promise. A few hours later I was summoned back to the Oval Office.

'Chuck, I want a commission appointed *now*,' he told me. 'I've been thinking about what those men said this morning. I ordered it a year ago and no one pays any attention. You do it. Break all the — china in this building but have an order for me to sign on my desk Monday morning.'

It was now 5 p.m. Friday. 'I don't know where to start,' I confessed to my secretary, Joan Hall. My staff in those days was just the two of us. John Ehrlichman, Nixon's chief domestic aide, was off skiing that week; Bob Finch, head of the Department of Health, Education, and Welfare, was vacationing in the South. One of Finch's assistants found the file for me; it had been buried under a stack of papers on a mid-level career man's desk.

I called the Department of Justice first; all executive orders are drafted and cleared there. But the assistant whose office handles such things curtly told me the department was closed for the weekend; he could not put anyone to work until Monday. *No wonder,* I thought, *the President explodes in frustration. He probably thinks he's running the government.* I thought about calling Mitchell, but even if he took my call he'd probably refuse to help.

And so on Friday night, digging out some old orders to use as models, I dictated the document to Joan, the beginning of a frantic two days.

The next morning I reached Finch. 'That's the thing the boss has been asking about, isn't it?' he asked, confessing he hadn't been able to locate it for months. When I told him the file was now on my desk, he gave me his approval. Then the White House operator found the budget director, calling him off a golf course. In an exasperated voice, he approved the money. Ehrlichman was on a Colorado slope and didn't return my several calls; his assistant was travelling and also unavailable. A strictly worded White House staff order required that Ehrlichman pass on all domestic matters. But the President had said Monday morning, and so Monday morning I placed the order on his desk.

When Mitchell and Ehrlichman discovered what had happened they were furious. It set off a minor uproar within the staid offices at 1600 Pennsylvania Avenue. Richard Nixon loved it. He had found someone to cut through red tape and 'break china.' Soon I was doing it in other areas, winning a vote for the ABM missile programme by finding a job for a senator's friend, arm twisting, making deals, leaking stories to cut down opponents and promote friends.

It wasn't long before I was very much a part of the workings of the Presidency. Soon after the 'executive order' weekend a black limousine was assigned to me. It was a heady experience to speed through the streets of Washington in my first motorcade, close behind the sleek bulletproof limousine with

Presidential flags flying from small staffs on the front fenders, on our way to the Capitol. On this occasion the chamber of the House of Representatives was packed – the Cabinet, the Supreme Court, the diplomatic corps and 535 elected members occupying every seat on the floor, the galleries overflowing.

I took my place standing along the wall just to the side of the Speaker's rostrum as the voice of Fishbait Miller, longtime doorkeeper of the House, bellowed through the chamber, 'Mr Speaker, the President of the United States.' A thunderous, almost deafening applause began and went on. And on. My boss made his way down the crowded aisle, smiling, shaking hands with old colleagues, then up onto the platform to begin his constitutionally mandated duty to 'give to the Congress [and, nowadays, millions of Americans watching on television] information on the State of the Union.'

But mostly there was gruelling hard work, dizzying rounds of meetings, and mounds of option papers detailing the conflicting views of government agencies on policy questions. *Nothing that gets this far is simple,* I remember discovering. Each paper demanded an opinion, a careful recommendation, but some days there was scarcely time to do more than react. Pressures were unrelenting, days vanishing into night, passing by like wisps of smoke. I never once doubted that I could get the job done, whatever it was. It was just straight ahead, pushing and driving, the simple formula I had followed all my life.

There were times, however, when I did have doubts – anxieties and even deep fears for the country and the government we were trying to run. It was in the aftermath of Nixon's controversial decision in the spring of 1970 to order an invasion – 'incursion,' we preferred to call it – of Cambodia that I first felt the full weight of being part of the Presidency. The President was convinced that the action was necessary to relieve the pressure on our armed forces in Vietnam and was also aware that such a decision would provoke a fresh round of domestic dissent and political backlash. 'We'll catch unshirted hell, no matter what we do so we'd better get on with it,' Nixon told Ehrlichman and me when we warned him that an all-out assault, as distinguished from a more limited military operation proposed by the Pentagon, could inflame the country.

Nixon's speech to the nation the night of April 30 gave our critics no quarter. 'The US would not be a pitiful, helpless giant,' he argued. Expressions of shock and outrage swept across the country from governors to local church leaders. Four senators – Mark Hatfield of Oregon, George McGovern of South Dakota, Harold Hughes of Iowa, and Charles Goodell of New York – bitterly assailed Nixon's decision and introduced legislation to cut off all funds for Vietnam.

But it was an event that took place on a sleepy college campus nestled in the hills of Middle America which set off shock waves around the world. On the afternoon of May 4 came the first flash bulletins from Ohio's Kent State University – the National Guard had fired on a student demonstration. Grim-faced White House aides, haunted by memories of the domestic violence which erupted after Martin Luther King's shooting two years earlier, clustered around the chattering ticker-tape machines in Ron Ziegler's press office as the ugly story unfolded: four dead, eleven wounded.

I was working late that evening and went to the White House staff mess for a quick dinner. In a corner of the small oak-panelled dining room on a large colour television set were scenes of National Guardsmen advancing through tear gas, volleys of shots fired, bleeding bodies of college students lying on the ground. There was the horrifying picture which remains in my consciousness, as vivid today as it was then, of a young girl screaming in anguish, kneeling over the body of a friend.

I looked around the crowded room. Like a scene from a stop-action camera nothing was moving: dinner plates were untouched, red-jacketed stewards stood frozen in place, White

House staffers sat in stunned silence, their eyes fixed on the grisly tragedy being replayed before them. Then on the screen appeared a sobbing grief-stricken face, the father of Allison Krause, who was dead. 'The President is to blame!' he cried out.

My first reaction was: How unfair! What a terrible *thing* to say. The President didn't have anything to do with Allison's death. And then I thought, *Supposing it were my Emily?* I, too, would lash out at the leader of the government, the symbol of authority against which my daughter was protesting. Maybe I'd do more.

Then the sickening thought crossed my mind that if his accusation was fair, even in part, then I, too, was responsible; I'd helped the President make the Cambodia decision. For one awful instant I felt that Mr Krause was right in that room, that his tear-filled eyes were looking straight into mine, and I felt unclean. I skipped dinner.

I learned in time that if I was to remain in the White House, advising the President on decisions which meant life or death to real people, I could afford no personal feelings. How easy it used to be to read history, to study someone else's decisions, to ponder the merits with detachment – how different to make and live with those decisions. When word came of prisoners taken in a raid we had ordered, the picture would flash into my mind of a man crouched in a bamboo cage, rats and spiders picking at his flesh; I could actually hear his cries of pain. They were daytime nightmares, real as life.

Soon I forced myself to think only in numbers; the larger the numbers, the more impersonal it all seemed. Comparative statistics were anaesthetising, too: only ten US servicemen killed in Vietnam last week compared with fifty the same week a year ago.

In the wake of the Kent State shooting, student and faculty strikes erupted on scores of campuses from Stanford to the University of Maryland. Two black students lay dead at Jackson

State campus in Mississippi, shot by state police. Mirroring a fear-gripped nation, the stock market plummeted 100 points. Independent-minded Secretary of the Interior Walter Hickel released a private letter to Nixon, chastising his chief for turning a deaf ear to the student protesters Nixon had in an unguarded moment labelled 'bums'. Publicly Nixon praised Hickel as 'courageous', privately vowing to fire him.

The Secretaries of State and Defence leaked to friends in the press the stories that they had opposed the President's decision. Some of Henry Kissinger's most valued brain trusters resigned, including longtime Vietnam expert Morton Halperin who with his close friend, Dr Daniel Ellsberg, drafted Nixon's first top-secret option paper on Southeast Asia, 'National Security Study Memorandum Number One'.

There were public calls for Nixon's removal from office by student leaders and the head of the Wholesale, Retail, and Office Workers Union. In the Capitol cloakrooms the first impeachment murmurs could be heard. Nixon had been President slightly more than fifteen months.

On the weekend of May 9 throngs of students, estimated at over 150,000, descended upon the nation's capital. Streets surrounding the White House that Saturday morning were cordoned off several blocks in all directions. My car was met at a checkpoint at Nineteenth and E Streets and escorted in by helmeted police. As an emergency precaution several hundred DC Transit buses were strung out, end to end, around the White House, blockading Pennsylvania Avenue to the north and the Ellipse to the south. Riot-squad police were stationed at key points behind the buses; in the EOB basement was a battalion of troops from the Eighty-first Airborne Division, soldiers in full combat dress with field packs and camouflage-covered helmets.

As I walked through the basement chatting with the troops, most of them bright-faced kids, some sprawled on the cold marble floor sleeping, others reading or playing cards, it was hauntingly reminiscent of what I had seen twice before in Central American countries: uniformed troops guarding the palace against its enemies. But here – in the strongest democracy in the world?

Later from an upstairs window as I watched the crowd filling the streets, I struggled with my thoughts. What holds our society together is not force or even laws but moral suasion. Presidents rule not by fiat, but by the sufferance of free men. Without the collective goodwill of 200 million Americans, glibly called 'public confidence,' government is impotent, anarchy – or worse – inescapable.

Yet as far as I could see in every direction were angry citizens shouting defiance. Whatever was right or wrong in our foreign policy was irrelevant if moral leadership could not be regained. Maybe we were the 'pitiful, helpless giant' Nixon spoke of – not our armies in battle as he meant it – but right here as the delicate fabric which binds a free people together was being stretched to its breaking point.

As the day passed the anxious expectancy inside the besieged White House mounted. In mid-afternoon a warning was flashed from the command post in the White House basement: a large gathering of demonstrators was moving toward the northwest corner of the grounds. Several rocks were thrown, shattering bus windows. I could hear the rustling of the troops in the basement – loosening rifle straps, fixing bayonets, laying out ammunition clips.

Suddenly there was the muffled thump, thump, thump of tear-gas guns firing canisters into the crowd, great puffs of smoke billowing in the air. Two of the buses crashed over on their sides. Police wearing gas masks and steel helmets began moving into the crowd – clubs swinging, men running, some falling. There were shouts and screams, the shattering of glass and steel. A gentle breeze from the west swept a mist of tear gas through the White House windows; I felt the acrid, burning sensation in my eyes and nose. Then all was quiet. The alarm ended as quickly as it had begun; the crowd routed, dispersed into small groups.

Nixon's tough decision to go all out to rout the North Vietnamese from their sanctuaries in 'neutral' Cambodia, and then his steadfastness in the face of mounting congressional protests and public demonstrations, seemed to pay off when great caches of enemy supplies were captured and destroyed. Hanoi's forces were badly crippled, American casualties reduced, and troop withdrawals speeded up.

In late May more than 100,000 construction workers and longshoremen marched through the streets of New York bearing placards urging 'support the troops,' their hard hats covered with Nixon stickers. Despite the opposition of most White House staffers, who saw the hard hat as the symbol of student oppression, Nixon had me telephone the march organiser, a burly two-fisted Bronx Irishman named Peter Brennan. Two days later a procession of hod carriers, bricklayers and iron-workers, wearing hard hats and flag pins on their coats, paraded through the Oval Office to meet a grinning, appreciative President. Photos of that meeting – which signalled an unprecedented political alliance between a Republican President and organised labour – flashed across the country.

Within days, telegrams of support were flooding the White House. Spirits buoyed, Nixon continued the momentum by inviting fifty Wall Street leaders to an elegant dinner in the State Dining Room. In two days the market jumped fifty points: stability seemed to be returning to the country, fears receding.

But the memory of May 9 would not be erased. Within the iron gates of the White House, quite unknowingly, a siege mentality was setting in. It was now 'us' against 'them.' Gradually as we drew the circle closer around us, the ranks of 'them' began to swell.

Nowhere did our animosity run deeper than toward the media. Responding to what we viewed as the daily attacks of

TV news commentators, the *New York Times*, and the *Washington Post* cryptic memoranda were circulated containing as one did in 1971, the blanket order: 'No one on the staff is to see any reporter from the *New York Times* for any purpose ever.'

One day I made the mistake of accepting an invitation to lunch with Joseph Kraft, a liberal syndicated columnist. Lyn Nofziger, a hard-line conservative on the White House staff, spotted us at the posh Sans Souci. Nofziger came by our table and with a churlish smile berated me for having lunch with a 'flaming liberal'. I thought it was in good fun, a little joshing for Kraft's benefit, until I was summoned to Haldeman's office that afternoon and dressed down: 'If you want to stay around here, stay away from that —,' he snapped. Stunned, I did.

In the fall of 1970 the President dispatched me to conduct 'quiet' visits in New York with the presidents of the three networks simply to discuss regulatory matters and the fairness of network coverage. All-powerful within their own corporate domains, but with their economic fortunes held on a tight tether by the Federal Communications Commission, the three men were unusually accommodating. The significance of my visit was not lost on them. We engineered a successful legal challenge to a 'loyal opposition' series giving free TV time to Democrats, and believed we had tamed our foes.

Vice-President Agnew's verbal assault on the press rallied the silent majority but unfortunately solidified the antagonism of most journalists toward us. As the networks became merciless in their nightly barrages against the Vietnam War and Nixon policies, we in turn lost our capacity to be objective, seeing ourselves more and more the victims of a conspiracy by the press. Our attitude hardened newsmen's convictions that we were bent on destroying the free press. Thus the cycle continued.

Early in 1971, after a year of meticulous staff work by John Ehrlichman's domestic council, the President launched, under the banner of the 'new American Revolution,' the first cohesive domestic initiative of the Nixon Administration. Revenue sharing, welfare reform, and government reorganisation turned out to have all the crowd-drawing power of a last-place baseball club in September. The quick demise of this ballyhooed domestic programme merely confirmed to us that Mr Nixon's Presidency would ride or fall on foreign policy.

The blueprint for realigning world power which Mr Nixon and his adviser, Henry Kissinger, conceived soon after the election was ambitious and farsighted. The President would announce at Guam in July 1969 that the United States could no longer be policeman of the world, and would help other nations only if they would help themselves. The speech's significance was understood in Moscow and Peking; there would be no more Vietnams. But Mr Nixon was also saying privately that he would begin squeezing the Soviet Union for an arms agreement and détente. By driving a wedge into the Communist world, pushing the Soviets, tempting the Chinese, he would strive for a new tripartite balance of power in world politics, one that would maintain its own peace-keeping equilibrium. *Linkage* was the key phrase; everything was interrelated, nuclear arms agreements, tensions in the Middle East, trade, and of course, the one big open sore – Vietnam.

To engineer the design from its first ingenious blueprint was quite another task and may, when the passions of this era subside, be recorded as one of the great diplomatic juggling acts in history. 'Buying time' for an honourable solution in Vietnam, as the President often described it to me, was critical to America's bargaining position in secret negotiations with China and Russia. The talks themselves had to be managed in utmost secrecy. Leaks were more dangerous than the skills of our adversaries. It was nerve-racking business.

In May 1971 the Kremlin relented on one key sticking point that had kept strategic arms negotiations deadlocked for over a year. A private message from Brezhnev was delivered to Nixon in mid-May, concluding four months of secret negotiations between Kissinger and Soviet Ambassador Anatoly Dobrynin. Both sides were serious now. An arms agreement could be concluded before year's end. Simultaneous announcements were scheduled for May 20 in Moscow and Washington. The wording was to be guarded, but even the fact that the United States and Soviet Union could agree on issuing statements was significant.

To celebrate this breakthrough the President invited Kissinger, Ehrlichman, Haldeman, and me to join him for dinner on the Presidential yacht *Sequoia* the night before the announcement. Cruising the gentle waters of the Potomac was one of the few ways Nixon had discovered to escape the crushing weight of the Presidency.

I rode with the President to the Navy Yard. In the soft-grey-velveted comfort of the big Cadillac, he talked steadily from the minute we left: how this strategic arms agreement would be the first building block of the new order. More was to come, peace in Vietnam within a few months – Henry was about to deliver a generous offer at the secret Paris negotiations – then détente, a new understanding with the Soviets and the Chinese, bright promises for America. Dreams coming true – and – for a change – good news to announce.

Twelve minutes later we were inside the grounds of the historic Naval Gun Factory, pulling up to a heavily guarded pier, the stately old yacht tied up alongside. Sailors in crisp starched whites snapped salutes. Nixon stopped at the head of the short gangplank, returned the captain's salute, then turned, faced the ship's stern, and with obvious feeling, saluted the flag. It wasn't a politician's showmanship; nobody but a few stone-faced sailors and his closest confidants would see him. But respect for the flag was deeply ingrained in the man. Later that evening, precisely at 8 p.m., Nixon led us all to the foredeck to stand at rigid attention while the colours were lowered at Mount Vernon in the distance. The *Sequoia's* ship's bell rang in salute.

It was a balmy evening, the air clear; even the polluted brown water of the Potomac looked refreshing as it rippled past the long, narrow white hull of the Presidential yacht. We sat on the top deck; Nixon, Kissinger, and I sipping Scotch and sodas, Haldeman and Ehrlichman drinking ginger ale. I proposed the toast to the President, then to Kissinger, who smiled appreciatively. It was a moment to savour.

Thoughts of triumph, however, brought to mind the critics who had been snapping so furiously at the President's heels. 'Maybe those — in Congress will give us a little time now,' Nixon mused. 'Do you suppose they will understand the meaning of this, Chuck?' Then before I could reply: 'No, I suppose not. All they can see is Vietnam. They'll never see what's at stake. Peace, real peace – an end to the arms race – hope for your kids and grandchildren.'

It was well after seven when we went below to the mahogany-walled main cabin to take our seats around the long table, the Navy's best sterling glistening on the stiff linen tablecloth. Nixon tucked his napkin into his collar and took his seat at the end of the table. I looked at him in surprise. *Why should a President care if he spills something on his tie?* I wondered, until I realised that this, too, like saluting the flag, was a part of the man. It was a vestige of his plain middle-class background, a habit from years of sitting at the kitchen table with Pat and the girls.

Over tender New York strip steaks and fresh corn on the cob, the President outlined his plans for détente with the Soviets. It was an extraordinary recitation, lucid despite the freely flowing wine, coldly analytical, brilliantly conceived. All at once he turned with a wink at me: 'Do you think, Chuck, you'll get me an SST to fly to China?'

It was a needling reference to my unsuccessful effort to mobilise public pressure on the Congress to fund the supersonic jet passenger plane. But Kissinger blanched, fearful that Nixon, his guard relaxed, was about to blurt out the details of the plans to visit China, fully known only to Kissinger and Haldeman. Nixon turned on Kissinger: 'Relax, relax. If those liberals on your staff, Henry, don't stop giving everything to the *New York Times*, I won't be going anywhere. The leaks, the leaks; that's what we've got to stop at any cost. Do you hear me, Henry?'

Kissinger, who often did not know when he was being kidded, launched into an impassioned defence of his own office. It was all coming from 'disloyal bureaucrats' in the State Department. Haldeman smiled. He and I knew, as did Nixon, that Henry himself was often the major source of leaks; not the serious ones, not ones that compromised security, but those that made Henry look good in the press, often at Nixon's expense.

The President continued to return to the subject of his critics. 'Chuck, your job is to hold off those madmen on the Hill long enough for Henry to finish his work in Paris. Then we go for the big play – China, Russia.'

One of the 'madmen' most nettlesome to Nixon was a freshman senator, Harold Hughes. The brawny ex-truck driver and self-confessed alcoholic was a particularly vocal leader of anti-Administration forces in the Senate and a candidate for the Democratic nomination to oppose Nixon in the next election. In March he had bitterly assailed Agnew as the 'most divisive man' in American politics. He was in the forefront of each new anti-war demonstration and a leading sponsor of every end-the-war amendment. On April 7 he had been one of six Democratic senators to participate in a nationally televised denunciation of Nixon's foreign policy, and two weeks before in a Law Day speech he'd accused the Administration of 'repression, wiretapping, bugging . . . surveillance . . . and attempts by government to intimidate the communications media'. Unaware of the Sony tape recorders hidden throughout the White House and the FBI wiretaps spread throughout the city, I dismissed Hughes's accusations as the paranoid prattlings of an ambitious politician.

The President's finger circled the top of his wineglass slowly. 'One day we will get them – we'll get them on the ground where we want them. And we'll stick our heels in, step on them hard and twist – right, Chuck, right?'

Then his eyes darted to Kissinger. 'Henry knows what I mean – just like you do it in the negotiations, Henry – get them on the floor and step on them, crush them, show no mercy.'

Kissinger smiled and nodded. Haldeman said not a word, but the look on his face was one of hand-rubbing expectation. I spoke for all three of us: 'You're right, sir, we'll get them.' Only Ehrlichman, expressionless and often a lonely voice of moderation, jerked his head back and stared at the ceiling.

And so on the *Sequoia* this balmy spring night, a Holy War was declared against the enemy – those who opposed the noble goals we sought of peace and stability in the world. *They* who differed with *us*, whatever their motives, must be vanquished. The seeds of destruction were by now already sown – not in them but in us.

4

The President's Night Out

Not that the job of a President's assistant was concerned exclusively with matters of national and international policy. I remember a night in early October 1971 when I was working late with Budget Director George Shultz, preparing for delicate negotiations with union leaders over wage-and-price-control policies. By 9 p.m. we had papers strewn all over Shultz's office.

The President had just finished a television address to the nation on the economy, which we had watched. I expected his call. He always wanted reactions from me and it was a part of my job to be on the alert for this and anything else twenty-four hours a day, seven days a week.

A few minutes after nine the phone rang. 'Well, what did you think of it, Chuck? How did you like the point I made about public co-operation? Remember, that's what you were so concerned about.' We rambled on. About four minutes into the conversation, he asked, 'Where is Eugene Ormandy tonight?'

'I don't know,' I answered, wondering what the conductor of the Philadelphia Symphony Orchestra had to do with an economic speech.

The President explained that Julie had been to the Kennedy

Centre a few days earlier for an Ormandy performance which she highly recommended. 'Find out if Ormandy is still at the Centre and call me back,' he asked.

Simple enough, I thought. But through the White House operators I discovered that staff members who usually handled such details had left for the day. Shultz's secretary, Barbara Otis, began thumbing through newspapers. There were performances listed for the two other theatres in the Kennedy Centre – the Opera House and the Eisenhower Theatre – but none for the Concert Hall nor any mention of Eugene Ormandy.

I was becoming a trifle concerned; four or five minutes had passed and the President would be getting restless. Recognising my distress, Shultz had abandoned the complex option papers that were spread out on his desk. All three of us – the director of the Office of Management and Budget, his secretary, and the President's Special Counsel – were flipping through newspapers and weekly entertainment magazines.

White House operators, who had never failed us in reaching anyone, anywhere, anytime, were frantically now trying every conceivable number at the Kennedy Centre: backstage phones, listings for the manager's office, emergency numbers – all to no avail. (We learned later that the Centre did not answer its phones after 9:00 p.m. when its box offices closed.)

Six minutes had elapsed since the President's call. As I feared would happen, he called again. He was very pleasant. 'Just wondered if you have found whether Ormandy is at the Kennedy Centre?'

'Not yet, sir. We're still searching.'

He made one of those indistinguishable muttering noises, cleared his throat, and suggested I call him back when I had the information.

I was getting nowhere in Shultz's office and decided to return to my own. My resourceful secretary, Joan Hall, would surely be able to handle this. Joan came up with a reasonable idea. She placed a call through the White House switchboard for Eugene Ormandy at his home in Philadelphia.

'Mr Ormandy, this is the White House calling.'

'Really.'

'Yes, the President is trying to find out if you are at the Kennedy Centre tonight.'

Long pause. 'No. I am here at home reading a book.'

'Oh. Well, thank you. Sorry to have disturbed you.'

Joan hung up a bit sheepishly. I have often wondered what thoughts went through Mr Ormandy's mind that evening about the President, and how well we were managing the nation's affairs.

Always before, in handling sensitive, special tasks for the President, I had remained cool. And never before had I been given such a simple request, although anything to do with his travel had always been handled by someone else. But in those few moments after his second call – it was now about 9:25 p.m. – I found myself on the verge of panic. What if he decided to go? Oh, no! How would I handle it?

At this point Patty called. 'When are you coming home?' she asked.

'Get your copy of the newspaper and find out what's playing at the Kennedy Centre,' I shouted into the telephone. 'Don't ask me any questions, just find out and call me. I'll explain later.'

I don't think she even replied. Patty would assume the worst, I knew. She had been urging me to take a rest. Meanwhile Joan continued making calls to the Social Office, the newspapers, the military aide's office, and elsewhere, trying to find out what in fact was playing at the Concert Hall. Harried, frustrated, I decided to send a message to the President through Manola, his valet.

'Manola, this is Mr Colson.'

'Yes, sir. Do you want to speak to the President?'

'No, no. Has he – er – retired for the night?'

'No, Mr Colson. He is walking around the Lincoln Room. He seems restless, sir.'

'Manola, please take him a note. Tell him that Mr Ormandy – Yes, ORMANDY – is not playing at the Kennedy Centre.'

I hoped that the note from Manola would satisfy the President. After all, it was now 9:30 p.m., really too late to go anywhere. Maybe – I hoped – he would just decide to read a good book. But it was not to be.

At 9:35 p.m. the President called again, his irritation quite evident in the tone of his voice. 'Well, Chuck, you found out that Ormandy wasn't at the Kennedy Centre, eh?'

'Yes, sir.'

'That's very good, Chuck, very good,' he replied. There was a short pause and then came the question I dreaded, 'Do you suppose, Chuck, you might find out what is playing there?'

I explained to him that none of the papers had been any help to us.

'Have you thought about calling the Kennedy Centre, or should I?' the President asked, deliberately measuring each word.

I told him that I had tried that, but the phones didn't answer, that I would keep trying and call him back.

He said, 'That is very good. You do that,' and hung up.

By now my tie was down and I was perspiring. My assistant, Dick Howard, was also in the office calling friends, seeking their help.

Then Joan signalled me. She had on the phone the head waitress from the Kennedy Centre restaurant, La Grande Scene. The young lady, Raquel Ramirez, was Spanish and did not speak very good English. Would I talk with her? Yes, I sure would.

'Miss Ramirez, my name is Charles Colson – Colson – COLSON. Yes, I am Special Counsel to the President. The President of the United States, that is – Yes, that's right – Mr Nixon.'

I loosened my tie further.

'Now, Miss Ramirez, the President would like to come to the Concert Hall tonight. But we cannot seem to discover what is playing there. Would you be kind enough to walk over to the Concert Hall and find out what is going on?'

This is utterly ridiculous, I thought to myself. *She will think I'm a nut, that this is a practical joke.*

'The President wants me to go over to the Concert Hall?' a wee voice said incredulously.

Carefully I went through it again. 'I'll wait on the line until you come back,' I said desperately.

La Grande Scene is on the fourth floor of the mammoth building at the far south end. Fortunately – the only break so far in the evening – the Concert Hall is also on the south end. It is a good ten-minute walk from one end of the Kennedy Centre to the other.

For some inexplicable reason that waitress believed me. I waited for what seemed like an eternity. Within a few minutes, she was back, explaining in broken English that the Concert Hall seemed to be filled with military officers in dress uniforms and a military band was playing. I asked her for one other small favour: to go backstage, find someone who looked like he might be in authority, and tell him that the President might be coming and to make necessary arrangements.

With this clue, Joan reached the duty officer at the Pentagon and learned that this was a formal black-tie affair for senior officers, plus a performance by the four military bands. With a sigh of relief I called the President at 9:53 p.m. to tell him it was a military concert, private, by invitation only.

'These are the same bands you hear at the White House, sir; I don't think you are missing anything. These bands will come and play for you any time you like.'

'Marvellous,' he replied, to my consternation. 'That is just what I feel like hearing tonight, but I'm not dressed. If it's black-tie, I'll have to change.'

'Do you really want to go to all that trouble – I mean, you must be tired,' I suggested meekly. I should have known better. That was the surest way to guarantee that he would go.

'Have the car at the South Entrance in five minutes, Chuck.'

I sat for a long instant in frozen horror. How did I start this process by which the President could have a night on the town? There were Secret Service men to notify and the problem of carrying that vital little black briefcase housing the nuclear-alert device. Doctors, the press, radio hookups. For the President to walk across the street involved assembling a small army. I'd never had anything to do with arranging his travel.

Fortunately, my assistant had been an advance man for a year and a half. He called W–16, the Secret Service control office in the White House basement. He would take care of getting the President to Kennedy Centre, Dick told me as he pushed me out the door. 'You get down to the Concert Hall and let someone know that the President is coming.'

Dashing out of the door like a scalded bird, I jumped into a White House limousine which Joan had called. 'Come on, step on it. The President is right behind us,' I shouted to the driver, forgetting to give him directions. The driver looked startled, then suspicious; for a moment I thought he was trying to get a whiff of my breath. Finally, when I told him our destination, we shot out of the driveway.

As we sped down Virginia Avenue toward the Kennedy Centre at seventy miles an hour, I could listen on the two way radio to the frantic calls from W–16 summoning agents back to the White House, calling for the President's car and an accompanying Secret Service car. All but two agents had retired for the night, I later learned.

For a few reflective moments, I thought about the silliness of the whole business. Over the years a system of total and unquestioning loyalty to Presidents had grown up. General Eisenhower's hard-nosed chief of staff, Sherman Adams, tolerated nothing less than heel-clicking obedience from a small, tightly disciplined staff. The era of the 'Imperial' Presidency came to full flower with John F. Kennedy who trusted only family and longtime Camelot worshippers around him. Stories still circulate about Lyndon Johnson's gruelling demands on his men who were drummed out for the slightest transgression and forever banished from the court.

I didn't have a chance to pursue these ruminations because of a sudden and sickening thought. *What if the Concert Hall performance was already over?* I had forgotten to check that. A cringing sensation began to rise from the bottom of my stomach as I imagined the President arriving at the Kennedy Centre only to find the crowd pouring out. We had been unable, except through the very accommodating waitress at La Grande Scene, to let anyone know that the President even might be on his way. Would they believe her? As I thought about it, I became even more mortified. Why should they believe her? I wouldn't have.

When we arrived at the southern entrance to the Kennedy Centre, I was relieved at least to see one of the President's own Secret Service agents there with a radio plug in his ear. The professionals had taken over! Backstage were a collection of stagehands, a tall and very distinguished man standing in the shadows, and the red-tunicked conductor of the Marine Band. Cheerily I gave him the news: 'The President is on his way to listen to your concert.'

He turned pale. 'It's too late. Tell him not to come. All four service bands are now playing together on the stage. It is the final medley. In six minutes the programme will be over.'

'The President will be here any moment. You'll have to play something. Play the medley over again,' I said firmly.

Marines follow orders. The conductor took a full breath, stared at me for an instant, still ashen, then turned and marched onto the stage. He began whispering into the ear of the Army conductor. It was like watching a silent movie.

The Marine nodded his head up and down vehemently.

The Army musician shook his head stonily from side to side.

More whispers. The same thing all over again. One head bobbing up and down – the other shaking side to side. *This whole performance will wind up in an interservice melee*, I groaned to myself.

Suddenly there was another flurry of whispering. Then the Army conductor began nodding his head up and down. I sighed in relief.

As the pantomime on stage was going on, I peered around the curtain into the cavernous, elegantly decorated Concert Hall. Men were in dark-blue dress uniforms, bedecked with gold braid and colourful ribbons; women were in long flowing gowns. The reflection of the stage lights on the glittering braid against the darkened backdrop of the hall was a magnificent sight. Then I began to think about the puzzlement that would soon sweep over the crowded hall when the exact same medley was replayed. It was the first humorous thought I had had all night.

The Marine conductor was now backstage with his colleagues from the Navy and Air Force, working out additional numbers that would extend the programme another half hour. It was then I recognised the tall, distinguished man nearby. He was William McCormick Blair, director of the Kennedy Centre, former ambassador to Denmark during the Kennedy Administration, married to Danish nobility and a prominent Washington socialite. He, along with much of the Washington establishment, viewed us Nixon men as uncultured intruders at *his* Centre.

I introduced myself to Blair, who dilated his nostrils and said, 'This is highly irregular, you know.' I explained that the President had a regular box at the Kennedy Centre. It was *the* Presidential Box and the President's prerogative to use it whenever he wanted. In the future some better communications should be arranged in the event the President again had a last-minute desire to attend a performance.

'I have had a very clear understanding with the White House that the President will always give us twenty-four hours' notice before he attends,' he said testily.

I decided I didn't have time to stand there arguing and was afraid, in my distraught condition, I might commit some violent act – like punching him in the nose. I did think about it, but only for a fleeting moment.

Expecting the President at any moment, I sped back down the passageway to the double fire doors which led back into the main lobby. I was running and there was no point in slowing down. So I hit the two bar-type release handles at full speed. *Pow!* The doors exploded open. Barely a foot away was a startled President and an agitated Secret Service man who had started for his gun. I had nearly knocked the President down!

'Well – Chuck!'

Recovering my composure, I noticed that the President was wearing a red smoking jacket with black lapels. I started to tell him he had forgotten to change, but wisely thought better of it. 'Everything is in order,' I said breathlessly. 'You can go directly to your box.'

'Where is the box?' the Secret Service agent asked.

'I'll lead the way,' I said nonchalantly, not knowing the location but hoping that I could bluff it through.

Halfway down the long passageway leading to the back of the hall, the President turned and said, 'Have you made arrangements for them to play the you-know-what, Chuck?' He tried to slough it off with a wave of his hand, not wanting to come right out and say, 'Hail to the Chief'. According to protocol, it had to be played when he entered the hall. Once more I sped backstage to find my good new friend, the Marine conductor, grateful that the Secret Service agent would now have to find the entrance to the President's box.

The Marine bandleader did not seem happy to see me. 'Watch for the President. When he appears in his box, have the band play "Hail to the Chief",' I panted.

The conductor looked startled. 'The four bands are still on stage. They have never played "Hail to the Chief" together, and I don't see how they could do it without rehearsing.'

I must have looked on the verge of apoplexy because he raised his hand. 'Wait a moment.' Another consultation. More pantomime. Then he was back. 'We'll have the Marine Band play it alone,' he said.

Back down the long hallway I loped until I found the President's box. To my relief, the Secret Service agent was guarding the door. The President was standing alone in the small anteroom which is between the open entrance hall of the mezzanine and his box. It is a lovely room with red velvet-covered walls, a private bath, and a refrigerator for use between the acts.

The scene is forever engraved in my consciousness. The President was standing facing the wall, about a foot away from it. He was staring into the red velvet, his arms hanging limply by his side in the most dejected posture I have ever witnessed. I imagined that he was either counting to ten or else repeating over and over to himself, 'Colson must go – Colson must go.'

I went into the box, brought out General Haig, who was using it that evening, opened the door wide so the Marine conductor would get the signal, and ushered the President in. The Marine Band then struck up 'Hail to the Chief' and the President began waving to the cheering crowd.

Slowly I returned to my waiting limousine. My legs were weak. On the way home I advised the Secret Service command post by radio that the President was in his box and they should do whatever they normally do to take the President home after the performance. I also left word that if he were to ask for me – a possibility I considered quite remote – I would be at my residence.

At home, halfway through the second Scotch, it did occur to me that I should let someone other than the Secret Service know that the President was at the Kennedy Centre. I called Press Secretary Ron Ziegler and crisply gave him the news.

'The President couldn't be there,' he said stiffly. 'Otherwise I would have been notified.'

When I briefly explained the rather unusual circumstances, Ziegler sputtered, 'The press corps will be very upset that no one let them know.'

I hung up with a rather terse parting two-word epithet which I thought a fitting ending to the evening.

The next day Haldeman summoned me to his office and dressed me down for breaking every rule in the book. 'You know, Chuck, this isn't funny. You could have put the President's life in jeopardy. The Secret Service wasn't prepared. It was a thoroughly stupid thing for you to do.'

I agreed it certainly had been stupid, but I asked Bob what I should do if it ever happened in the future.

'Just tell him he can't go, that's all. He rattles his cage all the time. You can't let him out.' While I pondered this startling metaphor, the usually stern Haldeman softened. 'The President enjoyed himself and it came out well. I guess that's what counts.'

The next time the President called me, to my relief it had to do with the war in Vietnam, inflation, and negotiations with Russia.

5

Hatchet Man

Dear Chuck:
Of course you know how proud I am of all that you are
doing. If that old Swede, my Dad, should come to life,
he would almost bust with pride over the success of his
grandson. Only in America could such a thing happen.

I put down the letter from my dad and turned slowly in my
chair to look at the view from the window. The long shadows
of the December afternoon fell over the tailored shrubs of the
South Lawn. From my room in the Executive Office Building
I looked across at the west wing, the large glistening glass
windows of the Oval Office curving outward.

When I had first come to the White House staff, an old
friend, who had been President Eisenhower's appointments
secretary, gave me a piece of wise counsel: 'Once in a while just
walk around, look at the beauty of the grounds and the
buildings, take deep breaths and sniff in the history. It will
help you to remember where you are and keep things in
perspective.'

I was aware of where I was, all right, but somehow the
perspective had not come. The past months had been too
frantic. There wasn't time to think much about anything

beyond postal strikes, Cambodia, student protests, the cliff-hanging battles with Congress over the Supreme Court nominations, and the 1970 congressional elections. I'd found myself in the thick of each one as the President's troubleshooter. We were too busy making history ourselves to think about the history that had been made here – sometimes too busy to think at all.

I could tell how impressed my dad had been when he visited here, two weeks before. My office had been redone for me by GSA, the Government housekeeping agency. The bright yellow draperies and deep-pile navy carpet was the same colour scheme as the Oval Office; massive, historic paintings from the National Gallery of Art adorned the white walls. It was a huge cubelike room with twenty-foot-high ceilings. Sometimes the wasted space bothered my Puritan frugality. The doors, ten feet high, were heavy hand-carved mahogany with gold-leaf hardware, forged with the seal of the agency first occupying the office. Mine had an old Navy Department crest.

Most important, my office was next to the President's working office, separated only by bookshelves constructed to wall off what had once been a doorway. I'd seen him there almost every day now, sometimes several times a day. The new office was only part of what had come with my promotion the end of the first year. I had been assigned a large staff of twenty people and was attending Cabinet meetings and early-morning senior staff meetings with Kissinger, Haldeman, Ehrlichman – the men who ran things in the government. Heady stuff for one whose grandparents had come to this country as immigrants.

I'd taken Dad to the ceremony in the State Dining Room when the President personally decorated the heroes of the Sontay raid, the daring but unsuccessful attempt to rescue prisoners of war behind North Vietnamese lines. He was dazzled by all of it, the President standing under the grand portrait of Abraham Lincoln while military bands blared martial music, the magnificent chandelier glittering in the bright lights of the TV cameras.

On our way back to my office I was showing Dad the Rose Garden when Steve Bull came running up. 'Mr Colson,' to my father, 'the President would like to see you.'

Mr Nixon had spotted the white-haired man with me and sent for us. We were ushered into the Oval Office, where Dad told the President he had voted for every Republican candidate since Coolidge, having been too young by one month to vote for Harding. The President, with his impressive knowledge of history, talked in depth about Coolidge and then told my dad how much he relied on his son's counsel. I thought my father's chest would explode. The White House photographer was summoned and that picture, Dad assured me in the letter, was now his most treasured possession.

Abruptly, I picked up the letter and thrust it into a drawer. I knew, as Dad did not, that if I was as valuable to the President as he said I was, it was because I was willing at times to blink at certain ethical standards, – to be ruthless in getting things done. It was earning me status and power, as this quote from *Newsweek* (September 6, 1971) indicated:

> . . . when the President walked from the Oval Office to his helipad to begin his trip . . . the figure talking rapidly into his left ear at every step was Chuck Colson. Washington hostesses have begun to reckon with his name, the mere mention of which 'makes the tensions come in like sheet rain' in the words of one government wife.

But that same drive – getting the job done for the President whatever the cost – earned me also the dubious title of Nixon's 'hatchet man'. The *Wall Street Journal* had this headline on October 15, 1971: NIXON HATCHET MAN CALL IT WHAT YOU WILL, CHUCK COLSON HANDLES PRESIDENT'S DIRTY WORK.

Buried in the *Journal* account was a seemingly tongue-in-cheek quip attributed to an unnamed former staff member of Senator Saltonstall: 'Colson would walk over his own grand-mother if he had to.' At the time it had seemed to me good for a passing chuckle; I was to hear a lot more from it in the years ahead.

As troubleshooter – or hatchet man – my axe-wielding skills were often called upon to deal with government officials who leaked classified information to the press while so many secret negotiations were going on with Hanoi, Peking, and Moscow.

On Monday, June 14, 1971, when I arrived at the White House for the early-morning briefing, Henry Kissinger was pacing the floor as angry as I had ever seen him. 'There can be no foreign policy in this government,' he began. 'No foreign policy, I tell you. We might just as well turn it all over to the Soviets and get it over with. These leaks are slowly and system-atically destroying us.' He pounded his outstretched palm on the antique Chippendale table, rattling pencils and coffee cups. 'Destroying us,' he shouted again.

I had seen Kissinger angry before, sharp flashes of temper which, like summer cloudbursts, quickly passed. But never like this. He turned to glare at Bob Haldeman. 'I tell you, Bob, the President must act – today. There is wholesale subver-sion of this government under way.'

Kissinger was referring to the leak of the top-secret Pentagon Papers, the first instalment of which the *New York Times* had published the day before. I had read Sunday's account, and it looked to me to be nothing more than a compendium of old memos, position papers, and cables detailing how John F. Kennedy's New Frontiersmen had gotten us involved in Vietnam in the first place. But as I listened to Henry roar on, I realised that the material being disclosed could torpedo our secret negotiations.

'I tell you, gentlemen, there are forces at work bent on destroying this government. Look at this.' He sent three single sheets of paper spinning across the table. 'Cables from Australia, Great Britain, and Canada. All the same – protests. They can't trust us. Why should they? If our allies can't trust us, how will we ever be able to negotiate with our enemies?'

Later that morning I met with Ehrlichman who was receiving similarly alarming reports from the Justice Department. Continued publication could seriously compromise vital national security secrets and US decoding capabilities, the National Security Agency warned. The identity of CIA agents in the field might be revealed. Reports of U-2 flights over China were contained in some of the as-yet-unpublished documents. While the Chinese knew of the flights, the disclosure would publicly embarrass them and force Peking to save face by cancelling Nixon's visit – then in the most delicate stage of final preparation.

What began in the morning as familiar Kissinger fulminations exploded by late day into a full-scale governmental crisis. The decision was made that afternoon to seek a court order to stop publication.

On Tuesday a federal district judge in New York ordered the *Times* to discontinue the series, but on Thursday the *Washington Post* picked up where the *Times* left off. The *Boston Globe,* then the *Los Angeles Times* followed. Copies of the Pentagon Papers were by now popping up everywhere, including, we learned to our horror, at the Soviet UN mission in New York. A few days later, a red-faced Ambassador Anatoly Dobrynin, anxious to avoid any incident that might upset the budding courtship between Nixon and Brezhnev, returned the set of papers to Kissinger's office. Why not? He could read it all in the *Times* and *Post*.

Next, a copy of 'National Security Study Memorandum Number One,' the highly classified document outlining strategy for Vietnam, turned up in a senator's office. We feared that the floodgates were about to swing wide open, that this was only the beginning of a campaign by dissidents to leak all manner of classified documents.

Behind all the mischief was one Daniel Ellsberg, the enigmatic young man who had worked for Kissinger in 1969, drawing up contingency plans for Vietnam. A former Marine officer and avowed hawk, who by his own admission once experimented with LSD, Ellsberg became overnight a folk hero of the anti-war movement. The press hailed him as a courageous champion of the 'public's right to know'.

The Attorney General concluded from FBI reports that Ellsberg was part of a Communist spy ring. The President viewed Ellsberg's conduct as nothing less than treason. 'I want him exposed, Chuck. I want the truth about him known. I don't care how you do it, but get it done. We're going to let the country know what kind of "hero" Mr Ellsberg is.' Nixon was pacing in front of the doors to the Rose Garden, jabbing his finger in the air and repeating, 'Do you understand me? That's an order.'

'Yes, sir, it will be done,' I replied. I needed no coaxing. As far as I was concerned, Ellsberg stood in the way of ending the war. Friends of mine were in Vietnam, like Bill Maloney, who had talked me into the Marine Corps and was now flying rescue missions behind the lines, shot at day and night.

Our effort to stop publication of the papers was eventually thwarted; happily the newspapers refrained from printing some of the most sensitive documents, and others did not follow Ellsberg's example, as we feared would happen. The Chinese and Soviet talks continued. But the controversy, set against the backdrop of a sagging economy and a seemingly endless war, cost us dearly. Gallup and Harris polls reported the lowest rating yet for the President. Ellsberg's actions gave fresh heart to the anti-war forces, too. New hearings were held; and on June 22 the Senate by a 57–42 vote for the first time adopted an end-the-war amendment, calling for unilateral withdrawal in nine months. Four days later North

Vietnamese negotiators in Paris rejected the peace proposal Kissinger had left on the table in May, more than just an unhappy coincidence, we concluded.

Ellsberg himself was only a name to me, a symbol of the villainous forces working to undermine our goals for peace in the world. So it was that I gathered my staff together one July day and told them to nail him in the press. Then with Nixon's words ringing in my ears, I happily gave an inquiring reporter damaging information about Ellsberg's attorney, compiled from secret FBI dossiers. Later I was to learn that the FBI had released the same information to a national news service which published it. This was a not uncommon use of the media by the bureau when they were investigating someone.

Next I called in friendly congressional staffers and urged a full-scale, well publicised investigation of Ellsberg, his motives and associates. I gave not a passing thought to the effect the hoped-for publicity might have on Ellsberg's upcoming trial on charges of stealing government documents.

During a late-night meeting with Haldeman and myself, Nixon for the first time was showing signs of personal strain. He exploded, pounding his fist on his desk and leaning forward in his chair, his face flushed. 'I don't care how it's done. I want these leaks stopped. Don't give me any excuses. Use any means. Bob, do we have one man here to do it? I want results. I want them now.'

At the time there did not seem to be overly much significance to the outburst. Richard Nixon had simply blown his top. Presidents are human and most do it once in a while. Yet it was at that moment that the Nixon Presidency passed a crossroads of sorts.

The 'one man' Mr Nixon wanted for the job of nailing Ellsberg turned out to be an ex-CIA operative by the name of E. Howard Hunt. Debonair, smooth talking, unobtrusive, Hunt was an ideal candidate. He knew foreign policy, but more important, was a conservative true believer, fanatically loyal. I met him when we worked together on Brown University alumni affairs.

Ironically, Hunt's name was at the bottom of a list of six candidates I myself had given Haldeman; the other five were unavailable or unacceptable. Hunt was hastily interviewed by Ehrlichman and hired as a $100-per-day part-time consultant. Little did I dream of the far-reaching role he was to play when I assigned him a tiny cubicle office in a remote third-floor corner of the EOB. 'Howard, your job will be to research the Pentagon Papers – beginning to end. Analyse the political opportunities we can salvage now that we've taken all these lumps. Work with the congressional committees investigating the leaks and this madman Ellsberg.'

Hunt, dressed in a sporty tweed jacket, just properly baggy, sat across from my polished rosewood desk, winking knowingly as I spoke. *What a relief,* I thought, *to get a professional in here to deal with such matters.*

I should have been wary of the spy business after Hunt's initial assignment, an interview with a CIA operative who'd been involved in the ill-fated Diem coup of 1963 which had plunged the US into Vietnam. A tape recorder was set up under a couch in a vacant office and the CIA man invited there for a Friday afternoon meeting. He would talk more freely, Hunt suggested, over a bottle of Scotch; it was standard procedure in the intelligence game, I learned. For two hours the two men guzzled a fifth of the White House's best, while I awaited the results in my office.

It was after six when Hunt reported, blurry-eyed, his tie loosened and stammering an apology. He'd taken no notes, and there was no tape. Secret Service had placed the recorder under a couch which Hunt by mistake had sat on, crushing the sensitive equipment.

In a few weeks Hunt was assigned to the special investigative unit set up under Egil 'Bud' Krogh, an intense, no-nonsense young assistant to John Ehrlichman. Hunt was joined by a steely-eyed ex-FBI agent named G. Gordon Liddy – like Hunt, fervently loyal. The unit, later to be known as 'the plumbers,' was given wide latitude to plug leaks of secret government information.

In late summer the Hunt-Liddy team burglarised the offices of a Los Angeles psychiatrist, seeking information that might be used against a former patient, Daniel Ellsberg. With our sense of fair play gone, there was no check on the methods of these two political idealists whose misguided adventures would soon explode into bizarre headlines.

Our fortress mentality plunged us across the moral divide, leading to 'enemy lists', a new refinement on the ancient spoils system of rewarding friends and punishing enemies. Other excuses came, as the shadowy form of the demon which would strike down the Thirty-seventh President of the United States was now slowly taking shape – like a genie drifting out of a bottle.

Meanwhile, with his trip to China announced and the peril of leaks averted for a time, Mr Nixon turned his attention to the nation's economic woes. Though the President was soon to reverse field on the government controls he'd spent a lifetime opposing, in late July he was still trying to rally public belief in an imminent upsurge of the economy. Nixon's Cabinet dutifully followed orders, speaking publicly in glowing terms about the recovery just around the corner.

Arthur Burns, however, longtime Nixon friend and adviser and now chairman of the prestigious Federal Reserve Board, refused to go along. He testified before the Joint Economic Committee of the Congress that the Administration's lack of progress in fighting rising wages and prices was a 'grave obstacle' to the hoped-for recovery.

The press played up Burns's implied criticism of Nixon, who lamented during a session with several of us that day, 'Why can't Arthur ever give us a little boost? We've got to pick up people's spirits; that's what the country needs – confidence. Arthur can be so dour at times.'

One official present, opposed to Burns's policies, said slyly, 'You know, Mr President, about Arthur's plan to increase the salary of the Federal Reserve Board chairman to the level of Cabinet officer?'

'What did you say?' Nixon demanded, sitting upright in his chair. 'You mean Arthur is preaching wage-and-price controls and he wants a pay raise?'

The official nodded.

'Well, how do you like that?' Nixon said, half-bemused, half-angry. Somehow I knew what was coming even before he turned to me. 'Get that out, Chuck. Get that into the papers.'

Mr President, you don't really mean it, I thought. Wall Street was shaky enough; we had to present a solid front to the public at least. Shooting at Burns in the papers was risky. I glanced at Haldeman and raised my eyebrows to ask whether to write it down or forget it. Haldeman nodded affirmatively.

The official later pointed out that Burns was recommending the increase to be effective for his successor; he would not personally profit. But it was too late for that minor detail now. The enthusiasm for 'knocking Arthur off his high horse' was not to be contained. I passed on the instructions to a staff member who dutifully relayed to a *Wall Street Journal* reporter that Burns was publicly pushing wage controls while privately seeking a raise in salary.

As happens with most bad ideas, a disaster of sorts followed. Burns shot a strong complaint to the White House about the dishonest report. Haldeman shrugged his shoulders, assuring the kindly one-time professor that 'no one around here would ever do such a thing.' Ziegler reported he had no knowledge of discussions between Nixon and Burns over a pay raise. *Time* Magazine, acting on a tip from a White House source, reported that the villain was Colson. Ziegler advised newsmen off-the-record that Colson had been acting on his own. Meanwhile, as feared, the ruckus sent tremors through Wall Street and the rest of the financial community. At his next press conference President Nixon praised the 'most responsible and statesmanlike' leadership in fiscal policies of his 'very good friend, Arthur Burns'.

The Burns fiasco touched off a new round of Colson-the-hatchet man stories, reviving old tales especially involving the rough tactics of the 1970 campaign for which I had been responsible. The welter of articles brought new demands for interviews. I turned them all down in the misguided belief that by avoiding reporters I'd discourage publicity. Actually, the more I evaded the press and shunned the social circuit, the more curiosity I aroused. Unwittingly I was becoming a mysterious, shadowy figure and incurring reporters' hostility to boot.

Through 1971 the White House staff was divided over political strategy. Ehrlichman, Mitchell, speech-writer Ray Price, and others argued for an appeal to traditional Republican suburbanites and to the liberal, uncommitted voters. An opposing group – speech writer Pat Buchanan; Mike Balzano, a talented young member of my staff; and I – argued the case for capturing the Middle America-Wallace vote. The winds of social change sweeping across the country were, we felt, changing minds and hearts to our position.

In August 1971 the President promised federal aid for parochial schools to a cheering, foot-stomping crowd at a New York Knights of Columbus dinner. Nixon's stand against liberalised abortion toughened; the crackdown on drugs intensified. We rode the issue of bussing for all it was worth, stealing the issue which propelled George Wallace to smashing victories in the Florida and Michigan primaries. Amnesty for draft dodgers became anathema to our new majority. Slowly we inched upward in the polls.

The law-and-order standard which Richard Nixon and his men first unfurled in the 1968 campaign was now as American as wearing a flag pin on one's lapel, while the 'era of permissiveness' became the enemy. Our Democratic contenders, their party machinery captured by reformers and liberals, were forced to equivocate over bussing, compromise on abortion, duck amnesty, and as we charged, go 'soft' on criminals and pot smokers. We were seizing the high ground, politically speaking, and what's more, believed in the rightness of our cause with a religious fervour.

In part, the choice of issues was hard-nosed politics, as I suspect it has been in varying degrees with most of the tough-minded men who make it to the top of the political heap. But beneath it were deeply held convictions. The President thirsted for a restoration of the old-fashioned values, something a restless nation could rely on and believe in. He once told me in the summer of 1970: 'If I do anything else as President, I'm going to restore respect for the American flag.' And in the fall of 1971, after a long arduous session with his domestic advisers, in which aid to parochial schools was again debated, Nixon confided a secret longing for something of 'enduring spiritual value'.

'You know, Chuck,' he said earnestly, 'I could be a Roman Catholic.' Just the two of us sat alone in the Oval Office; it was close to seven; we were tired, the President's dinner was waiting, but he seemed in no hurry. 'I honestly could. Except if I converted, everyone would say it was some political gimmick – Tricky Dick making a pitch for the Catholic vote. But you know,' he mused, speaking softly, wistfully, 'it's beautiful to think about, the fact that there is something you can really grab hold of, something real and meaningful. How I wish sometimes we could all have it – something really stable. All this business about Catholic schools, you know, it's not politics. I believe, I believe . . .'

By the autumn months of 1971 the campaign strategy for

1972 was firmly set: the Middle America appeal. The President had phoned me at home just before the last weekend in September. 'Chuck, get your wife and let's take a long weekend in Key Biscayne.'

It wasn't a command, but rather a personal invitation, a warm one at that. I rode for most of the flight with the President in his handsome private compartment on *Air Force One*, sitting across from one another with his folding desk between us. Later Mrs Nixon, Julie, Patty, the President, and I sat together in the forward section of the helicopter which whisked us from Homestead Air Force Base to the Key Biscayne helipad. Our Pats chatted away like any two housewives, while the President and I stared silently at the bright lights of Miami swiftly passing only a few hundred feet below.

As the steady thump, thump, thump of the giant bird's mighty engines pounded in my ears, I couldn't help but recall that day on Vieques when I'd clawed my way up an impossible cliff. Gone now was the anger and confusion of the past summer. Richard Nixon was at peace with himself and confident of his place in history. At long last we were in control of events. And Nixon's gesture – seemingly so casual – the two families riding together – was a signal to the staff and the press travelling with us: I was to be in charge of the political game plan. At that moment I felt a sense of victory and even immunity from the petty bickering and infighting in the White House. It was the last time I was to feel that kind of elation.

We entered election year 1972 neck and neck with Democratic front-runner, Edmund Muskie, the gangling senator from Maine. Catholic, articulate, handsome, he had earned plaudits as the Democratic Vice-Presidential candidate in 1968. Since then he had carefully straddled most issues, leaving him in the 'centre' of the Party. Having worked with him when he was a junior Senator in the late fifties, I knew his one vulnerability, a low flash point. It's a popular myth that Muskie's high-flying campaign collapsed with his own emotional response in the closing days of New Hampshire's primary after newspaper smears on his wife and the publication of the famed and apparently phoney Canuck Letter accusing him of an ethnic slur against French Canadians. (A member of my staff, Kenneth Clawson, was accused of originating the Canuck Letter in a banner headline in the *Washington Post*. If it was a White House inspired trick, it was never proven. I knew nothing of it and the Watergate Special Prosecutor, after the most exhaustive investigation, apparently found no evidence linking it to the Nixon campaign, since charges were never brought.)

Actually, the death blow to Muskie's candidacy was administered in January, the result of good old-fashioned slug-em-in-the-gut politics, the kind I had learned in earlier Massachusetts brawls. On January 25 Nixon, convinced that the North Vietnamese would not agree to a negotiated peace, gave up on the secret Paris negotiations. In a half-hour telecast he stunned the nation by disclosing one of our best-kept secrets, that for thirty months Kissinger had been journeying secretly to Paris making peace offers more generous even than those doves in Congress were pushing. Nixon announced a new proposal and publicly invited Hanoi to accept it and end the war. The President came off triumphantly as patient and long-suffering, enduring in statesmanlike silence the attacks of smaller men.

We looked eagerly about for some way to capitalise on this dramatic turn of public opinion and incredibly the usually cautious Muskie provided it. He interrupted his campaign to fly to Washington and laboured with his staff late into the night over a speech which he delivered early the next morning to an anti-war gathering at a local church. In it he bitterly denounced Nixon's proposals, then offered his own peace plan, even more generous to Hanoi. John Mitchell, still Attorney General but readying himself to take over the campaign, sent instructions through Jeb Magruder, a young ambitious Haldeman aide: ignore Muskie, any attack will only build him up. The President and I believed otherwise.

I phoned Bill Rogers, the amiable, dignified Secretary of State: 'Bill, you've got to take Muskie on for sabotaging the peace talks.' It has been a time-honoured unwritten rule that Secretaries of State stay out of partisan politics; but what Muskie had done went too far, I urged. The Secretary agreed, unprecedented though it would be.

The next morning Bill Rogers walked unannounced into the State Department press briefing room. The assemblage of staid old-time diplomatic correspondents sat in stunned silence as Rogers attacked Muskie's speech as 'harmful to the national interest'. His voice rising in anger, finger jabbing in the air, he charged that Muskie was undercutting our bargaining position. The North Vietnamese had not responded to Nixon's offer and would now be encouraged to wait out the election; after all, they would get a better deal if Muskie were elected.

It was tough stuff, all right, from such a usually mild-mannered gentleman. Roger's blistering of Muskie was reported in every foreign capital of the world. Reeling from the blow, Muskie was alternately self-doubting and then self-justifying to the press, so much so that political pros began to wonder aloud whether Muskie had the internal strength to be President. Muskie must have wondered, too; his next speeches were flat and bland.

Mitchell called me in a rage: 'I'm going to the President unless you promise never to attack Muskie again. Do you?'

'Of course, John,' I assured him. 'It won't be necessary.'

And it wasn't. That one episode, more than all the dirty tricks combined, started Ed Muskie's toboggan ride down from his position as the top Democratic Presidential contender.

Though it eliminated our chief rival, the incident deepened the rift between the Colson men and Mitchell men. Magruder, now at the campaign committee, protected his territory – as he later wrote – 'for fear Colson would take it over.' I kept Mitchell and Magruder out of the inner councils. The split was to cause much of our later grief.

Muskie's decline was accompanied by Nixon's visit to China. Televised live and watched by millions, the modern-day Marco Polo journey was a political as well as diplomatic tour de force. Our fortunes were rising fast.

Then came the spring offensive of the North Vietnamese which threatened not only the South Vietnamese Army but also the sixty thousand American troops still remaining.

With the election coming up, delicate negotiations going on with Peking, and a Moscow Summit Conference weeks away, the President faced the toughest decision of his Presidency. To do nothing might result in the collapse of South Vietnam and a President humiliated, bargaining in Moscow from a position of near impotence. To react could put the Summit in jeopardy, maybe risk a widened war. He made the hard choice: mine the Haiphong harbour and launch an all-out bombing attack right up to the China border.

When told the decision would infuriate the American people and perhaps cost him the election, now only five months away, I saw the President's jaw tighten. 'So what!' he snapped. 'It's the right thing to do. If I didn't do it, the Presidency wouldn't be worth getting re-elected to.'

Later he confided: 'Only Al and John understand. [Al Haig, then Kissinger's deputy, and John Connally, Secretary of the Treasury.] They're the only ones in the whole government, besides you and Bob, who favoured this decision.' Then wistfully he added, 'You know, Chuck, those are the only two men around here qualified to fill this job when I step down.'*

Sick of the Vietnam situation as I was, feeling from the beginning that the whole Asian venture had been a dreadful mistake, seeing my election plans being knocked askew, still I admired the President for a decision based on principle. To me, it was one of Richard Nixon's finest hours.

Criticism was heaped upon us from the press, television, and Capitol Hill, but the events of the next months not only vindicated Nixon's judgement but produced a windfall of dividends. The mining and bombing stopped the North Vietnam offensive, the Summit Conference took place as planned, and the public – our 'silent majority' – rallied behind the President so solidly that political analysts later described the decision as the pivotal turning point in the election. Certainly Nixon's courage and tough foreign-policy stand (along with our careful wooing) were big factors in bringing endorsements from scores of labour leaders and unions who had never before supported a Republican president.

By late May, with Alabama Governor George Wallace paralysed by a bullet wound and out of the race, with Senator George McGovern's long-haired supporters wresting the Democratic nomination away from the party regulars, and with Nixon riding the crest of his diplomatic triumphs, the President's re-election was all but wrapped up. Only the close circle inside the White House could not see it, so haunted were we by the memories of the close campaigns of 1960 and 1968, when early leads had slipped away.

*Editor's Note: On May 1, 1973, the day after Haldeman's resignation, Charles Colson wrote President Nixon to recommend that he bring in General Haig as chief of staff. On May 4, 1973, Haig was named to replace Haldeman. Colson also negotiated John Connally's switch to the Republican Party, pledging to him early in 1973 Richard Nixon's support for the Republican nomination for President in 1976. Connally was indicted by the Special Prosecutor's Grand Jury in July 1974 on charges of bribery in the milk scandal, then acquitted in March 1975.

* * *

On a sunny Saturday afternoon in June, I was about to take a quick swim in our pool at home when the White House phone rang. It was John Ehrlichman. 'Where is your friend Howard Hunt these days?' he asked.

'Working at the Re-election Committee, I think.' Hunt had gone off the White House payroll months before. 'Why?' I asked Ehrlichman. It seemed to me a curious question. On the car radio that day I caught a minor news item about a robbery at the offices of the Democratic National Committee located in a complex of offices and apartments known as Watergate. I'd been mildly amused, thinking of the disappointed expression when the thieves discovered an empty safe. Everybody knew the Democrats were broke.

Ehrlichman pressed the question. 'You are sure he is not working for us?'

'Positive,' I replied. 'Why do you ask?' It must have been the tone of John's voice, because I remember all at once something that felt like an iron hand clutching at my stomach.

'You've heard about the robbery at the Democratic Headquarters?' Ehrlichman asked. 'Well, one of the burglars had something in his pocket with Hunt's name on it. I'll let you know if I learn anything further.'

I walked away from the phone and sat alone at poolside, terrible thoughts racing through my head. One of the last times I saw Howard was when he had come by my office with Gordon Liddy some months before – was it in February? He and Liddy were working on an intelligence plan and trying to get Magruder to approve it. *But it couldn't be this, it just can't be*, I thought. Surely Hunt was too smart for anything this stupid. If Hunt should be involved though, the press would quickly draw me in since I was his sponsor and friend.

The next morning the *Washington Post* bannered the story: FIVE HELD IN PLOT TO BUG DEMOCRATIC PARTY OFFICE. There was no mention of Hunt. But by Monday, speculation about his involvement was being widely reported. The telephone lines into my office were flooded with press calls. White House Counsel John Dean was tensely looking for information about when Hunt had left the White House, and the President was called from Key Biscayne, furious that anyone connected with the campaign would be involved in anything so idiotic. The news plunged Nixon into such a fit of temper that he hurled an ashtray across his Key Biscayne living room.

By Tuesday the trail led from Hunt to me. The *Star* ran the headline in bold black type right across page one: COLSON AIDE – BARKER TIED. The Colson aide, of course, was Hunt; Barker was the Cuban who had led the break-in.

The President must have known how low I felt because he called me into his office that afternoon to reassure me. 'Don't let them get to you, Chuck. It is me they're after, not you.'

I told the President that I would like to give a sworn statement to the FBI and suggested that everyone in the White House do the same.* I never suspected for a moment that anyone in the White House, least of all the man I was talking to, would for a moment tolerate or cover up such bungling incompetence. This was not a moral judgement on my part; the burglary seemed too stupid by the standards we set.

The Democrats shouted and screamed about it; the press made the most of each new morsel of circumstantial evidence, inferring that Hunt shared my office and was my closest friend. Larry O'Brien brought a civil suit hauling many of us before the Democrats' lawyers for depositions – each one giving rise to a new round of publicity. Yet to the nation in the summer of 1972, Watergate was no more than a nettlesome distraction.

Editor's Note: The actual White House transcript of June 20, 1972, quotes Colson addressing the President as follows: 'Everybody [in the White House] is completely out of it . . . This is once when you'd like for our people to testify.' This tape was subpoenaed by the Special Prosecutor but not introduced in the Watergate trial. The transcript was made available for inspection by attorneys in the case.

Campaign spying was, as one analyst put it, 'like trying to steal the other team's signals from its huddle'.

Everything else, however, was breaking our way. Along with foreign policy glories, the economy was surging. Our opponent meanwhile was thrashing helplessly, undercut on Vietnam by Nixon's bold stroke in May, stunned by the AFL-CIO decision not to endorse him, embarrassed by his Vice-Presidential selection and forced to change running mates in midstream. By September McGovern was reeling from our blows, defending his hastily conceived $1,000-per-person welfare plan against steady attacks from Cabinet members whom I scheduled for press conferences each day. Nixon meanwhile remained safely perched on the Presidential pedestal. Victory was not to be denied by one campaign gaffe like Watergate.

But the Watergate break-in sent reporters digging into the newspaper morgues for old clippings about Mr Nixon's hatchet man. Most stories contained a rehash of all the old dirty-tricks charges and that I had once boasted I would run over my grandmother if necessary to elect Nixon. I tried to steer a few reporters back to the original *Wall Street Journal* article. 'I never said it,' I protested, but it made such colourful copy no one heard me.

It was late August when Granny, in fact, became something of a minor campaign issue. I returned from the Republican Convention on a Friday morning, discovering to my dismay that about half of my staff had apparently decided to take a long weekend. I kept a huge poster in my office with a dial showing the exact number of days until the election. I glanced over at it – seventy-one days left. We were well ahead in the campaign, but I was not one to take anything for granted. How could anyone take a long weekend this close to an election?

The more I thought about it, the angrier I got. Then a little genie with a pitchfork prodded me. I called into my office one of my junior secretaries, Holly Holm, a bright, attractive twenty-four-year-old from a small town in Indiana. 'We'll put an end to this nonsense,' I muttered, and my scorching series of instructions went something like this: 'No one is to leave town without my permission. There are only seventy-one days left and every one counts. Ask yourself every morning what you are going to do to help re-elect the President today. A campaign is a twenty-four-hours-a-day, seven-days-a-week job. If I hurt anyone's feelings, I'll apologise after the election.'

Having said this, I concluded by poking a little fun at myself. 'More erroneous things about me have found their way into print lately – but last week's UPI story that I was once reported to have said that 'I would walk over my grand-mother if necessary' is absolutely accurate.'

I felt better now and even managed a smile. Those who worked for me knew my penchant for sometimes outrageous statements to make a point. But my quiet young secretary was ashen-faced, her hand shaking as she wrote down these words. Then with a deep breath, Holly asked, 'Mr Colson, you don't really want this to go to all the staff, do you?'

'Of course, Holly. They'll know most of it is tongue-in-cheek, but it will make the point.'

It did all right – halfway around the world. Within twenty-four hours a copy was leaked to the *Washington Post* and printed in full, the whole bombastic memo. It was picked up by the networks, re-printed in scores of papers across the country, and even in the *Paris Herald Tribune*. It was the subject of a Sevareid commentary and two Art Buchwald columns.

My mother failed to see the humour in the whole affair, convinced that I was disparaging the memory of my father's mother. I received a flood of angry mail from grandmothers, some of whom threatened to form an organisation to protest. Even though both of my grandmothers had been dead for more than twenty-five years (I was very fond of both), two press conferences were called during the campaign by

'Charles Colson's grandmother' to announce her support for McGovern, one by an elderly black woman in Milwaukee who managed to draw a large crowd of newsmen before the joke was discovered.

Not surprisingly, the furore the memo kicked up served only to reinforce Nixon's respect for my loyalty. 'Colson – he'll do anything. He'll walk right through doors,' the President would brag to others.

In our small White House circle, machismo and toughness were equated with trust and loyalty; these were keys to the cherished kingdom guaranteeing continued closeness to the throne.

Hubris became the mark of the Nixon man because *hubris* was the quality Nixon admired most. Small wonder that ambitious young men like Magruder and Haldeman's other eager, unquestioning young lieutenants sought through tough talk and derring-do to prove their political virility to Nixon and those of us around him.

Maybe it was bald stupidity to expect to get away with breaking into one of the most heavily guarded office buildings in Washington, but it sure was *hubris*. As in time I was to realise, whether we – Colson, Mitchell, Ehrlichman, Haldeman, yes, even Richard Nixon – knew about Watergate in advance, might later be important as a legal distinction, but it made little moral difference. We had set in motion forces that would sooner or later make Watergate, or something like it, inevitable.

6

'Exhausted Volcano'

In the weeks following his smashing re-election victory Richard Nixon withdrew to the seclusion of Camp David. Haldeman and Ehrlichman also moved their offices there. On the wind-swept Catoctin mountaintop they would plan for the four years ahead.

On the Monday following the election I joined them at Aspen, the rustic Presidential lodge nestled under tall pines. During a sumptuous dinner the President toasted me again with his best vintage wine for my election strategy, while Haldeman and Ehrlichman sat in stony silence.

'Stay with us for the next term, Chuck,' the President asked genially. 'There'll be increased responsibilities – great things to be done.'

To the visible relief of my colleagues at the table, I declined again. 'I'm one of those burned-out volcanoes you talked about, Mr President.' Nothing had really changed in my thinking. I did agree to stay on for several months into the new year to help staff the new Administration and also, important to me, avoid the appearance that I was leaving because of Watergate.

Dick Howard, my shrewd young assistant, had picked up shoptalk among the lower-level staffers that Ehrlichman was telling friends the White House Watergate woes would go with

Colson when he departed. The eagerness of Bob and John to see me leave led to the uncomfortable suspicion that I was to be the scapegoat. The way I'd been targeted in the press, it was plausible enough.

Meanwhile, Haldeman and Ehrlichman were embarked on the most ambitious White House reorganisation in history, which not only streamlined the government's decision-making machinery but also drew all executive power into a tiny circle of six White House super-aides. The two men controlled all access to and from the President, summoning those Cabinet members to be removed, determining those whom Nixon would interview as their replacements, and keeping him away from such 'interferences' as demanding senators or staff members with contrary views. Nixon was rarely seen; the press camping on Catoctin Mountain in makeshift trailers began to complain. At the nearly abandoned White House the favourite gag, though repeated with a touch of bitterness, was that the President, now re-elected handsomely, had been kidnapped.

It was during a trip to the mountaintop late in November when I realised that my inner malaise needed more than just a few days' rest. Peter Brennan, the hard-hat union leader from New York whom I had recommended for Secretary of Labour, joined me aboard one of the President's choppers for the trip to Camp David. We climbed to 1,000 feet, following the Potomac River west, then once outside Washington headed north for the mountains. The pilot, a Marine veteran, kept his craft low as long as possible to reduce the buffeting from gusty head winds. It looked like we were headed right into a forested mountainside until the pilot pulled up sharply. We climbed the side of the mountain like a tram car on a cable, then roared over the peak, and quickly settled down into an open field cut into the dense forest.

Armed Marines dressed in combat fatigues were stationed as always on the outer edges of the landing area. A Navy commander opened the door of the chopper a second after the wheels hit the asphalt, snapped a salute, welcomed Brennan, and quickly walked us to a waiting limousine which sped us through the narrow tree-lined roads past more armed sentries, to one of the small guest cabins.

The commander instructed us to wait until Mr Haldeman arrived. 'No one without an escort is to walk outside,' he politely explained for Brennan's benefit. A cheery, white-hot fire was burning, warming the comfortable sitting room. Brennan was impressed, not only with the obvious comforts of Camp David, but the military split-second efficiency. 'This is really something,' he muttered, peering out the window for a look at the other buildings scattered through the woods.

'It's something all right, Pete, something right out of 1984,' I replied. Brennan and I had become good friends following those fearsome days in the spring of 1970 when he paraded his flag-bearing carpenters and ironworkers through the streets of New York – and later into the Oval Office.

'This place is not for me,' I said. 'I feel like I'm being watched all the time, guards everywhere, even hiding behind the trees. It's like one of those secret hideaways in a James Bond movie – eerie! I can't wait to get back to the city.'

Brennan was staring at me. 'Chuck, you need a rest. Something's bugging you.'

Something was bugging me all right. But what was it that I resisted here? There were Navy officers saluting every time I stepped out of the door, luxurious quarters, beautiful scenery, gourmet meals, power to order anything I wanted. But the only thing I wanted to order, despite Nixon always urging me to stay overnight, was a helicopter to take me home. Pete was right; something was wrong, and by now I was beginning to wonder what I'd have to do to shake it off. It should have been the most triumphant time of my life; yet inside I was miserable.

Haldeman soon joined us and we walked together to Aspen for a relaxed hour with Nixon. As soon as Peter accepted the position of Secretary of Labour, I asked for a chopper to take me back to Washington.

A new crisis in Vietnam that December took our minds off Watergate and the second term. When Henry Kissinger had returned from Paris on October 24 with a tentative peace agreement in hand, his feet were hardly touching the ground. Ending the war, Henry believed, would sew up the election. But the President had been convinced there should be no announcement before the election lest it be labelled by the press as a political gimmick.

'I gave just a little background information to Max Frankel,' Kissinger offhandedly told the President that next afternoon, referring to his friend on the *New York Times*.

The three of us were sitting alone in Nixon's office. I glanced at Nixon as Henry was talking. He did not explode as I feared, but I could tell the President was seething. He spoke slowly through clenched teeth, glaring at Henry. Henry seemed not to notice.

The next morning, Paris time, the middle of the night for us, the North Vietnamese announced the agreement. Whether the result of inquiries by the *Times* Paris Bureau or a conscious decision by Le Duc Tho to complicate our lives just before the election, the damage was done and the next morning after frantic briefings by the President, Haldeman, and me, Kissinger walked into the Press Room to deliver what Nixon insisted be a down-played explanation. But buried in his long monologue was the phrase 'peace is at hand' which, predictably enough, was bannered around the world. We worried for a few days that the overstatement would boomerang. Nixon in his next televised speech toned down Kissinger's words. To our pleasant surprise hardly anyone viewed it as a last-minute gimmick; even the sceptics knew we needed no desperation effort to rescue an election in which we were already twenty-five points ahead.

After the election in November the agreement had begun to come unstuck. Hanoi hedged on key provisions. President Thieu of South Vietnam demanded more assurances. In December when Kissinger returned to Paris, hopefully to conclude the agreement, he was given an icy rebuff. The first day he fired back an angry cable recommending that negotiations be broken off, massive bombing resumed, with Mr Nixon going on national television to explain it to the American people.

The President called me into his office to read the cable. 'Well, what do you think?' he demanded.

I studied the three-page document carefully while Nixon sat tapping his fingers impatiently. 'I'd tell Henry to keep negotiating; they are just trying to test us,' I finally answered.

'No, no,' Nixon interrupted, obviously not interested in my foreign-policy judgement. 'What do you think about going on TV?'

'I wouldn't advise it. It will look like the October announcement was a phoney. The country will never take it.'

Haldeman joined us shortly and echoed my sentiments. Later that morning Nixon cabled instructions back to Kissinger: 'Keep negotiating.'

Kissinger stayed at the table, but the North Vietnamese remained truculent and on December 14 Henry broke off negotiations, returning to Washington. The next day Nixon fired off a strongly worded cable to North Vietnam: return to the Paris negotiations in seventy-two hours or else. It was no bluff. When the ultimatum expired, wave after wave of B–52s began raining hundreds of tons of bombs on North Vietnamese targets. Nixon made no public statement for fear of hardening the negotiating position, making it tougher for Hanoi to come around.

The public reaction was predictable shock and outrage, followed by a torrent of editorial denunciation, all directed at Richard Nixon. Kissinger's friends in the Washington press corps simply could not believe that Henry would be party to what the *Washington Post* labelled 'the most savage and senseless act of war ever visited . . . by one sovereign people upon another.'

The reaction from the Congress, happily for us then out of session, was the most vitriolic. Sentiment began to mount on both sides of the aisle for a resolution terminating all funds for military operations in South East Asia. We took the threats from Congress seriously; we knew we were racing the clock. If the North Vietnamese did not cave in and agree to return to the conference table by the time the new Congress got under way in January, we faced stern action.

The President got less and less sleep as he took almost the full weight of the criticism. Physically, he was drained before the crisis. He had taken only one brief weekend rest after the election. Now I saw him ageing right before my eyes. Many days his speech was not entirely clear, a sign of the total exhaustion I had come to fear. The President always drove himself hard, but except in periods of tremendous stress his speech remained clear, his voice strong. When his words slurred, as they had two or three times in the past, I knew that he was pushing himself beyond the point of even his extra-ordinary endurance. He was giving little or no attention to other matters, such as restaffing the second Administration, a fact that was to plague him in the months ahead.

With Haldeman and Kissinger vacationing in California, the President and I maintained the vigil alone. I remembered tales of Lyndon Johnson getting up in the middle of the night, putting on bathrobe and slippers and walking down to the Situation Room, the National Security Council headquarters in the White House basement, to read the latest military reports from Vietnam. Johnson became so totally immersed in the battlefield situation, his intimates later reported, that he began to lose his perspective and aged visibly. Richard Nixon learned from Johnson's mistake, and to my knowledge never once visited the Situation Room. But I could understand what had happened to Johnson, because for a brief time in December it started to happen to Nixon. Hard as he tried to discipline himself, there was no way to escape the anxiety of awaiting each report from the military command in Saigon – how many bombers shot down, how many men killed and captured – while Hanoi remained stubbornly silent. The strain weakened him physically and mentally. He was limping badly from a toe he cracked on the edge of the swimming pool at Camp David; like the hay fever he would never admit he had, Nixon refused to let the doctor treat his injured foot.

At 4:30 in the afternoon on December 28, the President summoned me to his working office next to mine, greeting me with the kind of smile he usually saved for mass television audiences, 'Sit down, Chuck,' he said. 'I have something to tell you, but not another person in this building can know. This must not leak. The North Vietnamese have agreed to go back to the negotiating table on our terms. They can't take the bombing any longer. Our Air Force really did the job.' The smile never left his face and there was boyish excitement in his voice.

The bombing was to cease the next day – Friday. On Saturday a very low-keyed announcement was to be made by Deputy Press Secretary Jerry Warren that the bombing had ended and that negotiations would resume the following week. Nixon's instructions to me were precise: we must not crow over our success as this might give Hanoi a reason to back away.

The helicopter was already waiting on the South Lawn to take the President to Camp David for the New Year's weekend; his being away from Washington would help us underplay the big news. Henry had wanted to return for the announcement but Nixon insisted that he not, fearing such an action would signal more than we wanted to signal. It was best for Henry to remain in Palm Springs, out of reach of the press. The President wanted no repeat of the October gaffe.

'Walk with me to the chopper, Chuck,' he said, bounding out of the easy chair. I helped him into his overcoat and we walked briskly to the South Lawn where Mrs Nixon joined us, wearing slacks and a beige car coat. It was the first time I had ever seen her dressed casually, looking like any other housewife off for a weekend in the country. Nixon repeated his instructions about Saturday's announcement, then took Pat by the arm and started for the chopper. All at once she turned around, walked back a few steps, and saying not a word gave me a big hug. She knew her husband's agony was over.

The President's helicopter lifted slowly into the air, banked sharply to the right, and headed up the river. I stood alone for a few minutes in the cold, dry winter air. I longed to tell someone the news I had just heard, maybe the guard at the door, or John Scali of my staff, who had been very much a part of the long ordeal, but I knew I could share that moment with no one.

Warren's Saturday announcement was terse and press reports which followed were restrained. The President and I talked by phone several times that afternoon and evening. His spirits were high. He and I had both talked with Kissinger who assured us he would talk to no one in the press.

I was up early Sunday morning anxious to read the full press coverage. Before nine the calls started, the first one from Scali, a longtime journalist himself. 'Have you read Reston's column?' Scali roared. 'It's a disaster. It can scuttle the negotiations before they even start.'

I flipped quickly to the editorial page. Whatever James Reston, senior eminence of the *New York Times*, said soon became gospel among the rest of the pack. Reston painted a reluctant Kissinger, opposed to the bombing, ready to have settled for the October 26 agreement, dragged along by a President who had capriciously decided to bomb Hanoi to try to get a better deal. Was this an attempt by Kissinger friends to salvage Henry's good-guy reputation? The danger was that Hanoi might misread it and hang tough on their November demands, believing there was some split between Nixon and Kissinger.

I made the first mistake of the day by reading it to Nixon when he called half an hour later. He exploded, ordering me to call Kissinger at once. (It was then 6:30 a.m. in California.) 'I will not tolerate insubordination,' he barked into the telephone. 'You tell Henry he's to talk to no one, period! I mean no one. And tell him not to call me, I will accept no calls from him.' With that he slammed the receiver in my ear. Henry, when I got through to him, promised not to talk to anyone in the press. I relayed his assurance to Nixon.

Nixon normally could cool off in a hurry, but not this day. By nightfall he was still brooding, so glum, Manola told me later, that he couldn't even enjoy the Redskins' championship football game. During the last call of the day, he ordered me to have the Secret Service keep a record of all incoming and outgoing calls from Kissinger's heavily guarded villa in Palm Springs.

I carried out that order and that was my second mistake. Secret Service learned – and I reported – that after trying to reach the President unsuccessfully, Kissinger proceeded to call his old friend Joe Kraft, whose column in the *Washington Post* three days later described Kissinger's valiant role in opposing Nixon's 'twelve days of murder bombing.' Kraft charged that Nixon 'compromised' Kissinger's honour and unless Nixon now gave him 'a new mandate . . . like being made Secretary of State,' Kissinger should quit. (Two years later Kraft explained that he'd been misled by Kissinger.) That did it. Stories and rumours of a Nixon-Kissinger rift were by now running rampant through Washington. Most people thought the rift caused by disagreement over the bombing decision. It wasn't. It was over the rash of news stories by which Henry or his friends tried to extricate him from the unpopular decision. Either way, it was damaging.

The President remained angry, counting the days until Henry left to return to Harvard. He had told me one November night at Camp David, after an especially unfortunate egocentric interview which Henry gave an Italian journalist, 'Kissinger will be leaving in six or eight months; it's not good for a man to stay too long in that position; it will be better for Henry. Time for him to get back to other things.' I thought in November that Nixon was merely piqued over one column and in time would forget it. In January I knew better.

In its 'last hurrah', Vietnam managed to poison the relationship between these two unusually gifted men, a relationship which had led to some of the most spectacular American foreign-policy achievements in decades. Ironically, it would take the catastrophe of Watergate to force the two men back together, when Nixon would see in Kissinger's unsullied reputation with the Krafts and Restons a desperate last-resort weapon. Watergate would force Nixon's hand; by September of that year instead of shipping Henry back to academia, Nixon would make him Secretary of State, just as Kraft had demanded.

Thus it was that a small band of tired, dispirited, sometimes mean and petty men, bickering among themselves, wary and jealous of one another, launched the Thirty-seventh President's second term. The inaugural festivities were fittingly regal, even by Nixon and Haldeman standards. The President, moreover, thoroughly enjoyed his own party, dancing late into the night at one of his own jam-packed balls, calling me in at two in the morning to read some last minute changes he'd penned in his inaugural address.

Then, only three days later, came the final announcement that 'peace with honour', a phrase borrowed from two Nixon favourites, Disraeli and Woodrow Wilson, had been achieved. This was the moment Nixon had longed for more devoutly than even his own re-election. We lunched together in the privacy of Nixon's private office that day, indulging ourselves to the extent of two Dubonnets on the rocks before the standard fare of cottage cheese and pineapple. Why not? The speech wasn't to be until evening and he'd rehearsed its lines in dream after dream over four long years. 'It's been a tough road, Chuck, but we've come through it,' Nixon said, but without the exhilaration I had expected. He was subdued as he recalled one agony after another, once staring pensively into his glass as if seeking in the reflection the response that would tell him it was worth it all.

He added, his voice even softer now, 'How rough it's been. No telling how long this peace agreement will last – a year, two years maybe, who knows. But we kept our word, we'll get our prisoners home and well, the South Vietnamese – at least those poor devils will have a fighting chance.'

Quiet and fatalistic, those were the inner thoughts of a man who recognised full well that little had been achieved for all the turmoil, blood, and sweat. It was no triumphant V–E Day; there'd be no flags waving, no ticker-tape parades for the returning heroes. A warm welcome, surely, for the POWs but it would be followed by a great sigh of relief and 200 million Americans would turn away, erasing the past decade of riot and war as quickly as possible from their minds.

There were long creases in Nixon's face and the dark shadows under his eyes had deepened since the early days of December. The day in-day out pressures of the Presidency had taken a fearful toll even on this remarkably rugged man. Always before I'd marvelled at Nixon's resilience, the way he usually brought himself back, tougher and stronger than ever, after each gruelling experience. Not now. He was tired this time and there was no hiding it. It was on his face, in the melancholy of his voice, in the new specks of grey in his hair glistening in the midday sun that poured through the tall windows of the old Victorian building. I thought then that his worst problems were behind him.

Nixon talked on wistfully: 'Some day, people will

understand why it was so important for us to do it this way. Somebody in this chair some day will surely understand.' With that, Nixon got up, walked across the room to the fluffy sofa, loosened his tie and stretched out: 'Ask Manola to pull the drapes, Chuck. I need a little sleep before tonight. A big night.'

'Get some rest, Mr President. You deserve it.'

History will doubtless show that the President's gritty stand in December 1972 and the peace accord that followed was just another grizzly chapter in North Vietnam's unrelenting thirty-year drive to take over South Vietnam. At the time it seemed a major breakthrough in America's ten-year war in Asia, worth all of the President's mind-and-body-sapping efforts. But the more significant consequence of this stressful time was that it consumed so much of Richard Nixon and his Presidency as to wound him mortally for the greatest crisis yet to come.

As a final official act, the President asked me to travel to Moscow in February to pry open slightly, if I could, the jammed doors that were blocking the emigration of Jews from the Soviet Union. Congress, under pressure from labour and influential elements of the American Jewish community, was threatening not to approve the Summit trade agreements until the Russians relented. Detente was again in peril, this time over an issue the Soviets indignantly told us was none of our business.

I knew the President picked me to go in part because he thought the change would be good for me and Patty, who was accompanying me. When we returned, my resignation would become official and I could return to my law office, only a block away. We would remain close; he wanted me to head his 'kitchen cabinet' of outside advisers and friends.

One could not be mawkish and still part of the machismo cult we so fervently worshipped in the White House, yet I found myself close to tears as we said good-bye the day I was to fly to Moscow. He spared us both by thumping me on the back, saving his good-bye for a letter delivered later. (*See* next page.)

(*See* next page.)

Richard Nixon is a man of many parts, at times brutally cold, calculating, a manipulator of power as so many great leaders in history have been. But he is other things, too – at times an intensely compassionate human being who all his sixty-plus years held up his own mother as a saint and could never bring himself to point out to a secretary her misspellings. I once saw him re-dictate a letter to eliminate a troublesome word, rather than embarrass the secretary.

A very excited Patty was waiting in a White House limousine. As I held her hand in the back seat, she bubbled over with questions. Would someone meet us at the Moscow airport? How cold would it be? Was she wearing the right outfit?

I tried to share her excitement, but the familiar inner deadness was asserting itself once more. What challenges did life hold, now that I was leaving the White House? Was I perhaps afraid to slow down, afraid to get off the twenty-four-hours-a-day, seven-days-a-week merry-go-round, for fear of coming face-to-face with a certain inner poverty? Did I really know what was important?

Although the plane was warm I found myself shivering. There was a point only months ago when I would have been as thrilled as Patty about a trip to Russia. Now I found it hard to pay attention to the briefings of Steve Lazarus, the brilliant Soviet expert accompanying us.

It was shortly before 11 p.m. when our 707 touched down at Moscow's Sheremetyevo Airport. We were, the pilot told us, the only flight to make it in through the fog that night. As the plane taxied toward the terminal, at first I could make out only occasional lights through the thick grey mist. Then all at once in the middle of the runway appeared a landing ramp, bright lights, a swarm of people, dressed in fur hats and long bushy fur coats.

'What do I do now?' I asked Steve.

THE WHITE HOUSE
WASHINGTON

March 10, 1973

Dear Chuck:

It is with deepest regret that I now officially accept
your resignation as Special Counsel to the President.

I shall not dwell on my reluctance at seeing you go,
for you know how highly I value your remarkable record
of achievements during the past four years. Let me
simply say that our Administration has been served by
many outstanding men and women, but few can match - -
and none exceed - - the skill and dedication you
brought to the post of Special Counsel.

Our association over the past years has been marked by
a deep and abiding friendship. Even more gratifying,
however, has been the knowledge that we share a common
commitment - - to make these years the very best in
our Nation's history. I shall always cherish your
loyal friendship, and in equal measure, I shall always
treasure the superb work you did for our Party, our
Administration, and the people of this good land.

It is good to know that we may continue to call upon
you from time to time, and you may be certain that we
will take advantage of your generosity. As you return
to private life, Pat and I extend to your Pat and you
our heartfelt good wishes for the success and
happiness you both so richly deserve.

                    Sincerely,

                    [Richard Nixon]

Honorable Charles W. Colson
The White House
Washington, DC

'This is very good. The brass is here, which means they're going to treat these meetings seriously. Very interesting,' he muttered, staring out of the window.

'But what do I say?' I persisted, this being my first venture in international diplomacy.

'Anything,' Steve replied calmly, his eyes fixed on the crowd. 'At this hour it won't matter. Just smile.'

I took a deep breath and stepped into the cold, dank night. The Russians – the officials they sent to the airport anyway – weren't the lean steely-eyed Communists I'd expected, but warm, outgoing people, pleasantly plump most of them; with their great fur coats and generally round faces they looked like big friendly teddy bears. I even managed to get out a phrase or two of Russian I'd learned during cram sessions at the State Department.

But on the ride into the city, Acting US Ambassador 'Spike' Dubs, a hard-nosed Midwesterner and career State Department officer, leaned toward us. 'Never say anything anywhere, including in this car, that you don't want *them* to hear. Remember everything is bugged, even the ambassador's residence where you'll stay. Everything you say is recorded, that goes for you, too, Mrs Colson,' he stared unsmilingly at Patty.

Spaso House, the official residence of the United States ambassador, is a large white Victorian building on an out-of-the-way side street, surrounded by forbidding dirty brick buildings and equally forbidding Soviet soldiers in their long brown coats, red epaulettes, black boots, and fur hats. Inside the darkened house were only two servants, one smiling old Chinese man, Yang, who'd worked for our embassy since we recognised the Soviet Union in the thirties, and one hefty Russian butler.

'Agatha Christie would have a field day here,' I whispered to Patty as Yang led us through long dark corridors, floorboards creaking with each step, up a rickety old elevator and into the tastefully furnished guest suite. Along with Steve, we

were the only occupants of the house. Dubs, as acting ambassador, lived in the apartment building connected to the embassy.
We stared at the radiators, ceiling mouldings, paintings, wondering which concealed hidden microphones. Little did I
dream that I'd been working daily for over three years in a
building similarly equipped.

From Spaso House early next morning began a dizzying
week; for me a steady series of meetings morning and afternoon
with various Soviet officials, for Patty a grand tour of Moscow
in the company of a smiling but muscular blonde, Mrs
Ulyanova (whom we later learned was a KGB officer). 'The
Colonel', as we called her out of her hearing, never once let
Patty out of her sight, even for the necessities of life.

The preliminary meetings were but the prelude to my
scheduled encounter with Vasiliy Kuznetsov. Dubs, Lazarus,
an Assistant Secretary of State, some other functionaries, and
I were escorted into a cavernous conference room on the top
floor of the towerlike Foreign Ministry. Kuznetsov, a tall gaunt
man with deep penetrating eyes, entered a moment later trailed
by a bevy of aides in dark suits, all wearing the same solemn
expressions. Kuznetsov took his seat in the centre of the table
across from me, our respective delegations flanking us in precise
protocol order.

After brief amenities, Kuznetsov, speaking flawless English,
said that the Soviets were not interested in the domestic
political problems of the United States; that Congress' threat
to nullify the trade agreement between the two countries was
our concern, not theirs. The Russians *knew* Nixon could handle
his part of the bargain, couldn't he? He was staring at me,
waiting for my response. *Not a very agreeable fellow*, I thought.
I took a deep breath to try to slow down my racing heartbeat.

'Mr Minister, your confidence in President Nixon is well
founded. But you don't understand the American people. We
are all immigrants, a whole nation of them. One of my grand-
fathers came from Sweden, the other from England – you see,

to us the right of a person, Jew or Gentile, white or black, to emigrate is a fundamental human right. We can't bargain it away; it's non-negotiable. It's God-given to everyone.'

For an instant I thought I detected the hint of a smile in the leathery face of this old-line doctrinaire Communist. I pressed on, explaining how deeply our labour unions felt about the issue. Kuznetsov then launched into a tirade, right out of the Communist handbook. I came back with a civics-class lecture on human freedom. More than an hour of the give-and-take passed, then Kuznetsov raised himself up in his chair, his shoulders braced back, glanced at his colleagues to either side, and announced: 'Mr Colson, we will do our part. You can tell the President.' Curtly he shook hands with me, turned, and strode out of the room, the procession following.

'Did he mean something by that last statement? Did I hear him right?' I asked Steve.

'You sure did. Wow, I've sweat right through my shirt, but it was worth it. We got what we came for!'

Kuznetsov's parting words, brief though they were, had great meaning to seasoned diplomats in our group who watched for nuances of words and even the inflection of a voice; the world of diplomacy turns on such things, I learned.

(Following later visits by the Secretary of the Treasury and others, the quotas for emigrating Jews were increased; more than 30,000 Jews left the Soviet Union in the next year. The Soviets never gave in all the way, however, and in late 1974 the Congress, over Kissinger's vehement objections, passed an amendment restricting US-Soviet trade relations until the Soviets eliminated all Jewish emigration restrictions. The Soviets predictably renounced the trade agreement, unwilling to allow their internal policy to be decided by an act of the US Congress.)

My first solo flight in the rarefied air of foreign affairs jacked up my spirits – until our last day in Moscow when Spike Dubs scheduled a press conference open to Western newsmen, about thirty hardy souls who endured Spartan life within the Soviet Union in order to report to the world outside. After my guarded, watered-down account of the meetings and several general questions about the trade bill and Jewish emigration, a reporter fired a question I was not prepared for: 'Mr Colson, there is a report from Washington that you sent Howard Hunt to Denver to interview Dita Beard during the ITT affair. Is this true?'

I felt like the quarterback all set to pass who was suddenly hit from the blind side. Watergate had followed me halfway around the world. There had not been a single word about the scandal in the Soviet press and the Soviet officials who were aware of it were perplexed; wire-tapping and bugging is a way of life in their country. One or two indeed had told me to express their private sympathies to President Nixon that so much was being made of nothing. But the free-world press corps stationed in Moscow followed every unfolding revelation with keen interest. I tried to get rid of the question with a quip answer, but other Watergate questions followed. Dubs shrewdly and mercifully terminated the press conference.

Any elation I had felt over the success of my mission evaporated. Despite an interesting visit to Rumania, a courtesy call on President Ceausescu who had helped us open relations with China, and pleasant days in Vienna, the nagging restlessness returned. I just couldn't shake off persistent forebodings.

It was during a carefree afternoon in Vienna that Patty noticed the latest European edition of *Newsweek* in a tiny shop window. I made the mistake of purchasing it and there to my horror was a full page entitled 'Whispers on Colson,' an article charging me with every imaginable Watergate misdeed, including many I'd never heard of. (See page 658 for explanation of the source of this story.) As I stood on the crowded street corner in Vienna, reading each poisonous accusation, Patty looking on with sorrowful eyes, I could feel the noose tightening. There was no way to escape the demon. We cut the rest of our trip short by two days; I had to get back to Washington.

My forebodings were justified. It was not the same White House I had left three weeks earlier. Haldeman seemed distracted and preoccupied. When I told him of my concerns over Watergate and the need to clear it up, he tried to shrug it off with a flip remark; yet he was obviously worried. I met with John Dean the same day I returned, hoping to track down the sources of the *Newsweek* article. He barely gave me a chance to begin talking.

'Chuck, you wouldn't believe what's happened around here since you left. *He*,' gesturing deferentially towards the Oval Office, 'has been calling me in every day. I guess I've kind of picked up where you left off.'

I looked more closely at John. He had been one of the more obscure members of the staff handling all the knotty, small legal problems. Far from a Presidential confidant, his long hair, occasionally loud dress and bachelor's life-style never fitted him into the Nixon mould. Now he'd been asked for a photograph by *Time* magazine; he spread some glossy prints across his desk top and told me to select the most flattering one.

'Don't worry about the *Newsweek* article,' he said off-handedly. 'That's only a drop in the bucket. We're getting clobbered from all sides on this Watergate thing now . . . Do you like this picture?' Excited about his daily visits to the Oval Office and rising status, he was unable to pay much attention to the concern I expressed. I knew the feeling only too well.

Anyway, there was nothing left for me to do at the White House but pack up my personal files, dash off the final trip reports and thank you notes, and with Holly Holm, who was now my top secretary, move 'across the street' to the plush suite of offices my law partners had provided for me.

It would be good to be back with my close friend Charlie Morin; I'd missed him. And the new partners, including a gregarious, heavy-set Brooklyn-born trial lawyer of some renown – Dave Shapiro – had opened their hearts as well as their pocketbooks. The name of the twenty-five man firm was changed to COLSON AND SHAPIRO, and as a coming-home present they'd purchased a Lincoln Continental and hired a driver for me.

Clients were lining up at the doors, the result of a rash of articles like the feature piece in the *New York Times* describing 'the first *bona fide* member of the President's inner circle – well on his way to becoming one of the busiest and best-paid lawyers in Washington.' *All of this, the warm welcome, plenty of money; surely,* I thought, *would give me a new thrust.*

During my last meeting with the President as his Special Counsel, he was leaning back in his chair, crossed legs resting comfortably on his massive carved mahogany desk. We talked of the trip to Moscow and other things. Then I came to Watergate. 'Whoever did order Watergate, let it out!' I said emotionally. 'Let's get rid of it now, take our losses.'*

I barely had the words out before the President dropped his feet on the floor and came straight up in his chair. 'Who do you think did this? Mitchell? – Magruder? –' he was staring intently into my eyes, face flushed, anger in his voice. I had struck a raw nerve, but I was convinced at that moment that he was as much in the dark as I was.

For reasons I could not then fathom, Richard Nixon seemed almost paralysed by Watergate, unable or unwilling to face harsh realities as the net was being drawn tighter around all of us.

---

* Unpublished White House Transcripts of February 13, 1973, subpoenaed by the Watergate Special Prosecutor but not introduced in the trial. (Expletives deleted.)

7

The Long Hot Summer

A few weeks after my return to law practice, I was in New York to meet with the producers of a promising TV system which might in time give the networks tough competition. With me was a bright young lawyer, Fred Lowther, whom we had hired away from the government. A healthy fee was on the line.

We met in the offices of one of New York's old-line investment banking houses. Soon the company's president, chairman of the board, three vice-presidents, and two bankers were seated around a long boardroom table, peppering Lowther and me with facts, figures, statistics, information about their plans for the multimillion-dollar investments. They needed a competitive break against the networks which would come if a government study, soon to be approved and released by the White House, were to recognise their industry.

Lowther was eagerly taking notes. I could not. For the first time in my life I was not able to concentrate in a meeting; it was all I could do to appear interested, nodding, I hoped, at the right times.

Am I having a blackout? I asked myself. Something serious must be wrong with me physically; I can't still be tired. Once I imagined that someone had drawn a soundproof glass window right across the table, leaving the mouths on the other side moving soundlessly. At the end of the day I was exhausted from struggling to maintain a pretence of alertness. The company's president came to the point: 'Will you represent us, Mr Colson?'

'We'll be happy to,' I responded, naming a six-figure amount.

'It's a deal,' he grinned, then happily shook my hand and instructed a vice-president to have his limousine drive us to La Guardia where the company's corporate jet would whisk us back to Washington.

'Fred, did you take good notes?' I asked my young associate as we leaned back in the plush seats of the four-million-dollar Gulfstream II.

Lowther assured me he had.

'Would you write up a complete memo and have it on my desk Monday? I'm still a little tired from the trip to Europe, I guess.' With that I turned and stared out of the window, alone again with the same doubts and worries that had been my unwelcome companions for five months. In the old days, landing a big account was exhilarating, a cause for taking Patty to dinner to celebrate. *Where was the old competitive zest?* I asked myself.

Many men I knew encountered periods like this in their lives, especially in their forties – fears about the future, about self-worth. 'Male menopause' it's often called. Having read some about this subject, I went through a quick checklist. Marriage – happy. Alcohol – no problem. Career – fulfilled. Health – good. Still puzzled, I decided that the decompression from the tension-packed White House years to law practice was an adjustment that simply would take time.

There was one client I'd represented before whose return I welcomed: the Raytheon Company, an electronics manu-facturer and the largest employer in New England. In mid-March I flew to Boston for all-day meetings with the company's top executives. The executive vice-president, Brainerd Holmes, who once headed the government's manned-space programme, was an old friend. His boss, Tom Phillips, the company's president, had climbed to the top by shrewd wits and raw ability.

I met Brainerd first in the company's modern brick and glass headquarters overlooking Route 128, the busy beltway around Boston. Holmes, bubbling over with enthusiasm for Raytheon's new programmes and my return as their legal adviser, ran me through a series of meetings with engineers and vice-presidents. Later in the day Tom Phillips left word that he, too, wanted to see me before I departed.

As I started for the president's office, Brainerd stopped me. 'Chuck, maybe there's something I should tell you about Tom before you go in there. He's had quite a change – some kind of religious experience.' Brainerd paused, searching for the right words to explain it. 'I don't really understand it, but it is quite important to him. He – he might come on – well, you know, maybe a little strong.' Brainerd concluded with an embarrassed smile.

This was surprising news. Tom Phillips had always been such an aggressive businessman; it was hard for me to see him teaching Sunday school. Once he'd told me he was Congregational in the same way I labelled myself Episcopalian. Nothing important – just another membership. I thought that he might be involved in church fund raising, as the top executive of the state's biggest company would be expected to do for church and community.

When I entered his office it was the same old Tom, jet-black hair, athletic build, stripped down to shirt sleeves as always. But the smile was a lot warmer, radiant, in fact, and he looked more relaxed than I had ever seen him. In the old days though always genial, he had had a harried look – with phones ringing, secretaries running in and out of the office, his desk piled high with paper. Now there was something serene about his office as well as about Tom.

'Tell me about yourself, Chuck. How have you been doing?' he began.

An honest answer would have been, 'Thanks, I feel rotten,' but instead I said, 'I'm doing fine, a little tired.' I had to maintain a strong front; Tom was an important client.

'You really should get some rest, Chuck. It's important after what you've been through,' he said, and I had the curious sensation that rather than being surface talk, he genuinely meant it.

We reminisced about old times, then it was back to me. 'About this Watergate business, Chuck, are you okay? It looks to me like people are trying to drag you into it.'

I told Tom that I had no direct or indirect involvement in the burglary – despite the heat from the press. I was launched into a lengthy defensive explanation when Tom cut me off. 'Don't explain. If you tell me you weren't responsible, that's all I need to hear.'

We had talked for twenty minutes and nothing at all had been said about religion. Yet Tom was different. There was a new compassion in his eyes and a gentleness in his voice. 'Uh – Brainerd tells me that you have become very involved in some religious activities,' I said at last.

'Yes, that's true, Chuck. I have accepted Jesus Christ. I have committed my life to Him and it has been the most marvellous experience of my whole life'

My expression must have revealed my shock. I struggled for safe ground. 'Uh, maybe sometime you and I can discuss that, Tom.' If I hadn't restrained myself I would have blurted out, *What are you talking about? Jesus Christ lived two thousand years ago, a great moral leader, of course, and doubtless divinely inspired. But why would anyone 'accept' Him or 'commit one's life' to Him as if He were around today?*

The conversation turned to more comfortable subjects and then Tom walked me to the door of his office, his long arm around my shoulder. 'I'd like to tell you the whole story some day, Chuck. I had gotten to the point where I didn't think my life was worth anything. Now everything is changed – attitude, values, the whole bit.'

Phillips was boggling my mind. Life isn't worth anything, he says, when you're president of the biggest company in the state, have a beautiful home, a Mercedes, a great family, probably a quarter-million-a-year salary . . .

But he had struck a raw nerve – the empty life. It was what I was living with, though I couldn't admit that to Tom. I went back to Washington to struggle with my inner malaise – and Watergate – and Phillips's astonishing words.

Weeks before, John Dean had asked me to see Howard Hunt and find out his attitude toward the White House. Dave Shapiro shrewdly vetoed it and saw Hunt himself instead, learning on March 16 for the first time that Hunt was demanding money to remain silent. Hunt wanted me to pass his demands on to the White House. When Shapiro and I met to discuss Hunt's startling disclosures, he said, 'Chuck, you stay away from this or I'll break your neck. If you pass that message on, you are involved in an obstruction of justice. This is serious business and our friend the "Trick" is in deep trouble.'

Shapiro, a liberal Democrat, had no use for Nixon. Coming from a pro like Shapiro, the words *obstruction of justice* were ominous. I had never thought of Watergate in that light. I should have, of course, but in my mind the crime had been ordering the stupid break-in, whoever had done that. By now a Select Committee, headed by Senate-dean Sam Ervin, was gearing up for a full-scale investigation. The *Post* had been waging a ferocious campaign to unearth Watergate skeletons and federal agents were digging intently.

'If you want to help your friend, we'd better get him the best criminal lawyer in the business,' Dave concluded.

I passed the suggestion on to the President during a mid-March phone conversation. A week later Bob Haldeman called me. Could I come over to the White House? Bob was waiting for me in his office. 'Let's sit here,' he said, walking toward the comfortable chairs in front of his fireplace.

This was a switch. The crew-cut, stern-faced Haldeman never relaxed; he was always brusque, all business. I'd been in his office hundreds of times and almost always sat at his conference table under the windows.

'How's the law practice?' he asked smiling warmly. This wasn't the Haldeman I knew. He detested small talk. Was Bob worrying about me, doubting my loyalty, afraid of my new partner Shapiro?

'Chuck,' he continued, 'we have got to get rid of this Watergate mess. It is hanging like a dark cloud over the President. He trusts you and needs your best advice. What can we do? What are we doing wrong?'

'Bob, I told the President last week to hire a criminal lawyer, someone who can get all the facts, piece the whole mystery together and give the boss cold-blooded, hard advice. Then get rid of the culprits. It's the only way.'

Haldeman's expression never changed, although I now realise that with what he knew, my proposal was like suggesting he hire his own executioner.

'You lawyers are all alike,' he laughed. 'This is a public-relations problem. We've got too many lawyers now.'

Just then the phone rang and as Haldeman jerked the receiver towards him, he missed his ear and cracked the hard plastic against his forehead. It was the action of a man under tremendous pressure. *He's powerless*, I suddenly thought, *right in the midst of all this power*.

Later walking across the lawn toward the sentry box at the Northwest Gate, I felt a curious sense of relief at being *out* of the White House. In spite of exhaust fumes from the rush-hour traffic, the spring air felt wonderfully fresh as I smiled at the guard and passed through the massive iron gates.

A few days later the headline in the *Washington Post* ended my smugness. It read: MCCORD LINKS MITCHELL AND COLSON TO WATERGATE BUGGING PLANS. I scanned the story with sinking heart. It was based on a leak from testimony given to the Ervin Committee by James McCord, one of the Watergate burglars. McCord had heard through Hunt, it was reported, that Colson was 'knowledgeable' about Watergate. The article was written by the *Post's* crusading Watergate hunters, Bob Woodward and Carl Bernstein.

Across the breakfast table Patty looked up. 'What's the matter, honey?' she asked.

'Look at this.' I slapped the paper on the kitchen table. 'A man I've never met, never laid eyes on, has tied me right into the break-in. I didn't even know a James McCord existed until the Watergate burglary.'

It was a rotten way to begin what shaped up as a rough enough day as it was. A debate on 'Government and the Press' was scheduled during a National Press Club luncheon between myself and a bitterly anti-Nixon, prizewinning reporter, Clark Mollenhoff. National television was to cover it. When I arrived at the Press Building, reporters and a TV camera crew were waiting.

'Mr Colson, you have been named by James McCord as the man responsible for the Watergate break-in. Do you have any comment?'

I denied it but my words sounded hollow. The question made it headline news. No one paid any attention to denials.

During the debate Mollenhoff, with arms waving wildly in the air, and voice reverberating through the high-ceilinged ballroom, indicted Nixon and his men for every high crime short of treason. I roared back. The heated exchange delighted the packed hall, five hundred of the most influential newsmen in America. But no matter what I said, I was on the defensive, parrying the attacks on Nixon and myself.

As press assaults mounted over the next days, I found myself once again *the* prime Watergate culprit. One evening Dave

Shapiro came up with a suggestion. 'Take a lie-detector test, Chuck, with all the junk in the press it could help, might keep the prosecutors off your back.'

I shook my head. 'That's black magic. I'm not putting my life in the hands of some quack.' I had nothing to hide about Watergate, but I was getting so jumpy on the inside that I feared my collywobbles would show on the machine.

Over the next weekend, however, I studied material Shapiro gave me about polygraph tests and the impressive qualifications of Richard Arther, the New York specialist he wanted to use. 'It might be the only way to clear yourself,' Dave argued. Then with a smile, 'If you don't pass, no one would know. The test results are confidential.'

By Monday morning I had reluctantly come around. Both *Time and Newsweek* on the news stands that day featured the McCord charges prominently. I knew I was telling the truth. I only hoped that the machine would know it as well. Shapiro scheduled us for Arther's first available time, Wednesday noon.

New York's skyline was eclipsed by a low-hanging grey sky that morning as blinding sheets of rain angled in from the north east. Shapiro had taken a flight up the night before. I came in on the last shuttle before the airport was closed. We had agreed to meet at Arther's office.

As I climbed into a cab a man asked if he could share it with me. It was, of all people, a reporter from ABC news, Bill Gill. Though Bill was a friend, I dared not let him know even the address I was heading for, so I asked the cab driver to let me off at Fifty-fifth and Fifth Avenue, four blocks from Arther's office. I made it the rest of the way through ankle-deep puddles, dodging the outward spears of passing umbrellas. At one point I caught sight of myself in a store window; collar turned up, rain-drenched hat pulled down over my eyes. This whole episode was turning me into a criminal.

Arther's office is located in a run-down building on the edge of the theatre district, surrounded by old movie houses, delicatessens, and flashing neon lights. It had been years since I'd ridden in such an antique elevator, which the operator opened by pulling down on a large metal bar stretched across the inside of the grated door. We clanged and shook our way to the eleventh floor, stopping at each level to discharge short frizzled-hair ladies carrying shopping bags.

On the eleventh floor at last I walked down a long brown-and-black-tiled corridor, past rows of oak doors, each with lettering on a frosted glass window: SYDNEY FAYNE/PODIATRIST – WALTER RUBENSTEIN, D.D.S. It was straight out of a 1940 detective movie. The black lettering on the door to Arther's office read SCIENTIFIC DETECTION SERVICE, INC.

The door was locked. After I'd twisted nervously on the handle several times, a small man opened it, introducing himself as 'Mr Arther's assistant.' I was told to sit on a straight-backed chair in the tiny windowless reception room. What had I gotten myself into? Moodily I remembered that this was our tenth wedding anniversary. I should be home with Patty.

In a few minutes Dave Shapiro and Richard Arther, a smiling, round-faced man, came out of a back room. The two of them burst out laughing at the sight of the forlorn and very wet figure of the former Special Counsel to the President of the United States.

I drew Dave aside: 'I'm not going to do this. I didn't sleep last night. My stomach is turned inside out. I couldn't eat this morning, and this place . . .'

Shapiro's hefty jowls were still shaking with laughter. 'Dick is the best in the business – and don't worry if you fail.' His expression turned serious now. 'I'll still represent you. I've gotten guilty people off as many times as I've lost innocent ones.'

That hurt. So even Shapiro didn't believe me. Never before had I felt the awful frustration of knowing in my own heart what was true but being unable to persuade anyone, not even my lawyer.

'Wiring up' for the test was enough to start adrenalin flowing even if I had been relaxed at the outset. The victim is seated in a dentist-type chair while narrow strands of wire running from a big grey metal box are taped to each fingertip. Next a rubber pad is strapped around the left arm and inflated. A large metal chain was fitted around my chest, connected by another set of wires to the same grey box, on top of which little pencils suspended from metal arms would record a series of wavy lines on a moving roll of paper.

Arther did his best to relax me with small talk and calm reassurances about the reliability of the test, a statistical record of only .03 per cent error. If a person had sensitive reactions, particularly a hypertense individual like me, the test was unfailing. 'Tell me every lie you've ever told and anything you've done you are ashamed of,' Arther began.

'You're kidding. We'll be here all day.'

'No, it's important. You must begin with a clean slate, holding back nothing from your past.'

I would have gotten out of the chair except I was fearful of electrocuting myself.

'I have a graduate degree in psychology,' Arthur volunteered, apparently bewildered by my reluctance to bare my soul in an unfamiliar confessional. The preliminaries took an hour, with my recitation of prior indiscretions going back before college days, and Arther monitoring test runs on the machine. To demonstrate the sensitivity of the machine, he gave me plastic cards numbered one to fifteen, and told me to note one number to myself and answer falsely when he read the number I picked out. I did, and Arther, by checking his machine, pinpointed the card.

'Not bad,' I admitted. This eased my anxiety slightly, but I could feel my heartbeat pick up, my hands start shaking, when Arther began the critical questions.

'Did you order the Watergate break-in?'

'No.'

'Did you know about it in advance?'

'No.'

Six key questions. As each one was asked I felt a surge in my heart and a flush in my face. My skin was icy-cold. I imagined the little pencils bouncing all over the charts. The tests completed, I waited numbly while Arther disconnected me.

'I failed, didn't I?'

He was passing the long sheet of paper which had now spilled out on to the floor through his hands, staring thoughtfully at the chart of wiggly lines.

'Dunno, I'll have to study this and let you know.'

But of course my nervousness had ruined the test. Shapiro wanted me to wait, but I was going to catch the next train back to Washington. 'Call me when you find out, Dave.'

On the street the rain was still coming down in torrents. I didn't care. I stood waving vainly at passing cabs imagining the headlines once Messrs. Woodward and Bernstein heard about the results, as they somehow would. A cab was pulling over at last when I heard Shapiro's booming voice, 'Chuck, Chuck – stop.'

Shapiro in his shirt sleeves was lumbering toward me. 'You passed – flying colours – Dick just had to double-check the control question. No doubt that you are telling the truth.'

I stood there hugging Shapiro, a 250-pound hulk of a man, right there on the crowded corner of Fifty-seventh and Broadway. It was raining so hard he couldn't see the tears rolling down my cheeks.

Passing the lie-detector test gave me a feeling of confidence for a few weeks. Shapiro, with my consent, leaked the story to the *New York Times* and on Sunday, April 8, it ran on page one under a three column headline: COLSON REPORTED PASSING A LIE TEST ON WATERGATE. For a while at least I believed that truth could be found in little grey electronic boxes.

But my sense of security was short-lived. Within a few weeks the press found a way to use the tests for their own purposes.

The *New York Times* on April 19 observed: 'Charles Colson, formerly a special counsel to the President, took a lie detector test two weeks ago to certify that he had no foreknowledge of the Watergate plot – *the first overt sign of continuing concern about guilt and possible recrimination within the President's close circle of advisers*' (italics added).

On April 27 the *Post* headline bannered: AIDES SAY COLSON APPROVED BUGGING. It was a devastating and untrue story reprinted in hundreds of papers and leading the network news shows. 'Charles W. Colson, former Special Counsel to President Nixon, knew of the Watergate bugging plans before they were executed and urged that the electronic surveillance be expedited, Federal prosecutors have been told by two top officials of President Nixon's Re-election Campaign Committee,' the article began. The Woodward and Bernstein story, later discredited in the Watergate testimony, was based on an innocent phone call I made to Jeb Magruder at campaign headquarters early in 1972 – before the Watergate scheme, according to testimony, was even conceived. And I had been the one to report this conversation. It is almost impossible to counteract an untruthful press report that circulates the nation – like trying to retrieve feathers shaken loose from a pillow in a high wind.

My misery deepened as I remembered the untrue story I had leaked about Arthur Burns.

Camera crews now began to surround our quiet, secluded home in McLean almost daily. We were, as one ABC cameraman sheepishly explained, on their 'stake-out' list. Morning after morning we would be awakened by the sound of cars and camera trucks crunching down our gravel driveway, doors closing, metal cases being opened, stage whispers of reporters instructing cameramen where to set up their equipment. Then always the same tiresome questions – the same wearisome answers.

If we slept late on a weekend morning reporters would often

tire of waiting and knock on the door until we answered. Only Patty's love of people and unfailing sense of humour saved us. She would offer the cameramen coffee, kid me, break the tension. One morning as I was about to swing the front door open wide, stomp out in my night-clothes, and tell them all where to take their cameras, Patty began to giggle. 'Smile, you're on candid camera.' I laughed with her, got dressed, and gave the umpteenth interview.

Then John Dean began to talk to the prosecutors, and the White House went through another convulsion. The 'resignations' of Haldeman, Ehrlichman, and Attorney General Richard Kleindienst, and Nixon's half-hearted effort to placate the nation on April 30 did nothing to slow the onslaught.

To the outside world I preserved the tough-guy facade, but there were moments when my own weakness now surprised me. I often woke up in the middle of the night with a sick feeling in my stomach, my heart beating rapidly and wild fantasies racing through my mind – scenes of jail, cold cement floors, iron bars, and men in grey denim marching along steel walkways.

One day outside the Senate Office Building I was stopped and interviewed by a man from CBS News while the camera ground away. At the end, the reporter shook his head. 'I don't know how much of this you guys can take. I told my wife last night one of you is going to crack or commit suicide before this is over. Keep your chin up, Mr Colson.' There were days – and nights – when those words would return with a dreadful chill.

In late April Shapiro and another partner, Judah Best, began meeting with the prosecutors. The US Attorney's office for the District of Columbia labours under a hefty caseload of shop-lifting, narcotics traffic, rapes, and murders. Probing into the affairs of the President and his men was as unfamiliar territory for Chief Assistant Earl Silbert and his two harassed aides as it was for us who were their targets.

Best and Shapiro escorted me for a face-to-face confrontation one evening. Silbert tried to compensate for his lean boyish appearance by scowling constantly, peering owlishly through huge horn-rimmed glasses. The grilling lasted four hours. Point by point I answered his questions. 'You, of course, wrote the Canuck Letter which ruined Muskie's campaign,' he accused me at one point.

'No, I didn't, Mr Silbert. I had nothing to do with it.'

The prosecutor, his brow now furrowing deeper, sat staring at me in disbelief. When the questioning was completed, Dave and Judd asked me to wait in an adjoining office while they talked to Silbert. It was a bare-walled room crammed with steel government desks, their tops piled high with newspapers, Watergate clippings, assorted writs, complaints, warrants, and mounds of court documents. Like a hundred other rooms in the massive courthouse, it housed the clerks and court officers who each day handle the cumbersome mechanics that keep the wheels of justice slowly grinding. As a lawyer I'd often been in the high-ceilinged, austerely elegant courtrooms, the warmly furnished judges' chambers, the handsome lawyers' libraries, lined with neat rows of books and portraits of judicial greats – where the eloquent arguments are made over abstract legal principles. For the first time I was inside the drab quarters of the army of marshals, clerks, and investigators who enforce the law – where the law touches lives. I was beginning to sense how it felt to be personally caught in the cumbersome machinery.

The minutes dragged by. I paced about, stared at the misty black night outside, thought of Patty home alone and worried, flipped through the papers, then stared at the desks and saw in my mind the pathetic human problems which parade through this room every day.

Eventually Dave and Judd came out all smiles – the prosecutors believed me. But the trapped sensation I had felt in that room persisted for days, even after I was officially notified that I was not a target of Silbert's grand jury but would be a government witness.

It was an important night. I now had Mr Arther's grey box and three Washington prosecutors on my side. But it was not to last. The appointment of Harvard Professor Archibald Cox as Special Prosecutor changed everything. Cox, a longtime friend of the Kennedy family, immediately suspended the original prosecutors.

In their first meeting Silbert presented to Cox a detailed eighty-page memorandum on the status of the investigation. Among other things, it exonerated me. Cox skimmed through it, listening attentively to the young lawyer's briefing. When Silbert finished, I was told later that the thoughtful grey-haired professor, peering over his glasses, inquired, 'Is that all?' Silbert nodded it was. 'But where's Colson?' he asked.

Then in his first press conference Cox announced that a more exhaustive investigation was necessary into the role of Charles Colson. I was back on the griddle.

Patty and I were in New York during the first weekend in June attending the wedding of Charlie Morin's son when a call came from the President. 'Well, boy, how are you holding on?' It sounded like the old Nixon, firm, confident, deep, resonant tones in his voice, reassuring. 'I hear you are considering some TV interviews. You'd be tremendous – no one any better. Just be careful. Don't get caught in the line of fire yourself.'

I knew he was coaxing me on even as he spoke. Yet I felt a sudden surge of excitement – back in the fight. The President needs me.

'Howard Smith wants me to do a half-hour special,' I told him. 'I'll really give it to Dean.' I was sitting on the hotel bed Indian-style, with Patty watching, her face troubled as her warrior suited up for battle. I was positively obsequious, so thrilled was I that Nixon had called and needed my help.

'Chuck, you are still serving the Presidency,' he continued.

'Bring the truth out. Dean is lying. I am innocent. These are terrible things he is saying. You know that.'

'Yes, sir,' I replied. We talked for forty minutes. He was preparing me for combat and I was dutifully rehearsing my lines. It would be like the old days, the days of glory, fighting for a cause, believing in something. 'Hail to the Chief' might well have been playing in the background. That's what had been wrong these past months. I needed a cause and Nixon was my cause. There was the appeal to pride, too. I could defend the President. I would turn the tide.

For weeks I gave it everything I had. ABC ran a special half-hour broadcast on June 5. 'I know the President of the United States was not involved in the Watergate,' I affirmed as Smith nodded benignly. 'I know the President of the United States was not involved in the Watergate cover-up.' I was as emphatic in tone as I was in my heart; after all, *he* had told me so.

The President called to tell me that Julie had watched the Smith show and it was 'the best job she'd ever seen. Keep it up,' he added. Nixon would never – even to me – admit to watching television, but Manola later told me he'd wheeled a television set into Nixon's office so the President could view this one. Nixon's encouragement spurred me on.

The interviews continued through June. A full hour on CBS morning news – more ringing, unqualified defences of Richard Nixon, coupled with increasingly vigorous attacks on his chief accuser, John Dean. Spot interviews before the camera in my front yard, on the steps of my office building; lengthy newspaper interviews. At least twice, sometimes three times a week, I was on national network programmes. Meanwhile Shapiro kept calling the Ervin Committee demanding – to no avail – that I be allowed to appear.

Then came a gruelling full-hour interview with NCB's crack Watergate reporter, Carl Stern, on the 'To-day' show as I continued the assault on Dean and the stout defence of

Nixon. On 'Face the Nation' I said more prophetically than I knew, 'What happens to Charles Colson or Bob Haldeman or John Ehrlichman or John Mitchell or any of the others who served the President, is really very secondary. There is a fundamental question that is before the American people, and that is, was the President involved or wasn't he? I think it's imperative that the American people know immediately the truth about the President of the United States.' I was *the* Nixon defender.

Meanwhile, John Dean stepped up the attack, five days of testimony carried live by all three networks and watched by eighty million Americans. Dean's drumbeat was precise, almost mechanically so. His emotionless monotone ground away, ticking off dates of key meetings – March 13, March 21 – and accusing Nixon of being in the cover-up of Watergate from the beginning, of ordering the truth withheld. Specific charges which demanded specific answers.

But Nixon remained in silent seclusion, succumbing to pneumonia, the first illness of his Presidency, and thoughts of resignation which he discussed with me in a late-night phone conversation in July. It seemed he would not defend, he could not resign. Quitting was the act of ultimate dishonour in Nixon's book. There was another factor known only to a few of us – a local Baltimore prosecutor, Mr Nixon, my partners, and me. At the President's request we were handling a 'small' legal matter for the Vice-President. Spiro Agnew was being threatened with criminal charges and might not be around much longer to succeed to the Presidency. My mind grappled with the enormity of the crisis – a President and Vice-President crippled. But the thoughts were so horrendous I quickly blocked them out.

Though convinced of Nixon's innocence, I was forced to admit to myself that I had not been present at any of the meetings Dean testified about. The doubts were fleeting ones, however. Even if Dean *were* telling the truth and Nixon were lying (inconceivable though that was), did it really matter all that much? Not really. Nixon was the President and it had always been my duty to defend him. That's what being a White House aide is all about – loyalty is the one imperative. Presidents couldn't survive without loyal aides – and I'd been blindly so all along. There the gospel began, there it ended – with one simple and unchallenged message. Dean had broken the commandment; I was still living with it.

The possibility of misleading Smith, Stern, and millions of Americans (as events of the next year proved that I did, unwittingly or not) never crossed my mind. The immorality of that was in time to burden me with a sense of guilt and shame far greater than any of the assorted misdeeds of which I was accused while in the President's service.

As the President's chief defender, the opposition aimed their guns at me. Charges, real and imagined, were making daily headlines. June 9, *Washington Post*: COLSON SAID TO URGE BREAK-IN, ARSON – June 12, *Post*: COLSON ORDERED TO TESTIFY ON SEC – June 13, 14, *Washington Star*: COLSON PARTNER REGRETS MEMO – June 15, *Post*: COLSON SAYS HE ORDERED HUNT TRIP – June 15, *Times*: COLSON SAYS HE PUT HUNT ON ITT JOB – June 21, *Post*: HUNT SAYS COLSON ORDERED BREAK-IN OF BREMMER HOME – June 30, *Times*: COLSON CONFIRMS BACKING KENNEDY INQUIRY BUT DENIES KNOWING OF HUNT'S CIA AID.

In July the Ervin Committee's televised hearings reached their crescendo. On Monday, July 16, Washington was buzzing with rumours of a bombshell to explode during the hearings that day. Dave Shapiro and I were huddled before the television set when Alex Butterfield, Haldeman's deputy, made the startling admission – all the President's conversations – in both meetings and on the telephone – had been secretly tape-recorded since 1971. The existence of the taping system was known only to Nixon, Haldeman, and several of Bob's aides.

Shapiro turned to me, scowling suspiciously.

'I didn't know it,' I muttered, the colour draining from my face.

Dave's eyes were filled with disbelief at first, then sympathy. 'Some friend you've got,' he snorted.

Shock gave way to hurt. I could hardly believe the President would have hidden from me the existence of a taping system. Then I remembered occasions when I should have been suspicious: the time at Camp David when he walked from his office to the corridor to whisper to me sensitive information about another staff member; then once during a telephone conversation with the President there had been a clicking sound, probably the changing of tape reels. I had been so naive and blindly trusting.

Then hurt turned to sudden relief. The tapes will prove my non-involvement in Watergate! The tapes will show that I'm right and Dean is lying! My euphoria was short-lived. When I visited the White House the next day, the worried expressions indicated more and greater troubles were ahead. The tapes would be the subject of a new controversy. All the while, the President's credibility was going down every day.

Now Watergate's hateful venom was rushing through the veins of Washington. There was a pervasive fear, a sense of impending doom, an atmosphere of recrimination reminiscent of McCarthy days. Usually-smiling secretaries were harried and irritable. White House staffers were worried and fearful. Tempers quickly flared even among friends who could normally discuss their differing views on controversial issues with civility. The press reporting was harsh, attacks personal and bitter, political rhetoric increasingly shrill. As the debate became more rancorous, thoughts of violence were spawned in a few warped minds. The FBI was called in to investigate three bomb threats against my home and car which followed TV appearances.

The workings of government were becoming paralysed; senior policymakers were without direction; option papers went to the White House, but no decisions were returned. There were few in Washington not absorbed in the drama being played out in the Senate Caucus Room; TV sets were on all day in many government offices.

Late one afternoon Holly summoned me to the TV in our law firm's reception room. The scene, as every day, was the Senate Caucus Room. The cameras were trained on Connecticut Senator Lowell Weicker, junior Republican member of the Ervin Committee. 'Efforts are being made to pressure this committee,' he charged furiously, and then proceeded to read verbatim the text of criminal statutes that he told his national TV-viewing audience *I had violated* by planting stories about him in the press. The senator's face was flushed with anger and the students packed in the Caucus Room to watch Nixon's men be skewered one by one burst into thunderous applause at the end of Weicker's ten-minute-long harangue.

'What is he talking about?' Shapiro was ashen-faced.

'I don't know,' I stammered. 'Weicker is a beer-drinking buddy and neighbour of John Dean's. I've never met Weicker, but from all I know he's a reasonable fellow.' I recalled an interview I had with a *Star* reporter a week earlier. Weicker's name came up but nothing had been said to hurt him.

'Come on, Dave, only one thing to do. We'll call him, explain the misunderstanding, and I'm sure he'll retract this.'

The senator, however, would not take the call, insisting through his secretary that I appear in his office at 8 a.m. the next day. I knew the instant that Dave and I walked through the senator's door that trouble was ahead. There were five men in the large office, seated on both sides of the senator's desk. Weicker is a big man, 6'4" and 250 pounds, and he looked even angrier than he had on television, leaning forward across his desk on his elbows, fists pressed into his cheeks.

'Sit down, Mr Colson,' he said, barely rising enough to shake my outstretched hand.

I began with as cheery a voice as I could muster that early in the day. 'Senator, I appreciate your seeing me. I think there has been some mistake. I'm not the fellow who tried to stir up stories about you in the press.' Already that morning the newspapers had reported that the 'smear' Weicker accused me of was attempted through another former Nixon aide.

The senator brushed this off and tore into me about other White House actions. We had an exchange of words that increased in its intensity. Finally, leaning across his desk, he shouted, 'You guys in the White House make me sick. I don't know you – but I do know what you stand for, Mr Colson, and we live in two different worlds. I deal in hard-nosed politics; you deal in ———. You make me so mad I'd like to break your ——— nose.'

With that he came around the desk and stood not six inches away, like a baseball manager trying to provoke a fight with an umpire. 'You make me sick,' he roared. 'Get your ——— out of my office.' Hastily I followed Dave out the door.

Shapiro and I headed for the cafeteria in the Senate Office Building. Dave spilled his first cup of coffee, stuck his finger in the second. The sight of Shapiro unstrung by the encounter cheered me up momentarily. But within hours someone in Weicker's office distributed to the press a verbatim transcript of our meeting and that weekend produced a fresh torrent of devastating headlines and articles.

In the whole sordid Watergate struggle, the Weicker episode for me was the most unpleasant; being falsely accused before millions on national TV, then coming almost to blows with a United States senator. I was used to playing as rough as the next guy, but Watergate was creating a madness I had never witnessed in twenty years in Washington, reducing political morality to the level of bayonet warfare. I canceled the balance of my scheduled television shows. The feeling of emptiness was back as well, the questions about myself, my purpose, what my life was all about. The doubts which had invaded my consciousness in February hung over me like a shroud.

The meeting in March with Phillips, meanwhile, had remained vivid in my memory. His warmth, his kindness, the serenity of his face, the starling words, 'I have accepted Jesus Christ and committed my life.' I hadn't understood them, but they had a ring of simple, shameless sincerity. Tom represented everything Watergate and Washington were not: decency, openness, truth. I thought often of Tom's words during this stormy time; even more often I recalled the expression on his face, something radiant, peaceful, and very real. I envied it, whatever it was.

When my efforts to appear before the Ervin Committee were rebuffed again and the committee recessed on August 7, Patty and I decided to get away for a week on the Maine coast we loved so much. It would enable us to make a stop en route to visit my parents in Dover, just outside of Boston. Mom and Dad, now both in their seventies, were bewildered by all that was happening in Washington. Our visit might ease their apprehensions.

At the time I was not sure why I called Tom Phillips to seek another get-together while I was in Boston, but he welcomed the call. We agreed to meet Sunday night, August 12, at his home. I was surprised at how much I looked forward to seeing him again.

8

An Unforgettable Night

It was 8 p.m., a grey overcast evening, when I turned off the country road connecting two of Boston's most affluent suburbs, Wellesley and Weston. The towering gentle pines brought sudden darkness and quiet to the narrow macadam street. Another turn a few hundred yards later brought me into a long driveway leading to the Phillipses' big white clapboard Colonial home. As I parked the car I felt a touch of guilt at not telling Patty the truth when I had left her alone with my mother and dad in nearby Dover.

'Just business, honey,' had been my explanation. Patty was used to my working at odd times, even on this Sunday night at the start of a week's vacation.

The Phillipses' home is long and rambling. I made the mistake of going to the door nearest the driveway, which turned out to be the entrance to the kitchen. It didn't bother Gert Phillips, a tall smiling woman who greeted me like a long-lost relative even though we had never met before. 'Come in. I'm just cleaning up after supper.'

Supper. Such an unpretentious New England word. Gert escorted me into a large modern kitchen. 'I'll call Tom,' she said. 'He's playing tennis with the children.'

Tom arrived a minute later along with son Tommy, sixteen,

and daughter Debby, nineteen, two tanned, handsome young people. Gert fixed us all iced tea while Tom mopped himself dry with a towel. If Gert was aware of the importance of her husband's position as president of the state's biggest company, she certainly did not show it. In fact, she reminded me of a favourite aunt we used to visit in the country when I was a boy, who always wore an apron, smelled of freshly made bread and cookies, and had the gift of making everyone feel at home in her kitchen.

'You men have things to talk about and I've got work to do,' Gert said as she handed us tall glasses of iced tea. Tom, towel draped around his neck, led me through the comfortably furnished dining and living rooms to a screened-in porch at the far end of the house. It was an unusually hot night for New England, the humidity like a heavy blanket wrapped around me. At Tom's insistence, first the dark-grey business-suit jacket, then my tie came off. He pulled a wrought-iron ottoman close to the comfortable outdoor settee I sat on.

'Tell me, Chuck,' he began, 'are you okay?' It was the same question he had asked in March.

As the President's confidant and so-called big-shot Washington lawyer I was still keeping my guard up. 'I'm not doing too badly, I guess. All of this Watergate business, all the accusations – I suppose it's wearing me down some. But I'd rather talk about you, Tom. You've changed and I'd like to know what happened.'

Tom drank from his glass and sat back reflectively. Briefly he reviewed his past, the rapid rise to power at Raytheon: executive vice-president at thirty-seven, president when he was only forty. He had done it with hard work, day and night, non-stop.

'The success came all right, but something was missing,' he mused. 'I felt a terrible emptiness. Sometimes I would get up in the middle of the night and pace the floor of my bedroom or stare out into the darkness for hours at a time.'

'I don't understand it,' I interrupted. 'I knew you in those days Tom. You were a straight arrow, a good family life, successful, everything in fact going your way.'

'All that may be true, Chuck, but my life wasn't complete. I would go to the office each day and do my job, striving all the time to make the company succeed, but there was a big hole in my life. I began to read the Scriptures, looking for answers. Something made me realise I needed a personal relationship with God, forced me to search.'

A prickly feeling ran down my spine. Maybe what I had gone through in the past several months wasn't so unusual after all – except I had not sought spiritual answers. I had not even been aware that finding a personal relationship with God was possible. I pressed him to explain the apparent contradiction between the emptiness inside while seeming to enjoy the affluent life.

'It may be hard to understand,' Tom chuckled. 'But I didn't seem to have anything that mattered. It was all on the surface. All the material things in life are meaningless if a man hasn't discovered what's underneath them.'

We were both silent for a while as I groped for understanding. Outside, the first fireflies punctuated the mauve dusk. Tom got up and switched on two small lamps on end tables in the corners of the porch.

'One night I was in New York on business and noticed that Billy Graham was having a Crusade in Madison Square Garden,' Tom continued. 'I went – curious, I guess – hoping maybe I'd find some answers. What Graham said that night put it all into place for me. I saw what was missing, the personal relationship with Jesus Christ, the fact that I hadn't ever asked Him into my life, hadn't turned my life over to Him. So I did it – that very night at the Crusade.'

Tom's tall, gangling frame leaned towards me, silhouetted by the yellow light behind him. Though his face was shaded, I could see his eyes begin to glisten and his voice became softer.

'I asked Christ to come into my life and I could feel His presence with me, His peace within me. I could sense His Spirit there with me. Then I went out for a walk alone on the streets of New York. I never liked New York before, but this night it was beautiful. I walked for blocks and blocks, I guess. Everything seemed different to me. It was raining softly and the city lights created a golden glow. Something had happened to me and I knew it.'

'That's what you mean by accepting Christ – you just ask?' I was more puzzled than ever.

'That's it, as simple as that,' Tom replied. 'Of course, you have to want Jesus in your life, really want Him. That's the way it starts. And let me tell you, things then begin to change. Since then I have found a satisfaction and a joy about living that I simply never knew was possible.'

To me Jesus had always been an historical figure, but Tom explained that you could hardly invite Him into your life if you didn't believe that He is alive today and that His Spirit is a part of to-day's scene. I was moved by Tom's story even though I couldn't imagine how such a miraculous change could take place in such a simple way. Yet the excitement in Tom's voice as he described his experience was convincing and Tom was indeed different. More alive.

Then Tom turned the conversation again to my plight. I described some of the agonies of Watergate, the pressures I was under, how unfairly I thought the press was treating me. I was being defensive and when I ran out of explanations, Tom spoke gently but firmly.

'You know that I supported Nixon in this past election, but you guys made a serious mistake. You would have won the election without any of the hanky-panky. Watergate and the dirty tricks were so unnecessary. And it was wrong, just plain wrong. You didn't have to do it.'

Tom was leaning forward, elbows on his knees, his hands stretched forward almost as if he was trying to reach out for me. There was an urgent appeal in his eyes. 'Don't you under-stand that?' he asked with such genuine feeling that I couldn't take offence.

'If only you had believed in the rightness of your cause, none of this would have been necessary. None of this would have happened. The problem with all of you, including you, Chuck – you simply had to go for the other guy's jugular. You had to try to destroy your enemies. You had to destroy them because you couldn't trust in yourselves.'

The heat at that moment seemed unbearable as I wiped away drops of perspiration over my lip. The iced tea was soothing as I sipped it, although with Tom's points hitting home so painfully, I longed for a Scotch and soda. To myself I admitted that Tom was on target: the world of *us* against *them* as we saw it from our insulated White House enclave – the Nixon White House against the world. Insecure about our cause, our overkill approach was a way to play it safe. And yet . . .

'Tom, one thing you don't understand. In politics it's dog-eat-dog; you simply can't survive otherwise. I've been in the political business for twenty years, including several campaigns right here in Massachusetts. I know how things are done. Politics is like war. If you don't keep the enemy on the defensive, you'll be on the defensive yourself. Tom, this man Nixon has been under constant attack all of his life. The only way he could make it was to fight back. Look at the criticism he took over Vietnam. Yet he was right. We never would have made it if we hadn't fought the way we did, hitting our critics, never letting them get the best of us. We didn't have any choice.'

Even as I talked, the words sounded more and more empty to me. Tired old lines, I realised. I was describing the ways of the political world, all right, while suddenly wondering if there could be a better way.

Tom believed so, anyway. He was so gentle I couldn't resent what he said as he cut right through it all: 'Chuck, I hate to say this, but you guys brought it on yourselves. If you had put your faith in God, and if your cause were just, He would have guided you. And His help would have been a thousand times more powerful than all your phoney ads and shady schemes put together.'

With any other man the notion of relying on God would have seemed to me pure Pollyanna. Yet I had to be impressed with the way this man ran his company in the equally competitive world of business: ignoring his enemies, trying to follow God's ways. Since his conversion Raytheon had never done better, sales and profits soaring. Maybe there was something to it; anyway it's tough to argue with success.

'Chuck, I don't think you will understand what I'm saying about God until you are willing to face yourself honestly and squarely. This is the first step.' Tom reached to the corner table and picked up a small paperback book. I read the title: *Mere Christianity*, by C.S. Lewis.

'I suggest you take this with you and read it while you are on vacation.' Tom started to hand it to me, then paused. 'Let me read you one chapter.'

I leaned back, still on the defensive, my mind and emotions whirling.

There is one vice of which no man in the world is free; which everyone in the world loathes when he sees it in someone else; and of which hardly any people, except Christians, ever imagine that they are guilty themselves. I have heard people admit that they are bad-tempered, or that they cannot keep their heads about girls or drink, or even that they are cowards. I do not think I have ever heard anyone who was not a Christian accuse himself of this vice . . . There is no fault . . . which we are more unconscious of in ourselves. And the more we have it ourselves, the more we dislike it in others.

The vice I am talking of is Pride or Self-Conceit . . . Pride leads to every other vice: it is the complete anti-God state of mind.

As he read, I could feel a flush coming into my face and a curious burning sensation that made the night seem even warmer. Lewis's words seemed to pound straight at me.

. . . it is Pride which has been the chief cause of misery in every nation and every family since the world began. Other vices may sometimes bring people together: you may find good fellowship and jokes and friendliness among drunken people or unchaste people. But Pride always means enmity – it is enmity. And not only enmity between man and man, but enmity to God.

In God you come up against something which is in every respect immeasurably superior to yourself. Unless you know God as that – and, therefore, know yourself as nothing in comparison – you do not know God at all. As long as you are proud you cannot know God. A proud man is always looking down on things and people: and, of course, as long as you are looking down, you cannot see something that is above you.

Suddenly I felt naked and unclean, my bravado defences gone. I was exposed, unprotected, for Lewis's words were describing me. As he continued, one passage in particular seemed to sum up what had happened to all of us at the White House:

For Pride is spiritual cancer: it eats up the very possibility of love, or contentment, or even common sense.

Just as a man about to die is supposed to see flash before him, sequence by sequence, the high points of his life, so, as Tom's voice read on that August evening, key events in my life paraded before me as if projected on a screen. Things I hadn't thought about in years – my graduation speech at prep school – being 'good enough' for the Marines – my first marriage, into the 'right' family – sitting on the Jaycees' dais while civic leader after civic leader praised me as the outstanding young man of Boston – then to the White House – the clawing and straining for status and position – 'Mr Colson, the President is calling – Mr Colson, the President wants to see you right away.'

For some reason I thought of an incident after the 1972 election when a reporter, an old Nixon nemesis, came by my office and contritely asked me what he could do to get in the good graces of the White House. I suggested that he try 'slashing his wrists'. I meant it as a joke, of course, but also to make him squirm. It was the arrogance of the victor over an enemy brought to submission.

Now, sitting there on the dimly lit porch, my self-centred past was washing over me in waves. It was painful. Agony. Desperately I tried to defend myself. What about my sacrifices for government service, the giving up of a big income, putting my stocks into a blind trust? The truth, I saw in an instant, was that I'd wanted the position in the White House more than I'd wanted money. There was no sacrifice. And the more I had talked about my own sacrifices, the more I was really trying to build myself up in the eyes of others. I would eagerly have given up everything I'd ever earned to prove myself at the mountaintop of government. It was pride – Lewis's 'great sin' – that had propelled me through life.

Tom finished the chapter on pride and shut the book. I mumbled something noncommittal to the effect that 'I'll look forward to reading that.' But Lewis's torpedo had hit me amidships. I think Phillips knew it as he stared into my eyes. That one chapter ripped through the protective armour in which I had unknowingly encased myself for forty-two years. Of course, I had not known God. *How could I?* I had been concerned with myself. *I* had done this and that, *I* had achieved, *I* had succeeded and *I* had given God none of the credit, never once thanking Him for any of His gifts to me. I had never thought of anything being 'immeasurably superior' to myself, or if I had in fleeting moments thought about the infinite power of God, I had not related Him to my life. In those brief moments while Tom read, I saw myself as I never had before. And the picture was ugly.

'How about it, Chuck?' Tom's question jarred me out of my trance. I knew precisely what he meant. Was I ready to make the leap of faith as he had in New York, to 'accept' Christ?

'Tom, you've shaken me up. I'll admit that. That chapter describes me. But I can't tell you I'm ready to make the kind of commitment you did. I've got to be certain. I've got to learn a lot more, be sure all my reservations are satisfied. I've got a lot of intellectual hang-ups to get past.'

For a moment Tom looked disappointed, then he smiled. 'I understand, I understand.'

'You see,' I continued, 'I saw men turn to God in the Marine Corps; I did once myself. Then afterwards it's all forgotten and everything is back to normal. Foxhole religion is just a way of using God. How can I make a commitment now? My whole world is crashing down around me. How can I be sure I'm not just running for shelter and that when the crisis is over I'll forget it? I've got to answer all the intellectual arguments first and if I can do that, I'll be sure.'

'I understand,' Tom repeated quietly.

I was relieved he did, yet deep inside of me something wanted to tell Tom to press on. He was making so much sense, the first time anyone ever had in talking about God.

But Tom did not press on. He handed me his copy of *Mere Christianity*. 'Once you've read this, you might want to read the Book of John in the Bible.' I scribbled notes of the key passages he quoted. 'Also there's a man in Washington you should meet,' he continued, 'name of Doug Coe. He gets people together for Christian fellowship – prayer breakfasts and things like that. I'll ask him to contact you.'

Tom then reached for his Bible and read a few of his favourite psalms. The comforting words were like a cold soothing ointment. For the first time in my life, familiar verses I'd heard chanted lifelessly in church came alive. 'Trust in the Lord,' I remember Tom reading, and I wanted to, right that moment I wanted to – if only I knew how, if only I could be sure.

'Would you like to pray together, Chuck?' Tom asked, closing his Bible and putting it on the table beside him.

Startled, I emerged from my deep thoughts. 'Sure – I guess I would – Fine.' I'd never prayed with anyone before except when someone said grace before a meal. Tom bowed his head, folded his hands, and leaned forward on the edge of his seat. 'Lord,' he began, 'we pray for Chuck and his family, that You might open his heart and show him the light and the way . . .'

As Tom prayed, something began to flow into me – a kind of energy. Then came a wave of emotion which nearly brought tears. I fought them back. It sounded as if Tom were speaking directly and personally to God, almost as if He were sitting beside us. The only prayers I'd ever heard were formal and stereotyped, sprinkled with *Thees* and *Thous*.

When he finished, there was a long silence. I knew he expected me to pray but I didn't know what to say and was too self-conscious to try. We walked to the kitchen together where Gert was still at the big table, reading. I thanked her and Tom for their hospitality.

'Come back, won't you?' she said. Her smile convinced me she meant it.

'Take care of yourself, Chuck, and let me know what you think of that book, will you?' With that, Tom put his hand on my shoulder and grinned. 'I'll see you soon.'

I didn't say much; I was afraid my voice would crack, but I

had the strong feeling that I *would* see him soon. And I couldn't wait to read his little book.

Outside in the darkness, the iron grip I'd kept on my emotions began to relax. Tears welled up in my eyes as I groped in the darkness for the right key to start my car. Angrily I brushed them away and started the engine. 'What kind of weakness is this?' I said to nobody.

The tears spilled over and suddenly I knew I had to go back into the house and pray with Tom. I turned off the motor, got out of the car. As I did, the kitchen light went out, then the light in the dining room. Through the hall window I saw Tom stand aside as Gert started up the stairs ahead of him. Now the hall was in darkness. It was too late. I stood for a moment staring at the darkened house, only one light burning now in an upstairs bedroom. Why hadn't I prayed when he gave me the chance? I wanted to so badly. Now I was alone, really alone.

As I drove out of Tom's driveway, the tears were flowing uncontrollably. There were no street lights, no moonlight. The car headlights were flooding illumination before my eyes, but I was crying so hard it was like trying to swim under water. I pulled to the side of the road not more than a hundred yards from the entrance to Tom's driveway, the tyres sinking into soft mounds of pine needles.

I remember hoping that Tom and Gert wouldn't hear my sobbing, the only sound other than the chirping of crickets that penetrated the still of the night. With my face cupped in my hands, head leaning forward against the wheel, I forgot about machismo, about pretences, about fears of being weak. And as I did, I began to experience a wonderful feeling of being released. Then came the strange sensation that water was not only running down my cheeks, but surging through my whole body as well, cleansing and cooling as it went. They weren't tears of sadness and remorse, nor of joy – but somehow, tears of relief.

And then I prayed my first real prayer. 'God, I don't know

how to find You, but I'm going to try! I'm not much the way I am now, but somehow I want to give myself to You.' I didn't know how to say more, so I repeated over and over the words: *Take me*.

I had not 'accepted' Christ – I still didn't know who He was. My mind told me it was important to find that out first, to be sure that I knew what I was doing, that I meant it and would stay with it. Only, that night, something inside me was urging me to surrender – to what or to whom I did not know.

I stayed there in the car, wet-eyed, praying, thinking, for perhaps half an hour, perhaps longer, alone in the quiet of the dark night. Yet for the first time in my life I was not alone at all.

9

Cottage by the Sea

Mother and Dad were up early the next morning to see Patty and me off on our Maine vacation trip. Dad's worry-filled eyes told me what was coming when he suggested the two of us walk alone behind their house.

'You're positive, son, that no one told you anything about the break-in before it happened' he asked. We had talked about Watergate Sunday afternoon, but his lawyer's mind was still probing.

'Absolutely, Pop. I've thought back to every conversation. Nothing.'

Dad's steps were flagging as we walked up the gently sloping lawn. For the first time I realised how fast the years – seventy-three now – were overtaking him. Beneath his pure-white crew cut glistening in the morning sun were new furrows in his brow, deeper lines on his face.

'I read through all the Watergate material last night and I just don't see how you can be dragged in. You're sure you've told me everything?' he pressed one final time.

When I assured him I had, his warm grin returned. He and Mother hugged us and Patty and I backed our car out of their driveway and headed toward the Maine sea coast. Wearing a sweater, slacks, and an excited smile, Patty began chatting eagerly about lobsters, clams, and the scenes flashing by. It was our first time alone in months.

But I was too preoccupied to be good company. My thoughts were not on Watergate but on my visit with Tom Phillips the night before. I had expected to awaken feeling embarrassment for my uncontrolled outburst of emotion. Not so. The sense of freedom in my spirit was still there. Something important was happening, but what? Perhaps I'd find the answer in *Mere Christianity*.

What better place to search for answers than by the ocean. From boyhood when I used to walk the stony beach of Winthrop, Massachusetts, the sea had been important to me. Rejuvenation always came when I lost myself in the sea's vastness, feeling its power as the waves crashed in great sprays of foam on to moss-draped rocks.

When combined exhaustion and anxiety nearly paralysed me one day late in the 1960 Massachusetts election campaign, I left the campaign office and drove to a favourite spot in Gloucester. There on an overhanging cliff I felt renewed as I watched the raging seas smash against the rocks, then subside into a cluster of small eddies. I'd gone there later to be alone when I was searching for answers about my first marriage. Faced now with a major decision, the sea would again help me find the strength and clearness of mind I needed.

After a four-hour drive Patty and I arrived in Boothbay Harbour, a lovely old fishing village and sailing port 180 miles from Boston. The narrow streets of the village are lined with steep-roofed, grey-shingled houses nestled together. Cool breezes from the east fill the air with the briny odour of fish and sea peculiar to New England coastal towns. Old as it is, everything about Boothbay looks freshly scrubbed, even the native fishermen who walk through the streets in heavy slickers, high boots, caps shielding their leathery, wrinkled faces from the glare of the sun and sea.

Having made no reservation, we skirted the main part of

town, driving along a winding coastal road looking for an out-of-the-way spot. We were twelve miles from town when Patty spotted a small inn at the end of a long, narrow point of land jutting straight out into the Atlantic. 'Maybe no one will recognise us here,' I agreed, weary of curiosity seekers, auto-graph collectors, Nixon partisans and adversaries who were always happy to tell me exactly what they thought, often at length and with passion.

Cautiously we drove on to a narrow dirt road atop a man-made causeway built over the sea ten feet below. The causeway connected what was once a small rocky island to the mainland. The innkeeper was a stony-faced young man, tall and gaunt, who gave us the quizzical once-over so typical of cautious Down Easters and then showed us the one cottage which surprisingly was available for the week. It suited us perfectly. One huge room and a great open deck were suspended over the rocks and sea below.

Patty began unpacking, gleeful over our discovery, and I returned to the office. As I signed the register and waited, the innkeeper conferred in a corner with one of his employees. He returned and looked at me curiously. 'Colson, eh?'

'That's right.'

'From McLean. That near Washington?' He looked sus-piciously at the address I'd scribbled. My heart sank; Watergate was following us all the way to this craggy little spit of land.

'Friend here tells me you're famous.' He wasn't smiling.

'No, not really.'

'You been on TV?'

'Well, yes, a few times. This Watergate business, you know,' I admitted. *What was the sense in trying to hide it?*

'Eyuh,' followed by a pause and a stare. 'Watergate still going on?' The word *eyuh* is generally spoken by Down Easters with a heavy nasal twang and means 'Yes', 'Maybe', 'I don't know', 'That's interesting', and scores of other interpretations.

'Yes, it's still going on.'

'Well, I'll be – thought t'was over in June. My TV's been busted.' With that, still unsmiling, he handed me my key.

I couldn't wait to tell Patty. Hallelujah! We had found a spot where the TV was out of order. And the *sea*, the beautiful green-blue ocean, was roaring in under our picture window. 'What a great time to relax,' I told Patty. *What a great time to think about God*, I told myself.

That first night I unpacked Lewis's book and placed a yellow pad at my side to jot down key points, not unlike the way I prepared to argue a major case in court. In a moment of emotion the previous evening I had made a surrender of myself to something – or Someone. Now the habits of a lifetime rose in protest. All my training insisted that analysis precedes decision, that arguments be marshalled in two neat columns, pros and cons. I wondered if I could overcome my intellectual obstacles so as to believe in my mind what I had felt in my emotions.

On the top of the pad I wrote: Is there a God?

As I probed back in time, I remembered the night twenty years before when I stared into the vast darkness from the rail of the USS *Melette,* cruising off the coast of Guatemala. There was no possible explanation for how this whole magnificent universe, the glittering array of galaxies and stars, could remain in such perfect harmony without the direction of some awesome power which created it all in the first instance. That there is such a force greater than man seemed indisputable to me. And I had no trouble calling this force God.

Then I found myself remembering a curious shining moment seven years before. In the summer of 1966 I had bought a fourteen-foot sailboat for my two boys and hauled it to a friend's home on a lake in New Hampshire to teach them to sail. Christian, then ten, was so excited over having his own boat that even though a gentle summer rain was falling the day of our arrival, he was determined to try it out.

As the craft edged away from the dock, the only sound was the rippling of water under the hull and the flapping of the sail when puffs of wind fell from it. I was in the stern watching the tiller, Chris in the centre, dressed in an orange slicker, holding the sheet. As he realised that he was controlling the boat, the most marvellous look came over his cherubic face, the joy of new discovery in his eyes, the thrill of feeling the wind's power in his hands. I found myself in that one unforgettable moment quietly talking to God. I could even recall the precise words: 'Thank You, God, for giving me this son, for giving us this one wonderful moment. Just looking now into this boy's eyes fulfils my life. Whatever happens in the future, even if I die tomorrow, my life is complete and full. Thank You.'

Afterwards, I had been startled when I realised that I had spoken to God, since my mind did not assent to His existence as a Person. It had been a spontaneous expression of gratitude that simply bypassed the mind and took for granted what reason had never shown me. More – it assumed that personal communication with this unproven God was possible. Why else would I have spoken, unless deep down I felt that Someone, somewhere, was listening?

Perhaps, I thought, *it is on this intuitive, emotional level that C.S. Lewis approaches God.* I opened *Mere Christianity* and found myself instead face-to-face with an intellect so disciplined, so lucid, so relentlessly logical that I could only be grateful I had never faced him in a court of law. Soon I had covered two pages of yellow paper with *pros* to my query, 'Is there a God?'

On the *con* side were listed the conventional doubts so prevalent in our materialistic, science-has-all-the-answers society – we can't see, hear, or feel God.

Or can we?

What happened to me on Tom Phillips's porch? What was the emotion I had felt? Love? Some unseen force had stirred

560

inside me. And I had always felt that unseen forces were more powerful than visible ones.

A piston engine with 280 horsepower can move a precise number of pounds against the calculated resistance of friction, but not one pound more than known physical laws prescribe. The engine is made of hard steel, its existence evident to every sense. Yet love, which no one sees or touches, moves men and nations in limitless ways. Love caused one man to renounce a kingdom in my lifetime. Another kind of love causes a soldier to hurl his body over a grenade which has fallen into the midst of his buddies. Love has incomparably greater force than any engine of known horsepower.

I struggled on with this thought. A law is tangible in the sense that it is recorded somewhere on a piece of paper, but it exists only to the extent it causes men to do or not to do certain things. Its real force is then beyond the reach of that which we see or touch, made real by the extent people accept and believe.

As a lawyer I was impressed by Lewis's arguments about moral law, the existence of which he demonstrates is real, and which has been perceived with astonishing consistency in all times and places. It has not been man, I saw for the first time, that has perpetuated moral law; it has survived *despite* man's best attempts to defeat it. Its long existence therefore presupposes some other will behind it. Again, God.

I was back with Lewis, my yellow pads, and my questions early the next day. Patty was beginning to eye me a little strangely. Usually when we travelled to new places, I was active, restless, eager to see the sights; here I was sitting quietly engrossed in a book.

If there is a loving God, the automatic next question was, of course, 'If He is good, why does He preside over such an evil world?' Again my legal training suggested a useful parallel. In the beginning, God gave to mankind dominion over the earth He created (*see* Genesis 1:26–30). In other words, He made us, in lawyers' parlance, His agents.

The theory of *agency* in the law suggests a freedom of action, something beyond being a servant or mechanical robot. The agent is given the power to act within the *scope*, lawyers say, of authority – within certain set limits. The limits of this authority – the delegation as we call it in the law – God also laid out in Scripture.

But at the same time, He gave us free will. That is the point, of course; give someone less and he is no agent; the giver ends up doing it all himself. With a free will we can defy those limits and His instructions to us as readily as any agent exceeds the scope of his authority in civil law. And that happens each day; there are hundreds of law suits going on to prove it. As with the failure of agency in the law, so man often fails in discharging our Creator's agency.

History supports this view. Down through the years it has been man's abuse of God's authority, his malice toward his fellow men, which has created the preponderance of human grief. And probably we will go right on abusing it.

To understand this I came back to where Tom Phillips started: pride and ego. As Lewis put it, 'The moment you have a self at all, there is a possibility of putting yourself first – wanting to be the centre – wanting to be God . . .' How devastatingly I now saw that in my own life.

It was during this second day that I was emboldened to begin to tell Patty of the journey I'd begun. 'You believe in God, don't you, honey?' I asked. We were both sitting on the deck reading. Patty had inquired once about my little green and white paperback, which I explained merely as a book Tom Phillips had given me.

'You know I do,' she answered, with a hint of suspicion in her eyes – the latent, never spoken concern, perhaps, that some day I'd try to talk her out of her Roman Catholicism.

'But have you ever really thought about it – deeply, I mean? Like who is God and how does He watch over each of us and why did He create us, things like that?'

Patty's look of suspicion changed into one of pure baffle-ment. 'What's in that book you're reading?'

In the ten years we'd been married, I realised, we'd never discussed God; religion once in a while, what Patty felt about confession and Communion, the significance of the Mass. But these are procedural points. We'd never gone right to the substance, the living God, the faith down deep inside either one of us. We had done so much together but never touched on the essence of life itself. How much on the surface are even the closest of human relationships!

'I guess I'm looking for something,' I continued. 'I'm trying to find out what's real and what isn't – who we are – who I am in relation to God.' Then I told her something about my evening with Tom Phillips – not the tears, but the dismal self-discovery, all quite clinically, not wanting to admit how much my emotions had been touched. She looked dubious, but was fascinated by the story.

'You see, I'm looking for answers and this little book is terrific.'

'Maybe you should talk to a priest,' Patty suggested, now wanting (I could see it in the compassion in her eyes) to help me, knowing the struggle was genuine, no flip remark or banter to pass the time. Patty is the gentlest, most caring person I've ever known, taking others' problems as her own, feeling the full weight of every burden I ever had to bear. She hadn't quite expected this one – a search for God – but I sensed she was ready to share it with me.

I checked myself from voicing the critical statement, 'No priest or minister these forty years has ever explained any of this to me.' Who was I to point an accusing finger? I had never been looking, probably never really listening. Now for the first time Lewis's explanation and Phillips's example were opening a whole new world.

We talked into the night, while the bell buoy clanged,

guiding the lobstermen through the early evening fog, and the waves slapped against the rocks beneath us. It was a relief to have Patty know of my search to find new peace within myself, and to acquire an antidote for the disease inside which had been sucking life out of me, vampire-like, for eight long months ever since election night the year before. We ended by deciding to get out the family Bible when we returned home and begin reading it.

It was during the next morning, as I went on reading, underlining, making notes, that another important question was resolved for me. If God is listening to my prayers, how can He hear those being uttered at the same time by many millions of others?

That is a question which boggles the finite human mind. The difficulty is the same as when we try to understand where the universe ends, and if it does, what is beyond. Lewis shed light on this in a chapter entitled 'Time and Beyond Time': 'God [is] beyond all space and time.' And there is now a respectable body of scientific knowledge to establish that time is indeed relative, not the absolute measure we know.

Since the Creator of an infinite universe has no limitations in terms of hours or days, the fact that He could listen to four billion prayers at once was suddenly not the dazzling feat I with my limited mind had made it out to be. It was hard for me to accept this only so long as I struggled with my finite mind to understand a concept which is beyond finite limits. I can't explain it any better than I can explain what is beyond the stars, but simply knowing that man can't, provides an important answer.

All of this added to my conviction that there is a loving, infinite God, but left unanswered the question of what Tom really meant by the words *accept Christ*. How does Jesus Christ figure into all this? Hindus believe in God and that He can be worshipped in almost any way anyone pleases. All my analysing so far had only gotten me to Hinduism.

The central thesis of Lewis's book, and the essence of Christianity, is summed up in one mind-boggling sentence: *Jesus Christ is God* (*see* John 10:30). Not just part of God, or just sent by God, or just related to God. He *was* (and therefore, of course, *is*) *God*.

The more I grappled with those words, the more they began to explode before my eyes, blowing into smithereens a lot of comfortable old notions I had floated through life with, without thinking much about them. Lewis put it so bluntly that you can't slough it off: for Christ to have talked as He talked, lived as He lived, died as He died, He was either God or a raving lunatic.

There was my choice, as simple, stark, and frightening as that, no fine shadings, no gradations, no compromises. No one had ever thrust this truth at me in such a direct and unsettling way. I'd been content to think of Christ as an inspired prophet and teacher who walked the sands of the Holy Land 2,000 years ago – several cuts above other men of His time or, for that matter, any time. But if one thinks of Christ as no more than that, I reasoned, then Christianity is a simple palliative, like taking a sugar-coated placebo once a week on Sunday morning.

On this sunny morning on the Maine coast with fresh breezes picking up off the ocean, it was hard for me to grasp the enormity of this point – that Christ is the living God who promises us a day-to-day living relationship with Him and a personal one at that.

Each of the steps I'd laboured through was an essential building block to get to this point, but once I had, the others seemed almost irrelevant. Lewis's question was the heart of the matter. The words – both exciting and disturbing – pounded at me: Jesus Christ – lunatic or God?

Even atheists concede that Christ's coming changed the course of history. The year in which we live, for example, is based upon the date of His birth. He was a man without power in any worldly sense, no money, no armies, no weapons, and yet His coming altered the political alignments of nations. Millions upon millions of men have followed His promises and words. No work of literature has even begun to approach the endurance of the Scriptures which record Christ's life and have the same vitality to-day as they did nearly two thousand years ago. Magnificent churches, in which are invested centuries of labour and treasure, have been built as altars to Him. Could all this be the result of a lunatic's work, or even the result of one man's work? – The weight of evidence became more overwhelming to me the more I thought of it.

My legal training led me to another parallel. Our system of law is founded on the principle of *stare decisis*, that is, a court decision stands as a precedent with the same force of law as if it had one time been enacted or decreed; the whole system is built on precedents and presumptions which rest upon the foundation of earlier decisions. It is the key to giving stability to the law, a validation of history.

The most important decision of the Supreme Court, for example, studied intensively in law school, is *Marbury v. Madison*. Nowhere in the Constitution did the founding fathers give the Supreme Court the right to pass on the constitutionality of Acts of Congress. The Court acquired that power years later as a result of this famous case.

Today no one questions the Court's power of judicial review which it has exercised with dramatic effect thousands of times since. Even a neophyte law student would prefer to argue the validity of the case for *Marbury v. Madison*. There isn't much going for him with a contrary position, because of the way in which the doctrine has become so well established by its long history of acceptance.

So why should I worry as I once did about being accused of mindlessly following the pack by accepting Christ? And why struggle so hard with concepts about God when I wouldn't question legal principles which have far less historic validity than the one we have laid before our eyes in the life and impact of the Carpenter of Nazareth?

Once faced with the staggering proposition that He is God, I was cornered, all avenues of retreat blocked, no falling back to that comfortable middle ground about Jesus being a great moral teacher. If He is not God, He is nothing, least of all a great moral teacher. For what He taught includes the assertion that He is indeed God. And if He is not, that one statement alone would have to qualify as the most monstrous lie of all time – stripping Him at once of any possible moral platform.

I could not, I saw, take Him on a slightly lower plateau because it is easier to do so, less troublesome to my intellect, less demanding of my faith, less challenging to my life. That would be substituting my mind for His, using Christianity where it helped to buttress my *own* notions, ignoring it where it didn't.

I realised suddenly that there is less heresy in rejecting Him altogether, dismissing Him as a raving lunatic, to use Lewis's word, than to remake Him into something He wasn't (and isn't). Jesus said take it, all or nothing. If I was to believe in God at all, I had to take Him as He reveals Himself, not as I might wish Him to be.

Patty and I decided to spend Thursday evening in Boothbay Harbour. It was band-concert night on the steps of the town library, a venerable and colourful institution of the New England summer. The music might have sounded to Arthur Fiedler like someone scratching a fingernail across a blackboard, but we loved every discordant note blaring forth with mighty gusto.

The band came in all sizes and shapes – from a tot with a trumpet who couldn't have been more than twelve, to a sweet-faced teenage girl in pigtails on the drums, her face pock-marked with acne, wearing a straight, flowered dress which mostly covered her knobbly knees, to a man of eighty or more at the bass trombone, pure-white hair, a wrinkled, unsmiling face, and denim coveralls hanging from his rounded shoulders. Fifteen band members in all were lined along the wide wooden steps of the white clapboard building, the panes of its tall windows etched with century old swirls and bubbles shimmering in the glow of two big floodlights.

It was a Norman Rockwell *Saturday Evening Post* cover come to life, a priceless piece of rich Americana, unspoiled and untouched by what modern society calls progress. There were tourists sprawled on the green lawn, kids with spun candy on a stick, and a large number of townsfolk for whom the concert is the major outing of the week.

The strains of 'As the Saints Go Marching In' mixed with the fresh smell of salt in the night air. As I surveyed the faces in the crowd, something about them looked altogether different. Each one, including the kids with sticky sugar on their cheeks, looked like an individual, a separate human being, a child of God. Always before I'd seen crowds as blurs, a mass of humanity blending into an indistinct mosaic. Perhaps this new perception came from another Lewis passage, one that sent many of my cherished political ideals scattering like tenpins hit by a perfect strike:

> And immortality makes this other difference, which, by the by, had a connection with the difference between totalitarianism and democracy. If individuals live only seventy years, then a state, or a nation, or a civilisation, which may last for a thousand years, is more important than an individual. But if Christianity is true, then the individual is not only more important but incomparably more important, for he is everlasting and the life of a state or a civilisation, compared with his, is only a moment.

The lowliest individual was more important than a state or nation! I had to take a lot of deep breaths after that one. Yet I had always thought of myself as a Jeffersonian conservative, one who believed fervently that the state exists only to serve the individual, created and maintained only with the individual's consent. What had happened to me was obvious; everyone who spends time in government becomes to some degree a 'statist', dedicated to preserving the institutions of the state, often at all costs. Thus the paramount place of the individual in the scheme of things is gradually, unknowingly subordinated. Law-and-order legislation, for example, is aimed at maintaining the stability of the state – even if a few individuals have their rights trampled on in the process. Then, hard as it was to stomach, I had to admit that Dr Daniel Ellsberg's rights were more important than preserving state secrets.

The political convictions I had developed from reading Locke and Jefferson had proved pliable guidelines, subject to tempering adjustments as 'governmental crises' required, bending in the winds of the moment. But if Christ is real, if that fundamental decision is once made, then I am face-to-face with the very core of life itself, and with that I cannot tinker. Was Christ to change my view of life – and my neighbour, enemy, friend, and stranger alike – so drastically? My mind was whirling. Maybe it was the music, the nostalgia of the moment, the escape from the rest of the world one finds in Boothbay Harbour, Maine. Yet deep down I knew forces were at work which were demanding that I rethink every facet of my life.

Back at the inn doubts about my motives continued to nag at me. Was I seeking a safe port in the storm, a temporary hiding place? Was that what happened in Tom Phillips's driveway? Despite the arrow to the heart and my awakening on the Maine coast to the incredible realisation about Jesus Christ, was I somehow looking to religion as a last-gasp effort to save myself as everything else in my world was crashing down about me?

Did I hope that God would keep my world intact? Legitimate doubts, I suppose. Certainly many people would accuse me of copping out in time of trouble. But could I make a decision based on how the world might judge it?

No, I knew the time had come for me: I could not sidestep the central question Lewis (or God) had placed squarely before me. Was I to accept without reservations Jesus Christ as Lord of my life? It was like a gate before me. There was no way to walk round it. I would step through, or I would remain outside. A 'maybe' or 'I need more time' was kidding myself.

And as something pressed that question home, less and less was I troubled by the curious phrase 'accept Jesus Christ'. It had sounded at first both pious and mystical, language of the zealot, maybe black magic stuff. But 'to accept' means no more than 'to believe'. Did I believe what Jesus said? If I did, if I took it on faith or reason or both, then I accepted. Not mystical or weird at all, and with no in-between ground left. Either I would believe or I would not – and believe it all or none of it.

The search that began that week on the coast of Maine, as I pondered it, was not quite as important as I had thought. It simply returned me to where I had been when I asked God to 'take me' in that moment of surrender on the little country road in front of the Phillips's home. What I studied so intently all week opened a little wider the new world into which I had already taken my first halting, shaky steps. One week of study on the Maine coast would hardly qualify, even in the jet age, as much of an odyssey, but I felt as if I'd been on a journey of thousands of miles.

And so early that Friday morning, while I sat alone staring at the sea I love, words I had not been certain I could understand or say fell naturally from my lips: 'Lord Jesus, I believe You. I accept You. Please come into my life. I commit it to You.'

With these few words that morning, while the briny sea churned, came a sureness of mind that matched the depth of feeling in my heart. There came something more: strength and serenity, a wonderful new assurance about life, a fresh perception of myself and the world around me. In the process, I felt old fears, tensions, and animosities draining away. I was coming alive to things I'd never seen before; as if God was filling the barren void I'd known for so many months, filling it to its brim with a whole new kind of awareness.

I wrote Tom Phillips, telling him of the step I had taken, of my gratitude for his loving concern, and asked his prayers for the long and difficult journey I sensed lay ahead.

I could not possibly in my wildest dreams have imagined what it would involve. How fortunate it is that God does not allow us to see into the future.

10

Washington Revisited

At 7:30 a.m. I heard the crunch of tyres on gravel outside our home in McLean. As I opened the front door to greet our law firm's chauffeur, the smell of the Maine sea coast seemed far away. It was Monday morning and time to go to work.

Stocton Von Black flashed me a big grin. 'Good morning, Mr Colson. Good to have you back.' Stocton was always cheerful but I had never before noticed such warmth and kindness in his eyes. In my preoccupation I had usually managed only a 'grumph' in reply.

As he drove into the city, I found myself asking about his life and family. I also noticed how green and beautiful were the trees and shrubs lining the sides of the George Washington Parkway, how clear and blue the sky. The outline of the city was suddenly before us as we rounded the great curve following the Potomac River: the white marble and glass of the buildings glistening in the sun, with the majestic Capitol Dome perched atop a knoll as a backdrop.

'That's quite a sight, isn't it, Stocton?' I remarked and then noticed the puzzled expression on the chauffeur's face as he glanced back at me through the rear-view mirror. It was precisely the same view that had been there every morning all the months Stocton drove for me.

When the traffic closed in, bumper to bumper, I managed to get all the way through the *Washington Post* without a single profane outburst. If enjoying the green trees and the skyline was unusual for me, not crumpling the *Post* in an angrily clenched fist at least once was really a change. Even the people in the lobby of my office building seemed friendly, probably because I really looked at them for the first time. One can almost always spot a VIP in this city of power and protocol – the determined stride and the air of studied concern as he passes unseeing through the crowd signal the importance of the problems he shoulders.

Ordinarily I would have concluded that the week of vacation had rested me, provided renewed energy and a better outlook, but I knew, in fact, that it was much more than this. Everything *was* different, much different, from before – before Watergate, before any time I could remember.

One morning later that week Holly buzzed me on the intercom. 'There's a Mr Coe here. He wants to see you but he won't identify himself. He's probably a reporter; those guys are really something.' I remembered Tom Phillips had said a man named Doug Coe would be contacting me. He certainly hadn't wasted any time; Tom would barely have gotten my letter.

Holly, protective as Washington secretaries are trained to be, wanted to turn him off. 'You'll get yourself into something, if I don't.' I wanted to tell her that I'd already gotten myself 'into something'.

Doug Coe moved into my office as if we had known each other for years. He greeted me with a wide, friendly smile and had one arm around my shoulder before I could even invite him to sit down. 'This is just great, just great, what Tom has told me about you,' he said.

New Englanders are natively cautious about complete strangers. I usually took the first few minutes of any encounter to feel my way slowly and keep idle chatter going while I took full measure of a visitor – a little like the family dog circling around a new animal in the neighbourhood. But Doug in those first minutes broke through the usual amenities, tossed a rumpled raincoat on the corner table, plopped his gangling 6'1" frame into one of my leather chairs, draping one leg over its arm, and smiled continuously.

As we chatted I saw a strikingly handsome man, with short-cropped, curly black hair, dark dancing eyes, glistening white teeth, and always that instantly contagious smile. Within minutes I realised it was the same radiance and unpretentiousness I felt with Tom Phillips.

'Tom called me and – I hope you don't mind – read me your letter.' Doug Coe was studying my reactions.

I do mind, I thought. But there was such kindness in his eyes my resistance began to melt.

'So great to have it happen that way,' Doug said with a warmth that filled the room.

Still, what had happened was between me and God, I thought. You don't go around talking about such things, at least not with people you hardly know. But Doug Coe suddenly didn't seem to be a stranger. As we talked on I learned that Doug had come to Washington with Senator Mark Hatfield, an old friend from their Willamette University days in Oregon. He now worked with the Prayer Breakfast group in Washington, of which former Senator Frank Carlson of Kansas had been the prime mover. I should have known Doug; he'd been around the Senate for years. I did not. Still I felt as if I'd known him always.

Soon I found myself with growing excitement relating the story of my experience in Tom's driveway and the follow-up intellectual quest at a Maine cabin hideaway. 'And so, Doug, I've asked Christ into my life. Nothing held back.'

It was the first time I had articulated my commitment aloud to another person and the words startled me with their strangeness. Coe's smile broadened and his eyes shone as he repeated the words, 'That's so exciting, just tremendous . . .' Then Doug shifted ground. 'You'll want to meet Senator Hughes. Harold is a tremendous Christian.'

I laughed. 'Harold Hughes won't want to meet me. From what I've heard, he considers me the number-one menace to America. He's anti-war, anti-Nixon, anti-Colson and we couldn't be farther apart politically.'

'That doesn't matter now,' Doug continued with unabated exuberance.

'You are telling me that because I've accepted Christ, Harold Hughes, just like that, wants to be a friend?' I shook my head in disbelief.

'Wait and see, Chuck. Wait and see. You will have brothers all over this city, hundreds of them, men and women you don't even know who will want nothing more than to help you. Some of them know we are meeting and are praying for you right now.'

I stared at Doug. For months I had been battling Cox's army of investigators, the Ervin Committee, a dozen other congressional committees which were joining in the Watergate spectacular, plus hordes of newsmen and 90 per cent of the Washington establishment – or so it seemed. No one in the long months ever once asked if I needed anything – not even my old friends in the White House. Now Doug was telling me that perfect strangers cared about me. The idea almost paralysed my mind.

Then Doug suggested that we pray together at my desk. At first I was concerned what my partners would think if one of them burst through the door. But Doug was so natural and relaxed that I relaxed, too. He thanked the Lord for bringing us together in the bonds of fellowship, for letting us know His love. I stumbled and stammered through my prayer; it was the first time I had prayed aloud with anyone in my life.

My new friend then handed me a copy of the Phillips version of the New Testament, inscribed: *To Charles – It is better to fail in a cause that will ultimately succeed than to succeed in a cause*

that will ultimately fail – God bless you! Doug. Matthew 6:33.
How those words were to haunt and then lead me in the days
to come!

Doug recovered his balled-up raincoat, gripped my hand,
stared knowingly into my eyes for a long moment and then, as
quickly as he had come – with a cheery 'Bye, brother,' was
gone. Gone with him was the presence, the warmth that had
filled the room. The white-walled office looked sterile, cold,
businesslike again.

'Well, you certainly spent a long time with him. Who is he,
Chuck?' Holly, arms folded, was standing in the doorway,
mildly annoyed at the intrusion into our busy day. I hadn't
realised that over an hour had passed. 'A friend, Holly – a
good friend. He'll be coming by often, I hope. Yes, he will be,
I am sure.'

Doug meant it when he said that I had unknown friends in
the city. The next day Under Secretary of State Curtis Tarr
whom Nixon brought to Washington from the presidency of
Lawrence University, a strong personality whom I admired
greatly although I had met him only once, called. 'Anything I
can do for you Chuck, just call. I'm with you all the way. Just
keep it in mind. You've got a friend here.'

I was so taken aback I hardly knew how to answer. Some
of my erstwhile colleagues in the Nixon Administration, even
men I had placed in their high positions, had grown more
distant as the accusations increased. Men in politics always
watch their associations carefully and Watergate's ugly stain
was being spread on a lot of bystanders with a broad brush.
Yet in the days that followed, men whom I hardly knew did
not hesitate to ally themselves with me, each with the same
message spoken in a dozen ways: 'As brothers in Christ we
stand together.' There was, I discovered to my astonishment,
a veritable underground of Christ's men all through the
government.

* * *

The moral support could not have come at a better time, since my blunt talk and outspoken defence of the President had made me a prime target of the forty-odd lawyers, mostly liberal, Democratic, and honour graduates of Harvard, now part of Professor Cox's office. Dave Shapiro and Judd Best from our office gently broke the news to me one evening: the grand jury investigating the break-in at the office of Ellsberg's psychiatrist was hearing evidence on me.

'Let's go see them. Let me tell them what really happened.' I suggested with what now seems incredible naiveté.

'Okay, if you're sure you want to,' Shapiro said, 'but the orthodox way is to stay a mile away from a grand jury when you're a target; all you can do is give them more to use against you later in the . . .'

Dave stopped and I finished the sentence for him. 'Trial, Dave – okay, I understand but I'll never be happy if I don't try. Get me a chance to testify and there won't be any trial, you'll see.'

Dave, Judd, and I sought a hearing. A week or so later we climbed to the sixth floor of the US Courthouse, walked the dimly lit corridor past large menacing signs which warn: 'General public and media personnel not permitted beyond this point,' and entered bare-walled rooms where the Watergate special grand jury was meeting. We waited in an outer office while the Special Prosecutor's ace assistant, William Merrill, briefed the grand jury on the evidence it might expect from one Charles Colson. I had once met Merrill, a mild-mannered man in his late forties, at a conference in his office. Having been a Democratic candidate for Congress in Michigan and state chairman for the 'Robert Kennedy for President' campaign, his political sympathies obviously were not with me.

As I moved about the room restlessly, I reviewed what I remembered from law school about a witness coming before a grand jury – he appeared alone without counsel before some twenty-three citizens selected from the community. The sole function of a grand jury is to decide whether evidence presented by government prosecutors is sufficient to support charges against an individual and thus warrant a court trial. In theory it is to protect an individual against reckless or capricious prosecution.

Finally a young man emerged from an inner room and beckoned for me to follow. I walked through what appeared to be a metal-detection device, past a sleepy-eyed uniformed guard slumped in a chair at the door, and into Grand Jury Room No. 2. To the right was a benchlike table at which were seated two young assistant prosecutors. Immediately before me was another small table with a microphone, obviously for the witness. Beside it sat a court stenographer, her hands poised over a little black stenotype machine. In the rear were six rows of chairs, six abreast, each tier slightly elevated above the one before it. With a sinking feeling I could count only three white faces among the twenty-three representative citizens of the District of Columbia. The blacks had not exactly been Nixon supporters.

William Merrill stood in shirt sleeves before the grand jurors, reminding me of a kindly schoolteacher addressing his flock. 'If you are ready,' he said, smiling and peering over his half-moon reading glasses, 'we can now begin the questioning of Mr Colson.' The foreman of the grand jury administered the oath and Merrill turned to me.

'I should tell you for the record that you are here before this grand jury which is inquiring into the possibility of violations of the federal law relating to the break-in of Doctor Fielding's office in Los Angles, Doctor Fielding having been the psychiatrist for Daniel Ellsberg. I think I should tell you also that from evidence the grand jury has heard you are a prospective defendant in the violation of certain criminal statutes relating to that matter, that you therefore have the right to take the Fifth Amendment in answer to any question that I may give to you, that any answers that you do give here can obviously be used against you . . .'*

Under my shirt I could feel cold drops of perspiration forming. I started to reach for the small paper cup of water on the table, but discovered my hand was shaking so badly that I couldn't lift it without making my nervousness obvious.

Merrill turned, smiled at the grand jurors, then continued: 'It is also my understanding and should be made known to the grand jurors if it is correct, that you are here at your request. Are the things that I have said – do you understand them and are they accurate?'

'I understand them fully, Mr Merrill, and I am here at my own request because I have felt from the beginning that I would like to be in a position to tell as much as I know about the events, anywhere I can,' I replied.

I was relieved to hear my own words through the speaker, firm and clear; at least my voice would not betray me. After Merrill had dispensed with the preliminary questions – name, occupation, when I came to the White House, what I did for the President – one of the young men at the table beside him, passed him a note and I waited for the main line of questioning to get under way. He began: 'Do you ever recall a discussion with Mr Magruder about obtaining one hundred thousand letters for use in the New Hampshire primary to try to persuade Democrats to vote for Kennedy?'

The question had nothing to do with the Ellsberg matter, and I hoped that I did not look as stunned as I felt. No one in all the months since the Watergate investigation began had ever asked me about this mailing, our secret attempt to encourage a write-in campaign in the New Hampshire primary to flush out Ted Kennedy, to force him to declare or disavow his

* *Editor's Note*: All questions and answers in this colloquy are taken from the actual transcript of grand jury proceedings.

candidacy. It was a campaign 'dirty trick' of old-style politics that indeed I had been responsible for.

I tried to collect my thoughts. I had been prepared to give every detail of everything I knew about the Ellsberg case, but I hadn't thought about the Kennedy write-in. Nonetheless, I truthfully answered each of Merrill's questions, aware that the Kennedy family is revered by the vast majority of blacks in the District of Columbia. If the question was designed to put me on the defensive, it succeeded.

The morning questioning dealt almost entirely with the 1972 campaign, other non-Ellsberg matters and my attitude towards the Kennedys. Merrill pressed on: 'Did you ever have any knowledge or suggestion of an effort to recruit either individuals or a group of homosexuals to indicate support for McGovern?'

'No, sir,' I protested, while one of Merrill's young men shook his head in disbelief, to the obvious delight of several of the jurors. There was not a shred of truth to this well-publicised accusation. Merrill's assistants then took turns in the interrogation, each one seemingly competing to ask the most difficult and embarrassing question. I felt like I was facing a wall of angry faces.

At the lunch break Shapiro and Best tried hard to buck up my flagging spirits. I was both outraged and dejected; during two hours in the grand-jury room there had been hardly any questions about the case I volunteered to testify about.

After Shapiro had a talk with Merrill, the questioning focused on the matter before the grand jury, the Ellsberg break-in. As Merrill laboured over each piece of evidence, much of which I had earlier turned over voluntarily, the interest of the grand jury waned. Several jurors, I noticed, were reading newspapers. One very heavy-set woman in a starched-white maid's uniform seated in the front row kept dozing off, her head falling forward and chin thumping against her breast-bone. Just as I thought I was making a particularly telling point, she would reach the bottom on this seesaw and a titter would ripple through the room. Another man in the second row fought to stay awake, moaning loudly each time he yawned.

At one point Merrill did manage to get their attention: 'Did you ever tell anybody that you wanted to *paint Ellsberg black?*' Groaning to myself, I admitted using that phrase once in a memo. It was useless to plead that I meant no racial slur; merely by asking the question Merrill scored.

The next day was almost a repeat performance, the questions just as piercing, my attempts to get exculpatory matter into the record thwarted. With the novelty of my appearance gone, many of the grand jurors either left mid-way through the session or slept unashamedly.

Shapiro, Best, and I concluded that evening that I should stop the voluntary appearances. Whatever I said could not possibly help me with the grand jurors. Merrill knew the evidence; he was either going to recommend my indictment or not. And indeed, two days later Merrill contacted Shapiro: 'We are going to indict your client, probably next week.'

Late that same afternoon I sat alone in my office staring moodily out the window. How would I explain it all to Patty and the children? The stigma would be on them forever. Strangely though, the fears of early summer were gone. There would be a trial and if I lost I could go to prison. But somehow that thought, grim and black though it was, no longer seemed to be the end of life.

What bothered me most was the inner knowledge that events were moving inexorably forward, that bitterness and anger now tended to tip the scales of justice, and that there was no way I could turn back the onrushing tide. The evil of my pride had been exposed that night with Tom Phillips, but the process of ego slaying was still going on.

Just at that moment Doug Coe burst into my office with his usual, 'Hi-ya brother – just passing through the neighbourhood.' His sense of timing was uncanny. He always arrived, it seemed, when my spirits most needed a lift. As I explained the impending indictment, Doug listened with a look of growing concern.

'It's tough on you, Chuck – really tough,' he said. There was a period of silence. 'What really matters,' he continued, 'is not what Mr Cox or Bill Merrill think or do, but what God knows. He knows your sins; He knows mine. And He's always ready to forgive us. That's the beauty of having a loving Father. You can be open with God no matter what you've done.'

As we talked, the truth of Doug's point became clear. God does not promise to spare us the pain or punishment that comes from our mistakes, but He will always forgive us, love us, and provide the strength to see us through the most difficult experience. Doug's insights and our prayers together lifted my spirits.

Yet in the days which followed I learned how hard it is for a new Christian to turn himself over to God completely. Daily prayer and a study of Scripture helped, but the old self keeps fighting; the old ego and pride die hard. I worried about what others would think of my indictment. How could I ever prove my innocence to my friends? An indictment is a permanent scar no matter what happens in a trial. There were times, too, when I was just plain frightened.

But remarkable things were happening inside me. I felt less of the old animosity and bitterness toward my adversaries. At a dinner party in October with old White House friends I found myself suddenly uncomfortable when the others began to attack John Dean.

'He's got to live with himself,' I responded mildly.

Patty looked at me surprised. Previously the mention of his name would bring a hot flush to my face and angry words. I found I could no longer hate so easily and quickly as I once had.

Meanwhile Dave Shapiro became convinced that he and I

were too close personally for him to defend me in court. Ethical questions were raised as well, since the prosecutors indicated that Shapiro, who had met once with Howard Hunt, might be called as a witness at the trial. After several long talks, we decided to find a top trial lawyer to assist us if the case came to trial. Both of us agreed on the man – Jim St Clair, senior partner of a prestigious Boston firm. Twenty years earlier Jim had been the young understudy to Joe Welch, the wily old defence counsel whose homespun barbs made him the hero of the Army-McCarthy hearings. Over the years Jim St Clair had won the reputation of being one of the ablest trial lawyers in the country, as shrewd and canny as his one-time mentor.

Before agreeing to handle the case Jim insisted on knowing everything. He spent two days interrogating Shapiro and me, interviewing key witnesses, and combing through my files. Late the second day he met with me in my office to announce his decision. 'I'll represent you. In fact, I believe you are innocent of the Ellsberg charges. That isn't essential to my decision but it helps. As I see it, you can feel pretty good about this case; we have a 50 per cent chance.'

'You believe I'm innocent, and we have a good case, but I've only got a fifty-fifty chance?' I protested.

Jim leaned back in the black leather chair across from my desk, erupting with a low guffaw. 'Look, Chuck, when a prosecutor is out to get you – and these Cox guys are out to nail your hide to the wall – it's rough to beat it. The Feds have everything on their side, including sometimes the jury. It's uphill now for all you guys with Nixon.'

St Clair's big toothy grin, greying mane, and stocky frame which moves nimbly in the courtroom earned him the nickname of the Silver Fox. He stared at me, grinning: 'All prosecutors are cops, you see.' Jim's brutally frank words, the language of the criminal world which even a stuffy Boston lawyer uses after two decades as defence counsel, remained vivid in my consciousness in the months to come. I was fast confronting some of the harsher realities of life – such as how criminal defendants feel – that I had passed right by in my headlong rush for the top.

We were still awaiting the promised indictment when a new crisis was upon me. There was nothing I had wanted more through the long summer of 1973 than my turn at bat before the Ervin Committee. But time after time my appearance was postponed. We suspected that the committee counsel, Sam Dash, had no desire to let a free-swinging Nixon defender before the TV cameras until the case against Nixon was firmly made with the eighty million Americans in the viewing audience. Even in early September, Dash's lieutenants refused to confirm a date for my testimony. But two days after Merrill informed Shapiro of my 'imminent' indictment, Dash called to schedule my appearance. Shapiro explained the dilemma: I obviously could not testify about matters – the Ellsberg break-in in particular – that would be included in the indictment. Under committee rules, and with the guideline of a Supreme Court decision, they could not even inquire into those matters.

'But he hasn't been indicted yet,' Dash insisted.

'That's a technical distinction,' returned Shapiro. 'The prejudice would be the same. In the interest of justice the committee should postpone the Colson testimony for ten days. If not indicted by then, well, Colson may have to take his chances and testify.'

Dash could not argue the fairness of Dave's position. He would check the committee's desires and call back. Within hours he did; the committee was determined. 'Of course,' Dash concluded, 'Colson can always invoke his constitutional right against self-incrimination . . .'

The Fifth Amendment to me was the scarlet letter of American politics. Nothing creates the aura of guilt and stench of cowardice more than refusing to testify. Those accused of Communist ties during the McCarthy days who invoked the Fifth Amendment might just as well have said, 'I'm guilty as charged,' as far as public opinion was concerned. No one had done it in connection with Watergate, except Bud Krogh, the youthful head of the Plumbers, who invoked his right before an obscure House Committee.

'I won't do it, Dave. I absolutely will not take the Fifth,' I insisted, as Shapiro reported his conversations with Dash.

Shapiro, a lawyer who defended more Loyalty Review Board cases than anyone else in the McCarthy heyday, paced angrily in front of his desk, one moment railing at the committee and the next screaming at me for my stupidity. 'Chuck, you stick your neck out now and you're dead. Do you want to commit suicide? Have you got a death wish? The only place you testify now is in court. You can say nothing. We don't know what those guys in Cox's office will use against you and we aren't giving them more ammunition.' St Clair was in agreement with Dave as well as all my partners.

Ervin scheduled my appearance for the morning of September 19, behind closed doors. He was uncertain, as even Shapiro was, whether I'd testify or take the Fifth Amendment, and should I do the latter on national television, under prevailing Court decisions, that could cause any subsequent prosecution against me to be thrown out.

As the hour approached I was still wrestling with my dilemma. Every instinct within me argued that I should testify. I spent five years working in the Senate, almost four in the White House, over half of my adult life in government or in the military, and all the while believing fervently in what I was doing. Refusing to testify seemed like ducking combat duty, failing to heed 'our country's call'. Then there was my pride still clamouring to be on stage, to rise to the defence of my commander-in-chief, to carry the battle to our attackers.

Camera crews were stationed at every entrance to the Capitol Building when we arrived. 'Let's go in with our heads up,' I urged. Shapiro, a young associate in our firm, Ken Adams, and I were met at the car door by a rush of cameramen and reporters, lights flashing, microphones on long poles thrust in our faces. A cordon of burly Capitol policemen rescued us and burrowed a path through the melee, up the short flight of steps, through the revolving glass doors. The crowd inside the building was almost as large as outside.

I struggled vainly to escape the grip of two overly protective policemen clutching both arms; the photo of that would be terrible. Other blue-suited officers were now out front, pressing ahead in a flying wedge. We inched our way through throngs of staring tourists, past rows of rich-brown mahogany doors and paintings of great moments in American history, and into Room S-143.

While waiting in the anteroom, we reviewed our strategy: first, through a series of manoeuvres, try to get the committee to vote a ten-day delay. Maybe we'd get one Democrat – the laconic Georgia senator, Herman Talmadge, to vote with the Republicans, which would carry 4–3. If that failed, Shapiro was adamant about the Fifth Amendment. I wasn't sure I could force the words out even if I agreed.

The chairman opened the session with only the seven senators and a handful of staffers in the room. We were seated at the far end of a long conference table. Shapiro began reviewing all of my voluntary appearances over the prior sixteen months, the dilemma which the threatened indictment posed, deploring committee 'leaks', and begging the committee to protect his client's rights to a fair trial.

He pointed out that my appearance this day would be the same as parading us before live TV cameras, that the resulting publicity would be just as damaging. If I were to take the Fifth Amendment, this would certainly influence the grand jury now considering my indictment. If I refused to take the Fifth I was waiving future rights to remain silent, stripping my trial defence. Through the full ten minutes of his impassioned appeal, not a person stirred in the committee room and there was a long moment of silence when he finished.

Dash was the first to speak: 'I do want to confirm, Mr Shapiro . . . on my own inquiry of the Special Prosecutor's office, it is true that the current grand jury . . . does intend to come down fairly shortly . . . and I have been informed that Mr Colson is a very real target and most likely would be one of those indicted.'* It was support we hadn't expected.

Sam Ervin, proud of his reputation as the eminent constitutional scholar of the Senate, seemed affected by Shapiro's argument. 'We have granted other witnesses the use of immunity,' he mused, looking down thoughtfully at his fingers tapping on the tabletop.

'Mr Colson has been rather – uh, he has made statements freely and voluntarily and on TV programmes and in press interviews,' he said, indicating that my TV appearances had stung him. Although I hadn't criticised the chairman directly, I had knocked the committee's tactics, the torrent of leaks to the press, the berating of witnesses, the exclusion of Nixon defenders. All my efforts had not affected public opinion one whit – Nixon continued to plummet in the polls. But it had succeeded in bruising Sam Ervin who now had me where he wanted me; I was looking right down the barrel of his loaded howitzer – and squirming.

Shapiro and I were asked to leave the room while the committee debated in private. But voices were soon raised until we could hear them even through the closed door. Senator Baker was in spirited support of my requests for a delay, Senator Weicker shouting opposition. The hands of the clock ticking off ten minutes, then twenty, thirty, forty, gave us hope. If Ervin had the votes to defeat the delay, this much debate would be needless.

After an hour we were called back. The chairman asked us to be seated. Ervin was obviously uncomfortable, his facial

* *Editor's Note*: All quoted statements are from Executive Session transcripts of the Ervin Committee.

muscles twitching continuously, his jowls trembling, deep furrows across his brow as he squinted over his glasses. 'The committee has denied the request,' he announced. 'Stand up and raise your right hand.'

Shapiro protested, only for the record now, and then leaned over to me and whispered, 'You have to do it or you can get yourself another set of lawyers.'

I bit my lip and gripped the underside of the felt-topped table so hard my fingers went numb. Pride, pride, pride! How I had despised cowardice in any form. How I had scorned those whimpering bureaucrats who invoked the Fifth Amendment during the early fifties and the thugs who did the same thing during Senator McClellan's racket hearings of a few years later. Pride. I had so wanted to ride forth on a white horse and save President Nixon, to hear his grateful voice, 'Good job, boy – you really laid them back on their heels.'

'Mr Colson, are you acquainted with E. Howard Hunt?' Dash's words rang in my ears, cutting and sharp. I turned towards the chairman.

'Senator –' I stammered, my voice failing me for a moment, 'I wanted more than I can tell you to appear before this committee and to be able to testify. If I believed one-tenth of the things that have been printed about me, I would not deserve to be sitting here. I am proud of the service I have been to my country... I never thought I would be in this position where I felt that my own legal rights were being prejudiced and that I had to avail myself of my constitutional privilege. I do not like doing this. I very much dislike it; I hate it. I am going to, Mr Chairman, follow the instructions of my counsel which I have to say are not the instructions of my conscience.'

Then it was over, just three questions, three apologetic, feeble 'I decline to answer' responses that I could barely get past the big heavy lump clogging my throat. I wanted to push myself away from the table and run out of the room. For a moment there was an eerie silence. Even Senator Inouye's stern scowl was gone. His eyes seemed to be saying, 'I don't like you but I feel for you.'

Ervin continued to stare at me with a knowing, fatherly expression: the hurt in Howard Baker's heart was as obvious as the bold pattern of his tweed jacket: all of the venom and outrage was gone from Lowell Weicker as he sat motionless, staring out of the one window in the small room. Men in politics savour their moments of victory, but there is no joy among politicians in witnessing one of their own, even a bitter foe, not just defeated but helpless, shamed, the last vestige of self-respect stripped from him.

As we left the committee chambers, we saw Senator Ervin, surrounded by cameras and reporters, explaining that I had taken the Fifth! No inferences were to be drawn, he reminded them. But we knew what would happen the next day – and it did.

The *Washington Post* printed, above the fold on page one, a gigantic picture of the one-time 'tough guy'. Beneath the photo was the headline: COLSON WON'T REPLY TO WATERGATE QUIZ. One unnamed committee source described me as 'subdued and contrite'. All three networks and virtually every major paper in the country gave banner coverage to the political obituary of Nixon's last stalwart.

Tom Phillips had begun the process on that still, humid night in August when for the first time I came face-to-face with the person which years of striving for the successes of this world had created. The *old* was dying, all right, but not without pain, not without resistance, not without tears and sorrow. Though my eyes were being opened slowly to a whole bright world I'd not known before, I was still struggling to save what I should have known must be left behind. For some of us, at least for a while, the struggle continues for the riches of both worlds.

11

Brothers

My encounter with Senator Harold Hughes was arranged for an evening in late September. Harold, I later learned, had stoutly resisted the idea when Doug Coe first called him to suggest it.

'There isn't anyone I dislike more than Chuck Colson. I'm against everything he stands for. You know that, Doug,' he protested.

Before Hughes hung up, Doug gently suggested that the senator's attitude was hardly Christlike. The next day Hughes called back and with a weary sigh relented. 'All right, Doug. You set it up.'

Fearing that a one-on-one confrontation between Harold and myself might be too explosive, Doug decided to make it a quiet evening with wives, at the home of the soft-spoken veteran Minnesota Republican congressman, Al Quie. He invited as well a former Democratic congressman from Texas, Graham Purcell. That made it two Democrats, two Republicans, and Coe.

Harold Hughes is indeed an extraordinary man, I discovered while reading about his past. Raised on a small Iowa farm, he fought his way through the mud of Italy during World War II as an Army infantryman, narrowly escaping death. In the postwar period Hughes became a truck driver and an alcoholic, brawling his way from one bar to the next, sometimes gone from his young family for days on end, and often waking up from a drunken stupor to find himself in a strange hotel hundreds of miles from home. Alienated periodically from family, imprisoned by whisky, he often thought of suicide.

Alone late one night in 1954 Hughes cried out to God for help. When the fog lifted the next day from his whisky-soaked brain, everything around him seemed new. He never took another drink.

Hughes achieved moderate success with a small trucking business. He and his wife, Eva, become active in the church. At first involved in Young Republican politics, the fiercely independent Hughes switched in 1957 to the minority Democratic Party and was elected state commerce commissioner. In 1962 he ran for governor. When a whispering campaign began about his alcoholism, Hughes met the issue head-on. Politicians didn't usually admit such things but he was what he was, he explained publicly, among other things a recovered alcoholic. The state's traditionally Republican voters elected him governor by over 40,000 votes, and despite his outspoken liberalism, re-elected him twice, then sent him to the US Senate in 1968, replacing a conservative GOP stalwart.

Ignoring unwritten traditions that freshmen members of the Senate sit quietly in the back row to learn from their elders, Hughes was quickly championing liberal causes and within a few months became one of the most outspoken advocates of legislation to end the Vietnam War. This was when we in the Nixon White House put him high on the 'enemies' list.

Burning with idealism about the need for sweeping social reforms in American society, Hughes plunged into the race for the 1972 Democratic Presidential nomination. His charismatic personality won him some pockets of early support, but with no political base of his own, meagre campaign funds, and his blunt manner frightening many of the more orthodox politicians in his party, Hughes decided to withdraw from the race.

Meanwhile the senator was finding the demands of political life more and more in conflict with his own commitment to Christ. Though he was virtually certain of re-election, Hughes, in the summer of 1973 after deep soul-searching announced that at the end of his term in January 1975 he would retire from the Senate. The announcement left political observers and the voters of Iowa stunned. Hughes stated that he felt he could do more for his fellow man out of public life, serving only one Master.

After reviewing what I knew about Senator Hughes, I found myself intrigued by his gutsy approach to life. At the same time my political instincts were preparing me for battle.

Doug was on the phone a few days before the planned meeting. 'Brother, why don't I pick you up at your office?' he suggested. 'Say about 8 p.m.'

'Sounds good.' Patty was to take Doug's wife, Jan, in our car.

At the selected time and place I spotted Doug's battered blue Chevy station wagon. Realising someone was in the front seat, I climbed in the back. The someone was Senator Hughes!

I sat back and studied my longtime adversary. Hughes was dressed in a checkered sport shirt hanging loosely over a set of denim coveralls. His deliberate disdain of the attire considered proper by Washington standards had earned him the title of 'worst-dressed senator' in the year's annual poll of Senate staffers. It was this very casualness plus the warmth of his deep resonant voice that made me lower my guard.

Yet I sensed that the senator was not making the same instant re-evaluation of me. Every now and then he would shift his husky frame, turning to stare into the back seat. His sharp features, black hair, and deep-set eyes give him the appearance of American Indian heritage. His scowl as he measured me sent shivers through me. I noticed Doug's eyes glancing nervously first at me through the rear-view mirror, then sideways at the senator.

Feeling uncomfortable in my conservative blue business suit, I removed my coat. Conversation fumbled along in safe areas: family and the few mutual friends I could, only with considerable effort, think of. As we pulled up to the front door of Al Quie's white Colonial home nestled among old oak trees, I could sense Doug's relief. So far, so good.

The Quies – Al and Gretchen – greeted us warmly. Al, a tall, rugged, athletic man and a former dairy farmer, flashed a shy smile which gave him the appearance of being younger than his fifty years. Graham Purcell, grey-haired and rangy, and his vibrant, attractive wife, Nancy, arrived a few minutes later. We all gathered before a mammoth brick fireplace in the large panelled family room, its walls covered with trophies and awards won by Al and his prize horses.

It was also the first time that I met Jan Coe whom Doug married when they were both freshmen in college during the late forties. She is graceful and ageless like Doug, with the same effervescent personality. In fact, I was startled by how much they look alike.

Whenever two or more politicians gather together during a Washington social evening, the conversation quickly turns to the latest fight on Capitol Hill, upcoming elections, and the fall from or rise to power of the current political personality. The men congregate together, leaving the ladies to fend for themselves. It is important to get the first cocktail in hand quickly, followed by a second and a third. Each man tries to impress whomever will listen with how close he is to the real source of power. 'You know, my friends in the White House tell me . . .' The scene might be cast in Greenwich, Connecticut or Winnetka, Illinois, and the conversation about the latest gyrations of the stock market or who's on the way up the corporate ladder.

This night instead we sat in a large semicircle around the

fireplace, sipping iced tea and lemonade. Husbands and wives were together, and the talk was about Al's horses. We might as well, I realised, have been in the living room of the Quie farm 1,000 miles from the hubbub of the nation's capital. I marvelled at the warmth and hominess, all the while keeping a wary eye on Harold Hughes. Gretchen, even more a Scandinavian beauty with an apron around her waist, brought out piping hot, homemade apple pie and ice cream and smiled appreciatively as Harold devoured the first helping and asked for another.

It was all so new to me I found myself squirming in my chair a few times. We had come together for me to meet Senator Hughes and the others. They were also to expose me to the nebulous concept which Doug had called fellowship. I sensed that Hughes was becoming a little impatient, too, since he was not known for socialising, particularly without Eva, who was ill at home.

In one sense, Hughes and I were like two boxers in separate corners, restless, awaiting the moment we knew was coming when we would be sparring together. Everyone there knew the two of us would have our confrontation sooner or later, but I was not prepared to have Harold Hughes abruptly put me on stage.

'Chuck,' he said, 'they tell me you have had an encounter with Jesus Christ. Would you tell us about it?'

I was not ready for this – to talk about Christ to a roomful of people I hardly knew. Even Doug had not heard in detail what had happened at Tom Phillips's and later on in Maine. For a fleeting moment I considered ducking, then from inside me came reassurance. Harold's expression was open – not warm, not cold. Patty looked nervous. The rest seemed very friendly.

Though I considered myself a veteran speaker in the political arena, this was different. The words came out haltingly. But to my surprise there was no embarrassment, simply a feeling of inadequacy in talking about the most intimate experience of my life. In the middle, I almost bogged down as I wondered, *Are they going to think I'm some kind of nut? Do people really go around talking about their personal encounters with God?* I stopped momentarily and looked around the room. No one spoke but their expressions told me to keep going.

'That night with Tom Phillips broke down some kind of lifelong barrier,' I continued. 'Yet I had to wonder the next day if all the Watergate unpleasantness had left me so shell-shocked that I was just looking for a way out – any way out. It was the week in Boothbay where I put it together in my mind, not just in my emotions. I really was able to see who Jesus is and my need for Him – then I could give my life to Him.' Just saying the words brought the emotion back and I choked up for a minute. 'As a new Christian I have everything to learn, I know that I'm grateful for any help you can give me.'

For a moment there was silence. Harold, whose face had been enigmatic while I talked, suddenly lifted both hands in the air and brought them down hard on his knees. 'That's all I need to know. Chuck, you have accepted Jesus and He has forgiven you. I do the same. I love you now as my brother in Christ. I will stand with you, defend you anywhere, and trust you with anything I have.'

I was overwhelmed, so astonished, in fact, that I could only utter a feeble, 'Thank you.' In all my life no one had ever been so warm and loving to me outside of my family. And now it was coming from a man who had loathed me for years and whom I had known for barely two hours.

Then we were all on our knees – all nine of us – praying aloud together. As I got to my feet, Harold lumbered toward me, a smile slowly spreading over his face. As he wrapped his arms around me in a great bear hug, I needed no further explanation of what *fellowship* meant or what Paul meant when he wrote, 'Let us have real affection for one another as between brothers . . .' (Romans 12:10 PHILLIPS).

The others also offered their support and counsel. 'Politicians are wary of anyone who faces indictment, but Christians stand together,' said Graham Purcell, a judge in Texas before his election to Congress. 'That's right,' chimed in Al Quie. 'We'll be with you. Stand tall.'

When Patty and I said good-bye, I was marvelling not so much at what was said, but at the impact of non-verbal communication. Harold Hughes need not have said a word to me. I read him perfectly in my heart through his smile, his bear hug, and the caring look in his eyes.

The only question in my mind about this extraordinary evening was its effect on Patty. She had sat in wide-eyed amazement during much of it. As a Roman Catholic, she found God on Sunday morning in the solemn hush of church. Kneeling at a sofa in a living room was a strange experience for her. During nine years of marriage she had never heard me pray aloud until that night. In fact, it was only the third time I had. Nothing she said that night indicated anything but support for me. The expression on her face, however revealed the inner doubts. Non-verbal communication again. I decided that Patty and I needed to have an in-depth discussion about it as soon as possible. But the events that swirled about us postponed it for weeks.

My indictment did not come as expected in September. At first my law associates and I concluded that the threat to do so had been simply a ploy to keep me from testifying before the Ervin Committee, and humiliate me in the process. Or maybe it was the valiant defence Shapiro and St Clair were waging, meeting with Cox and his assistants, even once bringing me in for what turned out to be almost a friendly session.

Shapiro submitted briefs to the prosecutors, arguing that for years the FBI engaged in illegal 'entries', a euphemistic term for burglary for national-security reasons, that the Ellsberg case wasn't any different from what had happened hundreds of times. Nixon's lawyers argued that the White House files fully supported the national-security justification.

The President then entered the situation. In a brief bravado moment, his voice surging with confidence during one late-night phone call, Nixon said, 'I know they've been after you, Chuck, but it won't work. There is no way I am going to let them do it to you. You are innocent in this. I know that, and from now on the President is in charge.'

But events in Washington were now spinning wildly out of control. The President was soon calling me evenings about the problems of Vice-President Spiro Agnew. Serious charges – accepting bribes while governor of Maryland – were now being amassed by a Baltimore grand jury investigation. Our firm, representing the Vice-President, was in the thick of it.

At first Nixon wanted to help his two-time running mate. Then the evidence began to pile up and the President's attitude changed. Pressure from the White House came for me to ask an industrialist not to contribute to the Vice-President's defence fund and to encourage Agnew to resign. This put me in an awkward spot. 'He's got to go,' General Haig told me one night, 'for the country's sake'. To whom was my greater loyalty: client or country? What did my new faith have to say about this dilemma? It seemed that every day offered me a new test. I decided not to contact the industrialist. A partial answer to my problem was to step aside, turning the case over to other lawyers in our firm more skilled in criminal law.

Agnew's main line of defence was to force Congress to take up the charges on an impeachment resolution, thereby block-ing a criminal indictment in court. Agnew's men began drum-ming up support in the House of Representatives.

Then Nixon told me one night, 'Both Jerry Ford [then House Minority Leader] and Carl Albert [House Speaker] will oppose any impeachment resolution.' White House lobbyists had cut the ground out from under their own Vice-President! Nixon also informed me that the Justice Department was prepared to offer Agnew a way to escape prison if he would resign.

I agreed to present the harsh facts to the Vice-President, a painful experience for both of us. A proud and erect man, he sat stoically behind his king-sized polished desk as I pressed home the points why he should resign. I could see the hurt in his eyes when he realised that his own President had turned against him.

The Vice-President rejected the first proposals of the Justice Department and the pressure of his chief. A few weeks later he made the decision on his own. Entering the federal district court in Baltimore on that historic October day, he pleaded *nolo contendere* to one count of income tax evasion, while simultaneously a lawyer in our firm delivered the Vice-President's letter of resignation to the Secretary of State.

Spiro Agnew received a suspended sentence and a once powerful man was now disgraced. For the country – a Vice-President vanquished and a President under heavy assault. It was mind boggling. Frightening for me, too, since I had been close to each man.

Then, a few days later came the firing of Special Prosecutor Archibald Cox and the resignation of Attorney General Elliot Richardson in what was labelled the 'Saturday Night Massacre'. A storm of public outrage swept the nation. The impeachment machinery was unleashed amidst a rising clamour for Nixon's resignation. What was happening in the capital in the fall of 1973 seemed completely unreal.

Very real to me, however, were the discoveries I was making as a new Christian. One statement which Paul made to the Philippians was especially reassuring:

> . . . I look upon everything as loss compared with the overwhelming gain of knowing Christ Jesus my Lord. For his sake I did in fact suffer the loss of everything, but I

considered it mere garbage compared with being able to win Christ.

Philippians 3:8,9 PHILLIPS

I wondered: *Could I really lose all things gladly?* This passage kept coming back to me as I was drawn more and more into the Watergate net.

Then, too, I was learning how little I knew about some of my old friends. Ken Belieu, one of my colleagues in the Nixon White House, for one. When we met one day for lunch at the Sans Souci restaurant, he revealed that ever since 1947 Christ had been first in his life. All of the camaraderie we'd known in the past, working together through two decades at all levels of government, paled into insignificance compared to the bond that Ken and I had from that day on.

Then there was Fred Rhodes, deputy administrator of the Veterans Administration. Our careers had been close – on Capitol Hill, in the Nixon Administration, and over the years in Republican politics. I knew that Fred was vice-president of the Southern Baptist Convention and involved in church activities. Close as we had been, however, he never discussed his religion with me.

It was during a lunch at the Lawyer's Club that I decided to have some fun with my old friend. In the middle of a conversation about how badly the White House was handling the impeachment fight, I asked, 'Fred, besides all this Baptist work you do, have you really met Jesus Christ?' The suddenness of the words caused Fred to drop his fork noisily on the plate. He stared suspiciously at me while he groped for an answer.

'Well, you have to appreciate what that means, Chuck. Yes, I have, but you ought to know . . .'

He was winding up for a long ponderous explanation, when I interrupted: 'What would you say if I told you I had?'

'I'd shout, "Praise the Lord".' He was now smiling, though still suspicious. Another Colson practical joke, perhaps?

'Please don't do it here, Fred, or you'll shock some of these stuffy lawyers, but I have. I haven't told many people. It's very personal but I thought you might like to know.'

Later that afternoon, a messenger arrived in my office carrying a large box containing a copy of the Living Bible, Fred's own pocket edition of the New Testament, three Keith Miller books, some Baptist literature, and a huge red book containing four translations of the Bible. From that point, our friendship moved forward in ways we could never have suspected.

The seeds planted that sultry night in September when we gathered at Al Quie's home continued to germinate. In late September Hughes, Quie, Purcell, Doug, and myself began gathering for breakfast each Monday morning at 8:30 at Fellowship House. A plain, French Provincial building that might easily pass for just another of the large old residences on Embassy Row, Fellowship House is operated by a group of men and women volunteers who are followers of Jesus Christ. There is no identification on the front of the building, yet for years people in government, in the diplomatic corps, and those visiting from every country in the world have found their way there for quiet prayer and fellowship. In socially conscious, protocol-wise Washington, Fellowship House occupies a unique place. The foreign minister of South Africa may find himself praying with a young black Christian worker whose ministry takes him each day to a nearby Lorton Reformatory. The key to admittance is not politics, but commitment to Christ. Our group was just one of dozens which meet there each week.

The bonds between the five of us grew slowly but firmly. We would spend the first hour gathered around a coffee table in the library sharing personal problems and concerns, then turn to a selection from the Scriptures to read and discuss, ending always with the five of us on our knees praying for each other, our families, and for the men in government whose lives each day we touched. Often the fellowship was so strong, we'd embrace one another after our prayers. If an outsider were to look in on us, he would doubtless consider it a strange sight for a city so torn asunder in the bitterest and most divisive political struggle in a hundred years.

Ironic as it might have seemed, the liberal Democratic partisan Harold Hughes was the one who most often suggested that we pray for President Nixon and the men in the White House. One morning in late October the senator told me, 'If the President is innocent as you say he is, Chuck, it's going to shock a lot of my colleagues, but I, for one, will not vote for his impeachment. I'm really going to wrestle with this. The only commitment any of us have here is to God, and God is the Truth.' Then the wide furrows of his brow seemed to deepen. 'I wonder if we could get the President to pray with us.'

I agreed to ask the President if he would do so, even though I knew Richard Nixon considered his beliefs a very private matter. He had often spoken disdainfully of men in public life who used their religious affiliation for political advantage. The opportunity came during one of our telephone conversations following the Cox firing when the burdens of the President seemed overwhelming. 'Sir, would you consider meeting with a small group of us to pray through some of these problems?' I went on to describe our group.

My suggestion was followed by a long silence – his way of saying no. It was hard for Mr Nixon to understand that a commitment to Christ transcended all ideological differences, all partisan quibbling, everything. One day I pleaded with his secretary, Rose Mary Woods, hoping that her Catholic roots would produce support for the idea.

'I know this sounds strange, Rose, but trust me. I know what I am talking about. Harold Hughes really wants to pray with the President. He wants to help him. Just man-to-man, to give him some support.'

'You've got to be kidding, Chuck,' Rose replied. 'After the terrible things that man has said about the President, I'd never want to see them in the same room.'

The poison of Watergate had by now infected everything in Washington. So firmly entrenched were both sides, that no one seemed able to understand there was a healing force that might rescue both the nation and the combatants.

It was Hughes who suggested also that we meet with former Vice-President Agnew, offer him the strength of fellowship, help him perhaps to see that while his old world might have collapsed around him, there was a much more meaningful world that we might help him discover. Our invitation was declined. Agnew was so overcome with humiliation and dejection that he chose instead the isolation of the small community in eastern Maryland to which he had moved himself and his family.

Unsuccessful in getting these two men to join us, we continued to pray for them and all the others in power and out. As we took steps to strengthen one another in our own commitment to Christ, to share our burdens and to love the Lord together, our scheduled hour and a half often stretched into two, sometimes three hours. The Monday-morning session meant so much to me I would never hesitate to change an appointment or cut short a weekend for it. Hughes often missed scheduled business of the Senate, Quie returned early from visits to his congressional district, Purcell postponed business trips, and Doug was always there – patient, teaching, guiding, lifting us in his unobtrusive gentle ways.

We were such an unlikely combination of men, coming from opposing parties, different sections of the country, and widely varied backgrounds and education. Yet each week we drew closer together in Christian love for one another. We thought we knew it fully that fall, but were to discover in the months ahead that events would bring us even closer.

'I don't know what you have found, Chuck, but I sure wish

I had it,' Dave Shapiro confessed to me after a long day of jousting with press and prosecutors. Dave's voice was hoarse and his face haggard and drawn. 'I'm going to pieces over all the heat *you* are taking and there you sit calmly; nothing seems to be bothering you.'

Of course it did bother me; the suspense was agony, always expecting to wake up one morning to black headlines announcing my indictment. Or when Prosecutor Merrill called Shapiro as he did from time to time, my heart raced while I waited for Shapiro to conclude the conversation. Each day I'd think, *Maybe today*. But it didn't come, not in October, not in November, not in December.

In fact, all the work of the prosecution was slowed after the Cox firing. At one point we were heartened when Nixon, on the recommendation of his stalwart friend, John Connally, appointed ex-American Bar Association President, Leon Jaworski – like Connally a Texan – as the new Special Prosecutor. 'Unlike Cox, Jaworski is a realist,' Al Haig told me in mid-November. 'He's got a great respect for the office of President. We have a good understanding: it will be a good working relationship.' Haig's voice was buoyant.

Even after the implausible eighteen-and-a-half-minute tape gap was disclosed, Nixon's spirits seemed up. He called me several times those November days, each time expressing his concerns for 'poor Rose' so profusely I couldn't help but wonder if his long-time secretary was about to sacrifice herself by taking sole responsibility for a deliberate erasure.

The long vigil was hardest on Patty. One evening sitting in our den before a roaring fire the concerns surfaced. I began talking about my new faith. Her soft skin furrowed slightly. 'I think I understand. I – I'm just not sure how I fit into this new life of yours.'

'But, honey, you are a complete part of it. We are both Christians now, whereas before you were a Christian and I was not.'

'Will you be going to a church?'

'Yes, but I'm not sure which one yet.'

Patty's eyes were still cloudy, her voice apprehensive. 'Then you don't expect me to give up my Catholic faith to join you?'

So at last the real problem was out in the open. Somehow Patty had identified what was happening to me as a Protestant experience, rather than an across-the-board Christian one. The language of the Christians we were meeting nowadays frightened her, as well it might: 'Accepting Christ' – 'In Christ'. Unintentionally, they were creating a mystique about what is really the simplest decision each man or woman makes in life. But the language which is so meaningful to one who has made the decision can be as scary as the words of a secret-society initiation to those who haven't – and can sound spiritually arrogant. Patty was put off by it.

She mentioned another concern: 'What if the press finds out about this change in you, Chuck? Would this help or hurt?'

I had been giving this a lot of thought myself. 'I don't know – probably hurt – but I have no intention of telling them. It's not their business.'

I stared for a long moment into the crackling fire. I hadn't even told my children or my parents, nor Charlie Morin, my closest and oldest friend. No one but Tom Phillips, Doug, and a few others in the fellowship knew. *Better that way*, I mused. If it was a foxhole conversion, the drowning man grasping for a straw, and I slipped and fell when Watergate passed by – as someday it must – at least it would only be between God and me and a handful of others. That would be bad enough, of course, but I wouldn't be embarrassed in front of the whole world. And if word got out now, it would be labelled a gimmick for sure. 'Colson hiding behind God,' some wise-guy reporter would write.

Admit it, Colson, you still care about what others think, don't you? I confronted myself in the dancing white and orange flames. Pride? Yes, I suppose. Yet what was happening inside was so real, the prayers, the Monday-morning time with the other men. But private – between my brothers and me and Christ.

'No, honey,' I turned to Patty whose blue eyes sparkling in the fire's glow were filled with love. 'No, honey, I'm not about to go shouting from the rooftops.'

I could almost feel her relief.

But events – God, I believe now – had other things in store.

12

Christ in the Headlines

Each morning shortly after eight, the men of power in the executive branch of government assemble around a long antique mahogany table in the historic Roosevelt Room just across a narrow corridor from the President's Oval Office. For over three years I was always present, listening to Kissinger's briefing on whatever troubled area of the globe demanded our attention, joining in the discussion of pressing domestic issues with John Ehrlichman or George Shultz, jotting down notes about the President's schedule as Bob Haldeman reviewed it.

Small wonder, I suppose, that all through those frantic years I had not known that at the very same time, one morning every two weeks, another group was also meeting around a table in the basement of the White House west wing. Those present would include a departmental Under Secretary or two, sometimes a Cabinet member and a handful of White House staffers sharing their faith with one another, reading from the Scriptures and praying together. Even if I had known there was a White House prayer group, I would have considered myself too busy to attend.

Although President Nixon had refused to invite his arch foe Harold Hughes inside the executive mansion, the small group meeting bi-weekly in the basement was eager for the senator's fellowship. Harold accepted their invitation to attend a breakfast meeting scheduled for December 6. Since he had been inside the White House only once during Nixon's term, and since these were bitter days, with Washington divided into hostile camps, Harold and Doug suggested I go along. Perhaps I could help in case some over zealous Nixon partisan took offence at Hughes's mere presence there.

I arrived a minute before eight, walking briskly through the South-west Gate, past the familiar faces of the guards who waved cheerily. It was such a beautiful sunny day, and I felt so jubilant over the prospect of Hughes praying in the White House, that I even smiled at the sleepy-eyed reporters who were always about, making notes on everyone coming and going.

I walked through the basement door entrance to the west wing, down the low-ceilinged corridor lined with huge colour photographs of Nixon and his travels, past a door marked simply SITUATION ROOM, the nerve centre of the National Security Council, whose offices stretch through a subterranean labyrinth beneath the South Lawn. The breakfast was being held in the panelled Conference Dining Room, reserved for senior White House staffers and Cabinet members. This morning three tables had been pushed together and places set for fourteen. Already seated, with his back to the wall – I thought he chose it that way – was Harold Hughes looking stiff and uncomfortable, surrounded by a half dozen staunch Nixonites.

The senator looked up at my entrance, brightened noticeably, and shouted, 'Hi, brother!' I greeted my friends and took a seat at a far corner of the long table. One by one, others arrived, filling all of the chairs except the one immediately to my right. Under Secretary of Labour Dick Shubert was there, as was Ken Belieu, who had been coaxed out of retirement to help new Vice-President Gerald Ford organise his office. There were other old friends; most I had not known to be interested in this sort of thing the red-jacketed Filipino stewards began shuttling silver pots of hot coffee and trays of buns from the kitchen. We had started to eat when the door swung open and the chairman of the Federal Reserve Board, Arthur Burns, entered.

'What is Arthur Burns doing here?' I asked in astonishment to the man on my left, Father John McLaughlin, the Jesuit priest and staff speech writer for the President. Aware of the 'dirty trick' episode several years before when I falsely accused Burns of seeking a pay rise, Father John chuckled. 'Arthur is a regular participant in these breakfasts,' he told me.

'But he's Jewish,' I protested. Not that this really made any difference; it was simply the first thing I could think to say to explain my obvious distress. As I am sure McLaughlin realised, I dreaded the confrontation.

'He is not only Jewish,' McLaughlin went on, 'he is the chairman of this breakfast meeting.'

Burns looked just as uncomfortable at the sight of me, and even more so at the realisation, as his eyes quickly scanned the table, that the only empty chair was next to me. He hesitated for a moment, then leaned across the table to introduce himself to Hughes, greeted the others, and with the barest nod in my direction sat down.

Hughes proved to be more of an attraction than the organisers of the breakfast had expected. Soon the room which seats fifty was almost full sending the stewards scurrying to the kitchen for additional plates of scrambled eggs. But the turnout, though large, was scarcely welcoming; the atmosphere was charged with scepticism.

At 8:20 Burns, who had picked nervously at his breakfast, welcomed the overflow crowd and explained how happy the White House prayer group was to have Senator Hughes present to discuss his reasons for leaving the Senate to enter a full-time lay ministry. Then with none of the flowery superlatives normally passed among politicians at Washington gatherings, Burns turned the meeting over to Hughes.

After a few opening moments of uncharacteristic nervousness, Harold was in charge, his eloquent commanding self. For twenty minutes there was not another sound in the room other than his deep, powerful voice. He spoke with devastating honesty about his past, the power of Christ in his changed life, the conflicts he had faced as a Christian in government, and then for the final few minutes, how he had come to know his brother in Christ, Chuck Colson.

If it had not been such a moving moment, I would have laughed aloud at the astonished expressions around the room. Out of the corner of my eye I saw Arthur Burns sitting absolutely motionless, eyes fixed on Hughes, a soft shock of grey hair hanging over his brow, his mouth open. The pipe he had been smoking furiously at the outset now lay cold in his right hand.

'I've learned how wrong it is to hate,' Hughes went on. 'For years there were men towards whom I felt consuming bitterness. I wasn't hurting them, only myself. By hating I was shutting Christ's love out of my life. One of the men I hated most was Chuck Colson, but now that we share a commitment together in Christ, I love him as my brother. I would trust him with my life, my family, with everything I have.'

When he finished there was a long silence – no one could take his eyes off the senator. Seconds ticked by, a minute perhaps, almost as if the whole room was in silent prayer.

Arthur Burns, who was to close the meeting, seemed unable to find the words. Finally, he very deliberately laid his pipe on the table, stared at it for a moment, folded his hands in front of him, and slowly lifted his eyes. In a voice so low I doubted if those across the room could hear, he began. 'Senator – I just want to say – that is one of the most beautiful and moving things I have ever heard from any man.'

He cleared his throat and it was plain that he was choking back tears. 'I don't want to say anything else,' he said. 'Just this – on behalf of this group, would you please come back again?'

With that he arose, took my right hand in his left and said, 'Now I would like to ask Mr Colson to lead us in prayer.'

Everyone in the room joined hands. I was so surprised that it was a moment before I found my voice. There was no time to compose a prayer in my mind; I would have to depend on the Holy Spirit. The words which came out were a plea for all of us in the room, regardless of our position in government, to come before Him in humility and submission, in the knowledge that we were nothing, that He was everything, and that without His hand on our shoulders we could not possibly attend the affairs of our nation. As I ended the prayer, asking it all in the name of our Lord Jesus Christ, I felt Burns's grip tighten.

As many of the men left, they either embraced the senator or gripped his hand warmly, repeating Burns's invitation to return. Many also clasped me by the arm, welcoming me to a fraternal bond much closer than what we knew as White House men standing alone, we thought, against the world. It was an emotion-packed scene; I had never seen anything to match it in all my years in government service.

After saying good-bye to Harold, I jogged toward the basement entrance, hoping to catch Burns before he reached his waiting limousine. I found him in the little coat-room by the guard's desk, wrapping a scarf around his neck. 'Doctor Burns, I know you have good reason to hate the sight of me,' I said, 'but I want to apologise to you for planting that story. Someday I would like to come and see you.'

Though soft-spoken, Arthur Burns can be testy and cantankerous; those who challenged his economic policies are often met with fierce scowls, clouds of smoke rising from his pipe, and a stern lecture. This morning I found myself looking into the understanding eye of a patient, grey-haired professor. 'You don't need to apologise,' he said. 'There's no need for that now. All of that is behind us. I would like to see more of you, too.' Then he stammered, 'I've never, never felt – I've never known

– well, this has been quite a morning.' With that he squeezed my arm, turned, and walked into the bright sunlight outside.

I walked back to my office praising God.

The regular White House press briefing that morning was slated for 11 a.m. Jerry Warren, a former *San Diego Union* reporter and for the past five years Ron Ziegler's chief assistant, strode into the White House Press Room shortly after eleven, braced for the onslaught of Watergate questions. Reporters lounging in easy chairs at the back of the room ambled to the front, notebooks out, as Jerry leaned into the microphone to begin the routine announcements: the President will sign the Veterans Disability and Death Pension Act of 1973, a three o'clock meeting to be held with his economic advisers, a reception is planned for Vice-President Gerald Ford. Then as was customary he opened it up to questions. The following is taken directly from the transcript of the session (White House News Conference Transcript No. 1869, December 6, 1973) beginning with Dan Rather of CBS News:

> RATHER: Jerry, what is the President doing continuing to see Charles Colson?
>
> WARREN: I don't think he is.
>
> RATHER: What was Mr Colson doing at the White House today?
>
> WARREN: (pause) Well . . . (pause) he was attending a meeting in the dining room downstairs which is held every other Thursday. A group of White House staff members get together for a prayer breakfast and Mr Colson was attending that . . .
>
> UNIDENTIFIED VOICE: Prayer!
>
> ANOTHER UNIDENTIFIED VOICE: Is he going to be the next preacher?

Several minutes of the proceedings here became unintelligible because of the laughter which apparently rocked the room.

Jerry told me later there hadn't been such merriment in the Press Room since before Watergate began eighteen months earlier.

RATHER: I would like an answer
WARREN: That is the answer.
RATHER: That he was attending a prayer breakfast?

The transcript shows that Warren launched into a lengthy explanation about Senator Hughes's appearance at the breakfast that morning, those who attended, the frequency of the breakfasts, and the fact that former staff members such as myself did attend. The laughter evidently was gone.

RATHER: Jerry, isn't this a little unusual, to have a full-time paid lobbyist for very large occasions and individuals in and out of the White House to attend things such as a prayer breakfast?
WARREN: Dan, I don't think so at all. I think that is stretching it a great deal. When a group of individuals who have worked together, sit down together to practise what they believe in, and that is a prayer breakfast, I see just no connection at all. I think you are stretching it.
RATHER: If I may follow on this, let the record show I am not anti-prayer or prayer breakfasts or anything, but I do think there is a fairly important question involved here. While Charles Colson was, at one time, a member of the White House staff, he is now operating for people such as the Teamsters Union. Now we all know the way Washington works. These people ingratiate themselves with people in positions of power, and at such things as, yes, a prayer breakfast, they do their business. Isn't someone around here worried at least about the symbolism of this?
WARREN: No more than we are worried about the

612

symbolism of Senator Hughes being the main speaker.

QUESTION FROM UNIDENTIFIED VOICE: Is he representing some outside business interest?

QUESTION: What is the parallel?

WARREN: The parallel is that these are human beings who are expressing their belief together, and I see no problem with that whatsoever.

QUESTION: Senator Hughes is going to go into the clergy. Are you comparing that with the Teamsters Union? (laughter).

WARREN: I think this has gone far enough.

With that Warren turned and walked away from the podium, leaving a roomful of bemused reporters and only one news story of the day – Colson at a prayer breakfast.

Shortly before noon every button on my telephone lighted up at once. Nothing unusual. It happened often enough through the long night of Watergate. Whenever a new accusation was hurled my way, reporters reached for their phones to call for my comment, a standard practice. 'The *Chicago Tribune*, the *Post*, the *New York Times*, AP,' Holly reported. 'All of them calling at once.'

My heart raced. There had not been much about me in the press lately. Could it be the long-expected indictment? I took the *Chicago Tribune* call first, because I liked Aldo Beckman, its Washington Bureau chief who was on the line.

'There's a story moving on the wires, Chuck, about your attending a prayer meeting at the White House this morning, about you and Senator Harold Hughes of Iowa becoming close friends.' The scepticism in his voice increased: 'And then something else here about your having found religion.'

In a flush of anger I protested, 'Come on, Aldo, you guys have printed everything there is to print about me. But my religion is my own business and I'm not about to talk about it in the public press. Enough is enough.'

'Warren has announced that you were at a prayer breakfast this morning at the White House. It's already public.'

'Warren announced it?' I was stunned. 'Well, then let Warren tell you all about it.' With that I hung up.

By now the calls were coming in a torrent. 'What shall I tell them?' Holly asked.

'Tell them to . . .' And then I thought better of it. 'Just take down the names. Maybe I'll call back.'

I placed a call to Jerry Warren who explained what had happened. 'I guess someone saw you come in today, Chuck. These vultures are grabbing for every little straw. They had a field day with the prayer breakfast bit. You should have seen their faces,' he chuckled.

'But I've been in the White House over and over these past months, Jerry, and they've watched me come and go all the time. Why should they ask about it today?'

I called Doug Coe, who told me that reporters were calling Hughes and Fellowship House, too, and were piecing the story together. 'Just be careful, Chuck. Don't lose your temper,' Doug advised.

The question I had asked Jerry Warren began to plague me: 'Why today?' Dan Rather might have asked that question almost any day of the week over the prior nine months. There were times just before a major Presidential announcement, or after the 'Saturday Night Massacre', or when the Ervin Committee was in full swing when my visits should have drawn suspicious attention. They never had. Why now?

Was it possible that it wasn't chance at all? I was learning that the Lord works in mysterious ways – although it was hard for me to see how His purposes could be served by cynical articles about my conversion. Yet the thought persisted. Why had not Warren brushed Rather's question aside, said simply that I had not been to see Nixon? Or that he didn't know? Why bring in the prayer breakfast? That wasn't Warren's usual style.

And yet how could this be God's doing? Attention from the press was the last thing we wanted now; the lower my profile the better, my lawyers believed. And the cynics would have a circus; there would be a lot of snickering, especially from old friends. Finally, if the story ever came out with my verification, I'd be locked completely into a new life, no falling back into my old ways.

And suddenly I found myself remembering how Tom Phillips had proclaimed his faith to me. He risked embarrassment in doing so, but his courage helped change my life. The teaching of Scripture was as clear as the sparkle of sun now streaming in my office windows. 'Never be ashamed of bearing witness to our Lord,' Paul wrote to Timothy (*see* 2 Timothy 1:8 PHILLIPS). We had discussed this recently at a Monday meeting. Not to verify the story would be almost to deny the reality of what had happened to me. There was no other way, I concluded, no way to modify it, condition it, or call it something else, no socially acceptable middle ground.

The decision was made. If Rather's question was the result of a one-in-a-thousand coincidence, so be it. But if it was God's doing, I must do my part. So I called the reporters back and did my best to explain my commitment. Even as I listened to the words coming out of my mouth against the clattering of typewriter keys on the other end of the phone it sounded unreal: 'Accepting Christ . . . Jesus Christ in my life.' What this was going to look like in the stark black of printer's ink! The occasional titters, the 'Would you repeat that – more slowly – this time,' confirmed my worst fears.

'TOUGH GUY' COLSON HAS TURNED RELIGIOUS proclaimed the *Los Angeles Times*; COLSON HAS 'FOUND RELIGION' in the *New York Times*. Time magazine summed up the press reports the following week (December 17, 1973) under the heading 'Conversion':

Of all the Watergate cast, few had a reputation for being tougher, wilier, nastier or more tenaciously loyal to Richard Nixon than one-time Presidential Adviser Charles W. Colson. The former Marine captain is alleged by Jeb Stuart Magruder to have urged the original Watergate bugging and has been implicated in a host of other dirty tricks, including the forgery of a State Department cable. At the peak of his influence, he proudly boasted that his commitment to the re-election of the President was such that 'I would walk over my grandmother if necessary'.

At a White House staff prayer breakfast last week, Colson, 42, revealed a new aspect. He said that he has 'come to know Christ . . .' Suspecting that his newfound faith may go down hard with some, Tough-Guy Colson had a forthright response for scoffers. Said he: 'If anyone wants to be cynical about it, I'll pray for him.'

I regretted this widely reported remark – 'I'll pray for him.' I had not meant it to sound so patronising, so much like the old Colson arrogance. It was simply the first answer that had popped into mind when someone asked what I would say to those who doubted my sincerity.

The *Boston Globe* in a lead editorial entitled 'Amen, Brother' recited every real and imagined Colson misdeed and concluded: 'If Mr Colson can repent his sins, there just has to be hope for everybody.'

Syndicated columnist Harriet Van Horne was more direct: 'I cannot accept the sudden coming to Christ of Charles Colson. If he isn't embarrassed by this sudden excess of piety, then surely the Lord must be.'

And a Catholic priest, turned liberal philosopher journalist, Colman McCarthy, likened the Colson conversion to Rennie Davis's profession of faith in Guru Maharaj Ji of India. It was my willingness to speak publicly that offended McCarthy: 'In the history of authentic conversion . . . the new members of the faith always kept silence at first.' And so it continued for days and weeks to come.

I worried whether there had been something smug and self-righteous in saying 'I *have* been converted?' Can anyone really be sure that in fact he has been? Certainly I had accepted and fervently believed certain truths. Yet I was hardly a transformed person. All I could honestly say was that I was seeking, searching, trying, learning, failing and falling short, recovering and continuing to try – all the time reaching for a relationship with Jesus Christ. The change was in my spirit, in my attitudes, in the set of my will. Why should anyone believe me when I described it, and why should anyone accept my word that indeed the conversion was permanent? The sceptics had every right to say. 'Let him show us by his deeds not by words.'

I've discovered that the term *conversion* is misunderstood by many people. St Paul's experience on the Damascus Road is the best-known in all of history and books written about other conversions are similarly dramatic. Yet I am sure that most are simple, undramatic, and not newsworthy.

I was troubled, too, by the popular assumption that to be converted to Christ one must be driven to it by the most heinous and sinful past, one's conscience must be so guilt-ridden, his mischief so great that in an act of desperation he thrusts himself upon God's mercy. For days after the initial rash of stories, many, including the prosecutors, believed that I was on the verge of stepping forward to confess to all of the most dastardly sins of Watergate.

In a meeting that took place in Mr Jaworski's office in late December, attended by Mr Merrill and several young assistants, the subject of my much-publicised conversion was brought up.

'We've read about your experience,' Merrill said. 'We believe that you are sincere and that *now* you do want to come forward and tell us everything.'

Merrill was sitting across from me at the big conference table in Jaworski's office. He lowered his eyes as he spoke, as if he wanted to spare me the embarrassment of staring at me while I told all. I looked to my left at Leon Jaworski; there was a faint enigmatic smile on his round face.

I knew, of course, what they expected. If my conversion was real I should tell them how guilty I had really been all this time. The only difficulty was that I had been trying to tell them the truth from the outset. They didn't believe it and hoped perhaps that God had now joined the Special Prosecutor's force to open me up. They were also saying, or so it seemed to me, that I could only prove the sincerity of my religious conviction by confessing to something I had previously withheld.

Anger welled up in me. 'I didn't seek this publicity about my religion,' I responded to Merrill. 'And I don't intend to use it, but it shouldn't be used against me.' Merrill quickly changed the subject; but I knew then and there that the publicity about my conversion had further eroded what little was left of my credibility with the prosecutors.

The other reactions ran the whole gamut. My mother was irate. 'His father and I raised our boy as a good Christian. He was baptised and confirmed in the Episcopal Church. We taught him every Christian principle. Imagine saying he's just now become a Christian!' she lamented to a neighbour.

I tried to explain to my parents that while their efforts had been sincere, nothing had happened to me. It was my fault, not theirs.

One relative believed that the strain of Watergate had been too much. 'I'm afraid poor Chuck has snapped, gone over the edge. This kind of religious fervour is often the sign of mental instability,' she wrote a mutual friend.

The sharpest blow of all was inflicted on Wendell, then in his sophomore year at Princeton. He was, as he later recounted, studying quietly in his room when one of the girls down the hall (yes, coed dorms at Princeton), an active Campus Crusader, pounded excitedly on his door. 'I just saw your father on television!' she exclaimed. 'He is one of us; he has accepted Jesus Christ as his personal Saviour!'

It was for Wendell the last straw. It had been hard enough for a nineteen-year-old college student struggling for acceptability on campus to have his father accused day after day of one crime after another. But he was not prepared for this. Slapping his hand against his forehead he sighed, 'Oh, no! Dad's a Jesus freak.'

Dave Shapiro was predictably irate, storming into my office the morning after the first stories broke. 'You've done it this time, Colson, you've really done it. I hope He [I assumed he meant Christ] can save your butt now because I can't.'

'Calm yourself, Dave,' I said. 'I couldn't do a thing about it this time. We should have expected it one of these days.'

'Calm yourself!' he screamed, pounding his beefy fist on my desk. 'Just when I thought we had the Ellsberg thing licked, just when you've been out of the press for a month, now this. It looks like the biggest "dirty trick" you've ever pulled, the final big play for sympathy. It probably is. As far as I'm concerned they ought to indict you for this one.' With that he stomped out of my office past Holly, whose fingers were plugged in her ears.

Old friends had the toughest time understanding it. Brad Morse, under-secretary-general of the United Nations, who thought he knew me as well as anyone, was visited one day by Jonathan Moore, my assistant in Saltonstall days and best man when Patty and I were married. Brad glared at Jonathan. 'What's all this Jesus stuff about Colson: I have only been double-crossed twice in my life, both times by Christians. Do you think Chuck is okay?'

An intensely serious Harvard law student who had worked for me as an intern in the White House put it very bluntly: 'Some of us knew, admired, and respected the Colson that "was". All this conversion talk, in addition to being pontifical, I frankly resent.' The young man took it as a renunciation of my past, of which he considered himself a part.

Teamster President Frank Fitzsimmons, himself a deeply religious Catholic, was furious. 'Those – in the press, nothing is sacred, nothing. Writing about a man's religion; that is the dirtiest, lowest thing of all.'

And yet some of the press coverage was surprisingly sympathetic. Bill Greider, a reporter for the *Washington Post* authored a page-one feature article, detailing the history of my conversion, the relationship with Hughes and the Monday prayer group. The Lord's ways are mysterious indeed: it had to be my sworn enemies on the Post who would write the first serious treatment of the subject. 'Colson's spiritual awakening may not remedy any of his problems with the Watergate Grand Jury,' Greider wrote. 'but it does satisfy one group, the men who meet with him regularly for prayer at Harold Hughes' home.' The understanding Post article, along with a sympathetic UPI story written by a young Christian, Wes Pippert, were carried in hundreds of papers across the country.

On Monday, December 17, Eric Sevareid devoted his entire commentary on the CBS evening news to the blizzard which had struck Washington that day – and the Colson conversion. An act of God, the snowstorm, he opined, had done more to save energy and to cleanse Washington's air than all the conservation legislation Congress was then scrambling to enact. As for the conversion, the other act of God, he said, 'Mr Charles Colson, once the toughest of the White House tough-guys and a man believed by many to be standin' in the need of prayer as well as a good defence lawyer, Mr Colson has made page one with the news of his conversion to religion. He is not repenting of any alleged sin of a juridical nature, but he does confess that he was just too big for his breeches. The new Colson does not claim the capacity to walk on water, but he has given up walking on grandmothers. A good many people here, anxious to believe in something, are quite willing to take Colson's change of heart as real. After all, that kind of change is what innumerable critics have been demanding all along . . . Mr Colson is clearly on the right track in more ways than one. An act of Congress has its place, but it's a simple act of God that gets results.'

The Sevareid commentary, watched by perhaps thirty million Americans, and the Post and UPI stories reaching millions more, resulted in a powerful public testimony for Christ. I could never have anticipated such a thing – nor another reaction which for me at least was the most surprising of all.

Almost from the first day, large bundles of letters began to arrive in my office, some addressed to the Ervin Committee, some to the White House, some simply to Washington, DC, one in care of 'Watergate'. I tried to answer them all but in time it became impossible. They came from all parts of the country, some from abroad, as far away as Manila and New Delhi. Almost without exception the letters spoke of prayers that were being offered for me, of the writer's excitement over one person finding Christ, of Christian love. Many were from people who confessed their complete disdain for Mr Nixon's politics and mine, but who in the next breath welcomed me as a brother, pledging their complete prayers for me. Some were from people who said they had never written to a public figure before. All of them praised God.

I'd never thought about how many such people there must be, but the letters piled on my desk renewed my enthusiasm as I pored through them each evening. Late one afternoon, shortly after Christmas, I came upon a letter that was to continue to affect my view of my own goals for months and years to come. It was scrawled on a single sheet of lined white paper:

25 December 1973

Dear Sir:

This may seem to you as an unusual letter, however, after reading an article in the *Charleston Evening Post* on you I gathered that you were (in the past) an unusual person. I'm a S/Sgt. in the USAF. For 19 years I've been trying to find myself. I've went to church on several occasions but they (the pastors) didn't reach me. After reading your article it has helped me more than anything in my entire life. It is Christmas morning. I'm usually drunk or trying to get drunk by now, but here I am watching the children open up their presents and thinking about going to church somewhere, instead of the club or someone's house and get drunk. I didn't even buy any 'booze' this year. It's people in positions like you who confess their past (maybe not so good life – wrongs) or whatever it may be called. Sure do help people in a position like me. I truly feel free within my inner self this morning and I pray that God may help both of us in all of our trying efforts.

I am going to try and find that book MERE CHRISTIANITY down here and read it myself.

God blessing you,
S/SGT NATHANIEL GREEN

I didn't care who saw me in my office as the tears streamed down my cheeks while I read and re-read Sergeant Green's letter. He said it all. For eleven years of my life I'd driven with every ounce of energy in my body to do the things in government that I believed might make people's lives better. But in all that time I could not point to one single person, not one life, that had actually changed for the better. In fact, nothing I could reflect back on could compare to the feeling of joy I felt at the thought of one man re-united with his family on Christmas Day. And the means of reaching this staff sergeant had been the press, against which I'd harboured such resentment.

'The individual is . . . more important . . . for he is everlasting and the life of a state or a civilisation, compared with his, is only a moment,' C.S. Lewis had written.

If – as one of my friends called to tell me, 'Everybody in this town is laughing at you,' then let them laugh. *There are many Sergeant Greens out there*, I thought as I looked into the late afternoon darkness beyond my office windows. And there is also the Master, alive and working in ways that we never will understand. I thanked Him, thanked Him for Dan Rather's hostile questions, for Jerry Warren blundering into the whole prayer breakfast business, even for those who had written the barbed and cutting stories.

'It's worth it all, Holly,' I said as I passed her desk, watching a bewildered expression come across her face, 'worth it all.'

13

The Lonely House

The day after the CBS broadcast by Eric Sevareid, Steve Bull called from the White House: 'Chuck, the President would like to see you. Can you come right over?'

Just like the old days, I thought. I felt the same old flutter in the heart, the excitement of going to see the most important man in the world. Although we had talked on the phone regularly, we had avoided face-to-face meetings since I left his staff, nine months before, for fear that the Watergate bad-guy image which clung so firmly to me would be an embarrassment to him.

It must be important, I thought, grabbing my overcoat and excusing myself without explanation from several of my partners then meeting in my office. I made my way the half-block from my office to the Southwest Gate, tramping through the now-grey snow which, along with my conversion, Sevareid had philosophised about the night before.

Steve was at the gate. To avoid the press he led me up the long circular driveway of the South Lawn, across the open, grassed area where the President's helicopter lands and takes off, past Secret Service men stationed around the building, and in through the diplomatic entrance.

'What's up, Steve?' I asked once we were inside the reception room with handsome Early American murals covering the walls and a gigantic blue, white, and gold rug with the fifty state seals woven into its border.

'The boss needs to talk to you, Chuck. Watergate has made things rough. No one knows you're seeing him. He's upstairs in the Lincoln Sitting Room. Safer that way. Can't even trust the staff in the west wing anymore.' Steve shook his head in dismay. 'It's killing him. He's taking it all so hard. Cheer him up, Chuck, like you used to in the old days.'

As I walked up the wide red-carpeted staircase and across the marble-columned centre hall, I felt a chill. The White House seemed deserted. Usually there were Secret Service men around, staffers showing people through, military aides, lines of tourists. But today there was no sign of life anywhere; the only sound was my leather heels hitting the cold marble. For an uncanny moment I remembered the silence of that strange day after the election.

Even the door to the Lincoln Sitting Room on the second floor was unattended as I walked in. The President was slumped in an uncomfortably stiff-looking yellow brocade chair in the corner of the small room crammed with relics of the Lincoln Presidency. 'Good to see you, boy, good to see you.' Nixon was out of the chair and on his feet, a big grin on his face, grabbing my hand as he had never done before.

After seating me in one of the rosewood chairs purchased by Mrs Lincoln, he offered me one of his pipes. Following an inquiry about my family, Nixon got to what was on his mind. 'The lawyers tell me we shouldn't be seen together. This business goes too far. No reason two old friends can't get together. We'll talk about George Meany, labour issues, or something; no one can criticise us for that, can they?'

We had not been together since I learned of the White House taping system. Half in jest I asked, 'Mr President, is our conversation being recorded?'

'What do you mean, recorded? Who would do that to us?'

He sat upright in his chair, the smile gone, a flash of fear in his face. 'Would *they* do that?' he demanded.

I tried to explain that I was only curious as to whether he himself was still taping conversations. But he kept interrupting: 'Can I trust the Secret Service, Chuck? I don't know that I can. You don't suppose Jaworski would bug *this* room, do you?' Again I tried to assure the President that if *he* did not have the room bugged I was certain no one else did. But this did not satisfy him.

'The problem, Chuck, is that I don't think I can trust anybody. Not even the secretaries.'

What irony, I thought. For years the President had recorded every unsuspecting visitor to his office; now he was obsessed over the thought that someone was recording him. The man who for four years strode so confidently through the grand halls and offices of the White House, savouring every minute of the unparalleled power he enjoyed, was hiding out in a far corner of the nearly empty mansion, distrustful of everyone around him. I felt a surge of sympathy for my old friend. He looked different, somehow smaller, as if he had shrunk into a protective shell; his skin was sallow, the lines on his face deeper. The fatigue was more apparent than it had been during any of the crises I had lived through with him.

'The tapes,' he recounted slowly regaining his self-assurance, 'they were all Haldeman's idea. Stupid. I told Bob twice to have the system removed, but you know Bob. I forgot all about them. But there aren't any here now. I ordered every one removed. I saw to it myself. You can be sure of that.'

Then the President questioned me about the conversations we'd had together in the early part of 1973. He donned his horn-rimmed reading glasses and began studying a sheaf of papers resting in his lap. Tape transcripts? I decided not to ask. I repeated each conversation as I remembered it, while Nixon nodded approvingly, his eyes scanning one sheet of paper after another. Was he testing me to see how good my recollection was? Now and again he interrupted:

'You're sure of that, are you?' Then he'd return to the papers in his lap, puffing again on his meerschaum pipe.

'Are you sure you never asked me to grant clemency to Hunt, Chuck?' he asked when I had completed the recitation.

'Positive,' I replied, 'I started to once and you cut me off. I remember it well.'

'Good, good, so long as you are positive. Well, let's talk about more pleasant subjects.' Nixon took off his glasses, slid the papers back into a brown manila envelope and began to smile. *Surely he hasn't called me here for this*, I thought; we had discussed these conversations three times on the phone. The answers were always the same and he had all the tapes.

'Do you have any reason to think my memory is faulty?' I asked – as close as I dared come to asking him what was in those papers. 'No, no, boy. Can't be too careful nowadays, though. Jaworski wants all these tapes; I just have to be sure. Don't you worry about it. That was an interesting article in the Post about you.'

Now it had come out. This was the real reason, I surmised for the President wanting to see me – my conversion. Was he worried that my commitment to Christ or my friendship with Hughes would turn me against my old leader? Or – could he be looking for spiritual strength himself? Should I recount my experience, as Tom Phillips had with me? If I could speak boldly to sometimes hostile reporters, why would I retreat now?

The silence hung there. And I remained silent – retreat it was. He would not understand, I rationalised. Besides, why should he take sermonising from me? I was no Billy Graham. 'The papers will print anything nowadays,' I said lamely. 'Crazy times, Mr President.'

If the President was giving me the opportunity I'd sought weeks before, to meet and pray with him, I failed him completely. I had always been forthright with the President on other subjects. Why the timidity about my conversion? It was to haunt me for months.

The rest of the conversation was filled with nostalgic reminiscing. We were back living again in the golden days when the crowds in the streets, roaring their approval, pressed forward for a closer look at *the* President and his passing motorcade. Those were the days of victory when the polls showed us on our way to a massive record-breaking re-election victory, when an American President triumphantly toured the Kremlin and marched atop the Great Wall of China, signalling a new era of American diplomacy. Ending the twenty-five-year cold war, plus the hot one in Vietnam, was to usher in a 'generation of peace', Richard Nixon's most cherished dream. 'We must have been doing something right, Chuck, no matter what they say now, right?'

'Right, right, Mr President,' I was saying, though it was only the memories that lived. All else lay crumbled and broken in the wreckage of Watergate.

More than an hour passed before the President looked at his watch. 'I'd better get back,' he said. 'Nobody except Steve knows I'm here. I'll never forget you – the service you've given your country. Someday we'll set all this straight, you wait and see, Chuck.' He repeated it, as much to convince himself, so I thought, as to reassure me. 'You just wait and see. There'll come a time when we wipe the slate clean. Not yet, but it will come.'

I knew, of course, what he was alluding to: pardons for his loyal staff members facing criminal charges, as soon as he regained popular support. Somehow it was not reassuring. Deep in my heart I felt that the Watergate tide would not be turned away. As we walked together through the family quarters I felt the President knew it, too.

We said good-bye at the edge of the Rose Garden. I stood for a moment watching his back slightly hunched, fade into the December grey, two Secret Service men scampering ahead to open the doors to the west wing. For him it was a return to the world of missing tapes, of new accusations, of irregularities in his tax returns, of congressmen calling for his impeachment. For me – a return to grand juries, sessions with my lawyers, the constant probing of Jaworski's men, and the uncertainty of the future.

My phone rang shortly after 11:30 that night, waking Patty and me from a sound sleep. The voice of the White House operator: 'Mr Colson, it's the President.' Though I had been unsettled by our meeting, chagrined that I hadn't been bold enough to talk about Jesus Christ and alarmed by the tragic picture that lingered in my mind of my old friend, it had apparently been a tonic for Mr Nixon. 'Sorry to call so late, but it was so good to talk with you today. I just wanted to chat a few minutes longer if you don't mind.' It was a continuation of our conversation that afternoon, more reminiscing, more questions about our conversations the prior January, a good report he'd received that day from Kissinger about the Israelis' willingness to make concessions in the Middle East, how to handle the Ervin Committee demand for 600 Presidential tapes. In the midst of a discussion about the tapes, Nixon suddenly stopped.

'Let me ask you one more time. Why did you suggest today that the room might be bugged? Do you have some information that you didn't want to tell me?'

There was no way I could reassure him. The tone had changed completely! I was no longer listening to the strong, self-assured resonant voice I knew so well. Then he turned to the appeal now before the court over delivering to the prosecutors the White House tapes. 'You know, Chuck, I will have no choice but to resign if we lose this case. I simply must draw the line.' His voice rose, strong again for an instant, 'I will not preside over the destruction of the Presidency.'

The prospect of stepping down was weighing heavily on

the President's mind as it had the night he called late in July. 'What do you think will happen, Chuck, if I stick it out and there's an impeachment? You know that if I am impeached I'll be wiped out financially – no pension – and now with all I owe in taxes. Everybody thinks I've gotten rich, but it just isn't so.'

Self-interest? Or high patriotic motive? The two were inextricably woven together in this complex man. I struggled to muster an enthusiasm and confidence which I did not feel. 'Stop talking that way, Mr President, you'll fight and you'll win as you always have.'

Then came the question that still rings in my ears. 'I know Jaworski doesn't want to hurt the President; he's said so. But you don't suppose *they* would send me to jail do you, Chuck?'

For an instant I couldn't believe he was serious. 'Stop it, Mr President!' I exclaimed. 'That's the most absurd thing I've ever heard! and stop talking about quitting. The captain doesn't desert the ship.'

'I know all that,' he countered. 'But maybe the country should be spared all of this. Maybe what the country wants is a nice, clean Jerry Ford – the trouble is, Jerry isn't ready just yet. It would take him a year to get up to speed on all the international issues – and you know Jerry would have a tough time with Kissinger. I'm not sure he could control him, Chuck; you know Henry can be unstable at times – fly off in all directions. You remember what we had to go through last year during the December bombing, holding Henry down. You remember, Chuck. No, Jerry needs more time; he'll have to learn Henry's ways.'

The President was using me as a barometer to find out how bad the situation really was. He wanted total reassurance which I tried to give. He wasn't reflecting on Ford or Kissinger, merely assessing realities. Ford had been on the job less than a month and was unfamiliar with the volatile idiosyncrasies of Kissinger's genius. For five long years Nixon and Henry worked together intimately, aware of each other's strengths and weaknesses, dependent on one another like two tightrope walkers – high-powered foreign-policy manoeuvrings are every bit as precariously balanced.

Then Nixon made the most startling statement of the day: 'You know, Chuck, I get on my knees every night and just pray to God.'

I was stunned. For a man so proud he could never admit human weakness in any form – refusing to acknowledge a common cold even when his chest was so congested he could hardly talk – it was an amazing confession. From the tone of his voice I am convinced he was sincere. The statement came from nowhere, had nothing to do with anything we were talking about, but before I could say a word he leaped back to safe ground and strategy to be employed against House Judiciary Committee Chairman Peter Rodino. Knowing Nixon as I did, I knew he was embarrassed by his own frankness in opening up such a personal topic.

But again that day he had given me the opportunity to speak, to tell him how God could lead us out of this wilderness. And again I kept silent. Was it cowardice? Was it the Lord Himself keeping my lips sealed? All I know is that a second time that day I had failed him.

It was nearly 1 a.m. when I put the receiver down, pushed my desk chair back and fell to my knees in the quiet of my library. I asked God to forgive me for my lack of boldness, imploring Him to overlook my weakness and deal with the President in His way. After all, I was still seeking Him myself – He alone knew through what struggle and confusion.

In the weeks that followed I resumed my old battle station, now as the President's impeachment adviser. Of top concern was finding the right criminal trial lawyer. We went through a long list of possibilities. None was right. Most people think that all the President has to do is push a button and he can command the services of top specialists in every profession. It doesn't work that way. The top talent is often hard to find, even for White House service, more so in the shadow of Watergate than ever before. The pay is lower than in the business world, but the real deterrents are the punishment of long hours, a paucity of gratitude, and the ever-present possibility of finding your mistake a national news item.

Late in December I offered him my own lawyer, Jim St Clair, describing him as tough, adroit in the courtroom, respected. The President interviewed Jim the next day, and two days later St Clair phoned to ask me to release him. There was no emotion about it. Jim, coldly professional as always, seemed to feel no excitement over going to work for the President who was to him just another client.

The following week St Clair's appointment was announced with scarcely a word in the press about what I feared might become an embarrassment – the connection between the President, St Clair, and myself. So little escaped critical examination in the glare of Watergate that it was a rare bit of good fortune for Jim St Clair to move into the White House untarnished.

For a while it seemed like the good old days, Nixon and me together again for the big fight ahead. But it was not like it used to be. We had both changed. Nixon, flag, and country were no longer one and the same to me. I was beginning to see for the first time Richard Nixon, the man. This individual, the one out of 200 million who rose to the highest office in the land, was great in some ways, weak in others, limited as all mortals are. If anything, I cared more for him in a personal way than ever before, but the awe and reverence were gone.

Nor could I put out of my mind nagging doubts about the President's innocence. Why the curious summer-long silence while John Dean's charges were rocketing off the walls of the Senate Caucus Room? Why the almost obsessive worry over the tapes? Why that eighteen-and-a-half-minute gap and Nixon's protestations about 'poor, poor Rose'?

The situation in the White House had become almost chaotic. Petty intramural jealousies dominated the various echelons. Haig told me one night in early January he was quitting unless Nixon demoted Ziegler; I called Nixon to warn him and put myself squarely in the middle of a bitter feud. Young staff members were leaving as fast as they could find jobs outside; those on the wrong side of the warring internal factions soon found themselves forced to look elsewhere. Practically all who had been in the White House during the first term were being summoned regularly before grand juries and Jaworski's prosecutors. Many were gripped with fear that they might be the next target of prosecution; all were in debt, incurring heavy legal expenses.

The White House staff Christmas Party that year was like a wake. Steve Bull took me into a quiet corner to whisper his most private fears that 'no one around here is trying to save the President; everyone is knifing him, protecting themselves'. Ziegler refused to attend because Haig was scheduled to be there. In the end neither came, a slight the juniors felt. Nixon himself was increasingly withdrawn and reclusive. 'We never even see him walking around anymore,' a senior staffer complained. One young girl began to cry as I was reminiscing about the exciting, purposeful days of the 1972 campaign.

Gone was the sense of mission, the common dedication to a cause greater than oneself. Never had I seen liquor flow more freely or produce fewer smiles. According to my former assistant, Dick Howard, the White House was like Berlin in the last days when Hitler's once proud and haughty lieutenants, trapped, smelling death and defeat, turned bitterly on one another and indulged every hedonistic desire.

As I began to see the shallowness in my blind and unquestioning approach to the President – to any human being, for that matter – I began to think more and more about the 'causes that mattered' in Doug Coe's inscription in my

Bible. Some days, in fact, my own thoughts surprised me. I found myself caring more about wanting Christ to come into President Nixon's life than whether he could successfully parry the thrusts of his attackers.

New Year's weekend I found a breath of hope in a small news item from San Clemente, reporting that Nixon was reading a recently published book about Lincoln. I knew at once it was Elton Trueblood's work on Lincoln's spiritual life. Tom Phillips had given it to me in September to read and perhaps pass on to the President. I had found the book spiritually stimulating as it portrayed Lincoln's slow conversion in 1862, his gradual turning to the Almighty for guidance and strength. I had sent my copy to Nixon in November. The President had never acknowledged receiving it, and I had wondered if he felt I was pushing him. Now I knew he was reading it.

It was the evening before the National Prayer Breakfast in late January that Al Quie, Graham Purcell, Doug Coe, Harold Hughes and I met for prayer and dinner in the Capitol with Billy Graham and Senator Mark Hatfield. Mark Hatfield's outspoken opposition to Nixon's Vietnam policy had earned him a reputation as a leading Republican maverick. Mr Nixon had ranted about him many times and I had joined in the denunciation myself. To Senator Hatfield I was the embodiment of all that was misguided and evil in the Nixon White House.

Yet as we knelt in prayer together at the altar in the quiet of the tiny granite-walled prayer room located just off the massive domed rotunda of the Capitol Building, the animosity drained away. Much of Hatfield's prayer was devoted, in fact, to thanking God for my conversion and for bringing us together in Christ. At dinner we discussed helping Nixon as a human being and as a national leader – Senator Hughes, a political foe; Hatfield, a rebel within his party; Billy Graham and I, his friends – all pledging ourselves to pray for our beleaguered President.

That night the President called to ask me a host of questions about the National Prayer Breakfast upcoming the next morning. Though it was late, and earlier in the evening Nixon had delivered his State of the Union address to Congress over live television watched by millions of Americans, he was alert, probing, obviously preparing his remarks as he talked.

'You know, Chuck,' he mused, 'I've never been able to talk about my beliefs in God in public and I resent people using religion in politics. That's so hypocritical. Not the kind of thing I've ever done.' As he talked on, he was as unguarded as I'd ever known him. He spoke of his devout Quaker mother, and how he himself accepted God when he was a boy and found strength from his faith. I urged him to speak freely at the breakfast.

Billy Graham rode with Nixon the next morning from the White House to the Washington Hilton Hotel; he later told us that he and the President enjoyed the most frank discussion ever about Christ, Nixon's faith, and the need for the Lord's hand in guiding an embittered nation. Nixon's remarks before 3,000 men and women from all over the world left no doubt about the impact Abraham Lincoln's spiritual life had had on him.

Although he never belonged to a church, he probably prayed more than any man who has ever been in the White House . . . He did not have a feeling of arrogance about his side as compared to the other side. He did feel that America was destined to be united . . . He did believe that America had something to stand for, something to believe in, and something to do in the world bigger than itself. In other words, there was something other than Lincoln, the politician, the President, and the American people, each individual; there was what he called the Almighty, the Universal Being; sometimes he referred to him as God who guided the destiny of this nation.

As he spoke, Nixon came close to professing his own commitment, speaking more openly than ever before in his long political career.

> When I was eight or nine years old, I asked my grandmother, a very saintly woman, a little Quaker lady, who had nine children – I asked her why it was that Quakers believed in silent prayer. When we sat down to the table, we always had silent prayers; and often at church, while we sometimes had a minister or somebody got up when the spirit moved him, we often just went there and just sat, and we prayed. Her answer was very interesting, and perhaps it relates to why Lincoln prayed in silence. My grandmother spoke to me on this occasion, as she always did to her grandchildren and children, with the plain speech. She said, 'What thee must understand, Richard, is that the purpose of prayer is to listen to God, not to talk to God. The purpose of prayer is not to tell God what thee wants, but to find out from God what He wants from thee.'

Watching his face closely as he spoke, I noted the sudden relaxation of all the tense lines and tightly drawn muscles as he said: 'Too often we are a little too arrogant [when] we try to talk to God . . . [Let's] listen to God and find out what He wants for us and then we will all do the right thing.' His voice almost trailed off and he was through. It was not the flag-waving ending he always sought in his speeches, but an awkwardly humble and candid remark that told of the hunger of his heart.

I knew that morning what had happened to the 'old fire' inside me, the old drive I could not now muster to lead Mr Nixon's charge against his enemies. No longer could I be Mr Nixon's unquestioning political lieutenant, dealing in hand-to-hand combat, and at the same time help him – or anyone else for that matter – find a relationship with Christ. By wanting to do both for my old friend I wasn't doing either one. My causes had been mixed up, I realised, as Doug's inscription in my Bible paraded again through my mind: 'Better to fail in a cause that will ultimately succeed . . .' And being faithful to Christ I realised, meant living it with everyone I encountered, as well as believing it. For me it could no longer be a private luxury. Nor could I apply it selectively, but universally.

'The one thing I don't want to do, and certainly not for any newspaper story, is try to relate my own beliefs today with Watergate,' I had told a UPI reporter only a few weeks earlier. Knowing Christ in my heart, but dealing with the biggest moral crisis in generations as if nothing had happened was, I now knew, trying to straddle two worlds.

What if I were to try to step boldly from the old into the new?

14

Underground Movement

The Cox firing created a temporary lull while the Watergate prosecutors regrouped under Leon Jaworski. For me this time was important, a chance to breathe in the fresh air of the new world I was discovering.

There was a sharp contrast between my hours of tense defensiveness over my past life and the time spent with a whole new set of people I was meeting through taking a stand for Christ. It was like finding shafts of sunshine and blue sky in a murky overcast.

One of my first steps, I knew, was to try and make amends to those I had injured with various 'dirty tricks'. I had already offered a faltering apology to Arthur Burns as both of us were leaving the prayer meeting in the White House basement – but I owed him a more detailed account.

There was another reason for my seeking him out. His wife, Helen, intensely involved with her husband's career, had also been hurt by the episode. I could tell by her angry eyes which bored holes right through me when we had been seated next to each other at a White House dinner not long after the damaging story about her husband appeared in the newspapers. This, too, needed healing.

When I telephoned him, Burns suggested we meet at his

Watergate apartment after work the following Tuesday. It was Helen who greeted me at the door and seated me in a downy corner sofa in the Burns's tastefully furnished, homey apartment. Helen, petite and the gracious hostess, was soon serving Arthur and me hors d'oeuvres as I began recounting everything I could remember about the painful episode in the summer of 1971 when I leaked to the press an untrue item that Burns was publicly pushing wage controls while secretly trying to get his salary raised. Burns's face remained impassive as I spoke, but his penetrating eyes never left mine, even when he reached out to sip his drink.

'And so, Arthur,' I concluded, 'that is the unhappy story. I can't justify it, and I can never undo the harm it caused, but I thought I owed you this apology. I am very, very sorry.'

Burns kept puffing on his pipe, continuing to stare into my eyes. 'What hurt me most,' he said at last, 'is that I have never tried to accumulate wealth or possessions. All I have and all I've cared about is my own good name. The story implied that I was trying to feather my nest and it was the first time in my life anyone had questioned my integrity.'

Arthur Burns began to reminisce about his many years with Richard Nixon. There was not a trace of animosity toward his old friend as I feared there might have been. 'Political wars are cruel,' he said. 'I just wish we could find a way to help the President. He needs so much understanding and I don't think those around him are really helping.' He brought the subject back to me.

'Tell me about this experience of yours. This is what really matters.'

For an hour I shared with him what had happened to me in New England, the changes I was beginning to notice in my values and attitudes. 'That's beautiful,' he repeated over and over.

It was nearly eight o'clock before I noticed that Helen was preparing something in the kitchen. I apologised for staying so long and talking so much.

'Nonsense,' Burns protested. 'Have dinner with us.' I explained why I could not and stood up.

'Please,' Burns persisted. 'Sit down for just a minute longer. Perhaps we could have a prayer together.'

We did, leaning forward over the coffee table and thanking God for the healing of one ugly sore of the Nixon years. As I was leaving, Helen filled a shopping bag with fruit and insisted I take it to my family. The white-haired chairman of the Federal Reserve Board escorted me to the elevator, gripping my arm as we walked slowly along the carpeted corridor of the world's now most famous apartment building.

'Let's meet again sometime,' he suggested. 'And be firm in your faith. This has been a wonderful evening for me.'

God's Spirit was working in powerful ways all over strife-torn Washington. Each Monday morning when we met – Al, Graham, Doug, Harold, and I – someone would report another miracle, old adversaries coming together as brothers, new fellowships begun, prayer groups revived, unlikely men seeking a relationship with Christ.

Doug Coe, for example, had worked for years to interest a few judges he knew in meeting regularly for prayer and fellowship. Since most judges tend to be independent-minded and wary of efforts to bring God into public affairs, nothing had resulted. But in January a small judicial prayer group was convened. Soon judges from several courts, high and low, conservative and liberal in their personal philosophies, were joining the fellowship.

New prayer groups were springing up in a host of governmental apartments. A small band of young senators began meeting regularly for prayer and fellowship. Several new groups began meeting in the House of Representatives.

Early in 1974 Senator Hughes made his second appearance at a White House breakfast, the meeting this time chaired by Earl Butz, blunt-spoken Secretary of Agriculture, whose Senate confirmation was nearly blocked in 1971 by a coalition of anti-Administration senators led by Hughes.

'If I'd known you then as I do now, brother, I might have led your cheering section,' Hughes confessed.

'No regrets needed,' Butz replied. 'I feel guilty enough for all the negative thoughts I've had about you.' The exchange was in good fun – lighthearted banter, some thought – but there was something more behind it. Men of opposing political philosophy were experiencing the camaraderie of their common commitment to God and in the process being released from poisoned memories of past political encounters.

The fiercely conservative speech writer, Pat Buchanan, whose saucy and courageous assault on the Ervin Committee ignited a brief pro-Nixon rally in late September of 1973, also attended. Over the years Pat was the author of the most caustic attacks against Nixon's enemies, prominently including Hughes, yet Harold's second breakfast appearance drained much of the partisan fervour from him.

'What a man! What a morning!' was all Pat could say to me as he left the room, shaking his head in bewilderment.

In a nationally syndicated column on January 13, Washington reporter Nick Thimmesch described the growing number of prayer groups as an 'underground movement . . . spurred by Watergate, which might surprise some of our jaded folks . . . They meet in each other's homes,' Thimmesch reported, 'they meet at Prayer Breakfasts, they converse on the phone . . . a Brotherhood in belief . . . there are many here and more are forming . . . I am not about to say that virtue and nobility are about to envelop the nation's Capital – this is a tough, hard town. But Watergate has created a great introspection, especially over personal values and this underground prayer movement can provide some peace, and a better sense of direction to many afflicted with spiritual malaise.'

Early in 1974 I strode up the grey granite steps of the Pentagon, the huge vaultlike headquarters of the US military establishment. A year before, this visit would have seemed ludicrous. In the old days I entered this building to represent the President in political battles, like mapping strategy to rescue the anti-ballistic missile programme when Congress threatened to cut off funds. Now I had accepted an invitation – for a fellowship luncheon!

A veteran civilian employee, John Broger met me at the main entranceway to guide me through the mazelike corridors of the world's largest office building. We stopped to look in on the meditation room, a small windowless cubicle on an inside corridor. Inside, chairs were lined along three walls with a simple altar at the far end.

'This was build on the orders of Secretary Laird,' Broger explained.

'Mel Laird!' I exclaimed. 'What would that old fox be doing building a meditation room?' Laird was Secretary of Defence in the first Nixon Cabinet, a longtime Wisconsin congressman and House leader. His zest for bureaucratic intrigue earned him the reputation as one of the canniest politicians in Washington.

'Secretary Laird not only ordered the meditation room built,' Broger added, 'but he was in here often himself.' Laird I learned, was a regular participant in a small congressional fellowship which later included among others the then-Vice-President Gerald Ford, Al Quie, and House Minority Leader John Rhodes. But there is a deliberate attempt by the military to avoid publicity about any religious events in the Pentagon for fear it would arouse criticism over motives.

The luncheon was held in a small dining room seating fifty men. I spoke briefly, telling of the changes in my life. At the end we all bowed our heads and prayed aloud or silently as the Spirit moved us, simple moving prayers from privates, lieutenants, and admirals alike. From one jut-jawed Army sergeant – a ranger, I could tell from the insignia and ribbons which stretched from his breast pocket to his broad shoulder – came an eloquent prayer for peace among all men. The Holy Spirit, no respecter of rank or armour, pierced this soldier's tough exterior as no enemy bayonet could.

To my further surprise I learned that this luncheon was a regular event; that there were dozens of early-morning groups meeting for Bible study and prayer before beginning twelve-to fourteen-hour crisis-filled days.

To most people, of course, the sudden popularity of religion in a town like Washington remained a matter of scepticism. In my case, in fact, outright hilarity. 'Colson coming to Jesus' quips soon replaced 'Colson's grandmother' as fodder for the cocktail circuit. At the annual late-January congressional dinner of the National Press Club, Speaker of the House Carl Albert produced a roar of laughter when he described 1973 as 'the year when Chuck Colson joined the Jesus movement . . . and his grandmother said a prayer of thanks from her hospital bed'.

Art Buchwald, the nationally syndicated humourist, joined the merriment with a column entitled 'Getting right with Granny. Step on her hand and help her up.' Buchwald spoofed the conversation as follows:

When Charles Colson got religion the first person he wanted to break the news to was his grandmother – the very same grandmother he had vowed to run over in 1972 to get Richard Nixon re-elected President.

He knocked on the door and cried, 'Granny, it's me, Charles.'

'You go away, Charley,' his grandmother said, 'and take your car with you.'

'Granny, you don't understand. I'm not here to run over you. I've got religion now. I've come to pray with you.'

Colson's grandmother opened the door a couple inches. 'You're joshing me, Charley boy.'

'It's true, Granny, I'm no longer the mean, dirty rotten, unscrupulous trickster you used to bounce on your knee. I've been reborn, Granny.'

She hesitated, 'How do I know this ain't one of your tricks to get me out in the street so you can go vroom . . . vrooooommm with your motor again?'

'I have Senator Harold Hughes with me. He'll tell you I mean it.'

'That's right, Granny,' Senator Hughes said. 'Charley has made his peace and he's asking everyone to forgive him his sins.'

'I ain't so sure I'm ready to forgive him. You know I was flat on my back for six months after the 1972 election.'

'Granny, please let me in. I want to show you I'm a new man.'

'All right,' Colson's grandmother said, 'but leave your car keys out on the stoop.'

Colson came into the house with Senator Hughes.

'Shall we kneel together?' Colson asked.

'Not me,' his grandmother replied, 'I haven't been able to kneel since you screamed at me, 'Four more years!' and then put your Oldsmobile into drive . . .'

Some of the barbs shot at me hurt, yet a Watergate-weary Washington needed some laughs. Through it all was the issue of 'How much can a man change?' – and maybe an unintended witness.

Among the many calls for interviews and TV shows was one from Mike Wallace, the sharp-questioning host of the CBS popular 'Sixty Minutes' Sunday-evening documentary. Wallace wanted to interview Hughes and me together.

We discussed it one Monday breakfast. Doug saw it as a rare opportunity for a powerful Christian testimony to millions of Americans: two political opposites, brought together by Christ's love at a time of unprecedented national division.

Hughes was dubious; a tough, probing newsman, Wallace might turn it into a political circus. 'I told Mike,' Harold reported back later after one of Wallace's insistent calls, 'we'd do it with him if he would spend the necessary time with us to see what our fellowship was all about.'

Hughes went a step further: 'I'll work with you, Mike. We can meet for prayer. I'll even help instruct you if you are serious.' People had asked for large fees to appear on Wallace's programme, but this was surely the first time anyone had set such an unusual condition – that Wallace seek a closer relationship with God. That might have ended all discussions with anyone less persistent than Wallace; but after recovering his composure he agreed to try – and along with his producer, a pert redhead named Marion Goldin, actually began meeting with Hughes. The rest of us waited in ill-concealed suspense for the outcome.

And meanwhile every day was bringing its new encounter – some as humorous in their own way as anything appearing in print. I remember the middle-aged waitress at the stately old Sheraton Carlton who learned I was in the hotel's basement barbershop and came down to find me. Interrupting the chatter of Milt Pitts, my longtime friend and barber, she asked me to explain to her how she could 'find Christ'. While Milt's electric clippers droned on and the rest of the customers stared bewildered, I did my best to outline for her what I knew of the steps in salvation.

Or the night when I participated in a young people's Sunday-evening fellowship at Washington's Fourth Presbyterian Church. The first fresh scents of early spring 1974 were in the air when Patty and I arrived shortly before 8 p.m. at the entrance to the massive red-brick church. As we were exchanging greetings on the front steps with Pastor Dick Halverson and some of his parishioners, I noticed a beat-up white Buick convertible, fenders dented and rusting and canvas top flopping, pull over to the curb nearby. A long-haired young man in an open shirt and dungarees flung open the door and dashed towards us. Nervously I thought of the protesters who were again carrying placards on Pennsylvania Avenue.

I nudged Patty. 'Watch out, honey. This could be trouble.' With the impeachment drive building to a fever pitch, the streets of Washington were again being visited by carloads of young demonstrators. Bumper stickers like HONK IF YOU THINK HE'S GUILTY were sprouting like spring leaves. Was this guy going to start an argument here in front of the church?

'Mr Colson, Mr Colson,' the young man shouted, brushing past the others. 'I want to talk to you a minute.' Then he grabbed my hand and wrung it vigorously. As I listened with growing amazement, he stated that he worked in the dissension-ridden Department of Labour. 'It's fantastic the way you and Senator Hughes have become friends. It's been a real boost to our morale in the department. It's given us hope that we can work together, too. You can't imagine what's happened in Labour in the past weeks . . .'

As he talked on, I could only think of the months I had spent in the White House trying to work out a plan for reorganising the Labour Department. This old-line agency was so encased in a mouldy bureaucratic crust it could hardly function. All my fancy charts had produced nothing and were long forgotten. Now it seemed that my goal was being achieved – without my hand being in it in the slightest – another example of Christ's Spirit-sovereignty at work: changing lives, reviving atrophied bureaucracies.

He was at work in our home as well; one evening Patty announced that she had enrolled that day in the Bible-study course a group of women in McLean were organising. I tried not to let my excitement show. I knew this had to be something Patty would come to in her own time and way. I tried to be nonchalant about it, but underneath was a warm joy and a sureness that God was working in both our lives.

To some it may have seemed odd that I could stand up

before total strangers and proclaim my faith, while with my own family I was sometimes faltering, always reticent. I didn't understand it myself. I like to think it was the guidance of the Spirit urging boldness at one point and caution at another. More likely, as a new Christian I was just making the bucketful of mistakes which all excited freshmen believers do.

I realise now that those months in early 1974 were a time of spiritual preparation. It was a calm before the gathering storm, a period for re-affirmation of belief, while all around me the forces unloosed by Watergate were moving relentlessly ahead.

Bud Krogh was the first Nixon man indicted. After the Watergate entry was exposed in the summer of 1972, Bud had denied under oath any knowledge of this or of the Ellsberg burglary months before. Then in the spring of 1973 he admitted that he had ordered the break-in at the office of Ellsberg's psychiatrist.

It was a clear-cut case of perjury, against which Bud's only defence was that John Dean counselled him to lie under oath if necessary, for *national security* reasons. Bud, like myself, genuinely believed that the whole Ellsberg affair should have been properly cloaked in the protective shroud of those never-questioned magic words.

While awaiting a second indictment for ordering the break-in, Bud had obviously gone through a long, searching self-examination. In mid-December he stunned Washington with a surprise guilty plea – no bargaining with the prosecutors, no effort to soften the offence, just a straightforward admission of guilt along with sound advice to those who would follow in government service: 'Always ask yourself about every decision – "Is it right?"'

I had known Bud as an influential member of the White House Palace Guard, a heady post for a thirty-one-year-old Navy veteran with only one year of law practice. I also knew that Bud and his wife, Suzanne, had drifted apart, had actually been separated for a time. Now, the family was reunited, bonds between them seemingly stronger than ever as they faced the onslaught of cameras and reporters on the courthouse steps the day Bud pleaded guilty. He was sentenced to six months.

A week before Bud was scheduled to surrender to the marshals and begin his confinement at Allenwood Prison in Pennsylvania, Doug, Harold, Graham, Al, and I invited him to meet with us at Fellowship House. We wanted to encourage him, to let him know that we cared and that we shared the agonies he and Suzanne were enduring.

While awaiting his arrival, I could not subdue my own apprehensions. I was not yet indicted, but each day I lived with the suspenseful torment of expecting it. In this appearance of an old friend – wan, haggard, dejected – I imagined that I might well be looking into a mirror.

The Bud Krogh that arrived at Fellowship House that late January afternoon was not the person I expected to see. Lean and muscular, with strong angular Norwegian features, Krogh had always been a ruggedly handsome man. On this particular day he seemed more vibrant, filled with more enthusiasm than he had been, even in his energetic hard-driving White House days. While relieved, I wondered what his secret was. He did not leave us long in suspense.

'Suzanne and I have been spending several hours each day deep in the Scriptures,' Bud explained. 'It may sound a bit strange, but we really thank God for what has happened to us.'

We all sat in numbed silence. My carefully rehearsed words of encouragement seemed pallid after his. Graham and Al sat staring. Even Harold, who normally takes command of any gathering, was strangely subdued. What do you say to a man who is penniless, jobless, headed for prison, and yet has this kind of faith?

As we talked together, it was Bud encouraging us, just the reverse of what we had planned. 'The Lord takes care of things,'

Bud explained. 'As Suzanne and I were praying about how we would make ends meet while I am in prison, she was offered a teaching job at the school the kids are going to. It will be great for her and we have it all figured to the day; with "good time" I will be home by mid-June. A six months sentence,' Bud said, 'is not all that bad.'

As the six of us prayed together, I could tell that Bud was not putting on a brave front. The Lord had already responded to his prayers and provided him with the assurance that he would not be alone in prison. I walked with him down the short flight of steps in front of Fellowship House toward his car parked on the edge of the forested parkland which borders Embassy Row. 'Bud, please let me know if there is anything I can do for you or Suzanne while you are away.'

But what I really meant was, 'Please let me know how you can be so sure.' The spectre of prison haunted all of us who had been close to Richard Nixon; it even haunted the President, as I had discovered during our December meeting. It was not so much the fear of confinement itself, even the loss of status, career, resources, friends. There was something more that was seldom discussed, but which lay just beneath the surface. Prisons contain violent men, to whom government officials are 'the enemy'. Officials are part of the system which caught and sentenced these men. Indeed, our particular administration boasted about it; filling up the prisons was the mark of success for Nixon's disciples of law and order.

There is a continuous stream of unexplained deaths in penal institutions which are usually attributed to prison vengeance. Once that was merely a remote fact of life. Now the realisation was personal – and terrifying.

As I watched Bud drive away, the warmth of his faith lingered on for several minutes. Yet with it was a kind of premonition. Could the Lord be using Bud to help prepare for me the path ahead?

15

Accused

'Mr Colson, unless my staff can show me a lot more evidence I would not include you in the Watergate cover-up indictment.'

Leon Jaworski, Watergate Special Prosecutor, was smiling now for the first time in our gruelling two-hour session. The one-time Bar Association president was sitting in shirt sleeves at the head of a long conference table in his stark bare-walled office, flanked by Bill Merrill and other assistants. My lawyers, Dave Shapiro, Judd Best, Sid Dickstein, and I had asked for this showdown meeting, a last-ditch effort to persuade the Special Prosecutor and his staff of my ignorance of the Watergate break-in and to avert the long-delayed Ellsberg indictment.

The expression on Jaworski's round face was positively benign. 'Of course,' he continued after what seemed an interminable pause, 'even if you are not indicted for Watergate, there is still this Ellsberg thing.'

I stared at Jaworski, breathing easier for the first time, but waiting, pondering his tactics. No one had ever before suggested I might be indicted in the Watergate cover-up. The original prosecutors had cleared me. But for most of the meeting Jaworski was threatening two indictments! Was it a pressure play?

Jaworski looked away for a moment and then turned to Shapiro, 'Why don't you, Dave, get together with Bill here,' pointing to Merrill, 'and see if you can't work it out? I think Mr Colson really wants to wipe the slate clean, and look forward to a useful career as a citizen and as a *lawyer*.'

With that he stood up abruptly as if on cue, leaving Merrill and Shapiro to dispose of my fate while I, no doubt, was supposed to feel gratitude and relief at the fading of the dread spectre of two felony trials. To the man on the street such terms as *felony, misdemeanour, and plea bargain* are confusing legalese. But for me these terms were as real as food and water. Without saying so directly, the prosecution was asking for a plea bargain for me: for me to plead guilty to a lesser charge in exchange for my testimony against others. Such a plea would mean my being convicted of a misdemeanor which carries a maximum one-year sentence, usually resulting only in probation, and would enable me to continue the practice of law. Conviction of a felony normally means prison – up to five years – and dis-barment. Jaworski's reference to my future as a lawyer was a deliberate signal.

Jeb Magruder and John Dean, both of whom were slated to be key government witnesses against Haldeman, Ehrlichman, and Mitchell, had both agreed to plea bargains. The prosecution also needed someone like myself who had been in the inner circle, one of the four men who, as columnist Joseph Alsop wrote, held a 'dagger to the President's heart'.

As I left the Special Prosecutor's office that day, the painful choice was plain enough. To plea bargain meant my stating under oath that I was guilty of conspiring to break into the office of Daniel Ellsberg's psychiatrist. It also meant offering testimony in advance about other Watergate figures, telling Jaworski's men what they would be getting in return for their leniency to me. How can anyone ever be sure he isn't even subconsciously tempted to offer up testimony more to the prosecutor's liking than the facts really warrant? When a good deal is hanging in the balance, is it not human nature to do so? 'Aw, come on,' they say, 'it really happened this way, didn't it?' And who is strong enough to say *no* when *yes* means staying out of prison? I wasn't sure I was. Krogh had refused to plea bargain on these precise grounds.

But what a relief to get all of this over with, the chance for Patty and me to live a normal life again, to spend time with our children, the end of my parents' agony, especially for Dad whose health I was worried about. Such thoughts, as I drove home that evening, were like a seductive potion. It would be like having a gigantic suffocating cloud suddenly lift and there would be fresh air and sunshine.

That evening I told Patty only a little of what was happening. There was no sense in getting her hopes up, then having them dashed again, the destructive yo-yo cycle she had been through so often in the past year.

Shapiro continued to negotiate with Jaworski's men, haggling over the kind of plea which both sides could agree to and which would save my licence to practise law. Each time he would return with the same report – 'We're making progress.' Breaking out in an awkward little jig, he'd dance about the office. 'C'mon, smile. I'm going to walk you out of this – a free man!'

I could manage a smile, not so much at Dave's report, as at the sight of his ungainly 250-pound frame performing pirouettes like a bear cub being trained for a circus performance. 'Dave, I just don't know that I can do this,' I told him the night after his second meeting. My words fell on him like cold rain.

'Chuck, you gotta be off your rocker. You'll do it or I'll have you committed to the funny farm.'

'I'm serious, Dave,' I repeated. 'I just don't know.'

The answer, whatever it was, I knew I could not find alone. It was the following Saturday evening I joined Harold Hughes in the basement of his modest brick home a few minutes from ours. Harold and I were now meeting frequently in between our regular Monday breakfasts at Fellowship House.

'Brother, I need help,' I said as we sat alone in the basement room Harold had converted into his study. There was a hooked rug spread over the tiles, a crucifix on the mantel over a snapping fire, freshly cut logs piled alongside, big overstuffed chairs pulled close.

I laid out for Harold, step by step, exactly what my choices were. With each point the pain became more evident on his usually stoic face, his scowl deepening as he interrupted with tough questions. It was a bizarre situation. President Nixon's faithful lieutenant was seeking counsel from one of Nixon's most implacable foes about a decision that could seriously hurt the President. For while I still believed the President innocent and had no intention of testifying against him, I knew my action could set in motion other forces which could damage the President's case. By all political standards Hughes would be expected not only to urge me to plea bargain, but also help me sharpen up the stiletto. I doubt if it entered his mind – our duty as followers of Jesus Christ and our love for one another as brothers were the only issues.

'I don't know,' Hughes exclaimed when I finished. 'What can I say?' There were deep furrows across his brow. 'Are you guilty of what you'd have to plead to, Chuck?' he asked.

'Legally, no. I didn't order the burglary at the psychiatrist's. I didn't know about it until it was over. But I'm not sure there's much moral difference. I'd have done anything to stop Ellsberg, anything the President ordered,' I replied.

'That's not the point, Chuck. Is what you would have to say in court true in your own heart, I mean between you and God?'

'No,' I replied quietly, 'the misdemeanour plea would require me to say I knew and approved the break-in. This would not be true.' At that very moment I knew that no matter how long we talked, no matter how many different arguments were advanced, this was the central question and Hughes had pounced upon it.

'Well, you are going to have to ask Christ to give you the answer, brother,' he continued. 'If it were me, with my family involved and all the rest, I don't know if I could turn it down. No one knows until they have to face it. I can tell you the correct answer but I'm not sure I'd follow it myself, so how can I advise you?' Even as he said it I knew the decision was made.

We sat silently with only the sound of the fire crackling in our ears. I looked at Harold, this hulking combat veteran, truck driver and one-time two-fisted drinker, a flamboyant orator, but a compassionate man whom I had come to love very much. His face was buried in his hands. Harold knew, too.

It was important that Patty and the kids understand. Back home that night Patty wholeheartedly agreed that I should make no plea, although a wistful look in her eyes almost betrayed her once or twice in our conversation. The ordeal of anxious days stretching into months, now into its second year, was taking a more brutal toll on her than on me. Wendell was next, through a phone call to Princeton. His answer was as quick and decisive as Patty's. 'Do what is right, Dad.' Although I was working hard at slaying the dragon of pride, I couldn't help feeling a tinge of it in the character of my oldest son.

Next I flew to Boston. Driving from the airport in Chris's dented old Ford with Emily in the back seat, I broached the subject with a more careful explanation, convinced that a fifteen-year-old girl would not understand the difference between a felony and a misdemeanour. Partway into the discussion I asked Emily if she understood the terms.

'Sure,' she replied. 'A misdemeanour means only a one-year prison sentence.' Having her dad in the middle of Watergate had accelerated this aspect of her education at least.

I explained that one of the dangers of not pleading was that I might not get off so lightly later; indictment and conviction on a felony could mean several years in prison.

'Most of my friends already think you're in jail or are going to be, so that doesn't matter,' Chris replied.

'Do they give you a hard time about it?' I asked.

Chris just shrugged his shoulders, but I knew from his silence he was sparing me the hurt of the truth. *How unfair that these two kids are already bearing scars for things they had nothing to do with,* I thought. Chris in his casual way was telling me the damage was already done and to do what I had to.

Emily was slumped in the back seat, looking even more petite than normal, her long blonde straight hair hanging limply over her shoulders. Gone was the pixie's dance from her blue eyes, replaced this day by an unusual look of melancholy. She was following intently every word. 'Did you do what they want you to say you did?' she asked crisply, businesslike, as she sat upright and leaned over the front seat.

'No, I didn't,' I replied.

'Well, then don't say you did it,' she snapped. It wasn't advice, it was an order, her voice revealing a core of toughness I never realised this sweet, shy little girl capable of. What simple logic and refreshing honesty. 'I don't know where these kids got this kind of courage, but thank You, Lord,' I said to myself, looking out of the window so they could not see my emotion.

Dave Shapiro was angry, as I knew he would be when I told him my decision. The negotiations between Dave and the prosecutors were terminated, having achieved nothing but more aggravation between us. (The prosecutors later denied that I was ever offered a misdemeanour plea. Literally that is true. The only basis for the extensive negotiation, however, was a misdemeanour plea. My lawyers were left with the clear impression that it would be formally offered *if* I agreed to accept it. Shapiro and Ken Adams later so testified under oath. The question was mooted, however, since negotiations were broken off before they got to final stages.)

I did not feel self-righteous in the slightest about my decision; I simply could not do anything else, certainly not after Emily's reaction anyway.

As my long, anxious vigil resumed, I continued to wish for another way out. I began to see that defending my past day after day would make it increasingly difficult to live a full and free Christian life, especially since mine was so much in the public spotlight. This letter to the editor in the *Philadelphia Inquirer* stung me:

> So, Charles W. Colson has had some kind of religious experience, and now says he's 'seen the light.' I for one find it impossible to believe that he has accepted the spirit of goodness in any form while he still holds the knowledge of crimes in his heart, and remains unwilling to let the truth come to light.
>
> Until he does that, he's no more than a pious hypocrite, braying his prayers in public for no one's good but his own – he hopes they'll save his skin.
>
> Dan Tanner
> Debran N. J.

What were the crimes in my heart? In a state of agony I probed every action I had taken in the White House. There were tough ruthless political acts – 'dirty tricks', certainly, because they hurt people. Perhaps even worse in God's eyes, there had been arrogance and pride and ego. My all-out loyalty to the commander-in-chief had warped and blurred my sense of right and wrong, no question about that. But actual crimes as defined in the statutes? – no.

I could try, of course, to dismiss Tanner as an anti-Nixon zealot. But if his reactions were typical, wasn't I doing far more harm than good to the Christian cause by publicly taking a stand on my new faith?

The tension mounted. Hardly a day passed without a fresh round of press speculation about the long-awaited indictments – when they would be announced, who would be included, what would be the political impact on Mr Nixon's embattled Presidency. Richard Nixon's strength was steadily deteriorating while House impeachment investigators were methodically filling their arsenals for the expected summer offensive. Nixon's lawyers, St Clair and Fred Buzhardt, were engaged in an heroic effort to shore up the sagging bulwarks while the rest of the White House staff sank deeper into the morass, quibbling and swallowed up by petty jealousies. Haig was meeting regularly with Jaworski and reported that his attitude, once sympathetic, was souring as the political balance was shifting. There seemed to be an historic inevitability to the process, like watching a Greek tragedy's final act.

There were other shocks in store for me as well – like the day I was called to the White House and shown files on the CIA's involvement in Watergate. 'I'd be fired if anyone knew I let you see these,' one of the President's lieutenants whispered to me as he handed me two six-inch-thick bound folders with TOP SECRET stamped in bold blue letters across the front.

I sat there for two hours reading the carefully documented, but seldom discussed CIA role in the Watergate scandal. It disclosed that Howard Hunt was working for Robert R. Mullen and Company, ostensibly just another Washington public-relations firm, but which in fact was a CIA 'cover' outfit. The CIA had monitored all of Hunt's activities and appeared to be involved in events leading up to and following the Watergate break-in.

What jolted me most was the series of memoranda about efforts by Robert Bennett, president of the Mullen firm, to implicate me in Watergate, reportedly to take the heat off the CIA. Attached to a March 1, 1973 internal CIA memorandum was a Xerox copy of the same *Newsweek* article Patty and I had read in Vienna almost a year earlier. There followed page after page of reports showing how the CIA fed Washington reporters – including Robert Woodward of the *Post* – damaging information about me, much of it false.*

President Nixon discussed this report with me on two occasions and said he was determined to expose the agency's misconduct. Other voices, principally General Haig, later convinced him he should do nothing to injure the intelligence establishment. Shapiro took the information to the prosecutors who assured him it would be investigated. It never was, to our knowledge, until later revelations brought forth full-scale congressional hearings. Robert R. Mullen and Company was later disbanded.

Dave believed that the prosecutors might be persuaded not to indict me in the Ellsberg case if I took another lie-detector test, this time to establish I knew nothing in advance about the break-in of the psychiatrist's office. I trotted back to the dingy New York office of Richard Arther and passed my second test.

Dave was so impressed he arranged a third test, this one to prove I'd never promised Hunt or his lawyer clemency or a pardon to keep him quiet in the Watergate case. This was, Shapiro learned, the one allegation that could cause Jaworski to include me in the Watergate cover-up indictment.

By now I was almost adjusted to sneaking furtively in and out of Arther's building, rumpled hat over my eyes, glancing from side to side. Anyone so close to the criminal world, I realised, quickly gets used to its ways.

Maybe it was the forlorn expression on my face as Arther went through the now familiar ritual of wiring me up for the

---

Editor's Note: Material from this file was later quoted in Senator Howard Baker's supplementary report, filed as part of the Ervin Committee's final findings, July 1974. According to the Baker report, the CIA 'took relish in implicating Colson in Hunt's activities . . . It is further noted that Bennett was feeding stories to Bob Woodward who was "suitably grateful" . . . and who was protecting Bennett and Mullen and Company'.

test, maybe it was my pulse reading which he took three times that day, but after it was over, instead of telling me the results, Dick Arther advised me to take no more tests.

'Why? Did I fail?' I asked, a surge of adrenaline sending my heart racing and a hot flush across my face.

'No, you passed. I don't mind taking your money $350 per sitting, but you are tested out. I can tell you are telling me the truth without even hooking you up and if the prosecutors can't by now, you're wasting your time and putting yourself through this agony for nothing.'

It turned out that Arther was right. Merrill could not bring himself to believe the test results, even dispatching an FBI agent to New York to investigate Arther's test procedures.

And still we waited. I was asked again to appear before the grand jury, refused since I was clearly a target, and was served a subpoena. Shapiro protested the unusual procedure – but to no avail. For a second time I was forced to invoke the Fifth Amendment, this time appearing like a criminal hiding his sinful past before the twenty or so citizens who in a few days would vote on whether to indict me.

At last the Special Prosecutor announced that indictments would be filed Friday morning, March 1. All week long Washington was buzzing with 'hot' rumours. Every reporter had a different list. GBS's Dan Schorr called me Thursday evening: 'Sorry to give you the bad news, Chuck, you are one of forty-two on the list. Do you have a comment?'

That seemed preposterous – forty-two indicted – none of us could take it seriously. Jack Anderson, the relentless investigative reporter, called Thursday to say there were only five on the list; I was not one of them. My friends in the White House told me I was not on a list Jaworski had 'unofficially' reviewed with the President's chief-of-staff, Al Haig.

I could take my pick of these speculations and sometimes I felt I almost did not care. Anything would be better than the suspenseful waiting. Patty accompanied me to the office that

Friday to be there in case the worst came to pass. The press would demand a statement; she would be at my side. Deep down I knew I would be among those indicted. Everything that had happened pointed to it, but outwardly I kept smiling, hoping, reading the Twenty-seventh Psalm over and over:

> For in the time of trouble he shall hide me in his pavilion: in the secret of his tabernacle shall he hide me; he shall set me up upon a rock. And now shall mine head be lifted up above mine enemies round about me . . . Deliver me not over unto the will of mine enemies: for false witnesses are risen up against me, and such as breathe out cruelty . . . Wait on the Lord: be of good courage, and he shall strengthen thine heart: wait, I say, on the Lord.
>
> Psalm 27:5, 6, 12, 14 KJV

At 9:30 Shapiro walked into my office, lips curled down, eyes filled with sorrow and hurt. 'The prosecutor just called,' he began, and after a long pause, he simply turned his big thumb down: 'I'm sorry, I'm sorry.'

Holly began to cry and Judd Best embraced Patty who was fighting back tears, trying as hard as she knew how to keep that big radiant smile from which I always derived such strength.

Seven of us in all had been indicted in the Watergate cover-up case. Two hours later Merrill called: 'Next Thursday the Ellsberg indictment will be returned and your man will be in that one, too,' he told Shapiro. What began as a pressure play was now reality. Arraignment was scheduled for both cases on Saturday, March 9, at the federal district court.

When Sid Dickstein and I arrived by cab at the corner of the courthouse that Saturday morning we saw a mass of humanity pressing against a roped-off area around the main entrance. Jeering, shouting spectators were held back from the walkway to the court's doors by lines of helmeted police standing in front of ropes and sawhorses. It reminded me of the days when anti-war protesters surrounded the White House. *There are no sturdy iron gates protecting me now,* I thought with a flash of fear.

Television camera crews and reporters spotted us and galloped our way, elbowing ahead of each other, some with bright, hot lights held over their heads. A few policemen caught in the rush were running with them, stopping periodically in a futile effort to slow the stampede. One cameraman took a bad spill, falling over a low hedge on the border of the courthouse lawn. Another was nearly shoved in front of a car pulling up to the curb.

Within seconds we were surrounded, mikes on long booms thrust at us like spears, questions coming from all sides. I thought *it was a wonder that no one gets trampled in these melees.* The spectators, several hundred by press estimate, were angry, waving homemade placards with slogans like: THEY HUNG HORSE THIEVES and NIXON'S NEXT. Some made obscene gestures. One man wearing a giant papier-mâché mask of Nixon's head was arrested for stripping naked from the waist down and 'streaking' through the crowd. (He was later identified as the local radio broadcaster.)

The uproar was predictable: the press all week had been overpowering. *Newsweek's* cover contained four large pen sketches of the heads of Haldeman, Ehrlichman, Mitchell, and Colson. Across the top in bold red letters larger than the masthead was stamped like a modern-day scarlet letter the single word: INDICTED. Almost the entire evening TV network news was devoted to the story. AP ran a Wirephoto of a smiling Daniel Ellsberg expressing his delight. Many press accounts were laden with the heavy presumption of guilt, all of them ringing with condemnations. Indictment and conviction were without distinction; we were handy targets for fast-moving public passions.

The quiet inside Judge Sirica's courtroom was a welcome

relief to the noisy mob outside. The spectators' benches were filled to capacity with press. As each of the defendants walked in through the side door, whispers filled the room like a great whoosh of air; reporters busily scribbled their impressions, the glimpses of colour that would capture the drama of the long-awaited moment. The *Times* reporter saw me as 'self-assured', while the *Post* scribe detected in me an 'expression of haunted preoccupation'. John Mitchell 'sagged in his chair . . . face grey and drawn'. John Ehrlichman had a 'sweet and sour manner', Bob Haldeman wore 'a well-pressed and well-tailored light blue suit'. Quick, sweeping strokes of crayons on huge white pads created the caricatures that would flash across the screens of millions of TV sets that night.

As I walked towards John Mitchell, seated with his lawyers at a table across the room, I wondered how to be Christ's man. It had been many months since I had seen or talked with Mitchell, my old White House antagonist. The stony-faced ex-Attorney General looked at first stunned and then pleased when I gripped his shoulder, shook his hand, and wished him well. The reunion with Haldeman and Ehrlichman was also warm; no time for bitterness or grudges.

Gordon Strachan, Haldeman's assistant and only twenty-seven, was one of the three minor figures included in the indictment, committee lawyer, Kenneth Parkinson, and former Mitchell aide, Robert Mardian, the others. A tall good-looking lad with long blonde hair and big blue eyes, Strachan was struggling to hold back tears, his eyes glazed with a distant stare. My heart ached for him. Gordon had served powerful men like Haldeman blindly, believing the cause just. It was a feeling I knew so well. Now suddenly, unbelievably, he was standing in a courtroom as a criminal defendant, jostled by an angry mob, the eyes of an outraged nation upon him.

'I understand you are reading the Bible,' he said, a quick flash of brightness in his eyes.

'Yes, I am, Gordon,' I replied. Just discussing it seemed to steady him.

'I'd like to hear about your experience,' he said.

It was hardly the place, standing in that vast open pit with Leon Jaworski and his lieutenants filing in to sit at the prosecutors' table. 'I'd like to, when we can talk,' I told him. 'Hang in there, Gordon, God will give you strength if you ask.' Gordon smiled, then bit his lip.

'All persons having business before the Honourable Judge . . .' the bailiff's words commanded silence in the crowded courtroom. As we stood up, stern-faced Judge John Sirica in flowing black robes strode across the raised platform to the high-back leather chair from which he would preside. It was only the second time I had ever seen Judge Sirica, who only a few months earlier was named *Time* magazine's 'man of the year' after twenty years of obscure service on the DC bench. At a small cocktail party in 1971 we had chatted amiably, the judge recalling fondly his own days in Republican politics, telling me of his admiration for President Nixon. The mild man of that conversation bore no similarity to the determined jurist before me now who was so tenaciously prying loose the lid the White House had attempted to clamp on Watergate.

Sirica summoned the seven of us to walk forward, stand at the rail beneath his bench, and answer as the accusations were read against us. The words were chilling: 'The United States of America charges John Mitchell . . . Charles W. Colson. . . '

All my life the mere words *The United States* had set my spine tingling like martial music. Corny as it may sound to some, I have deeply loved my country, worn the Marine uniform with a sense of honour, and felt pride every time I saw the flag. Now the beloved words were the accuser, striking at me, filling me with shame. It wasn't the United States against me, I wanted to cry out, it was a group of politicised individuals. My own country was not accusing me – but of course it was. That frightful realisation, which until this very moment

I resisted, brought a feeling of nausea. Nothing that could be done to me – trials, prison, ruin – nothing would match the dreadful knowledge that the country I loved was charging me with a breach of my trust and duty.

And in other terms there was something almost as sobering. The government has boundless resources and power: forty well-trained lawyers in Jaworski's office with full subpoena power, gargantuan computers recording, preserving, and tabulating great mounds of evidence, armies of investigators all across the country. One hundred investigators were employed by the Ervin Committee alone, and it was only one of a dozen congressional committees digging into every corner and crevice of our lives. Orders went out to the FBI and IRS to check every lead that might give the prosecutors more ammunition.

The lawyers in our firm were no match for all this. We couldn't even keep track of what was being testified by the hundreds of people who'd been involved in the spreading scandal, and my bank account would be gone in a year. I knew now what it was like for one person to stand virtually alone against the vast powers of government. How calloused I'd been all those past years about the importance of one individual's rights.

Of course there would be trials and a chance to prove my innocence, but no vindication could erase the ugly stain of this day. I stared up at Judge Sirica's scolding eyes, his grim face silhouetted against the cold, black marble wall behind him. My mouth was so parched I wasn't certain my words could be heard: 'Not guilty to all counts.'

I lowered my eyes. 'Neither death, nor life, nor angels, nor principalities, nor powers can separate us from Jesus,' the Apostle Paul wrote to the Christians in Rome (*see* Romans 8:38, 39) Never had those words been more important to me than that moment in the courtroom. In that instant when I felt the full wrath of the principality I had worshipped now accusing me, I felt His presence, too – utterly dependable, utterly caring.

In the days ahead I was to learn how this reality could make all the difference.

16

Decision

The words of the indictment were still ringing in my ears the following Monday as I drove to Fellowship house for our early-morning meeting. The blast of worldwide publicity in the Sunday papers added to my state of shock.

Doug Coe met me with the usual merry twinkle in his eyes. 'Brother, look at it this way. It's good. We've got a Christian in the news.'

My return smile was sickly. To the four men gathered in the library, I put the hard question which had troubled me all weekend: 'In view of the indictments, shouldn't I withdraw from this fellowship? Two of you are in public office and this thing could hurt you.'

'We're brothers,' Quie snapped. 'If you're indicted, Chuck, we all are. We're together. That's the way it is.'

Hughes nodded. For both men such a commitment could be costly. Though Hughes was leaving politics, he was 'Mr Clean' to an enormous following across the country. Quie as a Republican had to stand for re-election in the fall in a Democratic state with all signs pointing to a Democratic landslide. Even though his own law practice could also be hurt, Graham Purcell was the most indignant over the suggestion. 'You're stuck with us, podner,' he pronounced in his best Texas drawl.

In the discussion and prayer that followed, the despair of the weekend passed as once again I discovered the strength of His presence. When I arrived at the office later that morning, I felt almost serene. Dave Shapiro looked at me through sleep-starved eyes and shook his head. 'How do you do it? This has been the worst weekend of my life. Two indictments, a lynch mob at the courthouse, everybody in town howling for your hide and you look like you've just gotten back from a vacation.'

I was ready this morning even to take on Shapiro. 'If you really want me to explain we'll have to start two thousand years ago. That's where you guys missed the boat.'

Shapiro grinned. 'Let's get to work. I'm gonna walk you right out of that courtroom, Chuck. Those indictments are paper-thin.'

Buoyed up by the prayer session and Shapiro's brave talk, I settled in for a long fight. First I withdrew from the law firm and the name was changed to DICKSTEIN, SHAPIRO, AND MORIN, though Holly and I kept our office there. Then I explained to each of my clients that they had no further obligation to retain me. To my surprise the secretary-treasurer of the Teamsters, Dusty Miller, chose almost the same words Quie had: 'In the labour movement, we are brothers. You're indicted – I'm indicted. That's that.' Brainerd Holmes and Tom Phillips of Raytheon offered support. 'We'll just work with others in the firm until you're back. It'll be soon,' Brainerd encouraged. Not a single client took his account elsewhere.

With St Clair no longer available and most of the best lawyers already committed to Watergate defendants, Dave Shapiro decided to head up my defence along with Dickstein and a bright young associate, Ken Adams. We consulted the Bar Association which gave us permission, since I was no longer a member of the firm and finding new lawyers would work a severe hardship.

Since the two trials were scheduled back to back – Ellsberg in July, Watergate in September – there was no possible way to prepare adequately for both. Besides, the trials would come right during the impeachment hearings, creating the worst possible public climate for our defence. A delay in one or both trials was essential, we felt, but with the rising clamour for 'swift justice', Judges Sirica and Gerhard Gesell, who was assigned the Ellsberg case, would be unlikely to grant it.

'We've only got one chance,' Ken Adams concluded after studying the cases. 'Let's collect every newspaper article that's accused you of anything over the past two years. We'll package them together, index them, and drop them in the judge's lap. That's the kind of solid proof of prejudice that might persuade him to delay.' The law clearly holds such delays appropriate when there is such overwhelming adverse publicity before a trial.

'You've got to be kidding,' I replied, 'There must be thousands of articles. We'd need fifty people full-time. It's impossible.'

Ken Adams began by mobilising most of the office staff. Secretaries volunteered to work without pay in the evenings, clipping articles from great mountains of newspapers piled high on the conference room table. Some of the lawyers' wives pitched in each evening as additional boxes of old *Posts* and *Stars* were opened. The task began to appear more and more hopeless, like shovelling snow in a blizzard; for each shovelful cleared away, two more fell. It was difficult at times even to keep abreast of the current day's rash of speculations about impeachment and the upcoming trials.

The results of a private survey we commissioned added new urgency to the task. According to pollster Albert E. Sindlinger, a staggering 91 per cent of the nation was aware of the indictments, as high a number as can in most national election polls identify the candidates for President. In publicity-soaked Washington, the total was even higher. Nationally, of those with opinions 75 per cent believed the defendants guilty, 7 per cent innocent; in Washington the ratio was 84 per cent to 2 per cent. In the Ellsberg case the Washington odds were even more overwhelming – 75 per cent to 1 per cent. It defied all laws of statistical probability to think an impartial jury could be picked. Winning a delay or removal of the trial to a city where the impeachment fever was less epidemic was our one hope. The press clippings were crucial to making our point.

Doug learned of our plight and arrived one evening with an energetic young ex-Marine named John Bishop. Bishop took command like the infantry captain he'd been. Two Fellowship House girls manned the phones. The next day they began arriving: secretaries from government agencies, college students, retired couples, a doctor and his wife, a minister, housewives. By the weekend almost eighty volunteers had signed on and were crowded into our offices – sitting on desks and tables, squatting Indian-style on the floor, cutting, pasting, and indexing. They divided into shifts, some working days, others evenings – and a late crew which often stayed until the dawn hours. One morning I arrived early to find several young men stretched out asleep on the library floor.

Before devouring the bags of sandwiches and pots of coffee brought into the office three times a day, little groups would gather to ask for the Lord's blessing. Often before beginning their work the volunteers would gather in a circle with hands joined, asking Christ to strengthen their fellowship and help them in their task. Once I joined a group praying in the room where Ken Adams, who is Jewish, and two of the firm's young secretaries were working.

'Sorry, Ken,' I said afterwards. 'Didn't mean to trap you.'

But Ken was smiling. 'That's okay. What these people are doing for you is so great I'm glad to be part of it.'

Bit by bit the mounds of paper were whittled away, replaced by neat little piles of pages pasted with clippings, colour coded and ready for copying and filing in one of the thirty-nine big black notebooks Adams had organised. The 'Christians for Colson', as the volunteers dubbed themselves, cheerfully attacked the impossible and after two weeks victory was in sight.

More important than the job itself, the invasion began to affect the whole law firm, the 'healthy infection' which C.S. Lewis writes about. 'I don't know what's going on in here,' Dave Shapiro muttered one evening, 'but whatever it is, it's unbelievable. I just talked with one of those kids. He told me he couldn't stand your politics, but he loved you. Now explain that, will you?'

A couple of secretaries who had been with the firm for years and were chronic grumblers, watched with wide-eyed disbelief as the volunteers dug away at the work, with never a complaining murmur, even when the air conditioning was turned off at night or when the sandwiches ran out or when, as often happened, something was prepared improperly and had to be scrapped and done over. The harder the work and greater the frustration, the more these Christians smiled and toiled on.

Gradually but perceptibly the morale of the busy law firm was lifted. One of the clerks in the office was undergoing personal difficulties at the time and late one evening poured his heart out to a young Fellowship House worker, as the two manned a Xerox machine together. Some weeks later the clerk began attending a Fellowship prayer group and a few months after that left the law firm to take a sales position which would put him in contact with others which he in turn could help. He explained to me that these two weeks had changed his life.

The motions were due in court May 1. On the last day of April it was still touch and go, with papers spread throughout the office and a massive duplicating job still to be done to meet the court's requirement of four copies of everything. Forty blurry-eyed volunteers worked feverishly through the final night and by early the next morning the bound volumes were ready for delivery in the back of a station wagon to the courthouse. Each set of books rose seven feet into the air and contained thousands of clippings.

A few days later Judges Gesell and Sirica dismissed the most impressive research undertaking of the trial, denying our motions. Sirica refused to disqualify himself and assign another judge to the case even though his prior public statements showed a disposition to expose the 'higher-ups' now scheduled for trial, and both judges refused to move the trials to another city, an accepted practice to avoid local hostility. It was a bitter disappointment. But for me no outcome in the courtroom could sour the sweet taste of Christ's love from eighty otherwise complete strangers. 'Worth it all,' I told Holly once again, and this time there was no quizzical look on her face. She was discovering it, too.

Meanwhile a half-block away the President was announcing over nationwide television the public release of quite a different set of volumes. These were also dark, bound notebooks, containing transcripts of forty-seven taped White House conversations. 'The documents,' Nixon assured millions of viewers, 'will once and for all show that what I knew and what I did with regard to the Watergate break-in and cover-up were just as I have described them to you from the very beginning.'

He said it with such confidence that I thought it might be another rug-pulling performance, like the January 1972 bombshell when he disclosed thirty months of secret negotiations over Vietnam. *At long last*, I thought, *he has the proof he told me he had all along*. As I watched the 'old' Nixon, a sense of elation swept over me. But why in the world had he waited so long?

Holly obtained an advance copy of the transcripts early the next morning. As I began eagerly flipping through the pages of the thick blue-bound book, Dave Shapiro came to look over my shoulder. The words before my eyes and Shapiro's loud groans in my ears made my heart sink. 'I don't believe it,' I muttered as on page after page the phrase *expletive deleted* was carving for Richard Nixon a place as the most profane President in history.

'He's dead in the Bible Belt,' I told Shapiro.

'He's dead, period,' Shapiro responded. 'And by the way, faithful Nixon servant, he's lied right through his teeth to you.'

As I read on, the hurt and the feeling of betrayal came. And with it the memory of a remark by Bob Haldeman near the end of the 1972 campaign: 'Richard Nixon will use anybody. Remember that. When he doesn't need you, he'll discard you.'

At the time I shrugged off the remark as an unfeeling Haldeman expressing his idea of how any President should handle his staff. Nor did I mind being expendable, I told myself then, if that was the price of serving the man and the goals I saw as being so noble. Yet the ego in me made me think I would somehow be immune.

Here in the transcripts Haldeman's words became real. Shapiro's eyes were piercing through me. There was no time for bitterness. 'Dave, what Nixon must do is resign. Go out gracefully. I've got to tell him.'

Shapiro thought it unwise for me to call; the prosecutors might make something out of it. Instead he carried my message to Jim St Clair who brushed it aside. The legal case, St Clair was convinced, would be strengthened by the released transcripts. But it is the ground swell of public opinion, not legal argument, which moves events and nations. The jury was to decide this case on moral issues and Nixon had returned the decisive verdict himself.

Beyond the 'expletives deleted', the raw transcripts exposed to public scrutiny an indecisive, vacillating, and shallow man, Richard Nixon's worst side. This was not the leader I had heard making courageous decisions in an effort to end the war in Vietnam, not the man speaking with gentle sensitivity of the feelings of others, not the idealist who dreamed aloud his visions for America and the world.

For a few moments I felt some personal vindication from the tapes. Not included in the transcripts were meetings with the President when I had argued the public exposure of whoever was involved; the President told me he did not know who they were. But now reading the tapes it seemed that he had known much more than he ever let on. While I was urging disclosure, he was telling Mitchell, Haldeman, and Dean to 'stonewall' the investigators.

But the more I studied them the more depressed I became. That Nixon had lied to me, that he had not exercised the strength of character I knew in the man was a blow, yet I still cared about him. What hurt now so deeply was the sickening lead-in-the-stomach awareness that I myself had helped create the demeaned White House which stood exposed to public view.

Not so much the profanity. The tough talk was our way of showing Nixon we were good enough to stand up against the world, lieutenants worthy of front-line service. The real problem was the moral decay inside an office which should have, if not nobility, at least a high sense of purpose. Memories of the selfless and inspiring words of Washington, Lincoln and Jefferson, who sat in those places before us, rendered our conversations shoddy and dirty by comparison. Yet all Presidents had a private side; Ike was profane, Truman salty, others had moral weaknesses; the public is shielded from much of this knowledge, for most of us want to believe the best of our leaders.

And so the devastating truth came home to me. I as much as anyone had defiled my own lofty – maybe unreal – visions of the Presidency, and thanks to the taping system it was recorded for evermore. Confronting that reality was as shattering as hearing the clerk read, 'The United States versus Charles Colson'. A second body blow in as many months.

On the heels of Nixon's release of the transcripts came yet another shock, this one from an unexpected quarter. 'Chuck, I've got to see you.' It was Dick Howard's troubled voice on the telephone, the young man who had served for two years as my superbly efficient administrative assistant in the White

House. A tall, handsome Californian in his early thirties, Dick was now about to leave the White House to accept a good position in private industry. He and his wife, Marcia, and twin four-year-old boys were almost like family to us.

'I've been told not to talk to you anymore,' he explained when we met in my office. Dick, always unflappable even in the heat of the worst crises, was pallid and unsmiling.

'Who said that?' I demanded.

'The prosecutors, They've told me I'm going to be indicted for perjury.' There was a quiver in his voice.

'For what?' My own voice was rising uncontrollably, my stomach starting a fast elevator ride down. Howard explained that he had been grilled by the prosecutor's staff about everything which had gone on in my office. It was standard procedure, I suppose, although I strongly questioned some of the tactics used.

One young girl who handled research assignments reported to me that she was considered 'uncooperative' when she failed to confirm a theory of the prosecution. The two young lawyers questioning her asked at the end of a long interrogation, 'How could a nice young woman like you have worked for such an evil man?' She and others like my White House secretary, Joan Hall, were dragged before different interrogators every few weeks, forcing them to incur thousands of dollars in legal bills.

Holly, the secretary closest to me during the preparation of my defence, was grilled hard one day by three prosecutors. After hours of going over and over the same questions, gentle, patient Holly finally had enough. 'We can sit here all day and do this,' she fired back, 'but I know what the truth is and that is all you are going to get.' She was not bothered again. While the prosecutors were after me, not them, it was costing these people dearly in time, money, and anxiety. As it turned out, the prosecution failed to turn up a single former member of my staff, which numbered close to thirty, who had testimony to give against me.

But now Dick was on the hot seat. An indictment would wreck his career. He had been questioned over and over about one alleged incident where I was supposed to have hired some thugs to beat up Ellsberg. Dick had denied it under oath, but the prosecutors would not believe him. He was told his own indictment would come in two weeks. 'Look, Dick, you are telling the truth,' I assured him. 'Just stick to the facts and you can't be indicted.'

But I felt far less confident than I tried to sound. The rest of the day I was unable to work, my mind turning again to Dick and the other innocent people caught up in the gathering storm. I left the office and went directly to Doug Coe's home.

'This certainly calls for some special prayer,' Doug answered sombrely after I had explained Dick's problem.

'Doug, I can't let this happen to Dick and his family. He has no money. His new job will fall through. He's told the White House he's resigning. If it will get Dick off the hook, I'll plead guilty. I'll say I did whatever they want me to say.' My agitation must have startled Doug.

'No, you can't do that. We must get the Lord's answer to this,' he replied. Doug then went on to describe King David's dilemma when God punished him for prideful disobedience by giving him his choice between a seven-year famine, a three-month defeat in battle, or a three-day plague on his people. 'The price of leadership can bring on terrible suffering,' Doug continued. 'But stop worrying about Dick. There are brothers who will help him. You are being tested. Now open yourself and God will supply the answer.'

Further help to me came in a letter from Michael Alison, a young member of the British House of Commons whom I had met at Fellowship House a month earlier. Alison recommended to me a 'short, pithy, crisis prayer' like the one David used in his ordeal with Absalom: '. . . O, Lord, I pray thee, turn the counsel of Ahithophel into foolishness' (2 Samuel 15:31 KJV).

'This prayer was instantly and dramatically answered,' Alison wrote. 'It is this prayer which I pray for you and I hope you will for yourself in regard to those opponents who are out to discredit you.'

Each day thereafter, as more reports filtered back to me of former staff members one by one summoned before Jaworski's men, the pressure intensifying, I repeated the same prayer: 'Lord Jesus, please turn the counsel of my enemies into foolishness. Help me find *Your* answers. Show me *Your* will.'

Like opening the floodgates for a fast-swelling river, the release of the White House Transcripts triggered a deluge of stories, television specials, and new leads for the prosecutors. Nixon's supporters were embarrassed, his opponents had a wealth of fresh ammunition. Republican Senate leader, Hugh Scott, branded the transcripts 'shabby'. Two House leaders demanded resignation. Vice-President Gerald Ford claimed the tapes cleared Mr Nixon; then as the uproar continued, back-tracked, acknowledging the 'grave situation'. On May 9 the gavel struck, opening the formal impeachment hearings of the House Judiciary Committee. The rush to judgement was a near stampede.

As the sound and fury of the Watergate investigations rose, I noticed a new and recurrent theme in my mail. Although the tone of the letters remained warm and encouraging, there were more and more exhortations to do my Christian duty. A letter from Dr Vernon Grose, a strong Republican and good friend, summed it up this way: 'Be forthright and utterly honest in your legal confrontations regarding Watergate and the associated allegations.'

Here again was the dilemma I had encountered so many times since my conversion – of trying to live in two worlds. As a Christian I yearned to tell all, to testify in the impeachment hearings, but my lawyers – representing the world's wisdom –

told me I had to keep quiet. My freedom was at stake, they advised; whatever I had to say should be kept for the trial and even then I was to testify only to things that would help my case. To make it worse, my courtroom defence when it came would concern my life *before* Jesus Christ entered it. The old Colson was on trial and there was a lot in this life I did not feel like defending. But how to separate the new and the old? How to live in two worlds?

In the midst of the mounting pressures, Harold announced one Monday morning that Mike Wallace was receptive and sympathetic, thus clearing the way for us to appear on 'Sixty Minutes'. Doug was elated at the chance for a powerful testimony to millions. I was not so certain, with the doubts now nagging at me about my ability to be a full-fledged public ambassador. The filming was scheduled for May 16 in the Hughes basement.

The very weather that day was ominous: hot and damp. When I arrived at Harold's house, it was already surrounded by CBS camera trucks. Thick black wires stretched across the front lawn, lights on tripods and metal boxes cluttered the driveway, neighbours stared from adjacent yards. Harold, dressed in a checked suit, the most conservative one in his nontraditional wardrobe, was perspiring profusely. Eva bounced up and down the stairs, carrying trays of coffee and cold drinks. Mike Wallace, so fierce on TV, seemed strangely gentle when he introduced himself.

'What you men are doing is great, just great,' he said with a disarming smile. I decided that Harold had really reached him.

Harold and I slipped away to his living room for a few minutes together asking God to take charge of the interview. In the basement we found that producer Marion Goldin and the CBS experts had fashioned a makeshift studio. Under the scorching lights Harold sat in his favourite rocker, I on the Early American sofa.

The words of Marion, 'Okay, Mike, cameras are rolling,' were to Wallace like the sound of the bell for a prizefighter. His lips curled, his eyes became piercing. The soft-spoken, easygoing fellow we had chatted so amiably with was now a snarling tiger about to pounce.

'Twenty million people will see this,' Wallace had told us earlier. *Fine*, I thought. Having made many television appearances, stage fright was no worry. How hot the lights were! Under the blinding white glare I could feel beads of perspiration popping out on my upper lip, like little crystals on the sand, I imagined.

Mike's words shot forth in short staccato bursts: 'Senator Hughes, this is the fellow who put you on the White House "enemies" list and here you are sitting together . . .'

Hughes turned the question to me and I tried to explain that I was not the one who prepared the 'enemies' list but that it didn't matter. Christ heals the wounds, He is the transcendent power. Score one for our witness.

Wallace came on hard after that: 'Have you done more than pray? Have you made a palpable witness? Have you tried to make it up to those you've hurt?'

'In my own heart,' I answered lamely.

'But have you tried to make it up? . . . Have you apologised?'

'There are a couple of instances . . .'

'With whom?' Wallace pressed.

When I didn't respond fast enough, Wallace listed the sins for me: the Burns smear, the effort to intimidate CBS before the Federal Communications Commission, public attacks on Jack Anderson. Wallace leaned back and mused, 'A new Christian, besides talking to his God, does he do no penance for deeds like that?'

Score several for Wallace as he drove home his points with sharp, biting words. My answer about Christ forgiving us — that all of us are sinners — seemed limp. Later came the most lethal exchange of the interview.

WALLACE: Let's turn then to the White House tapes. Do they show a morality in the Oval Office?

HUGHES: Not the standards that I would hope to see in the Oval Office, no.

WALLACE: Do they to you, Mr Colson?

COLSON: I'm not going to try to characterise how I look at those transcripts, because I don't think you can . . .

WALLACE: Well, wait . . .

COLSON: I've sat in many, many meetings in the Oval Office, Mike, and I did not know there was a recording system. I suppose . . .

WALLACE: Is that moral?

COLSON: I'm not going to try to draw a moral judgement on it . . .

WALLACE: Wait a minute. *Let me understand something about this new Christianity, then.* You say that you are a new man in Jesus Christ. It seems as though your prior faith takes precedence over your new faith.

With a satisfied smile, Wallace leaned back. Score more points, many more.

HUGHES: Mike, you are placing a burden on a man who is new in Christ – a baby in Christ is what we say – and that implies just what it is, a baby, not full maturity, not full understanding. I would say it's immoral to make the tapes. I say it's immoral to use the types of language that were involved, regardless of whether you're behind closed doors. And yet I would also say that I have been guilty of similar things in my lifetime while I have been in public office.

COLSON: I don't believe that when you accept Christ in your life or when you decide that you're going to live by the teachings of Christ, that you necessarily should set yourself up as a judge of others. As a matter of fact,

> Christ teaches us exactly the opposite. Only God really
> is our Judge.
>
> WALLACE: Well, I confess you leave me somewhat bewild-
> ered, then, as to the meaning of your faith.

That was it. I was impaled on the question about the White
House transcripts, driven right through the gut and then nailed
to the wall. I wanted to say, 'They are lousy, rotten, and I was
part of many other conversations just like them.' But I did
not, for I might have to defend some of them in court as I
tried to wriggle through the maze of legal technicalities that
lay before me.

I made no effort to wipe my face dry as Wallace wound up
the interview. The reality was exploding before me in the
blinding-white camera lights: I could not be a criminal defendant and a disciple for Christ at the same time. The painful
dilemma of how to live in two worlds had confronted me again,
this time in living colour on national TV.

After the Wallace filming I flew to Boston to be with Dad
in the hospital where he was making a slow recovery from his
second heart attack. For me it was a painful sight, tubes
running out of his arms, a small oxygen cap over his nose, and
a frightened look in his eyes. Everyone loved my dad for his
kindness, his concern for others, for the contagious smile
surrounded by pink cheeks and the close-cropped white hair.
This day the smile was still there, but he could not quite hide
his fear. I believed that brave talk would bolster him.

'Don't worry, Dad, we're going to lick these indictments.
The prosecutors won't get a conviction.'

It had no effect because the lawyer in him knew better. 'Are
you innocent of the charges?' he persisted. It finally penetrated
that what concerned him was what he had taught me as a boy:
always tell the truth. My assertion that I had not known in
advance of the Ellsberg break-in gave him more comfort than
the bravado. I had not lied; I had lived by the code he taught

me, I assured him. This was more important to him than a jury's verdict.

I gave him a copy of *Mere Christianity*, which he was eager to read. We prayed together before I left. I wanted to go deeper, to tell him about the question I was struggling with involving my Christian life, but he was in no condition for it. Someday I'd be able to explain.

The following Tuesday morning I was in Judge Gerhard Gesell's courtroom for the opening oral arguments on the critical pre-trial motions in the Ellsberg case. At issue was whether the national security argument would be allowed in the trial. It was a vital line of defence.

Dave Shapiro was soon prancing before Gesell's bench, his head bobbing up and down to punctuate key points, his voice rising and thundering through the room. At moments the judge looked as kind and gentle as my dad. At other moments his stern, squinting eyes pierced the hearts of those before him.

Suddenly Gesell interrupted. 'The whole purpose of this case, beyond its immediate objective,' he stated, 'is to direct some attention to the desirability of having a government of law, not a government of men. That is what it is about.' Then the judge – his white hair so neatly in place it looked like one of those wigs worn by English judges – proceeded to give Shapiro and the other lawyers a scolding lecture on the fundamentals of the Constitution.

It was something I remembered from Civics I in school. These were the cardinal principles of American government, the real bulwark against man-made tyranny. When a man's constitutional rights are in jeopardy, the violation, even cloaked in the time-honoured protective shroud of national security, is simply intolerable. I did not know whether Gesell was a religious man, but while he was speaking, Lewis's words about the individual being more important than the state kept echoing through my head. Lewis and Gesell were singing the same tune. So what if I had not known of the break-in ahead of time? If I could prove that legally, I would be acquitted – but was that the real issue? When I first learned of the break-in at the psychiatrist's office, I believed it was justified – almost anything was, to stop Ellsberg. So why should my guilt or innocence turn on the particular day I first learned of the misdeed? Legal niceties made moral nonsense.

God was dealing with me at that very moment. I went home that evening and fell into the deepest depression of all the dark days and nights that had gone before. Judge Gesell had not ruled on the motions; he would do that later in the week, but now somehow it did not matter. Nothing he would say could alter my own self-judgement. How smug I had been during those years in the executive mansion. What happened around me never bothered me so long as I kept myself clean. I was just another 'see no evil, hear no evil, speak no evil,' monkey. If I had sidestepped any direct involvement in the Ellsberg break-in, it was pure happenstance. I had tried to smear him just the way I was now being attacked in the press and in somewhat the same way the CIA had leaked stories about me.

If I had gotten away with it from the sanctuary of the White House, then no one was safe. I had not succeeded, of course, and I was not being charged with character defamation, but was it any less reprehensible than the burglary I *was* charged with? *Hardly*, I concluded. It was worse: damage to a man's spirit as against damage to property.

Dad's question from his hospital bed, the simple idealism in Judge Gesell's impromptu sermon, memories of my White House attitude of 'anything goes just short of breaking the law', Mike Wallace's questions and the realisation of my own crippled discipleship were pulling against me like great iron chains. I'd struggle, twist, tear at them, but I could not shake free. I was barely able to hold a conversation with Patty.

'What's eating you, Chuck?' she asked with a trace of annoyance in her voice, as I sat on the desk by our swimming pool gazing vacantly into the blue water.

'I'm just tired, honey,' I replied, but I knew it was much more than that. Somehow I had to be altogether free of the past.

As a favour to Doug some while back I had agreed to speak at the annual prayer breakfast in the small central-Michigan community of Owosso. It could not have come at a worse time – Thursday, May 23. Arguments were continuing over the motions. The trial would begin in less than four weeks and every minute was precious now. My lawyers and I could make it only by working day and night, weekends as well.

But I had made the date, so Thursday morning I was sitting in the Owosso YWCA auditorium, located on a quiet, tree-shaded street just up the hill from the centre of town. Friendly open-faced Midwesterners had risen at dawn to sit shoulder to shoulder at long folding tables. There were high-school students, middle-aged couples, older folks, a sprinkling of clergy. Next to the Fourth of July, the prayer breakfast was the most important event in the town. After we had consumed huge platters of baked eggs atop bread, there were official welcomes, an opening prayer, passage readings from the Old and New Testaments and then I was introduced.

I had discovered that when I ask the Spirit of God to speak through me, the pressure leaves. He takes over. This morning the words came out more boldly than ever before. Toward the end of my thirty-minute talk, I thought I owed some explanation for my indictments, that it was important for them to know the truth so they could better accept my testimony.

'I know in my own heart,' I explained, 'that I am innocent of many of the charges . . .'

The flow of words stopped as my mind took in what I had said. '*Many* of the charges' – *but not all?*

There was an awkward silence. I looked down at the notes before me, but they were no help. I had hardly glanced at my prepared text during the whole talk. The pause must have been as embarrassing to the audience as it was to me. A hot flush spread over my face. *The press is here* I thought to myself. *Better recover fast.*

'Er – innocent of all the charges I stand accused of,' I stammered. I continued, but the life was gone from my words.

No one else seemed to have noticed my slip. There was nothing about it in the press. But the words *many of the charges* throbbed with the pulse of the jet engines flying me back to Washington. Was it a Freudian slip? Or was it God using my voice? 'Many, *but not all* the charges, Chuck!'

My own words had clinched it. My conversion would remain incomplete so long as I was a criminal defendant, tangled in the Watergate quagmire. I had to put the past behind me completely. If it meant going to prison, so be it!

In his book *The Cost of Discipleship* Dietrich Bonhoeffer wrote of what he called the Great Divide: 'The first step which follows Christ's call cuts the disciple off from his previous existence. The call to follow at once produces a new situation. To stay in the old situation makes discipleship impossible.'

It had all looked so simple once, just getting in tune with God, finding out who Christ was and believing in Him. But whether I was ready for discipleship or not, here I was and there was no turning back.

Patty was the first one whose agreement I had to secure. We talked long into the night amid tears that would not stop. She was hurt. We had struggled through so much and now I was simply to step forward, plead guilty, and go to prison.

'Why? Why do you have to do it?' she kept asking. 'Dave says you'll be acquitted. Then our lives will be normal again. You'll be practising law. We can travel.'

'It will never be the same again, Patty. Trust me that this is the way things will get better. I just have to do it.' It was the most difficult thing I had ever asked her to do, but finally she did, aching heart and all.

Next came Harold. We talked in the familiar surroundings

of his basement den, where only ten days earlier we had filmed the 'Sixty Minutes' show. 'Harold, I've reached a decision,' I said. 'I'm going to plead guilty to something I did do, smearing Ellsberg while he was under indictment. I assume if I do, the prosecutors will drop the other charges. The plea should be good for the country; it should stop this kind of thing in the future.' Even as I spoke I could taste the new freedom that would soon be mine.

Harold's expression was grim. 'How much time will you get?'

'Five years is maximum.' Somehow the words did not chill me as they always had before.

'That's tough. I don't think I could do it.'

'I'm going to, Harold, unless you and the other brothers disagree. I'm convinced I must.'

Harold's rugged face relaxed and a wide grin spread across it. 'Hallelujah!' he shouted. 'I could never have advised you to do it, but I've been waiting for this day. It kills me, it hurts so much, but I'm swelling up with joy.'

Dave Shapiro's reaction was predictable and I held the receiver away from my ear as he exploded. 'You are nuts, crazy, you've gone *meshuga*, that's what.' And then he really let me have it.

'Dave, calm down. It's a decision I've reached and I know what I am doing.' I tried to keep my voice down. Dave and I often shouted at each other.

'Well, we'll see if the psychiatrist agrees that you know what you're doing. I'm taking you to a shrink Monday morning.'

'Dave, I want you to talk to the prosecutors Monday. See Bill Merrill. Tell him we want no deal, no strings. Just say I'm ready to plead guilty to disseminating derogatory information to the press about Daniel Ellsberg while he was a criminal defendant.'

'It's not a crime. How can I plead that for you? No one has ever been charged with that.'

'It ought to be. If I plead, it will be a precedent. That will stop it in the future.'

'You are an idiot and you are going to end up in the slammer.'

'I know.'

'I won't do it.'

'Then get me a lawyer who will.'

'Colson, you are nuts. I've suspected it all along but now I know it. Let's sleep on it. We'll talk tomorrow. Right now I'm going to have a big stiff drink.'

Shapiro can't drink. One knocks him flat. The thought of it provided the first good laugh I'd had in weeks.

17

Guilty, Your Honour

Dave Shapiro appeared Monday morning looking as if he were wearing a rubber mask. There were sagging ripples of flesh under his mournful eyes; his grey-tinted cheeks were in contrast to a stark-white forehead. I knew one reason he was hurting. Dave is usually a winner, especially in law suits. To him this was defeat.

'Are you sure you know what you're doing?' he asked one final time. It was the same question Patty had asked when I'd kissed her good-bye at the front door.

'I've never been more certain of anything in my life, Dave,' I assured him, discovering a confidence I'd not known in weeks. With that, Shapiro was off to see the assistant prosecutor, William Merrill.

Everything depended on Bill Merrill and Judge Gesell being in agreement. If they were not, there could be no guilty plea and the fact of my offer would hurt me badly in the trial, where it would be viewed as a sign of weakness prompted by the fear that I was going to be convicted. Here again I had to go ahead on faith.

Only Patty, Harold, Holly, and Dave knew what was afoot. Any premature disclosure could cause the prosecutors to back away. We'd consult the other brothers and the rest of the family only when we had the green light from the prosecution. Somehow I would find a way to let my old friend in the White House know, too, but it would be hard to explain. So besieged was the President that he would probably see my act as one of betrayal.

Bill Merrill was as shocked by the decision as Dave had been, I learned from Shapiro. For the prosecutors about to begin a trial, it was welcome news, simplifying the case against the other defendants, particularly John Ehrlichman. The two lawyers immediately placed a long-distance call to Judge Gesell, who was at his summer home in Maine for a week's rest. The judge would make no commitment over the phone.

'You understand, Mr Shapiro, *if* I accept this plea, that my policy with high government officials is to impose a prison sentence,' he warned.

'I understand, Your Honour, and Mr Colson does, too,' Shapiro replied.

'There can be no deal here,' the judge continued. 'There is no understanding in advance about sentence. You and Mr Colson are voluntarily coming before me with no limits on what I may do.'

Judge Gesell's words had a menacing ring. Bud Krogh, who had admitted responsibility for the Ellsberg break-in, had been given a six-month sentence. What I was pleading to was a lesser offence and should warrant a lesser punishment. But I was a higher-up target and a more likely candidate to be made a public example. On balance, we reasoned, Krogh's sentence would be the logical guideline. Still the judge's tone was ominous. Five years was possible.

Over the phone Judge Gesell also cautioned Shapiro and Merrill that he would have to be convinced that what I was pleading to was, in fact, a crime. The plea would be an important precedent. Shapiro thus began the anomalous task of researching legal arguments to persuade a judge that his client was actually guilty of a crime. Gesell would not make his decision until he returned to Washington the next week.

'Honey, will it really mean prison?' Patty asked on Wednesday evening.

'I'm afraid so,' I replied. 'But it won't be long, a few months probably, like Bud. He gets home in a couple of weeks. Four and a half months goes by like nothing.'

But both of us knew it was not just the length of time, but the element of danger, too. The reports from Bud's friends were mildly reassuring; he had adjusted well, was working hard driving a tractor at Allenwood. There had been no threats on his life that we knew about. Howard Hunt had had a rougher time, was attacked in his cell one night in the DC jail, and later suffered a mild stroke, apparently from working in the sub-zero cold shovelling manure at Allenwood's farm. Stories of homosexual rape in the DC jail appeared regularly in the press.

'I'm scared, Chuck. I don't know if I can go through with it.' Tears lurked behind her wide blue eyes as she gripped my hand. Patty was tough inside, one reason I loved her so much, but we had grown close and were now dependent on one another. Years before, I had decided never to leave her alone in our house which is surrounded by woods and isolated from neighbours. Whenever I travelled Holly stayed with her. Nightly calls kept us close and I never took long trips without her. We had not been apart more than a two-day stretch in our ten years of marriage. Despite her warm outgoing personality and the brave front she struggled to keep, I realised suddenly how frightened she was.

'Honey, let's pray about it; let's ask God to protect us both and help us face what we must.'

In Patty's eyes, while Christ was once a threat to our relationship, He was now becoming a source of strength. The months in Bible class had helped. She had also grown fond of the brothers and their families. Yet not wanting to press her into something she was not ready for, I did not ask her to pray aloud with me this evening. We both did so silently. Later we talked about some of the hard decisions ahead – who would stay with her, who would take care of the house, how to tell the children – all of this assuming that Judge Gesell agreed to my guilty plea.

There was a make-believe quality in our talks all week long, as if a miracle would intervene to rescue us. 'Well, it's just not going to happen, that's all,' was Patty's way of ending each conversation.

The tentative paperwork with the prosecutors was not completed before Saturday. Some of Jaworski's assistants wanted my testimony in advance. We insisted that public testimony be withheld until after sentencing, except for one affidavit which merely re-stated what I had testified to before.

We wanted to do nothing before that final judgement day that could be interpreted as currying favour with the judge.

Notified that we were in accord with the prosecutors, Judge Gesell scheduled Shapiro and Merrill in his chambers Monday morning at 8:30 sharp. If satisfied, at 9:30 he would accept my plea in open court.

There were two important pieces of unfinished business – the first an eyeball-to-eyeball confrontation between Bill Merrill and myself. Dave arranged it for his office Saturday afternoon. Merrill arrived shortly after 3:00 p.m. and thrust out his hand. 'Chuck, I admire what you are doing.' He was not smiling, there was almost sorrow in his eyes. *The conqueror can afford to be gracious with his vanquished*, I thought, but soon realised it went deeper than that.

'I wanted to see you face-to-face, Bill,' I began, 'so there would be no misunderstanding later. I'm not trading my testimony for anything. I just want to tell the truth.'

'That's all we want, the truth. I wouldn't ask you to do anything else.'

I felt a sense of clumsiness as I groped for an important but elusive thought. 'Once this is over, will you guys try to do something about the system, not just the people? There are abuses in the CIA and the FBI and the courts, too, as well as the White House. For the good of the country there's a lot of cleaning up to do.'

'I know what you're saying, Chuck,' he replied with real compassion in his voice. 'You think we're just out to get you and Nixon. I can't blame you, but I want you to know that some of us are in this thing because we really do want to make the system better, correct things that are wrong. We're going to stay with it, and what you are doing now is going to help.'

In the half-hour that followed, some of the ugly sores laid bare in the past months began to heal. Merrill's relentless pursuit and hard tactics had embittered me, but as we talked this day the anger drained away. He was another human being doing a nasty job, but with a capacity to care about those he felled as much as those he was charged with protecting. Christ, I discovered, was giving me the capacity to see that which the bitterness of the world hides from view.

The second and most important piece of unfinished business was to lay my decision before all four of my brothers. We met in my house on Sunday evening – all but Al Quie who had been speaking in Pennsylvania and was delayed by the storm which had lashed Washington all day.

Graham, Doug, Harold, and I went into my cherry-panelled study and pulled chairs around the ship's-wheel coffee table. Remembering how long and hard those men had prayed, how much Doug's volunteers had done, it was hard to say it: 'I have decided, providing Judge Gesell permits it and you all agree, to plead guilty in court tomorrow morning.'

Graham, who was staring at the pictures on the wall, wheeled around, 'You're what?' Doug was smiling, however, and something told me that he understood immediately. Harold sat there in quiet but obvious agreement.

I reviewed the steps that led to my decision: the slip of the tongue while speaking in Owosso, my frustration over not being able to testify in the impeachment hearings, and above all the realisation of my crippled witnessing for Christ. I could not continue muddling along the way I had during the Mike Wallace interview. 'I knew what I had to do after that interview,' I told them.

Graham was the first to speak. 'But what you are pleading to isn't any crime, nor do they have a case against you in either indictment. You can't just up and decide to go to prison. I don't think being a Christian requires you to do that.'

Harold shook his head. 'I have been praying all week long this would be the outcome, that Chuck wouldn't waver in this decision because I know in my heart it is right. This may lead others to do the same thing and, God knows, this agony has to end for this country.'

Doug concurred wholeheartedly, but Graham winced when I explained the possible sentence and that it would probably mean disbarment as a lawyer as well. 'You guys can't expect me to pray for the judge to accept this,' he said.

'That is just what I want you to do,' I replied, 'but only if you feel it in your heart. Shapiro says there is only a fifty-fifty chance that Gesell will go along. We need prayer.'

At Harold's suggestion we wrote out on my yellow pad exactly what I would say the next day, assuming the guilty plea would be accepted. Meanwhile Doug finally reached Quie on the phone. His judgement was swift. 'I think it's tremendous,' he told me. 'I have been expecting you to do this, and I'm with you all the way. God bless you, brother.'

Graham was the lone holdout, pacing about the room in front of the big stone fireplace, turning away often to conceal his emotion. The one-time Texas district judge could not shake from his mind the horrors of the dark concrete holes into which he himself had once ordered men to spend years of their lives. Finally he nodded his head. 'If this is what it takes to give you freedom of the spirit then I'm with you. But it hurts, man, it hurts.'

We prayed for a long while.

It was after midnight when the liberal Democratic senator from Iowa mentioned the political implications. 'What does this do to the President and his impeachment?' he asked as I walked him to his car.

'Helps some, hurts some,' I replied.

'That's what I thought,' Harold mused. He gripped my shoulder tightly, climbed into his car, and drove off.

At 9:00 a.m. Monday morning I was pushing papers around on my office desk, re-reading my statement, and staring at my phone waiting for the call. Patty was chatting with Holly in her little office outside. Five after nine and no call. Was Shapiro having trouble with Judge Gesell? Three miles west in the white cement provincial house near Embassy Row, I knew that Harold, Doug, Al, and Graham were praying for the Lord to be in charge of the decision.

At 9:12 the phone rang. Shapiro's voice was serious: 'Okay, come ahead; it was close. Now hurry.'

It is a fifteen-minute ride to the court downtown, but one call had to be made first. The familiar, cheery voice of the White House operator explained that the President had visitors in his office. 'Then get me Fred Buzhardt, please. It's urgent.'

Buzhardt was in a senior staff meeting, but in a few seconds he was on the line. 'Fred, please tell the President right now so he gets it from me first. I'm pleading guilty this morning, but I'm not turning against him. Only telling the truth.'

There was a gasp, a moment of silence, 'But why?'

'Just the truth, Fred, I have to. I'll explain later.'

The courtroom was filled with the familiar faces of reporters and cartoonists, plus assorted curiosity seekers, as I strode through the waist-high gate into the lawyers' area and to the defence-counsel table where a solemn Shapiro was waiting. Patty slipped unnoticed into the back-row spectators' bench.

John Ehrlichman, fingers gently stroking his chin, was standing nearby talking to his lawyers.

Seated at the table was the strangest of all the characters in the Watergate cast: Gordon Liddy, the Kamikaze mentality, ideologue, and original Plumber. Despite months of incarceration in the DC jail, and the twenty-year sentence Sirica had hung on him to make him talk, he remained stoically silent, fervently worshipping a self-conceived deity of high authority. At the sight of me Liddy bounded to his feet and saluted snappily. Adhering to his own vow of absolute courtroom silence, he said not a word, but his eyes showed the fire of defiance, sparkling against a drawn, pallid face. To him I was a high priest of the government order he revered because I had not turned on the President. How the demon of Watergate had warped men's values and lives! For only a few more minutes would I have this proud man's esteem.

'This Honourable Court . . .' the words of the crier snapped. Judge Gesell strode in from the corner entrance behind the bench. My heart raced. I knew what I was doing, but still it was a wrenching moment. This one man from his commanding perch had my life in his hands to do with as he alone saw fit. Throwing myself on the mercy of the court at that moment was more than a figurative term, so helpless is the defendant before such absolute power.

The judge announced that there was to be a 'disposition' before the subpoena issue was argued. The lawyers knew at once that this term could only mean a guilty plea; their eyes quickly scanned the room, speculating. When Judge Gesell ordered Prosecutor Merrill to step forward, there was a murmur of surprise.

Merrill presented the information (the formal term for charges not brought by a grand jury) against Charles W. Colson. Shapiro and I walked to the rostrum, standing just to the side as Merrill handed the documents to the clerk who passed them to the judge. Years of listening to sordid tales of theft, murder, and rape desensitises the dark-suited bailiffs and clerks, who have learned to discipline themselves to conscious indifference. Like mechanical men oblivious to emotion of the human world about them, they move about the court, passing papers, transcribing, escorting witnesses. But this day they, too, stopped and stared at me. In the unguarded moment of her shock, I was warmed by the compassion in one woman clerk's eyes.

The judge began a series of questions to me. Did I waive the grand jury?

'I do, Your Honour,' I replied, relieved to hear my own words strong, for my knees were like sponges.

Bill Merrill then read from a document: 'We charge here that Mr Colson is responsible for devising a scheme to obtain derogatory information about Daniel Ellsberg, to defame and destroy Mr Ellsberg's public image and credibility . . .' Only Merrill, Shapiro, and I knew that I had written the script, had supplied the material and asked to be charged with the words now reverberating with such sinister echoes through the room. '. . . to influence, obstruct, and impede the conduct and outcome of the Ellsberg trial.' Obstruction of justice is the charge of maximum dishonour for a lawyer. *Now I can be free from the past*, I had to remind myself as I recoiled with each word.

Judge Gesell turned to me sternly. 'With your plea of guilty, you understand that you waive those rights under the Constitution and that all is left is for the court to impose sentence?'

'Yes, sir,' I replied. Then came my statement. My voice like the rest of me was shaky now. 'I have come to believe in the very depths of my being that official threats to the right of fair trial for defendants such as those charged in this information must be stopped; and by this plea, Your Honour, I am prepared to take whatever consequences I must to help in stopping them.'

'Do you still wish to plead guilty?' Gesell asked, the final step in the ritual.

'Yes, I do, Your Honour.'

It had taken just under ten minutes. Sentencing was set for June 21. This was hardly enough time to obtain all the letters and recommendations that might help persuade the judge to be lenient. Speed was necessary. I would soon be a witness before the House Judiciary Committee and wanted to be sentenced first so that my testimony – even subconsciously – wouldn't be influenced by the impact it might have on the judge. Judge Gesell ordered me to report at once to the probation officer and with Merrill's agreement freed me without bond.

The press broke loose from the back of the courtroom and raced for telephones. I was the first of the President's inner circle to fall and there had not been a hint of it in advance. Though Washington had become case-hardened to the daily revelations of Watergate, this story I knew would cause new reverberations, hopefully some of them constructive.

Bill Merrill was the first to come over to me as I walked away from the bench. 'Good luck, Chuck. I mean it.' he said, grabbing my hand. St Clair was standing only a few steps behind him, the man who months earlier told me that while convinced I was innocent he could give me only a fifty-fifty chance and who now was engaged in a Herculean struggle to rescue Richard Nixon whose chances were even less. 'I wish you the best,' he said, struggling with his words.

Inside the small plain-walled probation office, the numbness passed and I began to feel the reality of what it was to be a convicted felon. Here a clerk would write up my report just as he did each day for street criminals, rapists, car thieves, and narcotics peddlers. I had put myself here, but that knowledge made it no more comfortable. I would now be in the hands of GS-7 probation clerks, marshals, prison guards. The loss of control of my body and life was a sensation I had not fully understood before.

I had kept myself in tight control, but the sight of Doug Coe, waving to me from the door blocked by two blue-suited officers, choked me up. He was always there, always when most needed. I asked the police to let Doug through and with him came a small group from the Fellowship, including Dr John Curry and his wife, Betsy, who had worked round the clock for weeks pasting up clippings in our office. As we embraced I wondered if the spectators could understand what it meant to have such friends.

18

Awaiting Judgement

As I read my statement to reporters outside the courthouse – that I had pleaded guilty so that I could be free to speak out the truth, whether it helped or hurt me or others – I had a feeling they were scarcely listening. Fred Graham of CBS posed the only question they cared about: 'Are you going to testify against the President?' All I could do was try to explain that it would be improper for me to make any statements until after I had been sentenced.

COLSON'S PLEA OF GUILTY SENDS SHUDDERS THROUGH WHITE HOUSE the *Boston Globe* announced the next morning. COLSON'S PLEA WORRIES WHITE HOUSE, reported the *Post*.

Columnist Mary McGrory interviewed Hughes, Quie, Purcell, and Coe, and then wrote of our Sunday-night meeting: 'The Prayer Meeting That Led to Guilty Plea'. In the last paragraph McGrory, whose vitriolic anti-Nixon reporting once earned her a high place on his 'enemies' list, concluded: 'To Richard Nixon, Colson's change of heart may be the worst thing that has happened since John Dean told everything he knew.'

The account of the prayer meeting triggered a fresh round of stories and cartoons. Oliphant of the *Denver Post* sketched me, garbed in priestly robes, parading in front of the White

House carrying a sign: REPENT! FOR LO, I AM ABOUT TO LAY IT ON THE HOUSE JUDICIARY COMMITTEE.

The prevailing assumption was that my religious conversion had prompted me to tell all, that I had been hiding all sorts of heinous, dark secrets. The validity of my conversion, I feared, would thus be measured in direct proportion to the number and foulness of past transgressions I would now confess.

Those who thought my decision represented a turn against my former chief were the most eager to give purity to my motives. Carl Rowan, for example, rejoiced: 'If the devil made Charles Colson do it and the good Lord made him confess, we could be close to the end of the Watergate nightmare . . . I have a sort of gut feeling that the guy we thought was one of the dirtiest characters ever to nest at 1600 Pennsylvania Avenue, just might turn out to be the one who in telling the dirty truth can help make this nation clean again.'

The *Boston Globe* which only months earlier harpooned my conversion editorially now welcomed it and praised Jaworski's 'skill' in bringing me to his side. Scores of other anti-Nixon papers followed suit.

The week following my guilty plea the House Democrats dispatched a member of the Rodino Committee to meet with a man they believed to be one of their own, Senator Harold Hughes. He would, they reasoned, tell them how they could use my testimony to skewer Mr Nixon. Hughes, faintly amused, told his colleague: 'Colson is not out to nail anyone's hide to the barn door. He is just going to tell the truth. If the chips fall in someone's back yard, that's tough, whether it's the President's or someone else's.' Hughes's compatriots in the Congress believed him no more than the press believed me.

When the President dispatched his top field commander, General Alexander Haig, to reconnoitre, I tried to convince him there were no dark motives or intent. 'I just want to be free to testify to the facts.'

On the day of the plea Nixon sent me a handwritten note (*see* page 701).

But by the next day Nixon's eyes were focused on impeachment strategy. He called me that evening shortly after nine. 'Tell your boys that they can be very proud of their father,' he began. 'It's a crime that Ellsberg should go scot-free while you plead guilty. You weren't involved in these things; you are innocent,' he declared.

The President seemed curiously insensitive to the moral forces at work across the landscape of American life, much of which he had unleashed with his own transcripts. I explained that I had done what I had pleaded to; each of us had to be guided by his own conscience. Though underestimating the strength of the forces arrayed against him, Nixon was keen and sharp as ever, clicking off each vote he could count on in the House Judiciary Committee considering possible impeachment, then – if need be – in the Senate.

Near the end of the conversation I told him that regardless of any mistakes he had made, it was because of his Presidency that my sons would not have to go to war. That to me outweighed the pain, even of prison. I meant it, too; his moral judgement had been blurred, yet I couldn't forget the courageous long-viewed way in which he set out to create a more stable order in the world. I did not know then that among the miles of magnetic tape stashed away in the bowels of the White House was the proof of deceptions that would soon mean the end for this man and his dreams.

The President took my remarks as a signal that I was still his fighting knight, that my plea was perhaps one last desperate act of loyalty, flinging myself on the sword. The next day White House aides were telling the press that Mr Nixon had nothing to fear from Colson's testimony.

As an accommodation to the House Judiciary Committee, Shapiro arranged with John Doar and his staff to have informal interviews with me in Dave's office. Question – answer;

THE WHITE HOUSE
WASHINGTON

Jan 3, 1974

Dear Chuck,

I know what a Terribly sad and difficult day this must be for you and your fine family.

I want you to know that in a very personal way it is an equally sad day for me.

You must however keep your faith in the fact that as time goes on your dedicated services to the nation will be remembered long after this incident has become only a footnote in history.

Always your friend,

[Richard Nixon]

701

question – answer. It lasted all day. 'When have you last heard from the President?' Bernie Nussbaum, John Doar's chief assistant, asked during the second day of the sessions.

'Last week,' I replied.

Nussbaum's eyebrows lifted: 'Oh?'

'He called me,' I explained and then repeated the substance of the phone conversation. Nussbaum stared at me incredulously. 'He also wrote me a letter,' I added.

Nussbaum asked to see it and I gave it to him. He stared at it for a long time in silence. Then he put it down on Shapiro's glass-topped coffee table and, looking puzzled, fixed his eyes on mine.

'But – but how can you still be friendly?'

That evening I learned that the Judiciary Committee struck me from its witness list.

When the news of the committee's decision not to use me reached the White House, St Clair immediately demanded that I be called as his witness. For the next two weeks the committee haggled over whose witness I would be. Meanwhile committee investigators continued to meet with me – over fifty hours – gleaning every last shred of knowledge I had on all the assorted allegations of Nixon wrong-doing. Not until the eve of the final round of hearings did the committee conclude that I should be called, *despite* the friendly feelings I maintained towards the President.

In the midst of my frustration over being pitched back and forth between the warring factions came one bit of welcome news. The prosecutors informed Dick Howard's lawyer that he was no longer a target of any grand jury prosecutions. Marcia Howard's jubilant and relieved voice on the other end of the phone was the happiest sound we had heard in months. One by one the other former staff members phoned to tell me similar good news.

But for me the painful suspense mounted. The suspended sentence given former Attorney General Richard Kleindienst on June 7 was an unsettling development. Kleindienst had lied to a congressional committee, then plea bargained for a misdemeanour. Judge Hart's leniency touched off a small uproar, triggering a wave of editorial denunciations and demands for harsher sentences. Though I was happy for Dick, I'd be the next Watergater up to bat.

Some days my hopes would soar as I heard about the many letters pouring in to Judge Gesell, many unsolicited, most urging leniency for me. *Perhaps Gesell would give me a suspended sentence.* One such letter came from a young black lad I'd represented five years earlier as a court-appointed attorney, a copy of which was sent to me:

Dear Judge Gesell:

Mr Colson helped me when I was in severe difficulty with the law, and my life was such that I needed guidance. I was charged as a juvenile with breaking and entering into a convent. At that time I was a poor student, took no interest in schoolwork, and had broken the law numerous times.

More important than what Mr Colson did for me legally (the charges were dropped) is what he did for me personally. After the Court proceedings, he made clear to me, as no one else had done before, that my life was headed to disaster. He spoke of honesty, truth, ambition, and obligation to others, in terms that since then I have heeded. I have never again been involved with the law. I am now married, gainfully employed and a responsible citizen.

Very truly yours,
Richard Austin.

I was also buoyed up by a draft of the presentence report obtained from the prosecutors which acknowledged that most of the charges against me were based on evidence I myself had supplied: 'Colson turned over to the prosecutors a number of documents in spite of the potentially incriminating nature of them . . . [Which] . . . the prosecutors might not ever have received . . . if Colson had not provided them.' The report concluded that my guilty plea would be 'of great national significance in helping to insure the sanctity of the judicial process' with respect to the rights of defendants in celebrated cases. That report almost sent Shapiro pirouetting again.

The prosecutor even acknowledged to the press: 'Colson's alleged roles in the cover-up and burglary would have been more difficult to prove than those of the other alleged conspirators . . . because this man was outside the main stream of the overt acts.' All this was little solace now. My decision had not rested on how good my case in court would have been.

All convicted criminal defendants must submit to interrogation by one of the court's probation officers whose report is supposed to be the foundation for the judge's sentence. The criminal is accompanied to the interview by as much family as he can gather around him. It is part of the ritual and supposed to help. I protested putting Patty through it, but Judd Best, our firm's expert on sentencing practices, insisted.

Patty, Judd, and I were ushered into an austere office occupied by Horace Smith, a ruddy-faced man in his mid-fifties, sitting in shirt sleeves behind a cluttered and scarred oak desk. We sat in three hard straight-backed chairs while the probation officer rocked back and forth in a squeaky wooden swivel chair. Smith is a big man, a chain-smoker, burdened and somewhat stooped from years of listening to tales of woe, exaggerated claims of hardship, and plaintive pleas for mercy.

He went down the list of routine questions. 'Describe the nature of the charges against you,' he said, coming to one of the blank lines on the multi-paged form. I did my best while Smith sat scratching his head, staring at the page before him, his pencil not moving. 'Don't know how to put this one down,' he said. 'It's a little unusual.' Next Patty answered questions about our homelife.

With the form nearly complete, Smith suddenly leaned back in his groaning chair and stared out of the curtainless window. 'Although this may seem a little unnecessary, since I've read so much about you in the newspapers – but tell me about your religious experience and Senator Hughes and the fellowship.'

There was nothing routine about this question. Something told me he was genuinely interested, but something else told me that I must not use my conversion to try to gain his sympathy. 'Well, it's not really relevant to what we're doing here, is it, Mr Smith?' I asked. 'If you're interested, maybe someday I can come back and tell you about it.'

'No, I'd like to know right now,' he said. 'Just explain it the way it happened.'

I began a rather abbreviated account, determined to make it unemotional so that I would not in any sense be 'using' my religion. When I came to what had happened in the Phillips driveway, Smith interrupted. 'Slow down, Mr Colson,' he said, 'I really want to know what this is about.'

Suddenly there in that bare room a rather strange thing happened. The leathery exterior of this case-hardened bureaucrat softened. The printed form was pushed aside. Here was a thirsty man looking for the Giver of fresh water. My role was to pass the cup. I finished the whole story twenty minutes later, during which Smith's eyes never left mine. 'That's the answer,' he said. 'It's the answer to all the ugly problems we have in the world.' His voice cracked as he added, 'You see, I understand fellowship. I'm a recovered alcoholic.'

The probation officer apologised for keeping us so long, wished me well, then said rather wistfully that he believed Senator Hughes could help him. The next day Harold and Horace Smith spent three hours together in talk and prayer.

Smith's report, as I learned later, contained a strong affirmation of the sincerity of my conversion, along with excerpts from nearly 150 strong and moving letters. The report concluded that prison was altogether unnecessary, but then recommended that because of the international attention focused on the case, defendant Colson should be sentenced nonetheless. My testimony had no effect on Smith's report, but Christ touched one man's life.

The brothers remained closer than ever through the eighteen days of suspense. We met frequently in Hughes's office, at Fellowship House, or individually as the men and their wives dropped by for a few quiet hours with Patty and me. Their prayers and their presence were reminders that the current situation was but a way-stop on the road I had chosen. Soon I would be free, the past behind me and the 'victory', as Harold always put it, was with Jesus.

Doug Coe relieved one of the pressing personal problems: his beautiful twenty-three-year-old daughter, Paula, and a college friend would move in with Patty come autumn when our boys would be back in college.

The Colson family closed ranks as well. Wendell, a star oarsman in the Princeton crew, was scheduled to go to Switzerland for the summer to row in international competition. Being chosen was heady stuff and Wendell had been eagerly anticipating the trip. Now without a word from Patty or me, he cancelled out and moved down to McLean for the summer. He would be on hand for the sentencing and whatever happened next, working full-time as a carpenter, taking over my chores around the house at night. Wendell carried a notebook with him, jotting down instructions from me as I thought about things that would need to be done while I was away.

Emily and Chris also flew to Washington. Emily had taken a lot of abuse from her tenth-grade classmates and a few anti-Nixon teachers. A sensitive child, she would be the most vulnerable, I feared. I arranged for her to return to her mother before the traumatic time of sentencing. Before I put her on the airplane for Boston, we walked to a quiet corner of the airport waiting room. 'Emily,' I said, 'I just hope you aren't ashamed of me. Don't let what anyone says bother you. I've done some wrong things, but now I'm sure trying to do what's right.'

'Daddy,' she snapped, 'I'm proud of you.' The little girl of fifteen threw her arms around me and for the first time the emotions we had both held in check were shaken loose. A good cry was in order for both of us. Chris, on the other hand, was unusually quiet and subdued, carrying his own hurt inside. While I didn't know it then, he was to suffer the most.

Support and help came from others, some from old friends but some from unlikely sources as well. Ken Belieu, my old political comrade, now a brother in Christ, called one evening: 'Chuck, no time to be maudlin. I just want you to know that we have a guest room for Patty, an extra car, and a few thousand in the bank. They are all yours if you want them.' I turned it down but the words my heart searched for wouldn't come.

Other friends made similar offers, including my one-time assistant, Mike Balzano, who tried to give me his life's savings.

Arthur Burns took a call from a reporter who was digging around for anti-Colson material for his syndicated column. The newsman wanted to rehash the Colson-smears-Burns episode of 1971 and thought that Burns might cooperate with some fresh new tidbits. Instead he was told of my apologies, our prayers together, our reconciliation, and Burns's opinion that my conversion was sincere. The startled columnist wrote it all, but was quick to add that there was a long list of other apologies still due from the ex-hatchet man. (*See* 'Charles Colson: Time for Apologies?' Tom Braden, *Washington Post*, May 18, 1974.)

Jack Anderson had blasted me for years in his syndicated column for all manner of misdeeds. At the White House we considered him our arch nemesis, and I once proposed an investigation of Anderson. Because the money would help, I accepted an offer to debate Jack on television. The debate was standard fare; it was what occurred backstage that I'll never forget. While I was being pasted with powder and rouge by the makeup man, Jack asked Patty if he could talk to her alone for a moment. 'Don't tell Chuck – he's too proud – but while he's away if you need money for the family, just call. The Lord has been good to me. You are decent folks. This could happen to anyone and if I can help, I want to.' I did not learn until later what a deeply religious man Jack Anderson is, a side he has kept out of the news.

As the days passed and such episodes multiplied, Shapiro became increasingly optimistic. 'The maximum as I see it is six months. It could go to nine, but my money is on six.' Patty still believed the sentence would be suspended altogether. No amount of sober talk on my part seemed to deflate her expectations. She was praying this way and I was troubled about what a tough sentence might do to her growing faith.

Bud Krogh was released from prison in mid-June and Patty and Suzanne set up a quiet evening for just the four of us. It was a sultry June night, muggy the way Washington is during most of the summer, when we arrived at the Krogh's Cape Cod-styled brick home on the edge of one of Washington's middle-class black residential areas. When Krogh joined the White House staff, one of his first assignments was liaison with the District of Columbia. With characteristic idealism Bud believed he should live in the location of his assignment.

Bud trotted down the front steps to our car when he saw us arrive. There was no sign of jailhouse pallor; his eyes were clear and bright, his grip steel-strong. Everything seemed back to normal in the Krogh home. The two children interrupted us at dinner a couple of times to ask permission to play at a neighbour's house, later to be read to by their mother. Suzanne served steak. I felt guilty about it, knowing how deeply in debt the Kroghs were.

'The time apart really wasn't too hard,' Suzanne reminisced

at dinner. She had been teaching at a local school and writing articles to earn enough to buy groceries and keep the mortgage paid up. Each weekend she and the children had taken the seven-hour round-trip drive to Allenwood in their old Volvo. The fatigue still showed on Suzanne's young face. 'Visiting is a strain,' she said. 'You're constantly being watched and the guards can be abusive. But Bud and I did a Bible course with that time. Each week we'd study the same lesson and then discuss it over the weekend. It really brought us closer.'

After dinner while Patty and Suzanne did the dishes, Bud and I sat together in the living room. 'Okay, friend, now that the girls can't hear us, tell me what it is really like,' I said.

'It's hell, Chuck. But you're tough; you'll do okay. Be careful whom you associate with. You'll see a lot of ugly things going on around you – a guy once had his skull crushed changing a TV station in the middle of a programme. Just stay out of it and keep to yourself. The blacks will test you. Stand up to them if you're threatened; if they find any weakness in you, your goose is cooked.'

The prosecutors had told me that I would be kept at Fort Holabird, an abandoned Army base in Baltimore as long as I was needed in Washington to testify. 'You'll hate it there,' Bud said. 'That fence with barbed wire is right up against the building and the place is full of rats – you know, guys who are informers. But it's better than the city jail. I was in the bull pen in Montgomery Country for the first twelve days. There were men in there waiting trail for murder, some real tough customers, twelve of us in one cell. I slept on the floor right next to the toilet and one night a dude urinated all over me. Could have been ugly, but I knew I was outnumbered so I just talked to him, and thank God it didn't happen again.'

Bud talked openly enough about prison, but was strangely silent on other subjects. It was obvious he had detached himself from the outside world, a kind of self-insulation. When we had turned on the news telecast earlier in the evening, he had left the room. I could not resist the question that was weighing heavily on my mind: 'Bud, why is it that you aren't following things on the outside? Seems like you've shut yourself off from the world.'

He pondered that for a moment. 'For me it seemed the thing to do, Chuck. I looked at prison as a cleansing time – and for self-examination. I needed it. If you look at it that way, it will do you good. But it means cutting off everything you leave behind, except family, of course. For me it was a conscious decision.'

Driving home that evening I asked Patty if she'd noticed any change in Bud.

'Sure did,' she replied. 'He seemed distant, a million miles away.'

'That really terrifies me, honey. I can't believe prison can do that in only a few months to a guy with an iron will like Krogh.'

It was not as if prison had broken Bud. In some ways he seemed stronger than ever, but it was as if he had drifted off on a cloud to a faraway place and was now living in his own world. Could that happen to me? *It must not, I told myself.*

For me that would be the slow death of soul and spirit. One day years earlier when the thought that I might ever go to prison was beyond my wildest fantasies, a close friend who worked with ex-convicts told me that men are never the same after confinement. 'A year does it,' he said, tapping his temple. 'They go stirry, locked up that way.'

That night, bothered as I was by the change I saw in Bud and the fears racing through my mind, I could not know how much of a struggle it would be.

19

Fall of the Gavel

Shortly after 9 a.m. on the morning of June 21, Patty and I arrived at Courtroom No. 6. An air of expectancy crackled through the room. The press were nearly crowded out by well-wishers, friends, the office staff from our law firm. The lawyer's dock was almost empty since there was to be no combat this day. Dave Shapiro would make one eleventh-hour appeal on my behalf. A few men from the prosecutor's office would listen silently. The judge would then announce his decision.

By arrangement with the clerk, Harold, Al, Doug, and Graham were allowed through the swinging gate into the area normally reserved for lawyers. By 9:15 they had arrived and sat solemnly together on a long bench.

I walked down the aisle attempting a cheery greeting to each friend. Some of the secretaries who had worked for me in the White House were there, also many of Patty's friends. Their expressions spoke of anxiety or sorrow. I spoke to Dick Howard and his wife, Marcia, whose dark eyes were sparkling with encouragement. Dick managed a weak smile.

Marion Goldin, Mike Wallace's producer, was seated in the back as a spectator. I wondered why, since she didn't cover news events. Could she possibly have sensed the part her show had played in all this?

Two of Patty's and my closest friends, Tom and Kay Easely from Boston, had wanted to be present, but I prevailed upon them not to come so that Kay could be at the hospital to keep Dad from learning about my sentence on television. I'd phone her and she could break the news gently.

Patty took a seat in the front row in space reserved for family. *Like the first pew at a funeral*, I thought grimly. Wendell was beside her. My older son had achieved in those weeks a maturity well beyond his twenty years. Dave Shapiro was sitting at the defence table, pawing through a thick black notebook and rehearsing his arguments one last time. Dave was so hopeful that his final words would move Gesell that in his last conference in chambers he had asked the judge not to rule immediately, but to recess briefly after Dave's argument, withdraw from the bench, and weigh the sentence one last time.

After the words of the crier, Judge Gesell strode majestically across the raised platform, pulling his black robe together as he took his place in the judge's high-backed chair. The courthouse gossips had said that much would depend on Gesell's mood on the day of sentencing, that he is volatile and can change his mind even as he walks into the courtroom. If true, we were starting out this day in trouble. The judge was scowling angrily as he took his seat, glanced once around the courtroom, announced brusquely the motions which would be argued later in the morning, and then snapped, 'All right, Mr Shapiro, would you and Mr Colson come forward?'

I began reading my statement, stating the reasons for my plea which I believed 'right as a matter of law, right as a matter of conscience'. I reviewed all of the circumstances surrounding the release of the Pentagon Papers, how Henry Kissinger, President Nixon, and I had viewed Ellsberg's conduct as 'treasonous', tracing step-by-step the chronology of my actions. Then I came to the act itself.

'The President on numerous occasions urged me to disseminate damaging information about Daniel Ellsberg,' I said –

712

which was not exactly news since I had testified to this before. But a murmur from the clusters of reporters rippled through the room. Little did I dream how that statement would rumble through Capitol Hill, bringing forth new cries for the President's impeachment. If I were guilty of this crime, so was Nixon, his antagonists would argue.

I concluded my statement by telling the judge, 'I regret what I have done and I will spend a lifetime trying to be a better man for it.'

Gesell nodded as if by reflex, started to smile but stopped, then turned to Shapiro: 'I understand that you wish to make a statement and you may now do so.'*

I returned to the defence table and sat down. Shapiro began softly at first. I looked at my brothers; their heads were down – in prayer, I hoped.

'I say Charles Colson was unfairly indicted,' Dave said, his voice rising with indignation. He argued that a prison sentence would be imposed only because of public expectations which were created in this case by 'fraud – fraud, Your Honour – the most pernicious kind of publicity linking this man's name to every conceivable type of act and dirty trick and for the most part they were created by deliberate government leaks – smear stories'. Shapiro had prepared a long recitation of every fallacious story that had been printed about me, hoping to persuade the judge that the public demand for a sentence was falsely created.

But Judge Gesell wanted none of it. 'You are barking up the wrong tree, Mr Shapiro,' he interrupted. 'I am not a bit interested in the public expectations. That has nothing to do with what I am about to do. You are beating a dead horse.' My stomach felt as if it were trying to escape through the bottom of my chair. Whatever Gesell was going to do, he had already decided and was plainly annoyed by Shapiro's statements.

*Editor's Note: All quotations are from the court transcripts.

Jolted by the judge's assault, Dave placed both hands on the lectern, his body rocking back and forth, his eyes filled with disbelief and astonishment.

Gesell subdued his impatience but not his annoyance. 'You may proceed,' he continued, 'but I want you to understand you are beating a dead horse . . . You represent this man and you can do whatever you wish to do – and I will listen – but I simply wanted you to understand.'

Shapiro tried to recover, but all passion and feeling had been sucked out of his voice. The last flickering glimmer of secretly harboured hope that maybe there would be no prison sentence was gone. The only question now was – how bad?

Six months? Nine months? Longer? Ten months was the maximum time Gesell had dished out, and that to a Watergater convicted of two perjury counts after a jury trial. Sentences after trial are usually stiffer than with voluntary pleas.

Yet I was the closest to Mr Nixon and during the skirmishes over pre-trial motions Gesell had unleashed angry outbursts against the President, charging him one day in open court with near obstruction of justice for failing to make available White House files. Then, too, he was the judge who heard the Nixon Administration's case against the *Washington Post* to restrain publication of the Pentagon Papers. Gesell ruled against us and for the *Post*. Still, he was known as the fairest man on the bench. *What had gone on before, I reasoned, would not affect him this day.*

Shapiro forged ahead ticking off one by one, clinically now, the false accusations that had been hurled at me day after day in the headlines, including the documented proof that the CIA had planted false stories about me (*see* page 658.) He concluded with words that should have been ringing with emotion, but instead were as icy as the chill which had come over the courtroom. 'If Your Honour believes with me that the highest duty of this court, indeed, the highest duty of any court, is to stand between the defendant and the mob, let it be known!'

When he had tried his argument out on me the week before, Shapiro had put so much drama into that last sentence that in his imagination there was the thunder of a foot-stomping crowd, trumpet music in the distance, and the judge leaning over the bench to shake his hand. But now there was only a deadly silence in the room. The judge summoned Shapiro and me to come forward again to the lectern. We now simply waited for the dreadful fall of the gavel.

Judge Gesell took no recess before deciding, telling us instead that another case was pending. His voice devoid of feeling, his manner surgical, he stated that the defendant's 'deliberate misconduct affected the conduct of a pending federal prosecution'. A shudder raced down my spine. I had never even been charged with that; the prosecutors only alleged that I tried to, but acknowledged that I had failed.

'Morality is a higher force than expediency,' he continued, glaring at notes before him. 'The court does recognise,' his tone softened slightly, 'that Mr Colson's public image has been somewhat distorted . . . a thorough review of Mr Colson's life . . . show instances of useful public service, often compassion for others in trouble, qualities of the defendant which have rightly endeared him to his family, his close friends, and to clients he has effectively served.'

I felt Shapiro's arm come around my back, squeezing me gently and holding on for what was coming. The kind words were to soften the blow. I was taking deep breaths now to control my emotions. *I must show none*, I thought, as my ears detected gentle sobbing behind me. The judge explained that he reached his decision using as his guide all other obstruction-of-justice sentences handed down in the past year.

Gesell lifted the gavel in the air. 'The court will impose a sentence of one to three years and fine of five thousand dollars.' Hardwood struck hardwood with an ear-splitting whack. A half-muffled scream came from the back of the room, a high-pitched voice crying, 'Oh, no!' Then absolute silence again. A tingling sensation swept through my body like needles jabbing into my flesh. Then a sharp feeling of nausea. Shapiro squeezed harder. I bit my lower lip, praying that it was not Patty's voice that had shouted out.

My mind blotted out the rest of the words Gesell now spoke – the penitentiary, date of surrender, dismissal of other charges. Dave kept squeezing as he replied to the judge, his own voice cracking and hoarse. The gavel fell again. Crack!

Judge Gesell strode from the platform. As I turned away, I saw Dornetha, a black secretary from the law office, doubled over in tears. Others were trying to comfort her; she had been the one to cry out. Then I caught Patty's look, filled with sadness but dry-eyed. Wendell's face was frozen in shock. My brothers were still seated with heads down. Others stood motionless.

There was no press stampede this time, the reporters filing out slowly. It would be newsworthy – the longest sentence yet imposed on a Watergate defendant – but a few minutes give or take against the afternoon deadline didn't matter now.

I walked back to the defence table to gather up my papers. Shapiro kept mumbling, 'I can't believe it, can't believe it.' Patty came through the swinging gate, walking fast, then half-running, trying as she always did to smile even as she was choking up. 'It'll be okay, honey, you'll see,' Patty said as she threw her arms around me.

The marshals made available to us a small windowless waiting room. The brothers, Patty, Wendell, and I were escorted into it just to be alone for a few minutes. There was little to say; words were not needed. A surprising feeling of love began to fill our hearts. Even Wendell, who before had squirmed when trapped in a praying group, seemed to be lifted as we asked for God's strength in this moment of pain.

Harold's concern that I not be bitter was unnecessary. 'For some strange reason I even feel a sense of understanding toward Judge Gesell,' I said quietly.

'What are you going to say to the press outside?' he asked.

'I honestly don't know.' I had prepared no statement and was not sure I could have read it if I had.

'Then we'll just ask the Holy Spirit to take over,' Harold concluded.

As we walked down the long marbled corridor we could see through the glass doors a crowd of people outside – cameras, lights, and an even-larger-than-usual throng of newsmen. The marshals escorting us offered an escape route through the garage, but I knew I must not duck the press now.

The array of microphones, cameras, and inquisitive faces seemed somehow less hostile than before. 'What happened in court today,' I heard myself say, 'was the court's will and the Lord's will – I have committed my life to Jesus Christ and I can work for Him in prison as well as out.'

Those were the words given me and with them a whole new chapter was to begin in my life.

20

The Slammer

I was awakened by the sound of camera crews setting up their equipment in the gravel drive in front of our home. It was July 8, the last morning for a year or longer that Patty and I would enjoy the privacy of our bedroom and a quiet breakfast together. Rubbing the sleep from my eyes and opening a front bedroom window, I shouted: 'I am not leaving until two this afternoon. Come back then. I won't avoid you. You have my word.'

A chubby, friendly faced ABC cameraman with an American-flag pin in his lapel gave me a big smile. 'Okay, Mr Colson, see you at two. Have a good morning.'

The crews packed up their equipment and drove off. In past stake-outs these men would have remained rooted to their positions. *Ironic*, I thought, *now that I was a criminal headed for prison, the hard-bitten cynics of the press suddenly believed me*.

We watched the 'Today' show during breakfast, the last of a three-part interview I had filmed the week earlier. Barbara Walters came on live at the end: 'These interviews with Mr Colson were filmed in our studios last week when he was here with his wife, Patty, a charming woman, so supportive of her husband. Sometimes we don't think of the personal tragedies involved, but I can't help but think about the Colsons this morning.' Looking straight into the camera, she continued: 'And so I say to you, Mr Colson, if you are where you can hear this, and especially to you, Mrs Colson, we do feel for you.'

Patty and I kept our own emotions in check trying to make this morning just like any other, but the compassion in Barbara's face caught us off guard for a moment. My wife had surprised me with her strength over the final days of my freedom, but she was no more stoic than I was.

Graham Purcell had volunteered to drive us to Baltimore where I would surrender to the marshal at the Fort Holabird prison facility. Promptly at the appointed hour he pulled into the driveway, looking drawn and nervous. I had long since learned that beneath his hardened Texas-cowboy hide is a heart as big and soft as a ripe melon. Along with Judd Best who made the arrangements for my surrender, Patty and I piled into Graham's big sedan and headed up the driveway toward the newsmen and cameras now blocking the entrance.

As the questions came flying at me from reporters, humour seemed in order. How did I feel about going to prison? Like the man Abe Lincoln once described who was tarred and feathered and driven out of town. When asked how he liked it, he responded, 'If it wasn't for the honour, I'd just as soon have walked.'

One reporter shouted, 'What books are you taking with you?'

'Just two editions of the Bible,' I replied. When that statement was published, it produced a deluge of Bibles through the mail which I later shared with other prison inmates. The exchange was good-humoured; gone was the rancour of past confrontations.

Graham, unnerved by the mob scene and the number of cars now so doggedly pursuing us, sped down narrow Ballantrae Lane at seventy miles an hour right into the middle of Route 123, the heavily travelled east-west artery through

McLean. The whole scene was hardly a time for merriment, but we had to chuckle over the thought of this headline in the next day's paper: COLSON IN NINE-CAR PILEUP ON WAY TO PRISON. Gallows humour, I think it is called.

As much as they could, government officials have tried to maintain an aura of secrecy about Fort Holabird, referring to it only as a 'detention facility in the Baltimore Washington area for government witnesses'. Since many of the prisoners detained there were crime-syndicate men who had agreed to testify against underworld figures, the need for a safe, secret hiding place was paramount. Holabird was designated as the temporary facility for all Watergate prisoners who would be testifying in upcoming trials.

Four federal marshals met us at a downtown Baltimore motel, where there was one final moment of confusion, picture taking by the camera crews which had followed us, and good-byes to Patty and my two friends. Now officially a federal prisoner under guard, I was squeezed into the back of an unmarked car, which raced through dingy back streets, under an old railroad trestle, and to the once-proud gates of the now nearly deserted Holabird Army Base.

When we drove inside I was reminded of a ghost town in an old Hollywood Western. World War I-vintage red-brick build-ings were mixed in with World War II soot-covered green wooden barracks. The vast sprawling base was slowly decaying, windows boarded over with plywood, tall grass and bushes surrounding most structures, including the line of stately old homes which had once been Officers' Row. The streets were empty.

Our car pulled up in front of one of the green buildings which was different from the others in two ways. There was a nine-foot-high chain link fence around it, topped by jagged strands of barbed wire. It was the one island of life in the otherwise deserted base.

From a small sentry booth two heavy-set men with .38s on

their hips, moved forward to unlock the tall gate. Between the fence and the prison facility was a small twenty-foot area of grass. I remembered Bud Krogh's statement, 'That fence keeps getting closer and closer.' We alighted from the car, walked through the gate which was slammed behind me. Dave Shapiro always referred to prison as 'the slammer'. Now I knew why.

The Army-style barracks was as depressing inside as it appeared on the outside. Paint was peeling from the walls, steam pipes ran down the long corridor through the centre of the building which was illuminated only by dim light bulbs dangling every thirty feet from the ceiling. A stale, greasy odour seeped from a tiny kitchen on the right. A small dining room was on the left immediately inside the hole-riddled front screen door.

The chief deputy led me to the Control Room, a glassed-in office in the centre of the first-floor corridor. Processing began: more fingerprints, Polaroid snapshots, inspection of my luggage and personal effects, a thorough shakedown for drugs and contraband, and the filling out of endless forms.

'What is your number?' the deputy asked.

'I don't have a number.'

'What do you mean you don't have a number? Every federal prisoner has a number.'

'Maybe you're supposed to give me one, sir.'

'Those people in Washington,' grumbled the deputy. 'Don't they know what kind of an establishment I'm running here?'

Then I made the mistake of asking, 'I don't. Can you tell me something about this place?'

'No! The important thing for you to remember is that you remember nothing. No one knows this place exists. You will meet some very unusual men here. Don't discuss your business with them and don't ask them about theirs. When you leave here forget you ever met them. You will only know them by their first names anyway. Obey the rules and mind your own business.'

I was then turned over to Joe, a swarthy man with shaggy black hair who spoke little English.* He showed me to my room, a nine-by-twelve cubicle tucked under the eaves on the second floor, furnished with a maple bed, a battered dresser, and a small wooden desk. The desk top was etched with graffiti by the generations who had passed through this room – from young Army lieutenants to federal prisoners. The temperature was over 100 degrees. Baltimore was in the grip of the worst heat wave of the year.

As other inmates drifted by, Joe introduced me. Pete, a young Italian, reported that he, too, had been a Marine; Angie, an outgoing, genial sort, was from New York's 'Little Italy'. Pat and Andy, I learned, were ex-syndicate operatives and central figures in a big narcotics ring. I was told that two young men named Eddie and Jimmy were kept apart from the others for the good reason that both were ex-Baltimore policemen. Former cops and gangsters crammed into the same little building made a strange mix.

There was Mike, a muscular brute with long, flowing blond hair and an unmistakable Boston accent. There were others representing a variety of nationalities: Italians, Cubans, Frenchmen, including one whose hairy body was colourfully tattooed from top to bottom.

When I asked Joe how to lock my door, he leaned back and roared with laughter. 'No locks here; just one happy family.' I had not seen the movie *The Godfather* – or his term *family* would have been even more unnerving.

There was one man at Holabird I had known before – Herb Kalmbach, the President's personal lawyer, who had surrendered the week before I did and like me was awaiting his turn to testify at the impeachment hearings. Joe pointed out his room. When I looked in, Herb, a tall, urbane, and

---

Editor's Note: Here and elsewhere to protect persons involved, names of inmates have been changed except where permission was obtained.

handsome man in his fifties, bounded from his chair. 'Am I glad to see you! Not here, of course, but it's so great to greet an old friend.' It was the renewal of a friendship that was to become important to us both.

I took the deputy's warning seriously and suppressed my curiosity about the other inmates. With no facilities for exercise, time dragged. The heat was oppressive. I was beginning to understand why Bud Krogh had made himself an island. Jimmy the young ex-cop who was in prison for taking bribes, helped lift the oppressiveness with his chatter, particularly at meals.

During dinner one night little Pete was quite noisy, his high-pitched voice reverberating through the room that twenty of us were crowded into. Jimmy whispered to me, 'Don't fool with him; he goes off his rocker once in a while. He was one of the top narcotics men in New York.'

'That little kid?' I asked.

'That little kid,' Jimmy responded, 'was one of the bosses. They say his testimony will bring down a hundred people. Leave him alone. He would think nothing of putting one of those knives right through your gut.' Jimmy nodded to the large bread knife in the centre of the table, glistening in the late-afternoon sun. Jimmy pointed to Mike. 'He was one of their "hit men", you know.'

'That one who never says anything? The big guy from Boston?' Mike across the room ate without expression, his eyes cold and steel-hard.

'I thought you knew all about Mike,' he continued. 'You're from Boston, aren't you? It was a big thing when he was pinched. They say he's knocked off twenty-eight.'

I stared at Jimmy in disbelief. 'People – twenty-eight people?'

'That's what a hit man does, you know. Kills people.' Jimmy's tone indicated I was not with it.

I had trouble suppressing a grin. The hit man and the

hatchet man – what a vaudeville team Mike and I would make! Serious again I asked, 'Why isn't anyone with twenty-eight murders on death row somewhere?'

Jimmy shrugged. 'They've got him here to protect him. He's more valuable to the government alive than dead.'

While trying to keep from staring at Mike, I began to long for a cell with a lock on it.

As the days dragged by, visits by Patty and the brothers were my faith strengtheners, even though the visiting conditions were awkward and restrictive. It was especially hard for Patty and me – the long days of separation interrupted by a few hours of make-believe normalcy, one eye always on the clock, then the pain of parting. Yet slowly over the months our conversations about faith had become more meaningful. We were making progress in our understanding of the Bible, but still I held back from asking her to pray with me.

One day late in July after a tense visit, Patty wrote me a letter: 'Darling, I prayed most of the way home for both of us and I think it might be nice if from now on we prayed together before leaving each other in the evening . . .'

I received the letter the next day and wanted to shout for joy! All that night I felt that tingling sensation, the worth-it-all feeling I had known before in some of my darkest hours. From that day forward we held hands and prayed aloud together every time she visited, whether in public or private. This spiritual unity would sustain us through harder days to come.

The fall of Mr Nixon's Presidency had been inevitable for many months. The man who stood in a steamy-hot school gymnasium one August day three years earlier, saying with passion, 'It isn't losing that is wrong, it is quitting,' fought a long and lonely struggle with himself. This was also the man who one night in July 1973 quietly mused about the country being better off 'if I step down', and then a few months later, 'Maybe

America wants a nice, clean Jerry Ford.' But the real Nixon was the man in the auditorium; one who was incapable of bringing himself to quit anything.

To me his resignation was not the act of a quitter. He had been gently eased out of his office when all but his own family, and two diehard aides, Ken Clawson and Rose Woods, recognised the imperative pressures which seemed to demand it. Al Haig, his chief of staff, had told me in January 1974, 'If impeachment is inevitable, then better we go peaceably. We must not take the whole government down with us.' Haig had been preparing for months, hoping for a miracle, but readying himself for the day which finally came in August.

'The system worked,' one politician after another proudly proclaimed when Nixon announced his resignation. I am not so sure. At the end, the formal governmental structures were powerless to move decisively, the Senate would have been ensnarled in months of haggling debate, the courts clogged, the Presidency impotent. Never, in my opinion, has the American government been in greater peril, not even when the Capitol was threatened by Lee's forces advancing across the Potomac.

While the entire government was drifting aimlessly, a four-star Army general spent the last days of Mr Nixon's Presidency taking almost full control of the governmental machinery, negotiating with his chief's successor, asking the Pentagon to disregard any order from its constitutionally designated commander, and in the final hours working sensitively behind the scenes so that the Secretary of State and congressional leaders could persuade the President to step aside. Similar circumstances in other countries have resulted in bloodless coups. Fortunately for America, General Haig is a man of responsibility and integrity.

And so it was that Mr Nixon, exhausted by his last desperate convulsions, was unable to the end to recognise the lie with which he had lived or the apocalyptic forces it had unleashed.

His own perceptions of the great good he had tried to achieve blotted from his mind the transgressions of certain staff members which he believed to be minor. Then like a man clinging to a rock in rushing rapids, his last ounce of strength gone, he heaved one final gasp, relaxed his iron grip, and was washed helplessly away in the swirling waters.

At his first inauguration Richard Nixon's hand rested on the outstretched pages of his family Bible, opened to the Book of Isaiah and a verse chosen as the guide for his peacemaking Presidency – *They shall beat their swords into plowshares* (*see* Isaiah 2:4 KJV). Tragic that neither he nor those of us who served him could see seven verses later this warning of things to come: *The lofty looks of man shall be humbled, and the haughtiness of men shall be bowed down* ... (V. 11 KJV). We had all failed. Whether Mr Nixon was purveyor of the evil spell which was cast across his Presidency – or its victim – seemed irrelevant those grim days of August. The grace and dignity with which he fell was fitting testimony to his noble visions for the Presidency and the side of Mr Nixon's character I so admired.

That the resignation was necessary made it no less terrifying, particularly watching it on a small television set, stockaded behind rows of barbed wire in an improvised prison. I could not help but believe that God's hand was in those final days, for the quirks of history might have positioned a man less honourable than General Haig to achieve far less noble results. I needed no more vivid demonstration that it is the hearts of men which for better or worse change the course of human history, not the man-made organs of government.

Heartsick as I was for the President in his moment of torment, those of us who had served him were going through our own peculiar agony. Many months before he had told me: 'The day will come when I will wipe the slate clean.' I knew what he meant: a commander doesn't abandon his troops in battle.

Once he regained the momentum he would pardon his aides who had been imprisoned for Watergate offences.

Our hopes were dashed when Nixon's helicopter rose from the South Lawn for the last time. Not a word had been spoken about those whose crimes were committed – not for personal profit, but in his defence. I was prepared to serve my time, and take my medicine, but there is a special torture in seeing freedom dangled before your eyes and then pulled away. After President Ford's startling announcement on September 8 that he was granting a full and unconditional pardon for Richard Nixon, rumours began circulating that we were next. Ford's press secretary announced two days later that full pardons for all were being studied.

The pardon of Richard Nixon produced another public outburst, reminiscent of the Cox firing. An instant NBC poll reported that by 2 to 1 the public opposed Ford's action. Our spirits sank. The next poll showed that more than 50 per cent now favoured our release. Our spirits rose.

Patty had never in her life done an interview on TV, but she bravely agreed to go on the 'Today' show in my behalf. The pardon issue had completely aroused the country. Friends in the press called – the decisions would come in hours: we'd be set free. The press staked out our home day and night to catch pictures of the jubilant homecoming. But the political heat was threatening Ford's one-month-old Presidency; he announced there would be no more pardons. Those in prison would stay, the Watergate trial would go forward. President Ford had not succeeded in putting Watergate behind him.

For Patty and the other wives, the up-and-down cycle was especially tough – excitement, soaring hopes, anxiety, and then crushing disappointment.

In the depth of my despair these words that I read some-where seemed to leap out at me: *The darker that all around us seems, the greater the despair in our temporal life, the more light that God shines upon us, the more we feel the power of the Holy Spirit within us.*

There it was again – another reference to the power of the Holy Spirit. I knew little about this Third Part of the Trinity, but I was beginning to feel a deep need for this power. Did the Holy Spirit come when in moments of great helplessness I called upon God's help? At times there had been real stirrings inside me since the decision in Maine. Did this mean that the Spirit was already at work? Or was it a new experience I should seek?

My need for special inner strength was heightened by my loneliness, my daily uneasy encounters with members of organised crime, and feelings of despair about the future. Always the threat of physical assault by another inmate hung over me. One night I was up late preparing for my testimony scheduled for the next day. It was near one o'clock when I staggered into bed, after drawing tight the venetian blinds to keep out the beams from spotlights hanging from the eaves and illuminating the entire yard area all night. Then there came a noise outside my door. As my eyes probed through the darkness I heard the door handle beginning to turn slowly. My heart began to race. A midnight assailant?

'Dear Lord,' I remember saying, 'spare me from this, or at least give me something to fight with.' I reached beside my bed. Patty had bought me a small plastic lamp weighing no more than a pound so that I could read by it at night. It was utterly useless as a weapon, but maybe as a missile it would startle my assailant and arouse the guards.

The door slowly swung open, and now I could see silhouetted against the dim light a hulking form. I was not dreaming; my heart was pounding and the adrenaline was shooting through my body. It was time for a decision. Call for help? Jump him suddenly? Throw the lamp?

The figure moved into the room, stopped for a moment, then started for my bed. I jumped up, grabbed the lamp, and shouted, 'Who is it?' The silhouette practically crumbled before my eyes. 'Oh, no!' he gasped. 'I'm sorry.'

I flipped on the light, and there, pale and trembling, stood one of the deputy marshals. In between the deep, sucking noises he was trying desperately to apologise. I had frightened him far more than he had frightened me. The thought must have crossed his mind – what if I had been Mike?

He explained that he was on the night shift, believed my room was vacant, and was trying to find an empty bed in which to catch a short nap. He had been walking stealthily to avoid being detected by the night supervisor. I shared the experience during the next meal with the other inmates. Told with humour, it made a good story with the crime-syndicate men staring at me. I thought a small lie was permissible and pictured myself as unafraid, ready to administer a mortal blow to the intruder.

Word filtered through one of the marshals that John Dean would be joining us at Holabird. Watergate had turned John and myself into arch foes: John, the President's accuser; I, his defender. During the first days of the Ervin hearings, anger would boil up inside me at the mention of his name. Did I still feel that way? As I grappled with Christ's admonition not only to forgive but love my enemies, the anger inside me seemed to leave. The forgiveness part was not too difficult. In fact, I became aware of a gut-level admiration of John's courage in pitting himself against the awesome power of the Presidency. But to love John, that was not so easy.

He arrived one night just after dark. I was in the dining room when John walked by, surrounded by five marshals. Taking no chances with their star witness, the Watergate prosecutors had issued special instructions that Dean was not to mix with the inmates at Holabird, that he was to be kept isolated, confined to his room at all times with a twenty-four-hour guard outside his door.

'They can't keep him in a room all day alone,' laughed young Pat. 'He'll go bananas.'

That thought broke down my last barrier toward John. Late that night Dean came to the kitchen with one pistol-toting marshal. I burst into the kitchen and stuck out my hand. 'Whatever's happened in the past, John, let's forget it. If there's any way I can help you, let me know.'

Dean was as startled as the marshal and was barely able to stammer a response: 'Chuck, I really appreciate that. Honest, I really do.' The marshal quickly separated us, but in those brief moments some old wounds were healed.

John and I began to spend time together whenever a friendly marshal could be persuaded to look the other way. Our conversation was not about the case or about what had gone on in the past, but about our lives and the future. I discovered that he had once worked on a graduate-school project for a modern revision of the Bible, and had read it thoroughly. Furthermore, his belief in God had been strengthened by the tumultuous experiences he was now going through. It was the beginning of a new relationship.

I was startled to find Patty in the waiting room one Monday morning. Visitors are never allowed inside the compound until four o'clock. The look of sorrow in her eyes forewarned me.

'It's Dad, isn't it?' I asked.

'Yes, Chuck, but he went very peacefully – this morning.'

I held her tight, fighting my emotions. She knew how close my father and I had been. A hundred thoughts tumbled through my mind at that moment. Grief that he was gone, gratitude that it had been peaceful and painless. Memories of the last time I saw him, when he was in the hospital and we talked about my pleading guilty. Concern for my mother, now all alone. But overall a deep remorse that my dad had left this world knowing that his only son was in prison. What a sharp contrast to that proud moment when he had listened to the

President praise his Special Counsel.

He died in my mother's arms as they had been packing – against doctor's orders – for a trip to visit me. The shock of what had happened to me was more of a burden than his weakened heart could take.

The phone lines between Washington and Holabird were humming that day as my request for a furlough to go to the funeral worked its way up and down the bureaucratic ladder. Late in the afternoon Washington denied the request. A father's death notwithstanding, it would be 'inappropriate' for a Watergate prisoner to be given a furlough. I could attend the funeral only if it were private and I were kept in constant custody of marshals. Two would be assigned to me, all at my expense.

One marshal travelled with Patty and me on the flight to Boston. At Logan Airport two broad-shouldered men boarded the plane and ushered us off into a waiting car. For the next few days these men were with us at all times, sleeping in our living room, watching us while we ate, and in some ways sharing our grief.

During this time, as I went through Dad's effects I learned more about him. I had worried about his seeing me in prison, fearful of the shock to his sensitive nature. To my surprise I discovered that he had taken great interest in prison reform in the late thirties even while working twelve hours a day to hold his job and still going to night school. In his papers were moving letters he had written to the governor on behalf of men imprisoned for minor offences. In some cases he was successful in getting their sentences commuted.

I was intrigued to find that he was responsible for the plan whereby debating societies were formed in a number of prisons. He was active in the reform-minded United Prison Association. As I looked through his files my mind leaped ahead. I certainly had every reason to carry on this part of his work, which for some strange reason we had never talked about much during his life.

The tragedy also helped my mother and me to become closer as we worked out the details of the funeral and planned for her future. The services were held in St John's Episcopal Church in Winthrop, the same church in which my dad and his sister and brother had been baptised. The small church was a little piece of New England – with elegant stained-glass windows, rugged stone sides, brown shingles, and the weathered look of the seacoast. It was tucked away on a narrow street in an old part of town between two- and three- storey frame houses.

My mother and I prayed together before my father's casket. In it I placed Dad's Masonic apron and the American flag which faithfully each morning he had raised in front of his home and lowered at sundown. Following the simple service my mother, Patty, and I stood by the graveside surrounded by a few close friends and the two marshals. We watched silently as the casket was lowered within sight of the high school my Dad had attended, and the baseball field on which he had starred as a youth. The gentle breezes brought fresh salt air off the nearby sea which had been so much a part of his life and mine. The closest friend I had known in life was gone, to a 'room in the Lord's mansion', I believed.

That night I was back in prison, reflecting on what the Apostle Paul meant when he warned his disciples against despair: '. . . it is "through many tribulations" that we must enter into the kingdom of God' (Acts 14:22 PHILLIPS). I felt close to those words. My beloved father was gone, the man I almost worshipped for four years had been forced out of office, and I was about to be transferred to a much tougher prison facility in Alabama.

I should have been utterly miserable, yet there was a surprising lightness in my spirit. Patty and I were closer than ever before, John Dean and I had become reconciled, and I sensed that in some way the Lord had a plan for my life which He would gradually reveal to me.

21

'Don't Get Involved'

My transfer from Fort Holabird to the prison camp at Maxwell Air Base went smoothly. The two marshals and I were met at the Montgomery airport by the local US marshal. I breathed more easily when I climbed into the back of his car and he made no effort to handcuff or chain me – the painful, animal-like process which prisoners endure when travelling. Our drive took us through the Montgomery Air Force Base, past several golf courses and a desolate wooded area up to a group of low stucco buildings. A large sign with white letters read, FEDERAL PRISON CAMP.

Outside the prison there was an open feeling, with attractive plantings, rosebushes, tall shade trees. Inside the administration buildings stern-faced, blue-shirted guards took charge marching me past two black steel doors, each with a small square opening covered with a steel mesh grille. A quick glimpse inside revealed dark bare-walled cells empty but for a bench and toilet. This was the 'hole', I was told, into which prisoners are thrust for disciplinary purposes. The sense of openness was gone.

Our destination was a sterile and windowless receiving room a few feet beyond the hole. In one corner was a shower; all new prisoners were scrubbed down to eliminate the lice they so frequently carried from local jails. In the other corner was a Polaroid camera. More mug shots and fingerprints followed. Across a wooden counter was a genial, smiling man, the clothing officer, Mr Bleven.

'Strip down,' he commanded. Narcotics smuggling in prison is rampant and prisoners have a knack for concealing 'junk' in the most obscure crevices of their bodies. Bleven started through each piece of clothing and every personal article I had carried with me. 'This goes, this goes – this – this,' he said, listing items which were to be shipped home.

'No,' he said after deliberating a moment with himself about a pair of my shorts. 'You can't bring these in, you can wear them only if you can't find a pair around here.' The list was now two pages long. Next came my wallet, all personal identification, pictures of Patty and the kids. How I hated to part with identification! 'All jewelry must be removed,' Bleven said almost apologetically now, looking at my class ring.

'I wear it as a wedding ring and I'm not sure I can get it off,' I protested. Patty had given it to me.

'Sorry. Regulations. I'll have to have it.'

I did not offer up the silver cross and dove, hanging from the chain on my neck. He didn't ask for them.

'Try these.' Bleven tossed me a pair of well-worn underpants with a series of numbers that had been stencilled across the front and crossed out. I tried not to think about how many men had worn them before me and was so glad to put something on that I said not a word about the shorts being too tight. Next came well-worn socks, a handkerchief, and finally a set of ill-fitting surplus Air Force work clothes, dyed chocolate-brown. The first step in the deliberate de-individualising process was complete. More was to come.

'Out here, Colson,' a voice from the hall commanded and I was led back into the Control Room, from which all corners of the prison can be surveyed at a glance through thick glass windows arching outward, turret-like. I had to wait now for assignments which would thereafter govern my daily life: Dormitory G and my prison number: 23226. The guard on duty, a massive man by the name of Prather, was busily barking out orders over the camp public-address system.

For a moment I had a chance to look through the windows into the prison compound. Various grassy areas were bordered by concrete walks and two rows of one-storey dormitories. At the far end was the mess hall. Two hundred and fifty men lived here, but watching them through the window was like watching a silent movie in slow motion. Droop-shouldered, sticklike figures of men were drifting aimlessly and slowly in the open area; others were propped up against the buildings and a few sitting in small clusters on benches. The figures just seemed to be floating ever so slowly. I was soon to learn that no one walks fast in prison.

Not only were all uniforms the same drab brown; so were the expressions on the faces. *Something strange here*. Then it struck me – *no one was smiling*. Although it was a clear day, there seemed to be no sunshine in the compound. All of the colours, like the expressions on the faces, blended into one sandy haze.

Prather's booming voice broke the eerie silence. 'Colson, put your address on that package,' he snapped, turning in his chair to point to my suitcase now covered in brown wrapping paper and lying on the floor behind me. I knelt over it, carefully spelling out Patty's name and our address, trying not to think about her or our home.

'Colson, you'll be okay here,' he said. 'Just take my advice. Keep your mind where your butt is. The time will go fast if you do; if you think of home and outside things, this place will be hell.'

I could only nod as a chill swept over me. Prather's advice, standard for new inmates, had come in a different way from Bud Krogh. Don't think. Conform. Build an island around

735

yourself. *No, thanks, Mr Prather*, I thought. *My mind will stay alive.*

Walking across the compound, I sensed that advance word about the Watergate personality had preceded me. As I passed little groups, conversation stopped; men stared. My halfway attempts to smile at the faces I passed were met by suspicious glances. I would have to earn my way.

On the outside, Dormitory G was like all the other buildings at Maxwell, a cream-coloured stucco structure with red-shingled roof, outwardly well maintained. Inside, the stench of body odours and stale tobacco struck me first. Dust was everywhere. The walls inside the narrow entranceway were lined with two tiers of small lockers for those few personal items prisoners were allowed. On one side were two dayrooms, one for reading and card playing, with tables piled high with girlie magazines and cleansing equipment stacked in the corners. The other was a larger room full of broken-down vinyl-covered chairs and one old black-and-white television set.

Past the cluttered entranceway was the open dorm area itself, with two rows of steel cots lining the walls and two rows head to head up the centre with a four-foot-high partition in between. Each bunk was separated by a metal night-stand. The open toilet area was in the far end.

At minimum-security institutions like Maxwell, inmates are now housed in dormitories instead of cells. This supposedly makes for more comfortable living, but I was soon to hear many prisoners disagree with this. In cells there is a privacy and a degree of quiet. In dormitories there is constant noise and crowding together. Recent studies have concluded – correctly – that prison dormitories do not offset the disadvantages. Dormitory living can be a 'horror to inmates', according to *Struggle for Justice*, published by the American Friends Service Committee.

It was laundry day and the mattresses were stripped bare. A

few men were sprawled on bunks, some sleeping, others staring blankly. A large whirring fan overhead in the centre was stirring more dust than air. On the grimy yellowish walls and ceilings were blotches of peeling paint, cracks running out from each like tiny rivulets. This would be my home for the next year or so.

Jimmy, a friendly young black, introduced himself as the 'houseman', a title covering a variety of supply and janitor functions. While helping me find my bunk, he began handing out friendly tips: 'The commissary is only open on Wednesday, so stock up. Never leave your watch out. Keep anything valuable locked in your locker.' Jimmy spotted the Bible as I unloaded my few personal effects. 'That's safe. Ain't nobody here gonna steal that from you.' He grinned, the first smile I had seen.

'Colson, Colson, report to Control,' a rasping voice over the loudspeaker commanded. Prather had warned me that failure to respond immediately could create an instant crisis: a special count of inmates would follow to ensure that no one had escaped. The detested loudspeaker screeched incessantly. I rushed across the compound to the Control Room and was told to wait on a bench; the warden would see me shortly. Glad for the moment's rest, I began to try to sort out the bits of advice thrown at me.

'You're Colson?' Standing beside me and thrusting his hand forward was a tall, balding man with a strong, self-assured look about him. But for his brown dungarees I might have mistaken him for the warden. Smiling, he introduced himself as 'Doc' Krenshaw. I had heard about him, a former official of the American Medical Association, serving time for securities fraud. He had been in prison nine months, he told me, but it had not beaten him down.

Doc's smile suddenly vanished : 'Prison will be hard on you for a while. Gotta be a man here. I'm getting 'short' [meaning a sentence is almost over], but let me give you some advice,' he said, squinting through thick glasses. 'Just expect anything. You will probably see a man die here. Have you ever seen a man die before?'

'Yes,' I told him, 'I've seen most everything in life.'

'Well, you haven't seen prison, Colson. You're going to be shocked by some of the things that happen to you and others. Remember one thing – *don't get involved.* Don't complain. Tend to your own affairs and you'll be okay. I've made it that way.'

'This way, Colson,' the guard was signalling me to the front office. I stared at Krenshaw for a moment and then trotted towards the administration building. Doc's words were still ringing in my ears : 'Don't get involved.' Krogh's warning had been to mind my own business. Inmates at Holabird had told me : 'Trust nobody with nothin'.' Prather said it the same way with reference to my anatomy, and now Doc had added his chilling words.

The advice was more than a prison cliché, it was obviously the formula for survival. I was up against violent men with a code of life all of their own. If I wanted to get home and rebuild my own life, I'd better listen to those made wise by the ways of prison.

I expected the warden's office to be as drab and cold as the rest of the prison. Not so. Neither Robert Grunska nor his office fitted the prison scene. A handsome, athletic man in his mid-fifties with greying hair, the warden greeted me cordially. 'Sit down here, Mr Colson – er, Colson – and make yourself comfortable,' pointing to a cushioned straight-back chair just inside the door of his panelled office.

'The count is low here now,' Grunska lamented, sitting erect behind his desk, fidgeting with a pencil in his hands. 'We have a contractual obligation to the Air Force to provide a hundred and fifty men per day for base labour in place of military personnel – grass cutting, clean-up details, that sort of thing.'

Grunska was groping for some common point of

identification between us. An explanation of the prison's function, its relationship to the Air Force base, and the warden's role seemed good starting points. I was later to discover that Maxwell is little more than a work camp, and that prison policies, furloughs, work programmes, and education – so important to inmates and their rehabilitation – are secondary to the base's need for 150 free labourers a day.

Then with a friendly smile he said, 'I want you to know I have an open-door policy. Any time you need to see me, you just let me know – come right in.'

I don't know what caused me to do it – the man was being quite decent with me – but I blurted out, 'Does that apply to all inmates?'

The warden looked surprised and shifted restlessly in his chair. 'Why, of course. I see anyone who wants to see me – as much as I can – this is a busy place.'

I explained that I would have a hard enough time being accepted by the inmates and that I wanted to be treated like everyone else. The conversation rambled on, more awkwardly now, with more explanations of prison functions, the moral problems, particularly over furlough policies. 'You'll hear a lot of grumbling over furloughs,' he said. 'Pay no attention. They are the same here as everywhere. If men need furloughs they get them. Now if you need one, when you have to make a court appearance, you . . .'

Grunska caught himself in mid-sentence. 'Don't worry; I will see that you are treated like everyone else. The press will be asking about you and that's what I'll tell them. We have very uniform regulations here. Only way you can run a place like this, you know.'

The conversation ended and the warden walked me to the door. He was nattily dressed in a freshly starched, blue-striped shirt, a bright blue tie, and creased knit trousers : I was trying to keep closed my tattered brown shirts with two buttons missing, tugging down on the brown pants which were two inches too short. He reached for the door handle and then stopped. 'A lot of people ask me about your Christianity – all the stories they've read. Anything you want me to tell them?' I had noticed that he was wearing a silver tie clasp in the simple outline of a fish, symbol of first-century Christians. He seemed pleased when I called attention to it.

I then explained that what he had read was true, that I considered myself a born-again Christian. 'I assume you have Bible-study programmes for the prisoners.'

'Yes, and you can help with these things,' Grunska replied. (During my first weeks at Maxwell, however, the only planned Christian activities I found were church services conducted twice a week by visiting ministers.)

While the warden appeared to me as a kind and gentle man, I had already heard him described as 'heartless', a 'cold-blooded tyrant', and a 'sadist'. I had also learned that while inmates tend to hate all prison officials, the warden is their main target. They see only a distant commanding figure strutting about the camp on daily inspections, a symbol of total authority over their lives. The human qualities of prison administrators which vary, as they do among any group of individuals, are irrelevant. 'They' – or the system – include lawyers, prosecutors, judges, juries, probation officers and finally – prison administrators. The system punishes, inflicts pain; it is 'out to get' the accused. Resentment is a powerful mortar for building the invisible brick wall separating inmates and officials.

Certainly I had more in common with the warden than most of the inmates but at the slightest suggestion of 'fraternising with the enemy' I knew I would be in deep trouble: 'rats' are dealt with harshly. From what Grunska had said I sensed that I could work as a clerk in the front office. I need only ask. But something inside told me *no*, to seek no special favours.

From the warden's office I was taken to one of the two harried caseworkers who handle the administrative and personal problems of the entire population. Ben Brown, a stocky, smiling man, gave me rapid-fire instructions and one emphatic warning: 'Don't practise law.' As one of the two lawyers in the prison, I'd be besieged by requests for help, he told me, but regulations forbid it. Brown's order seemed further confirmation of all the advice I'd gotten to keep a quiet low profile.

As I left the administration building, I noticed a young black inmate, a wide grin on his face, clutching a single sheet of paper. He was pacing back and forth while a secretary busily typed out for him a set of forms. No one in prison smiles like that, I discovered, except when he is being released. I learned later that this young man had that day been freed by President Ford's executive order discharging from prison all men convicted of desertion or draft evasion. Their cases would be reviewed by the Clemency Board, part of Ford's amnesty plan.

I was glad for the young man, happy to see anyone leave, but the irony hurt all the same. A former Marine captain who had spent half of his adult life in military or government service was replacing on the rolls of the Maxwell prison a deserter freed by Presidential order!

Outside, a hazy dusk was falling over the compound, the sultry heat of the day giving way to gentle breezes coming from the banks of the Alabama River which form one boundary of the prison. To learn more about the area, I walked past a softball field and then along a high chain fence behind the dormitories, ending up behind the administration building in the visiting area, a fenced-in yard under tall shade trees with metal tables and chairs arranged in neat rows. I was staring into the yard, my thoughts hundreds of miles away when the silence was shattered. 'Colson, get away from there.' A tall, scowling, blue-shirted guard was jogging toward me. 'Get out of here. The visiting area is out-of-bounds.'

At first I thought he was joking. No one had told me about areas out-of-bounds. The look on his face convinced me. 'Get out of here – now,' he snarled as he steered me back toward the compound. The regulation, I later learned, was to prevent prisoners from ogling the visitors' area, a temptation for inmates who yearned for contact with the outside world. I apologised for my mistake, but the guard was still scowling. 'Read the regulations, Colson,' he growled and turned away, shaking his head as he walked slowly back to the Control Room.

An inmate who had watched the encounter ambled over: 'Don't let that rotten "hack" bother you. He is one of the worst – in this place.' I had heard the term *hack* used for a prison guard, but thought it an unnecessary put-down. From then on I called them hacks, too. Inmates and guards alike are soon trapped together in ugly demeaning practices.

When night fell the full weight of what it really means to be imprisoned settled upon me. I felt closed in and fearfully alone even though surrounded by forty other men. I had known loneliness before – a brief stint in boarding school when I was twelve, long days and nights as a Marine in a far-away land, once when I thought I was lost in the woods. It was not homesickness which weighed on my heart, but the barrenness all around me, the empty shells of men, the pervasive feeling of despair that, like the stale air, filled the dusty dimly lit dormitory.

Men lay on their bunks with glazed eyes, staring at nothing. There was some idle chatter, but unlike any group of men I had been with before there was no laughter, no jokes nor good humour. A harsh epithet, an angry outburst, or the sounds of locker doors being opened and closed were the main sounds above a few pockets of conversation and the steady whining of the fan.

I sat on the edge of my bunk trying to describe it all in a letter to the brothers at Fellowship House. While I knew that the stark drabness of my dormitory would be burned into my consciousness forever, in time as my sensitivities dulled I would get used to it. 'I want you brothers to read this back to me when I am out of here and inclined to forget what the initial shock was like,' I wrote. 'I want to be reminded how great the need is for prisoners to establish their identity and dignity as human beings. My heart aches . . .'

After the letter was written, it was time to meet some of the men. The clothing officer, Mr Bleven, had given me some friendly advice: 'Find an old moonshiner, a "country fella", and talk to him the first night.' Word would then spread that I wasn't the arrogant big-shot type they had expected me to be. One young lad named Paul Kramer was in a bunk near the door. A clean-cut type, he wore a large cross around his neck, the mark of a Christian. I had talked with him briefly. I sensed we were to become friends but not this night. He was not the 'country' type.

Most of the blacks were gathered in the corner of the dorm nearest me, but they had not acknowledged my smiles. The head-on approach with them would not be safe; they would be distrustful. The older man in the next bunk was a likely prospect. White-haired, a strong, craggy face, rough sinewy hands, he was probably a bootlegger. Earlier he had firmly gripped my hand and told me that his name was Homer Welsh. Homer seemed wary or very shy, stepping backwards as we had spoken. Now he was asleep.

Across the dorm were some men whom I approached. They seemed open, particularly the wiry younger man named Jed who wore an old dirty cap tilted forward over his brow. Jed stood out from the others because he never stopped grinning at me, revealing some missing front teeth. With his tiny chin, he looked for all the world, smile and all, like Mortimer Snerd. We soon were deep in conversation and I found myself fascinated by his mountain stories. (Bleven's advice was good; the next day when the story of my talk with Jed circulated through the prison, there was less hostility toward me.)

Sleep was fitful. The snores, groans, and other body noises of the men continued throughout the night. Many prisoners have trouble sleeping and are up and down, some chain-smoking. There was a constant shuffling in the darkness. The air reeked of smoke, sweat, urine, and dust.

During the first night I was awakened every two hours by the guards clattering through the dormitory, flashing a bright beam in my eyes. It is part of the ritual of body counts which continues day and night; whistle shrieks, all inmates return from wherever they are to their bunks, each dormitory is counted, a report made to Control and the loudspeaker announces 'count cleared'. At first it was merely an annoying disruption. Soon it was part of the nerve-chafing tedium, like the Chinese water torture; one drop is nothing, but when it goes on day after day, each drop is like a thunderclap.

Once that first night I awoke totally disoriented, thinking it was all a bad dream. Only later did I discover that some men continue for months to experience this sudden bewilderment as they struggle with reality, waking up abruptly in the darkness believing that they are suddenly free.

There was one welcome break in the routine, the regular Tuesday-night visit of Brother Edmon Blow, a local Southern Baptist preacher. Thirty of us gathered in the auditorium where a portable red vinyl-covered altar was wheeled up to the front of the large barren room; on top of the altar was a lopsided steel cross with the words US GOVERNMENT etched onto the crossbar. An old piano was moved alongside.

Brother Blow is a tall, rawboned man who accepts literally the Scriptural instruction to speak one's faith boldly. There were more *Amens, Praise the Lords*, and *Hallelujahs* in that one hour than I'd heard in a lifetime. But to my surprise I found myself singing loudly and loving every minute of it.

'Oh, how I love Jesus Christ,' Brother Blow shouted at the top of his lungs, thrusting his arms upward in an outstretched position, his jacket, which looked too small to begin with, drawn tight across his chest. 'He is *my* Saviour – our Saviour.' His voice reached a trembling crescendo as he proclaimed,

'Thank You, Lord Jesus, for saving this poor wretched sinner.'

Then he dropped his arms limply to his side and bowed his head in silence, tears rolling from his closed eyes. *This man actually seems to be talking to Jesus*, I thought to myself. I had never seen the dignified pastors of my church do it this way, but before that hour was over I found myself shouting *Amen* right along with them.

As I was leaving, Brother Blow caught my eye. To my astonishment he charged over and gave me a bear hug. 'Hallelujah, of all the men to be here,' Blow exclaimed. 'Hallelujah and praise the Lord.' He drew the word *praise* out as long as I'd ever heard it. His protruding cheekbones highlighted his leathery face, the weathered look of rural Alabama, but his eyes were filled with warmth and love.

Brother Blow was to have a part in the surprising things that would be happening in the weeks to come. For this night it was enough that I found a brother when I needed him most.

22

No Favours, Please

There were plenty of jolts those days, but the biggest was yet to come. As I was passing through the cafeteria line later in the week, one of the messmen named Jerry leaned across the counter, glanced sideways, and whispered, 'I need to see you – for your own good.'

Something told me he was sincere. When I met Jerry outside the mess hall right after the noon meal, he pointed towards the softball field, one area where inmates could be sure that their conversation would not be overheard. As we began walking slowly in that direction, I studied him. Jerry was a slight, balding man perhaps in his late thirties; he said New Orleans was his home.

Once we were at a safe distance, Jerry slowed down his walk and asked, 'Do, you have any enemies here?'

'I don't know. Why?'

'I mean someone who is really out to get you?'

'You mean kill me?' My heart was racing, that prickly feeling again attacking my spine.

Jerry nodded. 'It's none of my business and I don't know why I'm doing this, but you seem like an okay dude, better than we thought you'd be.'

I wondered if this was some kind of set-up. A way of testing me? Prisoners make a fetish of not getting involved. Why was Jerry doing just that?

As if he sensed my thoughts, Jerry shrugged, 'I'm a dope to stick my nose into something like this, but anyway – I overheard this dude say to his friend that he wants to kill you. Guys talk like this sometimes, but this one sounded like he really meant it.'

'Can you point him out to me?' I asked.

'No way. I'm no rat.'

I had kept my eyes on his during the whole exchange. He seemed dead serious. If he was testing me, I'd best appear nonchalant. 'If I report this to the hacks, will you back me up?' I asked coldly.

Jerry looked unhappy, then he began kicking the sand underfoot. 'Look, Colson, I really could care less about you. I just felt I ought to warn you. That's it. You take it from here and I bow out. Okay?'

I smiled at him for the first time. 'Thanks, Jerry, for doing this. I know how to take care of myself.' As we silently walked back to the dormitory I wished I felt as confident as I had tried to sound. Who was it? Someone who felt violent toward Nixon? Shades of Mike, the hit man! Now I had another killer to think about. If Jerry was to be believed, this one was in earnest – and about *me*.

It was late afternoon before I was free from a temporary work detail and could get off by myself to think. I sat on the grass by the side of the dorm, my mind thrashing about restlessly. What was I to do about Jerry's warning?

I could talk to the lieutenant on duty right then, or sweat it out this night and see the warden the next day. But what could they do? Jerry would not talk. If it was a gag and I went running to the guards, the next year would be living hell for me. The guards could not protect me anyway; there was nothing to prevent any inmate from quietly coming into a darkened dormitory at night in order to finish off a man in his sleep. I had heard tales of it happening at Maxwell and elsewhere. There were plenty of opportunities to get your victim, even during daylight.

What good would reporting the threat do, anyway? The most likely result would be to ship me somewhere else. It was now in the press that I was at Maxwell; how would they explain my transfer? The Bureau of Prisons would probably be accused of favouritism, that I didn't like Maxwell and had pulled strings to get transferred. Worse yet, I might be put in a maximum-security prison under constant surveillance. That would be one way to get protection, but at what a cost!

There were no options I concluded. I'd have to gut it out and hope that the Lord would guide me. Once again He was making me turn to Him for help. Before attempting sleep that night I prayed for Christ's presence and protection. My faith obviously was still weak, for though physically exhausted I tossed and turned all night long, drifting into a light slumber only to awaken at the slightest noise. For tense moments, I would stare into the blackness, then close my eyes and try again. In the morning I was bleary-eyed and edgy.

To make it worse, the ever-probing eyes of both prison personnel and 250 inmates were constantly on me. I sensed it wherever I was. How was I reacting to the food which I found surprisingly good? Whom did I seek out as friends? How much mail did I receive? Were my letters opened and inspected like everyone else's? (They were.) What work assignment would I draw? This would indicate if I was manoeuvring for special treatment. The slightest sign of favouritism would be seized upon gleefully, for it would prove what most believed anyway, that the system is unfair, or that those coming from important positions can't take it, or both.

There was surprise when word spread that I had not asked for one of the sought-after inside jobs. It had been deliberate. I knew it was expected of me since all prisoners jockey for the better jobs, the prime objective to avoid heavy, outside work details and kitchen duty. Whenever the prison's classification committee met to hand out assignments, there were near epidemics of chronic back disorders, mysterious pains, and other debilitating ailments; otherwise-lethargic men could rise to heroic thespian performances.

I tore into each temporary work assignment, waxing floors, raking leaves, emptying garbage containers as if my life depended on it, which in some ways I thought it might. Winning 'acceptance' and proving myself was as important now, incongruous though the comparison might seem, as it had been thirty years earlier assaulting the Brahmin bastions of Boston, or later when I sought to be 'good enough' in the Marines. I'd have to earn my way – and this time it would be tougher than ever before. For it meant overcoming not only my press notoriety, but penetrating the stifling dense air of mistrust which pervades every prison.

Prison life is often compared to the military. There are certain similarities – the close barracks living, the group standards, the feeling of oppression by authority. But there are sharper differences. In prison the man you befriend may steal your clean socks. Inmates seldom relax their guard even with those they know well.

The sole aim in prison is to survive, make time pass, avoid trouble, and get out. Getting out is the most treasured goal of all and that is very much an individual proposition. Fellow inmates can interfere with a man's chances to win his freedom by involving him in their misconduct, but there is little they can do to help him get out. Men in the armed services, by contrast, are trained to work closely together. In battle they must rely on one another. Staying alive depends upon your buddy.

'Colson, you still don't want to tell us where you'd like to be assigned, eh?' Ben Brown, the caseworker with the round face and a perpetual half-smile was staring at me intensely from behind the conference table. He was flanked by the education officer, two lieutenants, and the other caseworker. The time had come for the classification committee to make its decision on me.

'No, sir. Wherever you decide.'

'This is your last chance to make a request.'

'I understand.'

Brown then asked me to wait outside. In a few minutes I was called back in. 'Colson, you will work in the laundry.' Then came instructions on what I could and could not do.

I was tempted to ask the education officer whether there was any connection between this assignment and the two days of aptitude tests I'd taken as all new inmates do. I had never even run our washing machine at home and anyone who had even seen me trying to lift the hood of a car knew I was a disaster around things mechanical. The more I thought about it, however, the more I was delighted. The prison administration had struck a compromise between a cushy front-office job and the hated garbage detail. My fellow inmates would now know, at least, that I was not one of the warden's pets.

The laundry was located in a big warehouse-style building which was ferociously hot in the summer and where there was endless sorting of sweat-soaked underwear and brown work uniforms, running washing machines, and handing out clean clothes each day to the inmates. But there were advantages: I would be working for Mr Bleven, the friendly man who processed me into the prison, and I'd be able to keep myself in clean clothes, an important factor in maintaining good health. On some days work details were called out into the compound to stand in ankle-deep water for up to ten minutes in driving, semi-tropical rains. Prisoners were issued no rain gear and only one towel, T-shirt, and pair of socks each day. One such drenching the second day gave me a severe cold which lasted two weeks.

As a laundryman I could also wash my own socks and underwear; other prisoners had to take what was handed to them each day. Such small benefits could be very important. My assignment to the laundry was also, I'm convinced, another step in my ego-busting process. There was a certain lesson in humility in washing the clothes of other people, not too far removed from washing their feet.

While this work assignment should have been a step forward in overcoming the hostility of inmates to me, if I was any closer to being accepted, I could not tell it from their reaction. The quips flew about my head: 'That White House big shot is washing my socks now,' was a typical rejoinder. There were a few new overtures of friendship, but most of the men were still wary of me. Starved for the fellowship and warm support I had experienced at Fellowship House, I remembered the young lad with the cross and sought him out.

Paul Kramer at twenty-seven was forthright, muscular, the star second baseman of the prison softball team. After a hitch with the Marines in Vietnam, he had attended college in his native town of Atlanta, Georgia. To make up for lost time and meet expenses, Paul tried to handle two jobs. There were domestic problems, too, with his young bride and in time all of it was too much for him. Paul started using and then selling narcotics, lasting four months in the business. Caught and arrested, he was sentenced to three years. While in the Texarkana prison, he told me he had faced up to his messed-up life and had 'accepted the Lord'.

'Paul, I wish we could start a little group here,' I suggested. 'Couldn't we get a couple of other Christians and meet a few times a week just to share our problems and pray together?'

Paul pondered this suggestion, 'I don't know, Chuck; they laugh at 'Jesus freaks' here. You can't carry a Bible around without people ribbing you. There just isn't anything like that here.'

'Come on, Paul, let's try,' I persisted. 'You'll have to start it.

I'm new and I don't want people to think I'm trying to take over. How about it?'

But he shook his head. 'No, it's not the kind of thing you organise. Maybe we should just pray about it and see what the Lord wants.'

I was surprised at the rebuff, but did not press it further. Together we prayed that night, the two of us alone in the darkness just outside Dormitory G, prayers for God to bring men together in prison, prayers which were to be answered in a way that was to shake me to the depths of my being.

All week long I had looked forward to Saturday and Patty's first visit. I was out of my bunk before 6 a.m., knowing that Patty would be standing at the visitors' gate when it opened at 8. After an extra-close shave, I laboured over the wrinkles in my set of borrowed browns. Helplessly, I kept pulling down the too-short green T-shirt as I stood in the open toilet area, staring into the mirror. Behind a week's accumulation of toothpaste and shaving-soap splatter was the image Patty would see. I hoped the worry lines on my face would not be too obvious.

Only three or four of us were up preparing for visitors, and I was a little self-conscious. Other men had been here for months, even years, and dreaded the weekends when time passed so slowly. Some prisoners actually preferred not to have visits from family and friends, not wanting to be seen in the dreary garb and surroundings of prison. Others believed that time passed faster without the emotional drain on them of the anticipation, the break in routine, and then the trauma of having to see loved ones depart. But for most prisoners the obstacle was economic: their families simply couldn't afford the cost of travel. These inmates had no choice but to glide along in their routines while minutes drifted into hours, hours into days, days into weeks – like one long night of sleep.

Patty and I had decided to spend every possible minute

together. Maybe it was easier to adjust to confinement by not living on the emotional roller coaster of weekend peaks and weekday pits, but I was far from ready to become a prison robot. A full hour before visiting time I was pacing about in the courtyard.

Visitors first checked into the outside entrance of the main administration building. There, according to regulations, each one was to be searched (although many were not). Visitors must have been approved in advance, each inmate submitting a list of those he would expect. Prisoners were allowed to take nothing into the visiting room without special permission and could accept nothing but four packs of cigarettes from a visitor. Nothing could be exchanged. There were two pages of rules and regulations for conduct in the visiting room, including an admonition against embracing, except upon arrival and departure. Once a prisoner was inside the visiting area, he could not return to the prison; if he did the visit was terminated. Visiting hours are over at 4 p.m.

Precisely at 8 a.m., the loudspeaker called out, 'Colson, Colson, you have a visitor.' As eager as a first grader on his way home from school. I ran toward the auditorium, forgetting to check in at the Control Room. An exasperated guard called me back and chewed me out, hands on his hips, drill-sergeant style.

Wearing a vivid green sweater and green slacks, Patty was radiant when I came bounding into the auditorium. Both of us had to fight back our emotions, as we did for the better part of that day. I told her nothing of the discomforts, or of the threat against my life, only that most men seemed to be like all other human beings we had met, victims of circumstance. Patty could not take her eyes off my ragged clothes, and I knew her heart was aching.

Later that morning one of the female visitors was asked to leave and the prisoner involved told to report to Control. 'What happened?' asked Patty, her eyes troubled.

'Hard to say. Probably caught trying to smuggle something inside.'

'What will happen to him?'

'He'll probably go in the hole.'

'The what?'

'It's a small cell – for solitary confinement.'

Patty was subdued for a while, but soon she brightened – there was so much to cover about our home, friends, the fellowship, Patty's Bible class. By afternoon we had met a number of other inmates and their wives and were joking about my green underwear and old brown khakis.

Even though an early fall chill was in the air, we sat outside all day at one of the round tables. We might have forgotten where we were but for the guards pacing back and forth through the visiting area. It was a relief to be with Patty those two days and a joy to attend church services together in the prison on Sunday morning. At the same time we were fast discovering the emotional strains Bud and Suzanne had talked about. Sunday night back in the dorm, and feeling the awful loneliness again, I wondered how many weekends like this we could take.

I would in time become used to many things: the roaches noisily flapping about inside the locker beside my head while I tried to sleep, the ever-present stench which permeated one's clothes after a few days, rats, both kinds – rodents and in-formers. But when I watched Patty's car pull out of the parking lot that Sunday afternoon, there was no way to avoid the depression of the aftermath. While Patty was only a few miles away in a motel, if she needed me I could not be with her. I could not reach for her and touch her, and I had to spend another week in the dismal unreality of prison, waiting expect-antly for another weekend.

During the visit with Patty, we had read some Scripture together – the first time I had opened the Bible since entering prison. Feeling convicted about this, I arose early Monday morning determined to begin the Navigators' 'Design for Discipleship' Bible course which Doug Coe had given me.

The first suggested reading was Hebrews, chapter 2, for what was described as 'valuable information about the humanity of Christ'.

What we see is Jesus, after being made temporarily inferior to the angels and so subject to death, in order that he should, by God's grace, taste death for every man, now crowned with glory and honour. It was right and proper that in bringing many sons to glory, God (from whom and by whom everything exists) should make the leader of their salvation perfect through his sufferings. *For the one who makes men holy and the men who are made holy share a common humanity. So that he is not ashamed to call them his brothers . . .* [*italics* added].

Hebrews 2:9–11 PHILLIPS

It is plain that for this purpose his concern is not for angels but for men, the sons of Abraham. It was imperative that he should be made like his brothers in every respect, if he were to become a High Priest both compassionate and faithful in the things of God . . . For by virtue of his own suffering under temptation he is able to help those who are exposed to temptation.

Hebrews 2: 16–18 PHILLIPS

As I read these words over and over for the first time ever, I had the conviction that God was speaking to me. I was in prison because I had to be there, an essential step, a price I had to pay to complete the shedding of my old life and to be free to live the new. He was preparing me, chastening me for the future perhaps, but for what purpose *now*? Then something inside of me in the most unmistakable terms told me that it was right there before my eyes – *Read it, think about it, it means something about how God came to understand His children, how He became for a time in the flesh of Christ a human so that He could know His sons as brothers. The example means something to you.*

All at once something wonderful and beautiful appeared to me from the words on that page. God, I had already reasoned, had created us as His agents, in His image. We were to be His instruments. But following the original act of disobedience in the Garden of Eden and through all of human history recorded in the Old Testament, men continued to fail to reach His expectations. So instead of inflicting His wrath upon them as He had in olden days, or revoking the agency relationship altogether, God became one of us. He lived among His agents, so to speak, so that He as Jesus could for a time be flesh, understand our sins and temptations, feel our fears as we feel them. He could speak to us in our own language, forgive us, and offer us the way of salvation. What an awesome thought – knowing God as our *Brother* through the Person of Christ! What incredible personal fellowship He made possible! Just the thought of it sent chills through my body.

For the first time the Trinity began to come alive for me. God was first the Creator and Father; then as Jesus – the Son – He lived with us; finally, experiencing our needs in the flesh, He gave us the Holy Spirit, as Christ's replacement, to remain with us as a Comforter and Helper. Up to now I had merely accepted the Trinity as gospel – the way it was – but I had only sampled this Third Part. Now I saw it more and more as the source of strength and power, very real and part of God's logical plan. Before, I had asked the Spirit to lead me and I felt He was, not really understanding what was happening to me. How clear it now appeared.

Then another even more personal thought struck me. Just as God felt it necessary to become man to help His children, could it be that I had to become a prisoner the better to understand suffering and deprivations? If God chose to come to earth to know us better as brothers, then maybe God's plan for me was to be in prison as a sinner, and to know men there as one of them. Could I ever understand the horrors of prison life by visiting a prison? The voice inside of me answered: *Of course not*. No one could understand this without being part of it, feeling the anxieties, knowing the helplessness, living in the desolation. On a tiny scale, it was the lesson of Jesus coming to us.

Of course, of course, of course, I thought to myself. *There is a purpose for my being here, perhaps a mission the Lord has called me to.* As a Christian I fervently believed in Lewis's point that one individual is infinitely more important than the state. This certainly includes the individual in prison.

For the rest of my life I would know and feel what it is like to be imprisoned, the steady, gradual corrosion of a man's soul, like radiation slowly burning away tissue. Just as God in the Person of Christ was not ashamed to call us His brothers, so it was that I should not be ashamed to call each of these fellow inmates my brothers. Furthermore, I was to love each one of them. And would I – if I had not been here? *Never,* I admitted to myself.

Out of these startling thoughts came the beginning of a revelation – that I was being given a prison ministry, both inside while serving as a prisoner and then someday later on the outside! Already I could see and feel that prison life did not provide the creative correction and training needed for a man to be able to make a new beginning on the outside. Instead it was geared to use the men as labour, punish them if necessary, and disregard their inner spirits as of no consequence.

The reading in Hebrews had jolted me, made me re-examine the involvement dilemma. It was the same conflict I had faced when I agonised over whether to plead guilty: the world's way or Christ's? At that point I had chosen the latter. Was I now slipping back to using the world's methods? Doc Krenshaw's advice did make sense, but was it a rationalisation on my part?

Then I remembered the words I had been given on the courthouse steps after Judge Gesell's sentence: 'I can work for Him in prison as well as out.'

If that was His direction – and it seemed this day unmistakable – I would have to be willing to become involved and trust Him for the wisdom and courage I would need.

23

When Two or More Gather

At 6 a.m. shrill bells and crackling loudspeakers pierced the pre-dawn silence. The prison camp seemed to heave and groan, slowly coming to life; lights flickered on from one dormitory to the next, men crowded into shower stalls, sleepy-eyed messmen turned up the steam in cafeteria serving counters, blue-shirted guards paced concrete walks in the compound.

It was the same each morning, but on Monday of the next week the camp seemed stiff and brittle with tension. It was in the air like static electricity, evident in the taut expressions and unnatural silence in the dorms and mess hall. What conversation there was concerned only one subject: the parole hearings scheduled to begin that day.

Once every two months three examiners, mid-level civil servants from Atlanta, spend four days at the camp to make decisions about the forty or so men eligible for parole. One by one in assembly-line fashion, prisoners are paraded past the examiners for interviews, and with the stroke of a pen three-year sentences are cut to one, men with five-year sentences are told to 'continue to expiration,' as the dreaded term is officially known.

There is good reason for anxiety. Under the general practice of indeterminate sentencing, a man is given both a minimum and maximum term – in my case, one to three years. Parole statutes prescribe that a prisoner be considered for parole at his minimum-sentence date, the intent being to release men who have good prison records and are not considered dangerous to society. But like every bureaucracy, the Parole Board has adopted a complex patchwork of standards – guidelines – setting minimum periods of confinement for specific offences. As a result, parole hearings can be a second sentencing, with parole not often given after one-third of the sentence. Standards constantly change, making the parole process one great guessing game, an excruciating uncertainty for every prisoner and a major cause of prison resentment and anxiety.

In the days before the arrival of the examiners, all attention is focused on upcoming cases. Inmates are remarkably well informed about the particulars of each one. The results are important, not only to those whose freedom is at stake but to the others who will in time be affected by the pattern of decisions.

When the examiners arrived that Monday and began the hearings, bits of information flashed through the prison network: 'The first three cases rejected; Pop is getting another hearing; Smitty was given only five minutes and rejected. The ——— guidelines are still fouling us up.'

By 4:00 p.m. the first day's results cast a dark pall over the prison. Only two of the first twelve men heard were granted parole. The forebodings of morning turned to despair of evening. I was shocked, for like 99 per cent of my profession, I had blithely assumed that parole was virtually automatic, particularly for the kind of 'light' offenders which populate a minimum-security institution.

If the dormitory was dark and depressing on my first night, that evening it was a black hole. Everything in the prison, including most of the men's nerves, seemed to be gripped in the same tense vice. It took little to unleash frayed nerves into swinging fists. A large number of men, even in places like

Maxwell, have records of violence. Most fights are over such things as the programme to be watched on television, the distance between bunks, since space is such a precious commodity, even the slamming of a locker door while another man is trying to sleep. Fights occur over petty thievery. I once listened to a huge strapping convict shriek that he would 'kill' the man who had stolen soap from his locker.

While I was packing things away in my locker that very night, a fight broke out between two young inmates nearby. I later learned that both had long criminal records. These young toughs, heavily tattooed, teeth missing, had plenty of scars to show for previous battles. It started with some friendly pushing and shoving, but soon they were swinging for real. I watched for a moment, frozen on the edge of my bunk. When the blows came vicious, I jumped between them. Instantly both turned on me. Both raised their fists. I smiled; they snarled.

A hush fell over the dorm, the other men sensing gore as sharks do – by vibrations in the water. Blood – mine – was about to be spilled. One spat on the floor, and rubbed his hands together. A shudder ran through me. Could one of these be the man who had threatened to kill me? If so, I had given him a perfect opportunity.

'What's the matter with you guys?' I snapped, hoping they couldn't hear my heart pounding against my rib cage. Nobody moved. No one was going to rescue me. 'Didn't you see the hack just outside the window? You'll both be in the hole tonight.' It was a lie, a purely self-protective device.

As the words rolled out, tightly clenched fists relaxed, both men's arms dropping limply to their sides. 'Why didn't ya tell us?' one asked as I stepped out of the middle. The fight was over. Both of them walked off, arms around one another, their heads shaking in bewilderment over my strange conduct. I returned to my bunk, knees trembling.

Why had I done it? It was instinctive – a direct violation of the don't-get-involved principle. Did my act spring from the

Spirit within me urging to prevent bloodshed? If so, it was hardly the Spirit which had me tell a lie to protect myself from injury. I reasoned that God would hardy violate the principle of truth.

The more I pondered the scene, the more I felt that my motive had been right in trying to prevent violence, but that I relied on the old Colson craftiness to get me out of trouble. The right way to have handled it, I concluded, would have been to trust God at the moment of danger by being completely honest with the two antagonists.

Trust. How much I had to learn about this principle. This would be the key to my getting released from anxiety-filled nights – trust in the Helper. He could help me throw off the fear of sudden attack from the unknown threatener. He could help me resist the temptation of daytime sleep, replacing fatigue with strength.

Sleep was a trap for many prisoners. One young lad near my bunk had a pathetic routine. He arose at the last possible moment in the morning. He would be back sprawled on his bunk after lunch until the afternoon work call at 12:30; he would again return to his bunk after the 4:00 p.m. meal, sleeping until perhaps 7:00. Then he might spend an hour or two reading pornographic magazines before dozing off for the night.

While marvelling at his ability to sleep so much, I saw that his strength was being sapped with each passing day. His walk slowed, his shoulders were hunched, and seldom did his sallow face reveal any emotion. When released from prison, I wondered if he could ever regain the ambition needed to cope even with the everyday necessities of life, let alone a job and family responsibilities.

His was not an isolated case; others in the dorm spent their idle hours simply lying in their bunks, if not sleeping, staring trancelike at the ceiling. Some spent hours on menial tasks, like shining a belt buckle over and over. 'Building time' it is called, the ways men find to pass their hollow days. Walking slowly, too, was part of prison life; particularly the 'sleepers' shuffling about as if acting out some role in slow motion. Like an invasion of locusts, the empty hours eat away at a man's very being. Soon there is near-total disorientation: staring at the clock, its hands never moving; losing track of time and place.

One sleeper was in the bunk by the entranceway. His name was Lee Corbin and he was assigned to one of the toughest grass-cutting details, swinging a heavy scythe all day and arriving in the dorm each night soaking wet and exhausted. When I saw him reading the Bible one evening, I introduced myself.

'I know you,' he replied. 'That was good about your conversion. I was a Christian once myself.'

'*Was* a Christian?'

He leaned his head back, a wide smile covering his round ruddy face. 'Ha, if you only knew. I really fell, man – there's no way for me to get back.'

I wanted to pursue it. It seemed hard to imagine that this genial, hardworking man could have committed the unforgivable sin. 'Let's talk about it sometime,' I suggested.

'I don't think it's worth your time, but I'd like to talk,' he replied. Yet each night when I passed his bunk, he was asleep. There would be a time, I knew.

As I watched those who appeared to be almost sleep-walking about the prison, somewhat like men in space, I made the conscious decision never to lie down during the day. I would get what sleep I could at night. There were days when I fought back heavy eyelids and the urge simply to fall into my bunk and let an hour or two pass. But I resisted, even when I knew I needed the sleep.

Later when I read Dietrich Bonhoeffer's *Letters and Papers From Prison,* I discovered that he had made the same decision. He wrote of his rigidly self-enforced schedule to awaken each morning early, take a cold bath, and work all day without sleep. When put into solitary confinement, he determined not to succumb to the reclining position, aware that doing so would aggravate his disorientation and bring him to the 'first stage of capitulation'.

The man who refuses to be a part of the system, however, and struggles instead to preserve his own identity, all too often can end up fighting everything simply for the sake of fighting. This usually becomes rebelliousness which then hardens into hatred, infecting the man's entire value structure, first about the prison system and then about society as a whole.

It takes only a slight provocation to tip such men over the edge; the inner turmoil can stretch to a snapping point the cords which bind a man together as a rational being. I saw it happen. His name was James Howard, a handsome man in his early thirties, with sparkling blue eyes, reddish blond hair, and an unusually bright, alert manner. Out of prison garb I could see him as a stockbroker or an enterprising young IBM executive. Since Paul Kramer and I had been having Bible talks together he asked me one evening to pray for Howard.

'He just hasn't been himself for a few days. Terrible burdens. Won't say much either,' was all Paul told me.

When I saw Howard sitting alone in the mess hall the next noon I sat with him. After the idle chatter and get-acquainted questions, there were long awkward lulls in the conversation. His one show of emotion was when he vigorously protested his innocence of stolen-car charges. I had the uncomfortable feeling through lunch that my words were going right past him, that his thoughts were completely disoriented.

Howard lived in Dr Krenshaw's dormitory. When I asked Doc about him, he gave me that don't-get-involved look: 'It's better not to talk about it, Chuck,' he said. 'It will be bad for him if the word gets out and people start ribbing him.'

'But I only want to help.'

With that, Doc looked pained and then explained that in

his opinion Howard had suffered a nervous breakdown. Receiving bad news on parole and a 'Dear John letter' from his wife on the same day was too much. 'Chuck, it could happen to anybody. I'm trying to get Hart [the prison paramedic] to admit him to the hospital just for observation, but Hart can't tell if a man has had a nervous breakdown. He thinks we're all crazy and he's probably right.'

Doc related that three nights earlier Howard awoke in the middle of the night screaming. No one paid any attention; nightmares were common in the dormitory of forty men. From then on, Howard had been in a daze, listless as if all life had been sucked out of him. 'What the man needs, Chuck, is psychiatric treatment, but that's not going to happen. They don't move anybody out of here unless it's feet first, or unless they cause trouble. Forget it. Just be kind to him.'

Some days later Howard was admitted to the two-bed infirmary. His condition was not diagnosed and he was returned to his dormitory. Again at lunch I tried to talk to him. Once he leaned across the table and whispered, 'What did you find in my files?'

I was startled: 'What files, Howard?'

Looking about cautiously, he whispered again, 'You know, the other night when you were up in the office and had my folder out. All of you guys were talking about it. What did you find?'

'Honest, Howard, I have never looked at your file. I swear to you I don't know anything about it.'

He nodded with a smug, knowing expression: 'I understand. You can't talk about it, can you?' My heart sank; paranoia possessed him. Krenshaw could do nothing; the administration would not. I vowed somehow to help Howard, but it was agony to watch this young man's body and mind drift further apart each day.

Very few prisoners, I discovered, were able to maintain a sense of personal identity, without becoming resentful of the injustice they saw about them. The causes of bitterness went beyond prison life and were deeply rooted in the system of criminal justice itself. For all my years at the bar, all my study of the ideals of the law, I was now coming to perceive the law's workings in an entirely new light. Prisoners exaggerate, of course; I was prepared to discount many of the stories I heard. Yet I had discovered to my dismay that many of the tragic tales from inmates were all too true.

There was a lad from rural North Carolina, for example, who years before had purchased an old tow truck. With that start, he had built a thriving auto-repair and gas-station complex. Late one night he cashed an eighty-four-dollar government paycheque for a customer. After the cheque bounced, the FBI visited the garage and warned him of his rights. It turned out that the cheque was stolen. Though this young businessman had never before been in trouble, he was convicted and sentenced to six months in prison. Gone were six thousand dollars in legal fees paid to a lawyer who confessed that he had never before been in federal court, eighty-four dollars from the bad cheque, and six months of his life.

The case is extreme but not unusual. One of my dormitory mates, a South Carolina small businessman, was convicted of three misdemeanours for failure to file excise-tax returns. He had, I learned, infuriated the trial judge with one defiant remark. This offence, which seldom if ever results in prison, cost my friend eighteen months in jail, with the judge writing the Parole Board to recommend denial. The board did so.

Another man whom I later befriended was doing three years for a four-thousand-dollar tax evasion. The IRS offered him a chance to plead guilty and accept a fine, but my friend insisted on his innocence. After years of trials and despite acquittal on most of the charges, an exhausted judge gave him a stiff sentence.

There may have been other factors involved in these cases – and many men who should be punished go free, I realise. But as the stories accumulated and I checked them out as best I could, it was easy to see why sentencing disparity is the chief cause of the pervasive bitterness in prison. The injustice of the system, so painful when one comes to know the victim face-to-face, spawns contempt for the law, even among those receiving deserved punishment.

I especially yearned to help the illiterate men with their pleas, but remembered the stern admonition not to practise law in prison. Lawyers who do this, I was told, are transferred immediately to other prisons. Krenshaw was not allowed to practise medicine even though there was a shortage of doctors on the base nearby and no doctor in the prison. Regulations are strict. I was soon to be tested on this as well.

To escape the depressing dormitory atmosphere on the first day of parole hearing, I headed for the library located in the rear of the Control Building. A small room, the library has one wall lined with tiny stalls for writing, while the other walls contain bookshelves crammed with old paperbacks, a tattered dictionary, outdated volumes of the criminal code, newspapers, and old news magazines. Inmates usually congregated around two large tables in the centre of the room, chattering about writs and appeals which some enterprising prisoner was preparing, playing cards, or reading. Even so, it was quieter than the dorms, more brightly lighted, and the white walls somehow made it seem cleaner. As the library clerk, Paul Kramer spent most of his evenings there.

When engrossed in my writing I could usually shut out the din of conversation around me. But this evening I became aware of a small group of men gathering around Paul in the corner of the room. Doing most of the talking was a man named Tex, a flamboyant character and one-time evangelist who had spent years travelling the revival circuit. He had left the ministry and the Lord to traffic in stolen automobiles. During his six-month sentence, he had recommitted himself to Christ with the fervour of a new convert.

Tex was a red-necked, red-headed edition of Popeye, with short bulging biceps and a jutting chin. Standing with him were two other prisoners. One, a tall, handsome black man with a commanding presence, had been active in halfway-house work in Columbus, Georgia. While on probation for a previous narcotics sentence, he was found with a sporting rifle in his possession. Probation was automatically revoked and he was back in prison for nine months. The other, a quiet man with a huge bush of curly hair, was often in the library, reading Scriptures, or working on Bible correspondence courses.

Tex in loud whispers was describing the plight of an inmate named Bob Ferguson who was up for parole hearing the next day. 'Bob is in terrible shape. He's crawling on his belly tonight. Oh – Praise the Lord – We gotta help him. Poor devil, wife and five kids and no money. If he doesn't get paroled, they ain't gonna survive. Praise God, we gotta help him. Maybe pray with him. He's going off his head.'

I walked over to the little group. 'Sorry, but I couldn't help hearing about this fellow Ferguson. I'd like to pray with him, too,' I volunteered.

Tex, his eyes sparkling, grabbing me hard by the arm. 'Come along, brother. Come along. Praise the Lord.' One of the men went to get Ferguson. Paul sent for his close friend Amos, a pharmacist from Atlanta, who was doing six months for filling a prescription on a doctor's orders which exceeded the permissible narcotics content. Within minutes seven of us were assembled. We caucused for a moment at the library door to decide where to go. The guards were always suspicious of small groups of prisoners gathered in dark areas, since this usually meant they were smoking marijuana. We could not pray in the library which was crowded with other inmates, as were the dorms. The auditorium was out-of-bounds. Paul had a key to two small classrooms just off the library, which were locked at night and also out-of-bounds.

The classrooms seemed the best choice. We filed in, locking the door behind us. Memories of my own days in elementary school flooded back. Three rows of simple polished wood tables, chairs neatly pulled up to each one, a teacher's desk in front of a large blackboard covered with chalk scratchings, 'See John run – John has a cat – The cat is brown.' Basic reading and writing were regularly taught to the 15 per cent or so of the prison population which was totally illiterate. These were largely mountain and rural folk, moonshiners from the tiny Appalachian communities of Alabama, Tennessee, Kentucky, and the Carolinas. By and large God-fearing men, their primitive understandings of right and wrong were no match for the intricacies of the Internal Revenue Code, the complex laws of society, and hordes of federal agents.

Ferguson was just such a rural person – a man in his thirties, half his front teeth missing, eyes reddened, and a confused and worried expression on his face. Ferguson didn't say a word. He didn't have to. His face was pleading for help. Paul, we discovered, was also scheduled for a parole hearing the next day. Tex began by grimly recounting the experiences of those who were given hearings earlier in the day. The prospects were no better for those coming up tomorrow; the Parole Board was showing little mercy, rigidly adhering to its guidelines.

The Bible student read several Psalms and then passages from the Book of John about Christ's work on our behalf. Tex then suggested we all pray silently or aloud as we wished, and the seven of us were soon on our knees on the cold tile floor. Tex began. In my mind, I could see him on a hot summer night, underneath a tent surrounded by a few dozen wide-eyed country folk, demanding in the name of Jesus that Satan depart, calling on all of the assembled sinners to come forward and confess their sins or be damned eternally to hell.

'Oh, Lord,' he cried out, 'just spare these men who are coming up for parole tomorrow. We just praise You, Lord. We ask it of You, dear Lord, in the name of Jesus. We are all sinners but we are here on our knees making our claim. We know, dear Lord, You will hear us. We love You, Jesus.' In between each rapid-fire petition, Tex would breathe in deeply, sign, and begin again, his voice trembling with emotion.

Paul followed with a short quiet prayer, as did the others. I was last: 'Lord, strip away the calluses on the hearts of these parole judges, hardened by years of dealing so impersonally with criminals,' I prayed. 'Please give them wisdom, love, and compassion.'

As each of us slowly got to his feet, I found myself hugging the big black. Tex was jumping from one foot to the other, praising God for filling him with the Holy Spirit. Ferguson was unashamedly in tears. We filed out quietly and returned in little groups of two or three to our dormitories just in time for the 10:15 count. No guard had intruded upon our little gathering. But what a strange sight it would have been to anyone who might have stumbled across us.

The next afternoon, news spread quickly through the camp: five men paroled, Ferguson among them. Few expected it; he wasn't eligible under the guidelines. The statistics were startling: five out of seven cases heard – a dramatic switch from the day before. It was the best day even the old-timers could remember. Wednesday was almost as good; well over half the cases heard won parole dates, including Paul.

Paul had not prepared for the hearing in the conventional way. No one had accompanied him. He had even volunteered the information that though he was married (that fact adds one point to a prisoner's rating score) he expected to be divorced. When asked about his future, Paul did not try to blow up his situation with an over-optimistic forecast; he simply explained that he had accepted the Lord and believed He would lead him. According to Paul the Parole Board examiners listened with perplexed expressions; nonetheless they scheduled a March hearing for him.

Paul returned to the dormitory that afternoon with a

stunned, far-away look: 'I can't believe it, Chuck, I can't believe it. I'm not eligible under the guidelines for two years. But they told me they would hear my case in the spring. If I keep my nose clean, I'll be released. It's too good to be true. I can't feel anything. I'm numb all over.'

It *was* too good to be true, all of it. The parole actions lifted the morale of the whole camp. The mess hall filled with smiling faces. Word of our Monday-night prayer session had also spread. Some of the seven were the butt of wisecracks on Tuesday, but by nightfall all kidding ceased. By Wednesday night even the most cynical non-believers were in awe of what happened in the little classroom on Monday. Many wanted to believe there was something to it, whatever it was.

The Bible began to enjoy a new respect, too. 'Be careful now; somebody might steal it,' Jimmy, the houseman, warned me with a smile.

24

A Helping Hand

'You guys meet each night to pray?' Standing before me outside the mess hall was Lee Corbin, who had confided to me one night that his sins were too great, that he had gone past the point of redemption. 'You know I really believe in what you guys are doing.' Corbin said wistfully.

'Come and join us,' I urged. That first session in the classroom had been so inspiring that Paul, Amos, and I met again the next night to pray for Tex who was being released that week. There were so many needs we just kept meeting.

I spent much of that night talking with Lee long after lights were out. 'I have swindled so many people,' he explained. 'Even if I had the money to pay them back, I could never find them all.' Corbin astonished me with the story of how he became an accomplished con artist. He began as a phony but successful preacher. With his deep resonant voice and command of the Scriptures, he was soon asked to broadcast a weekly sermon over several Alabama radio stations. 'I was not preaching Christ but Lee Corbin,' he confessed.

Soon he became so involved in business ventures that he dropped his clergy role entirely. There followed a series of get-rich schemes: bank loans to defunct corporations, phony vending-machine concessions, and false credit cards, with each new flim-flam becoming progressively more ingenious than the one before.

'It was wrong, Chuck and I knew it all the time, but I was hooked on my hundred-thousand-dollar house, the new cars, the yacht. It was so easy. I felt sorry for the poor people I was swindling and I hated myself, yet I couldn't stop.'

For seven years Lee crisscrossed the South, leaving behind a trail of bewildered, dejected and sometimes broke victims, and scores of angry police departments. Then it all began to collapse; there was a series of charges and he became a fugitive. When he was arrested, ironically it was while attending a revival session in South Carolina.

'The Lord picked me right out of the crowd. I deserved it.' he added.

Corbin faced an awesome array of charges: mail fraud, embezzlement, forgery. 'They could have put me away for life and I guess I would have had it coming,' he said. Surprisingly, Corbin was tried on only one count of mail fraud, sentenced to one year, and the other charges were dropped.

'But I can never repay all those people whose money I took,' he insisted. 'Not if I work for the rest of my life. So how can the Lord take me back until I do?'

We talked that night about forgiveness. Corbin had studied the Scriptures, but he seemed more knowledgeable about the Old Testament than the new. The admonition in Leviticus 6:2–5 – that when a man has taken property wrongly from another, he must restore it plus a 20 per cent fine – had burned itself into his consciousness.

I steered Lee to the Gospels and we focused on the fact that Jesus came to save sinners; He wiped the slate clean for each of us when He went to the cross. As we groped our way through the Scriptures that evening, both of us concluded that Jesus would demand from Lee only an open heart, a complete confession, restitution where possible, and a renewed commitment.

We found further illumination in chapter 7 of Romans, where Paul describes the dilemma of Old Testament men who knew the law and wanted to abide by it, but did precisely the opposite because they were unable to conquer their own human imperfections. 'For I do not do the good I want, but the evil I do not want is what I do. Now if I do what I do not want, it is no longer I that do it, but sin which dwells within me' (Romans 7:19, 20 RSV). Paul's point: trying to live by the law only creates in us the very sin we seek to avoid.

But it wasn't enough for Corbin to see the trap into which he had fallen. He needed to be freed from it. The key to this we found in the next chapter of Romans. 'For the law of the Spirit of life in Christ Jesus has set me free from the law of sin and death' (Romans 8:2 RSV).

This matter of asking the Holy Spirit to take over our lives was something I had been struggling with since the time of my acceptance of Christ. I had felt then the movement of His Spirit in me. Yet I did not fully understand how to get my sinful self out of the way so that this Spirit could take charge. Strange that it was in prison where I was to find this freedom.

Corbin began attending our evening prayer sessions. On our fourth night together Paul asked Lee to lay it all before God, to ask for forgiveness and for the Holy Spirit to come into his life again. Lee prayed as hard as any man I've known, begging the Lord to take him back and to cast Satan out of his life. At one point his prayer seemed to shift gears, the words were unfamiliar, reminding me of the Gregorian chant I'd once heard in a Catholic church. I had not experienced this praying in tongues, nor had I been with anyone before who did, but not for a minute did I doubt that the Spirit was in control of Lee Corbin. When he finished praying, it was just as if every bit of strength left his body and he fell limp.

I watched the change that took place in him in the days that followed. Corbin stopped sleeping his evenings away, reading instead from his Bible, filled with vitality, a renewed sense of purpose in his life. Whether I fully understood it in Scriptural or theological terms, I knew it was real. I would have gladly shared a foxhole with him in battle – Lee had suddenly become that tough, dependable, and loyal.

There were four of us now meeting to pray regularly. Emboldened by the strength of our fellowship, we decided to encourage others to join us. No matter whom we sat with in the mess hall, we agreed always to ask the Lord's blessing before beginning our meal. We would each pass through the cafeteria line with our trays, find an empty seat, and bow our heads for grace.

At first other inmates would stare at us. Yet there were no sneers or ribbing. Soon the blessing became contagious – a man here, another there, following this practice. To my surprise, whenever I would join a table, even if the others were in the midst of their meal they would stop talking and eating, bowing their heads with me. It was as if a beachhead was established at Maxwell for the Holy Spirit!

Although we met every night in the classroom, most of the newcomers chose to come Monday. Within a few weeks those Monday night meetings became a regular, organised Bible-study programme. With the warden's permission, Martin Gay, a Christian lay worker from Montgomery, joined us to lead the instruction.

Did the main group of prisoners consider us 'Jesus freaks'? Some did, perhaps. But it didn't matter. My priorities were changing. Then one evening during a cleanup period a tough young prisoner deliberately bumped into me as we were both running buffing machines across the floor. 'Never did this in the White House, huh?' he said.

I grinned at him. 'I did this kind of work before you were born.'

Surprised, he smiled faintly and returned to waxing the floor. One of the veterans took me aside. 'You don't have to knock yourself out the way you are,' he said. 'We know why you're doing it, but you don't have to. We've discussed it. You're okay.'

So it happened. *Okay* was the magic word. I had passed a test of sorts with the main group of prisoners. Nothing formal, of course, but a silent understanding which signalled their acceptance of me. It meant an end to the wisecracks, the curious stares, the suspicions. I would still have to contend with the loners, the men not part of the system. The threat on my life most likely came from one of them, a 'nut' perhaps. But at least now I would have some allies. The men in the main-stream would watch out for me, as much as prisoners ever watch out for one another. Ironic that this acceptance had come when I stopped striving so hard for it.

From my first week at Maxwell, I had wrestled inside over the warning that I was not to help my fellow inmates with legal problems. Perhaps there were good reasons for the rule, but with such a desperate need for legal assistance in prison, it seemed a misuse of a man's gifts. In the prisoner' eyes it was just one more example of planned dehumanisation; men stripped of self-worth and dignity are easier to control. On the other hand, my role in prison had changed after the revelation that came to me through reading the second chapter of Hebrews. Since then I had become involved.

It was Homer Welsh, the shy, white-haired man in the bunk next to mine, who helped me resolve this dilemma. Homer was such an insecure person he would jump up each time I spoke to him and called me sir even when I asked him not to. Piece by piece I pried from him these facts – he had been a construction labourer in the coal mines of eastern Tennessee, was devoted to his wife and grown-up children. He owned his own home. Unfortunately he had chosen whisky-making as his avocation.

Moonshining is considered by these mountain people an honourable, respected profession. The profits are usually small, certainly in relation to the backbreaking work required. Many older moonshiners know no other trade or profession; it is a skill passed down from one generation to the next. Staying ahead of the 'revenooers' is simply one challenge of their craft; they recognised its illegality, but do not consider it immoral. Many when caught do not go to jail because of an unwritten 'social compact' between local judges and lifelong moonshiners. Those imprisoned do not understand why they are put with men who lie, cheat, and steal – and yet have about the same length of sentence. Moonshiners are usually hardworking. Bible-reading, God-fearing men.

Homer was just such a man. He read at night from a well-worn leather-bound King James Version of the Bible. After I offered him my Phillips translation of the New Testament, he would borrow it, but only after very formally asking my permission each time. It was during one of our exchanges about my Bible that Homer summoned up all his courage to make another request.

'Mr Colson, if you don't want to do it, I'll understand, but do you suppose you could help me with a letter to my judge? He told me I'd only be here four months. I can't get to see my caseworker and I've been here four months already. I don't think I'm getting a parole like the judge said. I thought I ought to write him and maybe he'll straighten it out. I have a job in November if I can get out, but if I can't, they won't hold it for me. Could you help, sir?'

I explained the constraints upon me and he was instantly apologetic. 'Didn't mean to brother you, sir. I understand completely. I hope you didn't mind me asking.'

Homer's request lingered in my mind all that night. He was my bunkmate and a decent man. He obviously could not afford a lawyer and even if he could, the mechanics of getting one were probably beyond him. The caseworkers were too harassed to help him. And jobs for men his age were hard to find. And there was also the possibility he would lose his home. The next morning I suggested a solution to Homer. While I could not write the letter for him, if he would do a rough draft, I would look it over and give him my suggestions.

The old man's face brightened. 'Yes, sir. I'll write it. I'll go right to work on it today. Thank you, Mr Colson.'

Night after night Homer sat on the edge of his bunk labouring over a white lined pad of paper. *He must be producing a lengthy brief,* I thought to myself.

A week passed before I asked him how he was progressing. 'I think I've got it all down,' he said, reaching into his nightstand draw and pulling out a single sheet of white paper. The barely legible writing covered only half the page. It was a series of words, not even sentences. 'This is the best I can do,' he lamely explained. 'All the facts are here, anyway.'

How blind I had been! Homer could not write. He had been struggling pathetically night after night – simply to get words on paper – and was too embarrassed to tell me. We hurried off to the library together. Within twenty minutes I had written a letter to the judge, using simple language in the hopes it would look as if Homer himself wrote it. Paul typed it, and it was in the next morning's mail.

From that moment my new course was charted: I could not refuse those who needed help. These were my brothers. The Lord had shown the way and now I was following. Most of my evenings thereafter were consumed helping other prisoners write parole applications, furlough requests, and the assorted other appeals men pursue in an effort to secure their freedom or fair treatment. I drew the line in not preparing court documents or writs against the prison officials, which would be a clear violation.

One day while I was regulating the flow of laundry into the washing machines, a new inmate, a young man from Tennessee named Dan, came into the laundry asking for the 'louyah, the Watergate man'. Nettled by his lack of restraint within the hearing of guards, I told him I wasn't allowed to practise law. His beaming smile disappeared, replaced by such a pathetic sheep-dog look that I relented and told him to return after working hours for a talk. Dan's face lighted up again. 'Thank you. Thank you.'

That evening Dan was waiting in the doorway with that big broad smile. We found a quiet spot and I asked him to tell me his problem. 'Well, suh,' he began, 'I don't know what mah sentence is and I thought maybe – some of the fellas said you'd help me write to the judge.'

'Don't put me on,' I cut in impatiently. 'Everybody knows what his sentence is. What were you convicted of?'

'I don't know that either, suh, honest I don't,' he answered.

I was tired and must have appeared angry because Dan kept saying, 'Honest – honest.' After weeks of meeting victims of the system, men who had experienced the most bizarre encounters with the law, I should not have been surprised. 'Don't you have a lawyer?' I asked.

'The judge gave me one who told me what to do. He said he'd "copped" something for me with the prosecutor. Then we went back before the judge who looked so mean at me my knees wouldn't stop shakin'. I don't know what he said. Somethin' about four years. That didn't sound so good. Then he said somethin' about probation. That sounded good. My louyah said it was, anyway. But then two men took me away in handcuffs. I never saw the louyah again, and here I is.'

I stared at him in total dismay. Dan was, I believed telling me the truth. I knew that such things did happen, that some court-appointed lawyers found such cases a bother and nego- tiated quick guilty pleas with prosecutors, leaving the un- suspecting defendant to the mercy of the court. What stung me now was that I was face-to-face with a decent, fresh-faced young kid who was in prison and didn't even know why or for how long. When Dan later brought me his papers, I saw that he had been given a four-year sentence for purchasing a stolen car. It was hard to believe that such an offence could warrant that kind of punishment. I agreed to do what I could to help him.

The decision to abandon the Krenshaw advice produced some subtle changes in me. There was a further lessening of resentment towards the forces that put me in prison. I was seeing firsthand that injustice was a part of life. Being so involved, doing something about these sad cases, gave me less time to think about myself, and brought home to me an awareness of a great need in our society. Soon I had almost no time for myself, getting even less sleep as I would sit up after hours in a dimly lit smoke-filled dayroom, preparing papers, advising others.

For many days now I had lived with a threat over my head, sleeping fitfully, watching for those angry, hate-filled eyes which would give me a clue to my would-be assassin. With God's Spirit now so alive in the prison, I had been able to trust Him even about this. When the time was right I would have a face-to-face showdown with this man. Until then I had been given other work.

Another change in me was a new sense of gratitude for family and friends. I knew that there was a vast group of people outside who still hated the 'hatchet man'. But how much it meant to have the letters flood in from grass-roots Americans who wanted to lift my spirits. One family, the Charles Givlers of Beaver Falls, Pennsylvania, wrote to say that they had adopted me. Each week brought notes from the Givlers children, crayoned drawings, cheery cards, books, small thoughtful gifts, and always expressions of Christian love.

Patty's regular weekend visits were always the week's highlight. For my birthday she gave me a present I had wanted all these months in prison – a wedding band on which she had inscribed: 'April 4, 1964 – Forever.' This might seem a curious gift for a couple married so long, but this new band was to remind me daily of the bonds we had together, with the word *forever* now having a new meaning for us.

A letter was received from the former President, written on my birthday (*see* page 782).

A birthday visit from two friends and former law partners, Charlie Morin and George Fender, was memorable in a different way. As lawyers they were able to obtain special permission to visit during the week. Since the visiting yard was closed, we were shown into what was called the captain's office, a tastefully furnished room with a large wooden desk in the centre. Although fearing I might be developing my own case of prison paranoia, I could not shake off the suspicion that the captain's office was bugged. The room was used for disciplinary proceedings, which, it seemed logical, prison officers would want recorded.

I knew that all phone calls by prisoners were monitored and probably taped, since one of the inmates had seen the transcribing equipment. (Prisons vary in the telephone freedom they allow. At Maxwell we were permitted to make unlimited personal collect calls on the two public telephones installed, but only at designated hours during the day. With long lines of men always waiting, a ten-minute limit for each call was carefully observed. Making the telephone more available to prisoners has been an important morale factor.)

All outgoing and incoming mail, except from attorneys, was opened and read. This feeling of being watched and listened to all the time was one of the most unsettling aspects of prison life. While George Fender was at his effusive best, telling jokes and funny stories from the office, my mind was searching the room for hidden listening devices. Finally, I passed Charlie Morin a note: 'This room is probably bugged.'

Charlie read the note and nodded understandingly. George read it over Morin's shoulder and then attempted to lift the desk, only to find it bolted to the floor. He scribbled a note back: 'You're right – standard technique – microphone wires run through the bolted desk legs under the floor.'

October 16, 1974

Dear Chuck,

During the two months that we have been in California since the Resignation and during the time that I have been grounded by the doctors, I just wanted you to know that my thoughts and prayers have been with you through this difficult time.

When I think of the enormous service you rendered to the Administration, your loyalty to me personally, and your friendship, my heart really goes out to you in what I know must be a terribly trying time for you.

Fortunately, you are a young man, you're a strong man, and you are a good man, and in the end this will pass and we will all live to fight another day.

God bless you and let's keep in touch.

Sincerely,

[Richard Nixon]

Now I could not suppress my curiosity. I went into the adjacent office, ostensibly to ask the secretary which phone line Morin could use for a call. She appeared flustered, jumped up, and escorted me out of the room, but not before I caught a good look at a large tape recorder on her desk, reel slowly turning, obviously recording something.

Then I remembered that the only other visits I'd had during a weekday had been in this same room. Wally Henley, a local preacher who once served with me in the White House, had visited several times, always in this room. Together we had prayed about a dilemma I'd felt during my first days – if asked by the warden or some other prison official for information about another prisoner, how could I keep from 'ratting' on a fellow inmate and still be truthful? Although other prisoners had been pressured to 'rat', I never had. Was it because they had listened to our prayers?

Our time together was not the relaxed few hours we had hoped for. Seeing men in prison garb and unable to be myself only increased my friends' distress. Being with two good friends and knowing they could walk out unimpeded suddenly made me yearn for my freedom. The awareness that our conversation was probably being recorded further dampened our spirits. Then an idea was dropped in my mind.

Here might be our God-given opportunity to help Howard. To my friends' surprise, I suddenly became charged with righteous indignation: 'This prisoner, Jim Howard, has suffered a nervous breakdown in prison and none of the officials care. It's criminal,' I ranted on. 'Howard will never get out of here until he dies or commits suicide. It's nothing less than manslaughter – criminal negligence. The warden is so concerned with providing slave labour to the Air Force, he doesn't think about individuals. I can't do anything about it now, but I sure will when I get out of here.' Hoping that my words would be heard by the warden, I laid this burden on him as hard as I could. My friends quickly caught on to what

I was doing and played straight men to me.

The next morning while in the laundry, I heard Mr Bleven taking a call to process clothing and linens for a prisoner who was to be transferred immediately. He came out of his office shaking his head and mumbling. 'Can't understand what's going on around here. Must be something funny. They never move anybody this way.'

That afternoon, escorted by two marshals, Jim Howard was taken to the prison hospital in Atlanta. And that evening Paul, Amos, Lee, and I said heartfelt, thankful prayers together.

Patty was staying in Montgomery that week instead of commuting back to Washington. For years wives in the area had attended Brother Blow's services on Tuesday night and Methodist services on Thursday night. Inmates and their wives sat together, but wives left immediately after the service. I'd noticed the care with which each couple observed the rules. No visiting, just time to worship together.

Patty arrived Tuesday night shortly before seven in a torrential downpour, escorted by Brother Blow and his wife. Though the auditorium was cold and damp, the service quickly warmed us. The Southern Baptist preacher was in great form, and it was as exciting for Patty as it had been for me the first night. Word must have reached the authorities about Patty's attendance at the service because the next day I was summoned to the office. 'Wives of prisoners can't come to church here,' the officer on duty told me curtly.

'The men tell me that it has been going on for years,' I answered.

'Something is wrong,' the officer said. 'If wives have been coming to the church services, we'll put a stop to that right now.'

My heart sank. Had Patty and I spoiled it for everyone else?

'Men are here to be punished,' he snapped, slapping his right hand against the back of his left, a gesture which too often summed up the rehabilitative philosophy at Maxwell. 'When prisoners and their wives attend church together during the week, this is visiting,' he concluded.

An inmate who served as the base-chaplain's assistant took the case to the warden. 'You should come hear Brother Blow yourself, Mr Grunska. He is very close to God,' the man pleaded.

'He'd better be – he's going to need God when I get through with him,' Grunska stonily replied.

There were more stormy words. Then came the warden's decision: church services were a privilege not a right. Wives of inmates were an intrusion. I couldn't help but wonder if this overreaction was not related to the Howard matter.

Word quickly spread through the camp that wives had been banned from weekday church services. I was particularly depressed because most knew that it was Patty's attendance which had brought the longstanding practice to an end. The warden's edict struck a sharp blow to morale within the camp. Not that very many men shared worship services with their wives, but the denial of any privilege, no matter how small, was taken seriously. It was a threat to the delicately balanced relationship between the prison population and front office. It was also an omen of worse things to come.

From then on there was increased harassment of our visitors. One weekend Doug Coe and Fred Rhodes flew down from Washington, replacing an exhausted Patty. Fred, who was then the chairman of the US Postal Rate Commission, was stopped by one surly guard who brusquely searched his briefcase, snarling all the while at Fred who kept smiling throughout. The official's rudeness upset us, not the search which uncovered only some allowable food items.

Fred's conclusion was that some of the guards seemed more imprisoned than the inmates themselves. 'Let's pray for them, Chuck.' And we did so right there in the visitors' yard, probably the first time this particular guard had ever been prayed for, unless it was for his transfer to another prison. Later we continued this prayer in our prison fellowship.

Meanwhile Doug in his irrepressible way spent time with almost all the prisoners in the visiting area, encouraging, exhorting, winning friends. Fred singled out Lee Corbin for a quiet talk. Doug and Fred were then joined by Jim Hiskey, who had a ministry to professional golfers throughout the country. The three of them brought the spirit of love into the prison area despite all manner of obstacles. Later that week Lee Corbin sat up all one night making a string model of a sailing vessel, a beautiful piece of work which he sent to Fred Rhodes. Fred, in turn, mailed Lee a Scofield Bible. The chairman of the Postal Rate Commission and an inmate convicted of mail fraud were thus sharing their faith – through the mail.

That evening I wrote Doug: 'I can't tell you how much these visits have meant to me. I often feel like I am on a lonely frontier away from the spiritual home of our fellowship. I know this is the Lord's plan and I accept the mission with joy. But just as I miss my physical home with Patty, I miss my spiritual home with you and the brothers. The Lord is moving here in such a powerful way – and there are few places where His presence is more needed than in this colony of lost souls. There must be such a need in other prisons, too . . .'

Brother Blow had asked me when we first met to talk at one of the Tuesday night meetings. I declined, explaining that I wanted first to become accepted by the men. Events of the past week convinced me that the time had come to try to explain my conversion to my fellow prisoners. I agreed to speak the following Tuesday.

The warden's action barring the wives from prisoner services during the week had the effect of rallying the prisoners behind Brother Blow. Twice the number of inmates plus a large number of parishioners from his church were on hand the following Tuesday for our service, As the hour approached I became increasingly nervous and apprehensive. In describing my White House experiences I would have a hard time relating to these moonshiners and country folk. What could I say that would be helpful?

Brother Blow opened the service with his usual enthusiasm. After hymns, guitar playing by one of the inmates, and a short sermon by Blow, the pulpit was turned over to me.

I began by praying for the Lord to take charge. Then the words began to flow, haltingly at first, as I explained how I had been separated from God by my own pride and ego and imprisoned by my own sins. Now only eighteen months later and a federal prisoner, I was a free man in my spirit.

'Praise the Lord,' shouted Brother Blow and others in the audience. At first I found it awkward to speak through the *Amens* and *Hallelujahs*. Many times I had been heckled and jeered by hostile groups when I was in politics. The memory of an Irish dinner in New York during the 1972 campaign, when I was almost driven off the stage by IRA sympathisers, flashed through my mind. I had tried to outshout the crowd, then had lost my train of thought.

Yet now the more I shouted, the more enthusiastic Blow and his followers became. Then suddenly I found I was no longer being distracted. Instead I was moving right along with the rhythm. The words came out with more feeling and excitement than ever before. Love and joy and power were surging through the room. What began as a quiet testimony almost turned into a revival meeting. Some of the inmates were involved as well. As a windup I said, 'Praise the Lord that I am in prison and have this chance to be a witness for Jesus Christ.'

Brother Blow bounded out of his chair, rushed to the altar, and nearly smothered me in an embrace. His long arm around me, he prayed, then issued an altar call. 'Hallelujah,' he shouted out. 'Come forward or just raise your hand and you will receive right now the salvation of Jesus Christ and the washing of His blood at Calvary.

The final hymn of the night was sung so loudly that I imagined the warden himself might be able to hear us as he sat in the living room of his home several hundred yards beyond the prison entrance. The response from Brother Blow's parishioners who were present was enthusiastic, but I was not sure how the message had been received by the inmates. Had I spoken over their heads? Had I held myself out to be too important? Did they still look at me as one of them? I walked to the back of the room where most of the inmates were now congregated. Lee, Paul, and Amos were standing together, all flashing the biggest warmest smiles I had ever seen on any faces. Their expressions gave me the answer.

During the week that followed, interest in the prison fellowship grew. God had used the testimony. Men were seeking. The tension and anxiety would continue – I knew that – but for all the oppressiveness of prison life, I had felt that movement of God's Spirit among us. More and more I could see how the Lord was guiding my life. Just knowing this was a foundation of assurance for the rough days ahead.

25

Unexpected Gift

With the brisk chill of autumn in the air, Mr Bleven asked me to issue winter clothing to all the prisoners, chiefly surplus dark-brown Army field jackets. As we opened box after box, out fell the most threadbare collection of old rags I'd even seen; the jackets had long frayed strings hanging from the cuffs, elbows punched through, large gaping tears in the fabric. Whatever warmth the garments once contained had been so worn or washed out that there would be little protection against the damp, raw Alabama winter.

As we passed them out to the men, I looked again for the hostile eyes that might reveal my would-be assassin. It was useless. Most of the men were angry – but it was at the poor quality of winter clothing they were receiving.

That wasn't all we had to gripe about. In the warehouse we uncovered crates of surplus, but little-worn, down-filled officers' flight jackets which an enterprising supply officer had rescued from the Air Force dump. But we could not use them; they were a light green colour and prison regulations demanded that all clothing be deep chocolate-brown. Then we began experimenting by loading them two at a time into the washing machines, trying different dark dyes. Success. They came out limp and shrunken replicas of the originals, but a deep brown shade. Snugness was a small price to pay for keeping warm.

Dye was the next problem. It wasn't on the prison supply list and Bleven's petty-cash account was used up. Obtaining dye was all that stood between 250 fluffy warm jackets and 250 half-frozen prisoners. As word spread of the availability of jackets and my eagerness to dye them, inmates began appearing in the laundry room, usually on Monday mornings, carrying small brown boxes. Bleven was sympathetic, turning the other way as one prisoner after another slipped the contraband into my hand. By mid-October, it was a thriving nonprofit business. I was troubled that the dye had to be smuggled in, but getting around idiotic regulations had always stimulated me and helping the men was now my main purpose in life.

In my enthusiasm, I enlisted the service of Woodie, a well-educated, good-looking young man who had been given an eighteen-month sentence for buying and selling stolen cars. Eager to have a flight jacket, Woodie offered to help bring in the contraband.

On a mid-October weekend Patty reluctantly brought six packets of dye from Washington. During visiting hours Patty and I spent time with Woodie and his attractive young wife in the yard. Glancing around to be sure a guard wasn't watching, Woodie took two packets under the table from Patty, stuffing them into his trouser pockets. I felt no pangs of conscience; the more jackets I could get to the inmates, the better off they would be. Smuggling in personal items was a fairly routine practice, though risky. Prisoners caught at it were sometimes transferred; at the least it meant a couple of nights in the hole.

Patty was worried, but Woodie was completely uncon-cerned. He had insisted that he bring the dye in, assuring me that he would never be searched. The guards normally spot-check men going in and out of the visitors' area, usually searching only prisoners with narcotics convictions. At the end of the day Woodie and I left the visitors' area together heading straight for our familiar position overlooking the street to wave good-bye to our wives. Woodie was walking a few steps ahead as we passed the Control Room. All at once two guards stepped forward.

'In here,' one commanded. The other grabbed Woodie's arm and yanked him through the door.

I dared not stop, but slowed my walk long enough to hear one of the guards shout, 'Strip down!'

Was he being shoved into the hole? Had someone seen him take the box from Patty? Had someone 'ratted?' With sinking heart I realised that Woodie was due for a parole hearing next month. 'What have I done?' I muttered to myself, my stomach churning. If my young friend was in deep trouble, I was responsible. He was almost a kid; I was supposedly the mature one. The idea had been stupid and wrong. No matter how silly the rule seemed to me, it represented authority which I had pledged myself to honour.

I returned to the dormitory and sought out Paul, telling him the whole story. By now the dye had been found for sure and Woodie was in the hole. The next day was a Monday holiday; Woodie's wife would arrive at eight, anxious to be with her husband. I couldn't bear it – the look of pain on her sweet face when she found out. Her husband could very well be hauled off this night to the city jail where he would be held for later transfer. That was often done and families would be out of contact for weeks.

'Okay brother, what do I do?' I asked Paul. 'I have to take the responsibility. Should I go to the lieutenant and tell him everything?'

Paul shook his head. 'Spilling the story will only get you transferred and that won't help Woodie. The warden sure won't show any favouritism to you. Smuggling is serious with him. Let's see what's happened to Woodie first.'

Surely Woodie would come to our dormitory if he had been released. The minutes ticked slowly by. No sign of him. Now I was certain of the worst. We sat waiting right through dinner.

Paul volunteered to look in his dorm, just to be certain – and then go to the hole. If a decent guard was on duty, Paul might be allowed to talk with him. I was now resigned to my fate. If Woodie was in the hole, I'd turn myself in. It had to be that way.

Paul, downcast, returned ten minutes later with the dreaded report, 'He is in the hole, but he'd like to see you. They're going to ship him out.'

Those next few moments were agony. Why had I been so stupid as to destroy everything I had tried to build up at Maxwell? I had refused to heed the reminder in my diary that week – a note to myself to resist succumbing to the little temptations of prison life. 'As a Christian I cannot engage in the commonplace things inmates do to make life a little bit more bearable here,' I wrote. 'I must avoid the little bends and twists in the rules, the little lies.'

Looking at those words made me almost physically sick. How could I be so hypocritical as to say one thing to myself and do another? The truth is that to have a chance at a furlough, prisoners lie, enlarge the facts, create emergencies. The prison officials expect it – encourage it, in fact – to build the proper record in the files. Games are played this way in prison as elsewhere, both sides using the same rules.

Sitting there on my bunk, staring bleakly at Paul, a crushing new thought rammed into my consciousness. Did I learn nothing from Watergate? How could I forget that a series of little lies can eventually blur one's capacity to see moral distinctions about big things? Months before at a Monday session at Fellowship House we had concluded that little lies are as corrosive to a man's character as big ones; it is only a question of degree and how long it takes. Now I'd fallen into this trap myself.

I told Paul of my decision and we walked together from the dorm towards the lieutenant's office. All of the worst imaginable thoughts rushed through my mind. Paul was doing his best to console me: 'Maybe they'll give you a second chance, Chuck. Maybe you and Woodie will be shipped to the same joint.'

Halfway across the courtyard we passed in front of Woodie's dormitory. Paul grabbed my arm, an enigmatic look on his face. 'Let's go in here first, Chuck.'

'There's no point in postponing things, Paul. Let's get it over with,' I said grimly.

But Paul was persistent. Finally a big grin spread over his face. 'We'll get Woodie and then the two of you can turn yourselves in together.'

I stood staring, aware that all colour had drained from my face. 'You're kidding.'

'Come on,' he laughed. 'Woodie is taking a nap.'

My friend had made it through the shakedown. The guards were looking for narcotics and paid no attention to the dye he carried. Paul was laughing harder than I'd ever seen him before, pointing at my white face, and doubling over. I was too relieved to be angry, too emotionally drained to speak.

It was a lesson learned. How easy it is to backslide, to succumb unknowingly to temptations of the moment. I was concerned only with helping the other men – or so I thought – but in part it was the old Colson. *Chuck will get it done* was the phrase I so loved to hear in the White House.

Strange are the workings of a prison. When I announced that there would be no more smuggling of dye, Mr Bleven made arrangements to purchase all the dye we needed. In short order all inmates were outfitted with warm jackets.

The easy way I had slid into my old pattern of behaviour with the dye operation shook me deeply. How had it happened? I was part of a fellowship, praying together with Christians. Ordinarily one of the group should have checked me: 'Chuck, about this dye business. Is it really honest – what you are doing? I know it's for a good cause, but does one right and one wrong equal right?' The question would have stopped me cold. It was

Watergate all over again. The end justified the means. What a trap that philosophy can be!

There has to be another way to accomplish good besides slipping into grey morality. What does Christ suggest for this special power? In all my intense study of His life over the past fifteen months, He had given me the answer. Yet it was elusive. I went searching through my Bible again. There it was in the first chapter of Acts. Jesus said to his disciples, 'But when the Holy Spirit has come upon you, you will receive power . . .' (Acts 1:8 LB).

I had studied the Trinity, learned to understand how the Father, the Son, and the Holy Spirit are different, yet the same. I had asked for the Holy Spirit to guide and strengthen me. But it suddenly occurred to me that I had not asked the Holy Spirit to fill me with power.

And then came one of those marvellous demonstrations of God's timing. That very Monday night Martin Gay announced that the next lesson would be on the power of the Holy Spirit. 'It is possible,' the soft-spoken teacher explained, 'to ask in prayer for God to fill us with the Holy Spirit. It works,' he said. 'We merely have to turn ourselves over to Him.'

During the days before the next lesson I reviewed everything I knew about the Holy Spirit, starting with the Book of Acts. The disciples, I saw, had all been rather ineffective people until the Upper Room experience. Then there was this mighty wind and tongues of fire – and the disciples were filled with the Holy Spirit. Timid men suddenly became bold. Courage replaced fear. They had been given power to establish Christ's church.

Yet in the centuries that followed, the term Holy Ghost frightened more people than it helped, while the more acceptable words *Holy Spirit* became just a theological utterance in most churches. Then in recent years the charismatic (Holy Spirit) movement had burst upon our world, rocking churches, changing worship forms, making the term *pentecostal* more respectable. Once again Spirit-filled people were finding a new power and boldness to claim God's audacious promises. I had seen some of the gifts of the Spirit in operation, but I knew little about them. Lee Corbin had prayed in tongues and I had sensed power coming into his life. But there was so much I didn't know about the Spirit.

The following Monday night Martin Gay did not intellectualise about the subject. 'Ask for it,' he said, 'and the Holy Spirit can take total control of your life. He will take charge if you open yourselves and *seek* – like a personal relationship with Christ, but something far deeper than the mere acknowledgement of God.'

I bowed my head while Gay was fending off questions being tossed at him by two doubting and inquisitive men at the far end of the long table. 'Father,' I asked silently, 'please fill me with Your Spirit. Fill me so full there's room for nothing else, no hatred, no hurt, no bitterness, no exhaustion. Lift me above it all, Father . . .'

And there sitting on a bench in a bare classroom filled with people who were wrangling over theological terms, the most curious effervescent sensation rushed through my body. It was like the cleansing I had experienced in the Phillipses' driveway. It was persistent and I kept praying. If Gay had called on me to speak, I would have never heard him. Then the bubbling sensation turned into a tingling from head to foot, like fever chills but pleasant, comforting, and energising. Joy and new strength were welling up within me.

I kept my head down until Paul, sitting next to me, nudged me with his elbows. 'You asleep?' he whispered.

'If I am, you ought to try it.' I looked up to see Paul, his index finger up to his pursed lips. I realised I was speaking too loudly. Gay was peering at us through his thick glasses.

'Brother Gay, this is some lesson tonight,' I exclaimed, but said no more. The others around the table were still grappling and I must not frighten them off.

I'd often wondered how a person really knew when he was filled with the Spirit. There is no light which goes on or off like the warning light on a dashboard when seat belts are not fastened. This day I had no more doubts. As I wrote in the diary the next morning, 'It was almost like a conversion again – the black cloud passed; it was an incredible experience to have my spirit washed clean.'

I've heard of people who have experienced this power and were transformed overnight. An alcoholic completely loses his craving for alcohol; a drug addict is so changed and freed from bondage that he does not even go through a withdrawal period. I believe the power of the Holy Spirit can work dramatically this way in us. More often, I surmise, the Spirit resides in us as a great source of new power, but He serves more as a Helper while we develop our own spiritual disciplines.

From the moment of this infilling, I felt a new sharpness in my awareness of life about me. I felt more understanding for prison officials, more love for fellow inmates.

I did ask the Lord to tell me if I could forget the threat on my life, or to show me who it was. This had hung over me too long now. I still found myself face watching at odd moments. Now I brought Him into it directly – 'This one, Lord?' as I saw a glowering face across the table at breakfast. Or – 'He, Lord?' as I passed a prisoner in the yard who did not return my greeting.

Once I had awakened suddenly in the night, then bolted upright in my bunk, convinced danger was near. For long moments I sat there, heart pounding. All I saw were sleeping forms, snoring, coughing, muttering in their dreams.

At first I thought he was one of the blacks. As a group they had been deeply hostile to Nixon's policies. In prison the blacks usually kept to themselves. Some were quiet and sullen. But as time passed many became friends.

Several times I questioned Jerry to see if by chance he could have been playing a game with me. Each time he firmly repeated his story and just as firmly refused to reveal the one who threatened to kill me.

A few days after my experience in class, I was walking in the compound on my way to the dormitory. Ahead of me were two men walking side by side. One was a handsome black-haired young man who always wore dark sunglasses; the other was perhaps in his mid-forties, a muscular individual whose head squatted bull-like on his broad shoulders. They had bronzed complexions with dark piercing eyes, probably of Eastern European origin. The two – both ex-policemen I was told – were always together, always unsmiling. As I approached their backs, the inner voice seemed to say – 'Now, Chuck.'

I quickened my pace until I was alongside, and heard these words come from my lips: 'Did you want to talk to me?'

The older, heavyset man wheeled around, his face reddened, squinting eyes smouldering.

'I've been wanting to talk to you,' I said.

He stared speechless for a moment, but the scowl deepened. The tall, younger man turned to him and said, 'Go ahead and find out now. Ask him.'

The older man kept staring at me. Then in a deep, gruff voice he asked, 'Do you know what happened to me?'

'Maybe,' I replied. 'You're a busted cop, right?'

'No, a busted Chicago police lieutenant. And busted because of you politicians in Washington. Framed and hung by your lousy White House, that's what.'

'And you blame me?' I asked.

'Does that surprise you? You were the guy who ordered the Chicago investigation. It's true, isn't it?' His voice rose in anger at the bitter memories.

'Look, Lieutenant,' I spoke calmly, 'I know all about the Mayor Daley investigation. I know who started it. It wasn't the White House; it was the Justice Department. If there were political reasons, they didn't come from me. I had nothing to do with it. That's the truth; you can believe it or not.'

As I stared into his tense, angry face, I felt certain at long last that this was the man Jerry had overheard. 'And by the way,' I added, 'I know what it's like to be a political target. Believe me, I know how you feel.' The words came out with deep emotion.

'I guess you do. Yeah, I guess you do.' His voice was softening, but his eyes still bored into mine.

We swapped tales of the agonies of our prosecutions. His story was of evidence stacked against him, how others had lied and implicated him, how he could have gotten off by laying it on higher-ups, but had refused. I told him about the prosecutors, the angry, bitter questioning, the squeeze put on my staff, how I could have turned on Nixon but did not.

'I think you're levelling with me,' he said finally. And his steel grip as we shook hands told me that we were no longer enemies. How serious his threat had been I'll probably never know. But thanks to the work of the Holy Spirit, I had been able to seek out my oppressor and turn hostility into understanding.

26

Spiritual Warfare

The gentle white-haired mountaineer, Homer Welsh fell ill during the third week of October. The flu, we thought. For several days he was excused from work and lay in his bunk hour after hour. Homer had begun attending our evening prayer sessions, and after the fever struck we would adjourn early and pray with him at his bunk just before lights out. Paul brought him food which he rarely ate and cold drinks which he craved for a parched throat.

When Homer did not improve he was taken to the base hospital for tests and then to the tiny, bare two-bedded room just off the infirmary. There Welsh remained while his 103-degree fever stubbornly defied massive doses of antibiotics.

When the lab reports came back, one of the inmates in the infirmary whispered to us the discouraging news – a spot on Welsh's lung, pneumonia at best, and not a good sign for a man who'd spent much of his life in soot-filled mines. There was blood in his urine and his white corpuscle count was high. It was a grim prognosis.

During this same week in rapid succession began a series of setbacks, accidents, and outbursts of violence. It was devastating, bewildering, and brought me face-to-face with the unseen enemy. In my pre-Christian years any talk in my circles of the devil or Satan as an entity had been in a jocular vein. I reasoned that the evil men did was a part of man's nature. Even after my acceptance of Jesus as a Person and later awareness that His Spirit was with us today, I still viewed demonology as something akin to black magic.

My thinking changed in prison. I soon discovered that there was no clear distinction between good and evil men. Many who had a sense of decency and goodness in them had committed gross sins while in the grip of some kind of evil power. I no longer could accept the idea that some men simply had an evil nature. All men are sinners, Scripture taught me, struggling between the two forces: God and Satan, good and evil. It doesn't matter whether we imagine Satan as a man dressed in a red suit brandishing a pitchfork, or whether we think of him as an invisible force. Whatever you call him (or it), there is an evil power which works in the world touching the lives of men.

Doug Coe once explained that Satan doesn't waste his time on those unbelievers who follow the world's ways; in time they drift into his fold without much persuasion. But those who choose Jesus Christ are Satan's chief enemy and the real threat to his rule. Like any good battlefield commander, the devil saves his best firepower for his foes' best divisions. Thus have history's most stalwart believers been tested, tried, and forced to withstand Satan's fiercest onslaughts.

Obviously Satan had claimed Maxwell as his territory long ago and wasn't about to surrender it easily. He had not worried about a few religious services every now and then, but the changing of men's hearts was something to take seriously. As for inviting the Holy Spirit into Maxwell, and then bringing men together to pray for each other and for the prison officials – well, that called for an all-out counter-attack.

A small incident, hardly more than a college-type prank, opened the lid. Two inmates slipped out of their dorms one evening, found a can of yellow paint in one of the worksheds behind the compound, and went to work. Insulting epithets aimed at the warden were scrawled on the walls of buildings and on the side of the rickety prison bus. Early the next morning a tight-lipped warden was on the scene surveying the vandals' work. Barely able to contain his anger, he marched with long determined strides back to his office. Within an hour, over the loudspeaker came the first official reaction: 'From now on, all areas behind the dormitories and all grassed areas beyond the roadway are out-of-bounds after dark. This curfew will remain in effect until further notice.'

Despite an extensive investigation, the warden never found the inmates responsible. There is seldom any real détente between prisoners and officials. What passes as tranquillity is usually only an uneasy absence of confrontation. The pent-up anger which smoulders inside every prison now began to heat up fast.

That night two prisoners in another dorm started an argument over something trivial. Soon fists were flying, one man throwing the other across several bunks. No one broke it up until the guards arrived. Both men were taken to the hospital where a gash over the younger man's right eye required extensive stitches. Then they were tossed into the hole. The next day prison justice was administered. Who started the fight didn't seem to matter. There were no hearings, no appeals, no second chances. Both men were led out in chains and handed over that afternoon to US Marshals for delivery to other prisons.

Patty had met the young wife of one of these men. She discovered later that he was not allowed to call her, even though she was right there in Montgomery. It would be weeks before the young girl found her husband. Such is the way the PC (Prisoner Coordination) system operates for moving prisoners. The PC system sounds reasonable enough, but in fact is one of the harshest forms of punishment.

When a prisoner is to be moved, local officers notify

Washington where, in the headquarters of the US Marshal Service, the information is fed into a computer. Data about the movement of all marshals is similarly recorded in this computer. In machine fashion, prisoners and marshals are brought together. It may be economical and work fine in theory, but in fact prisoners are moved about like pieces of luggage, often 'lost' in local jails for weeks at a time waiting to be picked up by a marshal.

These temporary and unnecessary delays in open cement cells jammed full of violent criminals result in some devastating experiences for young or inexperienced prisoners. The Fulton County Jail in Georgia is a favourite dumping ground for men from Maxwell. There in the overcrowded hundred-year-old institution, broiling hot in the summer, icy cold in winter, sixteen men have sometimes been locked in one open twenty-foot-square cell for days. There is only one toilet, one wash-basin, no windows, and four tiers of wooden slabs for beds. The inmates may be drunken vagrants, murderers awaiting trial, or federal prisoners in transit. I met men who after a few days in such holes were in severe shock. Some had spent months in transit in the PC system subjected to indescribable horrors. Permanent scars are hard to avoid.

Several nights later, while we were still discussing ways to try and help the wives of the transferred prisoners, the loud-speaker blared: 'Return to your dormitories, count time.' Then the shrill whistle. Ten minutes went by, usually enough to complete the tally. Sensing something out of the ordinary, we gathered at the door and peered into the compound. In the yard the guards were frantically running back and forth shouting to the Control Room now ablaze with lights. A prisoner had gone over the fence.

We soon discovered that the missing inmate was a gaunt, silent black who had come from fifteen months in maximum-security prisons. Though he had but a few months to serve, something snapped. He could not take another day of confinement. When recaptured days later, years were added to his sentence.

Early that week Doc Krenshaw was scheduled for release. The day before his freedom he discovered that the necessary paperwork had not been completed. Standing before a prison official's desk, Doc flew into a screaming rage. 'I almost hit him, Chuck – I was almost out of control,' he told me that night. So overwhelming are the pressures during the last days of confinement that even someone as even tempered as Doc nearly snapped.

Tensions continued to mount, fed to a great extent by a prisoner named Knight, who had been given a one-year sentence for passing bad cheques. A bright, scrappy rebel, Knight set up his 'office' in the Maxwell library shortly after his arrival. Soon he was producing for himself and a dozen other inmates an array of writs to be filed in court. I watched him each night as he methodically prepared for the assault, counselling with other aggrieved prisoners, carefully studying the tattered legal-form book in the library, pecking away at an old typewriter, amassing logical challenges to the prison's furlough policy, its inadequate medical facilities, the parole process, the whole range of things governing a prisoner's life.

Knight took a perverse delight in antagonising the warden. During that same hectic week he typed out daily announcements describing the writs filed, the reactions of the camp administrators, and their repressive countermeasures. Each night he posted copies on the bulletin boards at the entrance of each dormitory. The guards would then sweep through the camp tearing them off the walls.

One day the warden himself came through each dorm. I watched him angrily fling open the glass door covering the bulletin board, snatch the paper off the wall, crumple it in his hands, slam the door shut, almost breaking the glass, and storm off. An inspection of all typewriters in the camp was ordered to locate the machine used. New regulations were then

published – typewriters could no longer be used for other than
official business.

Even honest efforts to communicate seemed ill-fated. I was
following a tall prisoner through the mess hall line one day.
Warden Grunska was behind the serving counter inspecting a
large pan of stew. When the man in front of me was across
from the warden, Grunska looked up. Their eyes met. 'How's
it going fella?' Grunska asked cheerily.

The man was so taken aback – he had probably never had
the chance to speak to the warden before – that he stammered
for a moment, then told the warden that the TV in his
dormitory had been broken for a week. 'Any chance of getting
it fixed?' he asked timidly.

The warden's smile vanished. 'As soon as people around here
start behaving themselves,' he snapped. With that he turned
and marched away leaving the young lad staring in bewilderment.

One prisoner thrown in the hole that week was a middle-
aged Texan by the name of Rodriguez. From the day he arrived
at Maxwell it was obvious that he was an alcoholic who needed
psychiatric and medical help. At night he would sit on his
bunk chain-smoking and shaking uncontrollably; then he
would pace nervously about the compound. Already he had
had two seizures.

Early that demoralising week Rodriguez passed out on
the dormitory floor. An ambulance was summoned from the
base hospital, and the two corpsmen carried him away on a
stretcher. He was placed under heavy sedation and returned
the next day to the prison. The next morning Rodriguez
became embroiled in an argument in the mess hall with a
huge fellow inmate who smashed Rodriguez across the side of
his head with his fist, knocking him to the floor. The incident
was reported to the Control Room and two guards carted
Rodriguez off to the hole. Nothing was done to his assailant
who was a favourite of the front office.

Rodriguez spent that day in the hole, most of the time crying in pain, peering out through the small steel mesh-covered opening in the door, calling for a doctor. No one paid any attention to his cries. Late that afternoon, a marshal's van was pulled up outside. Two muscular guards opened the door to Rodriguez's cell and handcuffed him. 'Where am I going?' he cried. Prisoners who are being removed for disciplinary reasons are generally not told, but one of the guards answered, 'The Montgomery city jail.'

'Oh, no,' Rodriguez was pleading. 'Get me a doctor. Can't you see my ear is bleeding?' A stream of deep red was running from inside his ear, over his earlobe and down his neck, soaking his torn collar.

The two guards looked at Rodriguez's ear, looked at one another, then shrugged. One snapped, 'There is no doctor on duty and we have orders to move you right now. The van is here. We can't keep the marshal waiting.' I was standing nearby and watched helplessly while the two men dragged the struggling prisoner to the door. Rodriguez turned to me with a frightened expression on his face and shouted, 'You see I'm bleeding, don't you, Colson?'

'Yes, I do,' I responded firmly. 'You need a doctor.'

Both guards stopped dead in their tracks, turned and stared at me. For a moment I thought they were going to bring Rodriguez back and take him down the hall to the infirmary. It was only a momentary pause. The two blue-shirted men put their hands under Rodriguez's armpits, lifted his feet off the floor and carried him to the waiting van. There was nothing left now but a few blood stains on the tile floor. I felt nauseous, helpless. Nor was I ever able to learn what happened to this pathetic man.

Late that same tumultuous week Paul found me in the laundry. His eyes were filled with hurt and saying not a word he thrust a small piece of paper into my hands. It was a short terse notice from the regional director of the Parole Board:

'There are no circumstances warranting a decision outside the "guidelines" established for your offence . . . continue to expiration. Parole denied.' That single sheet of paper went against the ruling given Paul only a few weeks ago and doomed him to another two years in prison.

Remembering how our prayers for Paul and Ferguson had been so miraculously answered, the thought flashed through both our minds: *Could God have now abandoned Paul? Could He revoke His own work?* Hardly. We were being tested.

'Don't worry, Paul. We'll appeal it and beat them,' I said. 'By now I'm the best jailhouse lawyer around.' Paul could not even manage a smile at my forced humour. The challenge to us was clear – with God's help, fight for Paul's freedom.

Next it was Lee Corbin. One night that week while in the library I saw him approach, ashen-faced, lips quivering, 'What's the matter, Lee?' I asked.

'Chuck, I've got to see you right away. I need help.' We walked into the darkness just outside the library door. 'Chuck, it's my wife. She wants to leave me. I don't know what to do.'

The big, burly ex-Marine was trembling all over, his shoulders heaving as he fought back the tears. It was painful as he slowly explained it all. When arrested he sold his big home in Atlanta and moved his wife and two small children back to a small town near Asheville, North Carolina, to be close to his relatives. Lee's wife took a job nights in a textile plant, making just enough to feed their children and keep up the payments on the trailer which Lee had purchased with his last dollars before entering prison. At first she wrote faithfully, then less frequently until the letters stopped altogether. She had not been able to visit him in prison because their old car had broken down. She had no phone. Worried, Lee had telephoned his brother-in-law who lived a few miles away. That's when he learned the bad news.

'I guess I deserve it,' he sobbed. 'It's not her fault. Her brother says she still loves me, and I love her so much. She is on her way to her parents' house now. I've got to get there or I will lose her. She and the little ones are all I have left in the world; they need me. If only I can get home, I can save my marriage.'

Surely the prison officials would recognise this situation as a bona fide *emergency,* I thought. In the regulations one of the stated reasons for furloughs is 'to maintain family ties'.

But when Lee asked the officer on duty for an emergency furlough, it was denied. 'If there's been a serious accident or someone is critically ill and the doctor calls, then I can phone the warden,' the lieutenant said tersely. 'Otherwise, I have no authority.'

Lee, sobered by the rebuff, turned to me, 'I'm going to leave tonight. I'm going over the fence. You shouldn't know anything about it because I don't want to get you into trouble. But I have to do it.'

Corbin was calm, his words measured and cold as steel. He had been in prison since early spring with not one disciplinary mark. Only a few months remained on his sentence. He knew the consequences of trying to escape, but at the moment nothing mattered beyond being with his family. Lee was big and tough; I couldn't hold him if I wanted to.

I said the only thing that might stop him: 'Lee, unless you give me your oath to God that you will not do that, I'm going back to the lieutenant and tell him exactly what you said. I'll have him put you in the hole tonight. I'm not going to let you ruin your life.'

Lee knew I meant it. 'Maybe we'd better do just that,' he said, 'I can't control myself. I gotta go in the hole.'

As Lee calmed down, I explained that if he turned himself in this way, he would lose any chance for furlough and would probably be transferred into a maximum-security prison. Just talking about it brought Corbin to his senses. We prayed together quietly for a few minutes; Lee then left to try to reach his wife on the phone.

Later Lee reported back that he had talked with his wife and asked her to pray with him over the phone. 'She told me to cut out all the religious stuff,' Lee said, 'but I had a feeling that the Lord was really working on her. She says she still loves me and won't do anything foolish until I can come home, if I can come soon.' The pressure was eased temporarily, although Lee's painful anxiety was to continue.

That night I was in the office when I saw a young man with pock-marked face and sunken cheeks approach Peyton, the official on duty. 'My brother has died. I got to get home for the funeral.' The young man's grief-filled eyes were pleading for help.

'What do you expect me to do?' Peyton growled. 'Go fill out the forms and bring them to me. I can't do anything without a proper written request. You should know that.'

There was no 'I'm sorry,' not even a sympathetic expression. As the young prisoner walked dejectedly away, Peyton shouted after him, 'And do it right the first time. There's nothing that annoys me more than having to do those forms over again.' Peyton's lanky frame was draped over the chair, his legs stretched out, his head shaking in disgust that the young man had been so inconsiderate of him.

I bit my tongue and turned away in anger. I couldn't look at Peyton. Christ said to love your oppressor, but I could only feel utter contempt for this guard and his arrogance – for the whole camp, in fact – for the whole ugly week that had just passed.

I wanted to shut it all out of my mind: the disease-ridden body of Welsh as he was taken to the hospital, the bloody, senseless fight which further messed up the lives of two prisoners and their families, the pathetic man who had gone over the fence, the callous treatment of Rodriguez, the hurt in Paul's eyes when parole was denied, the look of pain and anguish on Corbin's face when he feared he had lost his wife. Now the sickening exchange between Peyton and the young prisoner put the cap on this miserable, depressing week.

Thank God for my experience with the Holy Spirit the week before. Beset from all sides, I called upon the power of His Spirit to keep me from doing something foolish – to help me stand firm, to be an encourager to the others. Our foursome continued to meet each night in the classroom. At least they had not closed this off to us. We accepted the fact that prison is friendly terrain for Satan's warriors. As God is Love, so Satan is hate. Hate, hence Satan, abounds in every prison like a mildew-bred fungus, its spores nurtured by suspicion, jealousy, anger, depression. Hate was mushrooming at Maxwell during this terrible week, threatening to engulf all of us. We prayed that the sunshine of our faith would blot out this ugly spongy growth.

Our prayers were answered. It began with Paul. For a while he had been so dejected by the adverse parole ruling that he could do little but wallow in silence and self-pity. Late in the week he broke through the cloud over him. 'Chuck, I know this is a testing time for me and I'm not going to allow it to shake my faith.'

Something began to sing in me. Too many believe that merely by accepting Christ, they will henceforth be delivered from all hazards and dangers in life, that He will produce all good things from par golf scores to freedom from prison. The disappointments and defeats which inevitably come only make us even more vulnerable than before to Satan's attacks. Paul was learning to tough it out with the Lord. Once more in his quiet way he imparted strength to others, seeking out men in need. The following week he brought to the Lord one young man who was going through a period of great anxiety.

Lee Corbin then began to feel God's love working in him. He decided he could not leave prison with any resentment towards his wife. All he wanted when he was released was for them to be able to share together their love and their faith. Lee's whole demeanor changed. His smile became more radiant. Other inmates began to seek him out for help. During church services the next Tuesday he gave an eloquent spontaneous talk, admitting with a refreshing candour that he had once been a 'phoney preacher'. He had fallen but was now working his way back. That the prison continued to deny his furlough request did nothing to dim God's Spirit in him.

A standard battlefield tactic I learned in Marine basic training is to cut off your enemy from his main line of supply. Satan had done just that for a while; for days we were so preoccupied with all that was going wrong that we failed to use the power of the Spirit to check the assaults. Once we did, the clouds parted and the sun shone through. The bonds of the fellowship tightened. The power surged back.

Homer Welsh was showing no improvement. He was still lying in one of the infirmary hospital beds, his spirit slowly sinking, his fever uncontrolled. Paul and I took turns sitting with him, bringing him pitchers of cold drinks we'd purchased at the commissary. Homer would force a smile during our visits, but his pathetic fear-filled eyes stabbed us.

The first Saturday of November we knew Homer's condition was grave. Amos, the pharmacist, pointed out that a severe fever over a ten-day period could permanently damage an older man. He was not responding to antibiotics; a red rash had broken out all over his body. The chances of his getting decent medical care were slim. It could be another week before he would be transferred to the base hospital.

'Do each of you guys believe in Christ's power to heal?' I asked my three sombre-faced brothers.

Lee was the first to reply, 'I sure do.'

Paul thought for a moment and then nodded. Amos was more sceptical. 'I'm not sure about this faith-healing business, but I gotta admit that nothing else is working.'

I then described an earlier experience with Harold Hughes when, through all-out prayer and a total relinquishment of his ailment to the Lord, he was spared a serious operation. 'But,' I warned, 'each one of us must believe. If any of us has any doubts that Homer can be healed, let's speak them now. We must be as one in our hearts, agreeing totally that Jesus heals today, just as He did two thousand years ago.'

While I believed every word I was saying, inside I was just as frightened as my brothers. It is one thing to know the truth in abstract terms; it's something else again to trust, to be bold about it. There is always the fear of failure and embarrassment in the eyes of others. This time I decided I would rather be a fool if need be, than not try anything for the kindly white-haired man lying so helplessly in pools of his own sweat.

We decided to think it over for the next few hours. If there were reservations, the doubters would not participate. Otherwise, we agreed to meet in Welsh's room to pray for his healing at nine o'clock that night. I checked for a late report with one of the prison attendants who seemed to know his business. 'There has been no break in his fever and the tests overall were very negative. Don't tell him this, but the doctor at the base is concerned. Possible complications. Maybe a malignancy somewhere. They are talking about clemency – so he can go home to die.'

At nine o'clock the four of us gathered in Welsh's room. No dropouts. Homer was happy to see us, but so totally exhausted he would doze off even as we talked to him. We told him that we wanted to put complete faith in Christ's power to heal and that if he would do the same and pray with us, we believed in the depths of our hearts that he would be made well. Homer didn't need to be apprised of the medical reports; he knew that he was a desperately sick man. He looked first into my eyes, then around the bed at each of the brothers. No one spoke. Then he nodded and mumbled a faint 'Thank you.'

The four of us knelt beside the bed. Homer turned his body towards us and buried his face in his hands. Each of us prayed aloud. Corbin began – in the name of Jesus commanding Satan to come out of Homer's body. Then he asked for the power of the Holy Spirit to fill Homer and continued his prayer in tongues. I felt the Spirit flood into the room, as Corbin's chant gained in intensity and emotion.

'Lord,' I prayed, 'I thank You in advance for this healing.' Then I went on to claim the victory.

Paul, who always prayed in a hushed and subdued voice, boldly proclaimed that night his complete faith in the power of Jesus Christ to heal men's bodies just as He had healed our hearts. Amos thanked God for the miracle of the moment and dropped his head to the floor in total submission.

It would have been an incongruous sight had anyone walked in on us that evening – the former White House hatchet man on his knees beside an old coal miner from the hills of Tennessee; Corbin, a great hulking ex-con man crying out to Jesus and uttering thoroughly unintelligible sounds; Kramer, the young ex-cocaine peddler, in total submission, praising God – all three of us former tough, pragmatic Marines. Finally Amos, in his own quiet way radiating kindness, the humble but scientific-minded pharmacist.

We prayed for more than a half-hour. As we finished, I felt the same surge of joy I first experienced in the Bible study a week before. As if some force was lifting me to my feet, I bounded up and shouted, 'Hallelujah!' I had never done that before either, usually being pensive after prayer.

Corbin jumped to his feet grinning. Then he leaned over the bed and grabbed the startled wide-eyed mountaineer in his arms. For a moment I thought he might pull Homer right out of bed. Corbin kept hugging him, indifferent to Homer's soaking-wet body. We all stood there smiling as at a victory celebration. None of us doubted that a healing was under way.

The next morning I was up early to check our patient. Not wanting to wake Homer if he was sleeping. I quietly opened the door to the little room just a crack and peered in. Homer was sitting up in bed wide-awake. He looked towards the door, spotted me and shouted, 'Praise the Lord. I love you guys. I love you brothers.'

I stood in the door stunned. Even when he was well, Welsh was shy and reserved, usually talking in such a low voice that I had to strain to hear him. Now his voice was strong, firm, ringing through the room. He seemed totally changed, not only physically but in his personality as well. To my relief he no longer called me *sir*. Though still pale and drawn, a giant smile covered his face.

'The fever's gone,' he shouted. 'It's gone. It left me right after you fellows did last night. I slept like a baby for the first time in a week. I'm ready to get out of bed right now. The Lord has healed me.'

I was so excited I ran back to the dormitory, waking the others. They dressed and followed me back to Homer's room. My feet were hardly touching the ground as I found myself praising God for putting me in this prison. 'This place needs Your man, Lord, more than it needs a doctor. Thank You for letting me be here. Thank You, thank You. This moment is worth it all.'

That evening we visited and prayed again with Homer who was sitting up in bed beaming at us. On Tuesday he was examined at the base hospital. All of the tests – blood, urine, and X-rays – were negative, and the next day he was discharged and returned to the dormitory. 'We'll let Squibb and the doctors take all the credit,' Lee laughed, 'but we know better.'

That day I noticed the change in the prison. The angry, oppressive atmosphere was gone. The mood was more relaxed, less tense. Voices had lowered. Even the most melancholy of the men seemed brighter, more alive. The unseen battle between the strongest forces in the world was over – for now.

27

A Time to Be Free

My transfer back to Holabird Prison in Baltimore came unexpectedly in mid-November. Once again I was to be a
witness, this time in the Watergate trial of Bob Haldeman,
John Ehrlichman, and John Mitchell.

I left Maxwell with strangely mixed feelings, hating the place
but loving so many of the people. Saying good-bye to Paul,
Lee, Amos, Homer, and the others was a deeply emotional
time. Like the four at Fellowship House, these men were now
my Christian Brothers; even in a few months close ties had
been woven. We had been through a lot together; we cared
about each other.

Homer Welsh walked with me to the Control Room. Gone
was the obsequious deference he had always shown me. 'I'll be
praying for you, Chuck,' he said smiling.

'I'll need it more than ever the next few months,' I said –
more a prophet than I realised.

Homer stood by the driveway as I walked towards the
marshal's car. I looked back once to wave and saw the old
man's eyes glistening in the late autumn sun.

At Holabird there was little change. Some old faces gone, a
few new ones. Herb Kalmbach and John Dean greeted me

warmly. Jeb Magruder wasn't sure how to take me. The hostility that had once put us in opposing camps had abated somewhat, but there was a healing needed in our relationship.

My testimony at the Watergate trial in Washington was heatedly assailed – first by the prosecution, then by the defence. Though called as a defence witness, it was Mitchell's counsel who subjected me to the most searing cross-examination. The simple truth as I saw it did not fit either side's strategy for the case.

Mary McGory scorched me in her column, unable to comprehend that I now saw my only loyalty not to the prosecutors in whose chains I was held, not to men I once served, but to the truth. Some wrote that I unexpectedly turned on my former colleagues; others suggested that I helped Ehrlichman. Most were simply confused and baffled as they searched my motives. It mattered little. The prosecutors played miles of Presidential tapes to the endless delight of the jury and spectators. The defendants tried to rebut their own often inaudible words. The outcome was predictable: my one-time cohorts were being marched towards judgement as surely as members of the French aristocracy were made to kneel before the blade two hundred years earlier.

When the verdict of guilty was announced on New Year's Day, Dean bounded into my room, rubbing his hands. 'I've been vindicated.'

I stared silently at John. There could be no victories now, I felt, for anyone involved in Watergate; reporters might win prizes, a number of us would write books after prison, unknown politicians would be vaulted into the nation's spotlight as others fell in disgrace, but at what price? It was time for lessons to be learned, all right, but how I ached for my country to move on and for wounded men to rebuild their lives.

Though John Dean and I were not allies in the combat of the trial, we became close, spending long evenings talking, planning our futures, discussing the Bible sometimes, exchanging ideas about the books each of us planned. I valued John's keen intellect. Watergate matured him, changed his values, brought to him a stronger core of integrity than I had seen before Watergate broke over us both.

Herb Kalmbach and I had become warm friends. I marvelled at how Herb, at first unsure of himself and sometimes despondent, had steadily gained strength through the long ordeal.

Watergate had toughened Jeb Magruder, too. He had accepted Christ through the help of a covenant group at Washington's National Presbyterian Church and its indefatigable pastor, Louis Evans, Jr, who had visited him weekly. Sometimes Jeb and I would pray together.

Other wounds were being bound up, too. Senator Lowell Weicker began an independent investigation of CIA abuses. Through the marshals he asked if I would cooperate through a series of interviews. It was only a few months before that we had nearly come to blows. But that was behind us now. Believing that his investigation was needed, I agreed to help. During the hours we spent together, the old antagonisms dissolved and I saw a different side to the senator: painstaking conscientiousness over his responsibilities and a deep concern for the country.

Al, Graham, Doug, and Harold trekked to Baltimore as often as the marshals would allow the visits. Near the year's end, they came every Saturday morning. After three hours of fellowship and prayer, the four would file through the chain link gate, climb into the same blue Buick which had delivered me to the marshals six months earlier, and drive away. It was harder for them in some ways than for me, having to leave one of their own standing behind the gate, peering through the mesh and waving good-bye.

The prosecutors decided to keep the four fallen Nixon men at Holabird for as long as the trial continued. I was happy about this. I hadn't realised how fatiguing the months at

Maxwell had been, never sleeping in the daytime, sitting up late to talk to needy men. I slept twelve hours a night at Holabird until I reminded myself of Bonhoeffer's warning and put myself back on a more disciplined routine.

It was a break for Patty, too, a respite from the rigours of travelling to Alabama. And my mother, now alone, was able to visit. She did so frequently. Despite her age and poor health, she drove alone from Boston and spent long hours with several prisoners, her lively wit cheering us all.

Despite the somewhat easier living conditions at Holabird, however, I missed the brothers in Alabama. I could barely read Paul Kramer's first letter without choking up:

> Chuck, everyone asks when you are coming back . . . Our group has grown, in size and in spirit . . . Chuck, I want you to know we pray for you each night at fellowship. We still see you sitting there with us, shorts, T-shirt, and pipe . . . We are close these days also. Our group has been so personal. Just like you wanted it to be. We carry each other's burdens . . . We love and miss you more than you realise. God bless you, Chuck and Patty.
>
> Paul et al . . .

On Christmas Eve my heart was so heavy for the men at Maxwell in their lonely outpost that I spent much of the evening writing Paul and the others. Since we had been denied permission to attend midnight services at a local church in Baltimore, the four Watergate prisoners assembled in Dean's room. Jeb and I read aloud from the Scriptures about the birth of Christ. We prayed quietly for each other and our families and in the silence I asked an extra blessing for the men at Maxwell.

It was while the jury was still out in the Watergate trial after Christmas that serious rumours began trickling out about our imminent release. As is standard practice the four of us had filed motions asking for reduction of sentence; normally they are routinely rejected. But the judges had not yet acted on them. They were waiting for something, we knew, perhaps the trial's end. Our hopes grew as the speculation became epidemic.

Jeb and I became the activists, suggesting that we petition the Justice Department, flood President Ford with letters, file new motions with the judges. Dean, too, was mapping his campaign. Kalmbach was the first of us eligible for parole, but his application had been ensnarled in red tape. He had the most legitimate reason to be impatient. Instead he was the steadiest of the four.

'Look, fellows,' Herb said one evening, just after New Year, 'I've done what I can do; my lawyers are doing everything. I'm just going to trust the lawyers' – he paused, staring at me – 'and the Lord.'

Herb was right; his words were like dashing cold water on my face. I had slipped back into trying to do things *my* way. How easy it is to fall on your face in the Christian walk. Harold had brought me up short on this very point in December. 'Look, Chuck, until you surrender this to the Lord, really put your whole trust in Him, you are simply punishing yourself. Just thank Him for everything. Turn it all over to Him, trust Him and you'll be set free.'

'Sure,' I snapped back. 'It's easy enough for you to say that. You'll be home tonight. I go on day after day – the dreary endless sameness, the closed-in, trapped feeling. It is hell.' Harold was right. I knew it. But so desperately did I want my freedom that I was fighting again.

On one point the courthouse tipsters, the lawyers, and Herb, John, Jeb, and I were all agreed – the four of us would be released together or none of us would. Dan and Magruder were government witnesses, which had won them favour, but their offences were more severe than mine or Herb's. Our sentences were comparable and Kalmbach was overdue. No, if one went out, all would go out.

On January 8 I was in Washington for more interrogation on other cases at the prosecutor's office. Our meeting was interrupted mid-morning by an emergency phone call: Dean's lawyer calling me. He explained that John was at Holabird and could not call me but had asked him to do so. John wanted me to hear it from him first.

'What is it?' I asked impatiently.

'John has been released today by Judge Sirica,' the lawyer said. My heart began racing just the way it did when Ford announced that all of us were being considered for pardon. I waited for him to bring me the good news. 'John wanted to be sure you heard it from him, not over the radio,' he continued.

'Why?' I asked. 'It's great news.'

'Well – it is for John,' he replied, 'and for Jeb and Herb, too, but it's kind of tough on you.'

For a long moment I couldn't believe the words pounding into my ears. Magruder, Kalmbach and Dean – all sentenced by Judge Sirica – were set free. I was not. Sentenced by a different judge – Gerhard Gesell – my future was still much in doubt.

By the time I arrived back at Holabird, John, Herb, and Jeb had already left for home. A heavy pall hung over the ramshackle barracks that night. I walked down the hall and stared into Dean's room where each night the four of us had met. There was nothing but the bed, its dirty mattress bare, two chairs, and the small desk. It was quiet – an eerie silence. On my desk I found a hand-scribbled note:

Dear Chuck –

It is difficult to know what to say – other than I know you will soon be freed. Rest assured that I will be calling for your freedom when I'm first confronted by the press.

Also I will be in touch with you soon – to talk about it all.

My prayers are with you and my actions will do whatever I can to help —

Your friend,
John

The evening television news highlighted the release of the three men with scenes of the jubilant homecoming in the Magruder's front yard, neighbours gathered for the welcome, interviews with the families. For Patty, watching it was nearly unbearable. Each weekend she had visited with the other families. Patty, Gail Magruder, and Mo Dean were friends, enjoying the dubious camaraderie of being prison widows together.

The next morning I stayed in my room reading the Scriptures, waiting for the phone to ring on the marshal's desk with the news that I felt had to come. Fittingly, the lesson in my devotional literature, *Our Daily Bread*, for this gloomy day – January 9 – was entitled 'The Philosophy of Patience'. The key Scripture passage: 'Rest in the Lord, and wait patiently for him . . .' (Psalm 37:7 KJV).

The only call that day was from Shapiro. 'No news,' he said, 'and the scuttle from the courthouse ain't good. Gesell doesn't like to have anyone think he is being forced to follow Sirica's lead. Hang tough, my boy.'

The short days and long nights were without beginning or end. Time seemed to stand still. I stared out of my little room at the prickly strands of barbed wire, tried to read and write, but my mind wandered. The marshals were sympathetic, dropping almost all barriers between captor and captive. A lean, rawboned Southerner named Jack, an all-out believer, was the most helpful. 'The Lord will handle this,' he said confidently.

The visiting hours were precious now – but hard, too, as I watched Patty suffering the agony of the vigil, our hopes fading each day as freedom – and our own homecoming – seemed to be slipping further and further away. Our prayers together, more fervent now, sustained us.

On January 20 the Virginia Supreme Court announced that I was disbarred. It should not have been the shock it was. Most of the lawyers implicated in Watergate were targets of ceaseless cries for reform: 'Clean up the bar – Purge the scoundrels.' The Ervin Committee had sent to every State Bar Association computer printouts of every allegation – proven or not – affecting each of us.

I had built false hopes. Although unable to attend the hearing before the Supreme Court in Virginia, the members seemed sympathetic, according to Morin and Mason who argued for me. We had asked for a delay until I could appear personally, but now it was denied.

Two days later I was summoned to the prison office. 'It's your attorney,' the duty marshal told me as he handed me the phone. The trip-hammer went off inside me again. Stupidly I still believed every call would be the one telling me I was free.

'Chuck, are you ready for a tough one?' The voice on the other end was Ken Adams. *How many tough ones are left?* I wondered. 'Go ahead, Ken.'

'Your son Christian has been arrested for narcotics possession. He's in jail, but we'll have him out on bail in a few hours.'

I couldn't reply; my stomach went again, like someone had kicked me in the middle. Chris, now a freshman at the University of South Carolina, had never caused us any trouble, hardly any worry. He had the kind of personality that everybody loved. We'd talked about drugs, Chris and I, and I was certain he never used them. But it was all too true. Chris had taken school board money advanced to him during Christmas vacation and invested a hundred and fifty dollars in fifteen ounces of marijuana. He hoped to sell it for a quick profit and use the proceeds to replace his old car with one in better condition.

I thought I had been through all the tribulations one person could take. My son in prison seemed the worst blow of all. I knew that Chris had been soured by all that had happened to me, but I never dreamed that it might lead him to do this.

'Now you've got both of us,' Chris told the arresting officer in a quote that made the front pages of the papers. It was the frustrated outburst of an eighteen-year-old boy, embittered over what had happened to his dad. That I couldn't be at my son's side made the pain intense.

I never once thought, however, that God had forsaken me. More testing, yes, and more teaching from Him. I knew all the Scriptural references which tell us to praise Him no matter what, but alone by my bunk that cold, bleak January night I simply couldn't bring myself to do it. Surely God could not expect me to praise Him for my son's life being ruined!

And how long must the agony continue? My licence to practise law was gone, my son imprisoned, my dad gone, my compatriots freed and over two years of a three-year sentence still staring me in the face. Though I knew I could not give up, those next days were the most difficult of any that I had spent in prison, probably the most difficult of my life.

Word filtered through that during the first week of February I would be returned to Maxwell, that Holabird was to be closed. It would be good to be with my brothers there again, but I was deeply concerned now for Patty who had been through so much the past two years. How would she take many months of commuting to Alabama? Her sweet gentle nature was near the breaking point.

Charlie Morin had nearly abandoned his law practice, visiting me several times a week and organising a campaign to ask President Ford to pardon me. Ken Adams spent full time on motions and procedures for early parole. Both men visited often. The mail poured in, too, from warmhearted people across the country sympathising that the others were freed and I was still imprisoned. Their encouragement helped sustain me.

Along with Charlie and Ken, the brothers at Fellowship House rallied to my aid. On Tuesday, January 28, Al Quie called: 'Chuck, I've been thinking about what else we can do to help you. All of us today signed a letter to the President appealing for mercy, but is there anything else?' The voice on the other end didn't sound like Al; the words came slowly and seemed laden with sadness.

'Al, you guys are doing everything possible,' I told him, 'and I love you for it. I just don't know what else you can do.'

'There's got to be something else, Chuck. I have been thinking –' There was a long pause. 'There's an old statute someone told me about. I'm going to ask the President if I can serve the rest of your term for you.'

Stunned, I could only stammer a protest. Al Quie with twenty years in Congress, was the sixth-ranking Republican in the House, senior minority member of the Education and Labour Committee, and one of the most respected public figures in Washington. He could not be serious.

'I mean it, Chuck,' he said. 'I haven't come to this decision lightly.'

'I won't let you,' I said.

'Your family needs you, and I can't sleep while you're in prison; I think I'd be a lot happier being inside myself.' The lump in my throat made it impossible to tell Al how much his offer meant, but that I could not accept it.

That very day Doug Coe sent me a handwritten note. All the brothers would volunteer to serve my sentence, he explained, and then added:

These past three weeks you have been on my mind constantly . . . Chuck, a band of like-minded men is being formed by God around the world. The thing you always dreamed of doing for our country and for the people –

peace and a better life – can still take place – only now God will get the credit. God only needs men totally committed to Him – and then the mobilisation of His resources for the common good of all people can take place . . . If I could I would gladly give my life so you could use the wonderful gifts of God, that He has entrusted you with, to the Glory of God.

I love you, friend – all your companions love you – !!

As always,
Doug

It was almost more than I imagined possible, this love of one man for another. Christ's love. Al Quie would give up his whole career, Doug Coe would lay down his life, Graham and Harold, too. Isn't that what it's really all about? Isn't that the overwhelming gain of knowing Christ Jesus which makes all else as 'loss'? And this day I knew Him as never before. I'd felt his presence all right, but now I knew His power and love through the deep caring of four men. All the pain and agony to mind and body was small in comparison.

It was that night in the quiet of my room that I made the total surrender, completing what had begun in Tom Phillips's driveway eighteen long months before: 'Lord, if this is what it is all about,' I said, 'then I thank You. I praise You for leaving me in prison, for letting them take away my licence to practise law, yes – even for my son being arrested. I praise You for giving me your love through these men, for being God, for just letting me walk with Jesus.'

With those words came the greatest joy of all – the final release, turning it all over to God as my brother Harold had told me to do. And in the hours that followed I discovered more strength than I'd ever known before. This was the real mountaintop experience. Above and around me the world was filled with joy and love and beauty. For the first time I felt truly free, even as the fortunes of my life seemed at their lowest ebb.

Forty-eight hours later, five o'clock on Friday afternoon, Judge Gerhard Gesell phoned Dave Shapiro: because of family problems – what had happened to Chris – an order was being prepared to release Charles Colson from prison immediately.

Hours later Jack, the marshal who had been so sympathetic, ran over to us as Patty and I were standing at the front gate at Holabird, bidding good-bye to the small band of inmates.

'The Lord really takes care of His own men,' Jack said. 'I kind of knew He would set you free today.'

'Thank you, brother,' I said, 'but He did it two nights ago.'

Since Then . . .

Five days after his release from confinement, Charles Colson returned to Maxwell Prison to visit Paul Kramer and encourage the men he had been so close to while imprisoned there. This was the first of numerous visits to institutions all over the country which have led Chuck Colson into a full-scale prison ministry.

In June 1975 the Bureau of Prisons approved a proposal by Senator Harold Hughes and Colson to furlough men and women from selected federal institutions to attend fourteen-day retreats and training sessions in the Washington area. These furloughed inmates are selected not by prison officials but by members of Fellowship Foundation after careful interviews and investigation. The training, under the auspices of the Fellowship, focuses on leadership development, and Bible study.

The first group – twelve inmates from six federal prisons in the east – gathered together in Washington in early November 1975. The key-note was trust: the furloughed prisoners – ten men and two women (six whites, six blacks) – were driven to Washington in private cars and housed in the Good News Mission. There were no guards, but complete freedom to come and go.

The results more than reassured any sceptics. The training

sessions were businesslike, with much give-and-take. The prisoners volunteered to visit and witness to inmates at the nearby Arlington County Jail and at Lorton Reformatory. One of the group composed a song especially for those he met at Lorton. Singing and praise sessions dominated free periods. During one trip through Washington, two of the prisoners separated from the others, found their way back to the Good News Mission on their own – verification of the trust given them.

Following the two-week course, the inmates returned to their prisons trained to be disciples in serving God and their fellow men. Their key mission: to start prison fellowships. Continued friendship and guidance will be given them while they remain inside, while job opportunities await when they are released. Six similar training sessions are planned for the Washington area in 1976.

To develop this prison ministry, Charles Colson is donating to it his speaking fees and a portion of the income from this book. His longtime friend Fred Rhodes took an early retirement from the government in 1975 to give his full time to the Lord's work as Colson's special assistant.

Meanwhile, Paul Kramer continues to serve his sentence at Maxwell – and to serve his Lord through his leadership in the prison fellowship there. Homer Welsh and Lee Corbin have been released. Homer is healthy, employed, and joyfully gives his healing testimony at every opportunity. Lee Corbin, his life rebuilt, is once again at work as an evangelist.

The Lord is healing Watergate wounds in the Colson family, too. Chuck's son Christian was released from jail and enrolled in a youth counselling programme. After four months the state of South Carolina dropped all charges and Chris continues in college, his marks improving. The incident – for which Colson could not praise God at first – has brought father and son closer together.

The editor

With Gratitude . . .

Neither this book nor the story unfolded in its pages is mine alone. Without such a loving, caring wife I would not have had the strength to weather these years or tackle the task of committing the story to paper. Patty and I have shared times of tears, times of joy. We shared this book as well. Patty took dictation, typed reams of manuscript, suffered my many moods and demands for silence around our home – always with good humour.

Following Dad's death, my mother showed real grit, suffering the pains of my experience with me. I have been richly blessed with a wonderfully supportive family – Chris, Wendell, and Emily, each in his or her own way has given me great strength.

Len LeSourd's remarkable editing skill was a source of continual wonderment – and education. Even as Len left big hunks of my prose on the cutting-room floor (writers have good reason to resent editors), we came closer together in true fellowship. Len made all the work seem a joy. His wife, Catherine, and John and Elizabeth (Tibby) Sherrill, the other three of the Chosen Books team, gave constructive criticism and encouragement.

Tibby Sherrill's role is worth special note. She laboured for several weeks polishing the final draft with her gifted deftness. Tibby had been one of those who marched outside the White House in an anti-Vietnam protest back in 1971 while I sat inside, seething with resentment against all demonstrators. In the secular world a Tibby Sherrill could not stomach a Colson manuscript; nor would a Colson let a Tibby Sherrill within a hundred yards of his book. Because we now share a commitment to Christ we could work together with common purpose, our opposite political viewpoints often producing new insights and more clarity in the manuscript.

Along with Patty, there were many who typed – and retyped: Dotty Hellyer from Fellowship House, my secretary these past six months, who laboured tirelessly – days into nights – draft after draft; Holly Holm, with her sparkling personality and strength of character, who served so loyally through it all – the White House, Watergate, and into the beginning chapters of *Born Again*; Josephine Englat, an old friend who typed several of the early chapters; Patricia Owens, Charlie Morin's secretary and a valued and dear friend for many years; and Connie Otto, Harold Hughes's oldest daughter.

But for the support of 'brothers' – Doug Coe, Harold Hughes, Graham Purcell, and Al Quie – there, of course, might be no story to tell. They opened their hearts to me and remained steadfast when others were fleeing Watergate's spreading stain. Together we have come to know the richest bonds in life. Tom Phillips was the steady compass when all else in my life was spinning dizzily out of control. *Born Again* is a story of how God used men like Tom in mighty ways. For his part in the story and more importantly his part in my life, I shall be grateful always.

Born Again is also the tale of Paul Kramer and the other men I came to know and love in prison. They remain my brothers, an unforgettable chapter in my pilgrimage.

Two of the men in the Fellowship, Paul Temple and Winston Weaver, made available their vacation homes (in Spain and the

Virginia mountains respectively) to Patty and me when we needed a place of retreat. Ken Adams, Dave Shapiro, Arthur Mason, Judd Best, Charlie Morin, Sid Dickstein, Myron Mintz, Henry Cashen, and all the lawyers and employees of my old firm not only represented me admirably in my travails – but contributed to and encouraged this manuscript. To Ken Adams is owed a special debt. He not only represented me with devotion, but he took a great interest in this manuscript, helping in his spare time with research reviews, and comments.

Fred Rhodes, with whom I have worked side by side this year, spared me from many distractions while I wrote – and from our prayers together came sustaining strength for this and other work.

Much of the research for this book was made possible because of the indefatigable work of volunteers from Fellowship House who pasted and indexed thousands of clippings. Though the court motions for which the clippings were assembled were denied, their work was not in vain. So my thanks to John and Betsy Curry, Ruth McDaniel, and scores of others who gave of themselves to support a brother in need.

Charles Morin, whose companionship I have treasured for twenty years, reminds me each day of the meaning of true friendship. And so do many others: Mike Balzano, Jesse Calhoon, Frank Fitzsimmons, Brainerd Holmes, Dick Howard, Alexander Lankler, and Bill Maloney, to mention but a few.

Then there are all those – in Washington and across the country – the thousands of warmhearted believers who supported me through encouraging letters and by prayer. How can a man describe his feeling at knowing that hundreds of men and women, most of whom he will never meet on this earth, have been constantly praying on his behalf! Nothing did more to enrich my faith and spur me on.

So to all who have shared this journey with me, my deepest thanks.

Charles W. Colson

Afterword to the Film Edition

It is a miracle that *Born Again* has become a major Hollywood motion picture. From the outset obstacles were staggering.

- No modern conversion story has ever been filmed by a major commercial studio.
- Secular film distributors historically shun Christian films.
- Conventional financing sources are quick to back 'R' and 'X' rated movies, but not religious films. We knew the $3 million budget would have to be raised privately.
- Finally, Hollywood was famed for its swinging parties and permissive lifestyles. Could we find the actors, producers and writers to handle Christian material in a sensitive way?

When *Born Again* book sales soared miraculously – it was the fifth best-selling book in America in 1976 – several film makers approached me. There were some interesting proposals, but I was uneasy; I soon discovered that most were primarily interested in the Watergate issues or such human interest angles as old enemies Chuck Colson and Harold Hughes becoming friends. The Gospel was secondary at best. One prominent Hollywood personality suggested we delete all references to Christ, substituting the word 'God' in order to reach the 'bigger audience'. I knew this would destroy the main message of the book.

Then one autumn day in 1976, I met Pat Boone at the Dallas Prayer Conference. He suggested I contact a Hollywood advertising executive, Bob Munger, who had originated the idea for the highly successful film 'The Omen'. Pat assured me that Bob was a deeply committed brother in Christ.

My close companion Fred Rhodes and I met with Munger in December. At that time, he was struggling with his own future. His wife had been praying, we learned, that he would give up his lucrative business and go full-time into Christian film-making. But the risks were high. And until Pat Boone brought us together, Munger had not found any promising stories to film.

After several sessions of prayer, Fred and I felt God's leading; so did Munger. An option agreement was executed and a veteran script writer with a long string of successful credits, Walter Bloch, was signed on to write the screen treatment. Walter, a converted Jew with a fervent commitment to the Lord, poured his heart into the project.

For the next eight months, Walter and I struggled together through six drafts. He wrote; I re-wrote; he polished the drafts; I re-wrote. More polishing, more re-writes. The effort was intense. We were determined that the end product be as close to the book as possible. But there were major technical problems, such as the episodic nature of the story. Only two brothers working together in Christ could ever achieve the goal: a true Gospel message on the screen.

As we expected, financing was a hurdle. Munger and I contacted friends. Some responded at once; but when the budget was half committed, we began hitting a series of dead ends as sophisticated investors turned away, realizing that no overtly Christian film had ever succeeded in the secular market.

One Friday night in September of 1977 I realised that I had exhausted the list of those who might help. One and a half million more was needed in the next few days in order that production commitments could be made for a December filming. Other critical deadlines were upon us.

Bob Munger could not execute contracts without assurance of the funds. If the date slipped, the big studios would not be available; it was already almost too late for many casting decisions. It appeared hopeless.

I sat alone at my desk in my library and prayed, 'Lord, I give up. There is nothing more I can do. If you want this film produced, you'll have to raise up the people to provide the money.'

With that prayer, I felt a sudden peace. I had done my part. If there were to be no movie, so be it. If the Lord wanted it, it would come to pass.

The next day a young man met me at an airport in western North Carolina, to drive me to a speaking engagement at a Christian retreat centre. I'd never laid eyes on him before. I settled into the seat beside him and began studying my speech notes. The young man made idle conversation, then asked me about the film *Born Again*. I didn't look up from my papers . . .

'Oh, it probably isn't going to be a movie; we haven't raised the money,' I replied. I didn't try to hide my discouragement.

'How much are you asking each investor to put up?' he asked.

'One hundred and fifty,' I replied brusquely.

'I'll take one,' he snapped.

My head jerked up and I stared at the smiling young man. He was dressed in sports shirt and slacks, a college student I imagined.

As our car wound its way up a mountain road, I struggled with how to break the news gently. I had meant $150,000; obviously this eager young fellow thought I meant $150. I hated to shatter his enthusiasm.

There was an awkward full in conversation. Finally, I spoke. 'I'm sorry. I mean $150,000,' I said gently.

'I know,' he replied. 'I'll take one share.'

Three other individuals called that same weekend, two of whom were like my young driver, total strangers asking if they could invest. By Sunday night one of the original investors, with no prompting from me, agreed to underwrite the remaining $1 million needed. God most assuredly had answered prayer.

There were still other obstacles, like finding the right leading man. As Munger interviewed several big name professionals, it became clear that one key ingredient was missing: the spiritual sensitivity necessary to portray true conversion.

Actors can portray most emotions like sorrow, joy, fear – all common to the human experience. But Scripture tells us that 'Jesus is Lord' can be said only under the power of the Holy Spirit. We discovered how true that is. As late as August 1977, we had no leading man.

Meanwhile, an actor named Dean Jones and I had become friends. We had some things in common: we were the same age and had both experienced dramatic conversions at about the same time. Dean's life, before and after, was a study in contrast. He once was a heavy-drinking, free-living actor who defied death on his motorcycles and sports cars, racing over mountain roads. Now he was a gentle family man, devoted church-goer, deeply committed.

Dean believed so much in the movie that he offered to be on the set each day for prayer. He entertained no thoughts of playing my part: nor did we. Dean's highly successful career, built up in over thirty Walt Disney films, didn't seem to fit the White House tough guy role.

By late August Bob Munger had become convinced that *only* Dean could play the lead, notwithstanding his Disney image. But was he free to do it?

The story Dean told us when we approached him could only be regarded as total confirmation. Some weeks earlier, NBC had offered Dean a leading role in a new TV serial. The format was perfect for him: a clean wholesome family series. The price was right, too. The script fitted all of his requirements. His wife Lory, also a deeply committed believer, liked it too. Together they prayed one night seeking God's guidance.

The next morning, Dean and Lory both woke up deeply troubled. Neither had a feeling of peace about the project. They agreed it was not right.

Dean phoned his agent to announce his decision. The agent was incredulous. 'If you want more money, we'll get it,' the agent pressed impatiently.

'It's not money,' Dean replied. 'I prayed about it and it just isn't right.'

Days later when Munger offered him the lead in *Born Again*, Dean discovered why he had not been given peace about the new series. Had he accepted the NBC offer, he would not have been available for this film. Though his role in *Born Again* paid much less than what NBC offered, Dean readily accepted.

Filming began on schedule. The first morning Munger assembled the cast, directors, cameramen and technicians for a pre-drawn prayer session. Despite bewildered expressions on the faces of some of the crew, we were determined to commit the project totally to the Lord. An army of friends across America maintained daily prayer throughout.

Midway through production, God's hand upon this film again became unmistakably clear.

Bob Munger arrived in Director Irving Rapper's office one morning to confer on the casting of David Shapiro, the law partner who represented me through out Watergate. Several 'name' actors were being considered for this major role in the film.

As Munger passed through the reception room, his eyes fell on one of those waiting for an interview. The man bore some resemblance to Shapiro. He asked Rapper about him.

'Oh, that's Jay Robinson. He's here to try out for a minor part.'

'Get him in here,' Munger ordered. Bob somehow believed that Robinson was the man for the Shapiro part; it was either a wild hunch or an inspiration from the Lord.

Jay Robinson had played Caligula, the Mad Emperor, in the movie classic *The Robe.* His acting was rated 'one of the ten best performances of all time' by *New York Times* critic Bosley Crowther.

Only 22 then, he enjoyed overnight fame. Jay partied in splendour at the swank Beverly Hills Hotel. There was no end to social and professional invitations. But fame was a trap for Jay. Haunted by a feeling of emptiness in the material things of life, he began using drugs as an escape from his search for meaning and fulfilment.

A highly publicised drug arrest was followed by a sentence in Chino, a California prison. The bleak, depersonalising vacuum of prison replaced Jay Robinson's glamorous Hollywood surroundings.

Free after fourteen months in prison, he soon discovered he was an unwanted ex-con. Jay tried to support his family as a fry cook. Third-rate roles and bit pieces helped keep groceries on his table. Life was hard and unfriendly.

Jay shared his background with Munger. The stigma of being an ex-convict had cost him other roles when directors learned of his past.

'But for this picture,' Munger laughed, 'being an ex-con is an asset.'

While Jay stood by, wide-eyed, Munger turned to Director Rapper. 'Could he play the part?'

Rapper responded instantly. 'Jay could play any role. He's a brilliant actor.'

'That's it, then,' Munger exclaimed. 'Sign him.'

Jay Robinson was standing beside me on the set one day while I was giving an interview to two reporters. I was describing the horrors of prison life – the deadness, the sense of hopelessness, the pervasive bitterness – when I looked over at

Jay. In the glare of the bright lights, I saw a tear roll down his cheek.

'Is something the matter?' I asked after the reporter had gone.

Jay responded quietly. 'I was there once myself, remember?'

Later that same day while I was watching Jay overcome early jitters, I penned a note to him on a piece of scratch paper. It read simply, 'You are great – your fellow ex-con, Colson.'

Jay soon began asking questions about my faith. He talked first with Bob Munger, then with Harold Hughes who spent a week in Hollywood playing his own part in the film.

In one of the most memorable moments of the film, Dean Jones (Colson) tells Jay Robinson (Shapiro) of his decision to plead guilty. Jay is momentarily shattered because he was confident he could win an acquittal for his friend in court, but then his deeper emotions are unleashed. He is proud of his friend's decision and puts his arm around Dean's shoulder, saying in an obvious Jewish accent, 'Keep this up and you'll have *me* believing in your Jewish friend.'

It was brilliant play-acting, but the words were to be prophetic. Some days later Robinson was on his knees in Munger's office, asking Christ into his life.

He could not help remembering the day fifteen years earlier when in a solitary cell he had cried out 'God help me.' Now the long and painful journey was over for the man who had tried many philosophies and once starred as Caligula, persecutor of Christians.

Jay returned to Chino prison a few days later, this time as a born-again Christian, to film prison sequences of the film. A star was pinned to his dressing room door, and a banner at the prison entrance announced, 'WELCOME BACK, JAY ROBINSON – STAR.'

But stardom is now only second in Jay's life. He had discovered that *Born Again* is more than a movie title – it is the new life that ended his restless search for meaning.

It was no surprise when filming ended on schedule and within budget. That seldom happens in Hollywood, but then seldom is a movie made with God's hand so obviously upon it.

My prayer now is that God will use this film to touch the hearts of the countless millions who will see it – and that it might be the first of many Christian films produced by secular studios in Hollywood. If the film succeeds in the market place, it will be a precedent dramatically transforming the kind of movie Hollywood produces.

Sound impossible? Maybe so, but the making of *Born Again* is simply a fresh reminder that 'with God all things are possible'.

Charles W. Colson
June 15, 1978